Lecture Notes in Computer Science 15236

The series Lecture Notes in Computer Science (LNCS), including its subseries Lecture Notes in Artificial Intelligence (LNAI) and Lecture Notes in Bioinformatics (LNBI), has established itself as a medium for the publication of new developments in computer science and information technology research, teaching, and education.

LNCS enjoys close cooperation with the computer science R & D community, the series counts many renowned academics among its volume editors and paper authors, and collaborates with prestigious societies. Its mission is to serve this international community by providing an invaluable service, mainly focused on the publication of conference and workshop proceedings and postproceedings. LNCS commenced publication in 1973.

Sølvi Ystad · Richard Kronland-Martinet ·
Tetsuro Kitahara · Keiji Hirata · Mitsuko Aramaki
Editors

Music and Sound Generation in the AI Era

16th International Symposium, CMMR 2023
Tokyo, Japan, November 13–17, 2023
Revised Selected Papers

Springer

Editors
Sølvi Ystad
CNRS, Aix-Marseille University
Marseille, France

Richard Kronland-Martinet
CNRS, Aix-Marseille University
Marseille, France

Tetsuro Kitahara
Nihon University
Tokyo, Japan

Keiji Hirata
CNRS, Future University Hakodate
Hakodate, Japan

Mitsuko Aramaki
CNRS, Aix-Marseille University
Marseille, France

ISSN 0302-9743 ISSN 1611-3349 (electronic)
Lecture Notes in Computer Science
ISBN 978-3-032-02041-3 ISBN 978-3-032-02042-0 (eBook)
https://doi.org/10.1007/978-3-032-02042-0

This Springer imprint is published by the registered company Springer Nature Switzerland AG
The registered company address is: Gewerbestrasse 11, 6330 Cham, Switzerland

Preface

The 16th edition of the International Symposium on Computer Music Multidisciplinary Research (CMMR 2023), entitled "Music: Bridge after the Turmoil", took place from 13–17 November 2023 in Tokyo, Japan. This was the first in-person CMMR Symposium since the COVID-19 crisis. The theme, "Music: Bridge after the Turmoil", symbolized the reconnection of researchers who had been separated during the pandemic, as well as the bridging of past and future events, the various academic disciplines represented at CMMR, together with the integration of art and science through demonstrations, installations, musical performances and scientific presentations. As with the previous Symposium held remotely in 2021, the present event was chaired by Keiji Hirata (Future University Hakodate, Japan) with Satoshi Tojo (Asia University, Japan) serving as co-chair. Tetsuro Kitahara oversaw the scientific program in collaboration with the PRISM Laboratory (Perception, Representations, Image, Sound, Music), in Marseille, France. Six local institutions participated in the organization of the event, i.e. Future University Hakodate, JAIST, Nihon University, RIKEN, University of Tsukuba, and Tokyo University of Science. The music program was chaired by Takuro Shibayama (Tokyo Denki University, Japan).

The symposium received 83 submissions, each reviewed by two to three reviewers under a single-blind review process. The accepted contributions were presented in oral, poster, and demo sessions. A total of 36 submissions were accepted for oral presentation, corresponding to an acceptance rate of 43%. Among the nine oral sessions, three special sessions were organized. The first session focused on "Singing Information Processing", organized by Tomoyasu Nakano (National Institute of Advanced Industrial Science and Technology (AIST)), the second on "Music and Sound Generation: Emerging Approaches and Diverse Applications", organized by Taketo Akama (Sony Computer Science Laboratories, Inc.), and the third on "Computational Research on Music Evolution", organized by Eita Nakamura (Kyoto University). The other sessions addressed a broad range of CMMR topics such as music information retrieval, audio signal processing, HCI in music, computational musicology, cognitive science and skill science for music and creative music systems. In addition, three keynote presentations were given by the internationally renowned researchers Shigeki Sagayama (Visiting Professor, University of Electro-Communications, Japan), Yi-Hsuan Yang (Full Professor, the College of Electrical Engineering and Computer Science, National Taiwan University, Taiwan), and Tatsuya Daikoku (Project Assistant Professor, International Research Center for Neurointelligence, University of Tokyo, Japan). Three combined poster and demo sessions showcased over 50 works. The Best Paper Award was given to Eita Nakamura for his paper: Computational Analysis of Selection and Mutation Probabilities in the Evolution of Chord Progressions.

The post-proceedings edition of CMMR 2023 is the 16th CMMR publication by Springer Verlag in its Lecture Notes in Computer Sciences Series and complements the previous editions: LNCS 2771, 3310, 3902, 4969, 5493, 5954, 6684, 7172, 7900, 8905, 9617, 10525, 11265, 12631 and 13770.

This year's edition contains 37 peer-reviewed papers arranged in seven sections related to Artificial Intelligence, Music and Sound Generation, Computational Musicology, Music Recognition and Creation Tools, Music Information Retrieval, Audio Signal Processing and Human-Computer Interaction in Music.

We would like to express our gratitude to all the participants of CMMR 2023 who made this event possible. A special thanks goes to the local organizers at Tokyo University of Science, who did a great job coordinating all the different kinds of sessions, and who gladly shared their spare time to make this Symposium an unforgettable event, both scientifically and socially. Additionally, we would like to thank the Program and Music Committee members for their indispensable work in selecting the content.

Finally, we would like to thank Springer for agreeing to publish the CMMR 2023 post proceedings edition in their LNCS series.

June 2023

Mitsuko Aramaki
Keiji Hirata
Tetsuro Kitahara
Richard Kronland-Martinet
Sølvi Ystad

Organization

General Chair

Keiji Hirata	Future University Hakodate, Japan

General Co-chair

Satoshi Tojo	Asia University, Japan

Scientific Program and Proceedings Chairs

Tetsuro Kitahara	Nihon University, Japan
Aiko Uemura	Nihon University, Japan
Mitsuko Aramaki	PRISM, AMU-CNRS, France
Richard Kronland-Martinet	PRISM, AMU-CNRS, France
Sølvi Ystad	PRISM, AMU-CNRS, France

Music Program Chair

Takuro Shibayama	Tokyo Denki University, Japan

Demo Program Chair

Masatoshi Hamanaka	RIKEN, Japan

Public Relation Chairs

Masatoshi Hamanaka	RIKEN, Japan
Shun Sawada	Tokyo University of Science, Japan

Proceedings and Registration Chair

Aiko Uemura	Nihon University, Japan

Demo Program Committee

Masatoshi Hamanaka	RIKEN, Japan
Stefano Kalonaris	RIKEN, Japan
Hiroya Miura	RIKEN, Japan
Nami Iino	NII, Japan

Scientific Program Committee

Taketo Akama	Sony Computer Science Laboratories, Inc., Japan
Daichi Ando	Tokyo Metropolitan University, Japan
Mitsuko Aramaki	PRISM, AMU-CNRS, France
Mathieu Barthet	Queen Mary University of London, UK
Corentin Bernard	PRISM, AMU-CNRS, France
Gilberto Bernardes	University of Porto, Portugal
Tifanie Bouchara	CNAM, Paris, France
Marcelo Caetano	PRISM, AMU-CNRS, France
F. Amílcar Cardoso	University of Coimbra, Portugal
Roger Dannenberg	Carnegie Mellon University, USA
Georg Essl	University of Wisconsin - Milwaukee, USA
Ichiro Fujinaga	McGill University, Canada
Mylène Gioffredo	PRISM, AMU-CNRS, France
Masataka Goto	National Institute of Advanced Industrial Science and Technology, Japan
Masatoshi Hamanaka	RIKEN, Japan
Mitsuyo Hashida	University of Fukuchiyama, Japan
Rumi Hiraga	Tsukuba University of Technology, Japan
Tatsunori Hirai	Komazawa University, Japan
Shigeyuki Hirai	Kyoto Sangyo University, Japan
Keiji Hirata	Future University Hakodate, Japan
Akinori Ito	Tohoku University, Japan
Takayuki Itoh	Ochanomizu University, Japan
Katsutoshi Itoyama	Tokyo Institute of Technology, Japan
Haruhiro Katayose	Kwansei Gakuin University, Japan
Tetsuro Kitahara	Nihon University, Japan
Richard Kronland-Martinet	PRISM, AMU-CNRS, France

Luca Andrea Ludovico	University of Milan, Italy
Akira Maezawa	Yamaha Corporation, Japan
Sylvain Marchand	University of La Rochelle, France
Masaki Matsubara	University of Tsukuba, Japan
Andrew McPherson	Imperial College London, UK
Tomohiko Nakamura	National Institute of Advanced Industrial Science and Technology, Japan
Eita Nakamura	Kyoto University, Japan
Tomoyasu Nakano	National Institute of Advanced Industrial Science and Technology, Japan
Juhan Nam	Korea Advanced Institute of Science and Technology, South Korea
Marco Buongiorno Nardelli	University of North Texas, USA
Hidefumi Ohmura	Tokyo University of Science, Japan
Noriko Otani	Tokyo City University, Japan
Samuel Poirot	PRISM, AMU-CNRS, France
Marcelo Queiroz	University of São Paulo, Brazil
Jocelyn Rozé	PRISM, AMU-CNRS, France
Shinji Sako	Nagoya Institute of Technology, Japan
Charles de Paiva Santana	PRISM, AMU-CNRS, France
Ariane Stolfi	Universidade Federal do Sul da Bahia, Brazil
Bob Sturm	KTH Royal Institute of Technology, Sweden
Shinnosuke Takamichi	University of Tokyo, Japan
Satoshi Tojo	Asia University, Japan
Yudai Tsujino	Meiji University, Japan
Adrien Vidal	PRISM, AMU-CNRS, France
Marcelo Wanderley	McGill University, Canada
Anna Xambó	Queen Mary University of London, UK
Ryosuke Yamanishi	Kansai University, Japan
Nozomiko Yasui	National Institute of Technology, Japan
Kazuyoshi Yoshii	Kyoto University, Japan
Sølvi Ystad	PRISM, AMU-CNRS, France

Steering Committee

Mitsuko Aramaki	PRISM, AMU-CNRS, France
Mathieu Barthet	QMUL, UK
Keiji Hirata	Future University Hakodate, Japan
Richard Kronland-Martinet	PRISM, AMU-CNRS, France
Sølvi Ystad	PRISM, AMU-CNRS, France

Contents

Computational Musicology

Music Recognition and Creation Tools

Music Information Retrieval

Audio Signal Processing and HCI in Music

Artificial Intelligence, Cognitive Science and Skill Science for Sound and Music

Emergence of Creativity and Individuality in Music: Insights from Brain's Statistical Learning and Its Embodied Mechanisms

Tatsuya Daikoku(✉)

Graduate School of Information Science and Technology, The University of Tokyo, Tokyo, Japan
daikoku.tatsuya@mail.u-tokyo.ac.jp

Abstract. Music is a universal feature of human culture, linked to embodied cognitive functions that drive learning, action, and the emergence of creativity and individuality. Evidence highlights the critical role of statistical learning—an implicit cognitive process of the brain—in musical creativity and individuality. Despite its significance, the precise neural and computational mechanisms underpinning these dynamic and embodied cognitive processes remain poorly understood. This paper discusses how individuality and creativity emerge within the framework of the brain's statistical learning, drawing on a series of neural and computational studies. This work offers perspectives on the mechanisms driving the heterogeneous nature of statistical learning abilities and embodied mechanisms and provides a framework to explain the paradoxical phenomenon where individuals with specific cognitive traits that limit certain perceptual abilities excel in creative domains.

Keywords: hierarchy · dynamics · embodied cognition · interoception · prediction

1 Introduction

Music has been a fundamental aspect of human culture, deeply embedded in the embodied cognitive and emotional frameworks that define our species [1–3]. The connection between music, the brain, and the body extends beyond mere appreciation; it plays a critical role in learning, action, and the emergence of creativity and individuality [4].

Recent studies have suggested that the brain's implicit learning mechanism, called as "*statistical learning*" plays an important role in shaping musical creativity and individuality [5–7] and embodied cognition underlying musical emotion [8]. Statistical learning [9], which involves detecting patterns and regularities in sensory input, emerges as an innate capacity from early brain development [10] and continues to shape individual differences throughout life [11–13]. This adaptive process constructs unique frameworks based on the diversity of sensory experiences, effectively tailoring an individual's embodied cognitive capabilities. Such individuality influences not only how people engage with music but also how creativity manifests in their musical expressions [6, 14]. Despite the

S. Ystad et al. (Eds.): CMMR 2023, LNCS 15236, pp. 3–14, 2026.
https://doi.org/10.1007/978-3-032-02042-0_1

vital importance of statistical learning, its exact neural and computational mechanisms remain unclear, making it difficult to fully understand how it supports creativity and shapes individuality.

This paper discusses how individuality and creativity emerge within the framework of statistical learning of the brain, drawing on a series of neural and computational studies. Building on these interdisciplinary insights, this paper introduces a computational framework called as Hierarchical Bayesian Statistical Learning (HBSL) model [15], mimicking the brain's hierarchical processes of statistical learning. This provides a novel perspective on the diverse nature of statistical learning abilities and embodied cognitive mechanisms, shedding light on understanding how creativity and individuality could emerge through statistical learning processes.

2 Predictive Processing Based on Statistical Learning

The brain operates as a predictive system, constantly anticipating sensory inputs based on accumulated prior experiences [16]. This neural process relies on resolving differences between expected and actual sensory input through Bayesian inference, known as prediction errors [17]. The internal model is treated as prior probabilities, while sensory inputs serve as likelihoods. By integrating them, the brain generates the most plausible posterior predictions. Crucially, the regulation of prior predictions is modulated by perceptual uncertainty at higher hierarchical levels [18, 19], making predictive processing dynamic and adaptive [20].

Music provides a compelling framework to examine predictive processing [21, 22], particularly through the lens of statistical learning. Through this process, the brain extracts transitional probabilities from sequences such as music or language, enabling it to predict future stimuli. Neural and computational studies have shown evidence that the brain encodes transitional probabilities of music sequences, modulating neural responses to expected versus unexpected musical events [23–27]. For example, when a musical tone with high transitional probability is predicted, neural responses to the tone are attenuated (for review, see [28]). Remarkably, statistical learning enables even sleeping neonates and infants to identify and segment high-probability sound chunks, such as words or phrases, from speech, despite their lack of prior linguistic knowledge [9, 10].

Beyond perception, musical statistical learning plays a critical role in the emergence of embodied emotional engagement. For instance, musical syncopation—a deviation from expected rhythmic patterns—generates prediction errors that elicit motor impulses, such as foot-tapping, as the brain attempts to align internal and external rhythms [29]. This phenomenon, termed music active inference [21, 22], highlights the integration of sensory prediction and motor response in reducing perceptual uncertainty in music. Importantly, the complexity of rhythmic patterns influences the brain's capacity for active inference. Overly complex rhythms may inhibit the resolution of prediction errors, while rhythms of intermediate complexity—characterised by a balance of uncertainty and predictability—are more likely to evoke embodied responses [22]. This relationship is often described by an inverted-U shaped curve, where peak pleasure and engagement occur at optimal levels of uncertainty-weighted prediction error. A neuroimaging study reveals that such peak conditions activate reward-related brain regions, including the nucleus accumbens and the orbitofrontal cortex, alongside motor systems such as the basal ganglia and premotor cortex [30]. This principle applies not only to rhythm but also to harmonic progressions. A study demonstrated that specific combinations of uncertainty and surprise—where one is high and the other is low—correspond to peaks in the inverted-U curve of uncertainty-weighted prediction error. These peaks are associated with heightened activity in reward-related brain regions and greater musical enjoyment [31]. These findings illustrate how embodied musical cognition links prediction errors to both motor behavior and dopaminergic reward systems, fostering emotional and aesthetic experiences.

3 Three Key Insights into Individuality and Creativity

Here, to fully understand how statistical learning contributes to musical creativity and individuality, we propose three key elements: 1) Hierarchical processing: The brain integrates local and global patterns of music sequences, enabling the construction of coherent musical structures, 2) Temporal dynamics: Prediction and uncertainty fluctuate over time, driving adaptive learning and creative exploration, and 3) Embodied Cognition: Musical experiences engage both the brain and the body, with physical responses (e.g., chills, increased heart rate) enriching the aesthetic and emotional dimensions of music. The three components illuminate the interplay between predictive processing, statistical learning, individuality, and creativity in music. They highlight how the brain not only perceives and predicts music but also generates novel compositions and deeply emotional experiences through the dynamic modulation of uncertainty and prediction errors.

3.1 Hierarchy

A hierarchical structure is fundamental in language and music [32], reflecting the temporal and spectral organizations of sensory stimuli [33, 34]. For example, the hierarchical temporal structure of language rhythm consists of large rhythms around 2 Hz corresponding to prosody, under which rhythms around 4-12 Hz corresponding to syllables are nested, and further, rhythms around 12–30 Hz corresponding to phonemes and onsets of sounds exist [35]. A similar hierarchical structure is present in music rhythms [36], where, for example, at 120 BPM (beats per minute), rhythms corresponding to quarter notes at 2 Hz may include rhythms of eighth notes at 4 Hz (Fig. 1a, left). Such hierarchical structures can be visualized through the amplitude modulation envelope of sound waveforms (Fig. 1a, right). The hierarchical rhythm structures have been confirmed in various languages such as English [35], Japanese [37, 38], Spanish [39], Portuguese [40], French, and German [41], as well as in various musical genres [36]. This suggests that these structures are fundamental characteristics shared by both language and music.

Recent studies have demonstrated that the brain extracts and synchronizes with these hierarchical rhythms via phase coupling between neural oscillations and the corresponding frequency bands of auditory input [42, 43]. For instance, the brain's delta oscillations phase-synchronize with the prosodic rhythms of speech or the larger rhythms in music, while theta oscillations synchronize with syllabic or finer temporal structures

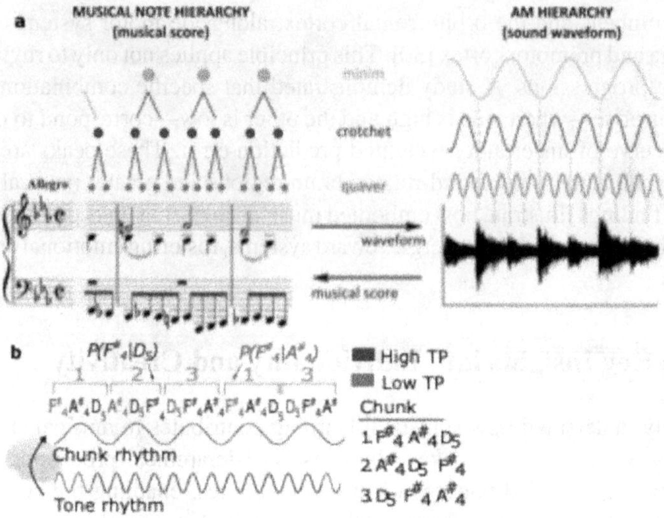

Fig. 1. Hierarchical structure of musical rhythm (a) and phase synchronization in the brain (b), reprinted from [36, 67]**.** Neural oscillators phase-synchronize with the hierarchical amplitude modulation inherent in the sound waveform (a). For example, when the duration of a single tone is 333 ms (3 Hz) in (b), the chunk frequency for a sequence of three tones is 1 Hz. When listening to a structured sequence (statistical learning), brain oscillations exhibit phase synchronization not only at the frequency of individual tones but also at the chunk frequency.

[44]. This synchronization facilitates the decomposition of complex auditory inputs into hierarchical components, supporting both perception and learning.

Interestingly, this process is not solely dependent on AM features of sound waveform. Even in the absence of explicit rhythmic cues in sound waveform, such as accents or strong onsets, the brain generates hierarchical structures by integrating lexical, syntactic, and statistical knowledge [45, 46]. For example, during statistical learning, neural oscillations initially synchronize with the frequencies of individual tones or syllables (Fig. 1b). As statistical learning progresses, these oscillations adapt to statistically chunked units, such as words or phrases, reflecting the hierarchical organization of learned patterns [47, 48]. The delta rhythm plays a crucial role in auditory learning during infancy. Studies have shown that neural oscillations in infants initially phase-synchronize delta rhythms before transitioning to theta-alpha rhythms, indicating a holistic-to-analytic progression in auditory learning [44]. Infant-directed speech (IDS) and music, characterized by prominent delta rhythms [36], may be more effective than adult-directed speech in facilitating this early learning process [49]. This suggests that hierarchical rhythms in music and IDS may be critical for the initial stages of music and language acquisition.

Hierarchical processing also contributes to creativity, particularly in music [5]. Statistical learning enables the brain to identify and chunk high-probability patterns, which form the basis for generating novel compositions. For example, jazz improvisation frequently incorporates common chord progressions, such as the II–V–I progression, which exhibit high transitional probability and low uncertainty. While these progressions represent shared knowledge at lower hierarchical levels, individual creativity emerges through unique combinations and manipulations of these chunked units (Fig. 1c). A comparative analysis of improvisations by renowned jazz pianists Bill Evans, Herbie Hancock, and McCoy Tyner revealed that lower-hierarchical statistical units were common across all three musicians, whereas higher-hierarchical units were distinct and reflected individual styles [50]. This indicates that while statistical learning provides a foundation for shared musical structures, hierarchical integration fosters individuality in creative expression.

The knowledge and chunk rhythms acquired through statistical learning are also utilized when generating new information. The author conducted simulation experiments using a corpus of child music (i.e., nursery rhymes) from Japan, France, Germany, Korea, and the UK to verify how hierarchical structures of rhythms are acquired through musical statistical learning and how the acquired knowledge is used to generate new music. This was achieved using the HBSL model [15]. This model integrates Bayesian estimation with Dirichlet prior distribution and Markov processes, allowing the calculation of confidence in probabilities from the inverse of the variance of the prior distribution of transition probabilities. By using normalized values of transition probabilities and confidence, chunking occurs when "confidence * probability" exceeds a constant α. The results of the simulation experiments showed that, through 15 trials of statistical learning, the number and hierarchy of chunks increased regardless of language or musical culture. Additionally, it was observed that the probabilistic components of the music generated by the model after learning gradually changed to new ones compared to the original music. Interestingly, it was found that the generated music increasingly contained rhythms in the delta band as learning progressed. This suggests that even without delta band rhythms as acoustic features of the learning information, the brain can chunk information through statistical learning, construct hierarchical rhythm structures internally, and generate information rich in delta band rhythms when generating new information. These results indicate that the statistical learning ability of the brain contributes to the formation of hierarchical structures and new information, which are important for the early development of language and music. This might also explain why nursery rhymes and IDS for children are rich in these rhythms [36].

Furthermore, I generated three HBSL models with different dependencies on sensory signals (hypo: sensory hypo-sensitivity, normal: typical sensitivity, hyper: sensory hyper-sensitivity) to verify how individual difference in sensory sensitivity transforms internal models through statistical learning of a nursery rhyme called "Yuuyake Koyake". Recently, the understanding of individual developmental characteristics based on the brain's predictive processing has been explained by sensitivity to bottom-up sensory signals from the external environment [51–53]. In this model, the hyper model exhibits fluctuations in the reliability of probabilities (variance of the prior distribution in the internal model) due to stimuli, while the hypo model shows less fluctuation in reliability even with new stimuli. Simulation results showed that hyper-sensitive models, which prioritize bottom-up sensory input, excel at chunking and learning hierarchical rhythms but tend to overfit existing patterns, limiting creative output. Conversely, hypo-sensitive models, less reliant on sensory input, exhibited reduced learning efficiency but generated more novel compositions. These findings underscore a trade-off between learning efficiency and creative generation, highlighting how individual differences in sensory sensitivity influence hierarchical processing and creativity.

Taken together, the hierarchical structures play a crucial role in music as well as language, supporting not only perception and learning but also creativity. Statistical learning contributes to internalizing these structures, enabling the emergence of creativity and individuality. Moreover, individual differences in sensory sensitivity influence the formation and utilization of hierarchical representations, suggesting a dynamic interplay between perceptual processing and creative expression. These insights deepen our understanding of how the brain processes structured auditory input and provide a foundation for exploring developmental and cross-cultural variations in music and language acquisition.

3.2 Temporal Dynamics of Predictability

Temporal dynamics of predictability, encompassing fluctuations in uncertainty and prediction error, play a critical role in shaping the creative and emotional dimensions of music [14, 54]. Unlike static predictability, these dynamic variations foster individuality, influencing both the perception and production of music. For instance, when a predictable chord follows an entirely predictable progression, the result may feel monotonous and uninspiring. Conversely, when a predictable chord follows an unpredictable progression, it often elicits a sense of relief or resolution, highlighting the brain's sensitivity to dynamic shifts in predictability.

In a recent study [8], the authors developed the HBSL model that decodes the relationship between perceptual uncertainty (i.e., entropy) and surprise (i.e., prediction error) in musicusing 80,000 chords from Billboard's US pop songs [55]. Using this model, we generated the eight types of chord progressions. Each type is characterized by varying degrees of temporal dynamics of uncertainty (red lines in Fig. 2) and surprise (blue lines in Fig. 2). After listening to each of these eight types of chord progressions, they assessed how they felt about creativity and beauty from the musical chords as well as valence and arousal, using the nine-point Likert scale [56]. The findings indicate that musical chord progressions characterized by the temporal dynamics of high uncertainty and surprise generated heightened feelings of creativity alongside increased arousal. However, the feelings of beauty and valence were more strongly influenced by the temporal dynamics of predictable, low-uncertainty progressions. These results suggest that the feelings of creativity may operate through a somewhat different cognitive mechanism than that of beauty and valence.

Such temporal dynamics evolve over a composer's lifetime, reflecting the progression of creative exploration. For example, an analysis of Beethoven's piano sonatas revealed a gradual increase in musical uncertainty over his lifetime [56]. This progression may suggest that Beethoven's evolving compositional style incorporated increasing levels of unpredictability, potentially as a means of sustaining novelty and complexity in his artwork. The temporal dynamics extend beyond individual lifetimes to influence musical creativity across historical eras. Using the HBSL model, fluctuations in uncertainty and prediction error were analyzed in a large corpus of jazz improvisations spanning 1925 to 2009 [58]. The results demonstrated distinct temporal characteristics in each era, indicating that the individuality of improvisational styles is shaped by epochal changes in musical creativity. These findings suggest that the brain's capacity for hierarchical statistical learning not only governs individual compositional styles but also underpins broader cultural and temporal shifts in music.

3.3 Embodied Cognition

The connection between bodily sensations and emotions can be better understood through the lens of the brain's predictive processing framework. The brain constructs emotions by minimizing the discrepancies between expected signals generated by its internal model and the sensory information received from exteroceptive, interoceptive, and proprioceptive sensations [59]. It has been proposed that interoception, or the perception of internal bodily states such as heart-beat acceleration, emerges from the ongoing refinement of these prediction errors [60–62]. For example, when a musical chord progression concludes abruptly with an unexpected modulation to a different key, this can result in a sudden increase in interoceptive prediction error, such as an accentuated heartbeat. This heightened prediction error may then be addressed by adjusting interoceptive priors, potentially facilitated through deep breathing.

By applying the bodily mapping assessment of emotion [63], the authors developed the new bodily mapping task [64] to investigate emotional responses and the distribution of subjective bodily sensations elicited by eight types of musical chords generated from the HBSL model [8] (Fig. 2). The results demonstrated that musical chords characterized by low uncertainty and high surprise elicited the positive valence, with sensations predominantly localized to the heart region on the bodily map. Furthermore, when a preceding sequence of chords induces prediction errors (i.e., low-probability chord sequences), the resulting pleasure diminished. In contrast, when the preceding sequences were easy to predict, it enhanced feelings of pleasure and beauty, along with interoceptive sensations related to the heart. Specific fluctuations in prediction and uncertainty may facilitate both interoceptive sensations linked to the heart and an enhanced musical emotion. Such embodied cognition may show individual difference depending on mental state and age [65, 66].

A recent study also explores the relationship between the experience of creativity and interoceptive bodily sensations, particularly in the heart and stomach regions [66]. The findings highlight the crucial role of heart-related sensations in fostering creative feelings (Fig. 2). This suggests the complex interplay between bodily sensations and feelings of creativity based on predictive processing. Further, using the same chord sequence that controls prediction error and uncertainty, a recent study involving participants aged 15 to over 80 investigated how bodily responses to music evolve over the human lifespan [66]. The findings indicate that heart and abdomen sensations peak around the age of 20, with a gradual decline and diffusion in older age groups. This may underscore the individual difference of embodied cognition of music based on developmental and age-related changes.

In summary, the embodied nature of musical cognition highlights the integral role of the body in shaping individual and creative experiences. By linking prediction errors to embodied cognition, music fosters a deep connection between cognitive processes and physical responses, enabling a richer understanding of creativity and individuality.

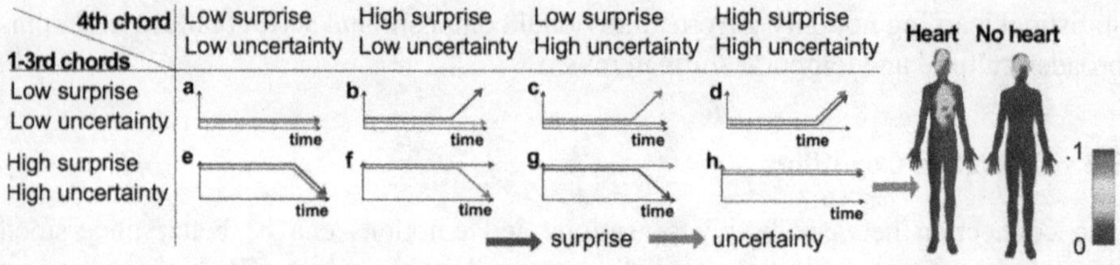

Fig. 2. Musical chord progressions with different surprise and uncertainty (left) and body map of the progression **h** in individuals with (Heart) vs. without (No heart) heart sensations (right). Reprinted from Daikoku et al., (2024) [56].

4 Summary

This paper sheds light on understanding how individuality and creativity emerge within the framework of the brain's statistical learning. Our findings suggest that musical experience is deeply embedded in predictive processing, where the brain continuously refines its internal model through musical exposure. This dynamic process facilitates not only perception and learning but also the emergence of creative expression and individuality.

One of the key insights is that hierarchical structures in music and language are fundamental to both cognitive organization and creative generation. Notably, our computational modeling demonstrated that hierarchical chunking occurs regardless of linguistic or cultural background, highlighting the universality of this process. The ability to extract and manipulate hierarchical structures allows for the flexible recombination of musical elements, a mechanism that underpins both improvisation and the evolution of musical styles. Moreover, our findings underscore the temporal dynamics of predictability in shaping musical experience. Creativity emerges not merely from static rule-based knowledge but through fluctuations in uncertainty and prediction errors over time. This perspective aligns with previous research indicating that composers progressively explore higher levels of unpredictability throughout their careers, fostering novel and expressive output [55]. The analysis of jazz improvisation and historical shifts in musical composition suggests that statistical learning operates at both individual and collective levels, driving stylistic evolution across time [56]. These insights contribute to a growing understanding of how predictive processing governs not only moment-to-moment musical perception but also long-term creative development. Furthermore, the role of embodied cognition in musical creativity was evident in our findings on interoceptive sensations [66]. These findings support the notion that musical creativity is not purely an abstract cognitive process but one that is grounded in the body's physiological and emotional states.

Taken together, our findings highlight the multifaceted nature of musical creativity, where hierarchical processing, temporal dynamics of predictability, and embodied cognition converge to shape individual and cultural expressions of music. The predictive brain not only perceives and interprets music but also actively generates new musical structures, driven by a balance of prediction error and uncertainty. This study provides a novel framework for understanding creativity as an emergent property of hierarchical statistical learning.

References

1. Cross, I.: Music, cognition, culture, and evolution. Ann. N. Y. Acad. Sci. **930**(1), 28–42 (2001)
2. Leman, M.: Embodied Music Cognition and Mediation Technology. MIT Press (2007)
3. Putkinen, V., et al.: Bodily maps of musical sensations across cultures. Proc. Natl. Acad. Sci. **121**(5), e2308859121 (2024)
4. Van Der Schyff, D., Schiavio, A., Walton, A., Velardo, V., Chemero, A.: Musical creativity and the embodied mind: exploring the possibilities of 4E cognition and dynamical systems theory. Music & science **1**, 2059204318792319 (2018)
5. Daikoku, T., Wiggins, G.A., Nagai, Y.: Statistical properties of musical creativity: roles of hierarchy and uncertainty in statistical learning. Front. Neurosci. **15**, 640412 (2021)
6. Zioga, I., Harrison, P.M., Pearce, M.T., Bhattacharya, J., Luft, C.D.B.: From learning to creativity: identifying the behavioural and neural correlates of learning to predict human judgements of musical creativity. Neuroimage **206**, 116311 (2020)
7. Daikoku, T.: Entropy, uncertainty, and the depth of implicit knowledge on musical creativity: computational study of improvisation in melody and rhythm. Front. Comput. Neurosci. **12**, 97 (2018)
8. Daikoku, T., Tanaka, M., Yamawaki, S.: Bodily maps of uncertainty and surprise in musical chord progression and the underlying emotional response. iScience **27**(4), 109498 (2024)
9. Saffran, J.R., Aslin, R.N., Newport, E.L.: Statistical learning by 8-month-old infants. Science **274**(5294), 1926–1928 (1996)
10. Teinonen, T., Fellman, V., Näätänen, R., Alku, P., Huotilainen, M.: Statistical language learning in neonates revealed by event-related brain potentials. BMC Neurosci. **10**, 1–8 (2009)
11. Siegelman, N., Bogaerts, L., Christiansen, M.H., Frost, R.: Towards a theory of individual differences in statistical learning. Philosophical Transactions of the Royal Society B: Biological Sciences **372**(1711), 20160059 (2017)
12. Kidd, E., Arciuli, J.: Individual differences in statistical learning predict children's comprehension of syntax. Child Dev. **87**(1), 184–193 (2016)
13. Misyak, J.B., Christiansen, M.H.: Statistical learning and language: an individual differences study. Lang. Learn. **62**(1), 302–331 (2012)
14. Daikoku, T.: Temporal dynamics of statistical learning in children's song contributes to phase entrainment and production of novel information in multiple cultures. Sci. Rep. **13**(1), 18041 (2023)
15. Daikoku, T., Kamermans, K., Minatoya, M.: Exploring cognitive individuality and the underlying creativity in statistical learning and phase entrainment. EXCLI J. **22**, 828 (2023)
16. Friston, K.: The free-energy principle: a unified brain theory? Nat. Rev. Neurosci. **11**(2), 127–138 (2010)
17. Friston, K.: A theory of cortical responses. Philosophical transactions of the Royal Society B: Biological sciences **360**(1456), 815–836 (2005)
18. Okano, T., Daikoku, T., Ugawa, Y., Kanai, K., Yumoto, M.: Perceptual uncertainty modulates auditory statistical learning: a magnetoencephalography study. Int. J. Psychophysiol. **168**, 65–71 (2021)
19. Daikoku, T., Yumoto, M.: Order of statistical learning depends on perceptive uncertainty. Current Research in Neurobiology **4**, 100080 (2023)
20. Daikoku, T., Yumoto, M.: Musical expertise facilitates statistical learning of rhythm and the perceptive uncertainty: a cross-cultural study. Neuropsychologia **146**, 107553 (2020)

21. Koelsch, S., Vuust, P., Friston, K.: Predictive processes and the peculiar case of music. Trends Cogn. Sci. **23**(1), 63–77 (2019)
22. Vuust, P., Heggli, O.A., Friston, K.J., Kringelbach, M.L.: Music in the brain. Nat. Rev. Neurosci. **23**(5), 287–305 (2022)
23. Daikoku, T., Yatomi, Y., Yumoto, M.: Statistical learning of music-and language-like sequences and tolerance for spectral shifts. Neurobiol. Learn. Mem. **118**, 8–19 (2015)
24. Daikoku, T., Yatomi, Y., Yumoto, M.: Pitch-class distribution modulates the statistical learning of atonal chord sequences. Brain Cogn. **108**, 1–10 (2016)
25. Pearce, M.T., Ruiz, M.H., Kapasi, S., Wiggins, G.A., Bhattacharya, J.: Unsupervised statistical learning underpins computational, behavioural, and neural manifestations of musical expectation. Neuroimage **50**(1), 302–313 (2010)
26. Pearce, M.T., Wiggins, G.A.: Auditory expectation: the information dynamics of music perception and cognition. Top. Cogn. Sci. **4**(4), 625–652 (2012)
27. Daikoku, T., et al.: Neural correlates of statistical learning in developmental dyslexia: an electroencephalography study. Biol. Psychol. **181**, 108592 (2023)
28. Daikoku, T.: Neurophysiological markers of statistical learning in music and language: hierarchy, entropy and uncertainty. Brain Sci. **8**(6), 114 (2018)
29. Witek, M.A., Clarke, E.F., Wallentin, M., Kringelbach, M.L., Vuust, P.: Syncopation, body-movement and pleasure in groove music. PLoS ONE **9**(4), e94446 (2014)
30. Matthews, T.E., Witek, M.A., Lund, T., Vuust, P., Penhune, V.B.: The sensation of groove engages motor and reward networks. Neuroimage **214**, 116768 (2020)
31. Cheung, V.K., Harrison, P.M., Meyer, L., Pearce, M.T., Haynes, J.D., Koelsch, S.: Uncertainty and surprise jointly predict musical pleasure and amygdala, hippocampus, and auditory cortex activity. Curr. Biol. **29**(23), 4084–4092 (2019)
32. Patel, A.D.: Language, music, syntax and the brain. Nat. Neurosci. **6**(7), 674–681 (2003)
33. Lerdahl, F., Jackendoff, R.: An overview of hierarchical structure in music. Music. Percept. **1**(2), 229–252 (1983)
34. Goswami, U.: A neural basis for phonological awareness? An oscillatory temporal-sampling perspective. Curr. Dir. Psychol. Sci. **27**(1), 56–63 (2018)
35. Leong, V., Goswami, U.: Acoustic-emergent phonology in the amplitude envelope of child-directed speech. PLoS ONE **10**(12), e0144411 (2015)
36. Daikoku, T., Goswami, U.: Hierarchical amplitude modulation structures and rhythm patterns: comparing Western musical genres, song, and nature sounds to Babytalk. PLoS ONE **17**(10), e0275631 (2022)
37. Daikoku, T., Kumagaya, S., Ayaya, S., Nagai, Y.: Non-autistic persons modulate their speech rhythm while talking to autistic individuals. PLoS ONE **18**(9), e0285591 (2023)
38. Daikoku, T., Goswami, U.: The Amplitude Modulation Structure of Japanese Infant- and Child-Directed Speech: Longitudinal Data Reveal Universal Acoustic Physical Structures Underpinning Moraic Timing. arXiv preprint arXiv: arXiv preprint arXiv:2503.05645 (2025)
39. Pérez-Navarro, J., Lallier, M., Clark, C., Flanagan, S., Goswami, U.: Local temporal regularities in child-directed speech in Spanish. J. Speech Lang. Hear. Res. **65**(10), 3776–3788 (2022)
40. Araújo, J., Flanagan, S., Castro-Caldas, A., Goswami, U.: The temporal modulation structure of illiterate versus literate adult speech. PLoS ONE **13**, e0205224 (2018)
41. Daikoku, T., Lee, C., Goswami, U.: Amplitude modulation structure in French and German poetry: universal acoustic physical structures underpin different poetic rhythm structures. Royal Society Open Science **11**(9), 232005 (2024)
42. Gross, J., et al.: Speech rhythms and multiplexed oscillatory sensory coding in the human brain. PLOS Biol. **11**, e1001752 (2013)
43. Poeppel, D., Assaneo, M.F.: Speech rhythms and their neural foundations. Nat. Rev. Neurosci. **21**(6), 322–334 (2020)

44. Attaheri, A., et al.: Delta-and theta-band cortical tracking and phase-amplitude coupling to sung speech by infants. Neuroimage **247**, 118698 (2022)
45. Ding, N., Melloni, L., Zhang, H., Tian, X., Poeppel, D.: Cortical tracking of hierarchical linguistic structures in connected speech. Nat. Neurosci. **19**(1), 158–164 (2016)
46. Baltzell, L.S., Srinivasan, R., Richards, V.: Hierarchical organization of melodic sequences is encoded by cortical entrainment. Neuroimage **200**, 490–500 (2019)
47. Smalle, E.H., Daikoku, T., Szmalec, A., Duyck, W., Mottonen, R.: Unlocking adults' implicit statistical learning by cognitive depletion. Proc. Natl. Acad. Sci. **119**(2), e2026011119 (2022)
48. Ringer, H., Sammler, D., Daikoku, T.: Neural tracking of auditory statistical regularities is reduced in adults with dyslexia. Cerabral Cortex **35**(2), bhaf042 (2025)
49. Leong, V., Kalashnikova, M., Burnham, D., Goswami, U.: The temporal modulation structure of infant-directed speech. Open Mind **1**(2), 78–90 (2017)
50. Daikoku, T.: Musical creativity and depth of implicit knowledge: spectral and temporal individualities in improvisation. Front. Comput. Neurosci. **12**, 89 (2018)
51. Pellicano, E., Burr, D.: When the world becomes 'too real': a Bayesian explanation of autistic perception. Trends Cogn. Sci. **16**, 504–510 (2012)
52. Lawson, R.P., Rees, G., Friston, K.J.: An aberrant precision account of autism. Front. Hum. Neurosci. **8**, 302 (2014)
53. Philippsen, A., Tsuji, S., Nagai, Y.: Simulating developmental and individual differences of drawing behavior in children using a predictive coding model. Front. Neurorobot. **16**, 856184 (2022)
54. Abdallah, S., Plumbley, M.: Information dynamics: patterns of expectation and surprise in the perception of music. Connect. Sci. **21**(2–3), 89–117 (2009)
55. Burgoyne, J.A., Wild, J., Fujinaga, I.: An expert ground truth set for audio chord recognition and music analysis. In ISMIR **11**, 633–638 (2011)
56. Daikoku, T., Tanaka, M.: Body Maps for Feeling of Creativity in Musical Chord Progression. arXiv preprint arXiv:2410.11885 (2024)
57. Daikoku, T.: Depth and the uncertainty of statistical knowledge on musical creativity fluctuate over a composer's lifetime. Front. Comput. Neurosci. **13**, 27 (2019)
58. Daikoku, T.: Temporal dynamics of uncertainty and prediction error in musical improvisation across different periods. Sci. Rep. **14**(1), 22297 (2024)
59. Seth, A.K.: Interoceptive inference, emotion, and the embodied self. Trends Cogn. Sci. **17**(11), 565–573 (2013)
60. Barrett, L.F., Simmons, W.K.: Interoceptive predictions in the brain. Nat. Rev. Neurosci. **16**(7), 419–429 (2015)
61. Khalsa, S.S., Craske, M.G., Li, W., Vangala, S., Strober, M., Feusner, J.D.: Altered interoceptive awareness in anorexia nervosa: Effects of meal anticipation, consumption and bodily arousal. Int. J. Eat. Disord. **48**(7), 889–897 (2015)
62. Ainley, V., Apps, M.A., Fotopoulou, A., Tsakiris, M.: Bodily precision': a predictive coding account of individual differences in interoceptive accuracy. Philosophical Transactions of the Royal Society B: Biological Sciences **371**(1708), 20160003 (2016)
63. Nummenmaa, L., Glerean, E., Hari, R., Hietanen, J.K.: Bodily maps of emotions. Proc. Natl. Acad. Sci. **111**(2), 646–651 (2014)
64. Daikoku, T., Tanaka, M.: Protocol to visualize a bodily map of musical uncertainty and prediction. STAR protocols **5**(4), 103473 (2024)
65. Tanaka, M., Daikoku, T.: Music-related Bodily Sensation Map in Individuals with Depressive Tendencies. bioRxiv, 2024.06. 14.599050 (2024). doi.org/https://doi.org/10.1101/2024.06.14.599050

66. Tanaka, M., Daikoku, T.: Lifetime changes in Body map based on music prediction, b bioRxiv 2025.02.02.636100 (2025). https://doi.org/10.1101/2025.02.02.636100
67. Daikoku, T.: Prediction, perception, and generation of rhythm and structure in sound sequences. Journal of the Acoustical Society of Japan **80**(1), 18–24 (2023)

Multimodal Hand Tracking for XR Musical Instruments Using Electromyography

Max Graf[1(✉)] and Mathieu Barthet[1,2]

[1] School of Electronic Engineering and Computer Science, Queen Mary University of London, London, UK
{max.graf,m.barthet}@qmul.ac.uk
[2] Aix-Marseille University CNRS PRISM, Marseille, France

Abstract. Hand tracking is a critical component of natural user interactions in extended reality (XR) environments, including extended reality musical instruments (XRMIs). However, self-occlusion remains a significant challenge for vision-based hand tracking systems, leading to inaccurate results and degraded user experiences. In this paper, we propose a multimodal hand tracking system that combines vision-based hand tracking with surface electromyography (sEMG) data for finger joint angle estimation. We validate the effectiveness of our system through a series of hand pose tasks designed to cover a wide range of gestures, including those prone to self-occlusion. By comparing the performance of our multimodal system to a baseline vision-based tracking method, we demonstrate that our multimodal approach significantly improves tracking accuracy for several finger joints prone to self-occlusion. These findings suggest that our system has the potential to enhance XR experiences by providing more accurate and robust hand tracking, especially in the presence of self-occlusion.

Keywords: extended reality · surface electromyography · hand tracking · deep learning · extended reality musical instruments

1 Introduction

Extended reality (XR) is an umbrella term encompassing virtual, augmented, and mixed reality (VR/AR/MR). In recent years, the increased popularity of XR technology has led to the establishment of extended reality musical instruments (*XRMIs*) as a research field [32]. Milgram et al. described the reality-virtuality continuum [27], along which digital applications can be placed. It stretches from real-world environments to fully virtual environments. Head-mounted XR devices bridge this continuum. They are capable of rendering three-dimensional imagery onto screens, removing the necessity for separate monitors or mobile displays, blending the real and virtual worlds together. The rapid development of XR technologies has opened up new possibilities for musical creation,

S. Ystad et al. (Eds.): CMMR 2023, LNCS 15236, pp. 15–39, 2026.
https://doi.org/10.1007/978-3-032-02042-0_2

performance, and interaction, with the emergence of various XR-based musical instruments and applications. Many XRMIs follow an embodied interaction paradigm. These instruments offer novel opportunities for artists to experiment with embodied interaction techniques, spatial sound design, and immersive performances, thus expanding the boundaries of traditional music making. XRMIs fall within the larger category of digital musical instruments (DMIs). [37] suggest that the control of DMIs can be made intimate (personal and familiar) by using appropriate control metaphors, low-latency action-to-sound, and continuous gesture recognition. This study is part of a larger project that aims to support control intimacy in XRMIs.

Based on the current state of XR technology and prior work in XRMIs [3,13,14], we highlight that gesture sensing errors on XR devices are a bottleneck for intimate musical control. Head-mounted XR devices (HMDs) rely on a set of sensors to record data and provide embodied control interfaces for users, e.g., head-tracking, hand tracking, and body pose detection. The transduction of these real-world sensor data to digital representations depends on computational methods. In this work, we focus on the problem of hand tracking, more specifically, accurate tracking of finger joints. Hand-tracking algorithms often use visual information from camera sensors in conjunction with machine learning techniques, for example, on the Meta Quest 2 device [16]. The accuracy of vision-based hand-tracking algorithms may be high [36], but current recognition rates do not reach 100%. Self-occlusion—the occlusion of finger joints by other parts of the hand—as well as challenging lighting situations, lead to failure cases in vision-based tracking systems. Such error cases may produce instances of jitter, tracking loss, or glitches in the virtual representation of the hands, which can have detrimental effects on the usability and user experience in XRMIs, as shown in a previous study [14].

This work aims to address such sensing-related issues through the use of surface electromyography (sEMG) sensors. EMG sensors measure the electrical potential produced during muscle contractions in the body. Surface electromyograms can be obtained through electrodes that are placed on the surface of the skin, above muscle tissue regions. We present an investigation of the potential of sEMG sensors and deep learning models to enhance hand-tracking accuracy in XRMIs. Our approach combines sEMG data and vision-based tracking methods to address sensing-related issues commonly encountered in XRMI performance. Thereby, we aim to improve the tracking accuracy and responsiveness of XR musical instruments, especially in situations where vision-based tracking falls short. Our contributions include:

1. Prototyping a deep learning model for real-time sEMG-based estimation of finger joint angles.
2. Multimodal hand tracking: development of a combined hand tracking approach that integrates sEMG data with vision-based tracking methods to address occlusion-related challenges in XRMIs.
3. Evaluation of the proposed multimodal system through an experimental comparison with traditional vision-based hand tracking methods.

We share our training data and code[1], fostering further research and innovation in the domain of sEMG-based neural interfaces.

The scope of this paper is limited to the exploration of sEMG and deep learning techniques for hand-tracking in XR musical instruments. Although our findings may have broader applications in other areas of XR interaction, the primary focus is on improving XRMI design and user experience. Through our work, we aim to contribute to the ongoing development of more accurate, intuitive, and expressive extended reality musical instruments.

2 Background

2.1 XR Musical Instruments

The development of XRMIs has attracted growing interest as VR, AR, and MR technologies continue to advance. Early studies in this domain focused on the design and evaluation of virtual interfaces for musical performance and interaction [12,25,28,32]. Several works investigated user experience [6,10,13], interaction techniques [2] and collaborative music making [15,26]. More recent studies have explored the creation of novel instruments and control schemes [3,4,6,14]. While there is no gold standard for XRMI design, many XRMIs rely on hand-tracking to facilitate embodied interaction with the instrument [4,12,14,28]. Various vision-based tracking methods are employed, including depth-sensing cameras [4,12,28], and machine learning-based approaches [16]. Despite the progress in hand tracking research, limitations such as occlusion, lighting issues, and computational complexity continue to pose challenges for hand-controlled XRMI applications.

2.2 Surface Electromyography

Surface electromyography is the method and process of recording electrical signals generated by muscle fibres during contraction via electrodes placed on the skin surface. Each muscle fibre's membrane potential fluctuates when that fibre is activated by the nervous system, and the aggregated signals from multiple fibres can be measured and digitised for analysis. In contrast to intramuscular EMG, which uses fine-wire or needle electrodes inserted directly into the muscle, sEMG is non-invasive and relatively easy to set up for research and interactive projects [9]. Its suitability for daily-wear scenarios and minimal discomfort make sEMG an appealing method for real-time gesture recognition in extended reality (XR) and new musical interfaces.

Typically, sEMG signals are in the range of a few hundred microvolts up to multiple millivolts. The raw signal must be amplified, filtered, and digitised (often at sampling rates of 500–2000 Hz in medical/lab setups, or around 50–200 Hz in consumer devices) [11,30]. Various processing steps—including rectification, smoothing, and feature extraction—are then applied, as described in later sections of this paper.

[1] https://github.com/maxgraf96/sEMG-myo-unity.

Because sEMG electrodes measure voltage differences on the skin, accurate placement is essential to pick up strong signals from the target muscles while minimising noise or crosstalk from adjacent muscles. Laboratory setups frequently use multiple electrode sites along the muscle belly, along with reference electrodes on bony landmarks or electrically neutral sites [17]. Crosstalk, which is the unintended contamination of one muscle group's signals by neighbouring muscles, is a known challenge in sEMG-based interfaces. Strategies such as precise electrode placement, high-density electrode arrays, and advanced signal processing can mitigate crosstalk [34]. Nonetheless, for wearable consumer devices that fix electrodes in a single circumference, it is often assumed that signals inevitably contain a mixture of muscle sources.

2.3 Hand Tracking Using Deep Learning with sEMG Data

Several studies have explored the use of sEMG data and deep learning architectures for hand gesture recognition [1,22–24] and prosthetics control [5,8,29,33]. These works have reported promising results, highlighting the potential of employing sEMG and deep learning models for precise finger movement estimation. However, some of these works depend on complex tracking setups [1] or leverage low-resolution tracking data for training [22].

A notable limitation of these studies is the lack of shared training data and code, hindering the reproducibility and comparability of the results across different research efforts. Several datasets on the topic of finger joint angle estimation through sEMG data have been published. However, they either require specialised sEMG measuring equipment [19–21,31], making the reproduction of results an expensive endeavour, or introduce temporal biases into the dataset due to lack of synchronisation during the recording procedure [18]. The absence of implementation details ([1,23,24]) makes it difficult for other researchers to build upon these works, potentially slowing down the progress in the field.

Here, we build on these findings by exploring the potential of combining sEMG data from a consumer-grade sEMG device with real-time vision-based tracking on a head-mounted XR device. This multimodal approach leverages the strengths of each sensor—local muscular activation plus external camera-based tracking—to deliver more reliable hand pose estimation for XR musical instruments.

3 Data Collection and Analysis

We have developed a software pipeline for data collection, feature extraction and modelling of sEMG data. We focus on eight finger joints that are prone to self-occlusion: the metacarpophalangeal (MCP) and proximal interphalangeal (PIP) joints of the index, middle, ring and pinky fingers. Specifically, we aim to model the rotations of the finger bones connected to these joints relative to the hand. Distal interphalangeal (DIP) joints are excluded from our investigation here, since they can be inferred from other joints, specifically the respective PIP

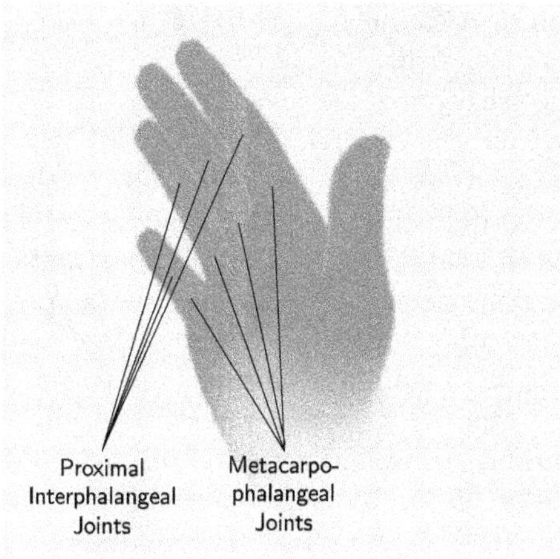

Fig. 1. The metacarpophalangeal (MCP) and proximal interphalangeal (PIP) joints of the right hand.

joints, with high accuracy [7]. The thumb is excluded from our investigation. Modelling thumb rotations with sEMG data is a hard problem, since the majority of muscles related to thumb movements are located in the hand, rather than the forearm. With that in mind, the goal of the model is to estimate the eight finger joint angles from a window of sEMG data. We now describe the nature of the data, our collection and feature extraction process, and the model architecture (Fig. 1).

We collect surface EMG signal measurements using the Thalmic Labs Myo armband and vision-based hand tracking data from the Meta Quest 2 XR headset. Both devices are employed simultaneously to capture the muscle activity and finger joint rotations, respectively. This approach allows users to capture data without the need for external tracking devices.

The Myo armband uses eight dry electrodes arranged around the forearm to capture sEMG signals generated by underlying muscle contractions. Each electrode measures the differential voltage between its location and an adjacent reference, sampling EMG signals at 50–200 Hz. The Myo's onboard firmware can apply hardware filtering to attenuate motion artifacts and powerline noise, followed by software rectification and smoothing to produce envelope signals reflecting muscle activation levels. These processed signals are streamed at 50 Hz via Bluetooth Low Energy. We obtain those filtered and rectified signals using the *PyoMyo* Python framework [35].

The Meta Quest 2 XR headset is equipped with four monochrome cameras that provide a wide field of view, enabling it to capture hand positions and movements. The built-in hand tracking algorithm [16] processes the camera data and estimates the 3D rotations of the user's hand joints in real time. In our system, we sample the hand joint rotations from the XR device at 50 Hz and synchronise them with the sEMG data from the Myo armband by aligning Unix timestamps from both devices during recording, with post-hoc interpolation to compensate for minor clock drift.

One researcher recorded hand gestures and movements in a controlled environment, with a focus on gestures relevant to XRMI interaction. This investigation should be seen as a proof-of-concept for our methodology. As such, the current work focused on data from the right hand only. The gestures included various finger flexions and extensions, as well as combinations of multiple finger movements. They were performed at different speeds, forces, and orientations. We conducted five data collection sessions across three days to account for the natural variability in sEMG readings, ensuring a more robust dataset. During the data collection process, the XR headset was strategically positioned in diverse locations and orientations to minimise self-occlusion of the hand. Data collection sessions lasted between ten and fifteen minutes, resulting in a substantial amount of synchronised sEMG and hand tracking data.

3.1 EMG Data Analysis

Table 1 shows summary statistics for all eight EMG channels, computed over a total of 93 251 frames in the dataset. Each channel contains rectified and smoothed sEMG values recorded at a sampling frequency of 50 Hz.

Table 1. Basic descriptive statistics for each EMG channel.

	Ch 1	Ch 2	Ch 3	Ch 4	Ch 5	Ch 6	Ch 7	Ch 8
Count	93251	93251	93251	93251	93251	93251	93251	93251
Mean	173.47	248.01	555.15	209.29	86.37	144.11	178.95	148.91
Std	194.59	142.51	301.19	143.02	50.36	90.05	138.03	98.95
Min	20	28	30	23	19	20	17	18
25%	71	152	307	101	51	76	78	84
50%	107	217	577	176	72	127	137	126
75%	176	313	781	278	105	190	236	185
Max	1533	1526	1492	1124	482	1336	1162	1220

All channels exhibit the same total sample count, showing consistent data capture across the dataset with no faulty data. The mean values differ notably by channel (ranging from around 86 for Channel 5 up to over 555 for Channel 3), likely corresponding to variations in forearm muscle activation patterns and electrode placement. Standard deviations (*std*) also vary, with Channel 3 showing the largest spread (301.19), suggesting that this channel captures a particularly wide range of muscle activity levels. Minimum and maximum values offer insight into the amplitude range of the smoothed EMG signals. Channel 1, for example, extends up to 1533, whereas Channel 5 peaks at 482. This discrepancy indicates

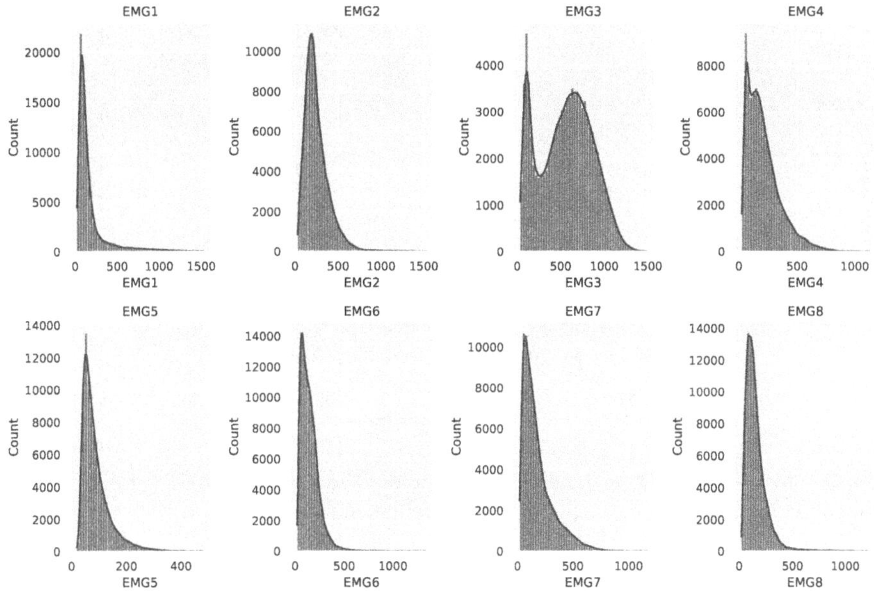

Fig. 2. Histogram and KDE distributions for each EMG channel.

that certain sensor locations (or muscle groups) may be more prone to higher activity levels.

These basic statistics indicate that the eight EMG channels do not capture identical distributions of signals: some channels exhibit consistently higher magnitudes (e.g., Channel 3), whereas others remain lower on average (e.g., Channel 5). Such channel-specific variability underscores the importance of feature extraction strategies when modelling and interpreting sEMG data for downstream tasks.

Distribution of EMG Channels. Figure 2 presents histograms overlaid with kernel density estimates (KDE) for each of the eight EMG channels. Horizontal subplot axes indicates EMG signal amplitudes (after rectification and smoothing), and the vertical axis shows the number of samples (i.e. occurrences) at each amplitude level. All eight channels exhibit highly right-skewed distributions, with a large proportion of samples clustering near the lower-amplitude end (near 0–200) and a long tail extending towards higher values. This pattern aligns with typical sEMG activity, in which muscle activity is predominantly low, with occasional spikes in amplitude when there are salient muscle movements.

Time Series Visualisation of EMG Channels. Figure 3 shows a time series plot of all eight EMG channels over the first 500 samples in our dataset, corresponding to 10 s of data (given a 50 Hz sampling rate). Each curve represents one EMG channel, enabling a direct comparison of their amplitude fluctuations

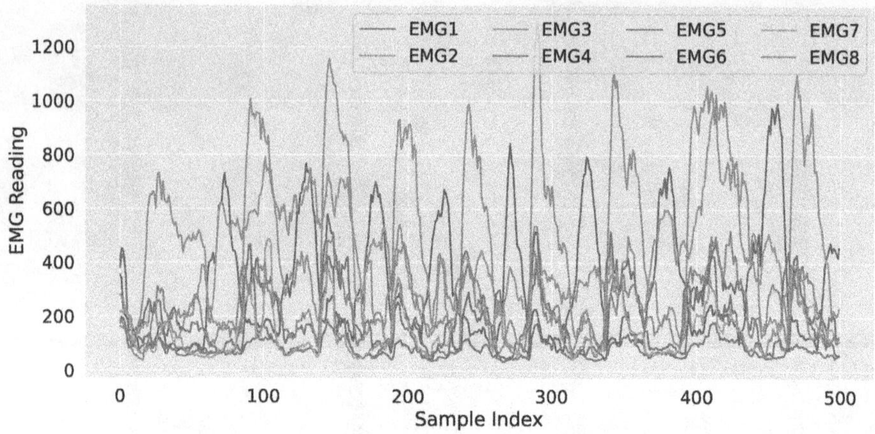

Fig. 3. EMG Channels over the first 500 samples (10 s). Each channel exhibits distinct amplitude modulations corresponding to different muscle activations.

over time. A few notable features stand out. Channel 3 (green) consistently reaches the highest peaks, at times exceeding 1000 in amplitude. Channel 1 (blue) and Channel 2 (orange) also show substantial bursts, though at slightly lower levels. This aligns with the previous histogram findings, where Channel 3 had a broad amplitude range and frequent high-intensity values. Several channels exhibit rapid spikes that quickly return to lower levels (e.g. Channel 3 around sample indices 100 and 200). Others, such as Channel 2, show broader plateaus of elevated activity, potentially reflecting sustained muscle contractions. Channels 4 and 5 (red and purple) remain relatively low for most of the plotted window, indicating that these sensor positions may capture moderate baseline activity, with fewer high-intensity bursts.

The time series plot highlights that muscle activation occurs intermittently rather than uniformly, giving rise to dynamic, channel-specific patterns of amplitude. Such periodic peaks are consistent with finger flexion/extension cycles during brief gestures. In subsequent analysis, correlating these amplitude patterns with finger joint angles will shed light on how each channel corresponds to particular types of hand movements.

Correlation Matrix of EMG Channels. Finally, Fig. 4 shows the pairwise correlation coefficients between the eight EMG channels, visualised as a heatmap. Each cell corresponds to the Pearson correlation coefficient between two channels, ranging from -1 (perfectly negative linear relationship) to 1 (perfectly positive). In terms of channel pairings, Channel 1 and 8 share a correlation of approximately 0.60, representing the highest overlap involving Channel 1 and suggesting that these two channels detect partially shared muscle activity. Channel 3, Channel 4, and Channel 5 form a group of moderate-to-strong correlations (0.61–0.78), implying that these electrodes capture signals from closely related muscle

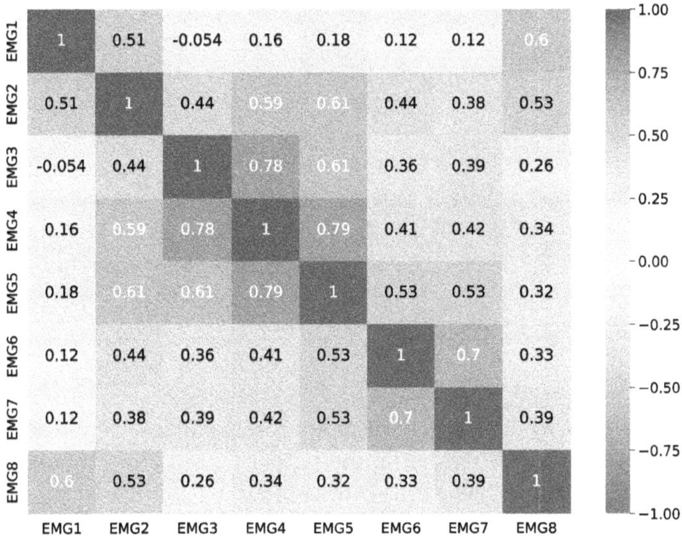

Fig. 4. Correlation matrix of EMG channels. Red indicates stronger positive correlation, whereas blue indicates negative correlation. (Color figure online)

regions or that they are often co-activated during common gestures. Channel 2 correlates moderately with Channel 4 and Channel 5 (0.59–0.61) but exhibits a weaker correlation (0.44) with Channel 3, while Channel 1 and Channel 3 show a near-zero value (−0.054) that suggests these channels measure different aspects of the forearm's muscle contractions. Channel 6 and Channel 7 display a higher correlation (0.70) compared to other channel pairs, indicating that they often track concurrent muscle activity. Overall, negative correlations are not prevalent, although Channel 1 and Channel 3 hint at a slightly inverse pattern. Certain channels form loosely defined clusters of higher correlation, while a few others remain partially independent. This pattern confirms that some channel pairs capture overlapping muscle groups, whereas others provide complementary information for downstream tasks.

3.2 Finger Joint Angle Data Analysis

To assess the typical rotation ranges and overall variability in the finger joints, we computed descriptive statistics for the eight angles tracked by the XR headset (MCP and PIP joints of the index, middle, ring, and pinky fingers). Table 2 presents the results, based on 93 251 samples.

The mean angles vary substantially across joints, with the *Index PIP* and *Ring PIP* averaging above 40°, whereas the *Pinky MCP* remains closer to 10°. Standard deviations also differ markedly; for example, *Index PIP* and *Middle PIP* each exceed 29° and 31°, respectively, pointing to broader ranges of flexion and extension in those joints. Negative minimum values (e.g. −13.36° for Index

Table 2. Descriptive statistics for the eight finger joint angles (in degrees).

	Index MCP	Index PIP	Middle MCP	Middle PIP	Ring MCP	Ring PIP	Pinky MCP	Pinky PIP
Count	93251	93251	93251	93251	93251	93251	93251	93251
Mean	28.32	40.06	35.83	41.83	33.93	43.16	10.92	29.26
Std	20.45	29.19	24.59	31.03	27.37	30.09	28.45	26.62
Min	−13.36	0.49	−8.54	−0.31	−10.16	1.77	−27.76	−1.33
25%	12.68	20.46	15.54	19.21	11.91	20.37	−10.53	13.61
50%	24.47	29.72	30.52	26.87	25.11	28.74	1.95	17.95
75%	41.30	45.88	54.53	66.98	54.27	66.20	25.93	30.09
Max	84.11	109.98	89.33	107.64	95.04	108.64	98.14	106.61

MCP or −27.76° for Pinky MCP) reflect specific postures or mild misalignment in joint angle estimation when the finger is hyperextended or at rest. The *25%* and *75%* quartiles reveal that many joints remain within moderate ranges (e.g., around 20° to 45° for most PIP joints), while maximum angles can extend above 100°, indicating occasionally deep finger flexions in the dataset. The variability shows the diversity of hand poses captured, ranging from relaxed half-bends to near-complete fist closures.

Distribution of Finger Joint Angles. To gain further insight into the typical ranges and shapes of each finger joint angle, we plotted histograms with overlaid KDEs for all eight joints. Figure 5 shows the distributions for the MCP and PIP joints of the index, middle, ring, and pinky fingers. Across all joints, we observe that lower angles (near 0° to 30°) generally dominate the distribution, consistent with a neutral or slightly flexed resting posture. The peak near 0° appears most pronounced for the MCP joints (e.g., *Pinky MCP*), suggesting that these joints remain near extension in a substantial number of samples. Meanwhile, joints such as *Index PIP* and *Ring PIP* exhibit secondary peaks above 50°, indicating more frequent deep flexions in these fingers. Several distributions reveal minor bumps or shoulders at intermediate angles (e.g., around 20° to 40° in the *Middle MCP*), suggesting transitions between different postural states. The PIP joints, in particular, often show a broader spread, extending up to or beyond 100°, consistent with the higher maximum values reported in the descriptive statistics. These histograms reinforce the idea that our dataset encompasses a wide range of finger postures, from near-extended (close to 0°) to deeply flexed (above 100°). The presence of pronounced sub-peaks shows that certain gestures or hand configurations are repeated often, while the long tails at higher angles underscore the occasional extremes of finger flexion.

Time Series of Finger Joint Angles (First 500 Samples). To observe the temporal evolution of each finger joint, we plotted the first 500 samples (10 s at 50 Hz) of the dataset for all eight joint angles (Fig. 6). Each curve corresponds to one joint, enabling a direct comparison of flexion and extension over time. A few

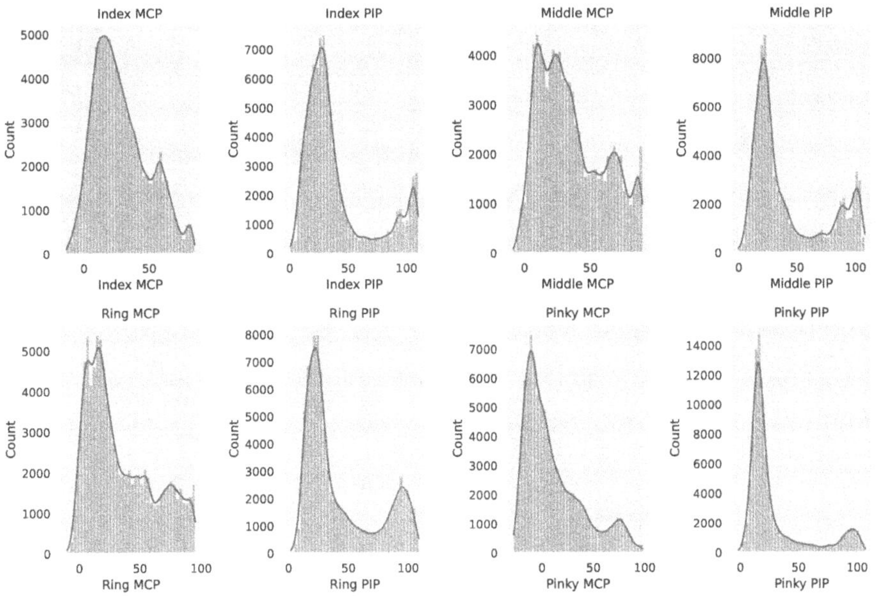

Fig. 5. Histogram and KDE distributions for the eight finger joints.

notable patterns emerge. First, the *PIP* joints clearly demonstrate the broadest swings, at times exceeding 100°, whereas the *MCP* joints vary more moderately. These differences among the MCP and PIP joints reflect the fact that the PIP joints often undergo more pronounced bending in typical hand motions. Second, the joint angles often rise and fall synchronously (e.g. around sample indices 75, 175, 275, etc.), illustrating the recorded gesture (flexion and extension of all fingers). The peaks near 100° indicate strongly flexed positions, whereas dips below 0° (e.g. near -10°) imply mild hyperextension or potentially minor sensor misalignment when the finger is extended.

Pairwise Correlation Among Finger Joint Angles. We next examined the linear relationships between all pairs of finger joints by computing the Pearson correlation coefficients (Fig. 7). Each cell in the heatmap represents the correlation between two joints, with values ranging from -1 to $+1$. Several trends emerge from the matrix. First, MCP and PIP joints in the same finger (e.g. *Index MCP* vs. *Index PIP*) are moderately to strongly correlated, consistent with their physical interdependence: when a finger flexes at the MCP, the PIP often flexes in tandem. By contrast, certain cross-finger relationships, such as *Index PIP* with *Ring MCP*, remain notably weaker, reflecting more independent motion across different digits.

More strikingly, *Middle MCP*, *Ring MCP*, and *Pinky MCP* form a relatively tight cluster (correlations around 0.75–0.80), suggesting that these metacarpophalangeal joints frequently move together—likely due to anatomical coupling

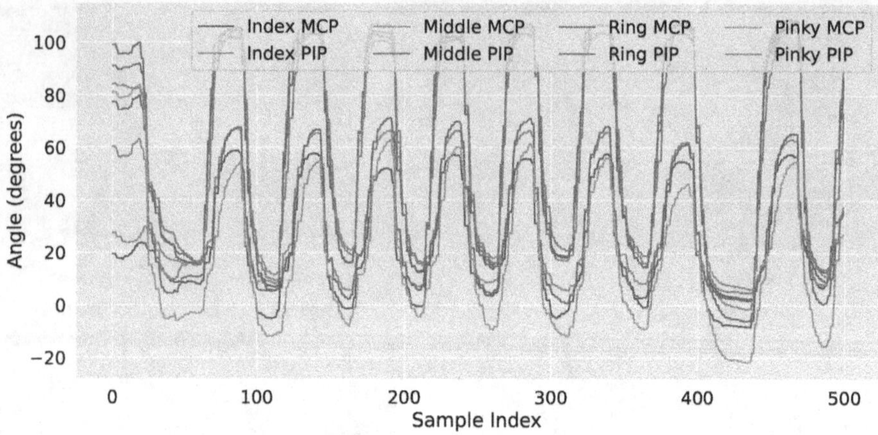

Fig. 6. Finger joint angles over the first 500 samples (10 s).

or common motion patterns in multi-finger gestures. Similarly, *Ring PIP* exhibits high correlations (above 0.7) with both *Middle MCP* and *Pinky MCP*, further demonstrating how the ring finger's proximal joints often flex in sync with its neighbouring digits. Meanwhile, smaller positive correlations (0.2–0.4) between *Index MCP* and pinky joints illustrate the relative independence of the index and pinky fingers.

These pairwise correlations confirm substantial co-activation among digits, especially within adjacent fingers and between MCP–PIP pairs on the same finger. Patterns where certain joints' movements partially constrain others are interesting to observe and can be advantageous for modelling, as consistent co-movement can help our models to learn anatomical constraints from the data.

3.3 Feature Extraction

Figure 8 illustrates the data flow in our pipeline. We employ methods described in the literature to inform our selection of features for each *2D window* of sEMG samples, where each window contains N time steps across C sEMG channels. Each windowed data segment is preprocessed to produce a feature vector for the subsequent modelling stages.

Time-Domain Features. For each channel, we compute:

$$\mathrm{MAV} = \frac{1}{N}\sum_{t=1}^{N}|x_t|, \quad \mathrm{RMS} = \sqrt{\frac{1}{N}\sum_{t=1}^{N}(x_t)^2}, \quad \mathrm{VAR} = \frac{1}{N-1}\sum_{t=1}^{N}(x_t - \bar{x})^2.$$

where the mean absolute value (MAV) is the average rectified amplitude, root mean square (RMS) emphasises higher-intensity contractions, and the variance (VAR) measures signal spread over the window.

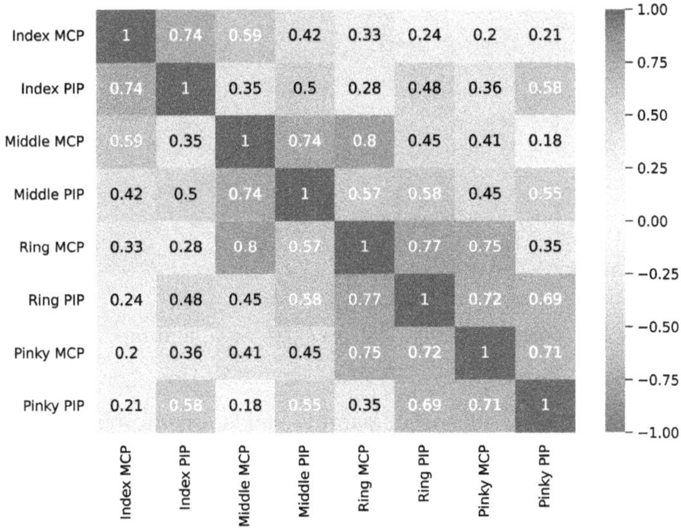

Fig. 7. Correlation matrix of finger joint angles. Warmer tones indicate stronger positive correlations, while cooler tones would indicate negative correlations.

Frequency-Domain Features. Following approaches in sEMG pattern recognition, we also estimate:

1. *Median Frequency (MDF)* and *Mean Frequency (MNF)*: derived via power spectral density (PSD) analysis, using Welch's method to compute PSD over the window. The MDF is identified as the frequency bin dividing the total spectral power in half, while the MNF is a weighted average of the PSD frequencies.
2. *Peak Frequency (PF)*: the frequency bin exhibiting the largest magnitude in the PSD, indicating the dominant oscillatory component in the signal.

Wavelet Coefficients. Finally, we capture a multi-resolution representation of the windowed sEMG signal via a discrete wavelet transform (DWT). As inspired by [1], the pipeline applies a level-4 *db2* wavelet decomposition (see wavelet online documentation) to each channel, concatenating the approximation (cA) and detail (cD) coefficients. Wavelet analysis allows us to capture localised variations in amplitude across multiple timescales.

We concatenate the above features row-wise for each channel into a single 2D array. Specifically, each row corresponds to either

- one of the time-domain or frequency-domain metrics (MAV, RMS, VAR, MDF, MNF, PF),
- a collection of wavelet coefficients,
- the last $\hat{N}$ samples of the filtered EMG signal, preserving the most recent, original time series,
- optionally, wrist angles, appended for context.

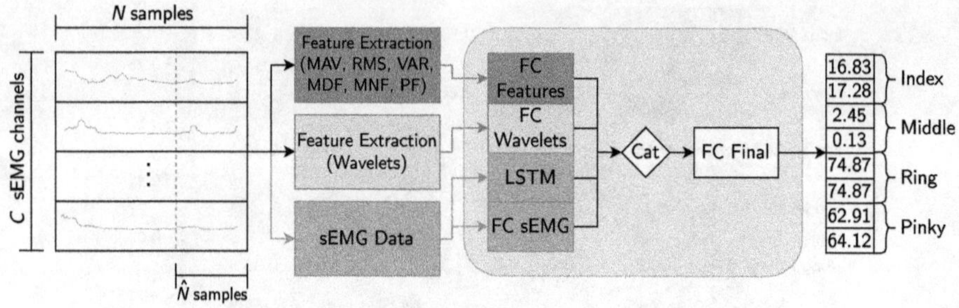

Fig. 8. Data preprocessing, feature extraction, and model pipeline

By stacking these components, each sample yields a comprehensive representation of the underlying muscle activity. Each sample is then stored, along with the associated finger joint angle labels, for use in training and validation.

This combined feature representation aims to capture essential information at multiple scales: local bursts of muscle activation (time-domain metrics), global frequency content (MDF, MNF, PF), and transient patterns (wavelets). These different representations can be useful for discriminating the subtle changes in hand poses. Moreover, by preserving a window of filtered EMG samples alongside these features, we allow a sequence model to discover additional temporal relationships that might not be captured by our computed features. The pipeline balances dimensionality with expressiveness: while the resulting feature array can be moderately large, initial user testing suggests that this multi-faceted approach effectively enhances finger joint angle estimation in the presence of self-occlusions or other sensor challenges.

Analysis of Feature Transforms. To illustrate the utility of our feature extraction pipeline, we investigate whether specific time-domain features—in this case, the MAV feature—correlate with particular finger joints. This step provides insights into which channels may be most helpful for predicting certain joints. We compute Pearson correlation coefficients between the MAV feature of each EMG channel and the final-frame angle of each finger joint window in our dataset. For each preprocessed sample in our training set, we extract the MAV for every channel, along with the final row of the joint angle labels. We then compute an 8×8 correlation matrix, where rows represent EMG channels and columns represent finger joints. We further identify the single `(channel, joint)` pair with the highest correlation and generate a scatter plot with a colour gradient to show how these data points evolve over time.

Figure 9 displays the resulting heatmap. Overall, most correlations remain modest, often ranging between about −0.6 and +0.5. Notably, Channel 1 shows a positive correlation (around 0.50) with the *Pinky PIP* angle, suggesting that higher MAV readings on Channel 1 tend to co-occur with deeper pinky flexion. Conversely, Channel 3 exhibits negative correlations with various middle-finger joints, hinting that its amplitude rises as those joints extend.

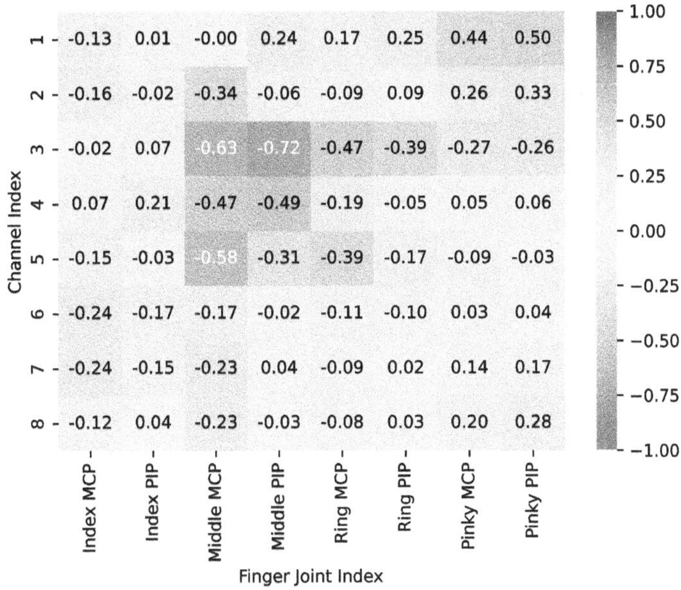

Fig. 9. Correlation matrix showing MAV(Channels) vs. Finger Joints (final frame).

To visualise the single strongest pair (Channel 1 vs. *Pinky PIP*), we plot a scatter diagram with a continuous colour scale representing the sample index, i.e. "time" (see Fig. 10). The cluster of values near the lower-left corner indicates sessions when the pinky was extended while Channel 1's MAV remained lower. Interestingly, we can trace the trajectory of the PIP bend in the first 2000 examples. We find one dark violet cluster in the bottom left, and one at the top, shifted slightly to the right. These two clusters correspond to two distinct pinky "states" (the lower left to a more extended state, and the top right to a more flexed state). Despite the Channel 1–Pinky PIP correlation, the overall results show that no single feature/channel alone can fully predict a given finger's posture. Nevertheless, the presence of slightly stronger relationships (e.g. $\approx$0.50) suggests that certain channels do indeed capture relevant muscle activations for specific joints. From a modelling perspective, combining all channels and multiple features, rather than relying on a single measure, should improve joint-angle estimation.

4 Model Architecture

Our model architecture is based on a combination of a bi-directional Long Short-Term Memory (LSTM) network and multiple separate sets of fully connected (FC) layers, aiming to capture both general trends in the sEMG signal data provided by the features and high-frequency characteristics of the signal. Formally,

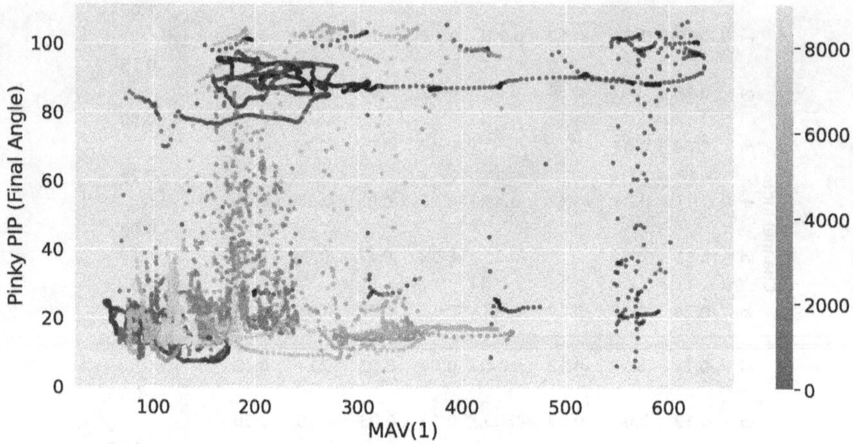

Fig. 10. Scatter plot of MAV (Channel 1) vs. Pinky PIP angle, with a continuous colour scale for sample index.

our model learns a mapping

$$F : \mathbb{R}^{N \times C} \rightarrow \mathbb{R}^{M} \tag{1}$$

where N denotes the number of sEMG samples, C represents the number of sEMG channels and M denotes the number of predicted joint angle values at every time step. More accurately, we learn a mapping

$$F(\mathbf{s}) = \phi_{\text{final}}\Big(\phi_{\text{lstm}}(\mathbf{s}_{\hat{N}}) \oplus \phi_{\text{feat}}(\psi_{\text{time-freq}}(\mathbf{s}_N)) \oplus \phi_{\text{wav}}(\psi_{\text{wavelet}}(\mathbf{s}_N)) \oplus \phi_{\text{filt}}(\mathbf{s}_{\hat{N}})\Big) \tag{2}$$

where

- $F(\mathbf{s})$ represents the mapping function that takes $N \times C$ sEMG samples ($\mathbf{s}$) and outputs M finger joint angles.
- $\mathbf{s}_N$ denotes all $N \times C$ sEMG samples.
- $\mathbf{s}_{\hat{N}}$ denotes the last $\hat{N} \times C$ sEMG samples in the data point.
- ϕ_{lstm} represent the LSTM layers, and ϕ_{feat}, ϕ_{wav} and ϕ_{filt} represent the fully connected layers processing time/frequency domain features, wavelet features and filtered EMG data respectively.
- ϕ_{final} denotes the final set of fully connected layers.
- $\psi_{\text{time-freq}}$ and $\psi_n$wavelet denote the feature extraction functions for time-frequency domain features and wavelet features, respectively.
- $\oplus$ represents the tensor concatenation operation.

The LSTM network, a type of recurrent neural network, operates on the subset $\mathbf{s}_{\hat{N}}$, which contains the last $\hat{N}$ samples of the sEMG data. In doing so, it captures temporal dependencies within the most recent portion of the filtered signal. Traditional feed-forward networks, when presented with sequential data, often lose track of the *time-varying* context that occurs across multiple frames. By contrast, LSTMs employ a gating mechanism (forget, input, and output gates) that enables them to selectively retain or discard information at each timestep, thus effectively learning medium-to-long-range dependencies in time-series data. This is critical for sEMG-based hand tracking, where subtle muscle activations (or relaxations) can unfold over hundreds of milliseconds and yield meaningful clues to impending finger movements.

In parallel, $\mathbf{s}_{\hat{N}}$ is also fed into a separate fully connected layer (rather than directly concatenating it with the LSTM outputs). Empirically, we found that providing a dedicated "shortcut" path for these recent EMG frames improves prediction accuracy, potentially because the model can disentangle fine-grained temporal details (through the LSTM) from higher-level amplitude trends (through the FC layer). The additional sets of fully connected layers process the time-domain (MAV, RMS, VAR), frequency-domain (MDF, MNF, PF), and wavelet features in parallel, yielding concise representations of broader spectral and statistical properties of each channel. By concatenating the outputs of the LSTM and these feature-specific layers, the model merges both temporal and non-temporal information streams, maximising its ability to capture short-lived bursts of activity as well as steady-state muscle contractions. This architecture thus takes advantage of both the LSTM's strength in managing time-dependent signals and the FC layers' ability to distill various feature channels into compact embeddings for finger joint angle estimation.

The outputs of the LSTM layers and the three sets of fully connected layers (time-frequency domain features, wavelet features, and $\hat{N}$ sEMG samples) are concatenated and passed to a final set of fully connected layers. The final output of the model is an estimation of the eight finger joint angles described above.

4.1 Model Implementation and Training

Our sEMG-based deep learning model was implemented using the PyTorch deep learning framework. The model is defined as a PyTorch Lightning[2] module that encapsulates the network architecture, the forward pass, and the training loop logic. By structuring the system this way, we ensure clear separation of concerns: the model code itself remains easy to read and debug, while the framework manages details such as scheduling learning rates and logging metrics.

We selected $N = 150$, which gives a sample window length of three seconds. Related works use window sizes of five seconds [23, 24]. During preliminary experiments with the model architecture, we found that a smaller window size of 150 samples did not reduce the quality of the predicted finger joint angles, whilst producing a significant speed-up in the real-time data processing pipeline during inference. $\hat{N} = 50$ was selected as a trade-off between LSTM accuracy and performance. Higher values for $\hat{N}$ produced slightly better results, but incurred a performance degradation, slowing down the model at inference time.

[2] https://lightning.ai/docs/pytorch/stable/.

The sEMG samples were separated into training and validation sets using a 95/5 ratio. During training, each mini-batch contains a set of preprocessed samples. Each sample is of shape $\left[\text{time steps} \times \text{channels}\right]$ to accommodate time/frequency features, wavelet decomposition rows, and a sliced set of the most recent raw EMG frames. The LSTM states are initialised to zero at the start of each sample. After the forward pass, the model's predicted angles are compared against the *final-frame* ground truth angles of the snippet. The mean squared error (MSE) is computed over all joint angles, and the sum of these MSE values is used as the primary loss. This aggregated loss is then backpropagated to update the network's parameters.

We adopt a step-based scheduler that decreases the learning rate $\gamma \approx 0.98$ each epoch, providing a gradual annealing of learning updates. Initially, we set a relatively high base learning rate (e.g. 3×10^{-3}) to encourage fast convergence, then reduce it slowly to refine final angles. During the first hundred epochs, the scheduler is stepped each epoch. The model monitors its validation loss and logs metrics such as the average training loss each epoch. Throughout the training process, we track and store the best-performing model parameters whenever the current epoch's average training loss sets a new record. Because sEMG signals can fluctuate over time, the best epoch might be one that balances a moderate learning rate with sufficient fine-tuning. By retaining a "running-best" checkpoint, we guarantee that if later epochs degrade performance (e.g., from overfitting), we can revert to the best state discovered up to that point. Dropout is enabled in multiple submodules (e.g. 0.5 in the LSTM and FC layers) to combat overfitting. Finally, the entire model is trained on a single NVIDIA RTX 2080 Ti GPU to enable mini-batch processing of up to 256 samples in parallel.

5 Multimodal Hand Tracking in XR

In this section, we present our approach to multimodal XR hand tracking by combining sEMG and vision-based tracking techniques. In our system, the vision-based tracking data provides information about the overall hand position and orientation in 3D space, while the sEMG-based model produces granular information about individual finger joint rotations. The hand position and orientation data are combined with the estimated finger joint angles to generate a complete hand pose representation.

The deep learning model is optimised for real-time performance, ensuring that the sEMG data can be processed with minimal latency. Our system operates at 50 Hz, which incurs a latency of 20 ms. For this work, data processing and model inference took place on a consumer notebook. The notebook concurrently runs a python server, responsible for sEMG data aggregation, preprocessing and model inference, and a 3D XR environment on the Unity platform. At every time step, the estimated finger joint angles are transferred from Python to Unity through the low-latency ZeroMQ framework[3]. A video demonstration

[3] https://zeromq.org/.

of our system is available online[4]. It shows a side-by-side comparison of the vision-based tracking system and our multimodal approach.

5.1 Evaluation

To validate the effectiveness of our multimodal hand tracking system, we conducted an experimental evaluation, comparing the multimodal tracking to the baseline vision-based hand tracking system provided by the XR device. We simultaneously collected tracking data from the vision-based tracking system and the multimodal tracking system. To establish a fair baseline for comparison, we used a Leap Motion sensor to acquire ground truth labels for finger joint angles. The Leap Motion is a high-precision vision-based hand tracking device that captures finger joint angles and hand position in 3D space. The ground truth labels were then compared to the results from both the vision-based and the multimodal tracking system.

The experimental setup included a series of hand pose tasks, designed to cover a wide range of hand movements, including gestures prone to occlusion. The tasks were selected with regard to their utility in playing a keyboard-inspired XRMI. The tasks were performed while wearing the Meta Quest 2 headset and the Myo armband. The Leap Motion sensor was placed on a table to record ground truth data. We recorded tasks under two conditions: 1) Full view of the hand - here, the XR headset was positioned at a 50cm distance, 45° above the hand to ensure optimal visual tracking conditions. 2) Self-occlusion of the hand - in this condition, the distance was kept identical, but the angle of the XR headset was lowered, such that the back of the hand occluded the fingers. Figure 11 illustrates the six hand pose tasks devised: (i) extending all fingers and making a fist; individual flexion and extension of the (ii) index, (iii) middle, (iv) ring and (v) pinky fingers; (vi) sequential flexion and extension of pinky, ring, middle and index fingers (similar to the gesture of drumming on a table while waiting for something). Each task involves the execution of the gesture at three different speeds: slow, over approximately two seconds, moderate (one second), and fast (half a second). To account for variability in the sEMG measurements, all tasks were executed three times, over two days, under identical lighting conditions.

To measure the degree of finger occlusion, we integrated a ray-casting system with the XR application[5]. Figures 12 (a) and (b) illustrate two occlusion scenarios: in the first, every ray from the camera to the finger colliders remains unobstructed (green lines), whereas in the second, some rays are blocked by the hand, causing those finger segments to register as occluded (red lines). We cast rays from the XR headset's 3D position to the eight finger bones whose rotations we measured every time a sample was taken. Rays intersecting other parts of the hand, e.g., the back of the hand, were used to mark the respective finger bones as occluded. This allowed us to quantify the level of occlusion per finger joint for every recording.

[4] https://www.youtube.com/watch?v=ivl2g2t2oaI.

[5] A short demonstration video is available here.

5.2 Analysis Methods and Results

After collecting the hand pose data, we quantified the absolute error (in degrees) of each system's joint angle predictions relative to the ground truth (Leap Motion) labels at every time step. Each task's errors were then aggregated across the three recorded sessions. Because preliminary checks using the Shapiro–Wilk test ($p < 0.001$) indicated non-normal distributions, we employed the Wilcoxon signed-rank test to compare errors from the vision-based (V) and multimodal (M) systems. Table 3 shows the results obtained from the Wilcoxon signed-rank tests, aggregated across all eight tracked joints per task for both conditions. The p-values indicate significant differences between the difference value matrices. Additionally, the table lists the average finger occlusion results obtained through the raycasting occlusion measure described above. The occlusion results describe the mean portion per task, in which the fingers were occluded by another part of the hand.

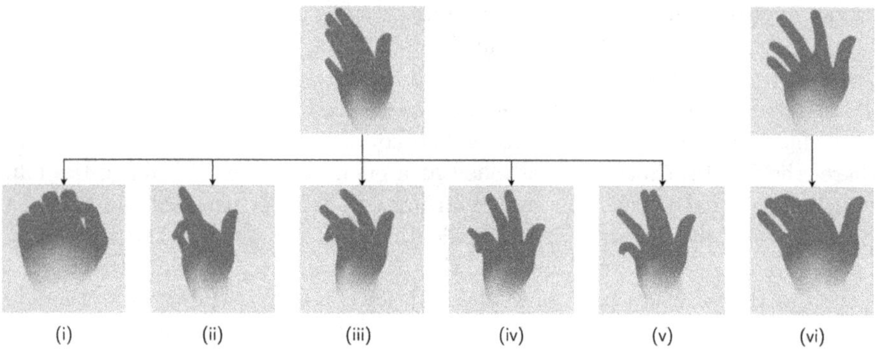

Fig. 11. Finger movements in the six hand pose tasks

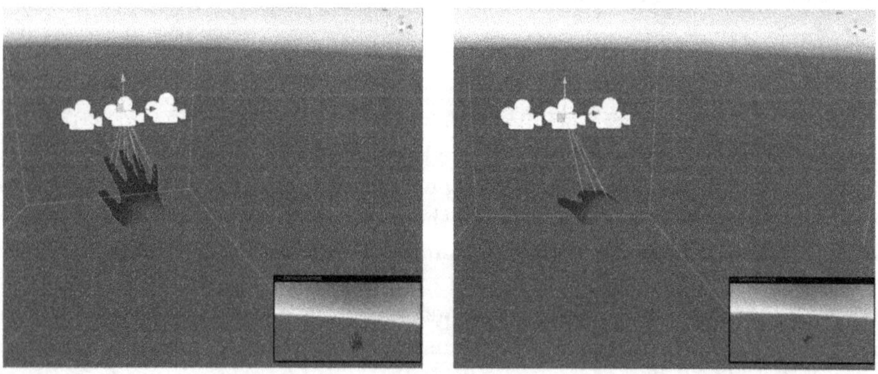

Fig. 12. Unity-based finger occlusion detection. (a) All finger rays successfully hit their respective colliders (green) when the fingers are fully visible. (b) Some rays are blocked by the hand mesh (red) when the fingers are partially occluded. (Color figure online)

Figure 13 illustrates the mean angle differences (with standard deviations as error bars) across six tasks—labelled (i) through (vi)—under both *Full View* (top row) and *Occluded* (bottom row) conditions. In the top row (Full View), the vision-based system and the multimodal approach show comparable performance: there are no statistically significant differences ($p = 1.0$). This is expected, as occlusion is minimal and vision-only tracking remains accurate. However, in the bottom row (Occluded), the multimodal method consistently outperforms vision-only tracking by approximately 5–15°, and these differences are statistically significant ($p < 0.001$) for all tasks.

Visually inspecting the bottom row reveals that the greatest improvements occur in tasks with more pronounced hand self-occlusions, such as (i) making a fist and (iv)/(v) flexing the ring/pinky fingers behind the palm. Here, the vision-based system often loses track of the occluded digits, resulting in higher errors. By contrast, the sEMG-based predictions remain stable because forearm muscle activation is captured even when the fingers are out of view. These findings confirm that our multimodal tracking system approaches vision-only performance in unobstructed settings and surpasses it significantly when the hand is occluded.

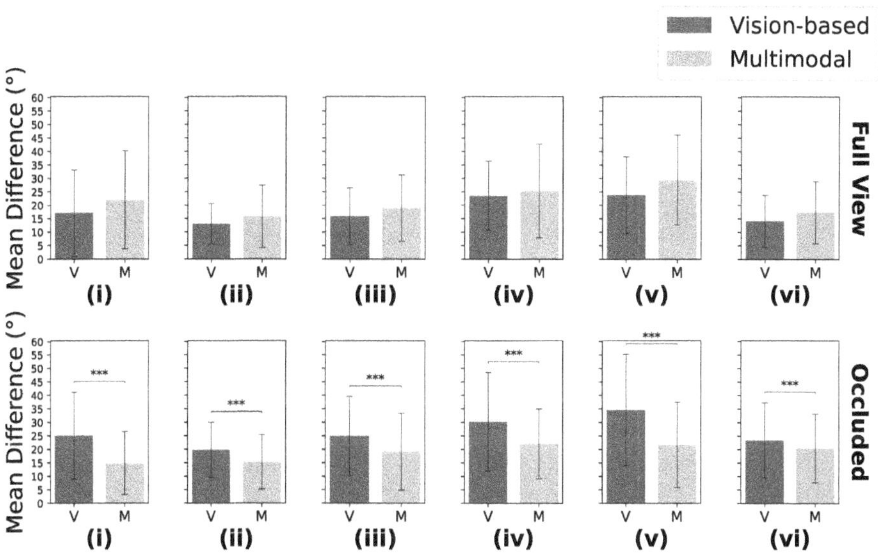

Fig. 13. Average deviation in degrees between the finger joint angles generated by the vision-based (V) and multimodal (M) tracking systems and the ground truth data for each task. Error bars show standard deviation; three asterisks indicate a significant difference between the V and M values ($p < .001$)

Table 3. P-values and average occlusion measurement results across tasks under both conditions

Tasks	Full view		Occluded	
	P-value	Occlusion (%)	P-value	Occlusion (%)
(i)	1.0	16.78	< .001	93.00
(ii)	1.0	2.65	< .001	70.58
(iii)	1.0	15.25	< .001	63.11
(iv)	1.0	16.78	< .001	53.02
(v)	1.0	27.94	< .001	78.82
(vi)	1.0	10.36	< .001	59.48

6 Discussion

Our evaluation shows that incorporating sEMG data can effectively address finger occlusion issues inherent in vision-based hand tracking. Specifically, when fingers are hidden behind the palm or partially out of view, the vision-only method tends to lose accuracy, whereas our multimodal system maintains tracking precision by relying on muscle-activation signals. This advantage is especially relevant for XR musical performance, where continuity of finger sensing is crucial to expressive control.

Nonetheless, there are several limitations. First, the present study involved only a single user, device, and experimental setting. As sEMG signals vary significantly with electrode placement, fatigue, and anatomical factors, wider tests across different users, hardware, and real-world conditions are needed to confirm generalisability. Second, while our current architecture uses a three-second window of sEMG data, exploring alternative time windows or network architectures may further improve reliability. Finally, seamless calibration routines or adaptive techniques could help mitigate variability in sEMG signals due to muscle fatigue and sensor drift.

In the future, additional sensing modalities—such as inertial measurement units (IMUs), depth cameras, or high-density EMG—may offer further resilience against occlusion and lighting changes. From a creative perspective, blending vision-driven hand position tracking with subtle physiological cues like muscle activity may unlock smoother, more nuanced musical performances in extended reality

7 Conclusion

We presented a multimodal hand tracking system that leverages both sEMG signals and camera-based vision tracking to mitigate finger occlusion issues in XR musical interactions. Empirical results confirm that the integrated approach reduces mean errors by 5–15° under occluded conditions while maintaining performance comparable to the accuracy of vision-only tracking in clear-view scenarios.

These findings suggest that augmenting camera-based methods with surface electromyography data can provide more robust and uninterrupted control for XR interaction. Looking ahead, multi-user evaluations, hardware diversification, and refined sEMG calibration will be important steps to broaden the system's applicability. By supplying an open-source pipeline, we hope to support further research and creative experimentation in hand tracking, ultimately enabling more expressive and reliable XR musical instruments.

Acknowledgements. This work was supported by the UKRI EPSRC AI & Music Centre for Doctoral Training (EP/S022694/1).

Disclosure of Interests. The authors have no competing interests to declare that are relevant to the content of this article.

References

1. Avian, C., Prakosa, S.W., Faisal, M., Leu, J.S.: Estimating finger joint angles on surface EMG using manifold learning and long short-term memory with attention mechanism. Biomed. Sig. Process. Control **71**, 103099 (2022). https://doi.org/10.1016/j.bspc.2021.103099
2. Berthaut, F.: 3D interaction techniques for musical expression. J. New Music Res. **49**(1), 60–72 (2020). https://doi.org/10.1080/09298215.2019.1706584
3. Bilbow, S.: Developing multisensory augmented reality as a medium for computational artists. In: Proceedings of the Fifteenth International Conference on Tangible, Embedded, and Embodied Interaction, pp. 1–7. No. 72, Association for Computing Machinery, New York, NY, USA (2021)
4. Bilbow, S.: Evaluating polaris - An audiovisual augmented reality experience built on open-source hardware and software. In: NIME 2022 (2022)
5. Boostani, R., Moradi, M.H.: Evaluation of the forearm EMG signal features for the control of a prosthetic hand. Physiol. Meas. **24**(2), 309 (2003). https://doi.org/10.1088/0967-3334/24/2/307
6. Çamcı, A., Vilaplana, M., Wang, R.: Exploring the affordances of VR for musical interaction design with VIMEs. In: Proceedings of the International Conference on New Interfaces for Musical Expression, pp. 121–126. Birmingham, UK (2020)
7. Chen Chen, F., Appendino, S., Battezzato, A., Favetto, A., Mousavi, M., Pescarmona, F.: Constraint study for a hand exoskeleton: human hand kinematics and dynamics. J. Robot. **2013**(1), 910961 (2013). https://doi.org/10.1155/2013/910961
8. Cipriani, C., Zaccone, F., Micera, S., Carrozza, M.C.: On the shared control of an EMG-controlled prosthetic hand: analysis of user-prosthesis interaction. IEEE Trans. Rob. **24**(1), 170–184 (2008). https://doi.org/10.1109/TRO.2007.910708
9. Criswell, E.: Cram's Introduction to Surface Electromyography. Jones & Bartlett Learning (2010)
10. Deacon, T., Stockman, T., Barthet, M.: User experience in an interactive music virtual reality system: an exploratory study. In: Aramaki, M., Kronland-Martinet, R., Ystad, S. (eds.) Bridging People and Sound, vol. 10525, pp. 192–216. Springer International Publishing, Cham (2017). https://doi.org/10.1007/978-3-319-67738-5_12

11. Delsys Europe, D.: Delsys EMG sensor placement technical note 101
12. Fillwalk, J.: ChromaChord: a virtual musical instrument. In: 2015 IEEE Symposium on 3D User Interfaces (3DUI), pp. 201–202 (2015). https://doi.org/10.1109/3DUI.2015.7131770
13. Graf, M., Barthet, M.: When XR meets AI: integrating interactive machine learning with an XR musical instrument. In: 1st AES International Symposium on AI and the Musician. AES (2024)
14. Graf, M., Barthet, M.: Mixed reality musical interface: exploring ergonomics and adaptive hand pose recognition for gestural control. In: International Conference on New Interfaces for Musical Expression (2022). https://doi.org/10.21428/92fbeb44.56ba9b93
15. Hamilton, R., Platz, C.: Gesture-based collaborative virtual reality performance in carillon. In: Proceedings of the 2016 International Computer Music Conference, p. 5. Utrecht, Netherlands (2016)
16. Han, S., et al.: MEgATrack: monochrome egocentric articulated hand-tracking for virtual reality. ACM Trans. Graph. **39**(4), 87:87:1–87:87:13 (2020). https://doi.org/10.1145/3386569.3392452
17. Hermens, H.J., Freriks, B., Disselhorst-Klug, C., Rau, G.: Development of recommendations for SEMG sensors and sensor placement procedures. J. Electromyogr. Kinesiol. **10**(5), 361–374 (2000). https://doi.org/10.1016/S1050-6411(00)00027-4
18. Hu, X., Song, A., Wang, J., Zeng, H., Wei, W.: Finger movement recognition via high-density electromyography of intrinsic and extrinsic hand muscles. Sci. Data **9**(1), 373 (2022). https://doi.org/10.1038/s41597-022-01484-2
19. Jarque-Bou, N.J., Vergara, M., Sancho-Bru, J.L., Gracia-Ibáñez, V., Roda-Sales, A.: A calibrated database of kinematics and EMG of the forearm and hand during activities of daily living. Sci. Data **6**(1), 270 (2019). https://doi.org/10.1038/s41597-019-0285-1
20. Jiang, N.: Gesture recognition and biometrics electromyography (GRABMyo) dataset (2022)
21. Kaczmarek, P., Mańkowski, T., Tomczyński, J.: PutEMG–a surface electromyography hand gesture recognition dataset. Sensors **19**(16), 3548 (2019). https://doi.org/10.3390/s19163548
22. Lee, H., Kim, D., Park, Y.L.: Explainable deep learning model for EMG-based finger angle estimation using attention. IEEE Trans. Neural Syst. Rehabil. Eng. **30**, 1877–1886 (2022). https://doi.org/10.1109/TNSRE.2022.3188275
23. Liu, Y., Lin, C., Li, Z.: WR-Hand: wearable armband can track user's hand. IN: Proceedings of the ACM on Interactive, Mobile, Wearable and Ubiquitous Technologies **5**(3), 118:1–118:27 (2021). https://doi.org/10.1145/3478112
24. Liu, Y., Zhang, S., Gowda, M.: NeuroPose: 3D hand pose tracking using EMG Wearables. In: Proceedings of the Web Conference 2021, pp. 1471–1482. WWW 2021, Association for Computing Machinery, New York, NY, USA (2021). https://doi.org/10.1145/3442381.3449890
25. Mäki-Patola, T., Laitinen, J., Kanerva, A., Takala, T.: Experiments with virtual reality instruments. In: Proceedings of the 2005 Conference on New Interfaces for Musical Expression, pp. 11–16. NIME 2005, National University of Singapore, SGP (2005)
26. Men, L., Bryan-Kinns, N.: LeMo: supporting collaborative music making in virtual reality. In: IEEE 4th VR Workshop on Sonic Interactions for Virtual Environments (SIVE) (2018). https://doi.org/10.13140/RG.2.2.27033.93289

27. Milgram, P., Takemura, H., Utsumi, A., Kishino, F.: Augmented reality: a class of displays on the reality-virtuality continuum. Telemanipulator and Telepresence Technol. **2351** (1994). https://doi.org/10.1117/12.197321
28. Moore, A.G., Howell, M.J., Stiles, A.W., Herrera, N.S., McMahan, R.P.: Wedge: a musical interface for building and playing composition-appropriate immersive environments. In: 2015 IEEE Symposium on 3D User Interfaces (3DUI), pp. 205–206. IEEE, Arles, France (2015). https://doi.org/10.1109/3DUI.2015.7131772
29. Nishikawa, D., Yu, W., Yokoi, H., Kakazu, Y.: EMG prosthetic hand controller using real-time learning method. In: IEEE SMC 1999 Conference Proceedings of the 1999 IEEE International Conference on Systems, Man, and Cybernetics (Cat. No.99CH37028), vol. 1, pp. 153–158 (1999). https://doi.org/10.1109/ICSMC.1999.814077
30. Rawat, S., Vats, S., Kumar, P.: Evaluating and exploring the MYO ARMBAND. In: 2016 International Conference System Modeling & Advancement in Research Trends (SMART), pp. 115–120 (2016). https://doi.org/10.1109/SYSMART.2016.7894501
31. Salter, S., et al.: Emg2pose: a Large and Diverse Benchmark for Surface Electromyographic Hand Pose Estimation. In: The Thirty-eight Conference on Neural Information Processing Systems Datasets and Benchmarks Track (2024)
32. Serafin, S., Erkut, C., Kojs, J., Nordahl, R., Nilsson, N.C.: Virtual reality musical instruments: Guidelines for multisensory interaction design. In: Proceedings of the Audio Mostly 2016, pp. 266–271. ACM, Norrköping Sweden (2016). https://doi.org/10.1145/2986416.2986431
33. Tenore, F., Ramos, A., Fahmy, A., Acharya, S., Etienne-Cummings, R., Thakor, N.V.: Towards the Control of Individual Fingers of a Prosthetic Hand Using Surface EMG Signals. In: 2007 29th Annual International Conference of the IEEE Engineering in Medicine and Biology Society, pp. 6145–6148 (2007). https://doi.org/10.1109/IEMBS.2007.4353752
34. Vugt, J.P.P., Dijk, J.G.: A convenient method to reduce crosstalk in surface EMG. Clin. Neurophysiol. **112**(4), 583–592 (2001). https://doi.org/10.1016/S1388-2457(01)00482-5
35. Walkington, P.: PyoMyo (2021). https://github.com/PerlinWarp/pyomyo
36. Weichert, F., Bachmann, D., Rudak, B., Fisseler, D.: Analysis of the accuracy and robustness of the leap motion controller. Sensors **13**(5), 6380–6393 (2013). https://doi.org/10.3390/s130506380
37. Wessel, D., Wright, M.: Problems and prospects for intimate musical control of computers. Comput. Music. J. **26**(3), 11–22 (2002). https://doi.org/10.1162/014892602320582945

Comprehensive Understanding of Patterns of Skill Acquisition and Forgetting in Music Games: Does Musical Experience Accelerate Forgetting?

Mio Matsuura[1], Ayanae Sasaki[1], Masaki Matsubara[2], Hiroki Watanabe[1], Yoshinari Takegawa[1(✉)], and Keiji Hirata[3]

[1] Future University Hakodate, Hakodate, Hokkaido 041-8655, Japan
yoshi@fun.ac.jp
[2] University of Tsukuba, Tsukuaba, Ibaraki 305-8550, Japan
[3] MIRAI SHARE, Hakodate, Mihara 041-0806, Japan

Abstract. This research aims at a comprehensive understanding, taking individual differences into account, of how the loss of skills acquired in a music game is influenced by factors such as the speed at which skills are learned and previous experience of music games. Using Sparebeat, an online music game, we conducted an experiment in which seven participants were each assigned a piece of music which they practiced every day, their scores being recorded, until they were determined to have reached a certain skill level. Then, they entered a 'non-training phase' in which they did not practice for one week, before playing their assigned piece again and having their score recorded. The state of skill loss was measured by repeatedly recording participants' scores at one-week intervals and comparing these to the scores at the end of the training phase. By analyzing the changes in score in the phases of skill acquisition and skill forgetting, we discovered two forgetting patterns, namely, maintenance of score and decrease in score. In addition, to study the influence of difficulty level on skill loss, we also analyzed the scores participants obtained on two pieces of music of different difficulty levels from their assigned pieces. Furthermore, we investigated participants' previous experience regarding playing music and music games. As a result, we found that participants with music game experience tended to maintain their scores, while the scores of participants with musical experience tended to decrease. This suggests the possibility that having musical experience accelerates skill loss.

Keywords: educational technology · human computer interaction · learning support system

1 Introduction

In recent years, advances in HCI technology have enabled the proposal of numerous learning support systems to assist in the acquisition skills involving physical

S. Ystad et al. (Eds.): CMMR 2023, LNCS 15236, pp. 40–58, 2026.
https://doi.org/10.1007/978-3-032-02042-0_3

movements, such as tennis [5], golf [7,10,11], calligraphy [4,19], playing musical instruments [17], and singing [12]. A common learning support framework involves lowering the difficulty of skill acquisition to suit the learner, providing a sense of accomplishment during training, leading the learner towards their goal and fostering motivation. For instance, attaching training wheels to a bicycle enables even someone who cannot ride a bicycle to pedal easily and move forward, while simultaneously giving them the target of becoming able to ride without training wheels, which motivates them to keep practicing. The main challenges lie in determining the extent to which the difficulty of acquiring the target skill should be lowered, and how to create stimuli and environments that promote sustained motivation to practice. It is well-known that the speed and efficiency with which skills are acquired varies from learner to learner, even if they carry out the same practice in the same environment [16]. Accordingly, there is much research that approaches skill acquirement from a cognitive perspective.

However, there are cases in which even a skill that has been acquired through a vast amount of time and effort gradually deteriorates and is ultimately lost if sufficient practice is not continued. We call this phenomenon 'skill forgetting'. Even if learners have attained the same skill level, the extent and manner of forgetting varies from person to person, thus it can be considered that a learner's cognitive aspects affect skill loss. By considering skill acquisition from two sides, learning and forgetting, we can expect to approach a more accurate cognitive model of skill acquisition.

Many preceding studies have investigated memorization and forgetting, but these studies have focused on tasks that do not involve physical actions, such as memorizing words. Ebbinghaus conducted an experiment related to forgetting, using himself as a subject and performing an experimental task of memorizing meaningless syllables [2]. Specifically, he carried out fixed-point observation by measuring the number of syllables that he was able to recall after one week, then after one month, demonstrated that the number gradually decreased, and proposed the Ebbinghaus forgetting curve. Even now, this theory is widely cited as basic research related to remembering symbolic information, and much research has been carried out relating to learning and forgetting in tasks that do not involve physical actions [1,3,8,13].

In the field of sports science, the relationship between sleep and memory consolidation through motor skill learning has been investigated in detail, focusing on professional athletes [9,18,20]. Such research, which takes the work of Ebbinghaus as a starting point, has fulfilled the important role of clarifying the mechanisms by which information is retained or forgotten. However, many aspects of said research differ from skill acquisition that involves physical activity, and the quantitative research that has been conducted so far has not sufficiently investigated patterns of forgetting related to physical actions. In the learning of physical skills such as sports, which involves physical actions, the sensory feedback obtained from body movement and kinesthesia is important and processes are involved that cannot be performed by symbolic memorization.

The music game targeted in our research provides a domain that combines the peculiarities of both symbolic learning and learning that involves physical actions. The notes that appear in the game (targets that represent sounds) are equivalent to the musical notation on a score in the domain of music, and it is necessary to memorize symbolic note patterns in order to increase one's ability to recognize melody patterns. At the same time, physical skill and procedural memory, which involve physical actions, are required to tap the screen reflexively when notes appear. Sufficient research has not yet been conducted to clarify, either quantitatively or qualitatively, the manner in which skills are acquired and forgotten in this complex domain that requires both physical action and symbolic memory.

Therefore, this research focuses on a music game and aims to conduct a qualitative study that will elucidate the condition of the acquisition and forgetting of the skills involved, through a long-term experiment. Specifically, we target beginners and intermediate players and aim to observe how the speed at which skills are acquired, as well as previous experience of music games, affects the condition of forgetting, and to comprehensively grasp various forgetting patterns considering individual differences. By 'considering individual differences' we mean, for example, taking into account how the manner of forgetting differs between people who quickly gain skills and those who are slower, or whether having music game experience makes a person less likely to forget. Furthermore, we intend to investigate whether learners have simply grown used to their assigned pieces, or whether they have progressed to a level at which they can also play other simple pieces, in order to establish whether skills are easily forgotten in the case in which a person is falsely determined to have acquired actual ability.

Stepping off from the above, this research poses the following questions.

RQ1: How does the manner of forgetting differ among players? Is this difference represented by a viewpoint such as music game experience, musical experience, difficulty of the assigned piece, or preferred kind of music?

RQ2: When measuring players' music game skills, how does the manner of forgetting differ depending on the establishment of actual ability?

Based on these research questions, we carry out analysis and classification of forgetting patterns, taking individual differences into account, and consider the effect of each factor on skill forgetting. This research presents various theoretical forgetting patterns to help determine what viewpoints an experiment plan should be based on when conducting quantitative research into skill forgetting. In addition, the research can be applied to future research on skill acquisition support systems using HCI, for example by presenting forgetting predictions, practice continuation strategies, etc. that are applicable to various manners of forgetting.

2 Related Research

Skill acquisition encompasses research from various fields and approaches. In golf, the trajectory of the golf club and the angle of the head of the club have a significant influence on the trajectory of the ball. Accordingly, research has been conducted on the trajectory and position of the club during a swing [7,10,11]. A golf club-shaped device is used, which generates torque to move the club, while held by the user, and correct its trajectory. In addition, Chen et al. [7] propose a method to change the angle of the head of a putter by switching between different weights. Nakamura et al. [11] demonstrated that using their proposed system enables users to perform efficient swing practice in a virtual reality golf environment.

In calligraphy, there is research that takes a different approach. Tanaka et al. [19] propose a learning support system that uses a tablet. When a calligraphy beginner writes a character while looking at an example, it is difficult for them to learn the characteristics of how to write the character, such as brush pressure, the speed of brushstrokes, and so on. This research verifies that using the proposed learning support system, which provides onomatopoeaic voice guidance, improves learners' technical accuracy and learning efficiency, when compared to a method that does not use onomatopoeia. Henmi and Yoshikawa [4] developed a calligraphy system that uses virtual reality technology to convey a teacher's sense of touch to a student. When the teacher draws a character, the position and trajectory of the brush are recorded and then, using a virtual piece of paper, the distance between brush and paper, and the way the brush is pressed down, are conveyed to the student.

In the field of music games, too, there has been research on supporting the improvement of skills. Liang/Ikeda proposed a method for automatically adjusting the content of an open source music game called OSU! to improve players' skills [6]. This work, using teacher-assisted learning, predicts the timing, type, and place of actions in the game. The system records a player's play log and analyzes what they are good and bad at, to automatically generate content that is suited to them. The system aims to adjust the content by analyzing the patterns in the original content that the player finds difficult and making the player practice those patterns intensively, then making the patterns even more difficult.

As the above shows, there are various approaches in research related to skill acquisition. However, as far as we know, there are no cases of measuring the long-term transition of skill acquisition and skill forgetting, as we do in our research. Nevertheless, the knowledge obtained in our research can be utilized in the above learning support research. For example, it could be applied to prompt learners to practice at the time when skills are most likely to be forgotten.

3 Experiment Plan

3.1 Music Game: Sparebeat

Sparebeat [15] was used in the experiment this time. Sparebeat runs in a web browser and is playable on PCs, smartphones, and tablets. The play screen, presented in Fig. 1, consists primarily of four black lanes upon which red, purple, blue, and green diamond-shaped icons, called notes, move from the distance towards the foreground. At the very front is a horizontal green line that cuts across the four lanes. The player must press the corresponding keys as the notes cross the green line to earn points. On a PC, the lanes, from left to right, correspond to the 'D', 'F', 'J', and 'K' keys, respectively. On a tablet or smartphone, the player taps the relevant lane. The points awarded are calculated according to the timing and accuracy of key presses.

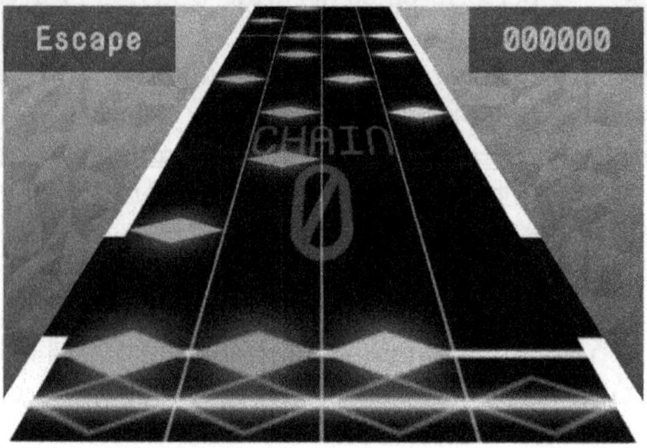

Fig. 1. Play screen

Figure 2 presents the Sparebeat difficulty selection screen. On this screen, the player can select the difficulty of the piece of music and set the speed and timing of notes. The difficulty of a piece is set as a number from 1 to 15. The higher the number, the harder the piece, and the lower the number, the easier the piece. However, one piece of music already has three difficulty levels: EASY, NORMAL, and HARD. Specifically, three musical scores (the set of notes to be pressed that will appear on the screen) are prepared for each piece, and they are designated easy, normal, and hard in the order of their difficulty, though the numerical value of each difficulty level differs according to the piece of music. Therefore, when comparing the difficulty of pieces in our experiment, we used not the indices of easy, normal and hard, but the numerical difficulty index.

Sparebeat has four types of timing judgement that are displayed in accordance with the timing of the player's key presses: Just, Rush, Cool, and Miss. Just is displayed when a key is pressed with accurate timing, Rush is displayed when the key is pressed a little earlier than the correct timing, Cool is displayed when the key is pressed a little late, and Miss is displayed when no key is pressed. Figure 3 presents detailed timing judgement values. The score in Sparebeat ranges from 0 points to 1,000,000 points.

3.2 Subjects and Difficulty Level Setting

The experiment targeted seven experiment participants, ranging from beginner players, who had never played a music game before, to intermediate players. We excluded advanced players who can obtain a score of over 800,000 points on even

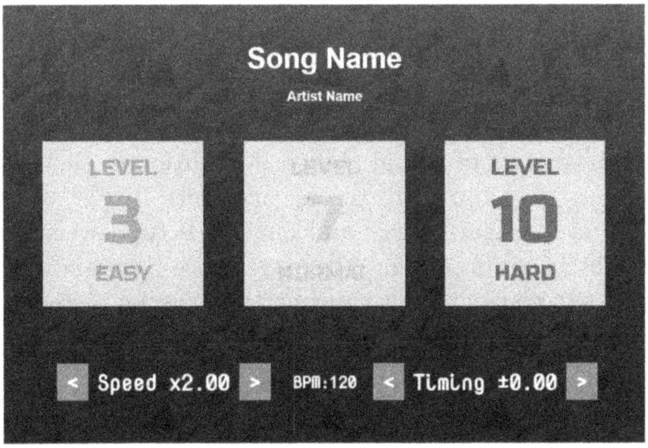

Fig. 2. Difficulty selection screen

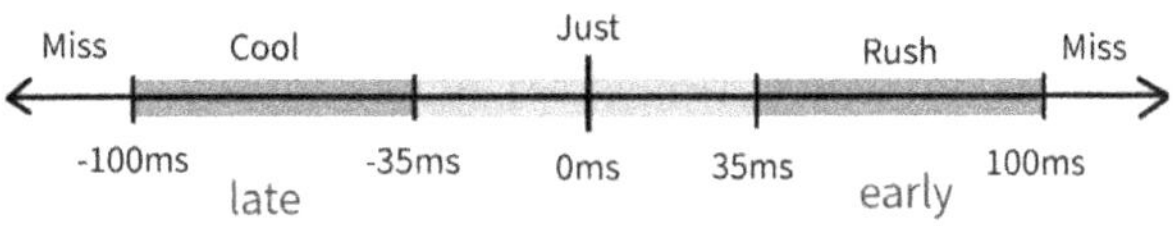

Fig. 3. Timing judgements

a difficult piece, as the state of their improvement is difficult to grasp. All the participants played Sparebeat for the first time in this experiment. The assigned pieces of music were selected according to each participant's ability. We had the participants play several pieces, changing the difficulty levels of the pieces, and selected, as assigned pieces, pieces for which the participants scored in the region of 650,000–700,000 points.

3.3 Experiment Procedure

Training Phase: During the training phase, each participant first begins each session by playing their assigned piece once from start to finish. Then they practice the assigned piece for 10 min. After practice, they are instructed to play the piece from start to finish once more. This process was designated as one training set and we had participants attempt one training set every day, when possible. When a participant became able to obtain a score of more than 900,000 points, they were deemed to have acquired skills and so transitioned to the non-training phase. This value was chosen because prior investigation revealed that a score of 900,000 points can only be achieved when there are almost no MISS timings and there is a high rate of JUST timing, thus a certain amount of practice is required.

Non-training Phase: Once they have moved into the non-training phase, a participant ceases practice for a period determined by the experimenters. Fixed-point observation was carried out to record the circumstance of forgetting. Once the designated non-training interval had elasped, each participant played their assigned piece once through without practicing before-hand and their scores were recorded. Then they did not practice for the same interval again, before playing their assigned piece through once. This process was performed repeatedly. To measure the establishment of actual ability, in addition to their assigned pieces, we had participants play two extra pieces: one piece two levels easier than the difficulty level of the assigned piece and one piece two levels harder than the assigned piece. Participants played each extra piece once and their scores were recorded. This was to clarify whether during the training phase each participant had acquired general music game skills or whether their skills were limited to their assigned piece.

3.4 Summary of Prior Research and Newly Added Processes

Previously, the authors' research group performed an experiment using five participants and classified three patterns of forgetting [14]. In the non-training phase described in our previous paper [14], participants played their assigned pieces once at intervals of one week, and their scores were recorded. As a result, the following three patterns were identified: a pattern in which the score is maintained for a while and then the skill is gradually forgotten, a pattern in which the score fluctuates wildly, and a pattern in which the skill is not easily forgotten. However, although forgetting patterns were observed, it was not possible to confirm a remarkable difference between patterns, thus it was necessary to reset the duration of the non-training intervals and investigate forgetting patterns again.

Hereafter, participants 1 to 5 are referred to as P1, P2, P3, and so on. Figure 4 shows the results of applying a linear approximation to the scores of participants 1 to 5 when the non-training interval was one week. These results show that scores generally do not decrease in a non-training interval of one week. In other words, the acquired skill is not easily forgotten in this interval. This may be because, just as a certain class may be taken once a week, for example, a non-training interval of one week may still constitute an ordinary practice schedule. Therefore, the non-training interval was extended to one month (Fig. 5). Accordingly, in this paper, we update the results of the previous experiment involving five participants, add two new participants, and set the non-training interval as one month. In addition, for participants who entered the non-training phase, we conducted a new experiment to confirm whether the ability to play the music game had been established, conducted an interview related to 'musical experience', 'music game experience' and 'awareness of fluctuation', and analyzed the results.

4 Experiment Results

4.1 Change in Score on Assigned Piece

In the training phase, we focus only on the post-training scores, in order to investigate the transition of scores until the skill is acquired. The experiment

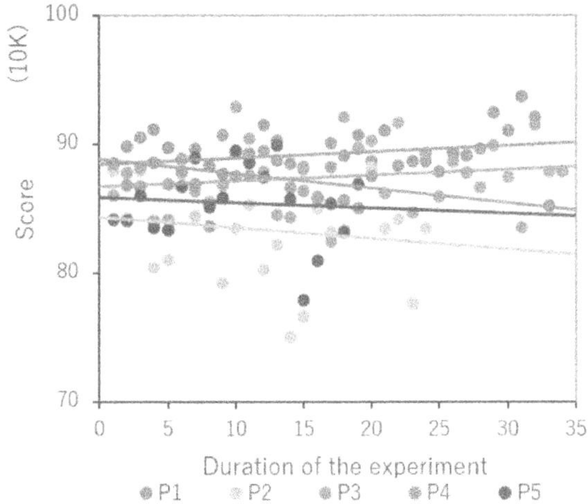

Fig. 4. Results of linear approximation of scores in one-week non-training interval

Table 1. Duration of experiment for each participant

participant	P1	P2	P3	P4	P5	P6	P7
Training phase	16 d	10 d	10 d	34 d	62 d	87 d	84 d
No. of sets	16	10	10	33	50	79	25
Non-training phase	459 d	420 d	422 d	438 d	431 d	-	152 d
No. of sets	39	31	40	26	25	-	4

results for all participants are presented in Fig. 6. The duration of the experiment for each participant and the number of sets performed by each participant are presented in Table 1. A set refers, in the training phase, to one set of practice and playthrough, and, in the non-training phase, to each time the assigned piece and the two additional pieces are all played. The duration of the training phase is different for each participant. The pink area in the left-hand side of the graph represents the training phase, while the white area on the right-hand side represents the non-training phase. To observe how scores changed after the end of the training phase, the final score in the training phase is taken as a value equivalent to 100%. In addition, to make score trends more visible, we take the four-interval moving average. On the horizontal axis, the last trial run is taken as the standard and is set as 0.

The results of linear approximation of the scores of all participants in the training phase are presented in Fig. 7. An upward trend was observed in which the score of every participant improved. In the case of P1, P2, P3, and P7, their scores improved more quickly the more they practiced, while the scores of the other participants increased gradually.

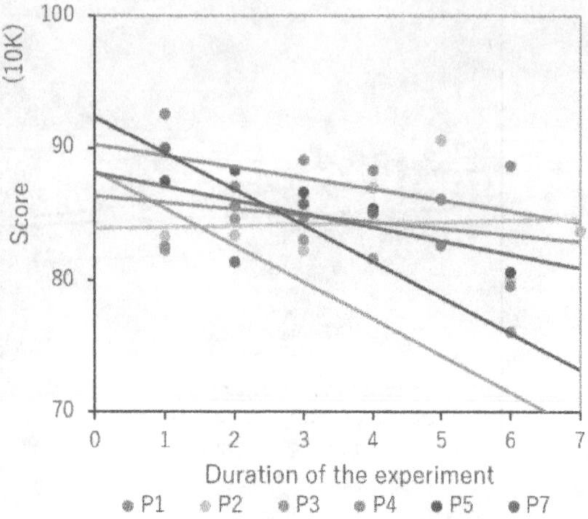

Fig. 5. Results of linear approximation of scores in one-month non-training interval

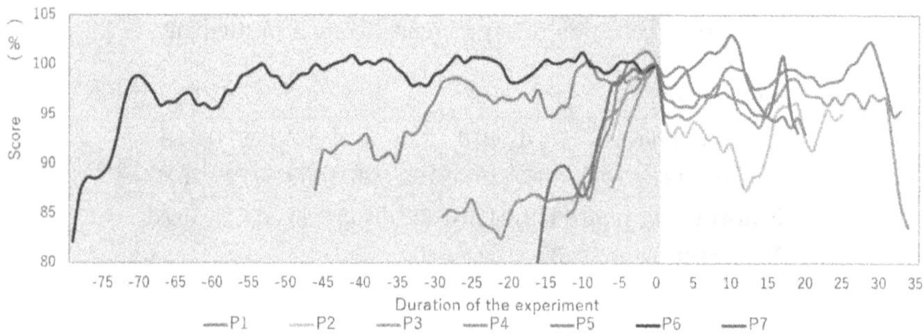

Fig. 6. Experiment results of all participants

From Fig. 6, it can be seen that P6 had a longer training phase than the other participants and ended the experiment before transitioning to the non-training phase. In contrast, the training phases of P1 - P3 were short. In the future, it will be necessary to investigate this difference in the results, based on the difficulty level of the assigned piece that is appropriate for each participant.

In Table 1, the first day of the non-training phase is the day after the day on which the training phase ended. The last day of the non-training phase is the day on which the experiment participant became unable to continue the experiment, due to personal circumstances. Accordingly, the total duration of the experiment for each participant is the sum of the number of days in their training phase and the number of days in their non-training phase.

Figure 5 presents the linear approximation of the scores of participants 1–5 and 7 when the non-training phase was changed to one month. From Fig. 4 and Fig. 5 it can be seen that the score decreases more in a non-training interval of

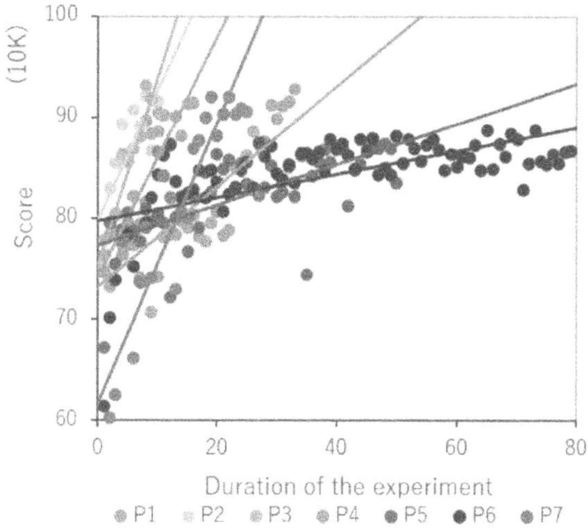

Fig. 7. Linear approximation of scores in the training phase

one month than of one week, and thus the participants are forgetting. From the inclination of the linear approximation graph, we classified patterns of forgetting.

4.2 Comparison of Scores of Assigned Piece and Two Additional Pieces

During each trial run in the non-training phase, each participant played their assigned piece through only once. However, in addition to this, they also played one piece that was more difficult than the assigned piece and one piece that was easier. The aim of this exercise was to measure whether they had genuinely acquired the ability to play music games. Supposing that a participant had acquired actual ability, their score should also be high on an easier piece (close to the 900,000 points scored on the assigned piece) and low on a more difficult piece (600,000–700,000 points). If, on the other hand, they were to score low on a piece that is easier than the assigned piece, this would be taken to mean that the player had not established actual ability but had merely grown used to the assigned piece.

These results are presented in Fig. 8. For most of the participants, the score of the assigned piece was highest. In addition, it was found that, depending on the participant, there were cases in which the score on the easy piece was close to the score on the assigned piece, and cases in which it was close to the score on the difficult piece. In the case of P2, P4, P5, and P7, the score on the easy piece was closer to the score on the assigned piece than the difficult piece, whereas, in the case of P1 and P3, the score on the easy piece was closer to the score on the difficult piece. Therefore, it is inferred that P2, P4, P5 and P7 established actual ability through practice, while P1 and P3 only grew accustomed to their assigned pieces without establishing actual ability.

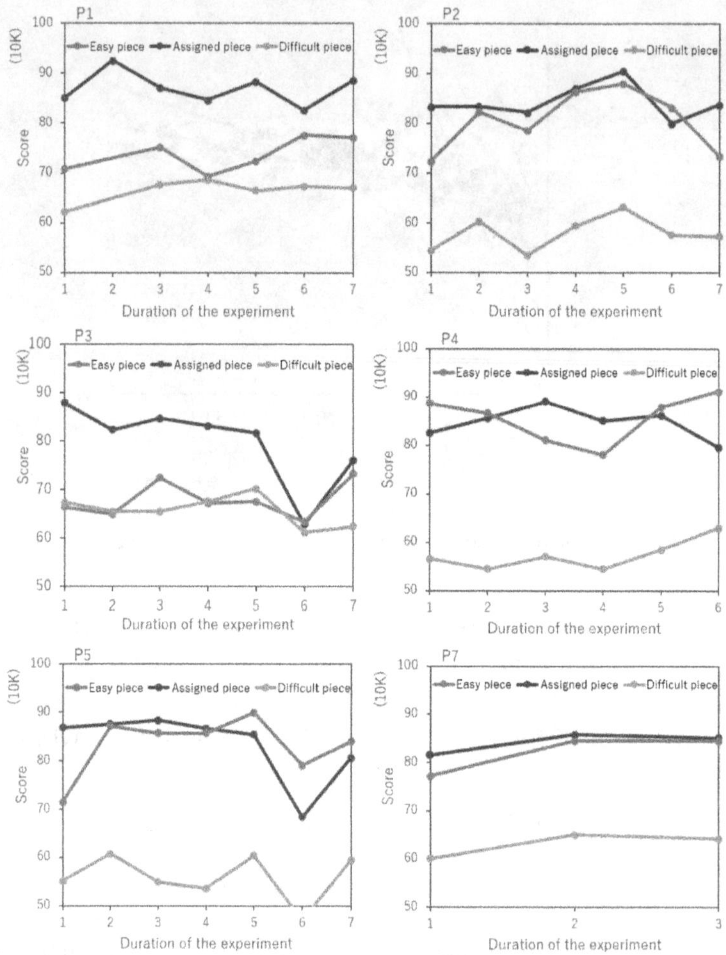

Fig. 8. Comparison of assigned piece and additional pieces for all participants

5 Considerations

5.1 Patterns Related to Forgetting

The four-interval moving average scores of P1 - P5 and P7 are presented in Fig. 9. This graph takes the four-interval moving average and takes the score on the last day of the training phase as a value equivalent to 1,000,000 points. The unbroken line represents the score when practice was stopped for one week, and the dotted line represents the score when practice was stopped for one month.

Regarding the scores in the non-training phase, as the participants are basically not practicing their assigned pieces, it is assumed that there will be no cases of the score continuing to grow higher than the score obtained directly before entering the non-training phase. Accordingly, we consider two patterns:

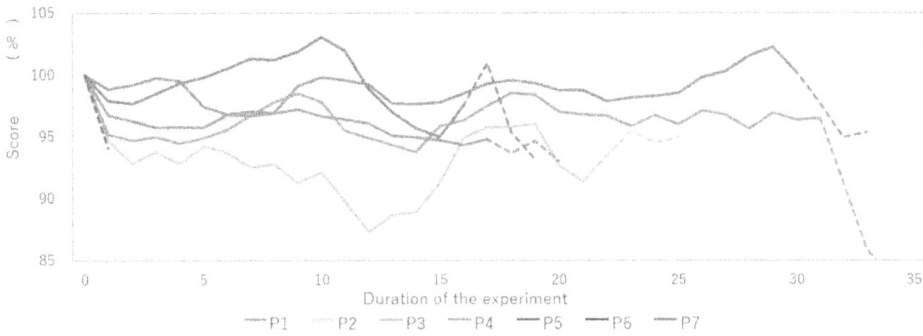

Fig. 9. Four-interval moving average scores in the non-training phase

a pattern in which the score decreases and a pattern in which the score is maintained. Then, we analyze the score transition trends to determine which pattern the transitions fall into. Specifically, when the score decreases, we must analyze whether the manner in which it decreases is sudden or gradual, or linear or fluctuating. On the other hand, when the score is maintained, it is necessary to analyze the extent to which the score is maintained.

Table 2 presents the linear approximation in the one-month non-training phase. As a result of analyzing and classifying score transitions in the non-training phase, the participants were divided as follows.

Score is maintained: P2, P4

Score decreases: P1, P3, P5, P7

This time, the upper and lower thresholds of the range of score increase/decrease were set to 5,000 and −5,000 respectively, and when the inclination was between −5,000 and 5,000 it was interpreted that the score was maintained, while an inclination smaller than −5,000 was taken to mean that the score decreased. As the number of samples was limited, the coefficient of determination was small, yet we consider that it is possible to grasp the state of forgetting. Further consideration is required regarding the valid coefficient of determination and the range of inclination related to maintaining score. The scores of P2 and P4 are still maintained when the non-training interval is changed to one month. Compared to the other participants, the score of P2 is maintained, despite some fluctuation, while the score of P4 is maintained with relative stability.

The scores of P1, P3, P5 and P7 are declining. These participants maintained their scores when the non-training interval was one week, but a change was observed after the non-training interval was altered to one month. The score of P1 began to decrease gradually after the non-training interval was changed, while the score of P3 suddenly began to decrease. The score of P5 gradually decreased throughout the non-training phase as a whole, although some fluctuation was observed. There was no remarkable variation after the non-training interval was altered. Although P7 only completed four trial runs, the score can be seen to gradually decrease.

The standard for determining fluctuation this time was the standard deviation of the degree of variability in the non-training phase. Table 3 presents the standard deviation of the degree of variability in the non-training phase for each participant. From Table 3, a score was determined to be fluctuating when the standard deviation of the degree of variability exceeded 0.050 (5.0%). As a result, the participants whose scores can be said to be fluctuating are P2, P3, P5 and P7, but the score of P7 was determined not to be fluctuating, as the non-training phase data of P7 are limited.

Table 2. Linear approximation in one-month non-training interval phase

	Coefficient of determination	Inclination	Intercept
P1	0.2075	−8,382.3	902,629
P2	0.0039	997.46	839,382
P3	0.4098	−27,906	882,090
P4	0.0799	−4,917.7	863,915
P5	0.4552	−27,325	923,780
P6	-	-	-
P7	0.1429	−10,270	881,532

Table 3. Standard deviation of degree of variability for each participant in the non-training phase

	Standard deviation of variability
P1	0.036
P2	0.056
P3	0.066
P4	0.030
P5	0.064
P6	-
P7	0.061

5.2 Scores of Pieces of Different Difficulty Levels from the Assigned Piece, and Patterns of Forgetting

Table 4 presents the level of the assigned piece, the forgetting pattern, and the relationship with the score of the easy piece. From the two additional pieces, we

Table 4. Difficulty level of assigned piece and score on easy piece

	Assigned piece level	Forgetting pattern	Score on easy piece
P1	6	Decrease	Close to difficult piece
P2	8	Maintain	Close to assigned piece
P3	6	Decrease	Close to difficult piece
P4	8	Maintain	Close to assigned piece
P5	8	Decrease	Close to assigned piece
P6	9	-	-
P7	8	Decrease	Close to assigned piece

Table 5. Summary of results of all participants

	Assigned piece level	Forgetting pattern	Establishment of actual ability	Musical experience	Music game experience	Group division
P1	6	Decrease	×	○	×	Group A
P2	8	Maintain	○	×	○	Group D
P3	6	Decrease	×	×	×	Group B
P4	8	Maintain	○	×	○	Group D
P5	8	Decrease	○	○	○	Group C
P6	9	-	-	○	○	-
P7	8	Decrease	○	○	○	Group C

analyze whether a participant has acquired general Sparebeat skills that constitute actual ability or whether they have simply grown used to their assigned piece.

An easy piece refers to a piece that has a low difficulty level on the 1–15 stage difficult index in Sparebeat and on which it is easy to obtain a high score. When the score of the assigned piece is higher than that of the easy piece, it is considered that the participant has grown used to the assigned piece, rather than having acquired general skills. Furthermore, the closer the score of the easy piece is to the score of the difficult piece, the more the participant can be said to have simply grown used to the assigned piece. In other words, the closer the score of the easy piece is to that of the assigned piece, the more the participant has learned general skills. However, even if a participant has acquired actual ability, we cannot say that the participant will definitely score highest on the easy piece. To investigate the relationship between the learning and forgetting of skills involved in music games, it is necessary to further improve aspects of the method of the training phase, such as the selection of the assigned pieces and the practice method.

For participants P2, P4, P5 and P7 the score on the easy piece was close to the score on the assigned piece, thus these participants can be said to have acquired actual ability. In contrast, P1 and P3, whose scores were close to the score on the difficult piece, can be said to have only become proficient at their assigned pieces.

5.3 Music Game Experience and Musical Experience

To investigate individual differences regarding music game experience, musical experience, awareness of score fluctuation, and impressions of gameplay, once the experiment was over, we presented the results to the seven participants and conducted semi-structured interviews with them.

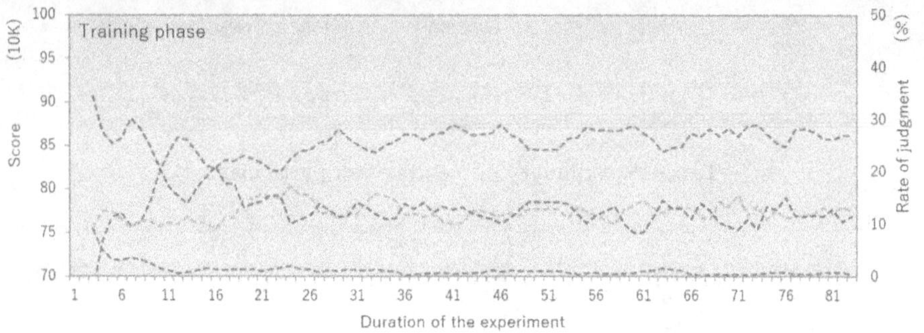

Fig. 10. Transition of score and judgements for P6

The results of the interviews related to musical experience and music game experience are presented in Table 5. Regarding musical experience, P1, P5, P6 and P7 had more than a year's worth of experience. Specifically, P1 and P7 had long-term experience, P5 had belonged to a music club at an elementary school that placed importance on music, and P6 had learned an instrument by self-teaching. On the other hand, P2, P3 and P4 had no musical experience beyond classes at school. Regarding music game experience, P2, P4, P5, P6 and P7 all had experience of music games, while P1 and P3 said that they had never played a music game.

Lastly, P2, P3 and P5, whose scores fluctuated in the non-training phase, were asked whether they were aware of the fluctuation. P2, giving a reason for the fluctuation, answered "I think it was because the tablet I used didn't respond to my fingers properly, and the screen closed down when I input four notes at the same time." It is thought that playing with swollen fingers prevented the tablet device from accurately recognizing the input, which caused the score to decrease. P2 also mentioned that the tablet settings caused the screen to shut down when four notes were input at the same time. Accordingly, we should have had participants use PCs in the experiment, or else instructed them to change the settings on their tablet devices. P3 commented "I think my mood on the day affected my score." P5 said "In cold periods like winter or the rainy season, my hands got stiff and I couldn't move them properly, so that might have caused my score to drop." Considering the above statements, it is possible that, for all the participants whose scores fluctuated in the non-training phase, the fluctuation was related not to forgetting but to external influences. Therefore, it is also possible that without these external influences the scores of those participants, like the scores of the other participants, would have either decreased or been maintained. From the above interview results, we will anaylze the relationship between music game experience and musical experience and the change in scores in the non-training phase.

5.4 Does Musical Experience Accelerate the Rate of Forgetting?

Looking at the interview results in Table 5, from the viewpoint of experience, the participants can be divided as follows.

Ⓐ **No music game experience & Some musical experience**: P1

Ⓑ **No music game experience & No musical experience**: P3

Ⓒ **Some music game experience & Some musical experience**: P5,P7

Ⓓ **Some music game experience & No musical experience**: P2, P4

In the case of P1 and P3, who correspond to Ⓐ and Ⓑ, respectively, the score on the assigned piece declined and, regarding the additional pieces, the score on the easy piece was close to that on the difficult piece, suggesting that these participants had only become proficient at playing their assigned pieces. In the case of P5 and P7, who correspond to Ⓒ, the score on the assigned piece declined and the score on the easy piece was close to the score on the assigned pieces, suggesting that they had acquired actual ability. P2 and P4, who correspond to Ⓓ, maintained the score on the assigned piece, and the score on the easy piece was close to the score on the assigned piece, suggesting that they had acquired actual ability. From the above, it can be inferred that the participants who had experience of music games tended to acquire actual ability.

In contrast, even when they had experience of music games, the participants who had musical experience tended to forget the skills they acquired. In other words, there emerged the hypothesis that musical experience hinders affects the ability to maintain one's score and accelerates the rate of forgetting. This is because a person with musical experience tends to memorize a musical score as combinations of symbols, whereas a person with music game experience has acquired the physical skills and motion skills unique to music games. In the case of the latter, it is thought that the skills are applicable even when aspects of the game-playing environment are changed, such as the frequency of playing and the pieces that are played.

Working on the basis that there is this difference, regarding forgetting patterns and the establishment of actual ability, between people who remember things symobolically and people who remember things physically, it is possible that by further clarifying the mechanism of acquiring and forgetting skills, in future research, the knowledge obtained could be utilized in the learning of other skills, such as dance and the performance of comic monologues.

Finally, we consider the reason P6 ended the experiment before entering the non-training phase. The transition of the three-interval moving average score and timing judgement of P6 are presented in Fig. 10. Regarding the change in the score of P6 in the training phase, in Fig. 10 it can be seen that the score increases steadily at the beginning of the experiment, but from around the 30th day the score stops increasing and remains stagnant at approximately 850,000 points for a long period. Compared to the other participants, P6 had a long training phase and little score variation. When asked about the reason for this stagnation, P6 answered “At first I enjoyed playing the game, but it gradually began to feel like a chore;” “My score didn’t increase, so my motivation decreased and I got tired of it.” This implies that in music games there is a relationship between score change and factors such as motivation and difficulty level.

6 Conclusion

In this research focusing on patterns of acquiring and forgetting skills in music games, we conducted an analysis, through a long-term experiment, of how the condition of forgetting is affected by factors such as experience of music games and the establishment of actual ability during skill acquisition. The experiment participants played assigned pieces in the music game until they achieved a certain score, then we investigated the extent to which they forgot the acquired skills once they stopped practicing, and the relationship between skill acquisition patterns and forgetting patterns. In addition, partway through the experiment, we extended the length of the non-training interval to one month and introduced additional pieces of music. As a result, we were able largely to divide the participants into two patterns, a pattern in which the score is maintained and a pattern in which the score decreases, and analyze how the scores transitioned. Furthermore, we compared the scores of the two additional pieces with the score of the assigned piece and determined whether each participant had simply grown used to their assigned piece or whether they had established a general ability to play the music game. After the experiment, we interviewed the participants to investigate their peculiarities and anything they noticed during the experiment. As a result, we found that it was possible that score fluctuation was not related to forgetting but to the influence of external factors, that having experience of music games may promote the establishment of actual ability, and that having musical experience may impede the maintenance of one’s score.

Our future intentions are as follows. This research adopted a hypothesis testing approach to gain a comprehensive understanding of skill-forgetting patterns. The results of the experiment and the interviews implied that each participant’s individual circumstances influence their patterns of skill acquisition and forgetting. It is thought that this knowledge will be useful for constructing theoretical samples when recruiting participants for the next experiment. In the future, to predict the acquisition and forgetting of skills, it will be necessary to verify the viewpoints and theories discovered in this research, by increasing the number of experiment participants and collecting a larger number of data. This time, there were participants who had a short training phase, such as P1 - P3, or who ended the experiment part way through. In the future, when conducting an experiment with new participants, it will be necessary to use stricter criteria for selecting assigned pieces and to adjust the procedure to bring a certain degree of coherence to the training phase.

Furthermore, in the analysis carried out in this research, we focused only on the factors of the score on the assigned piece, the breakdown of timing judgments, and the duration of the experiment. To clarify the acquisition and forgetting of skills, it is necessary to improve the experiment procedure of the training phase and investigate and incorporate factors related to skill, such as motivation, gaze, hand movement, and analysis of the parts of a piece of music that participants find easy or difficult.

In the classification of forgetting patterns, a slight variation in the score was interpreted as a measurement error and we judged that the score was being maintained. However, this does not constitute an accurate classification of patterns. Therefore, we must establish classification criteria, such as the degree to which the score has decreased and the length of the period for which the score varies. In so doing, we hope to quantify the prediction of the acquisition and forgetting of skills in music games, in order to support the mastery of those skills.

Acknowledgements. This research was supported by JSPS Grant-in-Aid for Research 22H0104 and JSPS Grant-in-Aid for Research 21K18518.

References

1. Alberini, C.M.: Mechanisms of memory stabilization: are consolidation and reconsolidation similar or distinct processes? Trends Neurosci. **28**(1), 51–56 (2005). https://doi.org/10.1016/j.tins.2004.11.001, https://www.sciencedirect.com/science/article/pii/S0166223604003558
2. Ebbinghaus, H.: Memory : a contribution to experimental psychology. Dover Publications (1987). https://ci.nii.ac.jp/ncid/BA14260604
3. Eysenck, M.W.: Attention and ArousalâĂŕ: Cognition and Performance. Springer, Berlin, Heidelberg (2012). https://doi.org/10.1007/978-3-642-68390-9
4. Henmi, K., Yoshikawa, T.: Virtual lesson and its application to virtual calligraphy system. In: Proceedings of the 1998 IEEE International Conference on Robotics and Automation (Cat. No.98CH36146), vol. 2, pp. 1275–1280 (1998). https://doi.org/10.1109/ROBOT.1998.677278
5. Kawamura, S., Ida, M., Wada, T., Wu, J.L.: Development of a virtual sports machine using a wire drive system-a trial of virtual tennis. In: Proceedings 1995 IEEE/RSJ International Conference on Intelligent Robots and Systems. Human Robot Interaction and Cooperative Robots, vol. 1, pp. 111–116 (1995). https://doi.org/10.1109/IROS.1995.525783
6. Liang, Y., Li, W., Ikeda, K.: Procedural content generation of rhythm games using deep learning methods. In: van der Spek, E., Göbel, S., Do, E.Y.-L., Clua, E., Baalsrud Hauge, J. (eds.) ICEC-JCSG 2019. LNCS, vol. 11863, pp. 134–145. Springer, Cham (2019). https://doi.org/10.1007/978-3-030-34644-7_11
7. Liao, C.C., Koike, H., Nakamura, T.: Realtime center of mass adjustment via weight switching device inside a golf putter. In: Extended Abstracts of the 2020 CHI Conference on Human Factors in Computing Systems, pp. 1–8. CHI EA 2020, Association for Computing Machinery, New York, NY, USA (2020). https://doi.org/10.1145/3334480.3383030
8. Mandler, G.: Organization and memory. Psychol. Learn. Motiv. **1**, 327–372 (1967)
9. Morita, Y., Ogawa, K., Uchida, S.: Napping after complex motor learning enhances juggling performance. Sleep Sci. **9**(2), 112–116 (2016). https://doi.org/10.1016/j.slsci.2016.04.002

10. Nakamura, T., Koike, H.: Golf club-type device with force feedback for modifying club posture. In: Extended Abstracts of the 2020 CHI Conference on Human Factors in Computing Systems, pp. 1–7. CHI EA 2020, Association for Computing Machinery, New York, NY, USA (2020). https://doi.org/10.1145/3334480.3383024
11. Nakamura, T., Saito, D., Wu, E., Koike, H.: Actuated club: modification of golf-club posture with force feedback and motion prediction in VR environment. In: ACM SIGGRAPH 2020 Emerging Technologies. SIGGRAPH 2020, Association for Computing Machinery, New York, NY, USA (2020). https://doi.org/10.1145/3388534.3407286
12. Nakano, T., Goto, M., Hiraga, Y.: MIRUSinger: a singing skill visualization interface using real-time feedback and music CD recordings as referential data. In: Ninth IEEE International Symposium on Multimedia Workshops (ISMW 2007), pp. 75–76 (2007). https://doi.org/10.1109/ISM.Workshops.2007.19
13. Ranganath, C., Blumenfeld, R.S.: Doubts about double dissociations between short- and long-term memory. Trends Cogn. Sci. **9**(8), 374–380 (2005)
14. Sasaki, A., Matsuura, M., Matsubara, M., Takegawa, Y., Hirata, K.: Exploring patterns of skill gain and loss on long-term training and non-training in rhythm game. In: Proceedings of the 16th International Symposium on Computer Music Multidisciplinary Research, pp. 66–77. Zenodo (2023). https://doi.org/10.5281/zenodo.10110049
15. suzukibakery: SpareBeat. https://sparebeat.com/, Accessed 20 Oct 2024
16. Takegawa, Y., Tayanagi, E., Tsubakimoto, M., Hirata, K.: Evaluation of a piano learning support system focusing on the learning process. In: Proceedings of World Conference on Educational Media and Technology (EdMedia2013), pp. 2306–2314 (2013)
17. Takegawa, Y., Tsukamoto, M., Terada, T.: Design and implementation of a piano practice support system using a real-time fingering recognition technique. In: Proceedings. 2011 International Computer Music Conference, pp. 1–8 (01 2011)
18. Tamaki, M., Matsuoka, T., Nittono, H., Hori, T.: Fast sleep spindle (13–15 Hz) activity correlates with sleep-dependent improvement in visuomotor performance. Sleep **31**(2), 204–211 (2008). https://doi.org/10.1093/sleep/31.2.204
19. Tanaka, S., Takegawa, Y., Hirata, K.: Proposal of a support system for learning brushstrokes in transcription for beginners. In: Proceedings of the 25th International Conference on Intelligent User Interfaces, pp. 352–356. IUI 2020, Association for Computing Machinery, New York, NY, USA (2020). https://doi.org/10.1145/3377325.3377534
20. Walker, M.P., Brakefield, T., Morgan, A., Hobson, J., Stickgold, R.: Practice with sleep makes perfect: Sleep-dependent motor skill learning. Neuron **35**(1), 205–211 (2002). https://doi.org/10.1016/S0896-6273(02)00746-8, https://www.sciencedirect.com/science/article/pii/S0896627302007468

Emotional Impact of Source Localization in Music Using Machine Learning and EEG
A Proof-of-Concept Study

Timothy Schmele[1,3(✉)], Eleonora De Filippi[2], Arijit Nandi[2], Alexandre Pereda Baños[2], and Adan Garriga[3]

[1] Institute for Music Informatics and Musicology (IMWI), University of Music, 76131 Karlsruhe, Germany
tim.schmele@eurecat.org

[2] Department of Big Data at Eurecat, Centre Tecnologic, 08005 Barcelona, Spain
eleonora.defilippi@eurecat.org

[3] Department of Multimedia at Eurecat, Center Tecnologic, 08005 Barcelona, Spain

Abstract. Little is currently known about how varied source locations affect a listener's emotional reaction to music. Here, using spectral features extracted from electrophysiology (EEG) data, we tested through machine learning whether four music source positions (front, back, left, and right) could be accurately distinguished according to the type of valence in a subject-wise manner. The findings demonstrate that distinct EEG correlates can reliably classify the four source locations and that the effect is stronger when music with a negative emotional valence is played outside of the listener's visual field. This proof-of-concept study may pave the way for advanced spatial audio analysis approaches in music information retrieval by considering the listener's emotional impact depending on the source direction of incidence.

Keywords: spatial music · emotion recognition · affective computing · EEG · machine learning · SVM · source localization

1 Introduction

Music's ability to modulate cognitive and emotional processes has been widely documented over the years [19,33,37,41], making it a relevant tool to investigate the brain correlates of emotional processes [22]. However, little is known about the impact of different sound-source locations on the emotional response to music, as only a few studies have addressed this issue [2,16,20]. In particular, the study conducted by Asutay et al. [2] provided evidence that the effects of spatial source location on attentional processes are mediated by the emotional information conveyed by the sound [2]. The authors also demonstrated that a sound source behind the participant led to a more robust affective response in the listeners [2]. In another work, Tajadura-Jiménez et al. concluded that sound sources

S. Ystad et al. (Eds.): CMMR 2023, LNCS 15236, pp. 59–71, 2026.
https://doi.org/10.1007/978-3-032-02042-0_4

outside the visual field produce emotional states of increased arousal [39], though these effects were more pronounced for natural sounds. Similarly, the work of Ekman and Kajastila showed that sounds are judged by the listener as scarier when they come from the back as compared to the front [16], although context has been found to be an important factor in eliciting the desired effect [20]. In a more detailed study using everyday sound events, Drossos et al. [12] showed that lateral positions do increase the listeners' affective state significantly, although this is dependent on the content of the audio sample used.

Moreover, there is a strong connection between space and music, as music can, in turn, evoke sensations of space and movement as a sense of *intrinsic space*, i.e. a metaphorical space, created by musical features in melody, harmony or rhythm, as opposed to the *literal, physical space* a sound source may occupy [11]. The most common effect is that of associating the perceived pitch with a sense of spatial height [35], although alternative spatial representations for the same also exist latently [15]. Furthermore, a correlation between the absolute pitch of a musical piece and emotional affect has been shown [21]. In a study conducted by Eitan et al. [14], in which participants were asked to associate music with imagined, spatial motions of a human character, it was shown that most musical parameters significantly affect the imaginary motion, indicating a strong correlation between music and space perception.

Here we investigated whether four different music source spatial locations (i.e., front, back, left, and right) are reflected in a distinct pattern of electrophysiological activity that can be captured by a machine-learning approach. Moreover, we explored the interaction between distinct music source locations and the emotional salience of the musical excerpts played. The dimensional model supports the idea that emotions can be modeled as combinations of a few fundamental and basic dimensions. Valence and arousal, sometimes known as the "circumplex model," are two fundamental qualities that researchers unanimously concur are necessary to understand emotions [23]. The valence level varies from unpleasant (negative) to pleasant (positive), while the arousal level, specifically, ranges from not aroused (low arousal) to thrilled (high arousal).

We recorded electrophysiological (EEG) data while participants were listening to musical excerpts characterized by either positive or negative valence, both with middle values of arousal, and occurring from different spatial source locations. To take into account individual differences, we performed subject-based classification between each pair of spatial locations, according to the type of valence. We hypothesized that when the music source was located outside the listener's visual field (i.e., back, right, left) it would lead to a different electrophysiological pattern and impact on the affective state as compared to frontal source localization. In order to choose which samples to use for this study, we categorized the musical excerpts into 3 groups of high, mid, and low values along each emotional dimension (valence and arousal), based on the static evaluation metric. To evaluate the effect of valence in this study, those samples that fell into the mid-arousal category were first selected and then separated into two categories of positive or negative valence. The error between the average dynamic and static rating served as an ordering mechanism, along which the final samples could be selected.

1.1 Experimental Design

The sequence of audio samples was arranged into blocks of 3 randomly selected musical excerpts without repetition. Random selection was done anew for each participant. First, from each category, i.e. positive or negative valence, the samples were shuffled and grouped into blocks of 3 musical excerpts. Each block was assigned a spatial position (front, back, left, or right) at random, representing each position equally. Then, the blocks from each category were combined in random order into a single sequence of $36 + 36 = 72$ samples.

The participant was first shown an introduction, explaining the experiment and the SAM questionnaire, followed by a short test if the participant has understood what the SAM represents. Then, a baseline rest period of 120s is recorded. After that, the main experiment started. In each block, 3 music samples from the same spatial position were played. Before each sample, a rest period of 5s was first presented to mentally reset the participant. At the end of each musical sample, the participant had to fill out the SAM questionnaire rating their emotional response to that particular musical stimulus. At the end of each block, another additional questionnaire was shown, where the participant answered how exhausted and attentive they felt.

The experiment ended after all blocks and their respective musical samples had been played to the participant. The EEG data were recorded using a 19-electrode Neuroelectrics® Instrument Controller (NIC2) at a sampling rate of 250 Hz. The subjects were informed about the experimental protocol, its approximate duration, and the meaning of the SAM scales. We instructed the participants not to move, particularly during playback of the stimulus, to reduce muscular artifacts in the EEG data. The experiment was conducted according to the Helsinki Declaration and all subjects signed the consent form.

1.2 Participants

We recruited a total of 20 healthy participants (10 males and 10 females) with a mean age of 28.66 years (SD = 5.53), no history of psychiatric or neurological disorders, and normal hearing. Furthermore, subjects had no prior experience or formal music training. Nearly all participants were right-handed, with only one participant being left-handed. After preprocessing the EEG signal, 3 participants were removed from the analysis due to excessive artifacts. Only 17 participants were included in the analysis, comprising 9 females and 8 males with a median age of 28 (20–38).

1.3 Experimental Setup

The room in which the experiment took place was acoustically treated, with acoustic diffusion panels on the walls and absorption panels on the ceiling, as well as acoustically isolated from the outside. The reverberation time was relatively short, with an RT_{60} of 0.398 s at 125 Hz to 0.253 s at 8 kHz. The average RT_{60} between 500 Hz and 1000 Hz is around 0.293 s. The audio stimuli were played from four positions: front, back, left, and right. A loudspeaker was placed in each position. The front and back loudspeakers were positioned at 3.2 m from the listener, while the side speakers were at 2.3 m.

To correct for the differences in distance between the loudspeakers, each loudspeaker was calibrated to 75 dBSPL using pink noise at −20 dBFS at the center listening position. The loudspeakers used were of the type Genelec 8040, fed by a Focusrite Scarlet 18i20 soundcard. The audio playback was done with the *sounddevice* module for Python, running on a Windows laptop computer.[1]

The interface was built for a web browser using HTML and CSS, with the functional elements programmed in Javascript and Jquery. The interface was designed with touch controls in mind, filtering accidental double taps and guiding the participant through the experiment. Whenever a button to continue was shown, the participant was also able to change their mind before sending off the result to be recorded. The Python script and the web front-end communicated using a simple socket connection over *localhost*. All activity on the touch screen was recorded over the socket connection.

1.4 EEG Preprocessing

EEG data were analyzed in an offline manner using the EEGLAB toolbox on Matlab R2019b (The Mathworks, Inc.). The preprocessing steps included down-sampling of the signal to 130 Hz and the application of a bandpass Butterworth filter ranging from 0.01 up to 40 Hz. To correct eye blinks and muscular artifacts, we used the Independent Component Analysis (ICA) algorithm. For each subject, we manually removed all components capturing artifacts. Afterward, we epoched the EEG data and created eight distinct datasets for each subject according to the experimental condition (i.e., spatial position and type of valence). Finally, we applied a spatial filter to reduce the volume conduction effect, using the surface Laplacian transform inspired by the spherical spline method described by [29–31].

1.5 Feature Extraction

To preserve information about the temporal dynamics, we transformed the EEG data into the time-frequency domain using Complex Morlet Wavelet convolution (CMW) [8]. We chose CMW instead of alternative approaches like the Short-time Fourier Transform or the Hilbert Transform, because CMW is a Gaussian-shaped wavelet in the frequency domain.

Since we were interested in all frequency bands, we selected a range of frequencies going from 1 Hz up to 40 Hz. Following the use of CMW convolution,

[1] https://github.com/multimedia-eurecat/Neuromuse.

we retrieved the power from the coefficients and then used a decibel-baseline normalization, utilizing all neutral trials as a baseline. We used a sliding-window strategy to reduce the time-frequency data for every trial in order to increase the sample size. There were a total of 39 windows in every trial, each lasting 1 s and overlapping by half a second.

Then, we calculated the average change in power compared to the neutral baseline for seven frequency bands (delta 1–4 Hz, theta 4–8 Hz, low alpha 8–10 Hz, high alpha 10–12 Hz, low beta 13–18 Hz, high beta 18–30 Hz, and gamma 31–40 Hz), which constitute the spectral features. Within each window and for all the 19 channels and the seven frequency bands, the features extracted were the mean power, the standard deviation of the mean, and the frontal alpha asymmetry (FAA). The FAA coefficients were calculated for the channel pairs Fp1-Fp2 and F3-F4 in both low-alpha (8–10 Hz) and high-alpha (10–12 Hz) bands. The resulting feature array consisted of 351 samples for each class with a total of 270 features.

1.6 Classification and Feature Selection

For data classification, we utilized MATLAB R2022a Statistics and the Machine Learning Toolbox. As a base classifier, the linear Support Vector Machine (SVM) supervised learning approach was chosen, which uses a hyperplane as a decision boundary to optimize the margin of separation between two classes. Herewith, SVMs give a metric that permits scaling the certainty with which a window sample is allocated to one of the two classes: the sample's distance from the separation hyperplane. To evaluate the classifier's performance robustly, we used 6-fold cross-validation to train and test the classifier, allocating all windows in one trial to the same fold. Having said that, we also ran the 6-fold cross-validation fifty times and averaged the results across different classification runs.

It is well known that feature extraction and selection strategies assist to reduce computing complexity and develop models with greater generalization capabilities, in addition to enhancing predictive power [1]. That is, we used the Bioinformatics toolbox of MATLAB R2022a to do feature selection due to the large dimensionality of our dataset. The goal was to improve the classifier's learning performance and find the most common discriminative characteristics shared by all participants. We rated the characteristics based on their importance between the classes, using the t-test as an independent criterion for binary classification. For each feature, the built-in function in MATLAB calculates the absolute value of the two-sample t-test with pooled variance estimate. Finally, we identified the top 20 characteristics for each topic and combined them to determine which features were shared by all participants.

Statistical Comparisons. We used the Wilcoxon rank-sum method to investigate if the SVM performances were significantly above chance, thus we statistically compared accuracy distributions of real-labeled data with surrogate data (i.e., randomly shuffled labels). Furthermore, data from the self-assessment

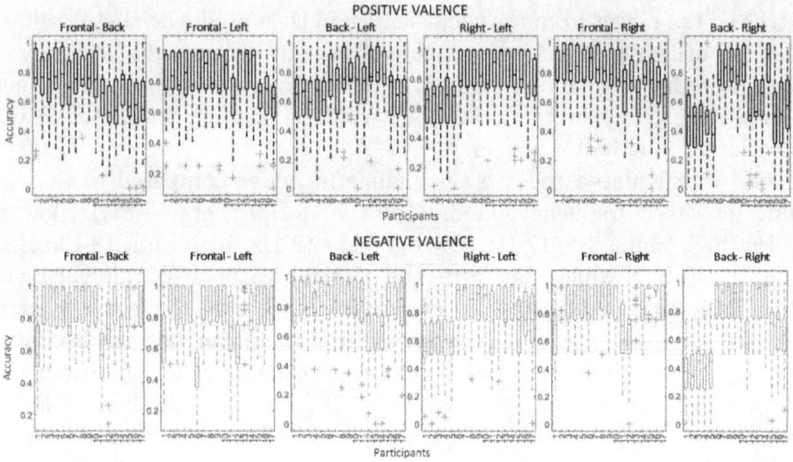

Fig. 1. Within-subject classification results of each binary classification between music position sources according to the type of valence. We performed 6-fold cross-validation 50 times, such that the boxplots depict the results of 50 classification runs for each participant.

SAM questionnaire were analyzed using a general linear model, the multivariate analysis of variance (MANOVA), on IBM SPSS Statistics.

2 Results

We investigated through machine learning whether the four music position sources could be accurately differentiated according to the type of valence in a subject-wise manner using spectral features extracted from EEG data cut into 1-second windows. The results of all cross-validation run for each participant are presented in Fig. 1. The corresponding accuracy averaged across subjects for each binary classification run is summarized in Table 1. For both positive and negative valence, we showed that the highest average accuracy was reached when classifying the frontal localization versus each of the three sources located outside the visual field. In particular, this effect was stronger when classifying pairs of source locations using events characterized by negative valence.

2.1 Highest-Ranked Features

To understand which channels and frequency bands were the most discriminative between the four location sources depending on the type of valence, we applied a feature selection algorithm and merged together the top twenty features for each subject. As represented in Fig. 2, the results of the feature selection procedure showed that the electrophysiological correlates of the difference between frontal location and the three sources located outside the visual field (i.e., back, right,

Table 1. Classification results averaged across participants for each pair of binary classification runs presented according to the valence type. An asterisk indicates that the average accuracy is significantly above the chance level (p<0.05).

	Pair of music source locations	Mean accuracy across subjects		Pair of music source locations	Mean accuracy across subjects
Positive valence	Frontal - Back	70%*	Negative valence	Frontal - Back	85%*
	Frontal - Left	80%*		Frontal - Left	82%*
	Back - Left	69%*		Back - Left	78%*
	Right - Left	76%*		Right - Left	74%*
	Frontal - Right	77%*		Frontal - Right	87%*
	Back - Right	61%*		Back - Right	67%*

left) rely on different activities of channels mainly located in frontal and central areas, especially in the highest frequencies. In particular, we found that when using musical excerpts with negative valence, the difference between frontal location and each of the three sources out of the field of view was based on activity in beta (low and high) and gamma bands in channels Fp1, F3, F4, Fz, Cz, and T8, and in FAA measures for pairs of channels Fp1-Fp2 and F3-F4. On the other side, when comparing the source locations using positive valence, we showed that also brain activity in the alpha band, together with beta and gamma was important for differentiating frontal position from each of the other three sources. Moreover, in the case of positive valence, channels from posterior sites, especially Pz, P7, and P8, as well as central, frontal sites and FAA, were relevant for the classification of source locations, indicating a more widespread involvement of different brain areas.

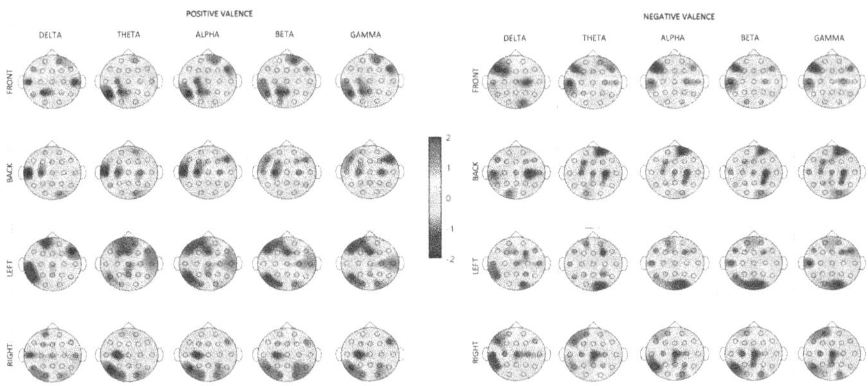

Fig. 2. Topoplots indicating brain activity for each of the main frequency bands according to the source locations (i.e., front, back, left, and right) and the type of valence (i.e., negative and positive). Colors in brain plots indicate the power in that specific channel and frequency band, with red showing the highest power and blue the lowest.

2.2 Self-assessment SAM Questionnaire

Results of self-reported ratings showed that there was a significant difference in arousal and valence ratings based on the type of event (source location and type of valence of musical excerpts), $F(14, 12428) = 28.133$, $p = 0.000$, $Wilk'slambda = 0.740$, partial eta squared = 0.14. The source locations depending on the type of valence had a significant effect both on reported levels of perceived arousal, $F(7, 1215) = 18.477$, $p = 0.000$, partial eta squared = 0.096, and valence, $F(7, 1215) = 47.886$, $p = 0.000$, partial eta squared = 0.216. Averaged reported levels of perceived arousal and valence are presented in Table 2.

Post-hoc analysis revealed that there were significant differences between trials with positive valence and negative valence within each source location ($p = 0.000$, Bonferroni corrected). In particular, musical excerpts characterized by positive valence elicited higher reported levels of arousal ($p = 0.000$) and valence ($p = 0.000$) for each of the four source locations. Differences between sources were not significant ($p > 0.05$) when comparing the same type of valence (i.e., either positive or negative), except the levels of reported arousal between the back and right when music with positive valence was played ($p = 0.03$, Bonferroni corrected).

Table 2. Average reported levels of arousal and valence by means of the SAM questionnaire on a Likert scale from 1 to 5.

Type of valence	Source location	Average SAM rating for arousal	Average SAM rating for valence
Positive	Frontal	3,41	3,25
	Back	3,57	3,21
	Left	3,22	3,17
	Right	3,45	3,36
Negative	Frontal	2,63	2,03
	Back	2,90	2,18
	Left	2,88	2,28
	Right	3,45	2,15

3 Discussion

In this work, we analyzed the impact of different source locations of music depending on the type of valence on the listener's affective brain processing by employing machine learning tools. The results demonstrate that frontal location can be accurately distinguished from each of the three sources (back, right, and left) located outside the listener's visual field. In particular, our results suggested that the emotional connotation of music (i.e., positive and negative valence) mediated the impact of the different source locations on the brain's electrophysiological signal, as reflected by music characterized with negative valence yielding higher classification performances in differentiating between the spatial sources as compared to musical excerpts characterized by positive valence.

Furthermore, by applying a feature selection procedure we showed that playing music from different source locations led to different electrophysiological brain responses in the highest frequencies (alpha, beta, and gamma) and in channels belonging to the frontal, central, and also parietal areas in the case of positive valence. The importance of beta and gamma bands that we found here is consistent with earlier research showing the significance of these bands for differentiating between various emotional states [24,25]. Moreover, a previous study has found that the alpha band in parietal channels was associated with the processing of auditory stimuli, while the gamma band activity was related to music awareness [27]. Interestingly, we found the FAA between pairs of channels Fp1-Fp2 and F3-F4 to be an important measure for distinguishing between different locations, both for positive and negative valence conditions. Alpha activity in the frontal site has been largely used as an index of emotional processing, reflecting motivation and dominance of perceived emotion. Indeed, in the literature, positive emotional stimuli have been related to a relative increase in left hemisphere activity, whereas negative emotional stimuli have been associated with a larger right hemisphere activity [10,32]. For example, a previous study has found that musical excerpts characterized by positive valence induced lower frontal alpha power in the left hemisphere [36]. In addition to valence and arousal, frontal asymmetry was also linked to other factors, such as self-reported dominance [34].

Music has generally been used in research as a tool to elicit emotional responses in participants and study emotional processes in the brain [7,40]. Recent applications of Brain-Computer Interfaces have used music as a way to convey information and/or feedback in a real-time manner to the subjects based on their own brain activity [9,13,18]. However, the difficulty of participants in engaging and sustaining genuine emotional states in an experimental context, particularly when trying to elicit complex emotions, has generally been a significant hurdle for neuroimaging and BCI studies based on affective processes. In this regard, the results of this study may pave the way for more effective use of music as a stimulus in experimental settings.

Moreover, the analysis of tones and their spatial orientation in relation to the listener is relevant in the context of *spatial music*. Here, spatial music refers to musical composition practices that specifically target spatial aspects of sound as a compositional parameter, such as the sound position or specific aspects of room acoustics [17,26]. Indeed, emotion elicited through spatial music listening is not an aspect that is not often considered in this context. The discussion around space in music tends to be often of philosophical [17], or conceptual nature [6,26] and often centers around aspects in electronics or hardware [5,6], technology [3,4] or taxonomy [38]. In a survey conducted in [28], composers are more often than not concerned with those spatial aspects in music that can be parameterized on a technical level and lesser with the emotional impact space can have on the listener. The results of this study indicate that an analysis of spatial music would need to take into account the correlation between the extracted emotional impact of the more traditional musical parameters, such as melody and rhythm, with the impact made by spatial features.

However, this study does present some limitations. Most importantly, the relatively small sample size may limit the generalization of our results. Also, despite having found a different brain pattern of activity in the EEG signal related to affective processing of music depending on the various source locations, this effect was not reflected in the analysis of subjective ratings of both arousal and valence. This may have been due to overthinking, rather than an immediate and intuitive reaction. When being asked how one would evaluate a piece of music, one would have to execute the said task by recollecting what was just heard. This evaluation will thus be skewed by the importance a subject might place on different musical aspects. Therefore, if a subject has little to no experience in associating spatial position with musical significance, then the recollection of the heard excerpt will most likely be focused on other aspects, filtering out the spatial direction from which the excerpt was heard. This means that mentally, i.e. in the inner ear, the music may have been heard *aspatially*. Future work may investigate the potential effect that musical training could have on the results in this context.

4 Conclusion

The present study has shown that machine learning methods are able to discern a listener's affective brain processing between different spatial positions of sound sources as a function of positive or negative affect. Annotated musical excerpts were classified into two groups of both median arousal and low or high valence values respectively. These samples were presented to the listener from the front, the lateral left or right positions, or the back, in random order. Our results showed that frontal location, compared to each of the other three sources located outside the visual field, is associated with different brain electrophysiological patterns related to emotional processing. In fact, we found a significant involvement of alpha, beta, and gamma frequency bands in frontal and central sites, together with FAA measures, in distinguishing between such source locations. These findings were not reflected in the subjective rating analysis, hinting that the subjects may have excluded the spatial aspect of the music when consciously evaluating the heard excerpts. While more analysis is necessary, these first results prove promising. Further analysis is necessary to understand how the source location is able to influence the emotional impact of music, particularly focusing on arousal. Also, it would be interesting assessing whether different types of music show divergence in the emotional impact depending on source location. Lastly, future work will also have to include the median plane to get a more comprehensive view of the effects of spatial source locations on the listener's affective state.

Disclosure of Interests. The authors have no competing interests to declare that are relevant to the content of this article.

References

1. Anthony, G., Ruther, H.: Comparison of feature selection techniques for SVM classification. In: 10th International Symposium on Physical Measurements and Signatures in Remote Sensing, pp. 1–6 (2007)
2. Asutay, E., Västfjäll, D.: Attentional and emotional prioritization of the sounds occurring outside the visual field. Emotion **15**(3), 281 (2015)
3. Baalman, M.A.: Spatial composition techniques and sound spatialisation technologies. Organised Sound **15**(3), 209–218 (2010)
4. Barrett, N.: Spatio-musical composition strategies. Organised sound **7**(3), 313–323 (2002)
5. Bates, E.: The composition and performance of spatial music. Ph.D. thesis, Trinity College Dublin (2009)
6. Brech, M., von Coler, H.: Aspects of space in Luigi Nono's Prometeo and the use of the Halaphon. In: Kompositionen für hörbaren Raum/Compositions for Audible Space, pp. 193–204. transcript Verlag (2015)
7. Brown, S., Martinez, M.J., Parsons, L.M.: Passive music listening spontaneously engages limbic and paralimbic systems. NeuroReport **15**(13), 2033–2037 (2004)
8. Cohen, M.X.: A better way to define and describe Morlet wavelets for time-frequency analysis. Neuroimage **199**, 81–86 (2019)
9. Daly, I., et al.: Affective brain-computer music interfacing. J. Neural Eng. **13**(4), 046022 (2016)
10. Davidson, R.J., Henriques, J.: Regional brain function in sadness and depression. In: The Neuropsychology of Emotion, pp. 269–297 (2000)
11. Di Bona, E.: Listening to the space of music. Rivista di estetica **66**, 93–105 (2017)
12. Drossos, K., Floros, A., Giannakoulopoulos, A., Kanellopoulos, N.: Investigating the impact of sound angular position on the listener affective state. IEEE Trans. Affect. Comput. **6**(1), 27–42 (2015)
13. Ehrlich, S.K., Agres, K.R., Guan, C., Cheng, G.: A closed-loop, music-based brain-computer interface for emotion mediation. PLoS ONE **14**(3), e0213516 (2019)
14. Eitan, Z., Granot, R.Y.: How music moves: musical parameters and listeners images of motion. Music. Percept. **23**(3), 221–248 (2006)
15. Eitan, Z., Timmers, R.: Beethoven's last piano sonata and those who follow crocodiles: cross-domain mappings of auditory pitch in a musical context. Cognition **114**(3), 405–422 (2010)
16. Ekman, I., Kajastila, R.: Localization cues affect emotional judgments–results from a user study on scary sound. In: Audio Engineering Society Conference: 35th International Conference: Audio for Games. Audio Engineering Society (2009)
17. Harley, M.A.: Space and spatialization in contemporary music: history and analysis, ideas and implementations. Ph.D. thesis, McGill Univeristy (1994)
18. Heo, J., Baek, H.J., Hong, S., Chang, M.H., Lee, J.S., Park, K.S.: Music and natural sounds in an auditory steady-state response based brain-computer interface to increase user acceptance. Comput. Biol. Med. **84**, 45–52 (2017)
19. Hou, Y., Chen, S.: Distinguishing different emotions evoked by music via electroencephalographic signals. Comput. Intell. Neurosci. **2019**, 3191903 (2019)

20. Hughes, S., Kearney, G.: Fear and localisation: emotional fine-tuning using multiple source directions. In: Audio Engineering Society Conference: 56th International Conference: Audio for Games. Audio Engineering Society (2015)
21. Jaquet, L., Danuser, B., Gomez, P.: Music and felt emotions: how systematic pitch level variations affect the experience of pleasantness and arousal. Psychol. Music **42**(1), 51–70 (2014)
22. Koelsch, S.: Brain correlates of music-evoked emotions. Nat. Rev. Neurosci. **15**(3), 170–180 (2014)
23. Lang, P.J., Greenwald, M.K., Bradley, M.M., Hamm, A.O.: Looking at pictures: affective, facial, visceral, and behavioral reactions. Psychophysiology **30**(3), 261–273 (1993)
24. Li, M., Lu, B.L.: Emotion classification based on gamma-band EEG. In: 2009 Annual International Conference of the IEEE Engineering in Medicine and Biology Society, pp. 1223–1226. IEEE (2009)
25. Li, P., et al.: EEG based emotion recognition by combining functional connectivity network and local activations. IEEE Trans. Biomed. Eng. **66**(10), 2869–2881 (2019)
26. Miller, P.: Stockhausen and the Serial shaping of Space. University of Rochester, Eastman School of Music (2009)
27. Mollakazemi, M.J., Biswal, D., Patwardhan, A.: Target frequency band of cognition and tempo of music: cardiac synchronous EEG. In: 2018 IEEE International Symposium on Signal Processing and Information Technology (ISSPIT), pp. 696–700. IEEE (2018)
28. Otondo, F.: Contemporary trends in the use of space in electroacoustic music. Organised Sound **13**(1), 77–81 (2008)
29. Perrin, F., Pernier, J., Bertnard, O., Giard, M.H., Echallier, J.: Mapping of scalp potentials by surface spline interpolation. Electroencephalogr. Clin. Neurophysiol. **66**(1), 75–81 (1987)
30. Perrin, F., Bertrand, O., Pernier, J.: Scalp current density mapping: value and estimation from potential data. IEEE Trans. Biomed. Eng. **4**, 283–288 (1987)
31. Perrin, F., Pernier, J., Bertrand, O., Echallier, J.: Spherical splines for scalp potential and current density mapping. Electroencephalogr. Clin. Neurophysiol. **72**(2), 184–187 (1989)
32. Poole, B.D., Gable, P.A.: Affective motivational direction drives asymmetric frontal hemisphere activation. Exp. Brain Res. **232**(7), 2121–2130 (2014). https://doi.org/10.1007/s00221-014-3902-4
33. Putkinen, V., et al.: Decoding music-evoked emotions in the auditory and motor cortex. Cereb. Cortex **31**(5), 2549–2560 (2021)
34. Reuderink, B., Mühl, C., Poel, M.: Valence, arousal and dominance in the EEG during game play. Int. J. Autonomous Adapt. Commun. Syst. **6**(1), 45–62 (2013)
35. Rusconi, E., Kwan, B., Giordano, B.L., Umilta, C., Butterworth, B.: Spatial representation of pitch height: the SMARC effect. Cognition **99**(2), 113–129 (2006)
36. Schmidt, L.A., Trainor, L.J.: Frontal brain electrical activity (EEG) distinguishes valence and intensity of musical emotions. Cognit. Emotion **15**(4), 487–500 (2001)
37. Sloboda, J.A.: Music structure and emotional response: some empirical findings. Psychol. Music **19**(2), 110–120 (1991)
38. Smalley, D.: Space-form and the acousmatic image. Organised sound **12**(1), 35–58 (2007)
39. Tajadura-Jiménez, A., Larsson, P., Väljamäe, A., Västfjäll, D., Kleiner, M.: When room size matters: acoustic influences on emotional responses to sounds. Emotion **10**(3), 416 (2010)

40. Trost, W., Ethofer, T., Zentner, M., Vuilleumier, P.: Mapping aesthetic musical emotions in the brain. Cereb. Cortex **22**(12), 2769–2783 (2012)
41. Vuust, P., Heggli, O.A., Friston, K.J., Kringelbach, M.L.: Music in the brain. Nat. Rev. Neurosci. **23**(5), 287–305 (2022)

A Quantitative Evaluation of a Musical Performance Support System Utilizing a Musical Sophistication Test Battery

Yasumasa Yamaguchi[1](✉), Taku Kawada[2], Toru Nagahama[3], and Tatsuya Horita[3]

[1] Sendai University, Miyagi, Japan
ys-yamaguchi@sendai-u.ac.jp
[2] Sendai Shirayuri Gakuen Elementary School, Sendai, Japan
[3] Graduate School of Information Sciences, Tohoku University, Sendai, Japan

Abstract. This article discusses the effects of a pitch feedback system integrated into Google Glass, called the MVP (Musical pitch Visualization Perception) support system, on the musical performance of wind instrumentalists. The study adopted the Goldsmith Musical Sophistication Index (Gold-MSI) to discuss the contribution of the MVP support system to the improvement of musical performance. The Gold-MSI is a popular tool in the field of music research that measures musical sophistication based on observable behaviors. The study reports the effects of the MVP support system from a quantitative standpoint, and the results show that the system had a positive impact on the participants' pitch accuracy.

Keywords: ICT · performance support · pitch feedback · performance evaluation · quantitative analysis

1 Introduction

The intonation of instrumentalists has been extensively discussed in the literature [1], with correct intonation being viewed as particularly important for novice instrumentalists when performing in an ensemble. Effective methods for improving intonation have been widely studied in music education research [2]. In recent years, many researchers have shown an interest in real-time pitch feedback systems, owing to the development of Information and Communication Technologies (ICT). For instance, Wang et al. [3] investigated the potential of real-time feedback for violinists. This study, however, will focus on wind instrumentalists who perform in a concert band or orchestra.

Instrumentalists must pay attention not only to their intonation but also to other crucial aspects of performance, such as sheet music, rhythm, dynamics, fingering, tempo, expression, ensemble, and conductor cues [4]. Information provided by the conductor is as essential as auditory information. However, during performances, some novice and student instrumentalists tend to rely on their tuner, which is typically placed on their music stand. This habit may cause fixation of gaze, narrowing of visual field, and poor posture. Therefore, Yamaguchi et al. [5, 6] proposed a pitch feedback system integrated

S. Ystad et al. (Eds.): CMMR 2023, LNCS 15236, pp. 72–79, 2026.
https://doi.org/10.1007/978-3-032-02042-0_5

into Google Glass as a Musical pitch Visualization Perception (MVP) support system to solve the problems mentioned above.

Yamaguchi et al. [5, 6] argue that the MVP support system has advantages over the conventional tuner in that it provides flexibility to the instrumentalist's physical and visual angle and reduces cognitive load during performance, according to usability tests and interview surveys. However, these qualitative methods have not escaped criticism, such as subjectivity and generalizability. Furthermore, these kinds of investigations do not fully represent the contribution of the musical performance system. The difficulty of quantitative analysis is an overall problem regarding musical performance research; however, evaluation of musical skill and ability have been conveniently defined by years of experience of musical activity. Yet these ideas should be dealt with as a multifaceted and complex concept. Thus, some of the convenient definitions are unworthy of trust. Controlling for musical sophistication, including skill and ability, is a major problem which still exists in the literature.

In this research, we report the effects of the MVP support system from a quantitative standpoint. To discuss the contribution of the MVP support system to the improvement of musical performance, we adopted the Goldsmith Musical Sophistication Index (Gold-MSI) [7, 15]. It is promising that the level of musical sophistication, such as skill and experience, will greatly affect the effectiveness of musical performance support systems.

2 MVP Support System

The MVP support system has been developed for wind instrumentalists. Although, the main concept was a pitch feedback system for them, it would also become a performance support system by utilizing Google Glass. The system can be defined as a glass-type tuner for instrumentalists and shows promise regarding the reduction of physical burden and the improvement of gaze flexibility and cognitive load during musical performances when compared to using a conventional tuner on a music stand [5, 6].

The feedback system utilized a three-tier scale rating system of "correct", "higher", or "lower" compared to the correct pitch, with the participant receiving real-time feedback through color indicators on the display. The correct pitch range was defined as the target, expressed in Hertz, $\pm$ 1% [5, 6]. The Glass Enterprise edition 2 by Google was used in the study. The reliability of the Google Glass system as a musical tuner was verified by a professional musician and the first author, who has experience conducting and training concert bands (for a detailed explanation, see [5]). The system was developed with four key standpoints: timeliness, ease of understanding, recordability, and stability [5]. To achieve this goal, the system utilized the ml5.js library [8], run in TensorFlow, which includes the PitchDetection package that implements the deep-learning-based CREPE algorithm [9, 10]. In this study, we also used the Glass Enterprise edition 2 by Google to send tonal pitch feedback to participants in real time. We also recorded the performance data and pitch estimate data in a CSV file, with the evaluation of the performance pitch stored in a separate column [5]. The schematic drawing of the MVP support system is shown in Fig. 1.

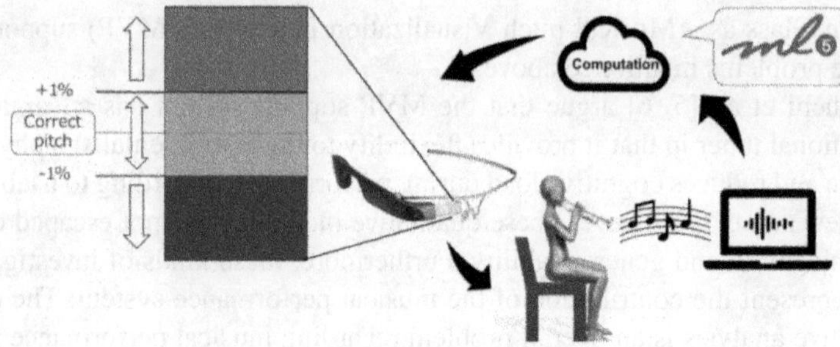

Fig. 1. The schematic of the MVP support system

3 Goldsmith Musical Sophistication Index

The Gold-MSI is a popular tool in the field of music research [7]. The term "musical sophistication" was introduced by Müllensiefen and colleagues as a more inclusive and neutral alternative to terms such as "talent" and "aptitude," and is based on observable behaviors. The Gold-MSI is composed of 38 self-report questions divided into five subscales: Active Engagement, Perceptual Abilities, Musical Training, Singing Abilities, and Emotions. These questions were carefully selected from a pool of 153 statements extracted from previous studies. The Gold-MSI has been validated by a large number of primarily English-speaking participants and has demonstrated good internal reliability for each subscale as well as the overall sophistication index, high test-retest reliability, and reliable correlation with a variety of objective listening ability tests.

The Gold-MSI has been widely used since its inception in 2014 and has been translated into various languages including Traditional Chinese, Simplified Chinese, Portuguese, German, and French [11–14]. These translations have shown high internal consistency and test-retest reliability, and the validation data collected from these studies indicate a good fit with the bifactor model structure proposed by the original Gold-MSI. These findings suggest that the structure and set of questions used to measure musical sophistication by the Gold-MSI are applicable to other cultures and languages.

The development of batteries for assessing musical abilities in Japan has resulted in the creation of several tests, including the Onken Musical Aptitude Test for Young Children [16], and the New Musical Aptitude Test [17]. Most of these tests are designed to assess the musical abilities of children. While there are few non-Japanese standardized tests that have been translated into Japanese, some, such as the Bentley Measure of Musical Abilities [18], have been translated and are available for use. However, there is currently no validated Japanese version of the Gold-MSI, which is widely used to assess musical sophistication.

Therefore, Sadakata et al. [15] translated the Gold-MSI into Japanese (Gold-MSI-J) and, after validating the translation with 689 Japanese speakers, it was found that the internal consistency and test-retest reliability were excellent. Furthermore, the confirmatory factor analysis showed that the bifactor model structure proposed by the original study of Gold-MSI is reasonably maintained in the data.

4 Method

4.1 Participants

We conducted the experiment which consisted of 22 student participants with an average age of 22.14 years (SD = 1.39). Students were selected from national universities' concert band and orchestra clubs. Their musical ability as wind instrumentalists was confirmed to be at an intermediate or advanced level by the Japanese version of Goldsmith Musical Sophistication Index (Gold-MSI-J) [15]. Their musical training factor score in Gold-MSI-J was 3 or more. The participants were 4 clarinet players, 4 trumpet players, 4 flute players, 3 French horn players, 2 saxophone players, 2 trombone players, 1 oboe player, and 1 bassoon player.

4.2 Procedure

The study comprised two distinct sections, namely a performance task section and a questionnaire and interview section. In the performance task section, the participants were instructed to perform the B-flat equal temperament major scale in long-tone while synchronizing with a metronome presented on the screen in front of them, set to a beat per minute (BPM) of 60. This long-tone scale task is the fundamental performance for wind instrumentalists in Japanese concert band societies. To gauge the efficacy of the Google Glass tuner system, a commercially available conventional tuner (YAMAHA TDM-70) which was placed on a music stand, was employed as a baseline. The order effects were counterbalanced for the performance task section. In both the baseline and Google Glass settings, the participants were advised to focus on their tempo and intonation while performing the task. There was no repetition and the duration of the experiment was approximately 30 min including explanation and warming up. After the performance section, we conducted a questionnaire survey regarding the musical sophistication using Gold-MSI-J. Finally, we ensured that all measurements were made using the same microphone, computer, browser, network environment and Google Glass system.

5 Results

Figure 2 shows the boxplots regarding the scores of the Gold-MSI-J subscales. Compared to the results of Sadakata et al. [15], these scores clearly show that musical sophistication of the participants is much higher than laypeople.

The median score of each factor in Gold-MSI-J was used as the threshold to divide participants into low and high groups for each factor, which were then used as between-participant factors. The tuner use condition, and the Google Glass use condition were defined as within-participant factors. Two-way repeated measures analysis of variance, for the effects of musical sophistication and the tuner system condition, was conducted on the pitch accuracy during the performance. Pitch accuracy was estimated by the recorded data of the MVP support system and transformed to angle data before analysis because it was ratio data by arcsine transformation. Table 1 shows the instrument of

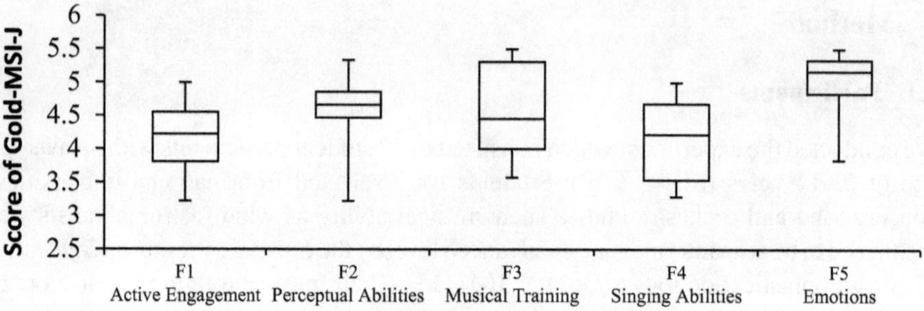

Fig. 2. The boxplots regarding the results of Gold-MSI-J

Table 1. List of participants and pitch accuracy data

ID	Instrument	Conventional tuner	Google Glass
1	Clarinet	78.52%	81.87%
2	French Horn	62.26%	91.93%
3	Euphonium	73.61%	86.70%
4	Trombone	75.65%	76.91%
5	Oboe	94.52%	96.58%
6	Flute	98.95%	97.75%
7	Trumpet	91.79%	95.16%
8	French Horn	84.67%	82.78%
9	Clarinet	54.88%	62.58%
10	French Horn	82.36%	92.86%
11	Flute	87.49%	96.18%
12	Trombone	54.66%	72.18%
13	Trumpet	85.56%	89.90%
14	Trumpet	93.68%	87.45%
15	Saxophone	71.54%	82.78%
16	Flute	95.32%	91.34%
17	Flute	97.63%	95.61%
18	Saxophone	87.59%	88.24%
19	Clarinet	94.70%	94.22%
20	Bassoon	95.46%	96.07%
21	Clarinet	94.37%	97.65%
22	Trumpet	76.15%	85.28%

each participant and the pitch accuracy under both conditions. The accuracy rate was calculated by dividing the length of time the performed pitch was within the correct pitch range by the total length of the performance.

The results show that there was no significant main effect between participant groups for the Active Engagement factor ($F(1,20) = 0.31$, *ns.*, $\eta_p{}^2 = 0.02$), and only the main effect of tuner system factors was significant ($F(1,20) = 9.68$, $p < .01$, $\eta_p{}^2 = 0.33$). There was no significant interaction between Active Engagement factor and tuner system factors ($F(1,20) = 2.68$, *ns.*, $\eta_p{}^2 = 0.19$). For the Perceptual Abilities factor, there was no significant main effect between participant groups ($F(1,20) = 1.90$, *ns.*, $\eta_p{}^2 = 0.09$), and only the main effect of tuner system factors was significant ($F(1,20) = 5.27, p < .05$, $\eta_p{}^2 = 0.21$). There was no significant interaction between Perceptual Abilities factor and tuner system factors ($F(1,20) = 3.27$, *ns.*, $\eta_p{}^2 = 0.14$). For the Musical Training factor, both the main effect between participant groups ($F(1,20) = 6.04, p < .05, \eta_p{}^2 = 0.23$) and the main effect of tuner system factors ($F(1,20) = 9.96, p < .01, \eta_p{}^2 = 0.31$) were significant. There was no significant interaction between Musical Training factor and tuner system factors ($F(1,20) = 2.44$, *ns.*, $\eta_p{}^2 = 0.11$). However, this factor can be hypothesized that it has an effect of the performance, we conducted exploratory testing of simple main effects. The result showed that pitch accuracy increased significantly only when the Google Glass tuner was used in the low group of between-participants factor ($F(1,20) = 8.92, p < .01, \eta_p{}^2 = 0.47$). For the Singing Abilities factor, there was no significant main effect between participant groups ($F(1,20) = 1.26$, *ns.*, $\eta_p{}^2 = 0.06$), and only the main effect of tuner system factors was significant (F $F(1,20) = 7.43, p < .05$, $\eta_p{}^2 = 0.27$). There was no significant interaction between Singing Abilities factor and tuner system factors ($F(1,20) = 2.68$, *ns.*, $\eta_p{}^2 = 0.03$). For the Emotions factor, there was no significant main effect between participant groups ($F(1,20) = 0.32$, *ns.*, $\eta_p{}^2 = 0.02$), and only the main effect of tuner system factors was significant ($F(1,20) = 6.32$, $p < .05$, $\eta_p{}^2 = 0.24$). There was no significant interaction between Emotions factor and tuner system factors ($F(1,20) = 2.26$, *ns.*, $\eta_p{}^2 = 0.10$).

For all analyses, the main effect of tuner system factors was significantly higher for Google Glass tuner conditions than for tuner conditions in terms of pitch accuracy. The main effect between participant groups for the Musical Training factor showed that the high group had significantly higher pitch accuracy than the low group. For this factor, the result of the test of simple main effects showed that the Google Glass conditions significantly improved pitch accuracy only in the low group.

6 Discussion

When using the Google Glass tuner, the accuracy of participant's pitch showed good values. Regarding the relationship with Gold-MSI-J, participants were divided into high and low groups based on their factor scores, and for all factors of Gold-MSI-J, the main effect of the tuner system was significant. On the other hand, the main effect between participant groups was significant only for the Musical Training factor. Furthermore, as a significant difference in pitch accuracy was observed only in the low group in the simple main effect test, it is suggested that the Google Glass tuners may have a strong effect as a performance support system for individuals with relatively low levels of musical training among instrument players. In the high musical training group, pitch accuracy was sufficiently high even under tuner use conditions, and there was no significant difference between the two conditions. However, the sample size is relatively small, so the statistical analysis was conducted with the aim of obtaining an overview of the data. Thus, we will have to conduct large-scale experiments for valid discussions, for example, the influence different instruments have on the results and the usablitity of the system. It will be also necessary to rely on qualitative analysis or subjective evaluations of participants, as described below, to understand how this system contributes to such individuals.

The results of this study show the effect of the MVP support system from each factor of musical sophistication by Gold-MSI-J. Compared with existing qualitative surveys, this method allowed a valid investigation regarding the individual performance and musical sophistication from multifaced standpoints. It should be noted that the present study also emphasized the effectiveness of the MVP support system. Further work in this area is underway to develop an effective pitch feedback system that is suitable to each instrumentalist. It is hoped that the outcome of this study will be of use for future empirical research regarding musical performance study.

References

1. Madsen, C.K., Geringer, J.M.: Preferences for trumpet tone quality versus intonation. Bull. Counc. Res. Music. Educ. **46**, 13–22 (1976)
2. Elliott, C.A.: Effect of vocalization on the sense of pitch of beginning band class students. J. Res. Music. Educ. **22**(2), 120–128 (1974)
3. Wang, J.H., Wang, S.A., Chen, W.C., Chang, K.N., Chen, H.Y.: Real-time pitch training system for violin learners. In: 2012 IEEE International Conference on Multimedia and Expo Workshops, pp. 163–168. IEEE (2012)
4. Drake, C., Palmer, C.: Skill acquisition in music performance: relations between planning and temporal control. Cognition **74**(1), 1–32 (2000)
5. Yamaguchi, Y., Kawada, T., Nagahama, T., Horita, T.: A pilot study of the MVP support system using google glass. In: EdMedia+ Innovate Learning.17–28. Association for the Advancement of Computing in Education (AACE) (2022)
6. Yamaguchi, Y., Kawada, T., Nagahama, T., Horita, T.: Development and evaluation of a musical instrument performance support system using smart glasses: from the subjective evaluation of form, gaze, and performance. Japan journal of Educational Technology **46**, 185–188 (2023)
7. Müllensiefen, D., Gingras, B., Musil, J., Stewart, L.: The musicality of non-musicians: an index for assessing musical sophistication in the general population. In Snyder, J. (ed.), PLoS ONE **9**(2), e89642 (2014). https://doi.org/10.1371/journal.pone.0089642
8. NYU. ITP "ml5js· Friendly Machine Learning for the Web." ml5js website. Accessed 16 March 2022. https://ml5js.org/. Accessed 4 May 2023
9. Kim, J.W., Salamon, J., Li, P., Bello, J.P.: Crepe: a convolutional representation for pitch estimation. In: 2018 IEEE International Conference on Acoustics, Speech and Signal Processing (ICASSP), pp. 161–165. IEEE (2018)
10. Mathieu, B., Essid, S., Fillon, T., Prado, J., Richard, G.: Yaafe, an easy to use and efficient audio feature extraction softwarem. In: Ismir (2010)
11. Degrave, P., Dedonder, J.: A French translation of the goldsmiths musical sophistication index, an instrument to assess self-reported musical skills, abilities and behaviours. Journal of New Music Research **48**(2), 138–144 (2019). https://doi.org/10.1080/09298215.2018.1499779

12. Lima, C.F., Correia, A.I., Müllensiefen, D., Castro, S.L.: Goldsmiths musical sophistication index (Gold-MSI): Portuguese version and associations with socio-demographic factors, personality and music preferences. Psychol. Music **48**(3), 376–388 (2020)
13. Lin, H.R., Kopiez, R., Müllensiefen, D., Wolf, A.: The Chinese version of the Gold-MSI: adaptation and validation of an inventory for the measurement of musical sophistication in a Taiwanese sample. Music. Sci. **25**(2), 226–251 (2021)
14. Schaal, N., Bauer, A.-K., Müllensiefen, D.:Der Gold-MSI: Replikation und Validierung eines Fragebogeninstrumentes zur Messung Musikalischer Erfahrenheit anhand einer deutschen Stichprobe. [The Gold-MSI: Replication and validation of a survey instrument for measuring musical sophistication with a German sample.] Musicae Scientiae **18**(4), 423–447 (2014). https://doi.org/10.1177/1029864914541851
15. Sadakata, M., et al.: The Japanese translation of the Gold-MSI: adaptation and validation of the self-report questionnaire of musical sophistication. Musicae Scientiae (2022). https://doi.org/10.1177/10298649221110089
16. Sho, O.S.K.: Onken-shiki Youji no ongaku tokusei tesuto [Onken's Musical Aptitudes Test for Young Children]. Nihon Bunka Kgakusha Co. Ltd. (1969)
17. Ogawa, Y., Murao, T., Mang, E.H.S.: Developing a music aptitude test for school children in Asia [Paper presentation], 10th International Conference for Music Perception and Cognition, Hokkaido, Japan (2008)
18. Furuichi, H., Umemoto, T.: Bentley ongaku nouryoku tesuto no hyoujun ka [The translation and standardization of the Bentley Measure of Musical Abilities]. Journal of the Musicological Society of Japan **21**, 65–77 (1975)

Music and Sound Generation: Emerging Approaches and Diverse Applications

Reconstructing Human Expressiveness in Piano Performances with a Transformer Network

Jingjing Tang[1(✉)], Geraint Wiggins[1,2], and György Fazekas[1]

[1] Center for Digital Music, Queen Mary University of London, London, UK
jingjing.tang@qmul.ac.uk
[2] Vrije Universiteit Brussel, Ixelles, Belgium

Abstract. Capturing intricate and subtle variations in human expressiveness in music performance using computational approaches is challenging. In this paper, we propose a novel approach for reconstructing human expressiveness in piano performance with a multi-layer bi-directional Transformer encoder. To address the needs for large amounts of accurately captured and score-aligned performance data in training neural networks, we use transcribed scores obtained from an existing transcription model to train our model. We integrate pianist identities to control the sampling process and explore the ability of our system to model variations in expressiveness for different pianists. The system is evaluated through statistical analysis of generated expressive performances and a listening test. Overall, the results suggest that our method achieves state-of-the-art in generating human-like piano performances from transcribed scores, while fully and consistently reconstructing human expressiveness poses further challenges. Our codes are released at https://github.com/tangjjbetsy/RHEPP-Transformer.

Keywords: expressive piano performance · music generation · transformer

1 Introduction

Expressive musical performances extend beyond merely playing notes as written in the score. Musicians interpret music by varying articulation, dynamics, and timing based on score annotations. These expressive modifications enable them to convey emotions and develop unique performance styles [7]. In computational modelling, expressive performance rendering often involves adjusting note velocity and timing to simulate human expressiveness [3]. This requires capturing subtle deviations from the score in tempo, timing, and dynamics. To effectively model different pianists' styles, systems must detect even the smallest perceptible variations in these expressive features.

Recent advancements in deep learning have significantly impacted music generation and representation learning. In particular, the Transformer architecture has proven effective for capturing long-range dependencies in sequential data, making it well-suited for modelling expressive performance attributes such as tempo and loudness. While most studies applying Transformers to music have focused on algorithmic composition [5, 11–13] and symbolic music representation learning [6, 31], few have specifically addressed modelling human performance expressiveness [2, 30].

S. Ystad et al. (Eds.): CMMR 2023, LNCS 15236, pp. 83–96, 2026.
https://doi.org/10.1007/978-3-032-02042-0_6

This paper introduces a novel approach for reconstructing human expressiveness using a multi-layer bidirectional Transformer encoder. Training such a model requires large, accurately aligned performance-score datasets, which remain scarce. However, with the emergence of a performance-to-score transcription system [18] and the transcribed expressive piano performance dataset ATEPP [33], we can leverage transcribed scores to train our model. This approach is particularly useful when canonical scores lack sufficient expressive details—such as in jazz improvisations or classical ornaments like trills, which may not be explicitly notated. Moreover, reconstructing human expressiveness from transcribed scores can aid research in musical style modelling, enabling performance reconstruction in a pianist's specific style. To evaluate our approach, we analyse the generated performances statistically and conduct a listening test comparing our model to state-of-the-art expressive performance rendering systems.

The remainder of this paper is structured as follows: Sect. 2 reviews deep learning approaches in expressive performance rendering and discusses relevant datasets. Section 3 details our dataset, feature extraction process, and model architecture. Section 4 describes our experimental setup, while Sect. 5 presents the results of our quantitative analysis and listening test. Finally, Sect. 6 summarises our findings.

2 Background

Deep learning techniques have demonstrated impressive results in expressive performance rendering. Various approaches, including Recurrent Neural Networks (RNN) [14], Graph Neural Networks (GNN) [15], Generative Adversarial Networks (GAN) [24], and diffusion models [32], have been explored. Transformers have also been employed to generate controlled expressions, particularly in modulating dynamics and tempo based on embedded performance directives [2,25]. Additionally, recent work [30] has used multiple Transformer models to predict note-wise features solely from onset and offset times extracted from music scores.

Despite advancements, existing models still face challenges with the need for large-scale, high-quality score-performance alignments. The most commonly used datasets, such as ASAP [9] and Vienna 4×22 Piano Corpus [10], are limited for models to handle complex playing techniques like pedalling and trills. The limited size of these datasets makes it challenging to learn sustained expressiveness over longer passages and to model individual performance styles [27]. While large-scale transcribed MIDI performance datasets exist [8,16,33], their application is often restricted by the need for precise annotations. However, with the support of a performance-to-score transcription system [18], introduced in Sect. 3.3, performances can be aligned with transcribed scores. This makes large-scale transcribed datasets more accessible for expressive performance modelling.

3 Methodology

3.1 Problem Definition

Expressive performance rendering (EPR) is commonly defined as *the task of generating human-like performances with music sheets as input*. Most existing work [2,14,15,25] proposes systems using recorded performances and canonical scores to solve the problem. All of these systems require alignment between the canonical scores and performances, which is limited in accuracy given the available datasets and alignment algorithms. With the purpose of reconstructing human expressiveness given a composition, we reformulate the task by relaxing the requirement for using conventional music sheets as input, in order to take advantage of the recent performance-to-score transcription algorithms [18] and large transcribed performance datasets [33]. We will provide more details about the transcription algorithm and the dataset used in this work in Sects. 3.2 and 3.3. As shown in Fig. 1, the EPR task, in our definition, is to take the transcribed scores as input and reconstruct human expressiveness by generating expressive performances that are similar to the transcribed human performances.

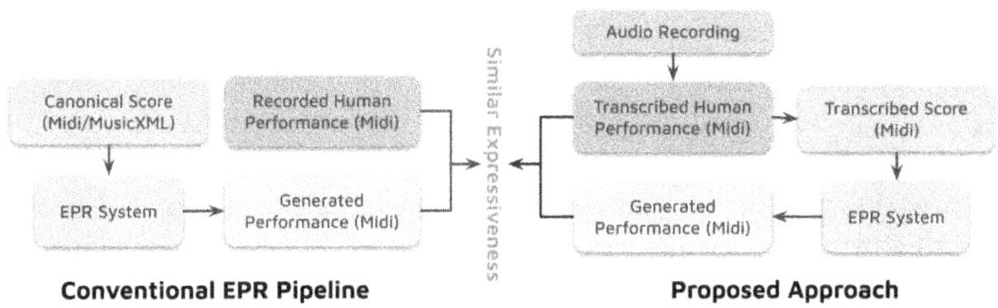

Fig. 1. Comparison of the conventional expressive performance rendering (EPR) pipeline with our proposed method

3.2 Dataset

The recently released ATEPP dataset [33] provides high-quality transcribed piano performances by world-renowned pianists. According to a listening test conducted by Zhang et al., the transcribed performance MIDIs reliably retain the expressiveness of performers. The dataset includes multiple performances of the same composition by different pianists, allowing comparison in expressiveness among different performers. However, the ATEPP dataset consists of albums from various performers, leading to a highly skewed distribution of recorded performances. Some pianists have an extensive number of recordings, while others have only a handful of albums. Additionally, there is variation in repertoire—some performers focus primarily on Romantic compositions by Schubert or Chopin, while others have a more diverse repertoire covering a wide range of composers and styles. This imbalance could introduce biases, as models trained on the full dataset may be disproportionately influenced by pianists with more recordings or specific stylistic tendencies. To mitigate these issues, we adapted a subset [23] that balances the number of performances across six pianists: Alfred Brendel, Claudio Arrau, Daniel Barenboim, Friedrich Gulda, Sviatoslav Richter, and Wilhelm Kempff. Compositions in this subset are mainly composed by Beethoven with only two pieces by Mozart. Each of the compositions corresponds to at least one performance by each pianist. Table 1 presents statistics of the subset in comparison with datasets used by other EPR systems.

Table 1. Comparison of datasets used in different EPR systems. *NN stands for the number of notes. † denotes that the information not provided.

Systems	Performances	Pianists	Compositions	Composer(s)	Total NN*
VirtuosoNet [14]	1052	/†	226	16	3301K
Sketching-Internal [25]	356	/	34	1	/
Sketching-External [25]	116	/	23	10	/
ScorePerformer [2]	937	/	212	15	/
Ours	457	6	36	2	1341K

3.3 Data Processing

Score Transcription. Similarly to other EPR systems [14,15,25], our method requires note-to-note alignment between the input score MIDI and the output performance MIDI. Despite the convincing alignment results of the state-of-the-art algorithm proposed by Nakamura et al. [21], the algorithm shows difficulty in dealing with repeated sections as well as trills in classical piano music, which causes unexpected loss of information during the alignment process. Instead of using the original or manually edited scores of the compositions, we obtained the transcribed scores of the performances through a performance-to-score transcription algorithm proposed by Liu et al. [18]. The transcribed score midi data can be aligned with the performances at the note level without losing any structural generality in the music [29].

The transcription algorithm performs rhythm quantisation through a convolutional-recurrent neural network and a beat tracking algorithm to remove expressive variations in timing, velocity, and pedalling. While expressiveness regarding velocity and pedalling is certainly erased through the process, how much expressiveness is remained in timing is implicit and will be discussed further in Sect. 5. A further constraint of this algorithm is its inability to retrieve performance directives like dynamics, phrase markings, and beam directions set by the composer. As a result, we were limited to leveraging only the note-related features the algorithm offered.

Data Augmentation. The transcribed scores are first scaled to the same length as the corresponding performances. We then augment the data by changing the tempo for both performances and the scores. For each pair of performance and score midis, the onset time, offset time and duration of each note are multiplied by a ratio $r_i \in [0.75, 1.25]$. In total, we have each pair augmented by multiplying 10 different ratios that are evenly spaced along the interval grid. This augmentation enhances model robustness by exposing it to variations in tempo, which are common in expressive human performances. By training on tempo-altered data, the model can better generalise to natural fluctuations in timing, reducing overfitting to rigid score-performance alignments.

Feature Encoding. Features related to performance expressiveness are extracted and tokenised to reduce the dimensionality of the input space. Following the tokenisation method OctupleMIDI, proposed by Zeng et al. [31], we encode note-level features,

Table 2. Vocabulary size of the tokenized note-level features

Features	Pitch	Velocity	Duration	Position	Bar
Size	89	66	4609	1537	518

including pitch, velocity, duration, bar, and position. Table 2 shows the vocabulary size of our tokens for each feature. We adopt OctupleMIDI for tokenisation due to its ability to efficiently encode note-level features by creating distinct vocabularies for each feature. This approach effectively reduces the overall vocabulary size, thereby enhancing model efficiency and promoting greater learning stability. With the OctupleMIDI tokenisation, the onset time of a note N_i is represented jointly by its bar number B_i and position number P_i, where $i = 1, 2, \ldots, n$ and n denotes the length of the note sequences. The position number P_i is calculated based on the resolution of 384 ticks per beat. Given that we assume 4 beats per bar, each bar contains $384 \times 4 = 1536$ discrete positions. Thus, the onset time of a note is computed as:

$$OT_i = B_i \times 1536 + P_i, \quad i = 1, 2, \ldots, n. \tag{1}$$

Given that we use a piano music dataset, we only consider pitches ranging from 21 to 109. The duration of notes is represented by a token value D_i, which is linearly proportional to the note's actual duration. Additionally, two note-level performance features, namely Inter-Onset Interval (IOI) and Duration Deviation (DD), are calculated to capture the expressiveness of piano performances, as commonly used in the literature [14,22,25].The Inter-Onset Interval (IOI) captures the tempo fluctuations in a performance, reflecting expressive timing variations such as rubato, accelerando, and ritardando. By analysing IOI, we are able to observe how performers adjust the timing of successive notes, shaping phrasing and musical expression. The Duration Deviation (DD), in contrast, provides insights into both tempo and articulation. It quantifies the difference between the duration token values of a note in the performance MIDI file and those in the score MIDI file. This feature accounts for expressive techniques, such as the elongation or shortening of note values, staccato, and legato articulations. Taken together, the IOI and DD features allow for the modelling of expressive nuances that extend beyond the literal score, thus providing a more comprehensive understanding of musical interpretation. The formal definitions of these features in our research are provided as follows:

- *Inter-Onset Interval*: the time interval between the onset time (OT) of the note N_i and that of the next note N_{i+1}:

$$IOI_i = \begin{cases} OT_{i+1} - OT_i, \ i = 1, 2, \ldots, n-1 \\ 0, \ i = n \end{cases} \tag{2}$$

  where $OT_i = B_i \times 1536 + P_i, \ i = 1, 2, \ldots, n$
- *Duration Deviation*: the difference between duration token values of a note in performance midi and score midi

$$DD_i = Dp_i - Ds_i, i = 1, 2, \ldots, n \tag{3}$$

where Dp is the duration obtained from the performance midi and Ds is that from the score midi.

3.4 Generation with Transformer Encoder

Input and Output Features. Input and output features are carefully designed to preserve the score content while allowing changes in the performance control of each note. The input features include pitch, velocity, duration, bar, position, and inter-onset interval from the score midis. As for the output, we infer values of three features including velocity, DD, and IOI in the performance midis. Following Eq. 2 and Eq. 3, we can calculate the predicted token values of duration, position, and bar for each note based on DD and IOI. Combined with the predicted token values for velocity, we can construct a performance MIDI file by reverting the process.

Model Architecture. Inspired by the MidiBert model proposed by Chou et al. [6], we design a multi-layer bi-directional Transformer encoder with 4 layers of multi-head self-attention where each has 4 heads and a hidden space dimension of 128. The pianist's identity is represented using a one-hot encoding embedding, which is then concatenated to the last hidden state before the final prediction, as shown in Fig. 2. Since velocity and timing are continuous, the interval between token values is crucial for distinguishing note performances. Most transformers trained for music generation [5,11–13] take different token values as independent classes which makes this information implicit to the model. Our system instead uses the tokens without creating embeddings, and predicts the token values for different features through regression. In addition, we add activation functions after the inference layer to clamp the predicted values, ensuring that they fall into the ranges of different features.

Loss Design. The losses $\mathcal{L}_v$, $\mathcal{L}_{dd}$, and $\mathcal{L}_{ioi}$ for velocity, DD, and IOI features are calculated respectively, following the loss function defined in Eq. 4 which represents the percentage of how much the predicted values y deviated from the target values $\hat{y}$. Masks are used to exclude loss calculations for padded tokens, ensuring that only valid tokens contribute to the loss computation.

$$\mathcal{L}_{feature} = \sum_{i=0}^{n} l(y_i)m_i, \tag{4}$$

where m_i represents the loss mask for the i-th note and

$$l(y_i) = \begin{cases} \frac{|y_i - \hat{y}_i|}{|\hat{y}_i|}, \text{ if } \hat{y}_i \neq 0 \\ \alpha|y - \hat{y}_i|, \text{ if } \hat{y}_i = 0 \end{cases}$$

The parameter α regularises the loss calculation when the target value is zero and is experimentally set to 0.001. The total loss is calculated by

$$\mathcal{L}_{total} = w_v\mathcal{L}_v + w_{dd}\mathcal{L}_{dd} + w_{ioi}\mathcal{L}_{ioi} \tag{5}$$

where weights are empirically initialised and assigned to each feature loss respectively.

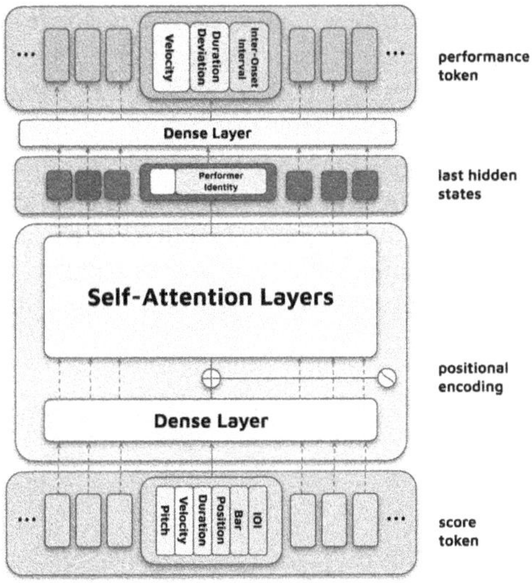

Fig. 2. Model architecture of the Transformer encoder

3.5 Evaluation

The system is objectively evaluated through the proposed objective metrics and statistical distributions of expressive parameters in generations, presented in Sect. 5.1. Additionally, we evaluate the perceived expressiveness of generated performances through a subjective listening test. As the aim of EPR task is to generate performances with human-like expressiveness [3], we assume that the more similar a model's output is to a human performance, the more effectively expressive it is. We recruit participants with experience in playing musical instruments and familiarity with classical music. These participants are asked to rate the expressiveness of the presented samples, considering factors such as how expressive, natural, and human-like the performances are. In other words, the participants are expected to evaluate the overall expressiveness by taking into account how well the performance conveys emotional depth, how closely it mirrors human playing, and how naturally it flows. The detailed experiment design and conditions and the results of the listening test are presented in Sect. 5.2.

4 Experimental Setup

We implement our model based on the PyTorch. We carefully divide the dataset so that 80% of both the composition pieces and performances are used for training, 10% for validation, and 10% for testing. We cut or pad the token sequences into sequences of 1000 notes before inputting into our transformer. The model is trained with a batch size of 16 sequences for at most 400 epochs, using the Adam optimizer with an initial learning rate of 1e−4 and a weight decay rate of 1e−7. We update the learning rate using the cosine annealing warm restart scheduler [20] since it has been shown to result in faster convergence during training, compared with other learning rate scheduling strategies. If the validation loss does not improve for 30 consecutive epochs, we stop the training process early. The training converges in 2 days on two RTX A5000 GPUs.

Different vocabulary sizes of expressive features shown in Table 2 result in different degrees of complexity when modelling. Consequently, we observed variations in the decrease of loss magnitudes and overfitting across different features during learning, despite assigning constant weights to each feature loss. To balance training and reduce overfitting, we optimize the training process using the GradNorm algorithm proposed by Zhao et al. [4] to dynamically update weights based on gradients calculated at the end of each training epoch.

5 Results

5.1 Quantitative Evaluation

Objective evaluation methods for expressive performance rendering are still evolving. One common approach [3] measures loss for key performance features: velocity, inter-onset interval (IOI), and duration deviation (DD). Building on the feature encoding and loss design outlined in Sect. 3, we estimate the average prediction errors in MIDI-quantised velocity values and seconds, as detailed in Table 3. Additionally, we incorporate recently proposed metrics [28]—Pearson correlation, dynamic time warping distance (DTWD), and Kullback-Leibler divergence (KLD)—to evaluate expressiveness. These metrics compare the tokenised predicted performance against the target performance, averaged across segments.

Our results are not directly comparable to existing works [14,15,25] due to several key differences in our approach. First, unlike previous methods that do not tokenise feature values, our system computes losses directly on tokenised values. Second, while most prior studies primarily rely on mean squared error (MSE) loss, we employ a broader set of metrics to assess expressiveness. Third, many existing works overlook certain features, particularly duration deviation (DD). Lastly, as discussed in Sect. 3.1, we use transcribed scores and performances as both input and target, whereas others typically use canonical scores and recorded human performances.

Table 3. Objective evaluation metrics for note-level expressive features on the test dataset

Feature	Loss	Avg. Error	Correlation	DTWD	KLD
Velocity	0.1267	±16.2048	0.7218 ± 0.0047	0.0570 ± (<0.0001)	0.0174 ± 0.0004
IOI	0.2389	±0.0183 s	0.4198 ± 0.0049	0.1430 ± 0.0030	0.0029 ± 0.0001
DD	0.6280	±0.0473 s	0.4279 ± 0.0083	0.0260 ± 0.0010	0.0008 ± (<0.0001)

The results indicate that the transformer model is capable of learning the patterns of expressive variations and reproducing them in the transcribed scores. However, the average errors at the note level in generations remain noticeable to human ears [19], and can affect the perceived expressiveness of the generated music compared to human performances. Human ears, depending on training, can detect timing differences as small as 25–45 milliseconds in musical performance. Consequently, even slight tempo discrepancies in the rendered performances may be perceptible, impacting the overall expressiveness and authenticity of the generated music.

Since the level of expressiveness regarding timing left in the transcribed scores is implicit as discussed in Sect. 3, we evaluate the ability of our system to reconstruct the expressiveness for individual pianists through the velocity distributions obtained from kernel density estimation [22,34].

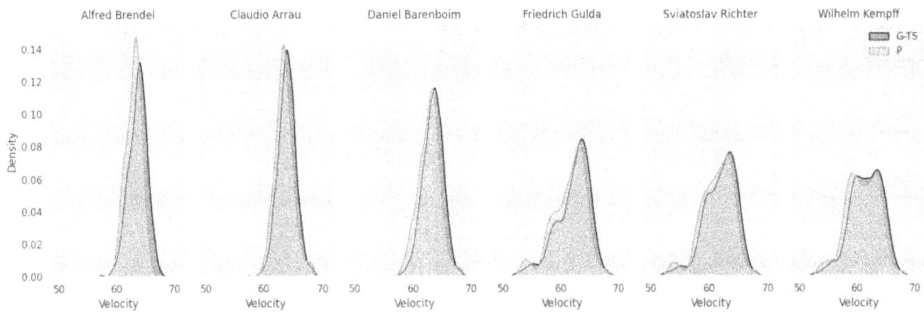

Fig. 3. Velocity distributions for the human performances (P) and the our generations (G-TS) on all pieces in the test set, grouped by different pianists.

As shown in Fig. 3, velocity distributions for each pianists are distinguishable, indicating different performing styles. However, performance recording environments may have impact on the transcribed velocity values [17] and contribute to differences of the distributions. The distributions of the generations based on transcribed scores (G-TS) and those of the human performances (P) have a high degree of overlap, providing evidence of learning individual expressiveness through the training.

5.2 Subjective Evaluation

A listening test was performed to evaluate the perceived expressiveness of our model's output. We recruited 19 people who had some level of music training through email. All participants have learned a musical instrument, while over half of our participants had been engaged with classical music for over 5 years. The participants completed the study anonymously.

The stimuli consisted of four 20 s classical piano excerpts detailed in Table 4. For each excerpt, the human performance (**P**) was provided as a reference to be compared with four MIDI renderings: the generation based on the transcribed score (**G-TS**), the generation by the state-of-the-art VirtuosoNet [14] using the canonical score (**V**), a direct rendering of the transcribed score (**TS**), and finally the canonical score (**S**) without expression. The human performances were transcribed piano performance MIDIs from the ATEPP dataset [33] and were included as one of the stimuli as well. All the

MIDIs were synthesised into audio recordings through GarageBand to ensure consistency in the listening experience. For each piano excerpt, six recordings, the reference plus 5 stimuli, were presented in the test[1].

Participants were asked to listen to five stimuli and rate the degree of expressiveness for each on a 100-point scale by comparing them with a reference human performance. We guided participants to focus on the expressive qualities of the performances, emphasising dynamics and tempo changes over compositional content. They were instructed to assess expressiveness by considering how effectively the performance conveyed emotional depth, mirrored human playing, and flowed naturally. During the test, we explicitly asked participants to concentrate on these performance features, encouraging them to use the full scale by rating the best sample higher than 80 and the worst lower than 20. We adopted the MUSHRA framework [26] to conduct the test using the Go Listen platform [1].

Table 4. Compositions used for the listening test

Annotation	Composer	Composition
Piece **A**	Beethoven	*Piano Sonata No. 19 in G Minor, Op. 49 No. 1: II. Rondo (Allegro)*
Piece **B**	Beethoven	*Piano Sonata No. 7 in D Major, Op. 10 No. 3: III. Menuetto (Allegro)*
Piece **C**	Haydn	*Piano Sonata in C Major, Hob. XVI:48: II. Rondo (Presto)*
Piece **D**	Bach	*French Suite No. 5 in G, BWV 816: 7. Gigue*

In total, 380 ratings from the 19 listeners were collected. We filtered out raters who could not identify the difference in expressiveness between the anchor (**S**) and the reference (**P**). Figure 4 shows the mean opinion scores (MOS) and the results of Wilcoxon signed rank test for the differences between: (a) **TS** versus **S**, (b) **G-TS** versus **V**, (c) **P** versus **G-TS**, (d) **P** versus **V**, (e) **G-TS** versus **TS**.

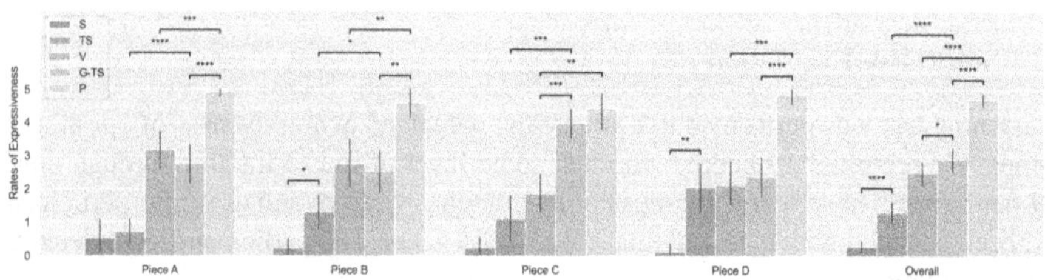

Fig. 4. Results of listening test. The mean opinion scores (converted to a 5-point scale) and 95% confidence intervals are presented for each test piece and the overall results. Wilcoxon signed-rank test are performed to test the significance of the differences. * ($0.01 < p < 0.05$), ** ($0.001 < p < 0.01$), *** ($0.0001 < p < 0.001$), **** ($p < 0.0001$)

[1] Listening samples are provided at https://drive.google.com/drive/folders/1nfaZ23vr8xZHlyhTAAppK2hl-aHQPigP?usp=sharing.

According to the results, human performances (**P**) are significantly different from generations of our model (**G-TS**) and VirtuosoNet (**V**) in most situations. The outputs of our model (**G-TS**) are overall preferred over the performances produced by VirtuosoNet (**V**) significantly ($p = 0.03167$, Cohen's $d \approx 74.52$), receiving trivially lower (not significant) ratings for piece **A** and **B** but higher (significant for **C** and not significant for **D**) ratings for the compositions that never appear in the training dataset. Comparing with canonical scores (**S**), transcribed scores (**TS**) get significantly higher ratings from listeners. Ratings of the generations by our system (**G-TS**) are significantly higher than those of the direct audio rendering of transcribed scores (**TS**) for most pieces except **D**.

These results suggest that our system achieves the state-of-the-art and even outperforms the VirtuosoNet [14] in some cases, although neither of the systems can consistently generate the same level of expressiveness as human performances. On the other hand, while the transcribed scores (**TS**) could have more expressiveness than the canonical scores (**S**), the generations from the transcribed scores (**G-TS**) are perceptually more expressive than the transcribed scores (**TS**) in most cases, indicating the success of reconstructing human expressiveness. The success has also been proven by the overall difference ($p = 0.03167$, Cohen's $d \approx 74.52$) in MOS between our generations (**G-TS**) and generations from the VirtuosoNet (**V**).

5.3 Case Study: Comparison in Dynamics and Duration

Building on the promising results of our system in the listening test of Piece **C**, we conducted a more detailed analysis to compare the expressive variations in dynamics and duration among human performances, system-generated performances, and scores. Specifically, in Fig. 5, we present the fluctuations in velocity and duration across the note sequences. Compared with the VirtuosoNet generation (**V**), the generation of our

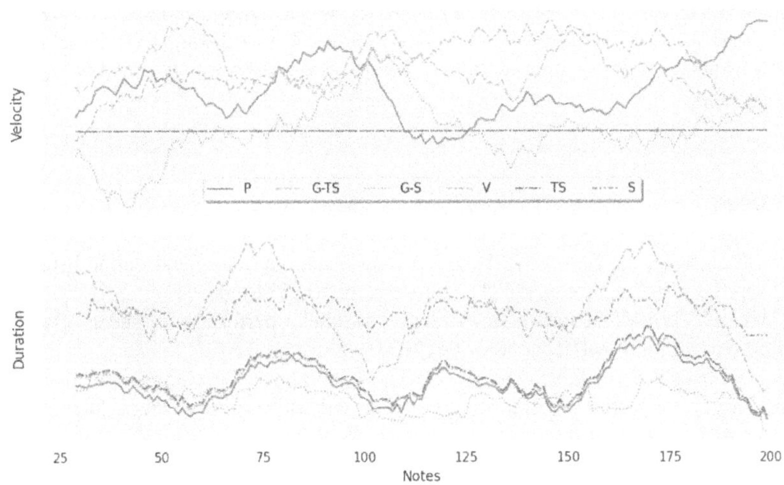

Fig. 5. Standardized and smoothed velocity and duration changes across note sequences from *Piano Sonata in C Major, Hob. XVI:48: II. Rondo (Presto)* for enhanced trend comparison. G-S represents the generation of our system based on the canonical scores.

system (**G-TS**) could capture both short-term and long-term velocity variations better. Even when inputting the unseen canonical score, the generation of our system (**G-S**) outperforms the other model in terms of reconstructing velocity variations. Meanwhile, the strong similarity between duration changes in the human performance (**P**) and transcribed score (**TS**) suggest that the transcription algorithm [18] alters the timing information of the notes cautiously with only limited modification of the duration. Therefore, the reconstruction of the expressive variations in timing through our system could be restricted. The limitation is also demonstrated by the duration changes of our system's generation based on the canonical score (**G-S**).

6 Conclusion

This paper presents a novel method for reconstructing human expressiveness in classical piano performances. Our expressive performance rendering system consists of a Transformer encoder trained on transcribed scores and performances. The quantitative evaluation and listening test show that the proposed method succeed in generating human-like expressive variations, especially for dynamics. Moreover, our method could be used for modelling the differences in expressiveness among individual pianists.

In future work, we will train our system with a mixture of the canonical scores and transcribed scores to create a more robust system. We will further improve the capacity of our system on modelling individual performance styles possibly through contrastive learning. In addition, we will consider a separate system to model pedalling techniques in performances or try to integrate the pedalling information into the current feature encoding.

Acknowledgments. This work is supported by the UKRI Centre for Doctoral Training in Artificial Intelligence and Music. J.Tang is a research student supported jointly by the China Scholarship Council and Queen Mary University of London. G. Wiggins received funding from the Flemish Government under the "Onderzoeksprogramma Artificiële Intelligentie (AI) Vlaanderen".We would like to thank Lele Liu, Jiawen Huang and the reviewers for their valuable feedback to improve our work.

References

1. Barry, D., Zhang, Q., Sun, P.W., Hines, A.: Go listen: an end-to-end online listening test platform. J. Open Res. Softw. (2021). http://doi.org/10.5334/jors.361
2. Borovik, I., Viro, V.: ScorePerformer: expressive piano performance rendering with fine-grained control. In: ISMIR, pp. 588–596 (2023)
3. Cancino-Chacón, C.E., Grachten, M., Goebl, W., Widmer, G.: Computational models of expressive music performance: a comprehensive and critical review. Front. Digit. Humanit. **5**, 25 (2018)
4. Chen, Z., Badrinarayanan, V., Lee, C.Y., Rabinovich, A.: GradNorm: gradient normalization for adaptive loss balancing in deep multitask networks. In: Dy, J., Krause, A. (eds.) Proceedings of the 35th International Conference on Machine Learning. Proceedings of Machine Learning Research, vol. 80, pp. 794–803. PMLR (2018). https://proceedings.mlr.press/v80/chen18a.html

5. Choi, K., Hawthorne, C., Simon, I., Dinculescu, M., Engel, J.: Encoding musical style with transformer autoencoders. In: III, H.D., Singh, A. (eds.) Proceedings of the 37th International Conference on Machine Learning. Proceedings of Machine Learning Research, vol. 119, pp. 1899–1908. PMLR (2020). https://proceedings.mlr.press/v119/choi20b.html
6. Chou, Y.H., Chen, I., Chang, C.J., Ching, J., Yang, Y.H., et al.: MidiBERT-piano: large-scale pre-training for symbolic music understanding. arXiv preprint arXiv:2107.05223 (2021)
7. Dai, S., Zhang, Z., Xia, G.G.: Music style transfer: a position paper. http://arxiv.org/abs/1803.06841
8. Edwards, D., Dixon, S., Benetos, E.: PIJAMA: piano jazz with automatic midi annotations. Trans. Int. Soc. Music Inf. Retrieval (2023)
9. Foscarin, F., Mcleod, A., Rigaux, P., Jacquemard, F., Sakai, M.: ASAP: a dataset of aligned scores and performances for piano transcription. In: Proceedings of the 21st International Society for Music Information Retrieval Conference, pp. 534–541. No. CONF (2020)
10. Goebl, W.: Melody lead in piano performance: expressive device or artifact? J. Acoust. Soc. Am. **110**(1), 563–572 (2001)
11. Hsiao, W.Y., Liu, J.Y., Yeh, Y.C., Yang, Y.H.: Compound word transformer: learning to compose full-song music over dynamic directed hypergraphs. In: Proceedings of the AAAI Conference on Artificial Intelligence, vol. 35, pp. 178–186 (2021)
12. Huang, C.Z.A., et al.: Music transformer: generating music with long-term structure. In: International Conference on Learning Representations (2018)
13. Huang, Y.S., Yang, Y.H.: Pop music transformer: Beat-based modeling and generation of expressive pop piano compositions. In: Proceedings of the 28th ACM International Conference on Multimedia, pp. 1180–1188 (2020)
14. Jeong, D., Kwon, T., Kim, Y., Lee, K., Nam, J.: VirtuoSonet: a hierarchical RNN-based system for modeling expressive piano performance. In: Proceedings of the 20th International Society for Music Information Retrieval Conference (2019)
15. Jeong, D., Kwon, T., Kim, Y., Nam, J.: Graph neural network for music score data and modeling expressive piano performance. In: International Conference on Machine Learning, pp. 3060–3070. PMLR (2019)
16. Kong, Q., Li, B., Chen, J., Wang, Y.: GiantMidi-piano: A large-scale midi dataset for classical piano music. Transactions of the International Society for Music Information Retrieval (2022). https://doi.org/10.5334/tismir.80
17. Kong, Q., Li, B., Song, X., Wan, Y., Wang, Y.: High-resolution piano transcription with pedals by regressing onset and offset times. IEEE/ACM Trans. Audio Speech Lang. Process. **29**, 3707–3717 (2021)
18. Liu, L., Kong, Q., Morfi, V., Benetos, E., et al.: Performance midi-to-score conversion by neural beat tracking. In: Proceedings of the 23rd International Society for Music Information Retrieval Conference (2022)
19. London, J.: Hearing in Time: Psychological Aspects of Musical Meter. Oxford University Press (2012)
20. Loshchilov, I., Hutter, F.: SGDR: stochastic gradient descent with warm restarts. In: International Conference on Learning Representations (2017). https://openreview.net/forum?id=Skq89Scxx
21. Nakamura, E., Yoshii, K., Katayose, H.: Performance error detection and post-processing for fast and accurate symbolic music alignment. In: Proceedings of the 18th International Society for Music Information Retrieval Conference (2017)
22. Rafee, S., Fazekas, G., Wiggins, G.: Performer identification from symbolic representation of music using statistical models. In: Proceedings of the International Computer Music Conference 2021, pp. 178–184 (2021). arXiv preprint

23. Rafee, S., Fazekas, G., Wiggins, G.: HIPI: a hierarchical performer identification model based on symbolic representation of music. In: IEEE International Conference on Acoustics, Speech, and Signal Processing (2023)
24. Renault, L., Mignot, R., Roebel, A.: Expressive piano performance rendering from unpaired data. In: International Conference on Digital Audio Effects (DAFx23) (2023)
25. Rhyu, S., Kim, S., Lee, K.: Sketching the expression: flexible rendering of expressive piano performance with self-supervised learning. In: International Society for Music Information Retrieval Conference, pp. 178–185 (2022). https://doi.org/10.5281/zenodo.7342916
26. Series, B.: Method for the subjective assessment of intermediate quality level of audio systems. Int. Telecommun. Union Radiocommun. Assembly **2** (2014)
27. Tang, J., Wiggins, G., Fazekas, G.: Pianist identification using convolutional neural networks. In: 4th International Symposium on the Internet of Sounds. pp. 1–6. IEEE (2023). https://internetofsounds.net/is2_2023/, 4th International Symposium on the Internet of Sounds ; Conference date: 26-09-2022 Through 27-10-2023
28. Tang, J., Cooper, E., Wang, X., Yamagishi, J., Fazekas, G.: Towards an integrated approach for expressive piano performance synthesis from music scores. arXiv preprint arXiv:2501.10222 (2025). https://doi.org/10.48550/arXiv.2501.10222, accepted by ICASSP 2025
29. Wiggins, G.A., Miranda, E., Smaill, A., Harris, M.: A framework for the evaluation of music representation systems. Comput. Music J. **17**(3), 31–42 (1993). http://www.soi.city.ac.uk/~geraint/papers/CMJ93.pdf
30. Worrall, K., Yin, Z., Collins, T.: Comparative evaluation in the wild: systems for the expressive rendering of music. IEEE Trans. Artif. Intell. **5** (2024)
31. Zeng, M., Tan, X., Wang, R., Ju, Z., Qin, T., Liu, T.Y.: MusicBERT: symbolic music understanding with large-scale pre-training. In: Findings of the Association for Computational Linguistics: ACL-IJCNLP 2021, pp. 791–800. Online (2021). https://aclanthology.org/2021.findings-acl.70
32. Zhang, H., Chowdhury, S., Cancino-Chacón, C.E., Liang, J., Dixon, S., Widmer, G.: Dexter: learning and controlling performance expression with diffusion models. Appl. Sci. (15) (2024). https://doi.org/10.3390/app14156543, https://www.mdpi.com/2076-3417/14/15/6543
33. Zhang, H., Tang, J., Rafee, S.R., Dixon, S., Fazekas, G., Wiggins, G.A.: ATEPP: a dataset of automatically transcribed expressive piano performance. In: International Society for Music Information Retrieval Conference, pp. 446–453 (2022). https://doi.org/10.5281/zenodo.7342764
34. Zhao, Y., Wang, C., Fazekas, G., Benetos, E., Sandler, M.: Violinist identification based on vibrato features. In: 2021 29th European Signal Processing Conference (EUSIPCO), pp. 381–385. IEEE (2021)

Spatially Situated Media and Spatial Sampler XR–Genealogy and Organology of a Family of Gestural and Spatial Musical Instruments in Mixed Reality

Grégory Beller[1(✉)], Jacob Sello[1], Georg Hajdu[1], and Thomas Görne[2]

[1] Ligeti Center, HfMT Hamburg, Hamburg, Germany
contact@gregbeller.com
[2] HAW Hamburg, Hamburg, Germany

Abstract. Spatial Sampler XR is a new musical instrument linking gesture capture to sound production. In the same way that a sampler is an empty keyboard filled with sounds, Spatial Sampler XR uses gesture capture to transform the surrounding physical space into an area of keys for, recording, indexing and playing back samples. Spatial Sampler XR let the musician arrange the sound around him or her through gesture, creating a spatialized and interactive soundstage. A virtual reality headset adds to the instrument the ability to visualize the layout of sounds. The 3D immersion greatly facilitates their organization and increases the precision of the interaction. Several modes of play are possible and the interaction modalities vary according to the type of performance and the number of performers. This article first introduces the Synekine project, a 10-year research project from which the concept of spatial sampling is derived. It presents the technical devices used, the instruments created, the different modes of play in performative situations. The instrument relies on movement to link time and space. Thus, the Spatial Sampler XR is particularly suitable for movement artists as well as for extra-musical applications.

Keywords: spatially situated media · spatial sampling · gestural interaction · new musical instrument · gesture and sound processing · interactive performance · movement computing

1 Introduction

For the past fourteen years, through residencies and artistic creations, *the Synekine Project has* invited performers to question the intimate relationship between vocal gestures and manual gestures, through the manipulation of scenic devices based on new technologies. Metaphorically, the preeminent neuromotor link between voice and gesture is closed by "creative prostheses" joining the capture of movement to the transformation of the voice by artificial intelligence. Linking space and time through movement then transforms the search for sound into a scenic exploration.

S. Ystad et al. (Eds.): CMMR 2023, LNCS 15236, pp. 97–112, 2026.
https://doi.org/10.1007/978-3-032-02042-0_7

This paper presents the Synekine Project according to several dimensions. After the exhibition of the scientific basis and the genesis of the project, the new organology developed is described in chronological relation with the artistic works produced. Although it generates devices that can be used in other fields of application such as therapeutic rehabilitation, commercial signage or even dance and music education, these corollary results are not presented in this article for the sake of clarity of presentation.

Researches on the augmented voice in the theater [8, 9, 11, 13] led to the instinctive, expressive and pleonastic relationship between vocality and gesturality. The faculty of speaking with the hands would not only result from cultural origins, but would also result from a deep neuronal relation connecting the speech to the gestures of the hands [22]. By analogy to synesthesia, a phenomenon by which two or more senses of perception are associated, "synekinesia" would reflect our ability to associate two or more motor senses.

There is ample evidence for the ubiquitous link between manual motor and speech systems, in infant development, in deictic pointing, and in repetitive tapping and speaking tasks [25]. So, it is obvious to most people to clap their hands with every syllable spoken when we speak. Metaphorically, the Synekine Project proposes to "complete" this neuronal loop by artificially establishing an "external" link between vocal gesture and manual gesture. The voice is conventionally captured by a microphone, while the positions and dynamics of the hands are informed by different movement capture processes, which have changed from one residence to another (glove-accelerometers, Genki Wave, LeapMotion, Kinect, Optitrack and Metaquest2, see Table 1). Between the two, different computer programs based on artificial intelligence, allow the direct manipulation of sound by gesture or the learning of temporal relationships between vocal and gestural. In both cases, the result is a new organology made up of different intangible musical instruments offering the user to spread her.his voice in space, to multiply it, to segment it or to manipulate it (Fig. 1).

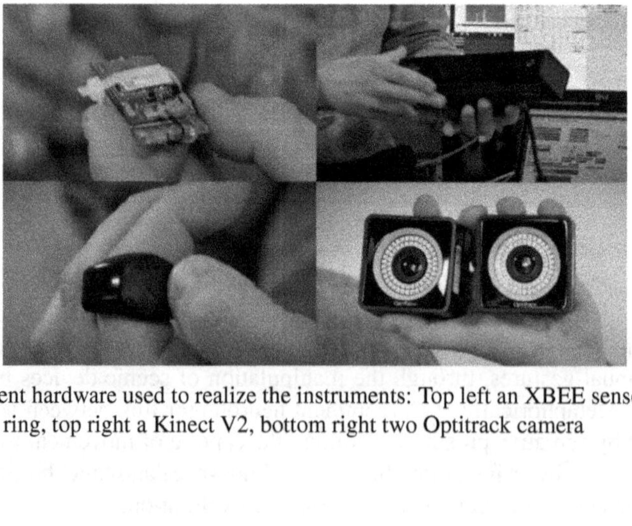

Fig. 1. Different hardware used to realize the instruments: Top left an XBEE sensor, bottom left a Genki Wave ring, top right a Kinect V2, bottom right two Optitrack camera

Table 1. Chronology of the works realized within the framework of the Synekine project presenting the various instruments elaborated from various technical devices.

Year	Work	Instrument	Gesture sensor / Button-trigger / Hand tracking	Link	Sound Mic.	Visualisation
2011	Luna Park	SpokHands	XBEE V1 / XBEE V1 / X	Wifi	Wireless headset	X
2013	Babil-on	Body Choir	XBEE V1 / XBEE V1 / Kinect V1	Wifi	Wireless headset	activity only
2014	TIIIME	Hand Sampling, Hyper Ball, Wired Gestures, Gesture Scape, Body Choir, Sound Space	XBEE V2 / XBEE V2 / Kinect V2	Wifi	Wireless headset	video for gesture scape
2015	Babil-on V2	Hand Sampling, Hyper Ball, Body Choir, Sound Space	XBEE V2 / XBEE V2 / Kinect V2	Wifi	Wireless headset	X
2017	TEDx Paris	Body Choir	X / X / Kinect V2	X	Wireless headset	X
2016	The Memory Palace - Installation	Sound Space	X / Kinect Gesture Recognition Kit / Kinect V2	X	Ambient mic	Projected 3D space
2016	The Memory Palace - Performance	Sound Space	XBEE V2 / XBEE V2 / Kinect V2	Wifi	Wireless headset	X
2017	Fissures	Hand Sampling, Body Choir, Sound Space	XBEE V2 / XBEE V2 / Kinect V2	Wifi	Wireless headset	X

(*continued*)

Table 1. (*continued*)

Year	Work	Instrument	Gesture sensor / Button-trigger / Hand tracking	Link	Sound Mic.	Visualisation
2020	Birth of a Tree	Spatial trigger, Spatial looper, Sound Space	Genki Wave / Genki Wave / Kinect V2	BLE	Wireless headset	X
2020	Air Sampling #001	Spatial trigger, Spatial looper, Sound Space	Genki Wave / Genki Wave / Kinect V2	BLE	Static mics	X
2021	Residency UME	Spatial trigger, Spatial looper, Sound Space	OptiTrack / Genki Wave / OptiTrack	BLE	Wireless headset	X
2022	Air Sampling #002	Spatial Sampler VR	Metaquest 2	Airlink	Static mics	VR + video
2022	The Vanishing Mirror	Spatial Sampler VR	Metaquest 2	Airlink	Static mics	VR only
2023	The Fault	Spatial Sampler VR	Metaquest 2	Airlink	Static mics	VR + video
2023	Air Sampling #003	Spatial Sampler VR	Metaquest 2	Airlink	headset + SM58	VR + video
2023	Air Sampling #004	Spatial Sampler VR	Metaquest 2	Airlink	Static mics	VR + video
2023	Air Sampling #005	Spatial Sampler VR	Metaquest 2	Airlink	Static mics	VR + video
2024	Air Sampling #006	Spatial Sampler VR	Metaquest 3	Airlink	Static mics	VR + video
2025	Air Sampling #007	Spatial Sampler XR	Metaquest 3	Wifi	Amp mic	VR + video

Taking advantage of the instinctive nature of the voice - gesture link, and taking advantage of new technologies allowing the joint capture of the sound of the voice and the coordinates of the gesture in real time, the Synekine Project has deployed across artistic productions and residencies, a new organology of sound, invisible and intangible instruments belonging to new Human-Computer Interactions. Motivated by artistic practice, the development of this organology is presented here in a genealogical form mixing innovations and creations.

2 Genesis: Expressivity, Sensors and Luna Park

On generative models of expressivity and their applications for speech and music, an artificial intelligence algorithm based on a corpus of expressive sentences, has been used to generate an "emotional" speech, by modulating the prosody of a "neutral" utterance [1–3]. During the development of this synthesizer of the emotion in the voice came the desire to control the prosody by the gesture. At the same time, instrumental gesture sensors were developed allowing the measurement of the dynamics of a bow by integrating small accelerometers and gyroscopes. The data related to movement is transmitted in real time by WIFI to a computer which triggers sounds and modulates effects according to the dynamics of the gesture [20]. In 2010, as part of the creation of *Luna Park*[1], a musical theater work by Georges Aperghis, these sensors have been integrated into gloves and a first instrument called ***SpokHands*** has been developed, which literally made it possible to speak with the hands [4–7].

SpokHands[2] *allows the triggering and modulation of voice samples by aerial percussion and hand elevation. Like a vocal Theremin, the instrument offers the performer the option of three-voice polyphony (her.his own and both hands) or control of text-to-speech parameters.*

In this case, the natural division of a conductor's brain is used, the left brain (right hand) for the segmental part, and the right brain (left hand) for expressivity. The percussive gestures of the right-hand trigger pre-selected syllables whose pitch and intensity are modulated by continuous gestures of the left hand. A particular aerial percussion technique aimed at triggering sounds in a temporally precise manner without hurting the self has been practiced by a percussionist. Indeed, the absence of haptic feedback from a physical object could cause, in the long run, pain in the handles which acted as a stop to the percussive movement. The research work on gestural control of speech synthesis has been pursued as part of an artistic research residency at IRCAM entitled The Synekine Project [10].

3 *Babil-On*: From Speech to Time

Babil-on, for solo and electronic voice is an augmented musical theatre performance. The composition benefited from IRCAM's artistic research residency program and the piece was premiered by Richard Dubelski in Marseille, at the Théâtre des Bernardines, in 2013, as part of CMMR 2013. Like a close-up, a "Speech" character discovers his own voice, cuts it up, superimposes it, spreads it around him, multiplies it, and reveals the emotional charge intrinsic to the language. A pair of button-rings have been added to the sensor-gloves allowing for the picking and erasing of voice samples on the fly. Thus, *SpokHands* and the triggering of pre-made sounds evolved into *Hand Sampling*, in which the vocal flow is cut and recombined in percussive gestures.

---

[1] http://www.gregbeller.com/2011/06/luna-park/.

[2] http://www.gregbeller.com/2011/06/spokhands/.

Hand Sampling*[3] *allows the performer to cut her.his voice in real time, and recombine immediately by the gesture. It involves percussive gestures that will segment and trigger vocal fragments.

The length of these fragments can vary from syllable to sentence. The order of the re-played segments can be sequential, random or palindromic, which allows different playing modes. In addition, the quality of the gesture influences the quality of the sound perceived, making the instrument expressive.

To the fast capture of the dynamics of the gesture by the accelerometer gloves has been added the relatively slow capture of the absolute position of the hands in space, by the use of depth cameras of the Kinect type [23]. This made it possible to obtain, in addition to the fine temporal precision of the percussive type triggering, the continuous control of sound processes according to the posture and the spatial position of the hands. On the other hand, the sensor brought other constraints such as a reduction in the playing area, a single performer possible, the need for a phase of calibration and detection of the skeleton, the risk of infrared disturbance by lights. The ***Body Choir*** uses the hand position to control a choir effect and the ***Hyper Ball*** to control a granular synthesizer.

Body Choir transforms a singer into a choir. This virtual choir accompanies the singer according to her.his gestures and the postures s.he adopts.

Singing involves movement of the body. This movement is captured and used to magnify the singer's musical intentions. The posture of the body and the sung note modulate in real time the harmony, the number of voices, or the spatial density of the choir.

Hyper Ball takes the form of a virtual sound ball, which the participant waters with her.his voice and modulates with her.his gesture.

The position, size and orientation of the ball influence the height, density and volume of the sound generated. This type of musical activity, by its constitution, causes choreographic movements.

In 2016 in Vancouver, Simon Fraser University, during ISEA2016, a new version Babil-on V2 has been premiered. The Kinect V2 replaced the V1 offering better acuity in capturing movement, greater flexibility of use and the possibility of following the hands of several people at the same time. Another pair of button-rings have been added to the sensor gloves.

From a compositional point of view, this second pair of button-rings offers free navigation in the structure of a work whose duration of each scene is flexible according to performer's own perception of time. From there, from the table to the stage, a change of writing paradigm takes place and we evolve in an open form that can break with the linearity of the pre-defined musical structure. Now, an improvised form can emerge from the dynamic choices made by the performers in a situation of comprovisation with these instruments.

[3] http://www.gregbeller.com/2014/02/hand-sampling/.

4 *TIIME*: From Time to Memory

TIIME stages three performers who play gestural, sound, visual and temporal mirror effects, in an apparent collective improvisation of which emerge from temporal themes: perception, memory, movement. The temporal relationship between vocal and manual gestures is modelled by artificial intelligence. On stage, a performer feeds a machine with his own vocal and gestural catalogue, then *Wired Gestures* restores fragments of this vocality in a way that is synchronous with the recognition and tracking of new gestures.

Wired Gestures *dynamically links voice to gesture, in an artificial way. The machine simultaneously records a voice gesture and a manual gesture* [21]. *It learns the temporal relationship between the two. Then it reproduces the voice, when the performer repeats the same gesture.*

The nuances of timing in the gesture are then heard as prosodic variations of the voice, and it becomes possible to break down the expressivity.

Visual extension, *Gesture Scape* records jointly and categorizes voice, gesture and video. Then new gestures, either manual or vocal will activate the visual and auditory archive. Video capture is introduced as a referential element of sound time. Not only does the manual gesture reproduce the sound of the voice, it can now also reproduce the image of the performer at the time of recording. Gesture Scape can be seen as the visual extension of Wired Gestures. The performer dances with her.his double, in a dialogue made of unison and counterpoint with the past, finding her.his inspiration in the lapsus of memory.

Gesture Scape *jointly records voice, gesture and video. Then, new gestures will activate this memory. The performer animates the video, by reproducing the same gesture, or by repeating the same associated sound.*

The performer dances with her.his double, in a dialogue made of unison and counterpoint, inspired by lapsus of memory. From the development of these two devices, based solely on the dynamics of the gesture and not on its location, was born the desire to be able to arrange and organize it in space. Symbolically, a wave of the hand, placed above the head, to say goodbye, differs from a refusal, however expressed by the same gesture, but located below the shoulder. From a performative point of view, the staging of learners manipulating learning machines has necessarily questioned the situation of memory.

5 *The Memory Palace*: From Memory to Process

Three installations and a choreographic performance, all entitled *The Memory Palace*, were created during the FACTS - Bordeaux and EXPERIMENTA - Grenoble festivals in 2017, with the support of IRCAM and ADAMI. This work cycle benefited from an artistic research residency at IDEX - University of Bordeaux, in scientific companionship with the LaBRI.

The Memory Palace is a mnemonic device practiced since antiquity allowing for memorizing long lists by arranging the elements of these in imaginary places [26]. The construction of an interior architecture sensitive, has been realized with the *Sound Space*, a choreographic musical instrument linking space and time through movement. The surrounding space becomes a key zone in which the voice can be deposited and awakened by the gesture.

***Sound Space** is a choreographic musical instrument which links space and time, through movement. It transforms the physical space surrounding the performer, into a zone in which s.he can place her.his voice and awaken it by gesture.*

By drawing her.his voice, s.he creates a unique soundstage, while evolving within it, in a creative process. The space then vibrates with a sound quality in line with the quality of movement. The *Sound Space* won the prize for technical excellence during the Guthman competition for new musical instruments.

Parable of the mnemonic, the installation transforms the place in which it is exhibited into a collective sound sculpture. Each participant is involved in the creation of a work of which s.he constitutes one of the many voices. Her.His gestures act as a reveler of the invisible sculpture. S.He can contribute to it by depositing elements of stories, sounds, or even songs that he can immediately recall in a creative process. A virtual but yet very audible forum, *The Memory Palace* acts as an indicator of the borders of the intimate, confronting the participant with the direct and immediate use of her.his voice imprint by others. In this mediation, the physical space, however empty, resonates with the different memories delivered by the participants in a temporal polyphony. Two sound installations based on the principle of *Sound Space* were presented.

The first uses a Kinect V2 for the localization and recognition of gestures, an ambient microphone as well as a video projection which materializes the sound traces of the participants on a screen. Two people were able to record sounds and play back the sounds of the others. The recording and erasing of sounds were controlled by gesture recognition (stone, leaf, scissors). The feedback showed that the main difficulty for the participants was to synchronize in order to avoid feedback (one playing while the other was recording). Finally, the representation on a 2D screen of the 3D space was a great help for the audience and made us want to use a 3D visual representation using holography or mixed reality.

The second uses the microphone and an ad hoc system of geo-localization in the confined space of mobile phones. This second version allows everyone to leave audio messages for others by simply wandering through the space with their phone, after installing a small dedicated application.

Within the former installation, the dancer Valencia James delivers a musical choreography involving personal memories, ancestral traces and imaginary characters. The choreographic process consists of the progressive materialization of a memory palace by the deployment at different points of the stage of characters combining sound quality and quality of movement. Then, a free wandering generates by interpolation a new sound space which in turn provokes new states of the body. Everything happens as if the dancer were making an improvisation with herself and the traces of memory that she has just placed on the stage.

This dramaturgical structure in three stages (discovery of a new device; development of an ad hoc language; expression of "something else" with this language) has the capacity to attract an audience and to take it somewhere to finally surprise it there. If "the something else" refers to the discovery, the device or the elaboration of language, this linear structure resonates and loops in mise en abyme generating meaning. This is the case, for example, in the musical theater solo *Fissures*, in which fragments of a text on amnesia are arranged in a spatial and repetitive cut-up.

6 *Birth of a Tree*: From Process to Notation

As part of a Scientiarum Musicae doctorate in the framework of the KiSS program - Kinetics in Sound and Space - at the Hochschule für Musik und Theater Hamburg, Germany, new technical gesture capture devices have been gradually being tested and integrated, such as the Genki Wave accelerometer rings, the Optitrack Motion Capture system or the Meta Quest 2 and 3 virtual reality Head Mounted Displays (HMDs).

In *Birth of a Tree*, percussionist Lin Chen, equipped with a microphone, two Genki Wave rings and a Kinect V2, builds an inverted chair while producing music with the various elements and tools, through the composed and notated use of gestures. The process of constructing the music goes hand in hand with the process of constructing the scenic element, again creating a mise en abyme.

For this artwork, Spatial Sampling paradigm has been developed [12, 14, 15]. The constantly renewed interest in the device *Sound Space* in different artistic configurations stems from its adaptability. Indeed, it is an empty and silent box at the start, just like the musical sampler. From the hybridization of the two concepts: Sampling and Spatially Situated Media, we derived a new instrumental paradigm.

The ***Spatial Sampler*** *substitutes the midi keyboard which classically indexes the samples, with spatial coordinates describing the positions of the hands. In our device, it includes three instruments: the sound space, the spatial trigger and the spatial looper.*

In the 1970s, the sampler revolutionized music production. This electronic music instrument, whose memory is empty at the beginning, allows the musician to create her.his own universe from percussion samples, ensembles, groups of instruments or orchestras and can also serve as a platform for musical creation.

Spatial Trigger *allows the automatic segmentation of a sound and its distribution in space by the gesture, then the selection of one of these fragments according to its position and its triggering by aerial percussion.*

Many musicians are now familiar with the "looper" or live looping. One of the main difficulties in this art is dealing with multiple layers of samples (usually dealt with a guitar pedal).

The ***Spatial Looper*** *allows the mixing of several sound loops according to the proximity of the hands, as well as the generation of music from the fragments distributed in space. It transforms the space surrounding the performer into a* ***Spatial Sequencer*** *and makes it easier to not only access the different layers but also to remember them.*

The *spatial sampler* is the basis of the creative improvisation process of the *Air Sampling* series. *Air Sampling* is a series of improvised performances in which one or multiple sound sources are sampled and distributed in space in real time. In the first performance #001, the sound source is given by Lin Chen on percussion and vocals. The author, playing the *Sound Space*, *Spatial Trigger* and *Spatial Looper* instruments, records and plays the samples in space. They perform with the percussionist an improvised musical choreography of which percussions are the only acoustic source. In order to better control the three play modes of the *spatial sampler*, and to organize sounds in space, our developments have been directed towards the integration of a graphic representation.

7 Air Sampling: From Notation to Interaction

VR versions of the *Sound Space*, *Spatial Trigger* and *Spatial Looper* instruments were created and tested in various performance situations involving one or more musicians, with or without a shared representation of what is recorded and played back [16–19]. Graham Wakefield's VR package for Max[4] is a toolkit that enables the rendering of virtual reality environments to head-mounted displays such as the Oculus Rift, Meta Quest and HTC Vive. This package enables the integration of immersive VR experiences into the Max/MSP/Jitter environment, allowing us to build interactive virtual worlds using our previously developed audio engine.

Air Sampling #002 uses the percussion sounds played by Lin Chen. *Air Sampling #003-Macht Macht Macht !* uses the sound of the voice of the sampler's player, as well as the sound of a microphone accessible to the audience, who can thus intervene in the co-improvisation. *Air Sampling #004 - Touching Spirits* and *Air Sampling #006 - Hybrid* are based on the sampling of a piano, as part of a composition in the former and as part of an improvisation with a prepared piano in the latter. *Air Sampling #005 – Si Xu* is a coimprovisation with a Guzheng player. *Vanishing mirror* is a composition for cello, piano, voice and spatial sampler VR where only the voice is been sampled. in *The Fault*, one intermezzo of the opera is the setting for organized ensemble sampling, with recordings of each musician in turn. Figure 2 shows the general performance setup used.

7.1 Shared Representation

An OpenGL representation allows the performer to visualize the position of the recorded sounds in a VR headset, which greatly facilitates the organization of the session and allows for greater spatio-temporal accuracy.

The graphical representation of the recorded sounds also offers the possibility to draw 3D structures in the virtual space. The *sound space* becomes a means of drawing 3D shapes with a line width relative to the sound volume. The automatically extracted segments of the *spatial trigger* and *spatial looper* are represented by cubes whose size is relative to the sound volume.

Several performance situations have been explored with or without sharing the representation of the 3D structure with the audience through video projection. On the one hand, showing the graphical representation to the other musicians gives them an additional piece of information about how the improvisation is being conducted. They can then see which sounds are being recorded and which are being played. In a way, co-improvisation revolves around a graphic structure co-constructed in real time. On the other hand, showing the representation to the public is a choice with multiple consequences. Making it visible facilitates the understanding of the instrument by the audience but unbalances the performance if other musicians contribute (whose scenic presence finds itself in competition with a screen). In a nominal concert situation, the musicians only show the scores and their interpretation choices through the sound produced. By sharing the visual representation of the instrument with the audience, the performer

[4] Wakefield, G. (n.d.). *VR: Virtual Reality HMDs for Max* (Version 1.0.1) [Software]. Cycling '74. Available at: https://cycling74.com/packages/vr.

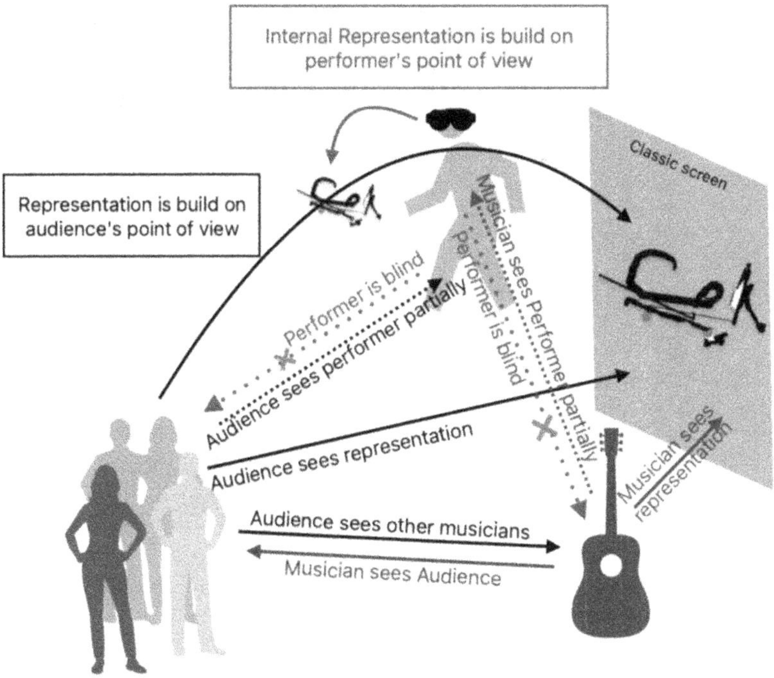

Fig. 2. Performance setup for *Air Sampling #002, #003, #004, #005, #006* and *The Fault*. The performer is completely immersed in a virtual environment, unable to see the real world, while the audience observes a digital representation that can be based either on the performer's perspective or their own.

shares a score that is being worked out in real time. The graphic element makes it easier to understand how the improvisation unfolds, but replaces the effects of memory, and also diminishes the visual impact of the performer, competing with a screen.

In *Vanishing Mirror*, the performer is the only one to visualize the recording of the sounds produced by a piano-cello-vocal trio. In *The fault* (see Fig. 4), on the other hand, the 3D structure on screen to the public is used for its own graphic quality, drawing a parallel with the activity of a sculptor on stage. In *Air Sampling #003 - Macht Macht Macht!* graphic representation is used as a medium for writing a message to the audience.

The prevalence of the visual medium over that of audio can present an important shift in the audience's perception of the instrument's purpose. Indeed, during a demonstration of the instrument to a young audience, the device was used more as a graphic tool for 3D drawing, rather than as a musical instrument. Similarly, the addition of a screen on stage can distort the perception of the scenic space and reduce the visual impact of the performer(s) on stage. Finally, the representation of the 3D structure can be made from the point of view of the performer (wearing the VR headset), resulting in significant camera movements, or from a fixed point of view at audience level, producing a static image of the structure being made.

Fig. 3. The author performing the spatial sampler VR. Recorded gestural sounds each have their own color. Each gesture is composed of circles arranged in space according to their xyzt coordinates, where t is relative to the sound frame. The size of each circle is defined by the sound volume of the frame.

Fig. 4. The *Fault*, Opera composed by the G. Beller, 2023, Hamburg, Germany. In the background, a representation of a 3D sculpture elaborated from the sounds of the instrumentalists.

7.2 Visual Occlusion

The occlusion caused by a VR headset worn by a performer on stage introduces significant challenges in live music settings (see Fig. 3). One of the primary issues is the loss of visual contact and communication with other musicians and the audience. In ensemble performances, musicians rely on visual cues for synchronization, such as gestures, facial expressions, or the conductor's direction. The lack of eye contact with the audience also diminishes emotional engagement, an essential aspect of live music. The presence of a VR headset obstructs the audience's view of the performer's facial expressions, which are crucial for conveying emotion in live performances. Additionally, ergonomic issues, such as headset weight and discomfort during extended performances, can impact the performer's endurance and concentration. This isolation can negatively affect the performer's expressiveness and real-time adaptability to the musical flow. And the physical constraints of VR - such as limited field of view and potential motion restrictions - can make navigation on stage difficult, increasing the risk of collisions or misalignment with co-performers.

7.3 Next Steps: Mixed Reality and Holographic Representation

Since holographic video technology is not yet fully mature, we propose a new performance setup for *Air Sampling #007 - Air Guitar (to be created)*. This setup (see Fig. 4) features a transparent gauze screen positioned in front of the performer, displaying a representation of the VR content from the audience's perspective (Fig. 5).

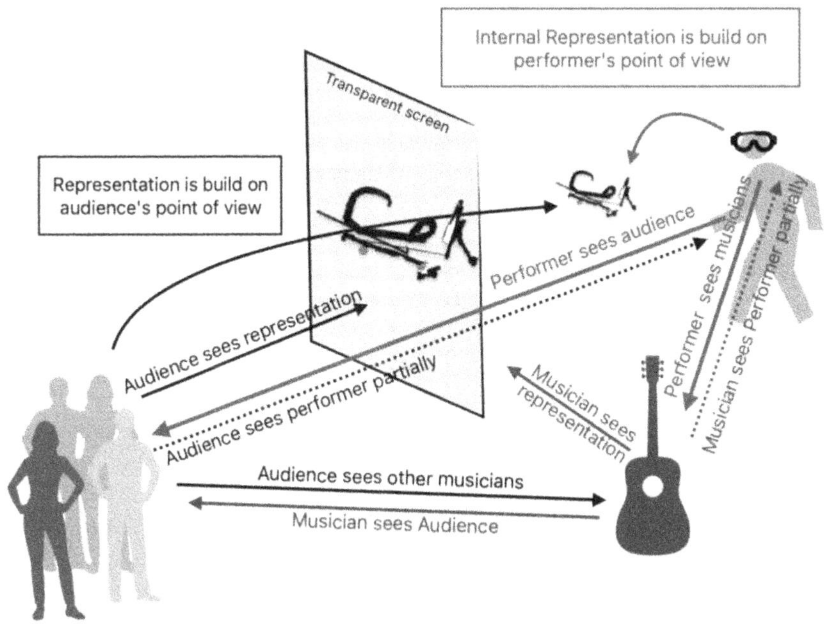

Fig. 5. Proposed performance setup for *Air Sampling #007 – Air guitar*. A transparent screen and a mixed reality headset allow the performer to see the audience while remaining in a virtual space, creating a dynamic blend between real and digital interactions.

To re-establish visual contact, at least from the performer's point of view with the audience and other musicians, a version for mixed reality headsets is under development. The evolution of the Spatial Sampler VR to the Spatial Sampler XR is currently being developed with the Meta Quest 3 mixed reality technology. An evolution which could implies the substitution of controllers by gesture recognition, thus adding the expressivity of the instrument by refining gesture processing. This evolution requires a refactoring of the instrument's visual component within the Unity environment, with a WiFi connection linking the MR headset to the sound engine—or even integrating the whole engine into an embedded application. Additionally, this change enables the improvement of the graphical representation of sounds, providing more information on timbre and pitch. Finally, the ability to manipulate samples in space, once recorded or imported, allows for their repositioning, editing, and arrangement. This process leads us toward the creation of a spatial sequencer, forming the foundation of a tool for editing spatially situated media - extending beyond audio to include images, text, code, and video.

8 Conclusion

The nexialist approach of *the Synekine Project* aims to establish protocols that generate creative processes in a holistic approach mixing Arts and Sciences. The path oscillates between meetings with scientific researchers, technical development phases, experimentation residencies of new scenic devices and crystallization of performative situations in shows or installations.

This article relates 14 years of research and artistic production accompanied by technological development. In chronological form, it exposes the development of the research theme of spatial sampling, the new musical instruments elaborated through the evolution of the technologies of gesture capture as well as the artistic stakes approached in different works. From the link between gesture and voice, the research has evolved towards the manipulation of spatially situated media. From *hand sampling* or *spatial sampler* to *sound space*, different instruments make movement the link between time and space. The technical developments are based on the evolution of technologies for capturing gestures. The fusion of data from the capture of the dynamics of the gesture, the position of the hands in the space and the sound, allows the elaboration of an interactive sound scene. In performance, improvisation, comprovisation or composition situations, different configurations are presented. The creation of about fifteen works with these instruments gives a context to the artistic stakes of spatial sampling.

Virtual reality allows to represent and manipulate "sounds located in space" in an environment comparable to that of a 3D painting software. The custom arrangement of media whose recording and playback is done on the fly inaugurates the possibility of "spatially situated media" editing. Compared to modern sequencers whose organization of windows and sounds is constrained by 2D, the possibility of freely organizing media content in 3D space seems to accelerate the work of the editor, who joins spatial memory to content memory. The use of the memory palace in the audio-visual editing activity can greatly facilitate the access to the contents and accelerate the work steps without requiring any particular cognitive dispositions of the user. While Virtual Reality allows for a better organization of the sounds recorded and produced, it has the unfortunate side effect of visually cutting the performer off from the other musicians as well as the audience. A new version using mixed reality is under development to enhance communication with musicians and audiences, to improve the graphical representation of sound and to allow for spatially situated media to be manipulated and edited in real time.

Acknowledgments. This research was partially funded under the Program "Innovative Hochschule" (innovative university) by the Federal Ministry for Education and Research (BMBF) of Germany (Grant No. 13IHS232C) and the City of Hamburg. The authors would like to thank all those who have contributed to this artistic research.

Disclosure of Interests. The authors have no competing interests to declare that are relevant to the content of this article.

References

1. Beller, G. : Analyse et Modèle Génératif de l'Expressivité: application à la parole et à l'interprétation musicale, Paris 6 – IRCAM (2009)
2. Beller, G.: Transformation of Expressivity in Speech. The Role of Prosody in the Expression of Emotions in English and in French, ed. Peter Lang (Peter Lang) (2009)
3. Beller, G.: Expresso: Transformation of Expressivity in Speech. Speech Prosody, Chicago (2010)
4. Beller, G., Aperghis, G.: Contrôle Gestuel de la Synthèse Concaténative en Temps Réel Dans Luna Park: rapport recherche (2011)
5. Beller, G., Aperghis, G.: Gestural Control of Real-Time Concatenative Synthesis in Luna Park, P3S, pp. 23–28. International Workshop on Performative Speech and Singing Synthesis, Vancouver (2011)
6. Beller, G.: Gestural Control Of Real Time Concatenative Synthesis. ICPhS, Hong Kong (2011)
7. Beller, G.: Gestural Control of Real-Time Speech Synthesis in Luna Park, SMC, Padova (2011)
8. Beller, G. : Arcane d'Un mage en été, Théâtre Publique, n° 200 (2011)
9. Beller, G. : In-vivo: laboratoire de recherche et d'expérimentation autour du son pour le théâtre, Towards a History of Sound in Theatre, Montreal (2012)
10. Beller, G.: The Synekine Project, MOCO 2014. IRCAM, Paris (2014)
11. Beller, G.: L'IRCAM et la voix augmentée au théâtre: Les nouvelles technologies sonores au service de la dramaturgie. L'Annuaire théâtral, Numéro **56–57**, 195–205 (2014)
12. Beller, G.: Sound Space and Spatial Sampler, MOCO 2015, SFU, Vancouver (2015)
13. Beller, G. : Spectacle vivant: des voix imaginaires aux monstres vocaux, InaGlobal, Paris, France (2017)
14. Beller, G. : Le Projet Synekine, Alternatives théâtrales, N° 146 – Les scènes du son – perspectives contemporaines (2022)
15. Beller, G.: The Synekine Project, KiSS Kinetics in Sounds and Space, Wolke-Verlag (2022)
16. Beller, G.: Air Sampling – Spatial Sampler XR, NIME, Mixed Realties as NIMEs workshop, Mexico City (2023)
17. Beller, G.: Spatial Sampling in Mixed Reality: A Review of Ten Years of Research and Creation», I3DA, Bologna, September (2023)
18. Beller, G.: Spatial Sampling in Mixed Reality, ICMC, Shenzhen, October (2023)
19. Beller, G., Sello, J., Hajdu, G., Görne, T.: Spatial Sampling in Mixed Reality An Overview of Ten Years of Research and Creation. CMMR, Tokyo, November (2023)

20. Bevilacqua, F., Rasamimanana, N., Fléty, E., Lemouton, S., Baschet, F.: The augmented violin project: research, composition and performance report. In: 6th International Conference on New Interfaces for Musical Expression (NIME 06), Paris (2006)
21. Françoise, J., Schnell, N., Borghesi, R., Bevilacqua, F. : Probabilistic models for designing motion and sound relationships. Proceedings of the 2014 International Conference on New Interfaces for Musical Expression, June (2014), London, UK, United Kingdom, pp. 287–292 (2014)
22. Iverson, J.M., Goldin-Meadow, S.: Why people gesture when they speak. Nature **396**, 228 (1998)
23. Kean, S., Hall, J.C., Perry, P.: Microsoft's kinect SDK. In: Meet the Kinect. Apress (2011). https://doi.org/10.1007/978-1-4302-3889-8_8
24. Laukka, P., Eerola, T., Thingujam, N.S., Yamasaki, T., Beller, G.: Universal and culture-specific factors in the recognition and performance of musical affect expressions. Emotion, American Psychological Association **13**(3), 434–449 (2013)
25. Parrell, B., Goldstein, L., Lee, S., Byrd, D.: Spatiotemporal coupling between speech and manual motor actions. J. Phon. **42**, 1–11 (2014)
26. Yates, F.: The Art of Memory. University of Chicago Press (1966)

JAZZVAR: A Dataset of Variations Found within Solo Piano Performances of Jazz Standards for Music Overpainting

Eleanor Row[(✉)], Jingjing Tang, and György Fazekas

Centre for Digital Music, Queen Mary University of London, London, E1 4NS, UK
{e.r.v.row,jingjing.tang,george.fazekas}@qmul.ac.uk

Abstract. Jazz pianists often uniquely interpret jazz standards. Passages from these interpretations can be viewed as sections of variation. We manually extracted such variations from solo jazz piano performances. The JAZZVAR dataset is a collection of 502 pairs of '*Original*' and '*Variation*' MIDI segments. Each *Variation* in the dataset is accompanied by a corresponding *Original* segment containing the melody and chords from the original jazz standard. Our approach differs from many existing jazz datasets in the Music Information Retrieval (MIR) community, which often focus on improvisation sections within jazz performances. In this paper, we outline the curation process for obtaining and sorting the repertoire, the pipeline for creating the *Original* and *Variation* pairs, and our analysis of the dataset. We also introduce a new generative music task, Music Overpainting, and present a baseline Transformer model trained on the JAZZVAR dataset for this task. Other potential applications of our dataset include expressive performance analysis and performer identification.

Keywords: jazz piano dataset · music generation · generative AI

1 Introduction

The growing interest in generative music models has led to the exploration of their potential in specialised music composition tasks. As current trends often focus on generating complete songs or music continuation tasks [2,3], there is a lack of datasets designed for specialised music tasks. However, these specialised music tasks, such as music infilling [4,17] and composition style transfer [16,24], could contribute to the development of artificial intelligence (AI) or generative AI (GenAI) tools in music composition.

We introduce Music Overpainting, a novel and specialised generative music task that creates new musical variations by rearranging a given music segment. Music Overpainting was inspired by the technique of overpainting in fine art and Liszt's compositional approaches to rearrangements in his piano transcriptions in classical music. While the task aims to reframe the musical context

S. Ystad et al. (Eds.): CMMR 2023, LNCS 15236, pp. 113–126, 2026.
https://doi.org/10.1007/978-3-032-02042-0_8

by changing elements such as rhythmic, harmonic, and melodic complexity and ornamentation, the core melodic and harmonic structure of the music segment is preserved. Compared to related music generation tasks such as compositional style transfer [5] and music infilling [17,22], Music Overpainting creates small variations within the same style and retains perceptible similarities in the underlying melodic contour and harmonic structure of the music segment. Outputs from Music Overpainting could be used in GenAI tools for music composition, to add variation and novelty to desired sections of music.

Our motivation for creating this dataset stems from the lack of available datasets for novel and specialised generative music tasks. Not only did we find that there was a lack of clean and high-quality MIDI data for investigating tasks such as Music Overpainting, but also in the context of solo jazz piano music in general. Most existing jazz datasets consist of transcriptions of improvised "solo" sections within a jazz performance or feature multiple instruments. Few datasets feature interpretations of the "head" section, containing the main musical theme, for solo piano only. Additionally, we found that many jazz datasets do not include performances from female musicians, so we are proud to include several extracts of performances from female jazz pianists within our dataset. Our dataset helps to fill this gap, while also providing insights into how jazz pianists rearrange standards for solo piano from a Music Information Retrieval (MIR) perspective.

Table 1. Overview of *Original* and *Variation* Segments.

Feature	Original	Variation
Segment length	4 bars	misc.
Location	"head" section	"head" section
File format	Manually-transcribed MIDI	Automatically-transcribed MIDI
Musical format	Melody and chords	Two-handed solo piano
Type	Lead sheet of jazz standard	Piano performance of jazz standard
Source	MuseScore	YouTube

The JAZZVAR dataset comprises of 502 pairs of *Original* and *Variation* MIDI segments from 22 jazz standards, 47 performances, and 35 pianists. An *Original* segment is 4-bars long and manually transcribed from a lead sheet of a jazz standard. A *Variation* segment is manually found from an automatically transcribed piano performance of the same jazz standard. We find *Variation* segments by searching for passages that are melodically and harmonically similar to *Original* segments. Figure 1 shows more details of the data curation pipeline. Table 1 provides more information about the *Original* and *Variation* segments. The jazz standards and the piano performances in our dataset are under copyright, therefore the JAZZVAR dataset has been made available for download under the Creative Commons Attribution, Non Commercial license for research purposes only[1].

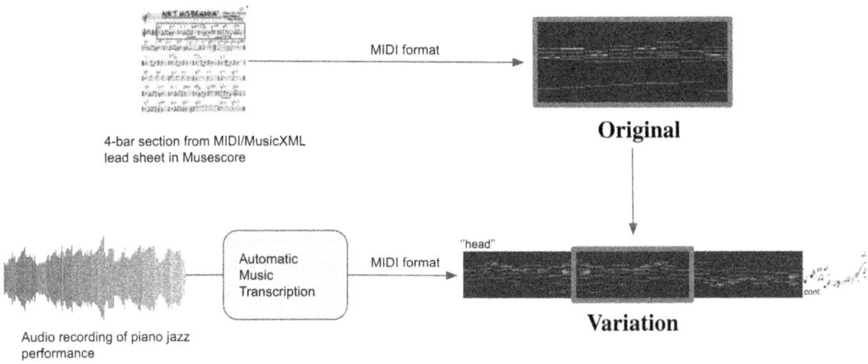

Fig. 1. The process of creating *Original* and *Variation* pairs. *Original* sections are MIDI segments from a lead sheet transcription of a jazz standard. Audio of a piano performance playing the same jazz standard is transcribed automatically into MIDI. A *Variation* is found by manually searching for passages that are melodically and harmonically similar to the *Original* in the "head" section of the piano performance.

The JAZZVAR dataset serves as a foundation for exploring the Music Overpainting task across genres. What we refer to as *Variations* are passages of music from a jazz standard that have been reinterpreted or rearranged by jazz pianists'. However, we can view these reinterpretations as variations on the melody and chords of the jazz standards. We use the *Original* and *Variation* pairs in the dataset to train a Music Transformer model to generate novel passages of variation from a simple MIDI primer. By presenting this novel dataset and introducing the Music Overpainting task, we aim to contribute to the field of generative music research and encourage further exploration of the relationship between composers and AI tools in various music genres.

The remainder of this paper is organised as follows: Sect. 2 provides an overview of related datasets in the field of generative music and MIR, Sects. 3 and 4 present an in-depth description and analysis of the JAZZVAR dataset, Sect. 5 introduces Music Overpainting as a generative music task and uses the JAZZVAR dataset to train the Music Transformer model for generation.

2 Related Works

Existing jazz datasets that can be used for MIR and Generative Music tasks often feature the improvisation or solo section only of the jazz performance. The Weimar Jazz Database (WDB) [18], consists of 456 manually transcribed solos

[1] Link to JAZZVAR dataset on Zenodo: https://zenodo.org/records/11264676.

by 78 performers and contains no solo piano performances. The DTL1000 dataset [6] from the "Dig That Lick" project is a set of 1750 automatically transcribed solos from 1060 tracks. However, it is not clear how many of these tracks are piano solo tracks.

The Million Song Dataset (MSD) [1] is a collection of audio features and metadata for one million contemporary popular music tracks. While the MSD does not specifically focus on jazz, it does include a substantial number of jazz recordings that could be used for comparative analysis. The Lakh MIDI Dataset (LMD) [14] is a collection of 176,581 unique MIDI files that are matched to songs within the Million Song Dataset using Dynamic Time Warping-based alignment methods [19]. Similarly, to the DTL1000 dataset, the MSD and the LMD have no specific focus on solo jazz piano performances.

3 JAZZVAR Dataset

3.1 Data Collection

Repertoire. A jazz standard is a well-known, and commonly played song in the jazz repertoire. Many popular songs composed in the early to mid-twentieth century for film, television, and musical theatre are now prominent jazz standards. Some of the more famous jazz standards include Gershwin's "Summertime" for the opera *Porgy and Bess* (1935) and "All the Things You Are" by Jerome Kern and Oscar Hammerstein II for the musical *Very Warm for May* (1939). These popular songs have been continually played and rearranged by jazz musicians for decades. Popular songs originating from these times contain a "refrain" section, which was the main theme of the song. In jazz music, the "head" section is often synonymous with these "refrain" sections. Many jazz musicians would learn the songs by ear, or through unofficial lead sheets, such as the ones circulated within the *Fake Real Book*. Some jazz musicians, such as the trumpeter Miles Davis (1926–1991) and Thelonious Monk (1917–1982), composed music themselves and these pieces have also become famous jazz standards.

Within this context, our goal was to find lead sheets of jazz standards and audio recordings of solo piano performances of jazz standards. The first publication dates of the jazz standards in our dataset range between 1918 and 1966, while the performances span from the mid-twentieth to the beginning of the twenty-first century.

Jazz Standard Lead Sheets. Lead sheets are condensed versions of song compositions that musicians have transcribed and passed through the community. They are presented as a single melodic line with accompanying chords.

We sourced MIDI and MusicXML lead sheets from MuseScore, created by users who often referenced the *Fake Real Book*. Candidate pieces were found using the following criteria:

1. To be entirely in 4/4 timing,
2. To be jazz standards mostly consisting of popular songs from the early to mid-twentieth century.

The lead sheets were cleaned and corrected by removing the introductions and verses from the songs, keeping only the refrain section. Songs with repeated refrains were further edited to include only the final repeat. We converted any MusicXML files to MIDI and made corrections by referencing chords from existing lead sheets. In some cases, the chords and melody were transcribed by ear from early recordings of popular songs. In other cases, the MIDI was completely rewritten, as many of the source files were corrupt. In total, we collected and cleaned 234 jazz standards, of which a subset of 22 appear within the JAZZVAR dataset.

Audio of Jazz Solo Piano Performances. To compile a list of solo piano performances of jazz standards, we manually searched for well-known jazz pianists' solo performances on Spotify and Youtube that matched the list of 234 MIDI lead sheets we had collected. We also used the *Solo piano jazz albums*[2] category on Wikipedia to help find performances. We gathered Spotify Metadata for these performances, which we used to collect the respective audio data. This approach allowed us to compile a diverse set of performances, including some by female pianists, and to capture the rich history of jazz piano performance.

3.2 Automatic Music Transcription of Jazz Audio

Automatic Music Transcription (AMT) algorithms such as [9,12] enable us to transcribe audio recordings into MIDI representations. According to results from a listening test conducted by Zhang et al. [25], the High-Resolution transcription system proposed by Kong et al. [12] is preferred over the other two systems by participants in terms of conserving the expressiveness of the performances. We used the Spotify metadata to download the jazz audio from Youtube and applied the High-Resolution model [12] to transcribe the downloaded jazz audios into MIDIs. In total, we collected and transcribed 760 audio recordings covering a wide range of performances from 148 albums by 101 jazz pianists, of which a subset of 47 performances appear within the JAZZVAR dataset.

3.3 Pair Matching Process

We segmented 4 bar sections from the MIDI lead sheets by taking into consideration the phrases in the main melody. As the jazz standards that we chose were all in 4/4 time, most of the phrases were contained within a 4-bar structure. We labeled these four bar sections as *Original* segments. We segmented 22 jazz standards and collected an average of 6 segments per standard. In order to create our *Variation* segments to form a data pair, we manually searched through the AMT solo jazz piano performances of the jazz standards and found segments that were melodically and harmonically similar to the *Original* segment for each jazz standard. To facilitate the matching process for finding *Original* and *Variation*

[2] See Wikipedia:https://tinyurl.com/solo-piano-jazz.

pairs, we created a Python application with a graphical user interface (GUI), which allowed us to view and listen to individual *Original* segments. We then searched through the AMT jazz performances and saved passages that closely corresponded to the *Original* segments melodically and harmonically.

4 Analysis

4.1 Experimental Dataset Analysis

We calculated several musical statistics across the dataset to provide insights into the dataset's musical content and structure according to [7]. We compared the differences between the *Original* and the *Variation* sections and summarise several characteristic features in Table 2.

Table 2. Means and standard deviations for various statistics for combined segments in *Original* and *Variation* sections.

Feature	Orig. Mean	Orig. SD	Var. Mean	Var. SD
Pitch Class Entropy	2.94	0.24	3.13	0.24
Pitch Range	36.44	3.60	47.20	10.91
Polyphony	5.30	0.28	5.01	2.08
Number of Pitches	16.08	0.28	29.42	8.05
Pitch in Scale	0.89	0.24	0.83	0.08

Pitch Class Entropy. The higher mean pitch class entropy in the *Variation* segments (3.13) compared to the *Original* segments (2.94) suggests that the jazz pianists in our dataset tended to introduce more diversity in pitch distribution when interpreting jazz standards. This increased complexity and unpredictability in the variations reflect the improvisational and creative nature of jazz music.

Pitch Range. The mean pitch range in the *Variation* segments (47.20) is considerably larger than in the *Original* segments (36.44), indicating that the jazz pianists in our dataset often expanded beyond the range of pitches used within a jazz standard. This expanded pitch range could contribute to a richer and more expressive musical experience in the variations.

Polyphony. Polyphony is defined as the mean number of pitches played simultaneously, evaluated only at time steps where at least one pitch is played. The mean polyphony is slightly lower in the *Variation* segments (5.01) compared to the *Original* segments (5.30). This suggests that the jazz pianists in our dataset may have used fewer simultaneous pitches on average in their reinterpretations. However, the higher standard deviation in the *Variation* segments (2.08) indicates that the polyphonic structures in these reinterpretations can be quite diverse.

Number of Pitches. The higher mean number of pitches in the *Variation* segments (29.42) compared to the *Original* segments (16.08) implies that the jazz pianists in our dataset tended to incorporate more distinct pitches when rearranging jazz standards. This increase in the number of pitches adds to the complexity and expressiveness of the variations.

Pitch in Scale. Pitch-in-scale rate is defined as the ratio of the number of notes in a certain scale to the total number of notes [7]. The slightly lower mean value of pitch in scale in the *Variation* segments (0.83) compared to the *Original* segments (0.89) indicates that the jazz pianists in our dataset may have been more inclined to use pitches outside the underlying scale in their reinterpretations. This could contribute to more adventurous and exploratory motifs in the variations.

In summary, the analysis of the JAZZVAR dataset reveals that the jazz pianists in our dataset often introduced greater complexity, diversity, and expressiveness when rearranging jazz standards for solo piano. Our findings highlight the dataset's potential for application in tasks such as Music Overpainting. Not only are these insights valuable for the development of specialised generative music models, but they also provide a better understanding of the creative process in jazz music.

4.2 Comparison of Multiple Pianists

Some of the jazz standards featured within the dataset are performed by multiple pianists. Therefore, there are some *Original* segments that are matched to multiple *Variation* segments from different pianists. To further highlight the diversity of variations within the dataset, we present a musical analysis of multiple pianists' interpretations of the same *Original* segment, from the jazz standard "All the Things You Are".

Melody. The melody from the *Original* segment was found and isolated within each *Variation* segment. To obtain accurate representations of the melodies, we manually extracted the melody lines from the *Variation* segments. This manual extraction process involved listening closely to the melody in the *Original* in order to carefully isolate the melody line within the performances note by note, ensuring higher accuracy and fidelity of melodic extraction in comparison to an automatic approach. We then compared the isolated melodies to find their pitch and duration deviation from the ground truth, the melody from the *Original* segment. We applied the Needleman-Wunsch [8,13] alignment algorithm which aligns melodies by minimizing the differences in pitch class and duration between the corresponding notes. Based on the alignment results, we calculate the average deviation score using the following equation:

$$\text{Average Deviation} = \frac{1}{n}\sum_{i=1}^{n}(PC_i + D_i) \tag{1}$$

where PC_i denotes the deviation of pitch class, D_i denotes the deviation of note duration, and i refers to the i-th note in the melody. We excluded the missing notes in the summation over the note sequences.

This average deviation score provides a measure of how similar the two melodies are, with lower scores indicating higher similarity. The deviation scores of the pianists' *Variation* from the *Original* melody can be found in Table 3. Our results show that different pianists' have unique and individual approaches to interpreting the *Original* melody. Some pianists, such as Leslie North, have a closer adherence to the *Original* melody, while others, like Bill Evans, exhibit greater differences.

Table 3. Average deviation from *Original* melody for different pianists.

Pianist	Average Deviation
Jim McNeely	1.60
McCoy Tyner	1.04
Roland Hanna	1.50
Lennie Tristiano	0.92
Elmo Hope	1.11
Leslie North	0.65
Bill Evans	2.68

We also mapped the melodic contours of the performances to further explore the differences between the interpretations, using the Contourviz[3] package as shown in Fig. 2. The visual representation of melodic contours allowed us to observe the overall structure and direction of the melody as it evolved throughout the performance. By comparing the melodic contours of different pianists, we found that some tended to be more experimental with their melodic choices, while others adhered more closely to the *Original* melody. This variation in melodic contours provides additional evidence of the rich diversity present in our dataset.

Harmony. The harmonies used within a performance can greatly impact the direction of the music and also the intention of the performer. To analyse some of the harmonic aspects of the dataset, we used Chordino and NNLS chroma [15]. We set out to find the rate of harmonic change across each performance. As shown in Fig. 3, we found that some pianists had a higher harmonic rhythm (the rate of chord changes in a chord progression) than others. Other pianists added more chords to the chord progression, which sped up the harmonic rhythm. We observed that most pianists played in the key of the *Original*, however, some transposed keys. Some pianists used the same chord progression as the *Original*

[3] Contourviz can be found in: https://github.com/cjwit/contourviz.

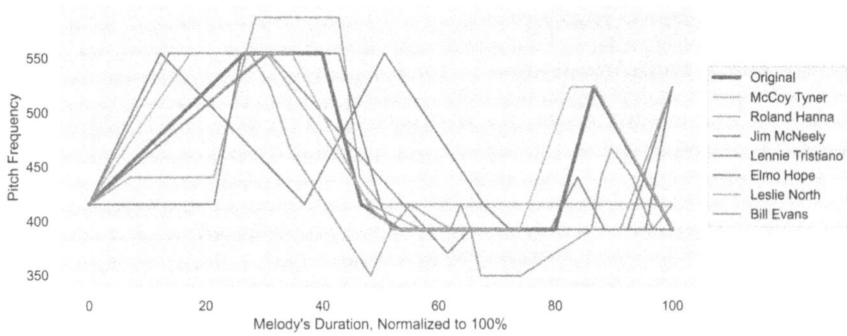

Fig. 2. The melodic contours of the melody taken from the jazz standard "All The Things You Are" (in Blue) and pianists' interpretations. (Color figure online)

but altered specific chords. For example, Jim McNeely used a similar chord progression to the *Original*, but modified a minor chord to major, resulting in a significant shift in the performance's intention and musical direction. We also observed that certain pianists used extended chords more extensively than others who played more closely to the *Original*. Other pianists added more chords to the chord progression, which sped up the harmonic rhythm.

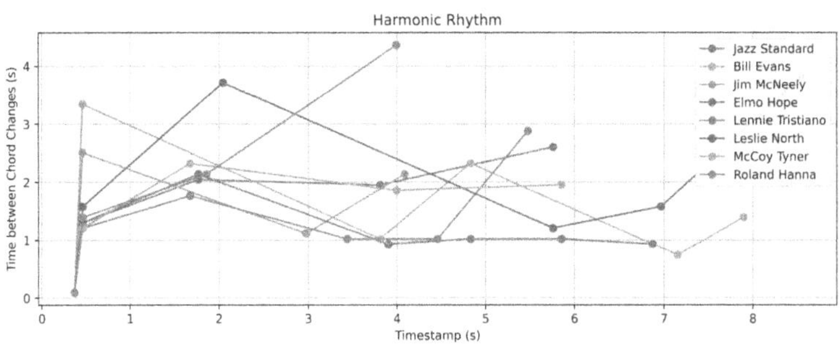

Fig. 3. A line graph comparison of the Harmonic Rhythm of the original melody (in Blue) and pianists' interpretations of the melody. (Color figure online)

Our analysis shows that the dataset contains a diverse range of interpretations, even when playing the same jazz standard. Within jazz, performers are individualistic and can be creative with their musical choices. The differences in melodic deviations, melodic contours, and harmonic rhythms between performances not only demonstrate the artistic freedom of each pianist but also indicates that the dataset could be a useful resource for those interested in expressive performance analysis or performer identification tasks.

5 Music Overpainting

5.1 Problem Definition

In this work, we introduce the task of Music Overpainting, where the goal is to generate creative interpretations of existing musical segments. We now formally define the task.

Definition 1 (Music Overpainting). *Music Overpainting is a generative music task that aims to create variations on pre-existing music sections. In the context of the JAZZVAR dataset, the task is defined as follows: given an Original jazz standard segment O and its corresponding Variation segment V, the goal is to determine a reinterpretation $I(O)$ such that*

$$V = I(O). \tag{2}$$

5.2 Generation with Music Transformer

Transformers have been widely applied to generate continuous music in genres such as pop, classical, and jazz [10,11,23]. Their convincing output demonstrates their capability of modelling musical structures and patterns. In this work, we adopted the design of Music Transformer, which uses music motifs as primers for conditional generation [10]. To train the transformer model, we concatenated the *Variation* segments to the end of the *Original* segments for each pair in the JAZZVAR dataset. In total, we obtained 502 concatenations and used 90% for training and 10% for validation. In inference, we treated the *Original* segment as a primer and conditionally generated a *Variation* segment, sampling from the probability distribution learned by the transformer model.

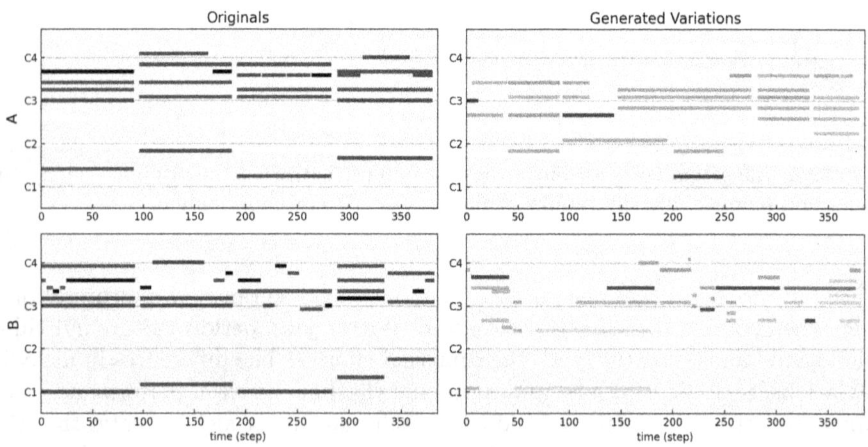

Fig. 4. Piano-rolls of two *Original* (left in Blue) and the corresponding generated *Variation* (right in Red) sections. The *Original* A is from the song "All the Things You Are", and the *Original* B is from the song "Alfie". (Color figure online)

5.3 Results

We present piano-rolls of two *Original* segments, referred to as **A** and **B**, and the corresponding generated *Variation* segments[4] with *Original* segments used as primers to the model in Fig. 4. We use the same pitch-related features calculated for the dataset in Table 2 to compare the *Original* segments and the corresponding generations. According to these results, we observe that the generated *Variation* segments are more complex and diverse in terms of the music features presented in Table 4, as well as the articulation and dynamics. By listening to the generations, we find that the model's ability to accurately preserve the melody and chord patterns of the *Original* segment in the generated output can be improved.

In this chapter, we initially presented the Music Overpainting task using the JAZZVAR dataset. Since then, we have extended this work to refine and improve the Music Overpainting task, exploring various transformer architecture configurations [20] and benchmarking the JAZZVAR dataset against a newly introduced dataset VAR4000 that supplements our work exploring Music Overpainting with transformers (see [21]).

Table 4. Comparison of musical features for the *Original* and the generated *Variation* segments.

Feature	Orig. A	Orig. B	Gen. Var. A	Gen. Var. B
Pitch Class Entropy	2.73	2.75	2.71	2.86
Pitch Range	28.00	36.00	34.00	36.00
Polyphony	3.98	2.74	4.88	4.68
Number of Pitches	12.00	17.00	13.00	14.00
Scale Consistency	1.00	0.90	1.00	0.98

6 Conclusion

We present the JAZZVAR dataset a collection of 502 MIDI pairs of *Variation* and *Original* segments. We evaluated the dataset with regard to several musical features and compared the melodic and harmonic features of *Variations* for different pianists performing the same *Original* jazz standard. Our results indicate the diversity and complexity of *Variation* in the dataset, which is one important component for successfully training a specialised generative music model. We introduced the Music Overpainting task, and trained a Music Transformer using the JAZZVAR dataset to generate *Variation* segments with the *Original* segments as primers.

[4] Listening samples of the generations can be found at https://tinyurl.com/jazzvar dataset.

Having a collection of *Variations* performed by different pianists on the same jazz standard allows us to apply the dataset to explore tasks such as performer identification and expressive performance analysis. As mentioned in 5.3, subsequent work has enabled us to expand the JAZZVAR dataset even further, with added AMT jazz piano performances [21]. This was achieved through a semi-automatic matching method, which allowed for a greater number of *Original* and *Variation* pairs to be produced (around 5400 pairs). However, we believe exploring deep generative music models for the Music Overpainting task specifically will still greatly benefit from much larger datasets. As AMT methods improve and are able to generate cleaner transcriptions, our future work looks to exploring the task with by training larger models with more data.

Acknowledgements. This work is supported by the UKRI Centre for Doctoral Training in Artificial Intelligence and Music, funded by UK Research and Innovation [grant number EP/S022694/1]. J. Tang is a research student also supported jointly by the China Scholarship Council and Queen Mary University of London. Special thanks to Max Graf, for his help in creating the GUI, and to both him, Huan Zhang, and Corey Ford, all from the Centre for Digital Music at Queen Mary University of London, for reviewing our paper.

Disclosure of Interests. The authors have no competing interests to declare that are relevant to the content of this article.

References

1. Bertin-Mahieux, T., Ellis, D.P., Whitman, B., Lamere, P.: The million song dataset. In: International Society for Music Information Retrieval conference (2011). tex.owner: thierry tex.timestamp: 2010.03.07
2. Briot, J.P.: From artificial neural networks to deep learning for music generation: history, concepts and trends. Neural Comput. Appl. **33**(1), 39–65 (2021). https://doi.org/10.1007/s00521-020-05399-0
3. Briot, J.P., Pachet, F.: Deep learning for music generation: challenges and directions. Neural Comput. Appl. **32**(4), 981–993 (2020). https://doi.org/10.1007/s00521-018-3813-6
4. Chang, C.J., Lee, C.Y., Yang, Y.H.: Variable-length music score infilling via XLNet and musically specialized positional encoding (ILM), pp. 97–104 (2021). http://arxiv.org/abs/2108.05064, _eprint: 2108.05064
5. Dai, S., Zhang, Z., Xia, G.G.: Music style transfer: a position paper. In: The 6th International Workshop on Musical Metacreation (2018). _eprint: 1803.06841
6. Dixon, S., et al.: History of recorded jazz: DTL **1000**, 1920–2020 (2022)
7. Dong, H.W., Hsiao, W.Y., Yang, L.C., Yang, Y.H.: MuseGAN: multi-track sequential generative adversarial networks for symbolic music generation and accompaniment. In: AAAI Conference on Artificial Intelligence (2018)
8. Gotoh, O.: An improved algorithm for matching biological sequences. J. Mol. Biol. **162**(3), 705–708 (1982). https://www.sciencedirect.com/science/article/pii/0022283682903989

9. Hawthorne, C., Simon, I., Swavely, R., Manilow, E., Engel, J.: Sequence-to-sequence piano transcription with transformers. In: International Society for Music Information Retrieval Conference (2021)
10. Huang, C.Z.A., et al.: Music transformer. In: International Conference on Learning Representations (2019). https://openreview.net/forum?id=rJe4ShAcF7
11. Huang, Y.S., Yang, Y.H.: Pop music transformer: beat-based modeling and generation of expressive pop piano compositions. In: Proceedings of the 28th ACM international conference on multimedia, pp. 1180–1188. MM 2020, Association for Computing Machinery, New York, NY, USA (2020). https://doi.org/10.1145/3394171.3413671, number of pages: 9 Place: Seattle, WA, USA
12. Kong, Q., Li, B., Chen, J., Wang, Y.: GiantMIDI-Piano: a large-scale MIDI dataset for classical piano music. Trans. Int. Soc. Music Inf. Retrieval (2022)
13. van Kranenburg, P., Volk, A., Wiering, F., Veltkamp, R.C.: Musical models for melody alignment. In: International Society for Music Information Retrieval Conference (2009)
14. Manilow, E., Wichern, G., Seetharaman, P., Roux, J.L.: Cutting music source separation some Slakh: a dataset to study the impact of training data quality and quantity. In: 2019 IEEE Workshop on Applications of Signal Processing to Audio and Acoustics (WASPAA), pp. 45–49 (2019)
15. Mauch, M., Dixon, S.: Approximate note transcription for the improved identification of difficult chords. In: International Society for Music Information Retrieval Conference (2010)
16. Mukherjee, S., Mulimani, M.: ComposeInStyle: music composition with and without style transfer. Expert Syst. Appl. **191**, 116195 (2021)
17. Pati, A., Lerch, A., Hadjeres, G.: Learning to traverse latent spaces for musical score inpainting. In: International Society for Music Information Retrieval conference (2019). event-place: Delft
18. Pfleiderer, M., Frieler, K., Abeßer, J., Zaddach, W.G., Burkhart, B. (eds.): Inside the Jazzomat - New Perspectives for Jazz Research. Schott Campus (2017)
19. Raffel, C., Ellis, D.P.W.: Optimizing DTW-based audio-to-MIDI alignment and matching. In: 2016 IEEE International Conference on Acoustics, Speech and Signal Processing (ICASSP), pp. 81–85 (2016)
20. Row, E., Fazekas, G.: Advancing AI in music composition: refining the generative music overpainting task. In: AES International Symposium on AI and the Musician (2024). https://qmro.qmul.ac.uk/xmlui/handle/123456789/98357, accepted: 2024-07-23T13:07:34Z
21. Row, E., Shanin, I., Fazekas, G.: Exploring transformer-based music overpainting for jazz piano variations. In: Late-breaking demo. San Francisco (CA), United States (2024). https://doi.org/10.48550/arXiv.2412.04610, accepted and presented as a Late-Breaking Demo at the 25th International Society for Music Information Retrieval (ISMIR) in San Francisco, US (2024)
22. Wei, S., Xia, G., Zhang, Y., Lin, L., Gao, W.: Music phrase inpainting using long-term representation and contrastive loss. In: ICASSP 2022 - 2022 IEEE International Conference on Acoustics, Speech and Signal Processing (ICASSP), pp. 186–190 (2022)
23. Wu, S.L., Yang, Y.H.: The jazz transformer on the front line: exploring the shortcomings of AI-composed music through quantitative measures. In: International Society for Music Information Retrieval Conference (2020)

24. Wu, X., Hu, Z., Sheng, L., Xu, D.: StyleFormer: real-time arbitrary style transfer via parametric style composition. In: 2021 IEEE/CVF International Conference on Computer Vision (ICCV), pp. 14598–14607 (2021)
25. Zhang, H., Tang, J., Rafee, S.R., Dixon, S., Fazekas, G., Wiggins, G.A.: ATEPP: a dataset of automatically transcribed expressive piano performance. In: International Society for Music Information Retrieval Conference, pp. 446–453 (2022). https://doi.org/10.5281/zenodo.7342764

A Live Performance Rule System Informed by Irish Traditional Dance Music

Marco Amerotti[1(✉)], Steve Benford[2(✉)], Bob L. T. Sturm[1(✉)], and Craig Vear[2(✉)]

[1] Speech, Music and Hearing, KTH Royal Institute of Technology, Stockholm, Sweden
{amerotti,bobs}@kth.se
[2] University of Nottingham, Nottingham, UK
{steve.benford,craig.vear}@nottingham.ac.uk

Abstract. This paper describes ongoing work in programming a live performance system for interpreting melodies in ways that mimic Irish traditional dance music practice and that allows plug-and-play human interaction. Existing performance systems are almost exclusively aimed at piano performance and classical music and few are aimed specifically at traditional music. We develop a rule-based approach using expert knowledge that converts a melody into control parameters to synthesize an expressive MIDI performance, focusing on ornamentation, dynamics and subtle time deviation. Furthermore, we make the system controllable (*e.g.*, via knobs or expression pedals) such that it can be controlled in real time by a musician. Our preliminary evaluations show the system can render expressive performances mimicking traditional practice and allows for engaging with Irish traditional dance music in new ways. We provide several examples online (See this website: https://www.kth.se/profile/bobs/page/research-data).

Keywords: music performance modeling · traditional music · Irish

1 Introduction

The performance of an Irish traditional dance tune involves ornamentation and variation over repetitions. Some practitioners employ small variations where the tune is always recognizable (*e.g.*, Irish accordionist Derek Hickey calls these "microvariations" of the "bones"[1]), while others move far away from the tune (*e.g.*, the fiddler Tommy Potts is well-known as an extreme example). The ornamentation and variation employed in a performance are often guided by the instrument one is playing, and certain choices are made based on the accessibility of pitches, physical constraints, range and so on. Irish traditional music is by and large an aural tradition, where notated music ("the dots on the page") is passed over in favor of listening to master musicians interpreting tunes and then

[1] Private communication in a lesson with author Sturm.

S. Ystad et al. (Eds.): CMMR 2023, LNCS 15236, pp. 127–139, 2026.
https://doi.org/10.1007/978-3-032-02042-0_9

imitating their creative choices. When Irish traditional dance music is notated, the convention is one of writing what one thinks are the most important notes, leaving ornamentation and variation to the performer. Computer playback of such notated music thus lacks important elements of the traditional music performance: how might we program a performance system so that its rendition is closer to real-life performance?

While there is much research on modeling expressive music performance, *e.g.*, classical piano, we find limited work devoted to traditional music. This paper presents a performance system focused on Irish traditional dance music aiming to render performances that mimic the practice. Our system operationalizes expert knowledge into a set of rules binding musical elements, such as ornamentation and dynamics, to performance parameters for controllable MIDI synthesis. The scarcity of explicit performance data in the context of Irish music motivates an expert-knowledge-driven, rule-based approach, which is both computationally efficient and sufficient to create at least a baseline model for Irish traditional music performance. Furthermore, since the performance of Irish traditional dance music can involve heterophony (multiple musicians playing their own versions of the same tune together), we make our system real-time and controllable such that one can play *with* it in a live performance scenario. In the next sections, we review existing work in music performance modeling, as well as conventions in Irish traditional music performance. We describe our system and how its components operationalize expert knowledge. We then provide some preliminary evaluation of its output and discuss its use in the context of a live performance. Future research is discussed in the conclusion.

2 Background

We now review research in the modeling of music performance. We then discuss specific characteristics of the performance of Irish traditional dance music.

2.1 Existing Work in Modeling Music Performance

Music performance modeling [4] is aimed at making machines perform music in expressive ways. This is accomplished by translating musical elements, such as pitches, phrases and timing, into expressive parameters, such as articulation, loudness, dynamics and phrasing. One example is the "KTH rule system" for musical performance [6], which applies a user-weighted rule-based estimation of expressive parameters for each note of a piece. The set of rules has been implemented in the software package *Director Musices* [7], which allows one to inspect the generated expressive contours.

Most work in music performance modeling is aimed at the performance of classical music, but a growing number of studies focus on popular music and jazz performance [4]. While there exists research in the analysis of traditional music practice [13,14,17,18], we find few approaches attempting to generate performances: Duggan [5] uses a case-based reasoning approach for modeling Irish flute performance creativity and Perez et al. [16] target Irish fiddle performance informed with multimodal data, such as violin bow movements. However, both systems generate *offline* performances, while our focus is on *online* (*e.g.* interactive and real-time) steerable performances of Irish traditional music.

The most commonly modeled parameters among performance systems include loudness, tempo, ornamentation and articulation, and so the MIDI protocol is often used since it allows some amount of modeling of the above through velocity, timing, pitch and control messages (*e.g.*, pitch bend). Expressive parameters are often modeled jointly since they can be highly related, *e.g.*, tempo and dynamics [19]. Moreover, since human performance can go beyond the written score, such as ornamentation and style-specific musical practices, some work has explored the modeling of such performance conventions, *e.g.*, ornamentation of lead sheets in the performance of jazz standards [8]. Another example is the MusicTransformer system [10], which can generate realistic accompaniments and performances given only melody input. Improvisation and variation are usually ignored when modeling classical music performance, but other styles (jazz and some folk traditions) consider them essential aspects of expressive performance.

2.2 Performance of Irish Traditional Dance Music

Irish traditional dance music has a history going back a few centuries at least [3,9,20]. A dance tune consists of parts, each typically built from simple musical ideas unfolding over two to four beats. These parts are often repeated in performance, as is the whole tune. Common dances are the reel, jig, hornpipe and polka, each executed with characteristic rhythms. Tunes are modal, most often in major, mixolydian, dorian or minor, and typically involve melodic motion that combines stepwise movement with arpeggiated chords. Ornamentation is an essential aspect of traditional performance, contributing to the rhythmic drive of a dance tune.

Irish traditional music is an aural practice, the expert performance of which does not involve playing tunes "as written". Figure 1 notates the A part of the well-known jig, *The Connachtman's Rambles*, as printed in "O'Neill's 1001" [15], along with a transcription of one of its repetitions performed by master musician Máirtín O'Connor. This shows his variation of the jig rhythm, playing with the timing of quavers within each beat. He uses a variety of "cuts" (a grace note ornament emphasizing the attack of the following note), some of which provide tonal value to establish a counter melody (bars 11–12).

O'Connor's performance of this tune demonstrates how the practice of the music involves "microvariations", which lends itself well to performance in "sessions" where musicians of varied abilities gather informally to play tunes together. While varying greatly, sessions tend to exhibit some common characteristics including [2] performers joining and leaving throughout, numerous and diverse melody instruments playing in unison (often accompanied by a few guitars, citterns and bouzoukis), musicians with different skills – from beginners to seasoned experts – playing alongside one another and playing and learning by ear more often than playing from printed music. Furthermore, sessions feature

Fig. 1. The A part of *The Connachtman's Rambles.* Top: as printed in "The Dance Music of Ireland: O'Neill's 1001". Middle: as performed by Máirtín O'Connor on accordion in 1979 (transposed down to D from Eb). Bottom: as interpreted by our performance model. The performance hyperparameters were set to create a performance similar to Máirtín O'Connor's.

tunes linked together in "sets" of two or more, each repeated a number of times. This structure allows tunes to be learned by ear or recalled to the fingers before then being embellished on subsequent repeats. There is also a degree of improvisation in selecting tunes that fit well together as sets and in guessing which tunes other players might or might not know and/or be able to pick up.

3 Performance System

We now present our performance system, which processes MIDI input and outputs control parameters to synthesize an expressive MIDI performance that can be exported on its own without human interaction, or input in real-time to any software or hardware with MIDI input capabilities. The resulting performance incorporates style-specific ornaments, time deviations and dynamics to reflect conventions of Irish traditional dance music practice. The performances of each of these three aspects (ornamentation, dynamics, tempo) are modeled with expert-knowledge-based rules and functions, user-specified performance parameters, and metadata in the MIDI file itself (*e.g.*, the key signature MIDI metamessage) (Fig. 2).

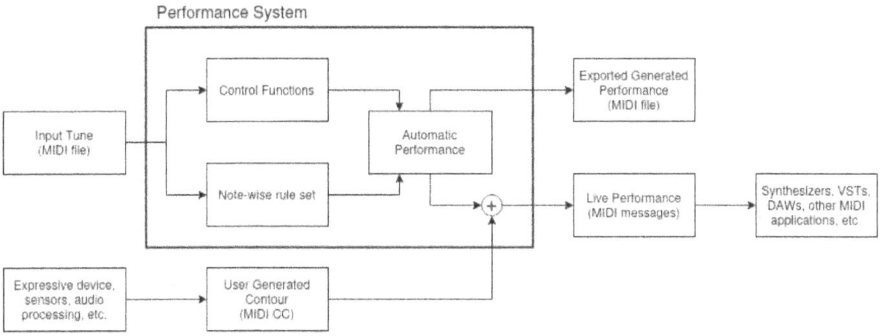

Fig. 2. The performance system pipeline. An input MIDI tune is processed by computing control functions to guide the performance and by evaluating rule-sets for each note (*e.g.* to generate ornamentation). The performance can be live and optionally steered in real-time, or otherwise exported to a MIDI file.

The expert-knowledge-based rules and functions are motivated not only by our own practical knowledge of Irish traditional dance music performance, but also that of noted Irish musician and theorist Tomás Ó Canainn [20]. In his analysis of Irish music, Ó Canainn presents a formalism of note importance in which he assigns points to each note appearing in a tune:

1) a note frequency count giving a point for each appearance of the note;
2) the addition of a further point (a) to a note that occurs on a strong beat, (b) to the highest note on its first appearance, (c) to the lowest note on its first appearance, (d) to a note proceeded to by a leap greater than a fifth, (e) to the first stressed note, (f) to a long note (*e.g.*, a dotted crotchet in a jig).

Inspired by Ó Canainn, our system assigns five scores to each note in a tune and then uses these to derive and apply control functions to guide the resulting performance. For each note-on event of a MIDI source, we compute the following scores:

1. a number of points equal to the number of occurrences of that pitch class in the entire tune (*frequency score*);
2. if the note occurs on a strong beat, it gets a number of points equal to the number of times the pitch occurs on a strong beat; otherwise zero (*beat score*);
3. a point if it is either the highest or the lowest pitch of the tune (*ambitus score*);
4. a point if the interval leading to it is greater or equal to a fifth (*leap score*);
5. a point if its duration is longer than the mode of the note durations of the tune (*length score*).

To generate control functions the system normalizes these scores and linearly combines them to manifest particular musical qualities relevant to the three modeled performance aspects. We hand-craft these linear combinations through a combination of formalizing our musical experiences and expectations, as well as trial and error, *e.g.*, that a cut is more likely to occur between a repetition of a pitch and on a strong beat. Table 1 shows the weightings involved, which have proven to be sufficient at this preliminary stage, but work is required to determine their sufficiency for modeling real performance. Finally, we apply smoothing to these functions to reduce extreme sudden variations that make the performance erratic. In particular, we employ a third-order Savitzky-Golay filter with a window size of 15 notes and use mean-value padding at the edges.

Table 1. Score weighting for computing control functions. For instance, the ornament score is given by the sum $0.2 \cdot \textit{frequency score} + 0.3 \cdot \textit{beat score} + 0.15 \cdot \textit{ambitus score} + 0.15 \cdot \textit{leap score} + 0.2 \cdot \textit{length score}$.

Control function	Frequency	Beat	Ambitus	Leap	Length
Ornaments	0.2	0.3	0.15	0.15	0.2
Dynamics	0.1	0.25	0.25	0.2	0.2
Tempo	0.25	0.1	0.3	0.25	0.1

To illustrate the procedure of generating control functions, consider the A part of *The Connachtman's Rambles* from Fig. 1. Figure 3 show the five series of scores derived using the above method. Figure 4 show the control functions resulting from the linear combination and smoothing for each performance model aspect. For each note in the input melody, the system uses the corresponding value of the control functions to affect its performance according to each modeled aspect.

Being intended not only as a performance generator but also as an agent capable of performing live with another musician, we make our system responsive to an external user-defined control signal to steer the performance, *e.g.*, an accompanying guitarist with an expression pedal. The following subsections describe how our system models each of the three performance aspects and how each of those is influenced by a control function.

3.1 Performing Ornamentation

Ornaments in Irish traditional music are partly dependent on the physical characteristics of the traditional instruments [20] (*e.g.*, sliding between pitches on the fiddle, "tapping" on the tin whistle to articulate repeated notes) and musical characteristics (*e.g.*, to accentuate beats in accordance with traditional dancing). On top of that, musicians may impose personal stylistic preferences and improvisational elements. We focus on the modeling of three of the most common ornaments which can be easily modeled with MIDI, and are not exclusive to particular instruments by and large. The particular ornaments performed by our system are slides, cuts and rolls:

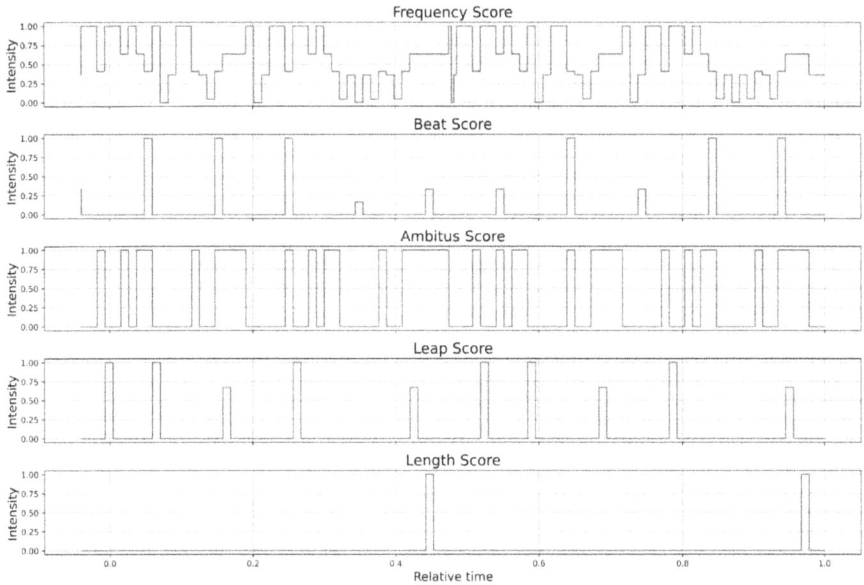

Fig. 3. Individual scores used to generate control functions for each modeled aspect for the A part of *The Connachtman's Rambles* (Fig. 1). The single note-wise scores are summed and weighted according to Table 1 to generate the control functions.

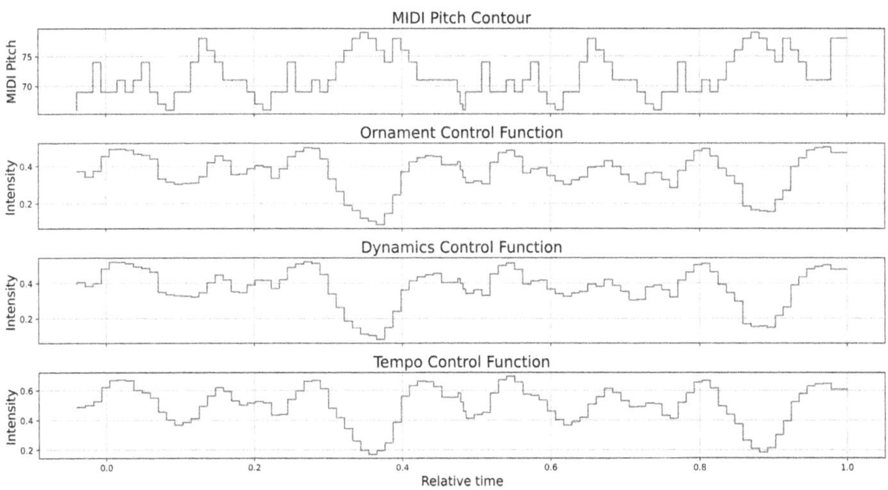

Fig. 4. From the top, MIDI Pitch contour and generated ornament, dynamics and tempo control functions for the A part of *The Connachtman's Rambles* (Fig. 1). The ornament control function is directly mapped to the probability of ornamenting a note; the dynamics control function is mapped to note velocity in the range [0, 127]; the tempo control function is mapped to a tempo drift percentage with 0.5 being the original tempo, higher/lower values meaning a faster/slower tempo.

- A slide entails approaching a note from a lower pitch. We create a slide ornament by using a series of MIDI pitch-bend messages between a note and the next lowest scale degree.
- A cut is like a grace note that emphasizes the attack of a note or separates repeated notes. We create a cut by adding a short note one scale degree above the note.
- A roll is a decoration of three quavers that involves separating each with cuts, similar to the classical "gruppetto" or "turn" and consists in approaching the pitch from above and then from below. We create a roll by adding the appropriate notes.

In our system, the pitches of rolls and cuts are drawn from the mode of the tune.

For each note of a MIDI file, the system determines if it is a candidate for ornamentation with a probability computed from the ornament control function and user-specified parameters. If it is a candidate, the system selects one of the ornaments, or possibly drops the note (a "humanizing" of the performance), at random.

3.2 Performing with Dynamics and Tempo Deviations

Our system models dynamics via MIDI note velocity using the dynamics control function, which is scaled to the range [0,127] and applied directly to the note velocity parameter. Notes falling on a beat are further accentuated by increasing their velocity. To humanize the performance, the system implements tempo deviations around a user-specified tempo by locally warping the performance tempo using the tempo control function. The motivating idea is that musicians will tend to speed up or slow down at times the melody has certain characteristics, *e.g.*, ornamentation, repeated notes and melodic leaps.

3.3 Human Interaction

Our system is capable of continuously reading an external MIDI control change signal on a specified MIDI control number during a performance with an accompanying musician. This signal is scaled to $[0, 1]$ and interpolated with the control functions with a user-defined weight. For instance, the musician can make the performance system play without ornamentation at first, and then gradually make it more adventurous. While basic, this approach can be quite versatile since any kind of user-generated control function can manipulate the MIDI control signal processed by the system. Possibilities include conventional controls, *e.g.*, MIDI pedals and knobs, but also unconventional ones such as body sensors.

4 Preliminary Evaluation

We now conduct a preliminary evaluation of our performance system to determine its effectiveness and chart future work for development. We first compare

Fig. 5. A tune generated by the model *Folktune-VAE* [1]. Top: original tune as generated by the model. Bottom: as interpreted by the performance system. A rolled note is notated with a tilde.

an expert performance of *The Connachtman's Rambles* (Fig. 1) with that of our system to determine acceptable parameters. We then apply the performance system to a novel tune generated by Folktune-VAE [1] – a model trained on Irish traditional music – and gauge its plausibility with respect to traditional practice. Audio examples of generated performances are available on our website.

Figure 1 shows transcriptions of two performances of the A part of *The Connachtman's Rambles*, one by an expert and another generated by our system. We see that the system is able to mimic some of the ornamentation of the expert, with a general difference in the pitch used to cut. Most of O'Connor's cuts are pitches a third above – which are convenient to do on the accordion because of the physical distribution of its pitches. Our system at this time is not instrument-specific and produces "generic" cuts within the mode of a tune. In terms of rhythm, our model accentuates the beats using cuts as in the human performance. Rhythmic swing is clear in the human performance (emphasizing the jig rhythm), while the performance system shows none since it is only subtly adjusting tempo at this time. The performance system stays with a steady tempo but introduces subtle drifts. While still far from the human performance, our system generates stylistically coherent elements that are more expressive than basic MIDI synthesis.

We now analyze how our system performs the machine-generated tune shown at top of Fig. 5. There is of course no reference performance for this tune, but we can gauge the stylistic coherence of our system's performance. The transcription, shown at the bottom of Fig. 5, shows the system mainly employs cuts and occasional slides and dropped notes. Cuts are placed appropriately, *e.g.*, at the start of bars or between repeated notes. The system generates a roll at the start of the B part on a dotted crotchet, which is also consistent with the practice. Listening to the performance, the reel rhythm is clear and the dynamics are varied throughout.

While preliminary, this evaluation shows our system shows some success in rendering a performance of melodies in ways that are consistent with the practice of Irish traditional dance music. Linking probabilistic decisions with higher-level control signals derived from the music content make expressive and varied renditions that are more interesting than straight MIDI playback. Furthermore, adding interactivity makes for a dynamic playing partner.

5 Discussion: The System as a Musician

The inspiration for our system arose from an ongoing project to explore how human and AI musicians might perform together. Our distinctive focus was on how humans might accompany AI, specifically on how a human guitarist might improvise an accompaniment to AI-generated and performed tunes. First, a human musician (Benford) used the *FolkRNN* system[2] to generate around twenty tunes, from which eight were selected and segued to form two sets – a set of four reels and a set of four jigs. While this yielded sets of tunes potentially interesting to accompany, the automated playback of the resulting MIDI files through a standard digital audio workstation was, unsurprisingly, flat and immediately striking for its lack of variation when tunes were repeated. There was no sense of the system pushing the performer or vice versa and the human accompanist was left to do all of the work in making the performance dynamic and interesting.

Our preliminary exploration involved a series of scripts generating ornamentation, micro timing and pitch errors[3] based on random chances alone; with those, a human musician generated twelve variations of each tune with different parameters (three levels of ornamentation, note pitch error, micro timing and three combinations of all of them with the scripts applied in sequence). The human musician listened to and compared these, selecting three versions of each tune to be sequenced together as part of the overall set. This process already led to some immediate insights and inspirations for further developments.

The traditional ornamentations of rolls, cuts and slides worked to introduce aesthetically pleasing variation. Timing errors and dropped notes on the other hand gave a sense of the agent struggling to play the tune, or being tentative, giving the impression that it was learning it or trying to recall it back to its fingers. Pitch errors were sometimes heard as mistakes, but sometimes as more as attempted "jazzy" (chromatic) improvisations, especially if the system was

[2] https://folkrnn.org.

[3] The pitch errors were not included in the system presented here as we felt that more work was needed in modeling this aspect.

otherwise performing fluidly (*e.g.*, was introducing odd pitches without obvious timing errors).

These observations led to the idea that the system might have a persona that would support a narrative through the performance that would make sense of their variations. For example, they might be a learner struggling to learn new tunes and/or to master their instrument, or alternatively, a skilled and proficient player quickly trying to recall "out of practice" tunes. The latter felt particularly appealing, as a skilled musician might conceivably play with various embellishments, but also errors depending on their situation, and might even be expected to vary these through a performance. The journey through such a narrative should be interactive, *i.e.* the human should be able to influence it. This inspired the idea of a simple control based on an expression of musical intensity; that the human musician should be able to signal that they would want their skilled AI collaborator to play with more or less intensity. This might be interpreted in various ways. Lowering intensity might signal the AI to back off, perhaps playing more solidly (if boringly) and ultimately more tentatively (as if trying to recall a tune). Raising intensity might cause it to introduce more traditional embellishments and eventually introduce jazzy improvisations or even take risks that would lead to mistakes. Intensity might be signaled explicitly (*e.g.* through the expression pedal) or perhaps detected automatically from the accompanist's own playing. In this case, our performance system allows us to hear a tune that is foreign to the tradition and which would have to be physically learned and played by a musician to be heard otherwise.

In summary, the variations introduced by our performance system felt potentially productive in inspiring accompaniment, but might benefit from the creation of an underlying musical persona and narrative for the system that would help make sense of them and enable them to be influenced during the performance. Our goal was to generate an authentic performance, more than an ideal one: such a performance cannot be modeled without having an underlying musician, or an idea of them.

6 Conclusion

We have operationalized expert knowledge to form a rule-based performance system that is able to render a melody expressed in MIDI as an expressive and dynamic performance that exemplifies conventions of the practice. Performance aspects that we have modeled include various ornaments, tempo variations and dynamics. Our preliminary evaluation demonstrates the effectiveness of our system and points to its usefulness in human-AI co-performance. The system has clear limitations, however. For example, its parameters and hyperparameters are currently set by trial and error, but could be estimated from expert performances. Another limitation is the performances it generates are not instrument-specific, possibly rendering a performance on a synthetic instrument that would not be typical or even possible on a real instrument. More work should thus be conducted to improve this baseline system, *e.g.*, further humanizing the performance, introducing melodic variation and extemporization and modeling specific instruments. Another aspect deserving of further work is the rendering of a *session* performance, where two or more artificial performers play a melody together.

While the task of creating a performance system presents common elements across styles, datasets and approaches [4], a main difference in the modeling of folk music performance is *performance creativity* [12], not limited to creativity in planning the performance, but ranging from adding ornamentation and micro timing to explicitly playing wrong notes and drifting in tempo. This is in contrast to the performance of classical music, where one must play a score as written without mistakes, but taking liberties with phrasing, dynamics, articulation and tempo. It might seem at first that modeling the performance of just a melody is a trivial matter, but the conventions of the practice of Irish traditional dance music bring subtle and interesting challenges. Folk music is more complex than it appears at first. The modeling of folk music performance presents challenges that are different from those when modeling other styles, and in our opinion should be pursued to enrich opportunities to engage with music traditions.

Of the performance systems dealing with performance creativity listed in [12], most of them present very limited evaluation, if any at all. An obvious way of evaluating a performance system is through listening tests, RENCON [11] being a key example. Our preliminary evaluation analyzes generated performances from an expert-knowledge-based perspective, but future work can conduct listening tests as done at RENCON, both of the system's output and its application in the context of human-AI co-performance. This latter aspect brings ambiguity, however: if a performance system is difficult to play with, it could be a bad performance system or a good emulation of a bad musician. Nonetheless, we aim to render performances that are expressive and faithfully reflect practical conventions.

Acknowledgements. Portions of this work are outcomes of projects that have received funding from the European Research Council under the European Union's Horizon 2020 research and innovation program: DigiScore (Grant agreement No. 101002086) and MUSAiC (Grant agreement No. 864189), and from the Engineering and Physical Sciences Research Council (EPSRC) under the UKRI Turing AI Fellowship: Somabotics—Creatively Embodying Artificial Intelligence (Grant agreement No. EP/Z534808/1).

Disclosure of Interests. The authors have no competing interests to declare that are relevant to the content of this article.

References

1. Amerotti, M.: Latent Representations for Traditional Music Analysis and Generation. Tesi di Laurea. Università di Bologna ((2022)
2. Breathnach, B.: Folk music and dances of Ireland: a comprehensive study examining the basic elements of Irish folk music and dance traditions. Ossian (1996)
3. Breand'an Breathnach: Folk music and dances of Ireland: a comprehensive study examining the basic elements of Irish folk music and dance traditions. Ossian (1971)
4. Cancino Chacón, C.E., Grachten, M., Goebl, W., Widmer, G.: Computational models of expressive music performance: a comprehensive and critical review. Front. Digit. Humanit. **5** (2018)
5. Duggan, B., Cui, Z., Cunningham, P.: MATT-A system for modelling creativity in traditional Irish flute playing. In: Third ECAI Workshop on Computational Creativity (2006)
6. Friberg, A., Bresin, R., Sundberg, J.: Overview of the KTH rule system for musical performance. Adv. Cogn. Psychol. **2**, 145–161 (2006)
7. Friberg, A., Colombo, V., Frydén, L., Sundberg, J.: Generating musical performances with director musices. Computer Music J. **24**(3), 23–29 (2000)
8. Giraldo, S., Ramírez, R.: A machine learning approach to ornamentation modeling and synthesis in jazz guitar. J. Math. Music **10**(2), 107–126 (2016)
9. ÓhAllmhuráin, G.: A Pocket History of Irish Traditional Music. The O'Brien Press (1998)
10. Huang, C.Z.A., et al.: Music transformer: generating music with long-term structure. arXiv preprint arXiv:1809.04281 (2018)
11. Katayose, H., Hashida, M., De Poli, G., Hirata, K.: On evaluating systems for generating expressive music performance: the RENCON experience. J. New Music Res. **41**, 299–310 (2012)
12. Kirke, A., Miranda, E.R.: Handbook of Artificial Intelligence for Music: Foundations, Advanced Approaches, and Developments for Creativity, Performance Creativity in Computer Systems for Expressive Performance of Music, pp. 521–584. Springer (2021). https://doi.org/10.1007/978-3-030-72116-9
13. Lerch, A., Arthur, C., Pati, A., Gururani, S.: An interdisciplinary review of music performance analysis. Trans. Int. Soc. Music Inf. Retrieval (2020)
14. Müller, M., Grosche, P., Wiering, F.: Automated analysis of performance variations in folk song recordings. In: Proceedings of International Conference on Multimedia Information Retrieval, pp. 247–256 (2010)
15. O'Neill, F.: The Dance Music of Ireland: O'Neill's 1001. Chicago (1907)
16. Perez, A., Maestre, E., Kersten, S., Ramirez, R.: Expressive Irish fiddle performance model informed with bowing. In: Proceedings of the International Computer Music Conference (2008)
17. Ramírez, R., Maestre, E., Perez, A., Serra, X.: Automatic performer identification in celtic violin audio recordings. J. New Music Res. **40**(2), 165–174 (2011)
18. Ren, Y., et al.: Feature analysis of repeated patterns in Dutch folk songs using principal component analysis. In: Proceedings of the 8th International Workshop on Folk Music Analysis, pp. 86–88 (2018)
19. Todd, N.P.M.: The dynamics of dynamics: a model of musical expression. J. Acoust. Soc. Am. **91**(6), 3540–3550 (1992)
20. Ó Canainn, T.: Traditional Music in Ireland. Routledge and Kegan Paul Ltd. (1978)

Benzaiten: A Non-Expert-Friendly Event of Automatic Melody Generation Contest

Yoshitaka Tomiyama[1,2], Tetsuro Kitahara[3(✉)], Taro Masuda[1,4], Koki Kitaya[1], Yuya Matsumura[1,5], Ayari Takezawa[1,6], Tsuyoshi Odaira[7], and Kanako Baba[8]

[1] MusicxAnalytics Meetup Steering Committee, Tokyo, Japan
[2] NABLAS Inc., Tokyo, Japan
[3] Nihon University, Tokyo, Japan
kitahara.tetsuro@nihon-u.ac.jp
[4] Nikkei Inc., Tokyo, Japan
[5] NOVASELL Inc., Tokyo, Japan
[6] Kyushu University, Fukuoka, Japan
[7] Tokyo, Japan
[8] Advanced Institute of Industrial Technology, Shinagawa, Japan

Abstract. This paper presents a contest-style music evaluation event called *Benzaiten*. There have been some attempts to evaluate different music generation systems with a unified criterion and/or platform, but it was not an event that non-experts could easily enjoy. At Benzaiten, we encouraged non-researcher people to join it as entrants by providing starter kits and communication channels. As well, we exercised ideas towards a high-quality entertainment event for laypeople to enjoy it. As a result, 15 people joined this event as entrants (eight of which moved to the main round), and more than 100 people participated as the audience.

Keywords: melody generation · evaluation · contest

1 Introduction

Whereas the research on automatic melody generation has a long history, the recent development of machine learning (ML) technologies has been rapidly increasing the number of attempts at automatic melody generation [1].

Evaluating melody generation systems/methods is still an important open problem in this field. Unlike speech recognition and image classification, the *correct* output (e.g., a melody) for a certain input (e.g., a chord progression) cannot be uniquely or objectively determined. We, therefore, have to conduct subjective quality tests on generated melodies employing music experts, but its methodology has not been necessarily established.

To provide a platform for evaluating different systems/methods on a unified criterion, some researchers made attempts to organize contest-based evaluation. Sturm et al. [3] organized the AI Music Generation Challenge 2000, in which they collected Irish double-jig pieces from entrants and hired experts to evaluate them. They also organized the 2021 edition focusing on Swedish traditional dance

T. Odaira—Freelance.

S. Ystad et al. (Eds.): CMMR 2023, LNCS 15236, pp. 140–148, 2026.
https://doi.org/10.1007/978-3-032-02042-0_10

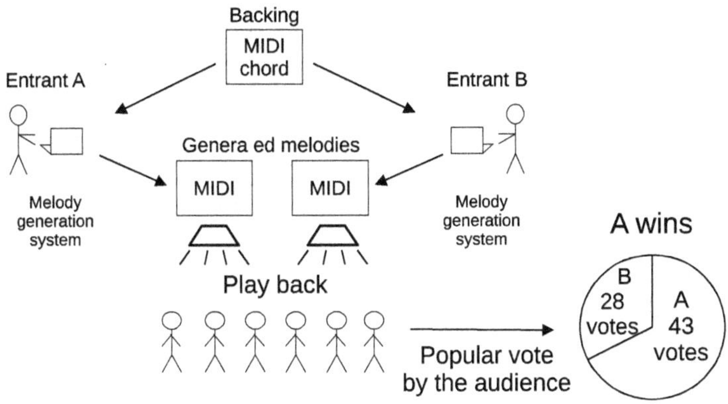

Fig. 1. Basic scheme of Benzaiten. Two entrants are given a backing track and generate melodies during the event. Then, the winner is determined according to popular votes by the audience.

music [4]. Katayose et al. [2] held Performance Rendering Contests (Rencon) to provide a subjective evaluation platform for researchers developing expressive music performance rendering systems. Yeh et al. [5] attempted on collaborative comparisons of harmonization systems developed by researchers from different institutes. However, these attempts have the following two problems:

- Because entrants are implicitly assumed to have skills or experiences in developing music generation systems/methods, there is no scheme for encouraging non-researcher people who have not tried such development.
- Because the primary purpose is to provide a unified platform for evaluation, they are not necessarily fun for laypeople as entertainment shows.

In this paper, we propose a novel contest-based music generation evaluation event, called *Benzaiten*. The most important policies in Benzaiten are *openness* and *fun* for non-experts. To develop the melody generation field furthermore, it is important to let a wide range of people have an interest in it. We, therefore, aim at an event that non-experts can enjoy as entrants and/or the audience. Benzaiten has the following features:

- To make it easy for novices to join it as entrants, we provided starter kits for developing melody generation systems and communication channels on Slack for sharing issues and ideas among potential entrants.
- To make it possible for laypeople to enjoy it as the audience, we exercised some ideas to make its quality as an entertainment show higher, including a popular vote and a one-on-one battle scheme.

2 Basic Policy and Event Design

Benzaiten (Fig. 1) is a contest-based melody generation evaluation event. Every entrant brings their melody generation system and generates a melody that fits a given backing track. The generated melody is played back within the event, then the winner is determined based on voting. As discussed in the Introduction, the basic policies in this event are *openness* and *fun* for non-experts as follows:

- *Openness to novices*: It is easy for various people to join this event as entrants, even if they are not ML and/or music experts.
- *Fun for laypeople*: Participants can enjoy this event as the audience even if they do not have music- or ML-related knowledge.

To achieve *openness to novices*, we make the following attempts:

- **Starter kits**: We developed two kinds of starter kits for this event, with which everyone can quickly try automatic melody generation.
- **Online tutorials**: We held online tutorials, in which the tutors taught the basic knowledge of MIDI and music as well as how to use the starter kits.
- **Community management of potential entrants**: We made a community of potential entrants, including those who had yet to determined entry. We encouraged communication among them by making a Slack channel and holding online meetings.

To achieve *fun for laypeople*, we introduce the following ideas to the event:

- **Popular vote**: The audience can get involved in determining the winner.
- **One-on-one battle scheme**: We adopted a tournament style based on a one-on-one battle scheme. This scheme makes the voting for each match simple, because all the participants have to do is to judge which is better of the presented two melodies.
- **Live melody generation**: For each match, the backing track is provided right when the match starts. Therefore, the entrants must generate melodies live during the event (they cannot generate melodies in advance).

3 Actions Before the Event

To encourage a wide range of people to join the event as entrants, we should promote this event widely and encourage as many people as possible to join the community of potential entrants. Therefore, we did the following (Fig. 2).

3.1 Release of Starter Kit (TensorFlow Edition)

To encourage people who are not familiar with automatic melody generation, we developed the Starter Kit TensorFlow Edition (Fig. 3 Left)[1], in which users can easily try melody generation based on LSTM-VAE. This starter kit provides the codes for:

[1] Available at the following URL (written in Japanese): https://docs.google.com/document/d/1CizJ6b9i2yZ9OIDPrBWUROyJahlZrlqe-naxh4brACQ/.

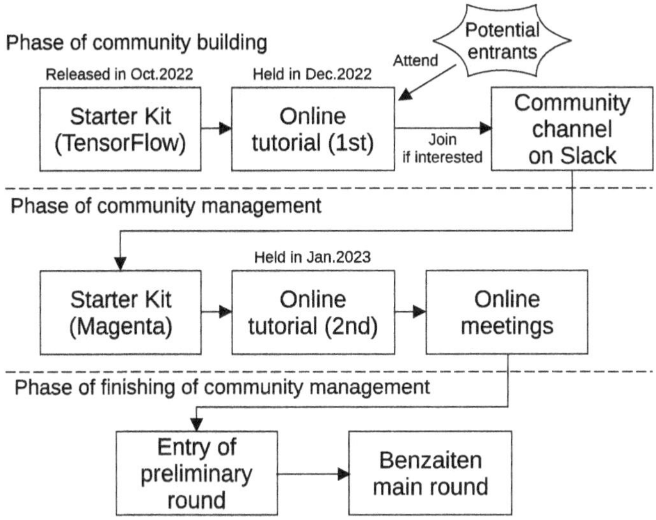

Fig. 2. Benzaiten's community management

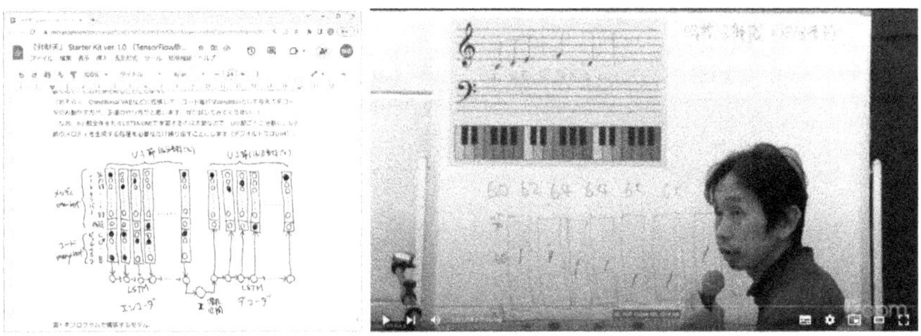

Fig. 3. Starter Kit (TensorFlow Edition) (left) and its tutorial (right)

- Reading MusicXML files taken from Charlie Parker's Omnibook MusicXML Data [6] and extracting melodies from them,
- Converting melodies to sequences of one-hot vectors,
- Training an LSTM-VAE model with prepared melodies using TensorFlow, and
- Generating a melody with the trained LSTM-VAE model in the MIDI format.

All codes are provided under the MIT License. As well, the starter kit provides several hints for extending those codes.

3.2 Tutorial on Starter Kit (TensorFlow Edition)

We conducted a tutorial aiming at allowing potential entrants to quickly understand the Starter Kit (TensorFlow Edition) on Zoom (Fig. 3 Right). We encouraged a wide range of people to participate in this tutorial, including those yet to determined to join Benzaiten as entrants. 124 people participated, and some of them expressed their interest in the entry. This tutorial was well-received because we explained general knowledge of MIDI, the harmony theory as well as the codes of the starter kit.

3.3 Encouraging Discussions on Slack

Because several participants of the above-mentioned tutorial expressed interest in joining Benzaiten as entrants, we invited them to the discussion channel for the community of potential entrants on Slack. We intended to let them exchange various information with each other and to foster a mood of friendly rivalry. They actually discussed some topics including: how to find publicly available datasets, and how to execute the starter kit's codes on a local computing resource with MacOS on an M1 chip.

3.4 Starter Kit (Magenta Edition) and Its Tutorial

We released the Starter Kit (Magenta Edition)[2], which illustrates how to generate melodies using ImprovRNN, included in Magenta [7]. Because this edition uses the pre-trained ImprovRNN model, unlike the TensorFlow edition, users can try melody generation more simply, even though improving the model is complex. Furthermore, we held a tutorial for explaining this starter kit. 13 potential entrants participated in this tutorial.

3.5 Online Meetings for Progress Sharing

We held online meetings twice to enable potential entrants to share each other's progress. 16 people participated in the first meeting, and 13 participated in the second one.

4 Preliminary Round

15 people (or teams) entered Benzaiten even though the number of acceptable entrants was limited to eight. We, therefore, held an online preliminary round. On the designated web page, participants listened to all melodies submitted by 15 entrants and rated them on a scale of 0 to 10. To avoid bias caused by the order etc., the web page lists the melodies anonymously in a random order. We promoted this preliminary round on Twitter, and ratings by 70 participants were collected. Finally, the eight entrants with high ratings moved into the main round.

[2] Available at the following URL (written in Japanese): https://colab.research.google.com/drive/1isnq_E2Mc-Fzeb8DKzYGL39l-B30AwZK.

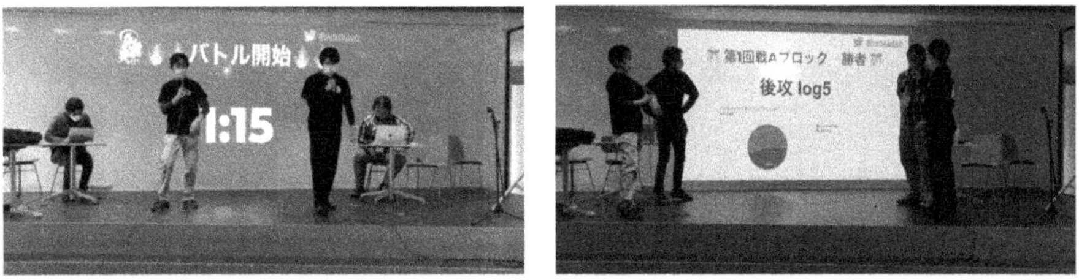

Fig. 4. Scene during a match (left) and winner announcement (right)

5 Implementation and Results of Benzaiten (Main Round)

5.1 Outline of the Event

Benzaiten adopts a single-elimination tournament style. Because we accepted eight entrants, the event consists of seven matches: four quarterfinals, two semifinals, and one final. The overall schedule is as follows:

14:00–14:10 Opening
14:10–15:30 Four quarterfinals (20 mins for each match)
15:30–16:00 Lightning talks by all entrants on the techniques they use
16:00–16:40 Two semifinals
16:40–16:55 Sponsors' lightning talks
16:55–17:15 The final
17:15–17:35 Long talk by T. Kitahara
17:35–18:00 Awards ceremony & Ending

Each match was conducted as follows (Fig. 4):

1. The two entrants go on the stage.
2. The organizer plays back the backing track for that match.
3. The backing track data (a MIDI file, a chord transcription file) is put into the online storage. The entrants are not permitted to download them before the match starts.
4. The match starts. The entrants must submit the generated melody's MIDI file before five minutes pass.
5. The melodies submitted by the two entrants are played back.
6. The popular vote starts. Google Forms is used as a voting platform.
7. The voting result (the winner) is announced.

5.2 Contest Rule

To achieve a fair contest, we carefully designed the contest rule and presented the rule book on the Web. A distinctive rule is to allow entrants to compare more than one generated melody by listening and choose one within a five-minute time limit. We also decided the length and the timbre (program change) of melodies; The entrants cannot change them to focus on the quality of the melodies. Chord transcriptions are given as a text file.

Table 1. Chord progressions and keys of backing tracks

Match	Round	Chord progression	Key
1	Quarter- finals	C |G/B |Bb |F/A |Fm/Ab|C/G |D/F# |G |C	C maj
2		C |C/E |F |G E |Am |C/G |D7/F#|Dm7G7|CM7	C maj
3		Am |F |G |C G |Am |F |G |E7 |Am	A min
4		C |G |G7 |C |C |Bb |F |C |C	C maj
5	Semi- finals	Am |DmEm|Am7 |DmEm|Am7 |DmEm|FM7 G|Am |Am	A min
6		Am |Am/F#|Dm |Bb |Am |Am/F#|Dm |Dm/B E7|Am	A min
7	Final	Dm7 F/G |CM7 FM7 |Dm/B E7 |A7 | Dm7 F/G |CM7 FM7 |Dm/B E7 |Am |Am	A min

5.3 Backing Tracks

To make this event successful, we consider it important to present high-quality backing tracks that include a variety of chord progressions. To achieve this, a professional musician joined our team and composed seven high-quality backing tracks with different chord progressions.

According to the contest rules, every backing track has nine measures with the key of C major or A minor. The used chord progressions and keys are listed in Table 1. Backing tracks for Matches 1, 4, and 6 contain chords with non-diatonic roots, which make appropriate melody generation slightly difficult.

The chord transcription file (in the CSV format) as well as the MIDI file of the backing track are given to the entrants at each match.

5.4 Entrants

The eight entrants are listed in Table 2. Two entrants (*log5* and *Dekoboko Friends*) improved the post-processing to avoid musically unnatural notes without improving the starter kits' ML model. On the other hands, two entrants (*yatszhash* and *nayopu*) adopted completely different approaches, that is, melody generation by ABC-notated text generation or notation image generation. The other entrants adopted well-known ML models such as a Conditional VAE, a CNN-VAE, and a Transformer.

5.5 Number of Participants

133 people (including the organizers) participated in Benzaiten on Zoom and about 40 to 50 people (including the organizers and entrants) participated on site. At each match, 54.7 votes were collected on average (max: 61, min: 51).

6 Discussions

6.1 Did We Succeed in Encouraging Non-experts to Participate?

Out of the eight entrants, five were non-music-related data scientists; they dealt with automatic MIDI generation for the first time. This fact shows that Benzaiten was able to reach out to a wide range of non-experts.

Table 2. Eight entrants and their melody generation techniques

No.	Name	Used techniques	Result
1	yatszhash	Generated a ABC-notated text with a language model	Champion
2	log5	Original post-processing based on music theory (with the unmodified ML model of the Starter Kit (TensorFlow))	
3	T. N.	Modified the Starter Kit (TensorFlow) to CNN-VAE	Semifinalist
4	nayopu	Generated notation images with DALL-E and converted it to the MIDI format	
5	AJI	Implemented Music Transformer with their original dataset	Semifinalist
6	M. Y.	Generated melodies with ImprovRNN and then reconstructed them with MusicVAE	
7	konumaru	Modified the Starter Kit (TensorFlow) to Conditional VAEs.	
8	Dekoboko Friends	Implemented post-processing to add grace notes and glissando (with the unmodified Starter Kit (Magenta))	Runner-up

6.2 Did Community Management Work Well?

Our community management allowed potential entrants to exchange various information including: codes for porting the starter kit to a local environment, publicly available MIDI datasets, and chord notation.

Sharing MIDI data generated by entrants at online meetings enabled us to check if the MIDI data met our rules. It was effective to avoid errors occurring when we played them back during the event. In fact, no entrants generated erroneous MIDI data.

6.3 Technical Trends in Entrants

As we mentioned, entrants had various approaches ranging from improvements of the starter kits' post-processing (*log5*, *Dekoboko Friends*) to completely novel ones (*nayopu*, *yatszhash*). The voting results showed that relatively *safe* melodies tended to win. In fact, melodies with some dissonant notes tended to be evaluated low.

Melodies generated by *log5* (the winner) and *Dekoboko Friends* (the runner-up) had different tendencies. The former was a sequence of close-packed short (e.g., 16th) notes, sometimes like arpeggios. The latter consisted of multiple phrases including rests between the phrases. Their system generated multiple melodies, and they selected one that included both notes and rests in a balanced way by checking them via piano rolls.

6.4 Future Challenge

One issue in our community management was that discussions among the entrants had not gathered momentum until the date of Benzaiten was approaching. On the other hand, at Kaggle [8], an online platform for data science competitions, entrants can identify their current ranks through the leaderboard. It gives them motivation for continuous improvement. Also in Benzaiten, we need a mechanism like the leaderboard, which makes entrants' current ranks public. If Benzaiten has such a mechanism, entrants should have more motivation for continuously improving their melody generation models, and hence they would participate in the discussion more actively.

7 Conclusion

In this paper, we presented an automatic melody generation contest called *Benzaiten*. This event's features are to encourage non-experts to join it as entrants with starter kits and community management and to aim at a high-quality entertainment event to allow laypeople to enjoy it. Through these attempts, we let many non-expert people have interest in automatic melody generation. In the future, we would like to extend this attempt to let various people, ranging from hobbyists and musicians to ML researchers, begin music generation development. We believe that it would bring remarkable findings, contributing to further progress in our music generation field.

Acknowledgments. This work was supported by JSPS Kakenhi JP22H03711.

References

1. Briot, J.-P., Hadjeres, G., Pachet, F.-D.: Deep learning techniques for music generation — A survey. arXiv:1709:01620 (2017)
2. Katayose, H., et al.: On evaluating systems for generating expressive music performance: the rencon experience. J. New Music Res. **41**(4), 299–310 (2012)
3. Sturm, B.L.T., Maruri-Aguilar, H.: The AI music generation challenge 2020: double jigs in the style of O'Neill's 1011. J. Creat. Music Syst. **5**(1) (2021)
4. Sturm, B.L.T.: The AI music generation challenge 2021: summary and results. In: Proceedings of the AIMC 2022 (2022)
5. Yeh, Y.-C., et al.: Automatic melody harmonization with triad chords: a comparative study. J. New Music Res. **50**(1), 37–51 (2021)
6. https://homepages.loria.fr/evincent/omnibook/
7. https://magenta.tensorflow.org/
8. https://www.kaggle.com/

Pitch Class and Octave-Based Pitch Embedding Training Strategies for Symbolic Music Generation

Yuqiang Li[1,2](✉), Shengchen Li[2], and György Fazekas[1]

[1] Queen Mary University of London, England, UK
y.j.li@se24.qmul.ac.uk, g.fazekas@qmul.ac.uk
[2] Xi'an Jiaotong-Liverpool University, Suzhou, Jiangsu, China
shengchen.li@xjtlu.edu.cn

Abstract. This paper presents two strategies to prevent the learned pitch representation from worsening so as to improve pitch and pitch class distributions in symbolic music generation. The first strategy is to switch the input pitch representation from the flat MIDI number representation to a hierarchical representation consisting of pitch class (chroma) and octave, which forces musically similar pitches to share part of the embedding vectors. The second strategy freezes the pitch embeddings during training according to the proposed evaluation metric of the pitch embedding space, maintaining the robustness of the embedding obtained in the first strategy. The experiments show that, when both strategies were applied to training an auto-regressive neural network for melody generation, the generated samples exhibited significant improvement in pitch class entropy (from 19% to 34% overlapping with the test dataset), and a modest but still significant improvement on pitch entropy (from 24% to 28%).

Keywords: music feature representation · pitch representation · symbolic music generation

1 Introduction

One of the key challenges in symbolic music generation is to design an effective input music representation that provides rich musical features while being computationally efficient. This is particularly challenging for neural sequence models, where various musical features must be serialised into sequences. Early MIDI event-like input representations such as [1,2] had the limitation of being exhaustive and too lengthy to be handled by the neural sequence models back then, and being implicit for models to reconstruct basic musical features (e.g. duration and metrical structures) [3]. Since then, domain knowledge-inspired solutions have been sequentially proposed to overcome these two problems, applying various structures, hierarchies and constraints to the input representation.

S. Ystad et al. (Eds.): CMMR 2023, LNCS 15236, pp. 149–167, 2026.
https://doi.org/10.1007/978-3-032-02042-0_11

The REMI representation [4] recommended explicitly encoded durational and metrical features over MIDI-like note-on/note-off events for sequential input representation, to enable transformer models [5] to better model rhythmic features. The Compound Word representation (CPW) [6] improved the maximum sequence length and generation quality by parallelizing the event-like token sequence into note-based super-tokens, introducing the inductive bias of hierarchically grouping note-wise musical features into a single time step. The recent Music Fundamental Embedding (MFE) [7] addressed a type of generation failure by encoding pitch, duration and metric position features as numeric features to ensure consistency of the implied relative musical features in the embedding space. These empirical studies revealed the general effectiveness of applying musical domain knowledge-based constraints to the input representation so that the model can benefit from explicit structures of musical features and their distinction.

Comparatively, the enhancement of pitch representations, nonetheless, is less researched in symbolic music generation, where most models empirically adopt MIDI number representation. Listening-wise, the limitation of this representation is often indicated by systems struggling with capturing slightly complicated pitch and harmonic features, e.g. lacking clear tonal centres, harmonic tension and releases. However, in both symbolic discriminative tasks (e.g. chord estimation, music style clustering and automatic harmonic analysis [8–10]) and the similar tasks in the audio domain, the pitch class, or chroma feature is used more often than MIDI pitch numbers, indicating its irreplaceable effectiveness. Therefore, we hypothesise the importance of the pitch class feature for symbolic music generation as well.

It is hypothesised that the hierarchical representation of pitch class and octave, is superior to the flat MIDI number representation for pitch-related modelling, which can be tested by (1) the generated pitch and pitch class distributions, and (2) the quality of the embedding space, evaluated by the proposed SLD metric. The proposed metric calculates the standard deviation of the magnitudes of interval vectors represented by different pitch vectors, to measure the inconsistency of the learned representations of intervals, which provides an alternative way to heuristically and efficiently examine the risk of poorly learned embedding space without needing to sampling melodies from the model. Two experiments were conducted. Experiment 1 tests whether pitch class and octave can improve the pitch distribution compared to MIDI number encoding. Experiment 2 is based on the results of experiment 1, testing whether freezing the pitch embeddings when the SLD metric reaches a local minimum can maintain high pitch performance during training.

In experiment 1, a Transformer-XL system was trained for melody generation with different pitch-unrelated hyper-parameters. For each hyper-parameter configuration, the control group used the MIDI number pitch representation and the experiment group used pitch class-octave representation. The results showed improved distributions of pitch and pitch class in the generated melodies from the pitch class-octave group, that the distributions had more overlapping with the test data distribution. The results also suggest that a lower SLD metric is a necessary condition for better pitch-related distributions.

Although the class-octave pitch encoding outperformed the MIDI number representation, they both suffered from the deterioration problem referred to as *representational degeneration* [11] over training. In our experiment, this problem was indicated by the aligned pace of decreasing SLD and better pitch performance in early training, followed by increasing SLD with accordingly declining pitch performance. Therefore, in experiment 2, the best hyper-parameter configuration of Experiment 1 was trained multiple times but the pitch embeddings were frozen at different epochs, respectively. The results reveal that the models with pitch embeddings frozen around the local minimum of SLD showed better performance over longer training.

The outcomes of the two experiments demonstrated the effectiveness of the pitch class and octave constraints on pitch representation, which informed the development of two practical pitch training strategies presented in this paper.

The rest of the paper will begin with a brief review of the previous methodologies in Sect. 2, followed by proposed methods in Sect. 3. The experiment and results are discussed in 4 and 5.

2 Related Work

2.1 Pitch Representations

The one-hot representation is a commonly used pitch representation in the literature [12,13]. It does not assume any pitch structure or proximity, as all the one-hot pitch vectors are equidistant. Mozer [14] argued that equidistant one-hot pitch vectors are problematic for music generation. He proposed a novel pitch representation named PHCCCF (pitch height, chroma circle and circle of fifth) based on the spiral model by [15] and psychoacoustic experiments on perceived pitch distance in 1979 [16,17]. While Mozer's results showed the system's ability to learn some structure of diatonic scales [12], the psychoacoustic experiments were limited to individual pitches without musical context, making the pitch representation less generalisable to music generation. Another limitation of the PHCCCF is the strong assumption that the perception of pitch does not change across octaves, which is less flexible than the mel-scale. For lack of a consensus on the best static pitch representation, in this work, we adopted the hierarchy of pitch class and octave, but only for tokenisation, combined with word embedding dynamically learned through backpropagation.

To the best of our knowledge, PiRhDy [18] is the only recent music generation work that employed pitch class and octave before the publication of our work, but the authors did not provide a comparison with the MIDI number encoding. Therefore, our work should be the first to compare these two different pitch encodings.

Alternative pitch encodings with domain knowledge have also been used in the symbolic music domain, but less frequently used in symbolic music generation. The tonnetz representation, proposed by Euler [19] in 1739, arranges pitch classes along major third, minor third, and perfect fifth dimensions. It has been successfully adopted for both feature extraction [20] and generative modelling in [21], but lacks smooth presentation of voice leading (namely the semitone or major second movements). Pitch class has also been effectively adopted in some discriminative tasks, e.g. chord classification [8] and style clustering [9,10], but pitch-class-only representations ignore octave information needed for precise pitch description in generation tasks. This work, as a result, combined the pitch class with the octave feature for comparison with the MIDI-number encoding.

2.2 Word Embedding Training Strategies

Word embedding as a deep learning technique generally suffers from the representation degeneration problem [11], i.e. the embedding vector distribution is gradually distorted into a narrow cone shape during training, increasing the similarity of the word vectors with decreasing performance. [22] explained that rare token embeddings are pushed by their gradients away from the non-rare tokens, causing degeneration. Likewise, our observations showed that the pitch embedding space was biased towards the imbalanced pitch and pitch class distributions in the dataset. To prevent degeneration, [22] proposed a gradient gating strategy that freezes the rare tokens at early training. This inspired our strategy two of freezing pitch embeddings to retain the performance.

Regarding poor numeracy performance of word embedding in language models [23], Gorishniy et al. [24] demonstrated the advantages of using the piecewise linear encoding (PLE) and sinusoidal activation functions (PAF) for numerical feature embedding. The FME [7], adopted a similar embedding scheme to embed pitch, duration and position features, ensuring the consistency of relative musical features such as intervals and durations in the embedding space. Instead of enhancing the numeracy of the pitch feature, our work investigated how the periodic nature of pitch class and octave contributes to the robustness of the pitch embedding.

3 Methods

3.1 Strategy 1: Use Pitch Class and Octave-Based Pitch Encoding

In the commonly used music representations, (e.g. the MIDI event representation and the REMI representation [4]), a pitch is encoded as a single token, indexed by the MIDI number, which we refer to as the MIDI number encoding. Being represented by one-hot vectors before embedding, the pitch vectors are flat, and homogeneous and contain no domain knowledge about frequency or pitch height as the dimensions are isotropic. This encoding is the baseline encoding.

The **class-octave** encoding is an alternative pitch encoding that carries pitch hierarchy, which is less used in generation models [18] and more commonly used in discriminative tasks as part of the input features [8–10,25,26]. This encoding first tokenises the pitch into its pitch class (0 to 11) and its octave number (0 to 9, (within the range of MIDI pitches). In a REMI-like implementation, which is used in this study, a pitch is serialised into two time steps in the sequence: the pitch class token of subscript ($p \mod 12$), followed by an octave token of subscript $\left\lfloor \frac{p}{12} \right\rfloor$. For instance, the pitch 60 (C4) is encoded into tokens p0 and o5, corresponding to two different embedding vectors, respectively[1]. One advantage of the class-octave encoding is its robustness to slight shifts in pitch, which aligns well with the perceived proximity before and after the shift. The pitch class-octave encoding is compared with the baseline encoding because it has a much smaller vocabulary size (12 + *the number of octaves to be encoded*), which reduces the chances of over-parameterisation. The pitch class-octave encoding also explicitly provides the constraints on the octave equivalency, i.e. all pitches that are one or multiple octaves apart share the same pitch class vector. Hence, it is expected to produce pitch embeddings that surpass those of the MIDI number encoding in effectiveness.

3.2 Strategy 2: Freezing Pitch Embedding in Early Training

Through empirical observations, the performance of pitch-related features tends to inevitably deteriorate over epochs even before any indicators of over-fitting appear. This suggests the possibility of pitch embedding deterioration. As proposed in [22], freezing the rare token embeddings at an early stage can alleviate the generation performance decline by preventing the embedding degeneration problem. In the music generation task of interest, most datasets have imbalanced pitch and pitch class distributions. Likewise, if the pitch embeddings are frozen at an appropriate moment before the representational degeneration problem intensifies, the pitch performance is expected to be accordingly better. Hence, we investigated freezing the pitch embeddings at different epochs of training.

3.3 Metrics

This study employed two types of evaluation metrics to examine whether the proposed strategies effectively alleviate the pitch performance issue caused by imbalanced pitch (and pitch class) distribution in the dataset. The first type evaluates the pitch embedding space itself and the second type focuses on the generation quality related to pitch and pitch-class distributions.

---

[1] If the class-octave encoding is implemented in other representations such as CPW [6], the pitch class token and the octave token will be separately embedded into two vectors, and then concatenated into a single super-token, which only accounts for one time step. In practice, CPW would clearly provide more benefits to class-octave encoding since the explicit note-wise feature grouping reduces the sequence length and requires less post-processing in decoding. In this study, the use of REMI-like representation for the experiments created a harsher condition for comparison where the class-octave representation did not benefit from the extra advantages of the feature grouping.

The Embedding Space Quality Metric. In order to consistently represent pitch interval vectors in the embedding space, the pitch vectors in the embedding space should follow certain geometric constraints. According to the concept of *translational invariance* discussed in [7], all pairs of pitch vectors $\{\mathbf{p}_{i+\delta} - \mathbf{p}_{j+\delta} | \delta \in \mathbb{Z}\}$ of the same interval size $|i - j|$ should have the same magnitude. In this study, the embedding space was not constrained to have such invariance, but we could still measure the consistency of the interval vectors as a heuristic evaluation of the quality. Therefore, we propose SLD, a metric that quantifies the violation of such invariance. The Standard deviation of L2 Dinstances of pitch vectors[2] in the embedding space is defined as follows:

$$\mathrm{SLD}(\mathbf{P}) := \sum_{\delta=1}^{\delta_{\max}} \left[\underset{i=1..n-\delta}{\mathrm{Std}} \left(|\mathbf{p}_{i+\delta} - \mathbf{p}_i| \right) \right]. \tag{1}$$

This metric captures the magnitude inconsistency of the same δ-semitone interval represented by different possible pairs of pitch vectors. $\delta_{\max}$ was empirically set to 24 here for two octaves, since larger intervals tend to produce more varied auditory experiences [27]. In [7], the SLD would be strictly zero as defined by their embedding scheme. Here, a better pitch embedding space would have a lower SLD closer to zero.

Generation Quality Metrics (Pitch-Related). Admittedly, it is not practical to conduct a subjective listening test when many models are to be compared, also because the differences in the generated pitch distributions can be too subtle to recognise by the listeners. Hence, objective metrics were adopted to evaluate the pitch performance in the generated samples. That is, the pitch class distribution entropy H(PC), and pitch distribution entropy H(P), as used in [28,29]. These two metrics can effectively capture the lack of pitch diversity, i.e. the repetitive use of very limited pitches when the H(P) is lower than that of the dataset, while H(PC) is an octave-agnostic version of H(P). The H(P) and H(PC) distributions of the test dataset are first approximated by Gaussian Kernel Density Estimation (KDE), and then compared with the KDEs of generated distributions. The overlapping area (OA) [30] between the generated and the true distributions was employed to score the generation quality, with the higher OA being the better.

4 Experiment Setup

4.1 Dataset

A cleaned version of the Wikifonia dataset[3] is used. Specifically, we only keep the songs with constant 4/4 time signatures. The training set (90%) contains 3,861

[2] The pitch vectors must be z-score transformed before SLD calculation, to remove the scaling factors along different dimensions.

[3] http://www.wikifonia.org.

songs, and the test set contains 429 songs. Note that quite some songs have key changes during the piece, so we did not balance the pitch class distribution e.g. by transposing songs into multiple keys for augmentation, which also avoided introducing sample-wise bias due to oversampling. The imbalanced pitch class distribution is plotted in Fig. 1. As can be seen, The frequent pitches come from the C major scales, the rest being rare in both subsets. The pitch class entropy H(PC) of the train set and dataset are 3.370 and 3.376 bits, respectively. Hence, the H(PC) of generated melodies should also be close to this dataset's average value.

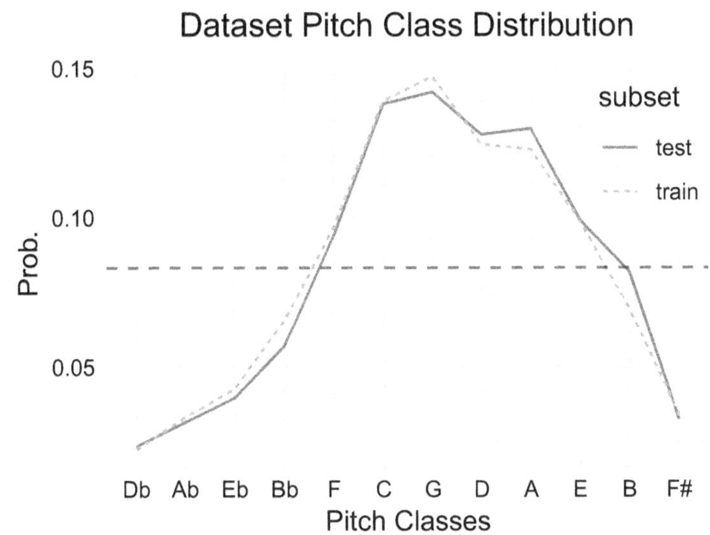

Fig. 1. Pitch Class Distributions of the Training Set and the Test Set

4.2 Data Representation

The input music representation resembles the REMI representation [4] because of the usage of duration, bar and position tokens. However, the melody-irrelevant features *chord*, *tempo* and *velocity* of REMI were excluded. In this work, the token vocabulary consists of *pitch*, *octave* (if used), *duration*, *bar* and *position* tokens[4]. We also varied beat-related tokenisation settings such as beat resolution and position token granularities (the number of rhythmic tokens to represent different subdivisions of the metrical position), to counterbalance the side effects of non-pitch hyper-parameters (e.g. a poor rhythm may negatively affect the model's prediction on the pitch) for a more robust analysis of the results.

[4] Miscellaneous tokens include a REST for silence that comes before duration, and PAD that pads the sequence.

4.3 Model and Training Specifications

A 4-layer transformer-XL network (proposed by [5] as used in [4,28]) was trained to generate melodies in a next-token-prediction manner. The parameter size of the network was also cut down to 4M from the original, 12-layer model of 150M parameters in order to reduce the risks of over-fitting on such a small symbolic music dataset. The reduced size also sped up the massive trials over the hyper-parameter grid.

The two models of each pair share the same hyper-parameters, except that the control group used the MIDI number pitch encoding and the experiment group used the pitch class-octave encoding. All models were trained with the cross-entropy loss, a 9:1 train-test split ratio, the AdamW optimiser [31], learning rate of 8e-4, batch size of 32 and the same number of epochs. Since the Transformer-XL architecture does not have a limit on the sequence length, the training sequence length is set to 1,024 tokens chunked into 8 segments of 128 tokens. We adopted the hugging face implementation of Transformer-XL[5], with PyTorch 1.9.0. With a single GeForce RTX 4090 graphics card, each instance took about 2 h of training. The model checkpoints were saved after every epoch.

Top-k sampling (at $k = 5$) with softmax temperature $\tau = 1.0$ was used for inference. 128 melodies were unconditionally sampled from each model to evaluate the generation quality. However, only 512 tokens were sampled for each melody based on empirical observations. According to our listening experience, longer sequences seemed to be over-repetitive and severely not listenable.

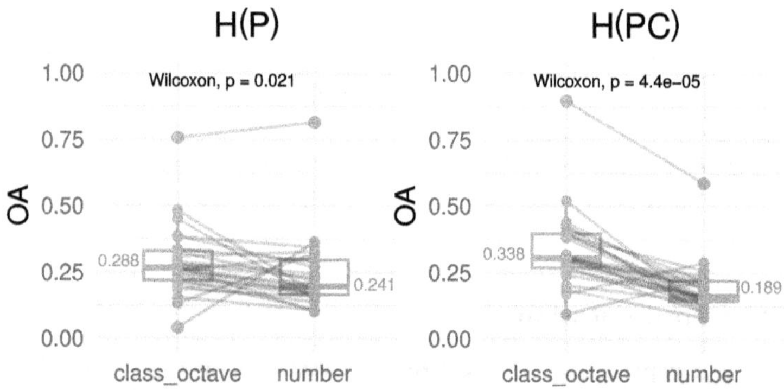

Fig. 2. Pairwise comparison of models using different pitch encoding, on the overlapping areas of two pitch-related metrics. Higher OA scores indicate better generated distributions.

[5] https://huggingface.co/docs/transformers/en/model_doc/transfo-xl.

5 Results and Discussions

5.1 Experiment 1 - Comparison of Pitch Encodings

In this experiment, models were trained in pairs for token-wise melody generation, with full teacher forcing. The two models in each pair shared the common dataset, and model architecture and only differed in the input pitch encoding: one being the MIDI number encoding and the other being the class-octave encoding. 24 such pairs were trained to compare the performance of two pitch encodings in different hyper-parameter configurations (e.g. the beat resolution). The only mismatch was that the class-octave encoding resulted in a doubled amount of pitch tokens compared to the other one, which potentially faced a more difficult learning process. However, it turned out not exceeding the capability of the Transformer-XL network at all.

The following comparison is two-fold, consisting of a conventional way based on distribution and a new approach focusing on the examination of embedding space.

Generation Result Metrics. 128 melodies were sampled from each model for evaluation. The distributions of pitch entropy H(P) and pitch class entropy H(PC) were calculated for all the samples for each model. The overlapping area (OA) between the generated distribution and the test data distribution was calculated (after KDE approximation) to measure the performance of a model on a specific metric. OA values closer to 1 indicate a better distribution.

For the two best models in terms of pitch class distribution OA H(PC), we observe a noticeable performance gap between them, where the class-octave model learned about 81% of the true H(PC) distribution while the number pitch mode only learned about 60%, exhibiting a clear weakness. However, the best performance of the class-octave group on pitch distribution, OA H(P), was modestly inferior to the number encoding. We account for this result to the fact that the number-encoding pitch encoding used more word vectors, which were directly and better fitted to pitch distributions.

In Fig. 2, each dot represents the overlapping area between the generated distribution of a model instance and the true distribution. Line-connected dots are pairs of models that only differed in non-pitch hyper-parameters. The class-octave group outperformed the number group in mean (two-sided Wilcoxon test, $p = 0.021$ for pitch entropy, and $p = 4.4 \times 10^{-5}$ for pitch class entropy). Only 5 out of 24 class-octave models, regarding pitch distribution, and 2 out of 24 models regarding pitch class distribution, were inferior to their paired model using MIDI number encoding.

Embedding Space Metrics. To better demonstrate how the proposed SLD metric associates with the model performance, we plotted the embedding spaces of the best models and the worst models for two pitch encodings, in terms of generation distribution quality (compared in the previous section), and provided corresponding SLD values in Fig. 3. PCA was used to reduce the dimensionality

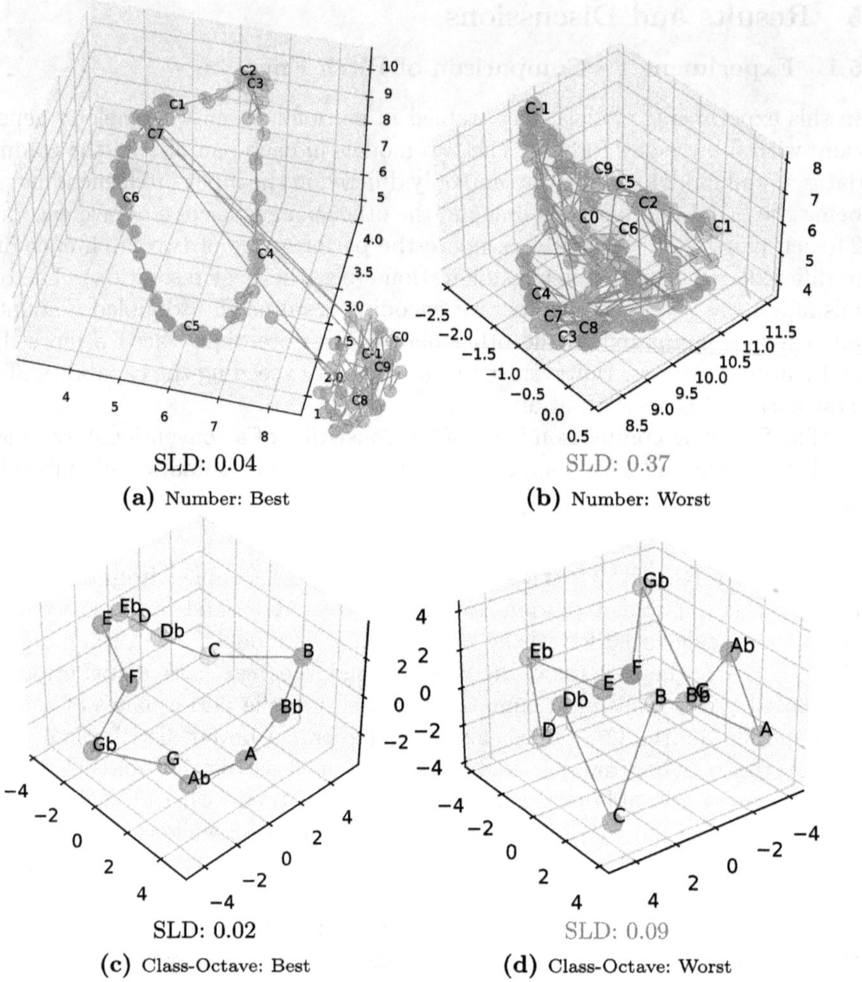

Fig. 3. The pitch/pitch class vectors are plotted as points, coloured by pitch classes. Octave vectors are not plotted for clarity. The red segments represent the semitone relationship. A clear invariance of magnitude of semitone segments is observable at low SLD values, but weaker when SLD is high. The low SLDs were consistent with the actual best generation performance on both pitch and pitch class. (Color figure online)

from 32 to the 3 principal components with the largest variances for visualisation. However, the two number pitch visualisations were produced by Uniform Manifold Approximation and Projection (UMAP) since the large number of pitch vectors were crowded in the PCA plots and UMAP zoomed in the local areas for clearer visual presentation.

Before calculating the SLD of a pitch-class octave embedding space, we first approximated the pitch vectors by adding the corresponding pitch class and octave vector and applying the SLD formula to the pitch vectors. Note that addition was just one of the possible ways to reconstruct the pitch feature, assuming that the learned pitch class and octave embedding vectors were semantic and they followed the additive analogy property of word embedding. The caveat is that addition can lead to different value ranges of SLDs compared with MIDI number pitch vectors, as the vector differences cancel out octave vectors if the two pitches are from the same octave. In practice, this approximation error was modest and did not dissipate SLD's ability to characterise the embedding space.

Overall, the visual distinction between the best cases (3a, 3c) and the worst cases (3b, 3d) in Fig. 3 revealed that the SLD of pitch embeddings greatly contributed to the model performance on pitch distributions. The two best cases demonstrate the success of modelling pitch distributions in early finished instances (some early stops were due to other hyper-parameters e.g. beat resolution that sped up the over-fitting), while the two worst cases indicate the degeneration of embedding space over time.

By comparing row 1 (Fig. 3a, 3c) and row 2 (3b, 3d), the class-octave encoding exhibited more robustness and suffered less from the rare-token degeneration problem. In the two MIDI number embedding spaces, the lowest and the highest pitches were almost all rare tokens, regardless of the data augmentation methods such as random transposition. As the training continued, these rare pitch tokens converged into a corner (as demonstrated in [22]), resulting in worse pitch performance.

In contrast, for the class-octave encoding, the rare pitches were represented by only a few octave tokens (e.g. `o0` to `o3`, `o8` to `o9`), and their pitch classes were no different from those of the non-rare pitches as they were shared. The degeneration problem could still be seen in 3d, i.e. the rare pitch classes $\{D\flat, E\flat, F\sharp, A\flat, B\flat\}$ (see Fig. 1), were extruding out, moving away from the non-rare pitch classes, causing worse pitch performance. Hence, the class-octave encoding alleviated the embedding degeneration problem.

Discussion. The visualisations revealed some commonalities between the learned pitch/pitch class representations and other pitch representations reported by previous works. Most noticeably in Fig. 3, the semitone relationship seemed to primarily define the neighbourhood for all pitches. Also, the cyclic structure did not appear to be closed, suggesting the extension towards the next or previous octave. This resembles the pitch helix model [15] where the chroma feature continuously increases in a spiral way. Alternative representations include the 4-d pitch representation reported by [17] where pitch classes in the context of tonal harmony are represented on a torus manifold, featuring the importance of fifths. Similarly, the concept of the cycle of fifth is important in terms of harmony, but the learned representations did not exhibit such a relationship, at least by observing the dimensions with the largest variances. We provide a possible explanation as to why the semitone-neighbourhood instead of fifth-based representation was learned in the current work. It is possible that the model was not able to learn harmony-related tasks in early training. Since no chord labels were used, the pitch representation was learned from scratch. Based on this, the task of modelling pitch relationship from scratch seems to be trivial in terms of semitones and non-trivial for fifths, if not provided with any harmony features.

Figure 3d displayed a degenerated pattern of the pitch embedding space, namely the structural change where the embedding of rare tokens converged to a corner, which could be explained by the imbalanced pitch class distribution. Here we provide another interpretation, that when the class-octave pitch embeddings were trained long enough, the learned relationship became more diatonic to C major (exactly because of dataset distribution). Despite the lower generation performance on pitch class diversity, the pattern was somehow related to what has been reported in [16] (Figs. 2 and 3 of their work), where in tonal context, the perceived diatonic pitch classes lied in a different layer than non-diatonic ones. This indicates that the modelling of diatonic relationship happened after the learning of semitone relationship in the current case. Hence, whether such diatonic pitch representation is desired for music generation remains an open question. It may have the advantage of aligning to perceived tonal context, but the weaker symmetry compared with a more chromatic representation tends to exhibit a lack of diversity. Further investigation can focus on how chromatic and diatonic pitch representation would influence the model's understanding of pitch and harmony, and how we should design a pitch representation where both chromatic and diatonic relationships coexist without compromising one over the other.

We would like to highlight that the effective use of SLD as a metric measuring the lack of transitional invariance of pitch embeddings does not imply that it can be simply used as a regularisation term in the loss function, because the SLD is based on the heuristic assumption of the magnitude invariance of interval vectors [7]. As discussed in the previous paragraph, whether such property is always desired remains to be answered, as it is not clear whether the magnitude, direction, angles or any other geometric feature is the best representation. Therefore, the problem depends on how strong the prior should be applied for the pitch representation, and how much freedom and flexibility the word embedding should have. We argue that for pitch features, a strong prior is necessary. The experiment showed that the homogeneous MIDI number representation, which does not use prior knowledge of pitch hierarchy, failed to be improved by the thousands of melodies of training data, and it is not likely to be improved because increased noise and over-representation of the dataset were observed as training continued.

To conclude, the class-octave encoding outperformed the MIDI number encoding because of the presence of pitch hierarchy, displaying stronger robustness and interpretability. The experiment showed that a low SLD is a necessary condition for models to be able to precisely capture pitch and pitch class distributions.

5.2 Experiment 2 - Freezing Pitch Embedding Space at Different Stages of Training

The previous experiment demonstrated the effectiveness of the hierarchical pitch representation compared to the homogeneous MIDI number representation, but the problem of embedding degeneration persisted as a barrier to better generation quality. In this experiment, we validated the existence of the optimal state of the pitch embeddings, by freezing the pitch embedding vectors at different epochs of training and continuing training, while keeping track of the SLD and the pitch performance.

Instead of exhaustively training all the hyper-parameters, this experiment selected the best set of non-pitch hyper-parameters[6] used in experiment 1. Specifically, both the MIDI number model and the class-octave model achieved their lowest test loss around epoch 5, which ended much earlier than other models that were trained for around 30 – 40 epochs.

It is worth reporting that the SLD of the number encoding model did not decrease (or it slightly decreased but rose up quickly at early training), which is a general problem regardless of most hyper-parameter settings. Contrarily, the SLD of the best class-octave model decreased in the first 5 epochs and started to increase, reaching the best OA H(PC) at epoch 5, too. Hence, this experiment is dedicated to the **class-octave** model where the SLD decreased noticeably at the beginning of training.

15 randomly initialised model instances were separately trained for 15 epochs from scratch, except that every time the pitch vectors are frozen 1 epoch later by zeroing out the gradients of pitch vectors. For each model, pitch embedding SLD was evaluated at each epoch until frozen. In the actual implementation, the embedding vectors would still slightly change despite being frozen because of the projection layer between the embedding output and the transformer input, which was not frozen as it is shared by all word vectors (including non-pitch vectors). In terms of the results, a slight increase in SLD was observed but it did not change the ranking of different SLDs (Fig. 4a and 4b).

Metric Results and Training Dynamics. We saved checkpoints for each model at the end of every epoch. After training, each of the 15 models was evaluated at two checkpoints: **Best**, at the lowest test loss, and **Last**, at the end of epoch 15. The embedding metric SLD evaluated of **Best** and the corresponding generated pitch performance metric (overlapping area OA H(PC)) are provided in Fig. 4a. Arrows near the metrics indicate whether higher or lower values are desired. A separate plot of the same SLD metric and generation pitch class performance is provided in Fig. 5 for visual clarity.

By studying the relationship between the moment of freezing pitch embedding and the resulting metrics of 15 models, we observed interesting 3-phase training dynamics about every 5 epochs.

[6] Hyper-parameters: A beat resolution of 8 subdivisions per quarter note, a position grid similar to REMI [4] but each bar now has $8 \times 4 = 32$ positions instead of 16 used by the authors.

Freezing Epoch	SLD Best ↓	H(PC) Last ↑	H(PC) Best ↑	Best Epoch
1	0.078	**0.788**	0.485	11
2	0.046	0.772	0.710	7
3	0.042	0.705	0.579	13
4	**0.039**	0.639	**0.792**	4
5	0.032	0.615	0.615	14
6	0.043	0.700	0.370	11
7	0.034	0.518	0.636	11
8	0.063	0.678	0.469	11
9	0.049	0.619	0.619	14
10	0.058	0.741	0.332	4
11	0.046	0.598	0.702	9
12	**0.039**	0.761	0.592	12
13	0.078	0.468	0.513	9
14	0.073	0.650	0.633	12
15	0.079	0.286	0.301	4

(a) The Embedding SLDs and Generation OA H(PC)s of 15 Models. SLDs are measured at model reaching lowest test error, not necessarily before or after the freezing moment.

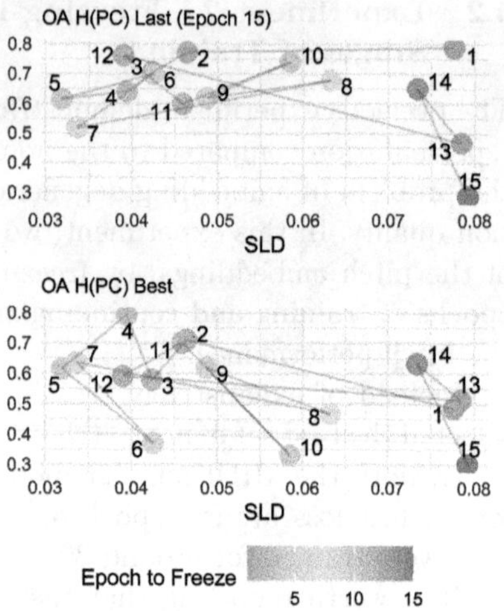

(b) The plot traces the pair of both OA H(PC) and SLD over epochs of freezing. Higher positions stand for better pitch class performance while lefter positions for better embedding quality.

Fig. 4. Models with Pitch Vectors Frozen at Different Epochs

- ∘ In phase 1, when frozen before epoch 5, the pitch embedding SLD decreased as expected. The OA H(PC) of the resulting best models climbed up, reaching the maximal performance of 0.79 at epoch 4. Models 1 to 4 at epoch 15 had OA H(PC) higher than 0.6, suggesting that the pitch embedding learned in early epochs sustained high performance over longer training.
- ∘ In phase 2, the freezing operation happened between epoch 6 and 9, when the SLD was higher. Both *last* and *best* OA H(PC) slightly decreased, especially for the best models when the OA H(PC) dropped below 0.4.
- ∘ In phase 3, from epoch 10 onward, the pitch performance became much more unstable. The SLD for around epochs 13 to 15 quickly increased, with decreasing OA H(PC) accordingly. Also notice that the values of "best epoch" below the dashed line in Fig. 4a are all smaller than the freezing epoch (the first column), indicating that further training did not improve the pitch performance at all, if freezing happened later than epoch 10.

The results first suggested the effectiveness of freezing pitch embeddings at low SLD values to retain pitch performance at higher levels for both the best and the last models. In addition, this strategy offers the benefit of being able to train a properly frozen embedding longer before over-fitting or stopping to improve.

Case Studies. Two representative samples were selected from the models of the highest and the lowest OA H(PC), respectively, and presented in Fig. 6.

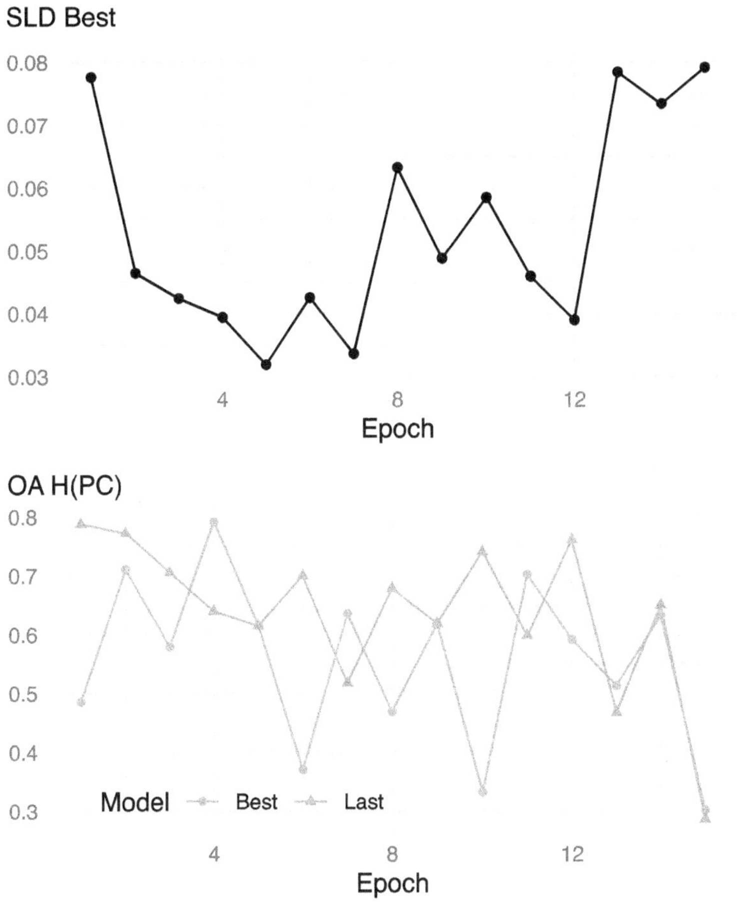

Fig. 5. The SLD metric and the corresponding generation pitch class performance were evaluated over epochs. The aggregated trend of SLD from 15 models suggests an empirical local minimum at epoch 5 when the translational invariance was the strongest, after which it held less. A weak negative correlation seems to exist between the SLD and the pitch class performance of the best models, suggesting an influence of pitch embedding structure on the generation performance.

Discussion. The multi-phase dynamics of the pitch embedding training process uncovered the phenomenon that more than one pitch representation was actually learned over back-propagation. Unlike word embedding for natural language word tokens, the learning process of pitch class tokens is much more interpretable in the musical context. When randomly initialised, all the pitch class vectors were unrelated, not forming a musical structure. The chromatic relationship was learned first in the first epochs, with a cyclic structure of chroma. After epoch 5, the original embedding gradually morphed towards the diatonic representation, where the generated melodies lacked pitch class diversity (with regard to

(a) Melody 1, H(P) = 2.58, H(PC) = 3.39, sampled from model 1 at epoch 15, pitch frozen since epoch 1. The beginning phrase clearly outlined a tonic chord of *G*♭ major. From pattern 1 on, the pitch development seemed to be trapped in the three-note motif (*F*, *E*♭, *D*♭). Bar 19 jumped out of pattern 1 with a new phrase. Bar 25 repeated the motif with the same rhythm but varied pitches. Even in the variation, the pitch classes were all chosen from the same major key, which is cohesive. The contour (annotated by segments under the notes) was also varied. Overall, in this excerpt, all pitch classes except *C*♭ (the fourth degree of the key) were used with a comparatively strong sense of tonality (see the annotated chord progression).

(b) Melody 2, H(P) = 1.20, H(PC) = 1.46, sampled from model 15 at epoch 15, pitch always being trained. With a degenerated pitch embedding space, the result exhibited low pitch class diversity and weak coherence in terms of tonality. Most notes are C (within the highlighted area in the staff), with occasional use of new pitch class (marked by short horizontal lines beneath the notes). The melody seemed to suggest an F major context but the abrupt use of *B*♮ and *D*♭ reduced the clarity. The phrases were more segmented and unrelated. Over-repetitiveness was also commonly observed in other samples of this model, indicating a model failure.

Fig. 6. Comparison of the Melody Samples

the true data distribution). When the invariance of interval vector magnitude almost dissipated eventually, the model failed.

This finding suggests an opportunity to further extend the current method to the examination of non-pitch musical features, such as rhythm and harmony. For instance, it is worth investigating how other musical features were learned, by proposing targeted embedding metrics to examine when the features were learned, and the pace and level of severity of the deterioration. Further research is also needed to elucidate how the different phases of learned musical feature embedding contribute to the generation, based on domain knowledge, visualisations and tools such as topological data analysis. Given the existing domain knowledge of musical structure, and a considerably smaller token vocabulary space compared to natural text, the interpretability of music embedding spaces should be much stronger. The potential latent structures obtained from the models can be reused for task-specific purposes as a strong prior.

6 Conclusion

Pitch representation plays a vital role in symbolic music generation. Motivated by the disconnection between the conventional static pitch representations and the problem of representational degeneration with deep word embedding technique, this work presented two strategies to improve the pitch performance of symbolic music generation. Both involve incorporating domain knowledge of pitch hierarchy that restricts the pitch representation in terms of feature encoding and feature representation, respectively, which effectively alleviates the problem of pitch performance deterioration.

Strategy 1 is to replace the flat and homogeneous MIDI number encoding with a hierarchical pitch tokenisation consisting of octave and pitch class, explicitly preserving the pitch proximity when encoded pitches share the common pitch class or octave. The comparison experiment suggested the advantage of this tokenisation method by significantly improved pitch and pitch class diversity.

With the proposed SLD metric, strategy 2 was based on the observed association between the over-learned diatonic embedding structure with weak translational invariance (indicated by higher SLD values), and the corresponding generation performance decline i.e. the lack of pitch and pitch class diversity. Experiment 2 demonstrated how SLD could be applied to estimate the training phase so as to alleviate the decline by freezing the pitch embedding.

This study also calls attention to the problem of insufficient use of prior knowledge when designing music generation models, that the learned representation without related constraints (e.g. translational invariance for the pitch embedding) can be easily biased to the dataset distribution, which negatively influences the generation performance as a result. In future works, strategy 1 can be extended to a new representation where both MIDI number, pitch class and octave coexist so as to fully exploit the use of domain knowledge. We plan to further address the problem of SLD being not appropriate for a loss function or regularisation term, by proposing new domain knowledge-based loss functions that explicitly the feature embedding. This approach is expected to generalise to advanced pitch features, such as intervals and harmony, or even non-pitch musical features.

References

1. Simon, I., Oore, S.: Performance rNN: generating music with expressive timing and dynamics (2017). https://magenta.tensorflow.org/performance-rnn
2. Meade, N., Barreyre, N., Lowe, S.C., Oore, S.: Exploring conditioning for generative music systems with human-interpretable controls. In: International Conference on Computational Creativity (2019)

3. Huang, C.Z.A., et al.: Music transformer. In: International Conference on Learning Representations (2019)
4. Huang, Y.S., Yang, Y.H.: Pop music transformer: beat-based modeling and generation of expressive pop piano compositions. In: Proceedings of the 28th ACM International Conference on Multimedia, pp. 1180–1188. Association for Computing Machinery, NY, USA (2020)
5. Dai, Z., Yang, Z., Yang, Y., Carbonell, J., Le, Q., Salakhutdinov, R.: Transformer-XL: attentive language models beyond a fixed-length context. In: Korhonen, A., Traum, D., Màrquez, L. (eds.) Proceedings of the 57th Annual Meeting of the Association for Computational Linguistics, pp. 2978–2988. Association for Computational Linguistics, Florence, Italy (2019). https://doi.org/10.18653/v1/P19-1285
6. Hsiao, W.Y., Liu, J.Y., Yeh, Y.C., Yang, Y.H.: Compound word transformer: learning to compose full-song music over dynamic directed hypergraphs. In: Proceedings of the AAAI Conference on Artificial Intelligence, vol. 35, no. 1, pp. 178–186 (2021). https://doi.org/10.1609/aaai.v35i1.16091
7. Guo, Z., Kang, J., Herremans, D.: A domain-knowledge-Inspired music embedding space and a novel attention mechanism for symbolic music modeling. In: Proceedings of the AAAI Conference on Artificial Intelligence, vol. 37(4), pp. 5070–5077 (2023). https://doi.org/10.1609/aaai.v37i4.25635
8. Laden, B., Keefe, D.H.: The representation of pitch in a neural net model of chord classification. Comput. Music. J. **13**(4), 12–26 (1989). https://doi.org/10.2307/3679550
9. Ens, J., Pasquier, P.: Quantifying musical style: ranking symbolic music based on similarity to a style (2020)
10. Yust, J., Lee, J., Pinsky, E.: A clustering-based approach to automatic harmonic analysis: an exploratory study of harmony and form in mozart's piano sonatas. Trans. Int. Soc. Music Inf. Retrieval **5**(1), 113–128 (2022). https://doi.org/10.5334/tismir.114
11. Gao, J., He, D., Tan, X., Qin, T., Wang, L., Liu, T.: Representation degeneration problem in training natural language generation models. In: International Conference on Learning Representations (2022)
12. Briot, J.P., Hadjeres, G., Pachet, F.D.: Deep learning techniques for music generation – A survey. In: Computational Synthesis and Creative Systems (2020)
13. Ji, S., Luo, J., Yang, X.: A comprehensive survey on deep music generation: multi-level representations, algorithms, evaluations, and future directions. arXiv:2011.06801 [cs, eess] (2020)
14. Mozer, M.C.: Connectionist music composition based on melodic, stylistic and psychophysical constraints. Comput. Sci. Tech. Rep. (476) (1990)
15. Shepard, R.N.: Geometrical approximations to the structure of musical pitch. Psychol. Rev. **89**, 305–333 (1982). https://doi.org/10.1037/0033-295X.89.4.305
16. Krumhansl, C.L.: The psychological representation of musical pitch in a tonal context. Cogn. Psychol. **11**(3), 346–374 (1979). https://doi.org/10.1016/0010-0285(79)90016-1
17. Krumhansl, C.L., Kessler, E.J.: Tracing the dynamic changes in perceived tonal organization in a spatial representation of musical keys. Psychol. Rev. **89**(4), 334–368 (1982)
18. Liang, H., Lei, W., Chan, P.Y., Yang, Z., Sun, M., Chua, T.S.: PiRhDy: learning pitch-, rhythm-, and dynamics-aware embeddings for symbolic music. In: Proceedings of the 28th ACM International Conference on Multimedia, pp. 574–582 (2020). https://doi.org/10.1145/3394171.3414032

19. Euler, L.: Tentamen novae theoriae musicae: ex certissimis harmoniae principiis dilucide expositae. Saint Petersburg Academy (1739)
20. Chuan, C.H., Herremans, D.: Modeling temporal tonal relations in polyphonic music through deep networks with a novel image-based representation. In: Proceedings of the AAAI Conference on Artificial Intelligence, vol. 32, no. 1 (2018). https://doi.org/10.1609/aaai.v32i1.11880
21. Lieck, R., Moss, F.C., Rohrmeier, M.: The tonal diffusion model. Trans. Int. Soc. Music Inf. Retrieval **3**(1), 153–164 (2020). https://doi.org/10.5334/tismir.46
22. Yu, S., Song, J., Kim, H., Lee, S.M., Ryu, W.J., Yoon, S.: Rare tokens degenerate all tokens: improving neural text generation via adaptive gradient gating for rare token embeddings. arXiv:2109.03127 (2022)
23. Wallace, E., Wang, Y., Li, S., Singh, S., Gardner, M.: Do NLP models know numbers? Probing numeracy in embeddings. In: Proceedings of the 2019 Conference on Empirical Methods in Natural Language Processing and the 9th International Joint Conference on Natural Language Processing (EMNLP-IJCNLP), pp. 5307–5315. Association for Computational Linguistics, Hong Kong, China (2019)
24. Gorishniy, Y., Rubachev, I., Babenko, A.: On embeddings for numerical features in tabular deep learning. In: Thirty-Sixth Conference on Neural Information Processing Systems. New Orleans (2022)
25. Lazzari, N., Poltronieri, A., Presutti, V.: Pitchclass2vec: symbolic music structure segmentation with chord embeddings. In: Workshop on Artificial Intelligence and Creativity, p. 17 (2022)
26. Chawin, D., Rom, U.B.: Sliding-window pitch-class histograms as a means of modeling musical form. Trans. Int. Soc. Music Inf. Retrieval **4**(1), 223–235 (2021). https://doi.org/10.5334/tismir.83
27. Moore, B.C.J.: An Introduction to the Psychology of Hearing. BRILL (2012)
28. Wu, S.L., Yang, Y.H.: The jazz transformer on the front line: exploring the shortcomings of AI-composed music through quantitative measures. In: The 21st International Society for Music Information Retrieval Conference. arXiv:2008.01307, Montréal, Canada (2020)
29. Dong, H.W., Chen, K., McAuley, J., Berg-Kirkpatrick, T.: MusPy: a toolkit for symbolic music generation. In: The 21st International Society for Music Information Retrieval Conference. arXiv:2008.01951, Montréal, Canada (2020)
30. Yang, L.C., Chou, S.Y., Yang, Y.H.: MidiNet: a convolutional generative adversarial network for symbolic-domain music generation. In: The 18th International Society for Music Information Retrieval Conference. Suzhou, China (2017)
31. Loshchilov, I., Hutter, F.: Decoupled weight decay regularization. In: International Conference on Learning Representations. arXiv:1711.05101 (2019)

VERSNIZ Audiovisual Worldbuilding Through Live Coding as a Performance Practice in the Metaverse

Damian Dziwis[1,2(✉)]

[1] TH Köln - University of Applied Sciences, Cologne, Germany
damian.dziwis@th-koeln.de

[2] Technische Universität Berlin, Berlin, Germany

Abstract. Even before the circumstances the global pandemic forced, a diverse ecosystem of technologies and artistic practices for performances in digital and virtual media was raising. Thus, not only is there a sustained interest in transferring existing performance practices into said media, but it also enables the emergence of new practices and art forms. In particular, immersive, networked, virtual multiuser environments (summarized under the term "metaverse") offer many possibilities for creating new art experiences that need to be explored. In this paper, we present VERSNIZ, a system for audiovisual worldbuilding, the spatial shaping of virtual environments, as a collaborative real-time performance or installation practice. It combines gamification concepts, known from popular sandbox video games, with the performance practice of live coding based on the esoteric programming language IBNIZ. We describe the technical implementation of the system, as well as the resulting artistic concepts and possibilities.

Keywords: live coding · esoteric programming languages · metaverse · music performance · virtual installations

1 Introduction

The term "metaverse" has become a real hype, and today all kinds of virtual and augmented reality (VR, AR) applications are often promoted as "metaverse". Used as a marketing term, the question of how these called metaverse applications differ from other VR/AR applications often remains unclear. Derived from the dystopian science fiction novel "Snow Crash" [37], the definition of the metaverse as "an interconnected web of social, networked immersive environments in persistent multiuser platforms" ([26], p. 1) seems to be gaining acceptance. According to this definition, the term metaverse environments is suitable for classifying online, multiuser, interactive, and interconnected virtual worlds, in contrast to other virtual applications. As virtual, freely experiential environments, metaverse worlds offer a high degree of immersion and many creative possibilities. The manifold ways of multimodal interaction via text, speech, and movement allow for diverse social exchange and self-expression [31]. Thus, they have many properties that make them suitable for art experiences [19], also in

S. Ystad et al. (Eds.): CMMR 2023, LNCS 15236, pp. 168–180, 2026.
https://doi.org/10.1007/978-3-032-02042-0_12

the context of music practice [42]. A particular challenge in the context of metaverse environments for art expression is real-time performances with multimedia content of music and visuals. Although there is a long history of realizations and concepts for live performances in metaverse environments [12], in recent years, they have come into focus for a broader audience due to the limitations imposed by the global pandemic. But as all related areas of the metaverse continue to grow and advance technologically, we can expect to see continued interest in these topics. Metaverse environments can provide an immersive environment for telematic/networked music performances (NMPs) [30] and are an environmentally friendly and barrier-free alternative for bringing together audiences and artists from around the world.

Here, not only the issue of suitable streaming technologies is in the foreground [35], but also the resulting artistic possibilities. It is not only about how to transfer existing performance practices into such virtual environments but also about which new practices can emerge from these environments.

Virtual environments, such as in VR, already allow for expanded possibilities in terms of virtual instruments, composition, and performance practice [20,22,43]. They also offer the possibility of creating entire worlds under the concept of worldbuilding/worldmaking [48,49]. The technological overlap with video games also allows for the incorporation of gamification elements for composing or performing in such environments [5,15].

In comparison to the above-mentioned virtual instruments or systems for performances in enclosed virtual environments, we present a system for real-time performances and installations incorporating the audience in online, multiuser, metaverse environments. Because they are shared virtual environments (SVEs) [50] that are also accessible to the public via the Internet, they enable audience participation in the virtual performance and composition processes and thus new art practices. How can the role of the performer, the stage, and the audience be redefined in this process? To explore the emerging possibilities of such environments, we combine the gamification concept of worldbuilding with the practice of live coding. As a result, we propose a performance and composition system that is only feasible in metaverse environments.

In the following, we describe the development of the metaverse environment "VERSNIZ" for audiovisual live coding using the IBNIZ programming language [17]. The implementation integrates the above-mentioned concepts, to dissolve conventional ideas of performer, audience, and stage and enable a new performance practice in metaverse environments.

2 Background

A long and wide-ranging history of virtual environments as a medium can be found in video games. The perspective of the recipient is significant here. Usually, the user does not take the passive role of a spectator, but is an active protagonist in narrative scenarios or collaborative games. In concepts like sandbox games,

Fig. 1. A screen capture from the VERSNIZ environment, showing a live coding object placed in the default virtual world. It is rendering music and an animated visual from an example algorithm.

such as the popular Minecraft [23], the player also takes on the role of the creator, creatively shaping the environment and the game experience. Here, players build virtual worlds by placing static or interactive elements as building blocks that shape the entire environment, referred to here as the concept of worldbuilding.

Thus, especially in the medium of virtual environments, the long practice of video games has led to a familiar blending of the recipient and the performing actor. The surrounding world is thereby both, the material as well as the stage for the creation of these experiences. When it comes to live performances of audio/visual content, there are a growing number of musical live performances in multiplayer games like Fortnite or metaverse environments such as VRChat [45] or Mozilla Hubs [25]. In its most basic application, these are concerts with 2D audio and video live streams on such platforms [4]. The experience, with the audience viewing a large virtual screen, is more akin to a public screening than an actual live performance. More complex approaches allow artists to perform as virtual avatars, partly based on motion capture [39]. High-quality, pre-recorded live performances with 3D sound and video are another form of virtual live performances.

This century has seen a rise in the concept of the composer-programmer, which manifests itself especially in the performance practice of live coding [28]. A practice in which the on-the-fly programming of algorithms for the generative composition of music and/or visuals is performed live in front of an audience [6,34]. As programming languages, these can also be embedded well in new technologies, such as web-based applications in the browser [18,29,33]. Therefore also into web-based metaverse environments. Embedding live coding into such environments allows live performances to be executed within the platform without the need to stream audio and video from local computers. For VERSNIZ we implemented an appropriate programming language for audiovisual live coding in metaverse environments and present a performance practice that combines the advantages of metaverse environments with the gamification concept of worldbuilding.

3 Concept

Our objective for VERSNIZ was to create a metaverse environment where multiple users can create a transforming virtual world as a collaborative performance or installation through audiovisual live coding. For this purpose, as in many worldbuilding video games, objects can be placed in virtual space by the user (see Fig. 1). These objects have a programming terminal and can be live-coded in the IBNIZ programming language. The algorithms simultaneously create the visual form, the animation, and the music. The placement and movement of the live coding objects, as well as the design of the acoustics of the virtual environment, allow for the additional application of spatial composition techniques [3].

Through movement in six degrees of freedom (6-DoF), the individual selection of what is seen (field-of-view) and heard is influenced by the head orientation and the position in space. Different visual details and a different "mix" of auditory components have a significant and individual influence on the perceived art experience.

Various criteria were considered during the implementation of a suitable system to meet the definition of a metaverse environment: along with the fundamental requirement of being a multiuser virtual platform, particular focus was put on the resulting immersion. In addition to the 3D rendering of the visual environment, special attention was also paid to the spatial audio rendering. Here, three-dimensional 6-DoF audio reproduction is realized with binaural synthesis for headphone-based auralization [24]. An adequate auditive room simulation was additionally implemented. Compliance with the WebXR [47] standard ensures the use of common VR/AR end devices. While compatibility with VR and AR devices using head-mounted displays (HMDs), controllers, hand or room tracking enables immersive experiences, the ability to use a conventional computer or mobile device ensures a low barrier to entry for the widest range of users.

As a web-based application, users do not need to perform platform-specific installations, and the environment is automatically networked as the metaverse concept intends. Integrating audio and video streaming or text-based chats enables additional forms of interaction and enhances the social component of the experience. In addition, the possibility of modifying the virtual environment

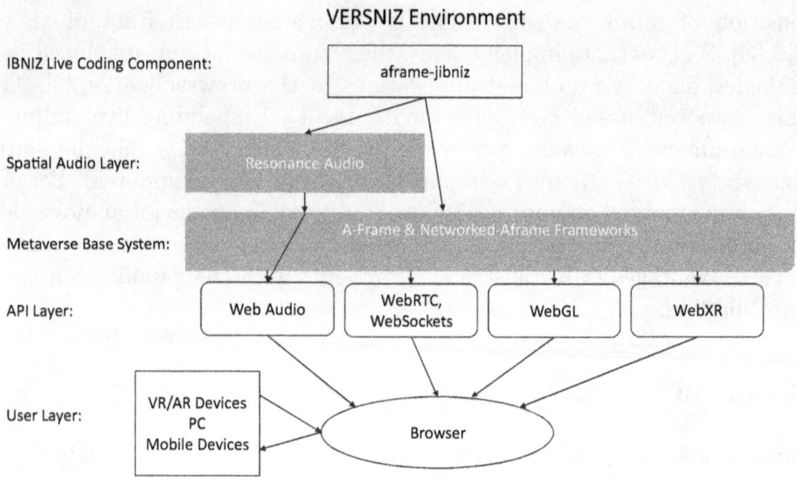

Fig. 2. The architecture of the VERSNIZ metaverse environment. The graphic shows the involved frameworks, libraries, and programming interfaces.

allows new types of stage and design concepts that can be realized with low effort compared to physical reality, and would otherwise be difficult or impossible to realize.

4 Implementation

Implementing a system with the mentioned features requires a complex interchange of various programming languages, frameworks, libraries, and interfaces (see Fig. 2).

To comply with the described requirements for a metaverse environment, a selection of suitable web technologies was made. Thus, the virtual environment was developed based on the A-Frame framework [2]. Together with the library Networked-Aframe [27], shared, multiuser virtual environments can be implemented. This combination is well established, being the basis of the popular Mozilla Hub metaverse systems. The binaural rendering of A-Frame was extended with an implementation of the Resonance Audio spatializer [32]. The most critical component for the audio-visual composition is the programming language for live coding. The programming language IBNIZ unites various features that are particularly beneficial for programming in VR or AR and enables simultaneous programming of audiovisual algorithms. The following describes the development of these elements in more detail.

Metaverse Base System. The web-based multiuser virtual environment was mainly realized with the A-Frame framework. A-Frame is a framework developed in JavaScript that enables the programming of virtual environments for VR and AR abstracted in HTML-like syntax. It is based on the JavaScript library Three.js [41] for programming WebGL applications. The HTML-like abstraction allows it to start designing 3D virtual worlds easily, while the access to Three.js makes it still very powerful. Embedding the WebXR application programming interface (API) enables integration with common VR/AR hardware and mobile devices - with stereoscopic rendering on HMDs and interaction via controllers and tracking. A-Frame applications can still be used with conventional computer hardware via screen, mouse, and keyboard. This allows most users to experience it without requiring special hardware. A-Frame provides various so-called "components" that can be used to program 3D geometries and models, materials, lights, shadows, and multimedia content such as images, videos, and sounds into a virtual environment. The framework is also arbitrarily extendable by programming custom A-Frame components in JavaScript.

The Networked-Aframe library builds on A-Frame and enables the programming of multiuser environments for VR and AR. Networked-Aframe offers various adapters for data exchange via WebRTC with a WebSockets fallback. The data is transferred from user to user in a so-called peer-to-peer (P2P) network. The integration of the WebRTC standard [13] enables the low-latency transmission of audio and video streams, so that video and audio chats can be realized. Text can also be transmitted in-between users, as can the parameters of all A-Frame components, including custom-developed ones. In addition to sharing data, Networked-Aframe also provides templates for implementing avatars and synchronized interaction with the environment to ensure interactivity and persistence of the virtual environment.

For VERSNIZ, Networked-Aframe was integrated using the default EasyRTC adapters. Besides the synchronization of avatars and user interaction, the IBNIZ source code of the audiovisual live coding objects is shared. The virtual world unfolds its immersive potential when immersive end devices are used [36]. Stereoscopic rendering on HMDs and tracking head and movement in the room, create the feeling of presence in virtual environments. Not only is the image rendered to match the user's perspective, but so is the sound. A-Frame, in combination with the Web Audio API [46], already creates a dynamic three-dimensional sound experience through binaural rendering for headphone playback using real-time convolution with head-related transfer functions [24]. Sound sources are rendered at the appropriate location depending on the head orientation and the user's position in the room. To increase acoustic plausibility, a spatial room simulation for reverberation that considers the material properties of reflective surfaces, was added. This makes it possible to match the visually designed environment acoustically and to increase audiovisual coherence [51]. As there is already an A-Frame port [8] of the Resonance Audio spatializer, and Resonance Audio can be considered an appropriate choice for web-based applications [21], the existing port was extended and implemented in conjunction with the IBNIZ live coding component [8]. Based on these technologies, any desired immersive world can be created to represent the stage in VERSNIZ.

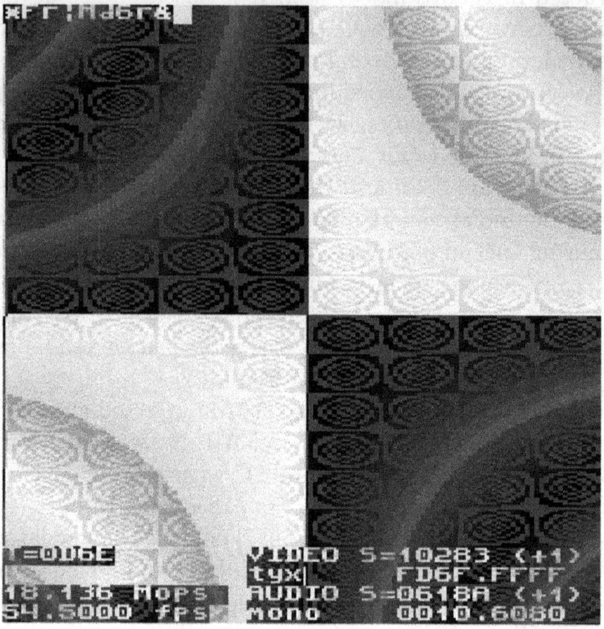

Fig. 3. A screen capture from the original IBNIZ code editor. It shows an example of the same algorithm from Fig. 1.

IBNIZ Live Coding Component. IBNIZ, "Ideally Bare Numeric Impression giZmo", is a virtual machine for low-level programming of audiovisual algorithms [17] which is closely related to the Bytebeat concept [16]. It was developed by Ville-Matias "Viznut" Heikkilä and is linked to ideas present in the Demoscene. This is reflected in the minimalistic design of the language, resulting in the reduced instruction set, consisting of only one character per instruction.

Through this minimalist approach, IBNIZ is often considered an esoteric programming language [40]. A kind of programming language developed out of the motivation to implement experimental, weird, or sometimes artistic concepts rather than to pursue a practical use. Here many results can be already considered software art themselves.

The language design of IBNIZ also has artistic characteristics in it, and it is at the same time a domain-specific language [44] for the programming of further 2D video and audio art (see Fig. 3).

The language's minimalism is not only ideal for live coding in real-time performances, allowing the artist to program expressive algorithms quickly and with few characters only, but also for typing with virtual keyboards on VR/AR devices. While the use of virtual keyboards in VR is often limited to short texts due to the difficulty of using them with the available input devices [14], the advantage of IBNIZ as the chosen language is particularly evident here. The entire instruction set can be placed on a single virtual keyboard view to code the desired algorithms quickly, even with controllers, the mouse, or hand tracking. Building on a web-based port 'jibniz' [1] in JavaScript, we realized an implementation of IBNIZ as an audiovisual live coding language for metaverse environments. The IBNIZ virtual machine is implemented as an A-Frame and Networked-Aframe compatible component 'aframe-jibniz' [7] using the Web Audio API. The resulting audio is linked to a Resonance Audio source and can be rendered spatially depending on its position in relation to the listener. The visual output serves as a displacement texture for arbitrary 3D geometries; in this way, using algorithms, an animated, constantly changing object is generated. In combination, three-dimensional audiovisual objects are created that continuously evolve in real-time. Each object can be programmed independently with a programming terminal and a virtual keyboard, implemented using the Aframe-Super-Keyboard component [38]. The written code and the objects' position are also synchronized P2P using Networked-Aframe with all other users. Since the rendering is client-based for each user, neither audio nor video needs to be streamed, only the text of the programmed code. This way, low bandwidth is used to transmit only text, enabling low-latency, real-time performances.

Fig. 4. A screen capture of a collaborative live coding scenario in VERSNIZ. Two people represented as a head point-cloud avatar performing together in the default environment setup.

5 Use Cases

With VERSNIZ we provide an exemplary template implementation of the 'aframe-jibniz' live coding component into an A-Frame/Networked-Aframe metaverse base system. Using this template, users can create arbitrary virtual worlds and art experiences. Within the possibilities offered by A-Frame, artists can freely design virtual environments, also specifically for use with VR or AR systems. It is intended for performances or installations using the proposed worldbuilding concept (see Sect. 3): the placement and live coding of multiple IBNIZ audiovisual objects in this environment, to enable the algorithmic composition of a constantly changing virtual world. The composition can then take place in real-time within the virtual experience, rather than being produced in advance. The resulting music and the 3D visualization of the objects change constantly depending on the algorithm. The location of their placement adds a spatial component to the composition and allows for extensive integration of spatial composition techniques. Placement and live coding can be done by any user or restricted to specific performers, allowing for different levels of audience engagement. The audience can not only simultaneously take on the role of the performer by live coding themselves, but they can also have their individual experience as passive spectators by interacting with the environment, for example by freely roaming around the world of various audiovisual objects. The recipient is free to move around the virtual environment at any time; the artist has no control over the time and place where the objects are experienced. This adds a spatial component to a time-continuous performance whose control is entirely in the hands of the recipient.

The above-mentioned properties allow a performance practice specifically tailored to the possibilities of metaverse environments, where all actors (performers and audience) come together in an immersive virtual world. The spatial aspect is important here; multiple IBNIZ live coding objects allow an audiovisual composition to be placed as individual fragments in space. This concept, inspired by worldbuilding videogames, allows different composition and performance concepts in combination with audiovisual live coding:

1. virtual worlds can be used as a shared playground for free-form audiovisual creation by different users
2. as a multiuser environment, it can be used for networked music performances in the form of collaborative improvisations or rehearsed compositions (see Fig. 4)
3. artists can create immersive, persistent audiovisual installations in virtual worlds (see Fig. 5)

With VERSNIZ, a new dimension is added to live coding as a performance practice, while the medium of virtual environments offers a high degree of freedom in designing artistic experiences. The gamification concept of worldbuilding allows for a new way of spatially distributed collaboration. A demo of the default VERSNIZ template implementation can be found at: https://versniz.glitch.me/

A video with a brief demonstration of the concept and mechanics is available at: https://youtu.be/O4TmE1-bth4

Fig. 5. A screen capture of multiple audiovisual objects composed into a sculpture, as an example for an audiovisual installation.

6 Conclusion and Future Work

With VERSNIZ we have created a metaverse environment for networked, collaborative live coding of audiovisual worlds. It allows for various novel performance and composition concepts characterized by their spatial aspects. This makes it possible to create art experiences that would be difficult or impossible to realize in physical reality. As an open-source environment, it allows artists a high degree of freedom in design, customization, and expansion. With the incorporation of the worldbuilding concept inspired by video games, we have described a specific performance practice that particularly benefits from the advantages of metaverse environments. The primary constraint is the programming language IBNIZ. While its minimalist design has significant advantages for programming in VR/AR, it is limited in stylistic variety. The properties of the IBNIZ virtual machine in terms of visual and audio resolution or the lack of external media integration, such as images and audio samples, limit the results to a lo-fi 8-bit-like aesthetic.

The current implementation of VERSNIZ works best for Chromium-based browsers and can be found at: https://github.com/AudioGroupCologne/VERSNIZ. However, it is still under continuous development to increase compatibility with browsers and end devices, improve the user experience, provide additional features for artists, and improve stability and performance. Referring to the limitations of IBNIZ mentioned above, also other systems for performances in metaverse environments [11] are being developed parallel to VERSNIZ. This includes additional programming languages for live coding [10], systems for programming and performing with virtual instruments, and performances using real-time streaming of volumetric audio and video [9].

Acknowledgements. I thank Christoph Pörschmann (TH Köln), Stefan Weinzierl and Henrik von Coler (TU Berlin) for supervision and support in carrying out the research and writing this paper.

Disclosure of Interests. This work and the described open-source software is without profit intentions, restrictions, conflicts or competing interests due to any associated funding.

References

1. Escot, L.: jibniz. https://github.com/flupe/jibniz. Accessed 15 Feb 2023
2. A-Frame: Homepage (2023). https://aframe.io. Accessed 15 Feb 2023
3. Baalman, M.A.: Spatial composition techniques and sound spatialisation technologies. Organised Sound **15**(3), 209–218 (2010). https://doi.org/10.1017/S1355771810000245
4. Champlin, A., Knotts, S., Chicau, J., Xambó, A., Saladino, I.: Community report : LivecoderA. In: 7th International Conference on Live Coding (ICLC), pp. 1–5 (2023)
5. Ciciliani, M.: Virtual 3D environments as composition and performance spaces. J. New Music Res. **49**(1), 104–113 (2020). https://doi.org/10.1080/09298215.2019.1703013
6. Collins, N., McLean, A., Rohrhuber, J., Ward, A.: Live coding in laptop performance. Organised Sound **8**(3), 321–330 (2003). https://doi.org/10.1017/S135577180300030X
7. Dziwis, D.: aframe-jibniz. https://github.com/AudioGroupCologne/aframe-jibniz. Accessed 06 Feb 2023
8. Dziwis, D.: A-frame resonance audio git repository (2023). https://github.com/AudioGroupCologne/aframe-resonance-audio-component. Accessed 15 Feb 2023
9. Dziwis, D., Coler, H.: The entanglement – Volumetric music performances in a virtual metaverse environment. .J. Netw. Music Arts **5**(1), 1–12 (2023)
10. Dziwis, D., von Coler, H., Porschmann, C.: Live coding in the metaverse. In: 2023 4th International Symposium on the Internet of Sounds, pp. 1–8 (2023). https://doi.org/10.1109/IEEECONF59510.2023.10335358
11. Dziwis, D., Coler, H., Pörschmann, C.: Orchestra: a toolbox for live music performances in a web-based metaverse. J. Audio Eng. Soc. **71**(11), 802–812 (2023)
12. Elen, R.: Music in the metaverse. J. Audio Eng. Soc. (16) (2008)
13. Google Developer: WebRTC (2023). https://webrtc.org/. Accessed 15 Feb 2023
14. Grubert, J., Witzani, L., Ofek, E., Pahud, M., Kranz, M., Kristensson, P.O.: Text entry in immersive head-mounted display-based virtual reality using standard keyboards. In: 25th IEEE Conference on Virtual Reality and 3D User Interfaces, VR 2018, pp. 159–166. IEEE (2018). https://doi.org/10.1109/VR.2018.8446059
15. Hamilton, R.: Collaborative and competitive futures for virtual reality music and sound. In: 2019 IEEE Conference on Virtual Reality and 3D User Interfaces (VR), pp. 1510–1512 (2019). https://doi.org/10.1109/VR.2019.8798166

16. Heikkilä, V.: Discovering novel computer music techniques by exploring the space of short computer programs. arXiv.org/abs/1112.1368 (2011)
17. Heikkilä, V.M.: Ideally bare numeric impression giZmo - IBNIZ. http://viznut.fi/ibniz/. Accessed 15 Feb 2023
18. Lan, Q., Jensenius, A.R.: QuaverSeries : a live coding environment for music performance using web technologies. In: Web Audio Conference WAC-2019 (2019)
19. Lee, L., et al.: When creators meet the metaverse: a survey on computational arts. CoRR arXiv:2111.13486 (2021)
20. Loveridge, B.: Networked music performance in virtual reality: current perspectives. J. Netw. Music Arts **2**(1), 2 (2020)
21. McArthur, A., Tonder, C.V., Gaston-Bird, L., Knight-Hill, A.: A survey of 3D audio through the browser: practitioner perspectives. In: 2021 Immersive and 3D Audio: From Architecture to Automotive, I3DA 2021. Institute of Electrical and Electronics Engineers Inc. (2021). https://doi.org/10.1109/I3DA48870.2021.9610839
22. Men, L., Bryan-Kinns, N.: Supporting Sonic Interaction in Creative, Shared Virtual Environments, pp. 237–267. Springer International Publishing, Cham (2023). https://doi.org/10.1007/978-3-031-04021-4_8
23. Microsoft: Minecraft (2023). https://www.minecraft.net/. Accessed 15 Feb 2023
24. Møller, H.: Fundamentals of binaural technology. Appl. Acoust. **36**(3–4), 171–218 (1992). https://doi.org/10.1016/0003-682X(92)90046-U
25. Mozilla Foundation: Mozilla Hubs (2023). https://hubs.mozilla.com/. Accessed 15 Feb 2023
26. Mystakidis, S.: Metaverse. Encyclopedia **2**(1), 486–497 (2022). https://doi.org/10.3390/encyclopedia2010031
27. Networked-Aframe: Git Repository (2023). https://github.com/networked-aframe. Accessed 15 Feb 2023
28. Nilson, C.: Live coding practice. In: NIME 2007, Proceedings of the 7th International Conference on New Interfaces for Musical Expression, pp. 112–117 (2007). https://doi.org/10.1145/1279740.1279760
29. Ogborn, D., Beverley, J., Navarro Del Angel, L., Tsabary, E., McLean, A.: Estuary: browser-based collaborative projectional live coding of musical patterns. In: International Conference on Live Coding (2017)
30. Oliveros, P., Weaver, S., Dresser, M., Pitcher, J., Braasch, J., Chafe, C.: Telematic music: six perspectives. Leonardo Music J. **19**, 95–96 (2009). https://doi.org/10.1162/lmj.2009.19.95
31. Park, S.M., Kim, Y.G.: A metaverse: taxonomy, components, applications, and open challenges. IEEE Access **10**, 4209–4251 (2022). https://doi.org/10.1109/ACCESS.2021.3140175
32. Resonance Audio: Git Homepage (2023). https://resonance-audio.github.io/resonance-audio/. Accessed 15 Feb 2023
33. Roberts, C., Kuchera-Morin, J.A.: Gibber: live coding audio in the browser. In: ICMC 2012: Non-Cochlear Sound - Proceedings of the International Computer Music Conference 2012, pp. 64–69 (2012)
34. Romero, J., Borgeat, P.: Live-coding – programming masterly music. In: TEDx KIT (2018). https://www.ted.com/talks/juan_romero_patrick_borgeat_live_coding_programming_masterly_music_jan_2018. Accessed 15 Feb 2023
35. Rottondi, C., Chafe, C., Allocchio, C., Sarti, A.: An overview on networked music performance technologies. IEEE Access **4**, 8823–8843 (2016). https://doi.org/10.1109/ACCESS.2016.2628440

36. Slater, M., Lotto, B., Arnold, M.M., Sanchez-Vives, M.V.: How we experience immersive virtual environments: the concept of presence and its measurement. Anuario de Psicologia **40**(2), 193–210 (2009)
37. Stephenson, N.: Snow Crash. Bantam Books, New York (1992)
38. Supermedium: Aframe-Super-Keyboard (2023). https://github.com/supermedium/aframe-super-keyboard. Accessed 15 Feb 2023
39. Scott, T.: Epic Games: Travis Scott and Fortnite present: astronomical (full event video) (2023). https://www.youtube.com/watch?v=wYeFAlVC8qU. Accessed 15 Feb 2023
40. Temkin, D.: Language without code: intentionally unusable, uncomputable, or conceptual programming languages. J. Sci. Technol. Arts **9**(3 Special Issue), 83–91 (2017). https://doi.org/10.7559/citarj.v9i3.432
41. Three.js: Homepage (2023). https://threejs.org/. Accessed 15 Feb 2023
42. Turchet, L.: Musical metaverse: vision, opportunities, and challenges. Pers. Ubiquit. Comput. (2023). https://doi.org/10.1007/s00779-023-01708-1
43. Turchet, L., Hamilton, R., Camci, A.: Music in extended realities. IEEE Access **9**, 15810–15832 (2021). https://doi.org/10.1109/ACCESS.2021.3052931
44. Voelter, M., et al.: DSL Engineering - Designing, implementing and using domain-specific languages (2013)
45. VRChat: Homepage (2023). https://hello.vrchat.com/. Accessed 15 Feb 2023
46. W3C: Web Audio (2023). https://www.w3.org/TR/webaudio/. Accessed 15 Feb 2023
47. W3C: WebXR (2023). https://immersiveweb.dev/. Accessed 15 Feb 2023
48. Wakefield, G., Ji, H.H.: Artificial nature: immersive world making. In: Giacobini, M., et al. (eds.) EvoWorkshops 2009. LNCS, vol. 5484, pp. 597–602. Springer, Heidelberg (2009). https://doi.org/10.1007/978-3-642-01129-0_68
49. Wakefield, G., Smith, W.: Cosm : a toolkit for composing immersive audio-visual worlds of agency and autonomy. In: Proceedings of the International Computer Music Conference (2011)
50. Waters, R., Barrus, J.: The rise of shared virtual environments. IEEE Spectrum **34**(3), 20–25 (2002). https://doi.org/10.1109/6.576004
51. Werner, S., Klein, F., Mayenfels, T., Brandenburg, K.: A summary on acoustic room divergence and its effect on externalization of auditory events. In: 2016 8th International Conference on Quality of Multimedia Experience, QoMEX 2016, pp. 1–6. IEEE (2016). https://doi.org/10.1109/QoMEX.2016.7498973

An Audio-to-Audio Approach to Generate Bass Lines from Guitar's Chord Backing

Tomoo Kouzai(✉) and Tetsuro Kitahara(✉)

Graduate School of Integrated Basic Sciences, Nihon University,Setagaya-ku, Japan
{kouzai,kitahara}@kthrlab.jp

Abstract. In this paper, we address a system that generates a bass line from a chord backing played on the electric guitar in an audio-to-audio manner. Yielding bass lines for guitar chord backings would be helpful for amateur musicians composing band music. Conventional music arrangement systems targeted MIDI-like symbolic music representations, but accurately obtaining symbolic representations from guitars takes work. To solve this problem, we attempt an audio-to-audio approach; Once the user gives an audio recording of the guitar's chord backing, the system extracts some audio features (spectrogram, mel-spectrogram, or chromagram) and then generates an audio signal of bass lines using a convolutional neural network. The experimental results showed that the model with chromagrams generates bass lines the most robustly.

Keywords: music · CNN · guitar · band arrangements · audio-to-audio

1 Introduction

The electric guitar is one of the central instruments in light music, especially in band music. Therefore many amateur guitarists enjoy playing in a band. When they try to play their original songs in a band, a particular member (such as the guitarist) often composes a melody and a chord progression. They often collaboratively decide the phrases of instrumental parts (e.g., bass, drums). However, it is a challenging task because it requires musical knowledge, like typical phrases of each instrument. If the phrases of each instrument part can be automatically decided on a computer and the band members can listen to them, creating original songs may be more efficient.

Most of the existing studies on automatic music arrangements have been for the piano, such as piano arrangement from band or orchestra pieces [7,8] and score reduction of piano pieces for beginners [10]. Although some studies targeting guitar, most of them are systems for arranging solo guitar scores, such as generating solo guitar scores from orchestral scores [1]and from audio signals [11]. No research has been done on band arrangements that add drums, bass, or other sounds from the guitar sound.

S. Ystad et al. (Eds.): CMMR 2023, LNCS 15236, pp. 181–189, 2026.
https://doi.org/10.1007/978-3-032-02042-0_13

Our goal is to develop a system that automatically makes band arrangements for a given song. This system is intended to be used by people who can play a simple backing for their original song on the guitar but cannot create phrases of other instruments, such as the bass and drums. As the first step, this paper addresses a system that generates a bass line for a given chord backing played on the guitar.

Most existing systems of music arrangement use MIDI-like symbol music representations, but it is not easy to accurately obtain a symbolic representation from recordings of guitar performances (Although there are commercial products of MIDI guitars, their audio-to-MIDI conversion is not necessarily accurate). We, therefore, adopt an audio-to-audio approach in which both inputs (guitar backings) and outputs (bass lines) are audio signals.

2 Proposed Method

Given an audio signal of a chord performance played on the electric guitar, our method generates an audio signal of a bass performance that fits the given guitar performance. For simplicity, the tempo and length are fixed (120 BPM and four measures in the current implementation). First, the given guitar signal is converted to a feature representation (i.e., spectrogram, mel-spectrogram, or chromagram). Then, it is segmented by 0.5 s, and each segment is input to a convolutional neural network (CNN), which generates a bass spectrogram. Finally, the bass spectrogram is converted to an audio signal. To train the CNN model, we use a pairwise dataset consisting of guitar feature representations and bass spectrograms.

2.1 Calculation of the Spectrogram of the Input Sound Source

The spectrogram is computed from a given guitar audio signal (and the bass source when learning) using the short-time Fourier transform (STFT) after downsampled to 22050 Hz. The Hann window is used. The window size is set to 2048, and the hop size is set to 1/1000 of the sampling frequency.

2.2 Feature Extraction

We attempt three different feature representations:

- Spectrogram: The amplitude spectrogram obtained in Sect. 2.1 is used without conversions.
- Mel-spectrogram: This is calculated from the spectrogram using Librosa.
- Chromagram: This is also calculated from the spectrogram using Librosa. The hop size for the chromagram is set to 512.

Below, the models with a spectrogram, a mel-spectrogram, and a chromagram are called the *STFT model*, *Mel model*, and *Chroma model*, respectively.

2.3 Generation of Bass Spectrogram

The feature representation (spectrogram, mel-spectrogram, or chromagram) of the given guitar signal is converted into a spectrogram of a bass performance using a CNN model, because CNNs are widely used for analyzing spectrograms [2–6,9]. Our CNN model (Fig. 1) consists of convolution layers and deconvolution layers as follows:

Convolution Layers. For the *STFT* model, the convolution layers consist of:

- 1st layer: The frequency axis of the guitar's feature representation is compressed to one dimension. The input spectrogram of dimension 1025×500 (frequency axis: 1025, time axis: 500) is compressed to a 1×500 matrix with a 1025×1 filter.
- 2nd layer: The 1×500 matrix is compressed to a 1×250 with a 1×2 filter.
- 3rd layer: The 1×250 matrix is compressed to a 1×50 with a 1×5 filter.
- 4th and later layers: A 1×2 filter and a 1×5 filter are alternately applied until a 1×5 matrix is obtained.

The number of filter channels in each layer is 1024. The stride is 1.No padding is used. A ReLU function is used for the activation.

For the *Mel* model, the filter size for the 1st layer is 128×1 because the input matrix size is 128×500. Apart from this, the same configurations are used.

For the *Chroma* model, the following convolution layers are used:

- 1st layer: The 12×22 chromagram is compressed to a 1×22 (filter size: 12×1).
- 2nd layer: The 1×22 matrix is compressed to a 1×11 matrix (filter size: 1×2).
- 3rd layer: The 1×11 matrix is compressed to a 1×2 matrix (filter size: 1×5).

Deconvolution Layers. The set of deconvolution layers generates a bass spectrogram independently of the feature representation used for guitar signals. It consists of:

- Multiple decomposition layers with filter sizes of 1×5 and 1×2 are alternatively applied. These layers converts a 1×5 matrix (a 1×2 matrix for the *Chroma* model) to a 1×500 matrix.
- After that, a deconvolution layer expanding the frequency axis is applied. This layer has a filter size of 1025×1, which converts a 1×500 matrix to a 1025×500 matrix. This matrix represents a bass spectrogram.

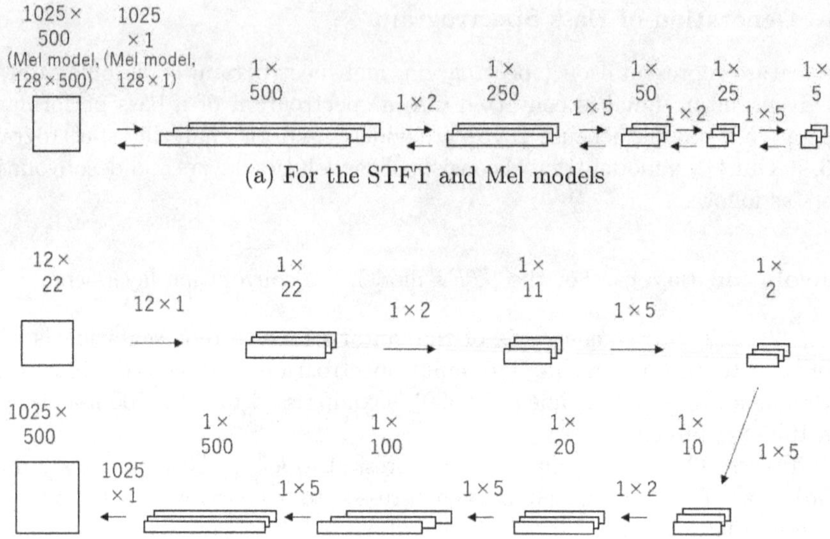

(a) For the STFT and Mel models

(b) For the Chroma model

Fig. 1. Architecture of the CNN model. The numbers above the rectangles represent the shape of the data, and the numbers above the arrows represent the shape of the filter. Right-pointing arrows indicate the convolution layer and left-pointing arrows indicate the inverse convolution layer.

2.4 Generation of the Bass's Audio Signals

The audio signal of the bass part is obtained by using inverse Fourier transform and phase restoration on the spectrogram generated from the CNN. The Griffin-Lim algorithm is used for phase restoration. The number of iterations is 32, the window size is 2048, and the hop size is $1/1000$ of the sampling frequency. To reduce impulsive noises, we use harmonic percussive source separation (HPSS) because impulsive noises are similar to percussive sounds.

3 Experiment

We conducted an experiment to confirm whether an appropriate bass sound can be generated in several conditions.

3.1 Dataset

We made MIDI sequences that consisted of the guitar chord performances and bass lines using Cakewalk by BandLab. For simplicity, we only used four-bar chord progressions that consisted of one chord per measure. The guitar and bass performances are a sequence of eighth notes (for the bass, root eighth notes).

Those MIDI sequences were converted to waveforms using software synthesizers (sforzando for the guitar and SI-Bass Guitar for the bass, included in Cakewalk by BandLab). The tempo for all sequences was set to 120 BPM. Based on these criteria, 20 pairs of guitar and bass signals were created. These pairs include those of the same chord progression but with different voicings. An example is shown in Fig. 2. Out of them, 10 were allocated for training and 10 for testing.

Fig. 2. Examples of guitar and bass scores created.

3.2 Experimental Conditions

The following three conditions were set.

Condition 1 The chord progressions or voicings are different between the training and test data, but all conditions in generating audio signals are the same.
Condition 2 In addition to Condition 1, the acoustic features are different between the training and test data. Specifically, a low-pass filter (setting: −3dB per octave increase) was applied to the test data.
Condition 3 The training data were those described above, while the test data was a recording of a performance by the first author on a real guitar. It was recorded using M-Audio's M-Track.

The generated bass signals were evaluated by calculating the ratio of *correct* frames. When the difference of the fundamental frequency (F0) at each frame from the signal given as the ground truth is lower than 50 cents, that frame is regarded as a *correct* frame. This ratio is called *accuracy* here. We also calculated *octave-ignored accuracy*, in which the difference of 1200 cents was considered correct.

3.3 Experimental Results

The experimental results, listed in Table 1, can be summarized below[1].

Table 1. Accuracy and Octave-ignored accuracy for each test data. The name of the test data represents the chord progression. The same chord progression used for training, but with different voicing, was given "_voicing".

Condition	Filename	Accuracy			Octave-ignored accuracy		
		STFT	Mel	Chroma	STFT	Mel	Chroma
Condition1	A♯CDmEm_voicing	0.37	0.32	0.66	0.55	0.65	0.83
	EABmC♯m_voicing	0.39	0.20	0.64	0.48	0.29	0.67
	CDEmAm_voicing	0.39	0.49	0.53	0.53	0.57	0.81
	GABmD_voicing	0.55	0.54	0.62	0.62	0.56	0.77
	GCDEm	0.58	0.56	0.62	0.76	0.57	0.83
	CDmEmDm	0.42	0.21	0.17	0.66	0.26	0.77
	DmEmAmEm	0.57	0.40	0.32	0.65	0.40	0.84
	EmAmFG	0.59	0.39	0.81	0.69	0.42	0.87
	AmFGC	0.70	0.54	0.79	0.81	0.58	0.88
	FAmGDm	0.58	0.35	0.63	0.69	0.38	0.90
	Average	0.51	0.40	0.58	0.65	0.47	0.82
Condition2	A♯CDmEm_voicing	0.29	0.26	0.58	0.53	0.58	0.78
	EABmC♯m_voicing	0.22	0.26	0.62	0.27	0.41	0.75
	CDEmAm_voicing	0.17	0.30	0.51	0.29	0.43	0.82
	GABmD_voicing	0.28	0.49	0.67	0.34	0.51	0.74
	GCDEm	0.24	0.31	0.52	0.32	0.34	0.78
	CDmEmDm	0.15	0.11	0.23	0.20	0.10	0.85
	DmEmAmEm	0.23	0.17	0.22	0.27	0.18	0.85
	EmAmFG	0.35	0.26	0.68	0.43	0.28	0.88
	AmFGC	0.17	0.35	0.76	0.21	0.39	0.79
	FAmGDm	0.41	0.42	0.58	0.43	0.46	0.83
	Average	0.25	0.29	0.54	0.33	0.37	0.81
Condition3	CDEmAm_Audio	0.20	0.09	0.35	0.21	0.11	0.69

Experimental Condition 1. The model with the highest average accuracy, both with and without octave ignorance, was the Chroma model, and the model with the lowest average accuracy was the Mel model. When the octave is not ignored, the Mel model had the lowest accuracy among the three models in 6 out of the 10 data. When the octave is ignored, the Mel model had the lowest accuracy among the three models in 8 out of the 10 data.

[1] Audio samples are available at: https://sites.google.com/kthrlab.jp/cmmr2023-kouzai.

Looking at Fig. 3, which shows generated bass lines' F0 with the highest and lowest accuracy in the Chroma model, we can see that F0 is moving up and down. This is because the estimated F0s often contain double-pitch errors. In fact, the octave-ignored accuracy for these data is 0.77 and 0.6, respectively. For data containing three or more minor chords, the STFT model showed higher accuracy than the Chroma model, but again, the octave-ignored accuracy was high with the Chroma model.

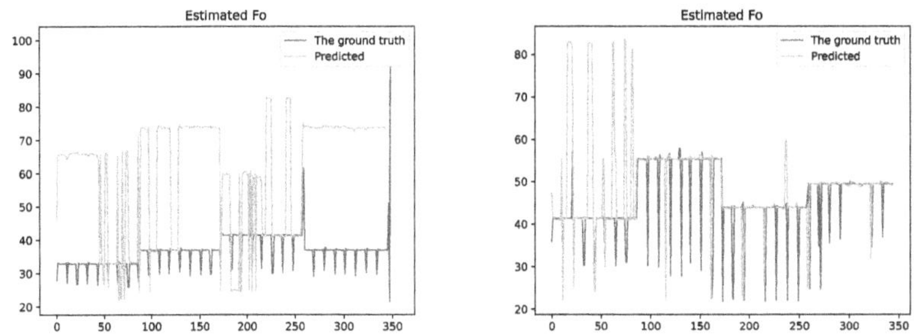

Fig. 3. Condition 1: F0 of generated bass lines with the Chroma model and the ground truth (Left: CDmEmD, the lowest accuracy; Right: EmAmFG, the highest accuracy).

Experimental Condition 2. As in Condition 1, the model with the highest average accuracy with and without octave ignorance was the Chroma model. Especially for the Chroma model, the average accuracy was almost the same as for Condition 1. On the other hand, the model with the lowest average accuracy with and without octaves ignorance was the STFT model.

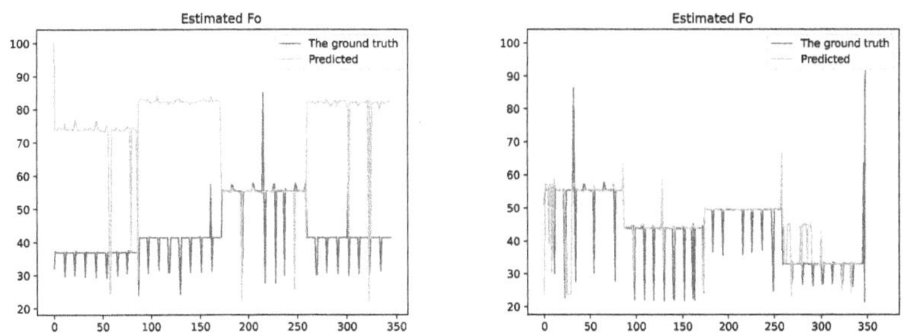

Fig. 4. Condition 2: F0 of generated bass lines with the Chroma model and the ground truth (Left: DmEmAmDm, the lowest accuracy; Right: AmFGC, the highest accuracy).

Compared to Condition 1, the average accuracy for the STFT model dropped by more than 0.2, while the average accuracy for the Chroma model did not drop as much. This would be because the chromagram is a robust feature to timbral changes caused by the low-pass filter. Compared to Condition 1, the accuracy for data with many minor chords was lower for all models, especially for the STFT model; the accuracy dropped to less than half of the accuracy in Condition 1.

Figure 4 showed that the F0 fluctuates less up and down than in Condition 1. Instead, for DmEmAmEm, the double pitch was stably estimated. This is why the octave-ignored accuracy is high (0.85) while the accuracy is low (0.22).

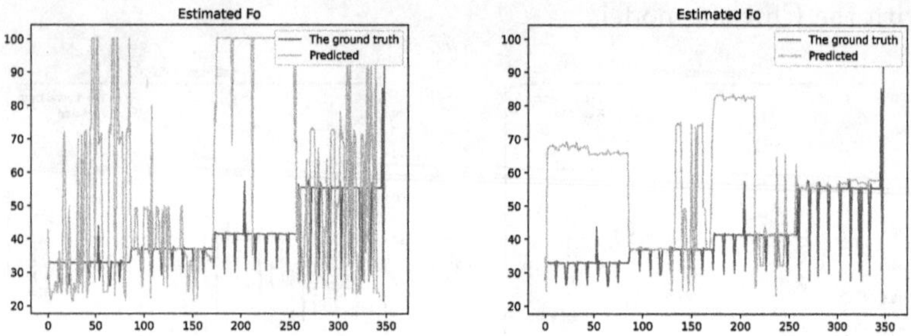

Fig. 5. Estimation of the fundamental frequency of CDEmAm_audio in the lowest accuracy Mel model and the highest accuracy Chroma model.

Although the accuracy was lower than in conditions 1 and 2, the model with the highest accuracy was the Chroma model, while the model with the lowest accuracy was the Mel model. The Mel model generated no harmonic tone in the first two measures. Because there were no harmonic tones, the F0 estimator showed erroneous values, as shown in Fig. 5. This is why this model showed the lowest accuracy. With the Chroma model, bass-like harmonic tones were generated but were slightly distorted. This distortion caused double-pitch errors in F0 estimation; in fact, the accuracy and octave-ignored accuracy had a large difference.

4 Conclusion

In this paper, we proposed a method for generating bass signals from given guitar signals using a convolutional neural network. The experimental results show that the accuracy of the model using the chromagram is the best in all conditions, while the accuracy of the model using the mel-spectrogram and STFT is considerably low for guitar signals with a low-pass filter.

However, these models have been tested only with simple bass lines that consist of only root notes. To enable to generate more complex bass lines, the models need to learn various bass lines, ranging from rhythmic to melodious ones, played in real songs. To achieve this, we must consider longer contexts in the models. Therefore, we would like to extend our models, for example by increasing context layers.

Acknowledments. This work was supported by JSPS Kakenhi Nos. JP22H03711 and JP21H03572.

Disclosure of Interests. The authors have no competing interests to declare that are relevant to the content of this article.

References

1. Ariga, S., Fukayama, S., Goto, M.: Song2guitar: a difficulty-aware arrangement system for generating guitar solo covers from polyphonic audio of popular music. In: International Society for Music Information Retrieval Conference (ISMIR), pp. 568–574 (2017)
2. Dong, M.: Convolutional neural network achieves human-level accuracy in music genre classification. arXiv 1802.09697 (2018)
3. Ferraro, A., Bogdanov, D., Serra, X., Jeon, J.H., Yoon, J.: How low can you go? reducing frequency and time resolution in current CNN architectures for music auto-tagging. In: European Signal Processing Conference (EUSIPCO) (2020)
4. Gong, Y., Khurana, S., Rouditchenko, A., Glass, J.: Cmkd: CNN/transformer-based cross-model knowledge distillation for audio classification. arXiv 2203.06760 (2022)
5. Ji, C., Pan, Y.: Infant vocal tract development analysis and diagnosis by cry signals with cnn age classification. In: Speech and Dialogue Conference (SpeD), pp. 37–41 (2021)
6. Jiang, G., Biswas, A., Bergler, C., Maier, A.: Inse-net: a perceptually coded audio quality model based on CNN. In: AES Convention (2021)
7. Nakamura, E., Sagayama, S.: Automatic piano reduction from ensemble scores based on merged-output hidden markov model. In: International Computer Music Conference (ICMC), pp. 298–305 (2015)
8. Onuma, S., Hamanaka, M.: Piano arrangement system based on composers' arrangement processes. In: International Computer Music Conference (ICMC), pp. 191–194 (2010)
9. Retta, E.A., et al.: Kinit classification in ethiopian chants, azmaris and modern music: a new dataset and CNN benchmark. arXiv 2201.08448 (2022)
10. Terao, M., Hiramatsu, Y., Ishizuka, R., Wu, Y., Yoshii, K.: Difficulty-aware neural band-to-piano score arrangement based on note-and statistic-level criteria. In: IEEE International Conference on Acoustics, Speech and Signal Processing (ICASSP), pp. 196–200 (2022)
11. Tuohy, D.R., Potter, W.D.: Ga-based music arranging for guitar. In: Congress on Evolutionary Computation, pp. 1065–1070 (2006)

Computational Research on Music Evolution

Historical Changes of Modes and Their Substructure Modeled as Pitch Distributions in Plainchant from the 1100 s to the 1500 s

Eita Nakamura[1(✉)], Tim Eipert[2], and Fabian C. Moss[2]

[1] Kyoto University, Kyoto, Japan
eita.nakamura@i.kyoto-u.ac.jp
[2] Julius-Maximilians-Universität Würzburg, Würzburg, Germany
{tim.eipert,fabian.moss}@uni-wuerzburg.de

Abstract. Large-scale quantitative investigations into the cultural evolution of music have mostly focused on only a limited range of time periods and genres. Here, we analyze more than 40 000 pieces of plainchant to better understand the evolution of modes and pitch distributions in a period of five centuries that saw the development of the Western modal practice. Specifically, we employ a hierarchical Markov mixture model to analyze the eight medieval modes and their substructure represented as pitch distributions and observe their historical changes. We found that the individual modes exhibit internal clusters, that the relative frequencies of the eight modes remained remarkably stable over time, and that there were comparatively large changes in the pitch distributions of individual modes. We discuss our results on the background of musicological insights and point to the need for further interdisciplinary work.

Keywords: computational musicology · cultural evolution · plainchant · statistical modeling · mode classification

1 Introduction

Quantitative analysis of music evolution has been gaining increasing attention in recent years. Previous studies have observed trends and regularities in musical styles in several cultural domains such as Western classical music [2,6,19,22,24,25] and popular music [13,16,18,21]. There are also several studies on evolution of folk and world music [17,20]. Such studies inherently rely on the availability of large-scale music data that also include information about the time of composition to be used for evolutionary analysis. Most studies using quantitative methods in the Western classical context have focused on music from the Renaissance, Baroque, Classical, or Romantic periods, and thus covered both modal and tonal practices [1]. However, this concentration on the period from approximately the 16th to the 19th centuries ignores several preceding centuries in which the Western modal practice developed. Here, we draw our attention to medieval monophony and its manifestation in chants [7], in order to shed light on our understanding of the development of pitch organization in Western music from its earliest beginnings.

S. Ystad et al. (Eds.): CMMR 2023, LNCS 15236, pp. 193–204, 2026.
https://doi.org/10.1007/978-3-032-02042-0_14

Table 1. The eight medieval modes. The reciting tone and range are represented in the standard pitch notation for clarity, but the pitches have only relative meanings here.

Number	Name	Type	Final	Reciting tone	Range
1	Dorian	authentic	D	A4	D4–D5
2	Hypodorian	plagal	D	F4	A3–A4
3	Phrygian	authentic	E	C5	E4–E5
4	Hypophrygian	plagal	E	A4	B3–B4
5	Lydian	authentic	F	C5	F4–F5
6	Hypolydian	plagal	F	A4	C4–C5
7	Mixolydian	authentic	G	D5	G4–G5
8	Hypomixolydian	plagal	G	C5	D4–D5

Arguably, the most fundamental concept of medieval music theory for the categorization of chants is that of a *mode*. In the liturgical practice since the eighth century, we can find so-called *tonaries*: books that categorize chants into eight modes [11]. These are then identified in later manuscripts with one of the *finals* D, E, F, and G, each coming in two variants: authentic (the final is usually the lowest note) and plagal (the final is usually the central note in terms of pitch height). The eight medieval modes are conventionally labeled with a number or a Greek name (Table 1). It is, however, not entirely clear whether the concept of mode was merely used as a classification system to organize existing musical material into distinct categories based on some set of shared features (e.g. pitch-related or other), or whether mode was, in contrast, a concept existing prior to composition, that allowed music to be sung "in a certain mode." It seems likely that these two conceptualizations were never strictly separated but that they are rather intricately entangled. Both the categorization and composition aspects probably played a role to varying degrees, as mode is a complex concept influenced by ancient music theory as well as medieval practice [3].

Commonly, the mode of a chant is determined on the basis of pitch-related features, e.g. which pitches are used in which frequency, which pitches are initial or final to a chant, etc. Consequently, modal characteristics should be reflected in pitch-distribution statistics, although it is not clear whether a mode can be modeled as a simple pitch distribution or a distribution with substructure reflecting other features such as the function of chant in liturgical use. These arguments indicate the importance of analyzing the evolution of modes and related pitch distributions and the need for addressing two major research questions: (i) How did the relative frequencies of modes change over time? (ii) How did the pitch distributions of individual modes change over time?

Our contribution shares a research interest with two prior studies on medieval mode. In their pioneering study on the pitch-class distributions of the eight modes, Huron and Veltman [12] found a 'supra-modal group' consisting of modes 3, 5, and 8 (sharing reciting tone c), and another group consisting of modes 1, 4, and 6 (sharing reciting tone A), and suggested that this polarization facilitated the major-minor bifurcation in the 17th century. There has also been some musicological criticism on this work. Specifically, Wiering [23] noted that the abstraction of a pitch class ignores the different functions of octave-equivalent tones in medieval music. Moreover, the assumption of chromatic transpositions contradicts the medieval practice (and virtually all musical practice prior to the Romantic era). It was also noted that the melodic aspects were also ignored in the pitch-class profile approach, which does not account for pitch transitions and cannot represent subtle distinctions of modes based on melodic motions.

In a more recent study, Cornelissen et al. [4] examined mode classification in medieval plainchant melodies using a distributional model that improved some of the shortcomings of the earlier study by including both pitch information (as opposed to pitch classes) and n-gram models. Using the tf-idf vectors of chants, their model achieved a classification F-score of 93–95% and maintained F-scores of 81–83% even without absolute pitch information. The result suggested that plainchant contains 'natural units' that lie somewhere between the levels of individual notes and complete phrases.

To address our two research questions about mode in medieval plainchant, we analyze a large corpus of monophonic melodies that were almost exclusively written for liturgical use (see Sect. 2.1). We analyze the historical changes in pitch distributions in the chants whose source manuscripts date back to the range between the 12th and the 16th centuries. To examine the substructure of modes, we go beyond the approaches in previous research and apply an elaborated technique of machine learning to infer internal clusters of pitch distribution from data. We formulate a hierarchical Markov mixture model for this purpose and study the inferred parameters in terms of mode classification ability and the relationship with chant genres. We then analyze the historical changes in the relative frequencies of these clusters to draw conclusions for our research questions.

2 Method

2.1 Data

Our data source is *Cantus* [14], a database for Latin ecclesiastical chant that was created with the goal of digitizing and distributing indices of medieval chant manuscripts and early printed books [15] (see Fig. 1a for an example). Developed by Steiner in the 1980s, the Cantus database continues to provide an essential resource for scholars and researchers studying the history and evolution of Latin ecclesiastical chant. The central focus of the Cantus database is the so-called *liturgical office*, which is, besides the eucharist (mass), an essential element of the liturgy in almost all Christian denominations. It is a shared act of prayer, typically sung, that involves reciting the psalms and other supplementary texts throughout the various times of day and days of the year (referred to as the canonical hours) [5].

For the present study, we draw on a publicly available data resource that contains a total of 63 628 chants from the Cantus database, including a rich set of metadata [4]. Three types of information are used in particular: melody, mode, and source date. We thus excluded in the following analyses chants with less than ten notes, without an annotated mode, or without source date information. Furthermore, we use the genre

Fig. 1. Three different representations of a responsory chant incipit in mode 8 from the Cantus database (https://cantus.uwaterloo.ca/chant/284929). (a) Detail of the manuscript scan with only one staff line indicating the position of pitch F. (b) Volpiano encoding of the responsory assigning pitches to letters a to p, and modern staff notation. (c) Pitches in standard notation (note name + octave).

metadata with labels such as antiphon, responsory, and responsory verse[1]. Melodies are represented by a string in *Volpiano* encoding [8] (Fig. 1b). The alphabets represent pitches in the ascending order, and dashes indicate the hierarchical segmentation into words, syllables, and neumes. Conversion from this format to the standard pitch notation is straightforward (Fig. 1c).

A chant's metadata often contains a mode attribute extracted from the containing manuscript or assigned by experts. A majority of annotated modes are a single number from 1 to 8 corresponding to the eight modes explained in Sect. 1; only chants classified in these modes are used for analysis. Some of the other chants are transposed chants, indicated with a T, or verses that are sung with a special melody, indicated with an S. There are also chants whose mode is unknown or uncertain, indicated with a question mark. The date of a source manuscript, if it is given, is represented as a year range (e.g. 1201–1300). We use the middle values of these ranges as the time stamps of contained chants. After these data selection steps, we were left with 41 158 chants in total used for the following analysis.

[1] An antiphon is a short, mostly syllabic refrain that was commonly sung before and after a psalm in the liturgical chant. A responsory typically follows a scripture reading and comprises a verse sung by a soloist or small group, succeeded by a response from the choir or congregation. Its melodic structure is often more intricate and melismatic than an antiphon, and its content closely aligns with the theme of the reading it accompanies.

2.2 Markov Mixture Model

We use a Markov model to parameterize the pitch distribution of a certain set of chants, e.g. chants in one of the eight modes. To analyze the substructure of modes, we formulate a Markov mixture model to find internal clusters of chants according to their pitch distributions. This model can also be used to represent the different pitch distributions of the eight modes and to automatically estimate the mode of an unseen piece.

We represent a piece as a sequence of pitches $\boldsymbol{x} = (x_\ell)_{\ell=1}^{L}$. A Markov model describes the generative probability of x_ℓ by the initial probability $\psi^{\text{ini}}(q) = P(x_1 = q)$ and the transition probabilities $\psi(q', q) = P(x_\ell = q | x_{\ell-1} = q')$ as

$$P(\boldsymbol{x}|\boldsymbol{\psi}) = \psi^{\text{ini}}(x_1) \prod_{\ell=2}^{L} \psi(x_{\ell-1}, x_\ell). \tag{1}$$

Given a set of pieces $(\boldsymbol{x}_n)_{n=1}^{N}$, the set of parameters $\boldsymbol{\psi} = \{\psi^{\text{ini}}(q), \psi(q', q)\}$ can be optimized for maximizing the likelihood $\prod_{n=1}^{N} P(\boldsymbol{x}_n|\boldsymbol{\psi})$. The parameters learned in this way represent the pitch distribution in these pieces.

In a Markov mixture model, we consider a set of K Markov models parameterized by $\boldsymbol{\psi}_k$ $(k = 1, \ldots, K)$, each representing the pitch distribution of a class of data, and a mixture probability π_k representing the relative frequency of the k-th class. The probability of a pitch sequence is given as

$$P(\boldsymbol{x}) = \sum_{k=1}^{K} \pi_k P(\boldsymbol{x}|\boldsymbol{\psi}_k). \tag{2}$$

This model is not to be confused with a hidden Markov model, in which each latent variable is introduced for each pitch. In the Markov mixture model, the latent variable k is introduced for each sequence.

Supervised and unsupervised training methods can be derived for estimating the parameters π_k and $\boldsymbol{\psi}_k$ from data. In the supervised setup, we consider that we have data divided into K classes. We can then estimate the mixture probability π_k from the relative frequencies of the individual classes and parameters $\boldsymbol{\psi}_k$ from the subset of data in the k-th class. For example, using the mode label in the present data, we can train the Markov mixture model with eight classes corresponding to the eight modes. In the unsupervised setup, we can train a Markov mixture model from a dataset of pitch sequences without class labels. In this case, the number K of classes is an adjustable hyperparameter that defines a resolution of the analysis. The EM algorithm can be applied to estimate the parameters π_k and $\boldsymbol{\psi}_k$.

Given a Markov mixture model with trained parameters, we can estimate the posterior probability of the class of an unseen piece by the following equation:

$$P(k|\boldsymbol{x}) = \frac{P(\boldsymbol{x}, k)}{P(\boldsymbol{x})} \propto \pi_k P(\boldsymbol{x}|\boldsymbol{\psi}_k). \tag{3}$$

We can then take the class $\hat{k}$ that maximizes the posterior probability as the estimated class for the piece.

In our analysis, we use the Markov mixture model in a hierarchical manner. We train a Markov mixture model with K_m classes from a subset of data in mode m, thus obtaining parameters $\pi_k^{(m)}$ and $\psi_k^{(m)}$. We combine the eight Markov mixture models to obtain a hierarchical Markov mixture model represented as

$$P(\boldsymbol{x}) = \sum_{m=1}^{8}\sum_{k=1}^{K_m} \pi_m \pi_k^{(m)} P(\boldsymbol{x}|\psi_k^{(m)}). \tag{4}$$

As in Eq. (3), we can use this model to estimate the posterior mode probability of a piece $\boldsymbol{x}$ as

$$P(m|\boldsymbol{x}) \propto \sum_{k=1}^{K_m} \pi_m \pi_k^{(m)} P(\boldsymbol{x}|\psi_k^{(m)}). \tag{5}$$

The Markov mixture model and its hierarchical version can be used for addressing our two research questions. First, since the mode-level mixture probabilities π_m represent the relative frequencies of modes, the first research question can be examined by analyzing the temporal changes in their values over time. Next, the component Markov models of the hierarchical Markov mixture model represent internal clusters within individual modes and can thus be used for analyzing the modes' substructure. Specifically, the second research question can be examined by analyzing the temporal changes in the relative frequencies of the internal clusters.

The set of pitches, or the state space of Markov models, was constructed from the Cantus database. There were 22 pitches ranging from the lowest pitch F3 to the highest pitch D6. To account for the specific statistical features of the last note of a piece, we also introduce an additional state 'end' in the Markov models so that the statistics of the last note is incorporated in the transition probabilities to the 'end' state. Therefore, the number of states of the Markov models was 23.

3 Result

3.1 Internal Clusters of Modes

We trained the hierarchical Markov mixture model with $K_m = 3$ for all modes m (Fig. 2). The obtained internal clusters of a mode are ordered in the average time of appearance weighted by the relative frequencies, from the earliest to the latest (see Sect. 3.3). We can observe that the three internal clusters exhibit notable differences in pitch-class transition probabilities in mode 1, 3, and 5, whereas the substructures are less visible in the other modes.

The result of hierarchical clustering of mode-level pitch distributions is also shown in Fig. 2. The same tree structure was obtained when the symmetric Kullback–Leibler divergence and the squared distance were used as the distance measure. This result is similar to the result of [12], which used a single source and a subset of the data we used. Therefore, the structure with two supra-modal groups, one with mode 1, 4, and 6 and the other one with mode 3, 5, and 8 as core members, is shown to be a general characteristic over the time period from the 12th century to the 16th century.

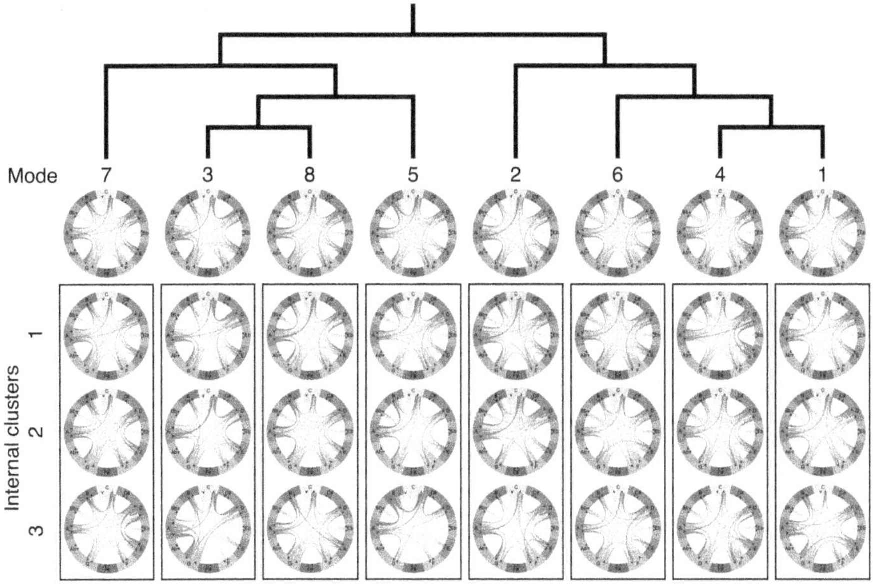

Fig. 2. Visualization of pitch distributions of the eight modes and their internal clusters. Here, the pitch bigram probabilities are reduced to pitch class bigram probabilities visualized as the band widths. The pitch classes are represented by different and arbitrary colors and the colors of the bands indicate the pitch class from which the corresponding pitch transitions occur. The dendrogram was obtained by complete-linkage hierarchical clustering.

To quantitatively measure the effect of the internal clusters for mode classification, we evaluated the accuracy of mode classification by the Markov mixture models with and without internal clusters. In this analysis, we randomly split the data into training (70%) and test (30%) data and used the former data for unsupervised training of the model and the latter data for evaluation. The accuracy was 84.0% without internal clusters and 85.3% with internal clusters, showing the positive effect of more precisely representing the distribution of pitch distributions using internal clusters. It was also confirmed that the accuracy further increased with $K_m = 4$ and 5, indicating the existence of finer-grained internal clusters. As a reference, a previous study [4] reported an F-score of 88–90% by a classification method using the pitch profile (unigram distribution) and 91–92% using pitch bigram features, evaluated on a smaller subset of data with a larger average piece length. We expect that the present Markov model without internal clusters has an equivalent classification ability with these methods when compared in the same setup since the pitch transition probabilities are generally more informative than the pitch profile and essentially equivalent to the bigram probabilities.

Figure 3 shows the confusion matrix of mode classification by the hierarchical Markov mixture model ($K_m = 3$). The result shows that the classification errors generally occur within each of the two supra-modal groups, as expected. We can also find relatively high error rates across these groups between pairs of modes sharing the final, that is, between modes 3 and 4 (final E) and between modes 5 and 6 (final F).

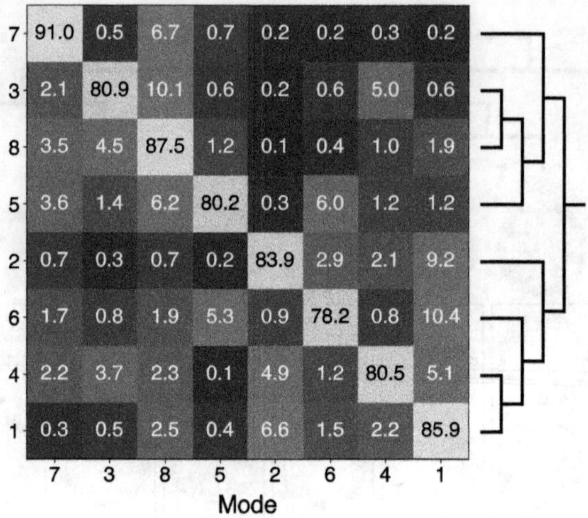

Fig. 3. Confusion matrix of mode classification rates (%) by the hierarchical Markov mixture model.

3.2 Internal Clusters and Genres

To investigate the relationship between the internal clusters and the genres of chants, we analyzed their correlations. We focus on the three main genres, antiphon, responsory, and responsory verse, which cover 91% of the data, and analyzed the proportion of genres $P(g|k)$ in each internal cluster k. More specifically, we used the posterior probability $P(k|n)$ of internal clusters k for piece n and its annotated genre g_n to calculate the genre probability $P(g) \propto \sum_n \delta(g_n, g)$, the conditional internal cluster probability $P(k|g) \propto \sum_n \delta(g_n, g)P(k|n)$, and the proportion of genres $P(g|k) \propto P(k|g)P(g)$ in internal cluster k.

The result in Fig. 4 shows that, for all modes, most of the pieces in genre 'responsory verse' belong to the third internal cluster. Since the labels for the internal clusters only indicate the order in the average time of appearance weighted by the relative frequencies, such a relationship indicates the heterogeneous time distributions of the genres as well as their distinctive features. The distinctive features of the genre 'responsory verse' are not surprising because its musical structure is fundamentally different from that of antiphon or responsory. For example, a responsory verse follows a psalm formula [10] and does not necessarily close with the mode's final. Additionally, all the modes except mode 6 have an internal cluster dominated by the genre 'antiphon' and another one dominated the genre 'responsory'. These results indicate that the three genres tend to have pitch distributions with different characteristics in most modes, and at the same time, that the internal clusters obtained by unsupervised learning do not perfectly match the genres.

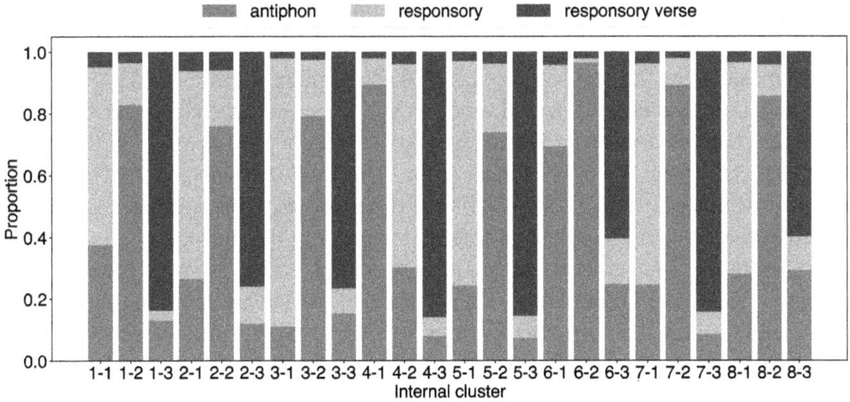

Fig. 4. Proportion of genres in each internal cluster. Internal cluster k of mode m is labeled as m-k.

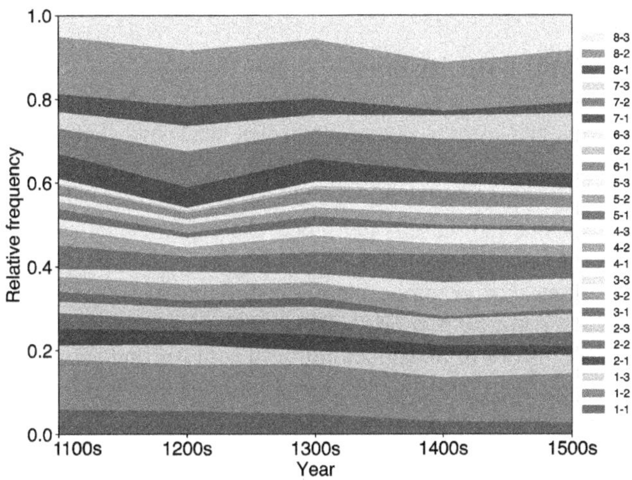

Fig. 5. Relative frequencies of modes and internal clusters over time.

3.3 Time Evolution of Mode Frequency

The time evolution of the relative frequencies of modes and internal clusters is shown in Fig. 5. To obtain this result, we first calculated the posterior probability $P(k|n)$ of internal clusters for each piece n using its mode annotation as a constraint, and used this probability and the time stamp t_n to calculate the relative frequency of internal clusters in each century.

Some interesting observations can be made from the result. First, we find that the changes in the mode frequencies are remarkably small throughout the analyzed time period. The largest relative changes can be observed between the 12th and 13th centuries and between the 13th and 14th centuries, but the relative changes of the mode frequencies are less than 100%. The observed stability of relative frequencies of clusters of musical styles is in stark contrast with the transitions of musical styles in Western classical music since the 16th century [22,25] and popular music [16,21].

Second, compared to the overall mode frequencies, the internal cluster frequencies have larger changes over time. For example, the frequency of cluster 3-3 increased by more than 100% from the 12th century to the 15th century, whereas the frequency of cluster 1-1 decreased by more than 50% in this period. With the result in Sect. 3.1, this means that there is some amount of internal changes in the average pitch distribution within each mode. We can also find some systematic tendencies across modes: the frequencies of the first internal clusters tend to decrease and those of the third internal clusters tend to increase. With the result in Sect. 3.2, we can relate these tendencies to the overall decrease of the proportion of genre ‘responsory’ and the overall increase of the proportion of genre ‘responsory verse’.

Finally, all internal clusters had a non-negligible frequency in the 11th century and emergences of new clusters were not observed. This means that there is no significant innovation in the pitch distribution in this data.

4 Discussion and Conclusions

We here summarize and discuss our results. First, we found that the eight medieval modes exhibit internal clusters of pitch distributions, which correlate with the three major chant genres (antiphon, responsory, and responsory verse). Although we focused on the case of three internal clusters per mode, the experimental result suggested the existence of finer-grained internal clusters, which are also expectable from musicological considerations. For example, there are different types of responsories, such as responsorium prolixum, responsorium breve, and responsorium graduale, that were sung on different occasions or in distinct liturgical contexts and have different melodic features [9]. Incorporating deeper musicological insights into specific genre forms and their implications on mode is likely to shed further light on the substructure of the medieval modes.

Second, we found that the mode frequencies remained remarkably stable over five centuries. This can be explained by the fact that the responsories and antiphons were seen as divine texts that should by all means be authentically preserved. Incidentally, this was also a main driving force behind the development of music notation in the West and the emergence of other genres such as sequences and tropes that granted greater creative flexibility. It would be interesting to further study the Cantus database to reveal how such stability was attained when chants were transmitted across different geographical locations in relation to notational practice. It is also important to examine possible reasons for the observed small variations in mode frequencies, such as changing preferences to write chants in certain modes, changes in categorization practices, and artifacts/biases of sampling manuscripts in different time periods. Such a study will be facilitated when more manuscripts will be digitized and made available for computational analyses.

Third, we found considerable changes in the frequencies of internal clusters, which are related to changes in the proportion of the chant genres in the data. Additionally, the analysis conducted at the resolution of three internal clusters per mode revealed a lack of substantial innovation in the pitch distribution. As a caveat, we note that the Cantus database has a limited number of manuscript sources, and further study should also inspect possible biases by employing strategies such as downsampling and generating synthetic pieces to ensure a more balanced analysis.

Moreover, this study demonstrates how researchers can employ large datasets and computational modeling for investigating music-theoretical concepts and their cultural evolution. Finally, our work points to the necessity of increasing collaboration and exchange between researchers from the humanities and computer science. This pertains not only to the interpretation of quantitative results *post factum*. Rather, it is important to engage in interdisciplinary dialog early on in the research process, in particular when constructing and evaluating computational models. We believe that the vibrant field of cultural evolution provides an ideal forum for such exchanges to take place.

Acknowledgments. This work was in part supported by JSPS KAKENHI Grant Numbers 21K12187, 21K02846, and 22H03661, and JST FOREST Program Grant Number JPMJPR226X.

References

1. Aldwell, E., Schachter, C., Cadwallader, A.: Harmony and Voice Leading. Cengage Learning, 4th ed. (2010)
2. Anzuoni, E., Ayhan, S., Dutto, F., McLeod, A., Moss, F.C., Rohrmeier, M.: A Historical analysis of harmonic progressions using chord embeddings. In. Proceedings of the 18th Sound and Music Computing Conference, pp. 284–291. Axea sas/SMC Network (2021)
3. Atkinson, C.M.: The Critical Nexus: Tone-System, Mode, and Notation in Early Medieval Music. Oxford University Press (2008)
4. Cornelissen, B., Zuidema, W., Burgoyne, J.A.: Mode classification and natural units in plainchant. In. Proceedings of the 21st International Society for Music Information Retrieval Conference, pp. 869–875. Association for Computing Machinery, New York (2020)
5. Dobszay, L.: Art. Offizium. MGG Online
6. Harasim, D., Moss, F.C., Ramirez, M., Rohrmeier, M.: Exploring the foundations of tonality: statistical cognitive modeling of modes in the history of western classical music. Humanit. Soc. Sci. Commun. **8**(5), 1–11 (2021)
7. Haug, A.: Singing from the book: the end of sacrifice and the rise of chant in the fourth century. Musical Q. **104**(3–4), 370–391 (2021)
8. Helsen, K., Lacoste, D.: A report on the encoding of melodic incipits in the CANTUS database with the music font 'Volpiano'. Plainsong Medieval Music **20**(1), 51–65 (2011)
9. Hiley, D.: Western Plainchant: A Handbook. Oxford University Press (1995)
10. Hucke, H., Hiley, D.: Art. Responsorium, Die Melodien der Responsoria prolixa. MGG Online (2016)
11. Huglo, M.: Tonary. Grove Music Online (2001)
12. Huron, D., Veltman, J.: A cognitive approach to medieval mode: evidence for an historical antecedent to the major/minor system. Empirical Musicology Rev. **1**(1), 33–55 (2006)
13. Interiano, M., Kazemi, K., Wang, L., Yang, J., Yu, Z., Komarova, N.L.: Musical trends and predictability of success in contemporary songs in and out of the top charts. R. Soc. Open Sci. **5**(5), 171274 (2018)

14. Lacoste, D., Bailey, T., Steiner, R.: Cantus: A Database for Latin Ecclesiastical Chant – Inventories of Chant Sources (2011)
15. Lacoste, D.: The cantus database: mining for medieval chant traditions. Digit. Medievalist **7** (2012)
16. Mauch, M., MacCallum, R.M., Levy, M., Leroi, A.M.: The evolution of popular music: USA 1960–2010. R. Soc. Open Sci. **2**(150081), 1–10 (2015)
17. McBride, J., Passmore, S., Tlusty, T.: Convergent evolution in a large cross-cultural database of musical scales. PsyArXiv (2021). https://doi.org/10.31234/osf.io/eh5b3
18. Moss, F.C., Souza, W.F., Rohrmeier, M.: Harmony and form in Brazilian Choro: a corpus-driven approach to musical style analysis. J. New Music Res. **49**(5), 416–437 (2020)
19. Nakamura, E., Kaneko, K.: Statistical evolutionary laws in music styles. Sci. Rep. **9**(1), 15993 (2019)
20. Savage, P.E., Passmore, S., Chiba, G., Currie, T.E., Suzuki, H., Atkinson, Q.D.: Sequence alignment of folk song melodies reveals cross-cultural regularities of musical evolution. Curr. Biol. **32**(6), 1395–1402 (2022)
21. Singh, R., Nakamura, E.: Dynamic cluster structure and predictive modelling of music creation style distributions. R. Soc. Open Sci. **9**(220516), 1–18 (2022)
22. Weiß, C., Mauch, M., Dixon, S., Müller, M.: Investigating style evolution of western classical music: a computational approach. Music Sci. **23**(4), 486–507 (2019)
23. Wiering, F.: Comment on Huron and Veltman: does a cognitive approach to medieval mode make sense? Empirical Musicology Rev. **1**(1), 56–60 (2006)
24. Yust, J.: Stylistic information in pitch-class distributions. J. New Music Res. **48**(3), 217–231 (2019)
25. Zivic, P.H.R., Shifres, F., Cecchi, G.A.: Perceptual basis of evolving western musical styles. Proc. Natl. Acad. Sci. USA **110**(24), 10034–10038 (2013)

Computational Analysis of Selection and Mutation Probabilities in the Evolution of Chord Progressions

Eita Nakamura(✉)

Kyoto University, Kyoto, Japan
eita.nakamura@i.kyoto-u.ac.jp

Abstract. We build a model of cultural evolution and study the properties of the process in which new chord progressions are repeatedly generated by referencing and modifying past chord progressions. As an extension of the models for biological molecular evolution, this model represents a stochastic process in which references are selected from an accumulating pool of chord segments and new chord segments are created by mutation including insertion, deletion, and substitution of chord symbols. We used a dataset of Japanese popular music and analyzed this evolutionary process by inferring the model parameters. A number of suggestive results regarding the evolution of the creative culture were obtained, including a strong recency bias, large mutation rates and large dynamic changes in mutation probabilities, and correlations between fluctuations and mutation probabilities and between the diffusedness of mutant chord segments and their mutation probabilities. Model-based predictions of new chord progressions were also made.

Keywords: cultural evolution · evolutionary model · symbolic music processing · chord progression · prediction of evolution · accumulating artifact pool

1 Introduction

Cultural development is a key aspect of human's intelligence, and musical culture provides a fruitful venue for studying its creative role. Quantitative studies on music evolution have revealed some interesting macroscopic phenomena. These include directional changes (trends) in average features continuing for decades [9,11,19] or centuries [13,14,24], punctuational short time periods with rapid changes [11,24,27], concurrent and transient cluster structure [11,19,24], and frequency-dependent selection bias [14,26]. Since individual musical pieces are produced by creators who learn to create music from previous creators or musical pieces, revealing the microscopic processes of knowledge transmission and modification is essential for understanding the mechanisms underlying these phenomena [4].

Transmission processes of musical knowledge can be classified into two types, direct and indirect. In direct transmission, a song or other musical data serves as a reference and is replicated for producing a new one. For example, folk songs are typically transmitted in this way [16]. Some models of direct transmission of musical scale

S. Ystad et al. (Eds.): CMMR 2023, LNCS 15236, pp. 205–217, 2026.
https://doi.org/10.1007/978-3-032-02042-0_15

[12] or music sampling [26] have been proposed for testing musicological hypotheses. Direct transmission of music is also studied in laboratory experiments [1,20]. In indirect transmission, on the other hand, knowledge for music creation is learned from a collection of past music or through teaching, and the acquired knowledge is used for creating (rather than replicating) new musical pieces. A dominant part of art music and popular music is considered to be created by indirectly transmitted knowledge, and there is some evidence from studies on automatic music composition showing the relevance of statistical learning [7]. Cultural evolution models incorporating indirect knowledge transmission have been studied to explain empirical laws found in music data [14,15].

Here we focus on the evolution of chord progressions in popular music. Chord progressions outline how accompaniments are played and are of prime importance in the composition process of tonal music. In popular music, they are usually notated together with the melodies, forming a type of musical score called lead sheet. Unlike melodies, chord progressions are very often reused with possible modifications, and there are books [17] and websites [8] listing commonly used chord progressions, suggesting that direct transmission is at work. It is commonly known and has been shown by a corpus analysis [5] that patterns of chord progressions have changed significantly over the last decades while new chord progressions have continuously been invented. Therefore, chord progressions are scientifically and practically interesting objects to study how a creative culture evolves by knowledge transmission and modification.

To reveal the basic characteristics of the transmission and modification processes of chord progressions, we construct a stochastic model of evolution and analyze a dataset of chord progressions in popular music songs. We view a chord progression as a sequence of chord symbols and consider chord segments (L-grams) as the unit of knowledge transmission. The process of creating a new chord segment by (i) choosing a reference from the 'artifact pool' of previously created chord segments (i.e. selection) and (ii) possibly modifying it (i.e. mutation) is akin to that of biological molecular evolution, where nucleotides or amino acids correspond to chord symbols.

We thus build a model similar to the models of molecular evolution [2,6], with extensions to incorporate essential factors of the cultural evolution. First, we formulate a model where created artifacts (chord segments) are accumulated in the artifact pool unlike individuals that are removed upon death from the population in biological models. Second, we incorporate in the selection process the recency and frequency-dependent biases, which are often relevant in cultural evolution [3,22]. Third, we consider in the mutation process insertions and deletions of chord symbols, which are often ignored in molecular evolution models [2], as well as substitutions. These features also make our model different from the one previously used for chord progression data [23], enabling us to harvest a number of suggestive results. Another study analyzed folk songs and estimated note-wise mutation probabilities using a dataset without time information [16]. With the use of mathematical model and data with proper time information, we here analyze more detailed properties of the evolutionary process such as dynamic changes of mutation probabilities, correlations between evolutionary parameters, and the characteristics of new chord segments that later become commonly used.

2 Method

2.1 Data Representation

We consider a dataset of chord progressions represented in a standard popular music notation, transposed to the natural key (C major or A minor), and labeled with a year of creation. The set of distinct chords in the data is denoted by Ω (e.g. $\Omega = \{\mathrm{C}, \mathrm{Am7}, \mathrm{FM9}, \ldots\}$). From each progression, we extract L-grams (also called chord segments), which are segments of L consecutive chords, where we remove repetitions of chords. An L-gram so obtained is assigned a time stamp, which is the same as the year of creation of its source progression. The collection of all L-grams obtained from progressions created in year t is denoted by $S_t^{(L)} = \{w_i | t_i = t\}$ and its index set by $I_t^{(L)} = \{i | t_i = t\}$, where i is used as an index for L-grams and $w_i = (w_{i\ell})_{\ell=1}^{L}$ ($w_{i\ell} \in \Omega$) denotes the corresponding L-gram. We also define $S_{<t}^{(L)} = \bigcup_{s=1}^{t-1} S_s^{(L)}$, where we take the starting time $t = 1$ as the earliest year of creation in the data. For simplicity of notation, we define $S_t = S_t^{(L)}$, $S_{<t} = S_{<t}^{(L)}$, $S_t^+ = S_t^{(L+1)}$, $S_t^- = S_t^{(L-1)}$, etc. For the result in Sect. 3, we consider the case $L = 4$.

2.2 Evolutionary Model

We consider that each L-gram $w \in S_t$ is stochastically generated by selecting a reference segment w' from past data and possibly mutating it. Three mutation modes are considered: substitution, deletion, and insertion. In the substitution mode, a reference w' is taken from the set $S_{<t}$ of L-grams and mutated by changing one or more component chords, from w'_ℓ to w_ℓ, according to the symbol-wise substitution probability $\pi_{\mathrm{sub}}(w_\ell | w'_\ell)$. The substitution probability from L-gram w' to w is defined as

$$P_{\mathrm{rep/sub}}(w|w') = \prod_{\ell=1}^{L} \pi_{\mathrm{sub}}(w_\ell | w'_\ell), \tag{1}$$

where we also include the pure replication case ($w_\ell = w'_\ell$ for all ℓ) in this probability. In the deletion mode, a reference w' is taken from the set $S_{<t}^+$ of $(L+1)$-grams and mutated by removing one of its components. Since a removal of the first or last chord in $w' \in S_{<t}^+$ produces an L-gram in $S_{<t}$, we exclude such a case. Then, the deletion probability can be defined as

$$P_{\mathrm{del}}(w|w') = \frac{1}{L-1} \sum_{\ell=2}^{L} \delta(w, w'_{1:(\ell-1)} w'_{(\ell+1):(L+1)}), \tag{2}$$

where $w_{\ell:\ell'} = w_\ell w_{\ell+1} \cdots w_{\ell'}$, and $\delta(w_1, w_2) = 1$ if $w_1 = w_2$ and 0 otherwise. In the insertion mode, a reference w' is taken from the set $S_{<t}^-$ of $(L-1)$-grams and mutated by inserting a chord a after one of its chords w'_ℓ according to the symbol-wise insertion probability $\pi_{\mathrm{ins}}(a|w'_\ell)$. The insertion probability is defined as

$$P_{\mathrm{ins}}(w|w') = \frac{1}{L-1} \sum_{\ell=1}^{L-1} \pi_{\mathrm{ins}}(w_{\ell+1}|w'_\ell) \delta(w, w'_{1:\ell} w_{\ell+1} w'_{(\ell+1):(L-1)}). \tag{3}$$

Note that the mutation probabilities considered here are among the simplest choices and we can generalize them to more elaborated models. For example, while we assumed that the symbol-wise substitution probabilities are context free, that is, the probability is independent of the preceding or succeeding chord symbols, it is possible to include context dependence by extending the probability $\pi_{\rm sub}(w_\ell|w'_\ell)$ to such forms as $\pi_{\rm sub}(w_\ell|w'_{\ell-1}, w'_\ell)$ and $\pi_{\rm sub}(w_\ell|w'_{\ell-1}, w'_\ell, w'_{\ell+1})$. Similarly, we can extend the insertion probability so that it also depends on the succeeding chord symbols. These refinements generally increase the complexity (the number of parameters) of the model and require a larger amount of data to reliably infer the parameters.

In the generative process, one of the mutation modes is first chosen according to the mutation mode probability $P(b) = \lambda_b$ where $b \in \{\text{rep/sub}, \text{del}, \text{ins}\}$. We again note that the pure replication case is included in the mode $b = \text{rep/sub}$. Next, in this case, a reference segment w is chosen from $S_{<t}$ according to the selection probability $P_{\rm sel}(w|S_{<t})$. We incorporate two biases in the selection probability to represent potential tendencies of creators. The first is the recency bias [22], which represents the creators' tendency to more likely choose a reference that appears in a recently created song. This bias can be represented by a weighting factor $\mathrm{e}^{-(t-t_i)/\tau}$ for a segment i, where the time constant τ represents the time scale for the bias. The second is the frequency-dependent bias [3], which represents the creators' tendency to more likely choose a reference that is more (or less) frequently used in $S_{<t}$. To formulate this bias, let $F(w; I_s) = \#\{j \in I_s | w_j = w\}/\#I_s$ denote the relative frequency of w in S_s. The frequency bias can be incorporated in a factor $[F(w; I_s)]^\alpha$ in the selection probability, where $\alpha > 1$ ($\alpha < 1$) represents a positive (negative) frequency-dependency bias.

The selection probability incorporating the two biases is then given as

$$P_{\rm sel}(w; S_{<t}) \propto \sum_{s=1}^{t-1} \mathrm{e}^{-(t-s)/\tau} [F(w; I_s)]^\alpha. \tag{4}$$

We note that this formulation removes a potential bias arising from the unbalanced numbers of chord segments created in individual years. Similarly, we define $P_{\rm sel}(w; S^+_{<t})$ and $P_{\rm sel}(w; S^-_{<t})$ for choosing a reference in the deletion and insertion modes, respectively, where the same α and τ are used.

We can summarize the generative probability of $w \in S_t$ as follows:

$$P(w; S_t) = \sum_{b \in \{\text{rep/sub},\text{del},\text{ins}\}} \lambda_b P_b(w; S_t), \tag{5}$$

$$P_{\text{rep/sub}}(w; S_t) = \sum_{w' \in S_{<t}} P_{\text{rep/sub}}(w|w') P_{\rm sel}(w'; S_{<t}), \tag{6}$$

$$P_{\rm del}(w; S_t) = \sum_{w' \in S^+_{<t}} P_{\rm del}(w|w') P_{\rm sel}(w'; S^+_{<t}), \tag{7}$$

$$P_{\rm ins}(w; S_t) = \sum_{w' \in S^-_{<t}} P_{\rm ins}(w|w') P_{\rm sel}(w'; S^-_{<t}). \tag{8}$$

We can also separately define the (pure) replication and substitution probabilities as

$$P_{\text{rep}}(w; S_t) = P_{\text{rep/sub}}(w|w) P_{\text{sel}}(w; S_{<t}), \tag{9}$$

$$\begin{aligned} P_{\text{sub}}(w; S_t) &= \sum_{w' \in S_{<t}, w' \neq w} P_{\text{rep/sub}}(w|w') P_{\text{sel}}(w'; S_{<t}) \\ &= P_{\text{rep/sub}}(w; S_t) - P_{\text{rep}}(w; S_t). \end{aligned} \tag{10}$$

2.3 Inference Method

The parameters of the evolutionary model, λ_b, $\pi_{\text{sub}}(a|a')$, $\pi_{\text{ins}}(a|a')$, τ, and α, can be estimated from the data by the maximum likelihood method. To estimate the first three sets of parameters, we apply the expectation-maximization (EM) algorithm by treating the mutation mode b and reference w' as latent variables for each observed w.

To estimate τ and α, we can apply a simple iterative grid search using the likelihood as the objective function. Since the optimal values of these parameters depend on the values of the other parameters and vice versa, we iterate the EM step and grid search step alternately until a convergence of the likelihood value. To evaluate their estimation variances, we can apply a Bayesian method based on Monte Carlo Markov Chain sampling. Specifically, we used the Metropolis method with a flat prior distribution and a log-normal distribution as the proposal distribution.

2.4 Posterior Analysis

Given the set of model parameters estimated as in Sect. 2.3, we can apply the method of posterior analysis for analyzing possible dynamic changes in the evolutionary parameters. First, given an L-gram w at time t, its posterior probability of mutation modes $\tilde{\lambda}_b(w,t) = P(b|w,t)$ ($b \in \{\text{rep}, \text{sub}, \text{del}, \text{ins}\}$) can be obtained as

$$\tilde{\lambda}_{\text{rep}}(w,t) = \lambda_{\text{rep/sub}} P_{\text{rep/sub}}(w|w) P_{\text{sel}}(w; S_{<t}) / P(w; S_t), \tag{11}$$

$$\tilde{\lambda}_{\text{del}}(w,t) = \lambda_{\text{del}} P_{\text{del}}(w; S_t) / P(w; S_t), \tag{12}$$

$$\tilde{\lambda}_{\text{ins}}(w,t) = \lambda_{\text{ins}} P_{\text{ins}}(w; S_t) / P(w; S_t), \tag{13}$$

$$\tilde{\lambda}_{\text{sub}}(w,t) = 1 - \tilde{\lambda}_{\text{rep}}(w,t) - \tilde{\lambda}_{\text{del}}(w,t) - \tilde{\lambda}_{\text{ins}}(w,t), \tag{14}$$

where the right-hand sides of these equations can be calculated using Eqs. (5) to (8) and the replication and substitution probabilities are separately defined here. Then, the mutation mode probabilities $\tilde{\lambda}_b(t)$ at time t can be estimated, for example, as

$$\tilde{\lambda}_{\text{sub}}(t) = \frac{1}{\#S_t} \sum_{w \in S_t} \tilde{\lambda}_{\text{sub}}(w,t).$$

We can also calculate the posterior probability $P(w'|w,t,b)$ of reference segments $w' \in S_{<t} \cup S_{<t}^{+} \cup S_{<t}^{-}$ in a similar way. For example, in the insertion mode,

$$P(w'|w,t,b = \text{ins}) \propto P_{\text{ins}}(w|w') P_{\text{sel}}(w'; S_{<t}^{-}).$$

The posterior probabilities obtained in this way can be used to estimate the mutation probabilities $\tilde{\pi}_{\text{sub}}(a|a';t)$ and $\tilde{\pi}_{\text{ins}}(a|a';t)$ at time t.

3 Result

3.1 Dataset

We used a dataset of Japanese popular music songs. The dataset was constructed by the author and comprised of 2419 songs. The songs were taken from top ranked songs in the Oricon yearly charts and from a compiled collection of historical popular songs [18]. The composition years spanned the range $[1927, 2019]$ and we applied the evolutionary model for analysis in a range of years $t \geq 1960$ (Fig. 1A).

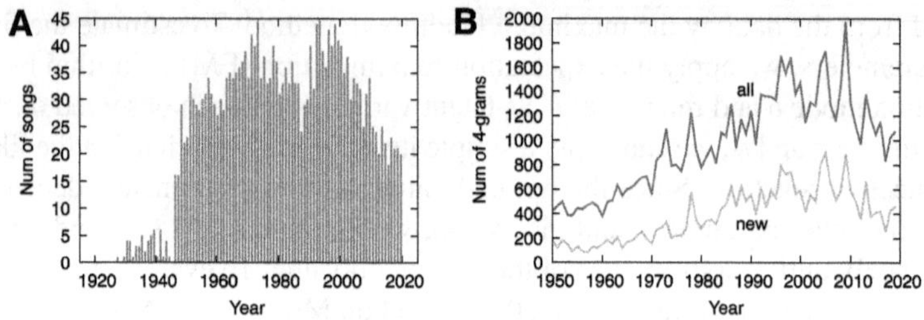

Fig. 1. A: The distribution of composition years in the dataset used. B: The yearly numbers of 4-grams (including duplications) and that of newly appeared 4-grams.

Before extracting L-grams of chords from a song, we transposed the song into the natural key, converted a consecutive repetition of the same chord into a single chord, and converted a slash chord into a normal chord by removing the bass note. The target of the analysis was 4-grams ($L = 4$). The number of distinct chord symbols was 232, from which approximately 2.9×10^9 distinct 4-grams can be created in principle. The numbers of distinct 3-grams, 4-grams, and 5-grams appearing in the dataset were 12 258, 27 237, and 44 204, respectively. Figure 1B shows the yearly numbers of 4-grams and those of newly appeared 4-grams; the average rate of new 4-grams was 39%.

3.2 Selection Biases

The inferred value of the time constant was $\tau = 2.61 \pm 0.53$. This means that the probability of a chord segment being chosen as a reference reduces by a factor of 10 in every 6.1 years, when other conditions are equal. The inferred value of the frequency-dependence parameter was $\alpha = 1.16 \pm 0.16$. The mean value indicates a slightly positive frequency-dependent bias, i.e., more common chord segments tend to be more frequently chosen as a reference than its frequency expected for random selection. However, the deviation of α from unity is small and the result is consistent with the frequency-independent bias within the range of statistical error.

3.3 Mutation Modes

The inferred values of mutation mode probabilities are listed in Table 1. We found that the probability of choosing the deletion mode tended to converge to zero. To understand this result, we note that the probability of each mutation mode is of the same order, $O(K^{-L})$ for $K = \#\Omega$, if we suppose a uniform distribution over all chord symbols. The result can then be explained by the fact that there are no tunable parameters for the deletion operation whereas the substitution and insertion probabilities, $\pi_{\rm sub}(a|a')$ and $\pi_{\rm ins}(a|a')$, are trained so that the likelihoods of these modes will increase in the course of statistical inference. Consequently, in our model, the main mutation modes are substitution and insertion.

Table 1. Inferred values of mutation mode probabilities.

$\lambda_{\rm rep}$	$\lambda_{\rm sub}$	$\lambda_{\rm del}$	$\lambda_{\rm ins}$
0.38	0.46	0.00	0.16

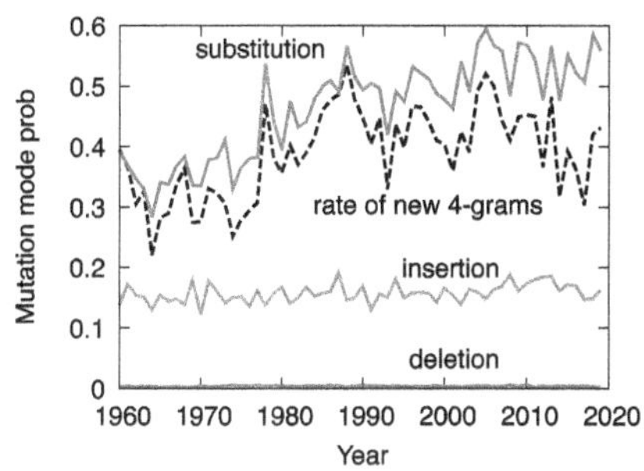

Fig. 2. Dynamic changes of mutation mode probabilities.

We see that the sum of mutation probabilities, which is equal to $1 - \lambda_{\rm rep}$, is 62% and larger than the average rate (39%) of new segments. This value is substantially larger than the mutation probabilities in typical biological evolution and leads to distinct characteristics. For example, a significant proportion (38%) of reappeared segments are estimated to be created through a mutation process according to the present model.

A posterior analysis over time showed that the substitution mode probability had some variations across years and a general trend of increase from the 1960s to the 1990s (Fig. 2). Its temporal changes highly correlated with the rate of new segments ($\rho = 0.86$, $p < 10^{-10}$). On the other hand, the insertion mode probability had small fluctuation and no notable trend was observed.

3.4 Symbol-Wise Substitution and Insertion Probabilities

The most frequent modes of symbol-wise substitution and insertion are shown in Fig. 3 with their yearly relative frequencies obtained by the posterior analysis. For substitution probabilities (Fig. 3A), we see that there are signifiant changes over years and the diversity of applied substitution modes considerably increased from the early period to the late period. There is also a tendency that substitutions involving less frequent chords such as FM7 and Gsus4 became more frequent in later periods. From the list of substitution modes, we can find that most substitutions occur between chords with the same harmonic function. These chords often share the root tone (e.g. E7 $\rightarrow$ Em, Dm $\rightarrow$ Dm7, F $\rightarrow$ FM7, and G $\rightarrow$ Gsus4) or share constituent pitches (e.g. Dm $\rightarrow$ F, C $\rightarrow$ Em, and Em7 $\rightarrow$ C). A similar relation between the substitutability of chords and the harmonic function was also found in an analysis using hidden Markov model [21].

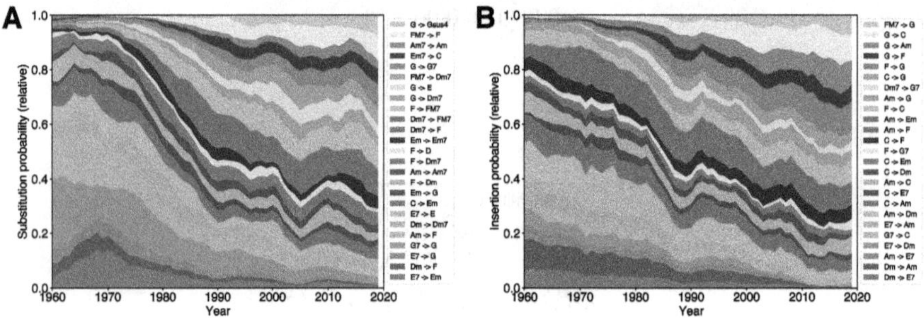

Fig. 3. Dynamic changes of symbol-wise substitution (A) and insertion (B) probabilities. In each panel, the relative frequencies of the 25 most frequent modes are shown, and a smoothing with a window of 5-year width is applied.

Significant changes over years were also found in the insertion probabilities (Fig. 3B). The list of insertion modes mostly consisted of common chord transitions (see also Sect. 3.5). We see a tendency that chord transitions used in the minor key (e.g. Dm $\rightarrow$ E7, E7 $\rightarrow$ Am, and Am $\rightarrow$ Dm) appear more frequently in the early period and those used in the major key (e.g. F $\rightarrow$ G, G $\rightarrow$ C, and FM7 $\rightarrow$ G) in the late period.

3.5 Correlation Between Fluctuation and Mutation Probabilities

We analyzed the correlations between evolutionary parameters to examine several expectations from the evolutionary theory. On the one hand, if new chord segments are stochastically generated by substitutions, we expect that the joint probability of different chord symbols $P_{\rm var}(a', a)$ in variants of segments related by a single substitution correlates with the joint probability of substitution $\pi_{\rm sub}(a' \rightarrow a) = P(a')\pi_{\rm sub}(a|a')$, where $P(a')$ is the prior probability of chord symbols. On the other hand, if we consider the implicit effect of social selection in the data, among potential creators who generate new segments with different substitution probabilities, successful creators would be those with substitution probabilities that are similar to the fluctuation probabilities of chord symbols in past data. This also suggests that the probability $\pi_{\text{sub}}(a' \to a)$ correlates with the fluctuation represented by the probability $P_{\text{var}}(a', a)$ in past data.

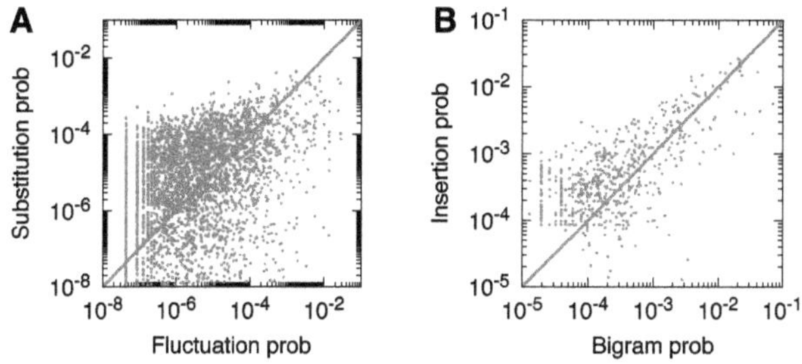

Fig. 4. Correlations between fluctuation and mutation probabilities. A: The fluctuation probability $P_{\text{var}}(a', a)$ and the joint substitution probability $\pi_{\text{sub}}(a' \to a)$. B: The bigram probability $P_{\text{bi}}(a', a)$ and the joint insertion probability $\pi_{\text{ins}}(a' \to a)$.

To examine this expectation, we analyzed the correlation between the joint substitution probability $\pi_{\text{sub}}(a' \to a)$ in a time range $[2010 : 2019]$ and the fluctuation $P_{\text{var}}(a', a)$ observed in a time range $[1927 : 2009]$. The result in Fig. 4A supports the expectation and shows a positive correlation ($\rho = 0.18$, $p < 10^{-10}$). We also see a significant amount of deviation: in particular, a high fluctuation probability does not always indicate a high substitution probability.

Similarly, we expect that the insertion probabilities are related to the corresponding fluctuation probabilities. More specifically, we expect that the joint probability of insertion $\pi_{\text{ins}}(a' \to a) = P(a')\pi_{\text{ins}}(a|a')$ correlates with the bigram probability $P_{\text{bi}}(a', a)$ of chord symbols in past data. The result in Fig. 4B supports the expectation and shows a high correlation ($\rho = 0.64$, $p < 10^{-10}$).

3.6 Diffusion of Mutants

Characterizing the conditions of new mutant chord segments that will diffuse and become commonly used is important for understanding the macroscopic evolution of chord progressions. For biological evolution, where mutations are rare, a similar problem of fixation has been studied, and the fitness of the mutant and the random sampling in a finite population are studied as two major factors [10]. Our case of cultural evolution has two features that lead to an evolutionary process distinct from the typical case of biological evolution. First, as we discussed in Sect. 3.3, the mutation rate is much larger than in biological evolution so that the chance that mutants of the same form are independently generated is not negligible. Second, the evolutionary process is an accumulated process so that mutant segments will not be removed from the artifact pool.

Based on this consideration, we expect that the accumulation of independent mutants is relevant for the diffusion of a new chord segment. As a measure of diffusion of a segment w, we can use its probability of replication. More specifically, we define the diffusedness $D^{10\mathrm{yr}}(w, t_w^\star)$ of a mutant segment w first appeared in year $t_w^\star$ as

$$D^{10\mathrm{yr}}(w, t_w^\star) = \frac{1}{10} \sum_{t=t_w^\star+1}^{t=t_w^\star+10} \lambda_{\mathrm{rep/sub}} P_{\mathrm{rep}}(w, t), \tag{15}$$

where the replication probability $P_{\mathrm{rep}}(w, t)$ is given in Eq. (9). Our hypothesis is that a mutant with a larger mutation probability $P(w; S_{t_w^\star})$ has a higher chance of repeatedly introduced to the artifact pool and consequently has a higher diffusedness on average.

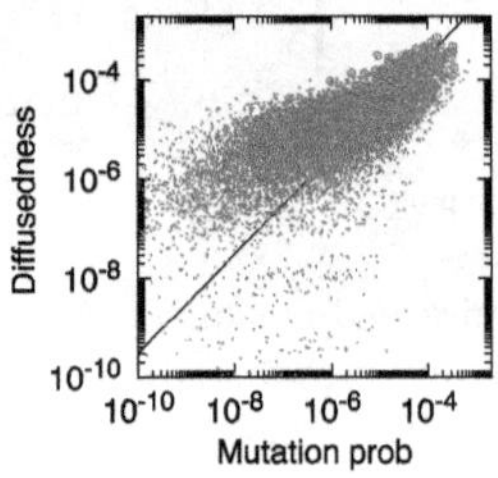

Fig. 5. Diffusedness $D^{10\mathrm{yr}}(w, t_w^\star)$ and mutation probability $P(w; S_{t_w^\star})$ for mutant segments w with the year of first appearance $t_w^\star \in [1960 : 2009]$. Segments that appeared four or more times within ten years after the first appearance are indicated by red circles. A linear function $y \propto x$ (black line) is shown as a guide for the eyes.

The relationship between the diffusedness and mutation probability analyzed for all mutant segments that first appeared in years between 1960 and 2009 is shown in Fig. 5. The observed high correlation ($\rho = 0.57$, $p < 10^{-10}$) supports our hypothesis, and the linear relation is particularly clear for mutant segments with highest diffusedness (marked in red circles in Fig. 5). The deviation from the linear relation in the small mutation probability regime can be explained by the finite size effect. We can also see that there is a variation of $O(10^1–10^2)$ in the diffusedness for those samples with a mutation probability $\sim 10^{-6}$, which indicates that the mutation probability cannot be the only factor that determines the diffusedness.

3.7 Predictions

The present evolutionary model can be used for predicting new segments to appear in the future. To examine its potential, we trained the model with a subset of the data of segments created in 1999 or before and evaluated its predictive ability using as test data the remaining data of segments created in years 2000–2019. We randomly generated 10^6 4-grams by the model and obtained approximately 2.6×10^5 segments after removing duplications and the samples already appearing in the training data. The generated 4-grams were sorted by the mutation probability in the decreasing order. We compared the predicted data with the test data by measuring the precision, recall, and F-score.

The recall achieved 48% on the whole predicted data (Fig. 6A). The precision was approximately 2%, which is much larger than the expectation value of 0.0004% by random sampling. Examples of predicted segments with highest mutation probabilities that were not included in the analyzed dataset are shown in Fig. 6B.

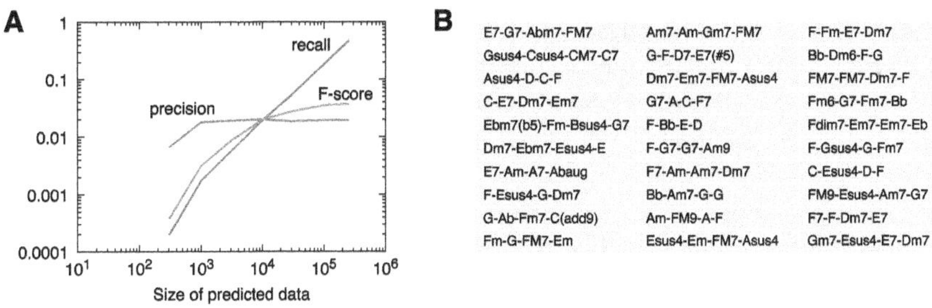

Fig. 6. Predictive ability of the evolutionary model. A: Prediction accuracies for varying sizes of predicted data. B: Most probable predictions by the evolutionary model.

4 Conclusion and Discussion

In this paper, we have studied the evolution of chord progressions based on a stochastic model of cultural evolution incorporating the selection and mutation processes. We summarize the main findings and discuss implications. First, the inferred selection biases showed a strong recency effect with a time constant of 2.61 yrs. This indicates that while chord segments are accumulated in the artifact pool, they will be effectively removed from the pool after some decades in the sense that their chance of being chosen as a reference will decrease significantly in that time interval. On the other hand, no significant sign of frequency dependence was observed.

Second, the analysis revealed large mutation rates and large dynamic changes in the substitution and insertion probabilities. The first feature reminds us of an interesting phenomenon known as the survival-of-the-flattest effect [25], which suggests the possibility that a chord segment with a high probability of replication can be outcompeted by segments that have lower probabilities of selection but are robust in usability against mutations. The second feature also suggests a selective advantage of chord segments that are robust in usability against mutations toward multiple directions. While the significance of this effect depends on the mutation rate and other model configurations, this observation may provide a new perspective on understanding why certain chord segments are more popular than others.

Third, the correlations found between fluctuation and mutation probabilities and between diffusedness and mutation probabilities support expectations from the evolutionary theory and may be useful for predicting the features of the evolutionary process. It is also important to seek for possible explanations for the observed deviations of $O(10^1\text{–}10^2)$ in the mutation probabilities for similar values of fluctuation probabilities.

We remark that although the present evolutionary model was build upon empirical knowledge on the process of music creation, the results of this study do not verify that the assumed process is correct. We can think of other processes of creating chord progressions, for example, a process involving data generation through statistical learning. To formulate a more realistic model, we should incorporate the multilevel structure of music, consisting of chord segments, musical piece, composer, etc.; reference and selection can occur at each of these levels. Japanese popular music is not a closed system and some chord progressions should have been imported from Western musical cultures; such migrations were treated as mutations in this study. Future work should experimentally test the model with other possibilities and address the aforementioned theoretical issues. The present evolutionary model can also be applied to analyzing the origins and relationships of chord segments in a similar way as the stochastic models of molecular evolution are applied to phylogenetic analysis.

Acknowledgments. The author thanks Hitomi Kaneko and Daichi Kamakura for useful discussions. This work was in part supported by JSPS KAKENHI Grant Numbers 21K12187, 21K02846, and 22H03661, and JST FOREST Program Grant Number JPMJPR226X.

References

1. Anglada-Tort, M., et al.: Large-scale iterated singing experiments reveal oral transmission mechanisms underlying music evolution. Curr. Biol. **33**(8), 1472-1486.e12 (2023)
2. Arenas, M.: Trends in substitution models of molecular evolution. Front. Genet. **6**(319), 1–9 (2015)
3. Boyd, R., Richerson, P.J.: Culture and the Evolutionary Process. The University of Chicago Press, Chicago (1985)
4. Cavalli-Sforza, L.L., Feldman, M.W.: Cultural Transmission and Evolution. Princeton University Press, Princeton (1981)
5. de Clercq, T., Temperley, D.: A corpus analysis of rock harmony. Pop. Music **30**(1), 47–70 (2011)
6. Felsenstein, J.: Evolutionary trees from DNA sequences: a maximum likelihood approach. J. Mol. Evol. **17**, 368–376 (1981)
7. Fernández, J.D., Vico, F.: AI methods in algorithmic composition: a comprehensive survey. J. Artif. Intell. Res. **48**, 513–582 (2013)
8. Hooktheory: Popular Chord Progressions. https://www.hooktheory.com/theorytab/common-chord-progressions
9. Interiano, M., et al.: Musical trends and predictability of success in contemporary songs in and out of the top charts. R. Soc. Open Sci. **5**(171274), 1–16 (2018)
10. Kimura, M.: On the probability of fixation of mutant genes in a population. Genetics **47**(6), 713–719 (1962)
11. Mauch, M., et al.: The evolution of popular music: USA 1960–2010. R. Soc. Open Sci. **2**(150081), 1–10 (2015)
12. McBride, J.M., Tlusty, T.: Cross-cultural data shows musical scales evolved to maximise imperfect fifths. Preprint https://doi.org/10.48550/arXiv.1906.06171 (2019)
13. Moss, F.C., Neuwirth, M., Rohrmeier, M.: The line of fifths and the co-evolution of tonal pitch-classes. J. Math. Music (2022)

14. Nakamura, E., Kaneko, K.: Statistical evolutionary laws in music styles. Sci. Rep. **9**(15993), 1–11 (2019)
15. Nakamura, E.: Conjugate distribution laws in cultural evolution via statistical learning. Phys. Rev. E **104**(034309), 1–13 (2021)
16. Savage, P.E., et al.: Sequence alignment of folk song melodies reveals cross-cultural regularities of musical evolution. Curr. Biol. **32**(6), 1395-1402.e8 (2022)
17. Scott, R.: Chord Progressions for Songwriters. iUniverse, Bloomington (2003)
18. Shiiba, K., Kubo, S. (eds.): Japanese Songs, vol. 3–9 (in Japanese). Nobarasha, Tokyo (1998/1999/2001/2004/2014)
19. Singh, R., Nakamura, E.: Dynamic cluster structure and predictive modelling of music creation style distributions. R. Soc. Open Sci. **9**(220516), 1–18 (2022)
20. Ravignani, A., Delgado, T., Kirby, S.: Musical evolution in the lab exhibits rhythmic universals. Nat. Hum. Behav. **1**(0007), 1–7 (2016)
21. Uehara, Y., Nakamura, E., Tojo, S.: Chord function identification with modulation detection based on HMM. In: Proceedings of the CMMR, pp. 59–70. The Laboratory PRISM, Marseille (2019)
22. Wang, D., Song, C., Barabási, A.L.: Quantifying long-term scientific impact. Science **342**(6154), 127–132 (2013)
23. Warrell, J., Salichos, L., Gerstein, M.: Latent evolutionary signatures: A general framework for analyzing music and cultural evolution. Preprint bioRxiv https://doi.org/10.1101/2020.10.23.352930 (2020)
24. Weiß, C., et al.: Investigating style evolution of Western classical music: a computational approach. Music Sci. **23**(4), 486–507 (2019)
25. Wilke, C.O., et al.: Evolution of digital organisms at high mutation rates leads to survival of the flattest. Nature **412**, 331–333 (2001)
26. Youngblood, M.: Conformity bias in the cultural transmission of music sampling traditions. R. Soc. Open Sci. **6**(191149), 1–8 (2019)
27. Zivic, P.H.R., Shifres, F., Cecchi, G.A.: Perceptual basis of evolving Western musical styles. Proc. Natl. Acad. Sci. USA **110**(24), 10034–10038 (2013)

Bipartite Network Analysis of the Stylistic Evolution of Sample-Based Music

Dongju Park and Juyong Park(✉)

Graduate School of Culture Technology, Korea Advanced Institute of Science and Technology, Daejeon, Republic of Korea
{pdj333,juyongp}@kaist.ac.kr

Abstract. In this study we present a network analysis of the communities of artists based on sampling. We construct a bipartite network between the artists who perform the sampling and the samples, then detect communities of the artists and the samples. We find that sample-based music has a clear community structure where each community features artists (nodes) with high centralities, allowing us to determine its musical style. We also define and visualize the similarities between communities representing distinct generations to observe how sample-based musical styles have evolved or been "handed off" to posterity. This study not only enhances our understanding of sampling-based music but also presents a novel application of network community structure to a creative enterprise such as music.

Keywords: sample-based music · bipartite network analysis · community detection · music style evolution

1 Introduction

Musical sampling is a technique used in popular music where one borrows some parts of existing recordings and incorporates them into new musical creations. Sampling can involve using any portion of a song, including the melody, drum parts, and vocals. While experimental music first began using sampling in the mid-20th century [10], it has since become extensively used in hip-hop, electronic, and pop music, particularly since the 1980s. The identity of sample-based music is profoundly related to the songs that were sampled. For instance, G-Funk, the dominant subgenre in West Coast hip-hop during the 90s, created its own rhythm by sampling George Clinton and other funk musicians [12]. Electronic music subgenres such as Jungle and Drum'n'Bass are built on the foundation of one of the most sampled songs in the world, "Amen, Brother." [8] As such, the sampling practice of an artist reflects the characteristics of the subgenre or the music community to which the artist belongs. Therefore, analyzing sampling relationships can help us comprehend the different musical styles in the in sample-based musical scene.

S. Ystad et al. (Eds.): CMMR 2023, LNCS 15236, pp. 218–226, 2026.
https://doi.org/10.1007/978-3-032-02042-0_16

Music sampling data is a form of metadata about music that represents the sampling relationships between songs. It is relational data that can be analyzed using network analysis. Many studies have used network analysis to quantitatively analyze musical metadata. Notably, Bryan and Wang [3] created a musical influence network of songs based on sampling relationships and analyzed the network to identify the most influential songs in sample-based music. In another study that analyzed musical sampling using network methodology, Youngblood [13] utilized a network diffusion model to verify the hypothesis that the diffusion of drum breaks, which play a significant role as key samples in sample-based music, occurred through collaborative networks. Unlike this study that focused on drum breaks, our study considers the relationships of all samples with artists, analyzing the community structure of sample-based music that goes further beyond the influence between individual pairs of songs.

Community detection is one of the most standard methods of network analysis. It can also be applied to an influence network based on sampling relationships to discover groups within sample-based music. To do this, we take a cue from studies on citation networks. Musical sampling and academic citation are comparable in that they credit past works for the production of current works [7]. The concept of Author Bibliographic Coupling (ABC) exists in citation analysis [14], a measure of similarity between two authors who cite the same paper. When the author is replaced with an artist and the paper with a song, the similarity between two artists who sampled the same song can be defined in the same fashion.

In this study, we analyze the community structure of sample-based music by constructing an artist-sample bipartite network. The community detected in this network can be understood as reflecting a style in the sample-based musical scene. Furthermore, we define similarities between generations of communities to investigate the stylistic evolution of sample-based music, which we then visualize.

2 Materials and Methods

2.1 Data and Network Construction

Our data set consists of a total of 333 090 sampling cases between 1980 and 2019 procured from WhoSampled.com. Each case consists of the sampling relationship between song pairs and their metadata (artist, genre, year of release). The total number of songs included in the dataset is 296 456. Each artist's genre is set to be the most common one among the artist's songs in the data set. Since there can be many styles within a genre, it is impossible to specify an artist's musical style by the genre tag alone. To overcome this, we collected the style tags shown on the artists' pages on Allmusic.com. Of the 42 969 sampling artists included in the sampling data, 14 124 style tags were collected. This low coverage is due to many of the artists who are relatively obscure not having been tagged.

In this study, the 40-year period from 1980 to 2019 was divided into five-year intervals, yielding a total of eight generations. The songs in the data set were assigned a generation by the year they were created. Then we constructed artist-sample bipartite networks inside each generation. The bipartite networks comprise two distinct node groups (artists and songs) with edges exclusively linking nodes between the opposing groups. Since an artist may sample a song multiple times, the network is weighted.

2.2 Community Detection

When dealing with bipartite networks, community detection is often performed on the one-mode projection of the bipartite network into a unipartite network [15]. Alternatively, community detection can be performed without such projection, preventing the loss of data but is not as widely used. Various modifications of 'modularity' have been proposed for bipartite networks, where modularity maximization is a popular method for community detection in unipartite networks. Modularity is an index that quantifies how many more connections are inside the community compared to random expectation. Here we utilized Barber's bimodularity [2], allowing both artist and sample nodes to be members of the same community, given as

$$Q = \frac{1}{w} \sum_{i} \sum_{j} \left(B_{ij} - \frac{d_{1,i} d_{2,j}}{w} \right) \delta_{c_{1,i}, c_{2,j}}, \qquad (1)$$

where B is the biadjacency matrix of the network, and w is the sum of the weights of all edges in the network. $d_{1,i}$, $d_{2,j}$ each denotes the degree of a node i of type 1 and j of type 2. And $\delta_{c_{1,i}, c_{2,j}}$ is 1 when the node i of type 1 and j of type 2 are in the same community, and 0 otherwise.

To maximize Barber's bimodularity, we used the biLouvain algorithm [9], a bipartite variant of the Louvain algorithm. The Louvain algorithm is a heuristic algorithm applicable to weighted networks and is computationally efficient. In this study, the communities can contain both artists and samples in them.

2.3 Defining Similarities Between Communities in Different Generations

The identity of the community can be determined from its samples; artists resample previously sampled songs to acquire sounds similar to previous works or to demonstrate respect for senior artists. Consequently, if two communities from distinct generations share samples, it is likely that the two communities show a similar style. The similarity between two communities of distinct generations can be computed based on this idea.

A community is a bipartite network consisting of artist nodes, sample nodes, and the edges connecting them. A network centrality can be utilized to determine the importance of the samples. The degree centrality is the most fundamental centrality, but it only takes into account the local network information and has trouble differentiating nodes with the same degree due to being an integer value. The HITS (Hypertext Induced Topic Selection) score is a centrality that incorporates nonlocal network information, and in this study, we employ the bipartite version of the HITS algorithm. HITS is a scoring algorithm for directed unipartite networks consisting of the 'hub' score and the 'authority' score. The hub score is the sum of the authority scores of nodes that the corresponding node points to, while the authority score is the sum of the hub scores of nodes that point to the corresponding node. This can be extended to the bipartite networks [6] where the score for each node can be defined as the sum of the scores of the nodes it is connected to. This can be expressed using the formula below, given as

$$p_j = \sum_{j=1}^{|U|} B_{ij} u_i ; u_i = \sum_{i=1}^{|P|} B_{ij} p_j, \tag{2}$$

where B is the biadjacency matrix of the network, and U and P are separate node sets. The final scores are normalized to 1.

To determine the similarity between two communities, we first identify the shared samples. Then we merge the two communities into a single network and calculate their HITS scores. Then we compute similarity between the two communities as the sum of the HITS scores of the shared samples:

$$HITS\_Sim(C_1, C_2) = \sum_{s \in S_1 \cap S_2} HITS_{\cup C}(s), \tag{3}$$

where $C_1 = \{A_1 \cup S_1, E_1\}$ and $C_2 = \{A_2 \cup S_2, E_2\}$. A_1 and A_2 are sets of artists and S_1 and S_2 are sets of samples. $\cup C$ is a union of communities C_1 and C_2.

3 Results

Table 1 shows the information on the networks belonging to the different five-year-long generations. While the numbers of nodes in each group exhibit an upward trend over time, the number of edges exhibits a greater degree of variation. Detection results indicate that the number of identified communities increases over time. Bimodularity, quantifying the strength of the community

Table 1. Network information and community detection results for each generation.

Generation	# of artists	# of samples	# of edges	# of communities	bimodularity
1980–1984	1060	2362	3460	465	0.884
1985–1989	3108	5614	19975	511	0.481
1990–1994	7871	14034	53916	966	0.491
1995–1999	9964	19196	46215	1761	0.667
2000–2004	8603	20874	36254	2521	0.784
2005–2009	9691	24147	41635	2785	0.777
2010–2014	14680	34469	63569	3805	0.757
2015–2019	15185	31002	53140	4369	0.827

structure, is comparatively low during the generations of 1985–1989 and 1990–1994 but increases subsequently.

The communities we derive from this study consist of artists and samples. Thus, a community is not simply a group of artists but can be considered as representing sample-based musical styles. We also identified artists and samples that played a significant role in the community (style) by calculating degree centrality, as the community evolved into another bipartite network. To better comprehend the musical styles of each community, we compiled the Allmusic style tags of each community's artists and designated the five most common tags as the community's main subgenres.

To investigate the evolution of sample-based music styles, we created a network of similarity between communities from successive generations. First, we see that the primary communities of each generation consist of more than 1% of the network's total nodes. The similarity between the primary communities of successive generations was then computed using the similarity index defined earlier. Finally, we constructed a network consisting of the primary communities of each generation as nodes and their similarity as edge weights. We set a threshold for the edge weights to visualize only connections above a certain level of similarity. Figure 1 depicts the network visualization resulting from a threshold value of 0.2. In terms of node labeling, for instance, '2_9599' represents the 2nd community of the 1995–1999 generation. The main subgenres of the primary communities visualized in Fig. 1 are presented in Table 2.

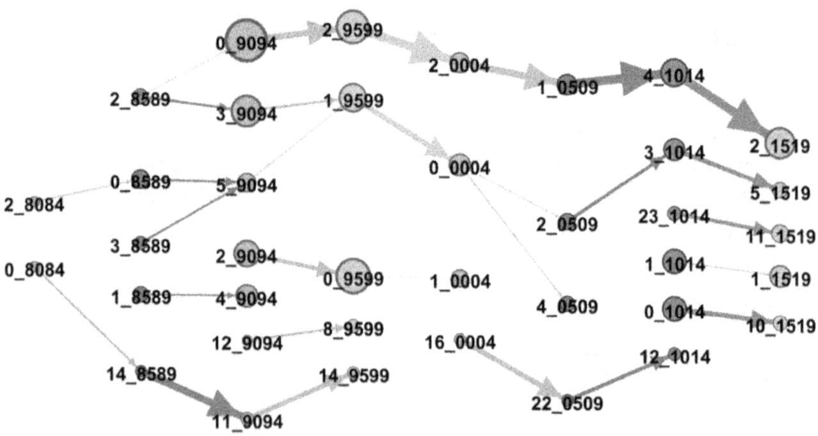

Fig. 1. Similarity network of primary communities in each generation. Edges exceeding the threshold 0.2 were excluded from visualization. The node size is proportional to the number of artists belonging to each community, and the thickness of the edge is proportional to the inter-community similarity. The color of nodes signifies the generation to which they belong. In terms of node labeling, for instance, '2_9599' represents the 2nd community of the 1995–1999 generation. (Color figure online)

Table 2. Main subgenres are the visualized primary communities in Fig. 1. The main subgenre of each community is determined by counting the style tags of artists belonging to the community.

comm.	main subgenre
0_8084	Dancehall, Roots Reggae, Ragga, Contemporary Reggae, Lovers Rock
2_8084	Golden Age, Old-School Rap, Electro, Alternative Pop/Rock, French
0_8589	Golden Age, Old-School Rap, Hardcore Rap, East Coast Rap, Club/Dance
1_8589	Club/Dance, House, Acid House, Dance-Pop, Techno
2_8589	Pop-Rap, Golden Age, East Coast Rap, Party Rap, Hardcore Rap
3_8589	Party Rap, Club/Dance, Bass Music, Quiet Storm, Modern Electric Blues
14_8589	Dancehall, Ragga, Roots Reggae, Contemporary Reggae, Lovers Rock
0_9094	Club/Dance, Jungle/Drum'n'Bass, Techno, House, Rave
2_9094	Gangsta Rap, Hardcore Rap, West Coast Rap, G-Funk, East Coast Rap
3_9094	Hardcore Rap, Pop-Rap, Golden Age, Contemporary R&B, East Coast Rap
4_9094	Club/Dance, House, Dance-Pop, Acid House, Euro-Dance
5_9094	Club/Dance, Party Rap, Bass Music, Southern Rap, Pop-Rap
11_9094	Dancehall, Ragga, Contemporary Reggae, Reggae-Pop, Club/Dance
12_9094	Hardcore Rap, Gangsta Rap, Southern Rap, Underground Rap, Dirty South
0_9599	Gangsta Rap, Hardcore Rap, West Coast Rap, G-Funk, Pop-Rap
1_9599	Club/Dance, Turntablism, Underground Rap, Hardcore Rap, East Coast Rap
2_9599	Club/Dance, Jungle/Drum'n'Bass, Techno, Hardcore Techno, Electronica
8_9599	Hardcore Rap, Gangsta Rap, Dirty South, Southern Rap, Adult Contemporary
14_9599	Dancehall, Contemporary Reggae, Ragga, Alternative Pop/Rock, Roots Reggae
0_0004	Alternative Rap, Hardcore Rap, Underground Rap, East Coast Rap, Turntablism
1_0004	Hardcore Rap, East Coast Rap, Gangsta Rap, Pop-Rap, West Coast Rap
2_0004	Jungle/Drum'n'Bass, Club/Dance, Techno, Electronica, IDM
16_0004	Contemporary R&B, Club/Dance, House, French House, Pop
1_0509	Jungle/Drum'n'Bass, Club/Dance, Garage, Breakcore, Dubstep
2_0509	Hardcore Rap, Alternative Rap, Alternative/Indie Rock, Underground Rap, French Rap
4_0509	Hardcore Rap, East Coast Rap, Alternative Rap, Trip-Hop, Club/Dance
22_0509	Pop, Dance-Pop, Adult Contemporary, Teen Pop, Contemporary R&B
0_1014	Southern Rap, Hardcore Rap, Pop-Rap, Gangsta Rap, East Coast Rap
1_1014	Pop, Alternative/Indie Rock, Club/Dance, Indie Electronic, EDM
3_1014	Hardcore Rap, East Coast Rap, Political Rap, Golden Age, Heavy Metal
4_1014	Club/Dance, Jungle/Drum'n'Bass, Dubstep, Garage, House
12_1014	Midwest Rap, Hardcore Rap, Left-Field Rap, Alternative Rap, French Rap
23_1014	Club/Dance, House, EDM, Dubstep, Pop-Rap
1_1519	Pop, Dance-Pop, Alternative Rap, Left-Field Rap, Acappella
2_1519	Club/Dance, Jungle/Drum'n'Bass, Dubstep, House, Garage
5_1519	Polish, Hardcore Rap, Central European Traditions, East Coast Rap, Political Rap
10_1519	West Coast Rap, Contemporary R&B, Left-Field Rap, Pop-Rap, Gangsta Rap
11_1519	Club/Dance, EDM, Pop, House, Downtempo

In Fig. 1, a significant path is observed from 0_9094 to 2_1519 (top of the figure). These communities represent Jungle and Drum'n'Bass, which are breakbeat-based subgenres of electronic music ('Jungle/Drum'n'Bass') [8]. Since these communities represent the largest electronic music samples of each generation, we can intuitively see that breakbeat-based music dominates sample-based electronic music. Breakbeat uses drum breaks included in funk, jazz, and R&B music, and the most famous drum break is "Amen, Brother" released by The Winstons. This song has been sampled the most across all communities on path. Other prominent drum breaks, such as those from Lyn Collins' "Think (About It)," Bobby Byrd's "Hot Pants," and Incredible Bongo Band's "Apache," are commonly found on each community's list of the top samples. Thus, the drum break, utilized primarily in breakbeat-based music, is fixed and can be seen to have been utilized throughout time.

Community 1_9599 is notable as well. The predecessors of Community 1_9599 refer to those that represent the old-school hip-hop style, including samples such as Beside's "Change the Beat (Female Version)" and James Brown's "Funky Drummer." Specifically, "Change the Beat (Female Version)" is the most sampled song in the world and can be considered an iconic old-school hip-hop sample utilized in DJ scratch performances [5]. Community 1_9599 represents turntablism and underground hip-hop styles focused on famous hip-hop DJs ('Turntablism', 'Underground Rap') and illustrates the success of turntablism music in the late 1990s [4]. The successors of 1_9599 can be considered to be the genres that retain the essence of classic hip-hop. Therefore, it is notable that the path following Community 2_0509 is dominated by Polish hip-hop artists [1]. In recent years, artists inheriting the old-school hip-hop style have emerged more frequently in Europe, especially Poland, than in the U.S.

Also identified is a path connecting 0_8084 → 14_8589 → 11_9094 → 14_9599 (bottom left of the figure). These communities are synonymous with reggae music. Reggae is also a sampling-based music genre, like hip-hop and electronic music, primarily sampling prior reggae music [11]. Before 1980, when hip-hop was born, reggae was the major music type. Reggae songs such as "Funaany" by Admiral Bailey, "Full Up", "Drum Song" by Jackie Mittoo, and "Real Rock" by Sound Dimension were frequently sampled in each community. The fact that this path was cut off in the 1995–1999 generation suggests that the sampling reggae became much less popular in the 00's.

4 Conclusions

In this study we investigated the community structure of sample-based music post-1980 using bipartite network analysis. We constructed the sampling networks for each of the eight five-year-long generations and then conducted community detection. The communities established in this manner were shown to be representing a style.

Our analysis focused on two significant sample-based music genres, electronic music and hip-hop. Jungle and Drum'n'Bass are the subgenres of electronic music that use a style that incorporates breakbeats. Since there are only a few types of breakbeats, we showed that the Jungle/Drum'n'Bass communities in each generation have strong ties. We also observed that the old-school hip-hop style, which has persisted since the 1980s, is diverging into multiple branches and that non-European artists, such as those from Poland, continue to use this style into the 2000s.

In the future we intend to increase our understanding of sample-based music styles by conducting a more comprehensive analysis of the artists and genre information of the derived communities. We may also vary the time unit used to divide generations in order to conduct analyses on a different scale. Moreover, by varying the edge weight threshold when visualizing the similarity network of consecutive primary communities, we may observe the evolution of sample-based music genres in more detail. Lastly, we could investigate generation-skipping transmission of musical styles by analyzing the similarity between two communities separated by more than one generation, which could show how the phenomenon of "revival" of musical styles occurs.

Acknowledgments. This research was supported by Korea Creative Content Agency (RS-2023-00270043), the National Research Foundation of Korea Grant (RS-2023-00245361 and NRF-2020S1A5C2A03093177), KAIST Post-AI Research Grant, and BK 21 FOUR Program for Content Science.

Disclosure of Interests. The authors have no competing interests to declare that are relevant to the content of this article.

References

1. Aniskiewicz, A.G.: Cultural remix: Polish hip-hop and the sampling of heritage. Ph.D. dissertation, University of Michigan (2019)
2. Barber, M.J.: Modularity and community detection in bipartite networks. Phys. Rev. E **76**(6) (2007)
3. Bryan, N., Wang, G.: Musical influence network analysis and rank of sample-based music. In: Proceedings of the 12th International Society for Music Information Retrieval Conference, ISMIR 2011, pp. 329–334 (2011)
4. Greasley, A.E., Prior, H.M.: Mixtapes and turntablism: DJs' perspectives on musical shape. Empir. Musicol. Rev., 23–43 (2013)
5. Hansen, K.F.: The basics of scratching. J. New Music Res. **31**(4), 357–65 (2002)
6. He, X., Gao, M., Kan, M.Y., Wang, D.: BiRank: towards ranking on bipartite graphs. IEEE Trans. Knowl. Data Eng. **29**(1), 57–71 (2016)
7. Hess, M.: Was Foucault a plagiarist? Hip-hop sampling and academic citation. Comput. Compos. **23**(3), 280–295 (2006)
8. Hockman, J., Davies, M., Fujinaga, I.: One in the jungle: downbeat detection in hardcore, jungle, and drum and bass. In: Proceedings of the 13th International Society for Music Information Retrieval (ISMIR), Porto (2012)
9. Pesantez-Cabrera, P., Kalyanaraman, A.: Detecting communities in biological bipartite networks. In: Proceedings of the 7th ACM International Conference on Bioinformatics, Computational Biology, and Health Informatics (2016)

10. Roads, C.: Early electronic music instruments: time line 1899-1950. Comput. Music J. **20**(3) (1996)
11. Veal, M.: Dub: Soundscapes and Shattered Songs in Jamaican Reggae. Wesleyan University Press, Middletown (2013)
12. Williams, J.A.: You never been on a ride like this Befo': Los Angeles, automotive listening, and Dr. Dre's 'G-Funk'. Popular Music History **4**(2) (2010)
13. Youngblood, M.: Cultural transmission modes of music sampling traditions remain stable despite delocalization in the digital age. PLoS ONE **14**(2), e0211860 (2019)
14. Zhao, D., Strotmann, A.: Evolution of research activities and intellectual influences in information science 1996–2005: introducing author bibliographic-coupling analysis. J. Am. Soc. Inform. Sci. Technol. **59**(13), 2070–86 (2008)
15. Zhou, T., Ren, J., Medo, M., Zhang, Y.C.: Bipartite network projection and personal recommendation. Phys. Rev. E **76**(4) (2007)

On the Analysis of Voicing Novelty in Classical Piano Music

Halla Kim and Juyong Park(✉)

Graduate School of Culture Technology (GSCT), Korea Advanced Institute of Science and Technology (KAIST), 291 Daehak-ro, Yuseong-gu, Daejeon 34141, Republic of South Korea
{kimhalla,juyongp}@kaist.ac.kr

Abstract. Musical composition can be viewed as an act of conditional problem solving, the realization of musical ideas by arranging notes spatially and temporally. The resulting creations may constitute the unique style of the composer. In this paper we focus on how chord voicing – the expression of chords by choosing and stacking musical notes – has evolved in western classial piano music using large-scale music datasets. Our results shows that the level and variety of voicing novelty have increased throughout history. We also find that some composers exhibit a high level of voicing novelty due to the utilization of innovative pitch class sets, while others actually have pushed the boundaries of voicing with traditional pitch class sets. This study helps us to probe the emergence of expression of musical style on note level and to understand the evolutionary pattern of note arrangements.

Keywords: musical style · voicing · evolution · novelty

1 Introduction

Musical composition can be viewed as a process of conditional problem solving: Composers' creations reflect their musical ideas by way of the selection and arrangements of such musical elements as melody, rhythm, harmony, and structure, which results the creations manifesting their particular musical styles [7]. In this paper we investigate in particular chord voicing – how musical notes are vertically arranged to express a given harmonic scheme – which is the core element of harmonic progression often called the fundamental task in Western musical composition [4]. For example, a fundamental voice-leading rules in classical music of dominant to tonic chord is realized in different ways: A Pitch Class set (hereafter PC-set) movement from $\{G, B, D\}$ to $\{C, E\}$ can be written either as $(G3, D4, B4)$ followed by $(C3, E4, C5)$ or $(B2, G3, D5)$ followed by $(C3, E3, C5)$ chosen by the composer.

By uncovering the historical compositional patterns of voicing, here we inspect how they developed over time. Previous works on musical novelty showed the stylistic evolution or the sweetspot in terms of success, including Park et

S. Ystad et al. (Eds.): CMMR 2023, LNCS 15236, pp. 227–235, 2026.
https://doi.org/10.1007/978-3-032-02042-0_17

al. [13] who showed that musical periods can be characterized by the novelty and influence of composers of each era. Similarly, the predictability of subsequent chords is measured by exploring chord transition probability [9], whereas the time of musical revolutions can be traced where novelty of harmonic and timbre properties change drastically [8]. Other symbolic features such as melodic intervals [12] or triads [14] are also shown to be effective for identifying styles and distinguishing musical eras. Weiß et al. [15] observed that the frequency of tritones and tonal complexity have steadily increased over the history of Western classical music. Nakamura and Kaneko [10] developed a statistical evolutionary model that fits the frequency data of tritones and that of non-diatonic motions where the creators and the evaluators coevolve through a function of novelty and typicality in a process of social selection. Finally, O'Toole and Horvát [11] used audio features to evaluate novelty and asserted that optimal level of differentiation is needed to become the most popular song. Few, however, have explicitly examined chord voicing (the vertical placement of pc-sets), with Harrison and Pearce [4] being an exception who introduced a computational framework of voicing. They suggested a mathematical model to calculate the probability of choosing the next voicing given current voicing according to pre-defined perceptual rules of chord voicing. In this paper, we try to investigate the very fundamental aspect of voicing; we hypothesize that novel ways of placing notes have been developed that characterize the style of composer and musical era.

2 Methodology

2.1 Dataset

The data used in our analysis were collected mainly from three online sources[1], and consist of 1 017 piano compositions by 40 historically prominent composers in MIDI format. We follow the common convention of dividing the history of classical music into the following five periods: Baroque, Classical, Romantic, Post-Romantic, and Modern, and specifically use All Music Guide[2] to tag the year of compositions and the era to which the composers belong.

2.2 Key Normalization

The objective of key normalization is to treat the notes equally that serve identical harmonic functions, irrespective of their absolute pitch, to promote consistency. For example, the harmonic role of the chord $C = \{C, E, G\}$ in C major is identical to that of the chord $F = \{F, A, C\}$ in F major. The key of each composition in the dataset was estimated using the Krumhansl-Schmuckler key detection algorithm [6]. This algorithm compares the pitch class distribution of a given piece of music with the key profiles obtained from music-cognitive experiments [5], and selects the key with the highest Pearson correlation among the

[1] http://www.piano-midi.de, https://www.classicalarchives.com, http://www.kunstderfuge.com.

[2] http://www.allmusic.com.

24 possible keys. If the highest Pearson correlation coefficient value refers to an outlier among the values for the whole song, key normalization was not performed since the algorithm's key estimation is unreliable. Any number that falls outside of the first quartile (Q1) or above the third quartile (Q3) by more than 1.5 times the interquartile range (IQR=Q3-Q1) was considered an outlier. After the key of each composition was estimated, all non-outlier major compositions were transposed to C major, and minor compositions to A minor (Fig. 1). It is clear from Fig. 1 that the comparatively high non-diatonic frequency is a result of outlier songs that would have chromatic scales or key modulation.

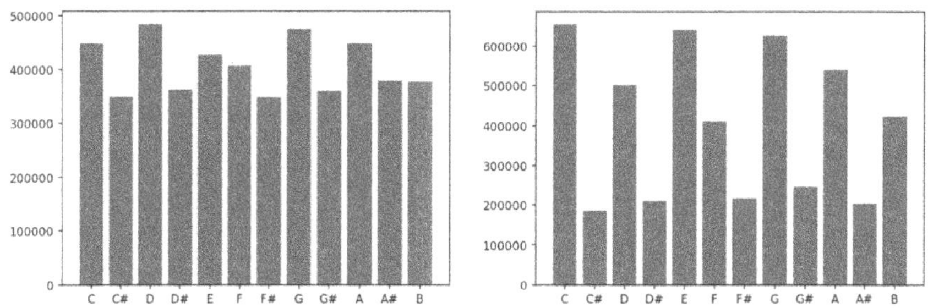

Fig. 1. Pitch class distribution of the dataset before and after key normalization.

2.3 Encoding of Voicing

Voicing refers to the simultaneous vertical placement of notes in relation to each other [2][3].or assigning pitch heights to pitch classes [4]. To conduct voicing analysis, we first encode each musical composition as a series of group of notes played simultaneously (which we call codewords) [1]. Next, we focus on the voicing of each codeword to calculate the novelty of the voicing used by composers. While there is an issue of not being able to clearly distinguish between voicing and harmonic skeleton [4], here we model a composer as choosing the pc-set first then subsequently determining the voicing as an elaboration or an embellishment.

Voicing Encoding Given a PC-Set. When regarding the voicing as an implementation of a pitch class set, we can express the probability of choosing a voicing v_i given a pitch class set s_i, as

$$P(v_i|s_i) = \frac{z(s_i \rightarrow v_i) + \alpha(s_i \rightarrow v_i)}{\sum_{v \in V(s_i)} z(s_i \rightarrow v) + \alpha(s_i \rightarrow v)}, v_i \in V(s_i) \tag{1}$$

where $V(s_i)$ is the set of all possible voicings for a pc-set s_i, $z(s_i \rightarrow v_i)$ the number of occurrences of voicings v_i that have a pc-set s_i, and α is a constant

[3] Another definition of voicing, a placement of notes among various instruments, does not fit to our analysis since we only address musical pieces for piano solo.

representing an uninformed prior, a type of additive Laplace smoothing. Setting $\alpha = 1$ means that every conceivable voicing element in $V(s_i)$ has a finite chance of being chosen [13]. Let us take an example of a pc-set $s_i = \{C, E, G\}$. This pc-set's possible voicings $V(s_i)$ includes $v_i = (C4, E4, G4), (E4, G4, C5), (C3, E3, G3)$ etc. The total number of all possible voicings is equal to the number of piano key combinations available in a given pc-set. Note that the two voicings $(C4, E4, G4)$ and $(C3, E3, G3)$ differ by an octave. To discard octave position and only handle the relative spacing between notes, we use the voicing notation as the pitch interval between adjacent notes starting from the bass note (Fig. 2).

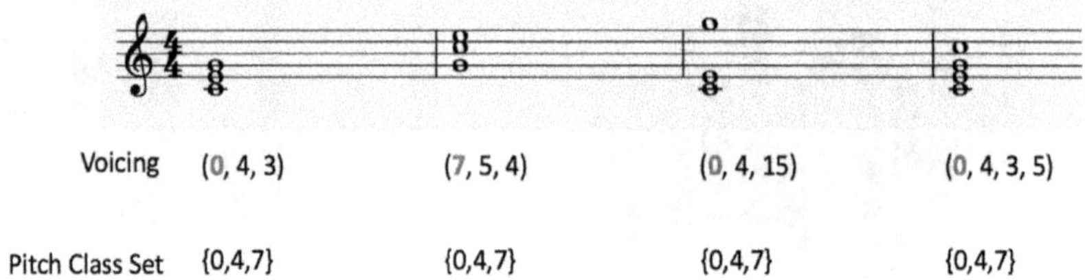

Fig. 2. Example of voicing and pc-set notation

2.4 Calculating Voicing Novelty

To see how the voicing style has evolved, we first measure the novelty of voicing. Representing a composition as a sequence of codewords (configuration of voicings) $\zeta = \{v_1, v_2, \ldots, v_m\}$, we can write the generation probability of ζ as first-order Markov chain

$$\Pi(\zeta) = P(v_1|s_1)P(v_2|s_2)\ldots P(v_m|s_m) \tag{2}$$

Its log inverse is the magnitude of surprise in information theory. We can thus quantify the novelty in voicing as an average unexpectedness of all voicings in a composition normalized by the length of a composition m:

$$Novelty(\zeta) = \frac{1}{m} log \frac{1}{\Pi(\zeta)} = \frac{1}{m}\left[\sum_{k=1}^{m} log \frac{1}{P(v_k|s_k)}\right] \tag{3}$$

2.5 Calculating PC-Set Novelty

Here we discuss the pc-set and compare it with voicing novelty. PC-set novelty measures how novel the current codeword's pc-set is when the preceding codeword's pc-set is given. Representing a composition as a sequence of codewords' pc-set, $\zeta = \{s_1, s_2, \ldots, s_m\}$,the probability of choosing a pc-set s_{i+1} after a pc-set s_i is written as,

$$P(s_{i+1}|s_i) = \frac{z(s_i \rightarrow s_{i+1}) + \alpha(s_i \rightarrow s_{i+1})}{\sum_{k \in S} z(s_i \rightarrow k) + \alpha(s_i \rightarrow k)}, s_i \in S \quad (4)$$

where S is the set of all possible pc-sets, $z(s_i \rightarrow s_{i+1})$ the number of occurrences of pc-set transition from s_i to s_{i+1}. Then the pc-set novelty can be acquired by plugging Eq. 5 into Eq. 6.

$$\Pi(\zeta) = P(s_1)P(s_2|s_1)\dots P(s_m|s_{m-1}) \quad (5)$$

$$Novelty(\zeta) = \frac{1}{m} log \frac{1}{\Pi(\zeta)} = \frac{1}{m}\left[log \frac{1}{P(s_1)} + \sum_{k=1}^{m-1} log \frac{1}{P(s_{k+1}|s_k)}\right] \quad (6)$$

3 Results

By examining the usage patterns of both the pc-set and the voicing of codewords, we investigate the composing style of Western classical composers. In the dataset the total number of codewords is 1 230 441, and its unique number of pc-set and voicing set were 4 071 and 209 439, respectively. Note that we only include codewords that consist of at least two notes. PC-set distribution is significantly skewed, which suggests that only a tiny portion of pc-set are employed for composition while the majority is rarely used (Fig. 3). The distribution of voicing is less skewed than that of the pc-set; the maximum frequency of voicing usage is less than 10^2 whereas the highest frequency of the pc-set is much more than 10^4. We decide to display the voicings of both {0,4,7} and {0,4,9} since they are the tonic chords of the normalized key and are included in the top five most often used pc-sets (Table 1). The second column shows the top five voicings of pc-set {0,4,7} (i.e. {C,E,G}) and the third column shows the top five voicings of pc-set {0,4,9}, i.e. {C,E,A}.

Table 1. Top five frequently used pitch class sets and voicings of two representative pitch class sets.

Rank	Pitch class set	Voicing of {0,4,7}	Voicing of {0,4,9}
1	{0,4,7}	(4,3,5)	(0,4,5)
2	{0,4}	(0,4,3)	(9,3,4)
3	{0,4,9}	(7,5,4)	(4,5,3)
4	{0,7}	(0,7,9)	(9,3,4,5)
5	{4,7}	(0,4,3,5)	(9,7,8)

The heterogeneity in the use of pc-sets provides clues for interpreting the two novelties that we ultimately seek to analyze. Figure 4 displays pc-set novelty

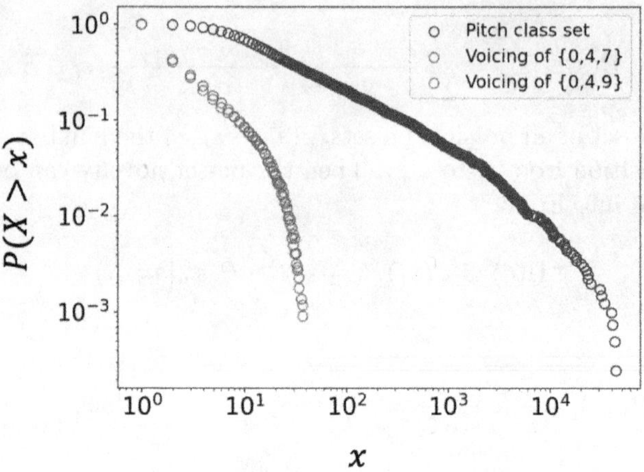

Fig. 3. The cumulative distribution on a log-log scale of the occurrences of pc-sets, voicing of {0,4,7}, and voicing of {0,4,9}. The frequency of pc-sets or voicing is represented on the horizontal axis, while the cumulative probability is represented on the vertical axis.

and voicing novelty for composers, arranged chronologically based on the average years of birth and death. Composers like Couperin and Handel showed a high level of pc-set novelty in their works due to the advantages of their time, and this remained consistent until later composers such as Elgar, Berg, Schoenberg, and Messiaen introduced new pc-sets, leading to greater variation. This figure agrees with Fig. 1(a) of Nakamura and Kaneko [10] which depicts the steadily increasing mean and standard deviation of tritone frequency, as tritone is one of the examples of historically important pc-sets. Similarly, increasing voicing novelty in later generations is a noticeable trend, with some prominent composers exemplifying it. When several new pc-sets are employed, the voicing novelty can rise only by virtue of the pc-set itself, or it can also increase if unique vertical arrangements are made using traditional pc-sets. These are the two scenarios where voicing novelty can be high. In order to identify the driving cause behind high voicing novelty, we computed the new pc-set ratio and new voicing ratio for each song. New pc-set ratio is the unique number of new pc-sets that were not used in the previous songs divided by the total unique number of pc-sets in a given song. It refers to the ratio of innovative pc-sets that the composer has chosen. New voicing ratio is the unique number of voicings for which the pc-set has already been used in previous songs but the present voicing is used for the first time in a given song, divided by the total unique number of voicings in a given song. The new voicing ratio serves as a metric to gauge the extent of reconfiguration undergone by existing pc-sets, as it specifically signifies the proportion of instances involving entirely novel voicings. According to Fig. 4, while Handel exhibited the highest degree of pc-set novelty among all composers, benefiting from an early temporal advantage, Bach, despite sharing a similar advantage, displayed significantly lower pc-set novelty. This observation highlights Bach's propensity for predominantly composing using existing pc-sets. Composers such as Elgar, Berg, and Schoenberg, despite being situated in subsequent eras, stand out as instances where both the new pc-set ratio and new voicing ratio are elevated, resulting in pronounced levels of pc-set novelty and voicing novelty. With the exception of a few later composers who introduced a significant number of new pc-sets, the majority enhanced the novelty of chordal expressions by creatively reconfiguring existing pc-set tones. Brahms compared to Beethoven serve as an example. Despite using a smaller percentage of new pc-set than Beethoven, Brahms had a greater new voicing ratio than Beethoven, which resulted in a higher level of voicing novelty (Fig. 4). In this way, through the comparison of the ratios and novelty values of new pc-sets and voicings in each composition, it becomes possible to explore how the chordal expression in Western classical piano music has evolved uniquely for each composer.

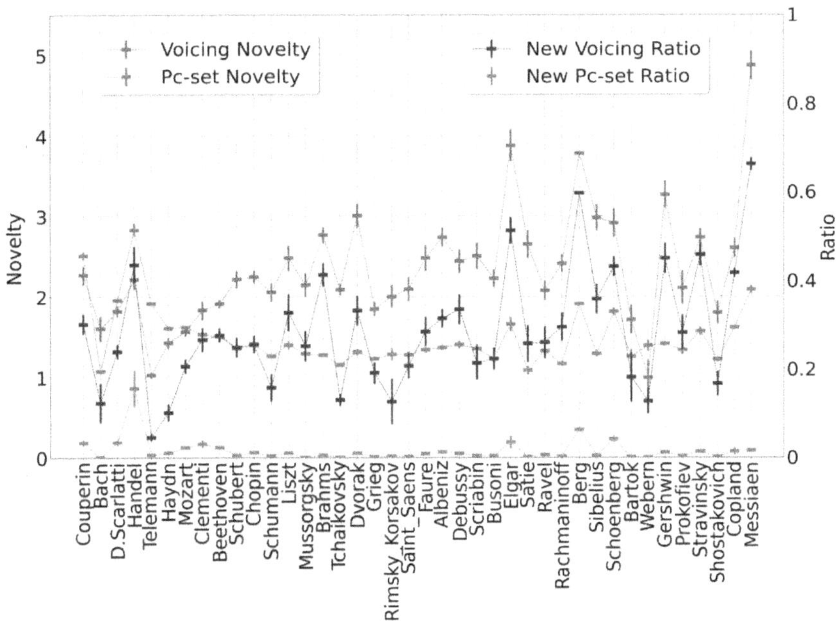

Fig. 4. Voicing novelty scores of all composers. A jackknife resampling error is indicated by an error bar. The mean of the birth year and death year was used to determine the representative year of composers on the x-axis.

4 Conclusion

In this paper, we studied the compositional style of Western classical piano pieces, with a particular focus on chord voicing – the vertical arrangement of notes within a set of pitch classes. Despite using the same set of pitch classes, altering the octave's location, the arrangement's sequence, or the distance between notes might result in a significantly different sound. We first encoded the voicing for each codeword, computed the voicing novelty, and then looked at the historical evolution of voicings to understand how composers chose and arranged notes. In Western classical piano music, voicing novelty exhibited a consistent upward trend over time, accompanied by an increasing divergence among composers. Early composers introduced a number of popular pc-sets that were widely used by later composers. Later composers mainly increased the novelty of the song by vertically arranging the pre-existing pc-set, with the exception of Elgar, Berg, and Schoenberg who used a sizable portion of novel pc-sets. Our examination of compositional trends among different composers reveals distinct patterns of novelty in their approach to chordal expression in Western classical piano music. As our study continues, we plan to explore the historical evolution of compositional style and how composers create their unique styles through influence scores of voicing, contributing to the understanding of musical styles at the note level using symbolic music data.

Acknowledgements. This research was supported by Korea Creative Content Agency funded by the Korean Government (RS-2023-00270043) and the National Research Foundation of Korea (NRF-2020S1A5C2A03093177 and RS-2023-00245361).

Disclosure of Interests. The authors declare that they have no competing interests.

References

1. Conklin, D.: Representation and discovery of vertical patterns in music. In: Anagnostopoulou, C., Ferrand, M., Smaill, A. (eds.) ICMAI 2002. LNCS (LNAI), vol. 2445, pp. 32–42. Springer, Heidelberg (2002). https://doi.org/10.1007/3-540-45722-4_5
2. Corozine, V.: Arranging Music for the Real World. Mel Bay Publications (2015)
3. Hanford, L., A theory of Voice Leading for Music of the Classical Period. Yale University (1984)
4. Harrison, P.M., Pearce, M.T.: A computational cognitive model for the analysis and generation of voice leadings. Music. Percept. **37**(3), 208–224 (2020)
5. Krumhansl, C.L., Kessler, E.J.: Tracing the dynamic changes in perceived tonal organization in a spatial representation of musical keys. Psychol. Rev. **89**(4), 334 (1982)
6. Krumhansl, C.L.: Cognitive Foundations of Musical Pitch. Oxford University Press, New York (1990)
7. LaRue, J.: On style analysis. J. Music Theory **6**(1), 91–107 (1962)
8. Mauch, M., MacCallum, R.M., Levy, M., Leroi, A.M.: The evolution of popular music: USA 1960–2010. R Soc. Open Sci. **2**, 150081 (2015)
9. Moss, F.C., Neuwirth, M., Harasim, D., Rohrmeier, M.: Statistical characteristics of tonal harmony: a corpus study of Beethoven's string quartets. PLoS ONE **14**(6), e0217242 (2019)
10. Nakamura, E., Kaneko, K.: Statistical evolutionary laws in music styles. Sci. Rep. **9**(1), 15993 (2019)

11. O'Toole, K., Horvát, E.Á.: Novelty and cultural evolution in modern popular music. EPJ Data Sci. **12**(1), 3 (2023)
12. Rodriguez Zivic, P.H., Shifres, F., Cecchi, G.A.: Perceptual basis of evolving Western musical styles. Proc. Natl. Acad. Sci. **110**(24), 10034–10038 (2013)
13. Park, D., Nam, J., Park, J.: Novelty and influence of creative works, and quantifying patterns of advances based on probabilistic references networks. EPJ Data Sci. **9**(1), 1–15 (2020). https://doi.org/10.1140/epjds/s13688-019-0214-8
14. Weiß, C., Mauch, M., Dixon, S.: Timbre-invariant audio features for style analysis of classical music (2014)
15. Weiß, C., Mauch, M., Dixon, S., Müller, M.: Investigating style evolution of Western classical music: a computational approach. Music Sci. **23**(4), 486–507 (2019)

Computational Musicology

Interpretable Rule Learning and Evaluation of Early Twentieth-Century Music Styles

Christofer Julio[1,3], Feng-Hsu Lee[2], and Li Su[3(✉)]

[1] Social Networks and Human-Centered Computing, Taiwan International Graduate Program, Taipei, Taiwan

[2] Faculty of Creative Arts, University of Malaya, Kuala Lumpur, Malaysia
fenghsulee@um.edu.my

[3] Institute of Information Science, Academia Sinica, Taipei City, Taiwan
lisu@iis.sinica.edu.tw

Abstract. The paper discusses the classification of four music styles, Serialism, Impressionism, Neoclassicism, and Nationalism, of early-twentieth-century music using interpretable rule learning techniques. Three interpretable rule learning techniques are considered: decision tree, minimum description length (MDL) rule list, and rule set (the skope-rule algorithm). The features of the classifiers are fundamental musical elements based on pitch and interval distributions. Objective evaluation based on the F1 score and subjective evaluation using user study is conducted to understand the result of our classifiers from the musicians' point of view. The results show that a rule set is preferred as the algorithm attained the highest scores for objective and subjective evaluations. The rule set can also generate rules which support music theory and provide new insights regarding the musical characteristics of early twentieth-century music.

Keywords: early twentieth-century music · interpretable AI · rule learning · evaluation · music information retrieval

1 Introduction

The studies regarding the classification task of classical music have undergone major development in the last few years. Multiple machine learning classifiers, from transparent models such as decision trees [12] to black-box models such as support vector machines [11,12,24] and more sophisticated neural networks [15,16,18,23,27], have been utilized and have effectively classified classical music across periods. In addition to focusing on good performance, another research endeavor has focused on interpretability, that is, the extent to which the process by which a model arrives at its decision is transparent and understandable by humans [12,28].

Despite abundant research on classical music classification, few studies include composers from the early twentieth century. Instead of labeling the early twentieth-century compositions based on their respective styles, most researchers

S. Ystad et al. (Eds.): CMMR 2023, LNCS 15236, pp. 239–251, 2026.
https://doi.org/10.1007/978-3-032-02042-0_18

label the composers around this period as "modern" [23,25]. This "modern" label may not be enough to become an accurate representation. The early twentieth-century period in classical music consists of various musical genres âĂŞ each highly distinctive from the others. Musicologists often categorize these styles as *-isms* [4,7].

Indeed, early twentieth-century music has a few common concepts. For instance, the composers avoid constructed melodies from the previous periods and do not follow the standard tonal harmony [4,5]. However, the approaches that each style made differ significantly from one another. Serialism, for instance, focuses on utilizing pitch set series or tone rows [1,4]. Impressionism does not neglect tonality but maximizes the utilization of timbres, layers, underdeveloped motifs, unresolved harmony, and exotic music scales [4,5]. Nonetheless, Neoclassicism combines the characteristics of music in the previous periods with modern melody and dissonance treatments. [8,17]. Conducting the classification tasks over these music styles would be insightful due to the unique characteristics of early twentieth-century music and the scarcity of study for this period.

Instead of focusing on performance alone, this study aims more into the interpretability of the result [21]. We want to see whether there is any new insight regarding the characteristics of early twentieth-century music, which may not be found using conventional music analysis. Our research objectives are motivated by the previous studies that have shown the potential to find new insights into classical music, such as the difference in pitch distribution between Mozart and Haydn's string quartet works [11] or the differences in interval utilization between Beethoven and the composers before him, such as Haydn and Bach [12]. On the contrary, the interpretable deep learning approaches for music classification and analysis [13,26] mostly focus on *post hoc* interpretation [21] over the learned representations and still require decision trees, rules, and linear models to explain it under specific situations [10]. Therefore, we take the approach of rule-based, transparent, and *simulatable* (i.e., humans can reason about the entire decision-making process of the model [21]) models instead of black-box ones. Moreover, in this paper, we extensively study various categories of rule-based models, including rule tree, rule list, and rule set [20]. Besides the well-known decision tree, it should be noted that the rule list and rule set models we employed have yet to be considered in music classification problems [9,22]. For evaluating the result, we perform not only objective evaluation but also subjective evaluation to understand the human's perceptions regarding the rules generated by the models.

To our knowledge, this paper is the first attempt to machine learning classification of early twentieth-century music. This paper has three major aims. First, we propose a new dataset regarding early-twentieth-century music in symbolic format. Second, we investigate various rule-based machine learning models for music style classification on this new dataset. Lastly, the interpretability of the classification results and the selected rules and features are analyzed and discussed with both objective and subjective aspects.

Table 1. The proposed dataset for classification of the early 20th-century music styles. The number of samples of each composer and each style in the dataset are shown.

Styles	Composers	# of samples		Styles	Composers	# of samples	
Serialism	Arnold Schoenberg	22	48	Neoclassicism	Maurice Ravel	11	104
	Alban Berg	2			Paul Hindemith	86	
	Anton Webern	5			Béla Bartók	7	
	Hanns Eisler	19		Nationalism	Béla Bartók	247	304
Impressionism	Claude Debussy	87	110		Leoš Janáček	43	
	Maurice Ravel	23			Manuel de Falla	14	

2 Data

Since the repertoires of early twentieth-century music are wide and complicated, we imposed several restrictions in choosing the works for the dataset. The subject of this research is limited to early twentieth-century composers' piano works, as we tend to use homogeneous data to avoid any potential problems related to instrumentation. This approach has also been used in previous studies, where the researchers limited their choice of instruments to only string quartet [11,14,24], the melody of the violin [6], piano solo [23,25], and orchestra [25]. We included the first 20 measures (approximately one page) of every composition to prevent the imbalance of the dataset. Besides, we chose the styles and composers based on the number of piano pieces for each composer and the availability of the scores. Composers who only have a few piano works were not selected. In addition, we only choose the works in the public domain. Hence, the dataset consists of four styles and ten composers, see Table 1.

Except for Béla Bartók and Maurice Ravel, each composer's compositions are classified in one style. Ravel's works are divided into Impressionism and Neoclassicism, as Ravel had distinctive styles during his early and late period [4]. In addition, Bartók's works with Nationalism style are chosen manually based on existing literature due to his unique approaches between the traditional and modernistic style [4]. Besides Nationalism, a few of Bartók's piano works are also separated into Neoclassicism due to the use of classical forms. Other Bartók's piano works, which do not fall into these two styles (such as Night music), are not included. Lastly, the pre-serialism works from Serialism composers, such as Schoenberg's late romantic works, are not incorporated into the dataset.

The dataset of the early twentieth-century music in this study utilizes note events derived from musicXML, as it can save more information compared to MIDI. We collected the data from the Petrucci music library (imslp.org) and manually converted them to the MusicXML format. Note events, including pitch value, onset time, and duration, are then extracted. The dataset will be publicly announced after this paper is accepted.

3 Method

3.1 Data Representation

We consider pitch-related features and intervals as the data representation, as our pilot study demonstrated that they are more relevant than other music features for classifying our early twentieth-century dataset. [2]. Given a music piece $\{x_i\}_{i=1}^{N}$ with N notes, the pitch value (in MIDI number) of the ith note being p_i, the pitch range (r_p), pitch mean (μ_p), and pitch standard deviation (σ_p) over all time steps are

$$r_p := \max_i(p_i) - \min_i(p_i)\,; \quad \mu_p := \frac{1}{N}\sum_{i=0}^{N} p_i\,; \quad \sigma_p := \sqrt{\frac{\sum(p_i - \mu_p)^2}{N}}\,. \tag{1}$$

Then, vertical interval features are calculated to understand the harmony of the repertoire. For simplicity, the positions of notes are grouped based on the beats. By normalizing all the data to 4/4 m, a *beat* refers to all notes within a quarter note duration. For example, given a music excerpt with Y beats, the position of a note x_i is y, $1 \leq y \leq Y$, if its onset is in the interval $[y, y+1)$, i.e., between the yth and the $(y+1)$th beat of the music piece. For any two notes x_i and x_j at the same beat y, assuming $p_i \geq p_j$, the vertical interval between x_i and x_j at y is 12 if $p_i - p_j = 12n$, $n \in \mathbb{N}$, and is $p_i - p_j \pmod{12}$ for other cases. That means a vertical interval is a value ranging from 0 (unison) to 12 (perfect octave). The distribution of the vertical intervals over all time steps is then represented as a 13-dimensional vector, obtained by aggregating the counts of each interval class over all the time steps. The final vertical interval feature (denoted as $\bar{v}$) is a min-max scale normalization over this distribution.

In addition, we employ another feature based on the horizontal interval for understanding the relationship between neighboring notes. For the horizontal features, we consider two groups of notes by m beats apart from each other. where Following the *skip-gram* technique in the field of natural language processing, m is the number of *skips*, and $m = 0$ represents no skip. Similar to vertical interval, the horizontal interval of x_i and x_{i+m+1} (assuming $p_i > p_{i+m+1}$), is 12 if $p_i - p_{i+m+1} = 12n$, $n \in \mathbb{N}$, and is $p_i - p_{i+m+1} \pmod{12}$ for other cases. Similar to the normalized distribution of vertical intervals, the normalized distribution of m-skip horizontal intervals (denoted as $\bar{h}^{(m)}$) is also a 13-dimensional vector by aggregating the counts of each interval and min-max normalization.

The straightforward way of calculating the vertical and horizontal interval features is demonstrated by an example in Fig. 1. There are three beats (indicated by the yellow boxes) in this example. The vertical interval calculations are shown in the blue lines. At the first beat, for the intervals from the note C♯3, we calculate every possible interval in the same time stamp. Here, calculations are made from C♯3 to E3 (i.e., a minor third, also denoted as "V-m3") and from A♯2 to C♯3 (i.e., minor third or V-m3). The rest of the notes are treated similarly without repetitions; for example, at this beat, we also have an interval between A♯2 and E3 (diminished fifth or V-d5). Summing up the vertical intervals over

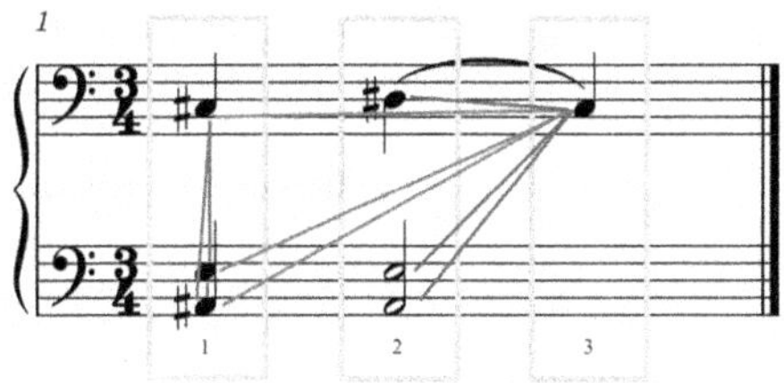

Fig. 1. The example of horizontal and vertical interval feature calculation. Excerpt taken from Bartók's *9 Little Pieces for Piano no.5*.

all the timestamps in Fig. 1, we have in total one V-m2, two V-m3, two V-d5 and one V-P5, so the distribution is $[0, 1, 0, 2, 0, 0, 2, 1, 0, 0, 0, 0, 0]$ and the min-max-normalized distribution is $\bar{v} = [0, 0.5, 0, 1, 0, 0, 1, 0.5, 0, 0, 0, 0, 0]$. Meanwhile, the red lines show the calculation of horizontal intervals without any skip. Our example here calculates the horizontal intervals between the second and the third beats, which result in three intervals: D♯3 to C♯3 (major second, or denoted as H-M2), C♯3 to E3 (H-m3), and A♯2 to C♯3 (H-P5). Lastly, the green line indicates the horizontal interval calculation with skips. In this example, we only demonstrate the interval calculation with one skip, i.e., between the first and third beats. The calculation results in three intervals: C♯3 to C♯3 (H-P1), C♯3 to E3 (H-m2), and A♯2 to C♯3 (H-m3). The method of summing up different timestamps is similar to the case of vertical intervals.

In the remainder of this paper, the number of skips is not specified if it is zero. To summarize, we consider the pitch features (pitch range, pitch mean, and pitch standard deviation, totaling three dimensions), vertical interval features (13 dimensions), and horizontal interval features with skips from 0 to 2 ($13 \times 3 = 39$ dimensions). This results in a total feature dimension of 55.

3.2 Classifiers

We consider three categories of rule-based algorithms: rule trees (i.e., decision trees), rule lists, and rule sets. These three are interpretable in that they are all constructed with conditional statements (i.e., if-then-else rules) of the input features and the corresponding outcomes [10]. In decision tree, the if-then-else rules form a tree structure in which the internal nodes represent conditions of features, and each leaf node represents a class label. In rule lists and rule sets, each condition of an if-then clause can incorporate multiple input variables. Specifically, in rule lists, rules are the conditions ordered in nested if-else statements, while in rule sets, rules are unordered and independent from each other in that the else statements do not connect the rules [10]. As for visual representation, rule trees are often illustrated in tree graphs, while rule lists and rule sets tend to have textual or tabular representation. Hence, rule trees, rule lists and rule sets are not equivalent and are different in multiple aspects.

Table 2. Classification results using the three rule-based classifiers on the four styles of early 20th-century music. Precision (P), recall (R) and F1-score (F1) values are shown.

	rule tree			rule list			rule set		
	P	R	F1	P	R	F1	P	R	F1
Serialism	0.80	0.59	0.68	0.68	0.68	0.68	0.99	0.73	0.84
Neoclassicism	0.60	0.60	0.60	0.52	0.42	0.47	0.84	0.56	0.67
Impressionism	0.56	0.57	0.57	0.55	0.27	0.37	0.68	0.63	0.66
Nationalism	0.62	0.67	0.64	0.57	0.97	0.71	0.83	0.58	0.68
Average	0.65	0.61	0.62	0.58	0.59	0.56	0.84	0.63	0.71

The rule tree classifier we adopt is the decision tree with the optimized CART Algorithm [3], available from the scikit-learn library.[1] For the rule list classifier, we utilize the minimum description length (MDL) rule list, a probabilistic multi-class classifier algorithm. MDL rule list is designed using the minimum description length principle, which chooses the best model based on the ability to compress the data [22].[2] The MDL Rule list requires only a few hyperparameters to work and can acquire competitive accuracy [22]. Lastly, for the rule set classifier, we utilize skope-rules.[3] Similar to Rulefit [20], the rules from Skope-rules are chosen by extracting the path of the tree from multiple decision trees. However, the difference lies in establishing the final rules. Skope-rules filter the rules using out-of-bag (OOB) precision and recall thresholds and the semantic deduplication method for maintaining the diversity of the rules [20].

The hyperparameters utilized in this study are described as follows. For decision tree, we use a maximum depth of four, gini impurity as the criterion, and minimum sample split as two. The rest are followed by the default settings of Scikit-learn's Decision Tree. Meanwhile, the parameters used for the MDL rule list classifier is elaborated as follows: static data discretization, the maximum size of each rule description being 4, the number of cut point of each variable being 1, minimum support being 0.1, and alpha gain being 0. Lastly, for Skope-rules, we utilize similar hyperparameters with Decision Tree, except that we limit the estimated number of the generated tree to 72.

4 Experiments

4.1 Experimental Settings

Before training the classifiers, data augmentation has to be done since the size of the dataset is considered small. In this case, a normalization process is performed as suggested by [11], converting every sample's key into C major and a minor. However, these adjustments are strictly for tonal music, and this conversion

[1] https://scikit-learn.org/stable/modules/tree.html.

[2] https://github.com/HMProenca/MDLRuleLists.

[3] Source code available at https://github.com/scikit-learn-contrib/skope-rules.

Table 3. The extracted rule set of four classes

Rules 1	Rules 2	Rules 3	Rules 4	Class
Pitch Range > 45.5	H-M7 (2 skip) > 0.17	V-m7 ≤ 0.39	V-P8 ≤ 0.8	Impressionism
Pitch Range ≤ 52.5	V-P1 > 0.15	V-P8 > 0.23	H-m2 > 0.05	Nationalism
H-P8 ≤ 0.004	H-M7 (1 skip) > 0.05	H-M6 (2 skip) > 0.15	VI 4 > 0.49	Serialism
H-A4 ≤ 0.5	H-P8 > 0.01	V-m7 > 0.4	V-M7 > 0.3	Neoclassicism

step is skipped for atonal works. Then, we perform pitch shifting from -5 to 6 semitones for each work. To balance the dataset, we randomly select 35% of Nationalism samples due to their larger number. The dataset is then divided into training and testing sets with the 80:20 ratio. Lastly, considering the number of samples, 5-fold cross-validation (CV) is performed for each experiment to obtain stable classification results. The test-set precision, recall, and F1-score values averaged over the 5-fold CV are reported and compared.

4.2 Objective Evaluation

Table 2 shows the classification result of decision tree, MDL rule list, and Skope-rules. Skope-rules achieves an average F1-score at 0.71, outperforming both decision tree (F1-score = 0.62) and MDL rule list (F1-score = 0.56) by a wide margin. Meanwhile, we have slightly different results for the F1-score of each class. Skope-rules still dominate in Serialism, Neoclassicism, and Impressionism classes, followed by decision tree. However, for Nationalism, the MDL rule list achieves a better result than the other two, with F1-score = 0.71. Lastly, the results of both Neoclassicism and Impressionism of the MDL rule list are underwhelming, with the F1-score less than 0.5.

4.3 Subjective Evaluation

A user study in the form of a questionnaire is utilized to understand the interpretability of the models for musicologists, musicians, composers, and other music-related researchers. The questionnaire of our subjective evaluation contains two parts, *visualization test* and *content test*. The first part evaluates the subjective response to the *visualization* quality of the rules. Rule tree is visualized with a decision tree graph (e.g., Fig. 2) while rule list is represented by text, consisting of the if, else-if, and else rules (e.g., Fig. 3). Lastly, rule set is represented by a table (e.g., Fig. 3). The questions then aim to understand the most favorable representation of the visualization results based on the opinions of respondents. Since the 5-fold CV generates five different lists, trees, and sets, we decided to take the best graphs or rules based on the best F1-score of the folds for the questionnaire questions.

The second part of the subjective test evaluates the *content* of the generated rules of each class. In the second part of the subjective test, we present $C_2^4 = 6$

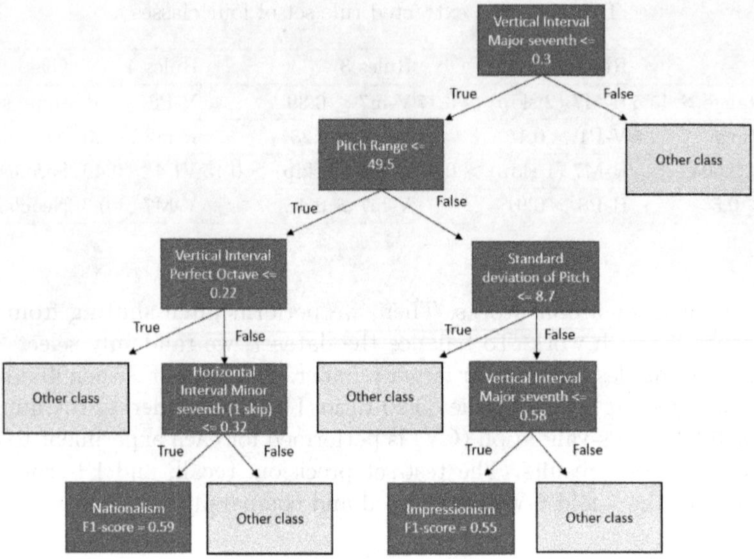

Fig. 2. Partially extracted tree of Nationalism and Impressionism class. "Other class" denotes the weak or irrelevant class which is neither Nationalism nor Impressionism.

question sets of rule tree, rule list, and rule set based on the binary classification; the six sets contain each of the two styles selected from the four musical styles for pairwise comparison. Each set consists of four questions. They are (Q1) From the three options, which one gives the best result according to current music theory? (Q2) From the three options, which one gives the worst result according to current music theory? (Q3) From the three options, which one gives the most unusual rules? (Q4) From the three options, which one gives the least unusual rules?

20 participants joined the subjective test. 18 of them have a degree in music. Among the participants, 13 have more than 11 years of experience in music. On a scale of 1–5, 7 participants are very familiar with early twentieth-century music (scale 4–5), while 10 participants are familiar with early twentieth-century music (scale 3). Only 3 participants are quite unfamiliar with early twentieth-century music (scale 2).

The left-hand side of Fig. 4 shows the result of the subjective test. For the visualization test, rule tree is the model representation that is easiest to read, followed by rule set. Meanwhile, rule list is the hardest to read. Similarly, among the three models, the rule tree is also the most comprehensible, followed by rule set and rule list.

The right-hand side of Fig. 4 shows the result of the content. In line with the result of the visualization test, the answers to Q1 and Q2 of the content test show that most participants favor rule set and rule tree over rule list. However,

↘19 list of ELSE IF with low impact results

➢ELSE IF Pitch Range < 43.0 AND Vertical Interval Perfect Octave >= 0.36 AND Horizontal Interval Perfect Fourth (2 skip) >= 0.4 AND Vertical Interval Minor Second < 1.0 THEN Probability of Nationalism = 1.0

↘12 list of ELSE IF with low impact results

➢ELSE THEN Probability of Impressionism = 0.96; Probability of Neoclassicism = 0.04

Fig. 3. The extracted rule list of Nationalism and Impressionism Class. The hidden lists contain other n rules which have low impacts to the classification decisions.

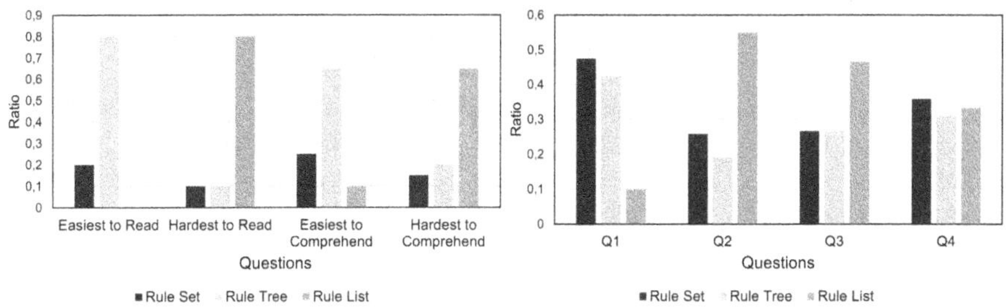

Fig. 4. Results of the subjective tests. Left: visualization test. Right: content test.

unique results are seen based on the answer of Q3. Even though rule set has the highest ratio in Q1, it turns out rule set also occupies second place in Q3. It means that although rule set has rules strongly similar to current music theory, some are also considered unusual.

5 Discussion

5.1 The Subjective and Objective Evaluation Analysis

The objective and subjective evaluations conducted in this study show several similar trends. The visualization and content test show identical results regarding the most accurate classifier among the three representations. Skope-rules appears to be the best classifier with the F1-score = 0.71, and the classifier shows the best result for the current music theory based on the *content* test (see Q1 and Q2 in Fig. 4). Meanwhile, the rule tree comes second with F1-score = 0.62, with the second-best accuracy towards the current music theory. On the other hand, the rule list becomes the worst classifier among these trees with the lowest F1-score, lowest Q1, and highest Q2 value of *content* test. The Q3 answers show that rule list generates the most unusual rules compared to others. There may be two possible explanations regarding this matter. First, the unusual rules may be the signs of the new possible finding regarding the theory of musicology. Second, the rules from rule list may not be accurate because it occupies the lowest F1-score in objective evaluation. However, at the current state of the study, we are unable to identify whether these found rules from the rule list are truly insightful, and further investigations are required. Lastly, based on the Q4 of the content test, no clear trend was found.

Meanwhile, regarding the interpretability of the rules, we still observe contrasting outcomes in between visualization tests Based on the result of the visualization test (Fig. 4), rule tree offers better comprehensibility and readability compared to rule list and rule set. Rule set comes second despite having the highest precision, recall, and F1-score on the objective evaluation. The result in our case shows that a higher F1-score does not always imply better interpretability. This is possibly due to data representation: the tree data structure in rule tree has the advantage of showing the relationship between the classes. For instance, in Fig. 2, the readers can easily notice the distinctions of Nationalism and Impressionism classes directly from the ramification on the first depth onward. Meanwhile, for the rule list and rule set, the readers need to compare each rule one by one. In addition, the rules generated from the rule tree always show at least one related feature of both classes (see Fig. 2) since, in the tree model, two child nodes always have at least one shared parent node. On the contrary, in both rule list and rule set, there are possibilities that all features of both classes are distinctive. Readers may be confused in comparing the rules if all the rules between classes are unrelated.

The rule list shows the most inferior performance from both the subjective and objective perspectives: The average F1-score is only 0.56 (although it performs the best in Nationalism), and it is the hardest to read, comprehend, and the worst according to music theory. This might be due to data representation: there is a possibility that even though the rule list may produce reasonable rules, the subjective evaluation participants tend to choose other models due to the unfamiliarity of the respondents with the IF-ELSE concept in Fig. 3, which are computer science rather than musical knowledge.

Based on the subjective and objective evaluation results, rule set shows the best accuracy in the F1-score and the content test while the outcome of the visualization test still indicates the potential of the rule tree as a good representation that favors music practitioners and musicologists. Besides, the results of the rule list are least favorable.

5.2 Case Study

In this part, we perform a case study to see how the learned rules work on real-world music examples. We randomly select four excerpts from our dataset to represent each respective style. The music pieces are the excerpts chosen from Claude Debussy's *Nocturne*, Béla Bartók's *Nine Little Pieces for Piano*, Arnold Schoenberg's *Suite for Piano* and Paul Hindemith's *Ludus Tonalis*.

The rule set on Table 3 is utilized in the case study since rule set is the most recommended algorithm according to our previous discussion. The details of the chosen excerpts and the values of those features which appear in the rules on

Table 4. The features of the four random-chosen excerpts. The green color shows that the feature fits the rule set and the red color shows that the feature unfits the rule set.

	Example (Composer)	C. Debussy	B. Bartók	A. Schoenberg	P. Hindemith
	Class	Impressionism	Nationalism	Serialism	Neoclassicism
Impression	Pitch range > 45.5	73	43	63	72
	H-M7 (2 skip) > 0.17	0	0.12	0.13	0
	V-m7 ≤ 0.39	[illegible]	0.06	1	[illegible]
	V-P8 ≤ 0.8	1	0.16	0	0.74
National	Pitch range ≤ 52.5	73	43	63	72
	V-P1 > 0.15	[illegible]	0	[illegible]	[illegible]
	V-P8 > 0.23	1	0.16	[illegible]	0.74
	H-m2 > 0.05	0.17	[illegible]	0.99	0.39
Serialism	H-P8 ≤ 0.004	[illegible]	0	[illegible]	[illegible]
	H-M7 (1 skip) > 0.05	[illegible]	[illegible]	[illegible]	[illegible]
	H-M6 (2 skip) > 0.15	0.46	[illegible]	[illegible]	[illegible]
	V-M3 > 0.49	0.65	[illegible]	[illegible]	0.84
Neoclassic	H-A4 ≤ 0.5	0.21	0.38	[illegible]	[illegible]
	H-P8 > 0.01	0.74	[illegible]	[illegible]	[illegible]
	V-m7 > 0.4	[illegible]	[illegible]	1	[illegible]
	V-M7 > 0.3	[illegible]	[illegible]	0.54	[illegible]

Table 3 can be seen in Table 4. Although the statements of feature in the rule set are combined with the logical AND, we discuss the feature separately for convenience. For example, the pitch range of Debussy's *Nocturne* fits the rule "Pitch range > 45.5" for Impressionism since its value is 73. In addition, the pitch range of Bartók's piece also fits this rule since it is non-Impressionism, and its value, 43, is smaller than 45.5. As a result, the value with the green color in Table 4 indicates that it fits the rule description of the music style, while the value with the red color shows that it does not fit the rules.

The results in Table 4 indicate promising outcomes. For Debussy's *Nocturne* (Impressionism) and Bartók's *Moderato* (Nationalism), two out of the four rules predict the style label correctly Meanwhile, for Schoenberg's *Präludium* (Serialism) and Paul Hindemith's *Preludio* (Neoclassicism), all the rules are correct. It should be noted that current music theory does support certain generated rules on Table 3. For instance, the pitch range of Impressionism is supposed to be larger than 45.5 semitones, and Debussy's *Nocturne* fulfills the requirements. The requirement of such a wide pitch range may be correlated with the main characteristics of Impressionism piano works; among them are "open chord, wide spacing, and extreme register" [19, p. 169].

Meanwhile, some other results demonstrate unusual rules based on the perspective of musicology. For instance, the rule from the rule set shows the importance of V-M3 (major third) in Serialism composition. However, Serialism works do not stress the utilization of the major third since Serialism composition utilizes intervals based on the tone rows [4]. Lastly, another issue that concerns us is that some rules generated by the rule set are very weak. For instance, one of the Neoclassicism rules states that the normalized value of H-P8 (perfect octave) needs to be larger than 0.01, a very small lower threshold. Therefore, such a rule may not be as insightful since any music piece that merely utilizes a few numbers of the horizontal perfect octave interval might satisfy it. Hence, in certain parts, such rules do not highlight the important characteristics of the styles but are redundant. However, certain weak rules are still able to show some insights. For example, the rule H-M7 (skip 1) > 0.05 seems weak given that 0.05 is a small lower threshold. However, based on observations, the excerpts in the other three styles have this feature smaller than 0.05, meaning that the horizontal major seventh interval with skip 1 rarely appears except in Serialism.

6 Conclusion

To conclude, the systematic study of rule-based interpretable algorithms for classifying the styles of early twentieth-century music indicates that the rule-set-based algorithm, Skope-rules, shows the best performance in the precision, recall, and F1-score of the objective evaluation and also offers decent comprehensibility and consistency of music theory in the subjective tests. In addition, the chosen algorithm with our feature design can find the rules in line with the current music theory, as well as the promising unusual rules which may show new insights regarding early twentieth-century music. Rule tree, on the other hand, is able to provide the best result in visualization test, yet is unable to outperform rule set in other evaluation sections. Thus, while the previous studies on rule-based interpretable music AI mostly considered decision trees, we suggest using rule-set-based algorithms for related research directions.

References

1. Auner, J.: A Schoenberg Reader: Documents of a Life (2003)
2. Author, A.: (Anonymized for double-blind review). Master's thesis, Anonymous school (2022)
3. Breiman, L., Friedman, J.H., Olshen, R.A., Stone, C.J.: CART: Classification and Regression Trees. Routledge (1984)
4. Burkholder, J.P., Grout, D.J., Palisca, C.V.: A History of Western Music, 10th edn. W.W Norton & Company, New York (2019)
5. Clark, N.A., Heflin, T., Kluball, J., Kramer, E.: Understanding music: Past and present. University System of Georgia, University Press of North Georgia (2015)
6. De Carvalho Junior, A.D., Batista, L.V.: Composer classification in symbolic data using PPM. In: 11th International Conference on Machine Learning and Applications, vol. 2, pp. 345–350. IEEE (2012)
7. Frisch, W.: Music in the Twentieth and Twenty-First Centuries. W.W Norton & Company, New York (2013)
8. Gabriela, V.: Baroque reflections in Ludus Tonalis by Paul Hindemith. In: 11th WSEAS International Conference on Acoustics & Music: Theory & Applications (AMTA'10), vol. 1 (2010)

9. Gardin, F., Gautier, R., Goix, N., Ndiaye, B., Schertzer, J.M.: Skope-rules. https://github.com/scikit-learn-contrib/skope-rules
10. Guidotti, R., Monreale, A., Ruggieri, S., Turini, F., Giannotti, F., Pedreschi, D.: A survey of methods for explaining black box models. ACM Comput. Surv. **51**(5) (2018). https://doi.org/10.1145/3236009, https://doi.org/10.1145/3236009
11. Herlands, W., Der, R., Greenberg, Y., Levin, S.: A machine learning approach to musically meaningful homogeneous style classification. In: AAAI Conference on Artificial Intelligence, vol. 28 (2014)
12. Herremans, D., Martens, D., Sörensen, K.: Composer classification models for music-theory building. In: Computational Music Analysis, pp. 369–392. Springer (2016)
13. Kelz, R., Widmer, G.: Towards interpretable polyphonic transcription with invertible neural networks. arXiv preprint arXiv:1909.01622 (2019)
14. Kempfert, K.C., Wong, S.W.: Where does Haydn end and Mozart begin? Composer classification of string quartets. J. New Music Res. **49**(5), 457–476 (2020)
15. Kim, S., Lee, H., Park, S., Lee, J., Choi, K.: Deep composer classification using symbolic representation. arXiv preprint arXiv:2010.00823 (2020)
16. Kong, Q., Choi, K., Wang, Y.: Large-scale MIDI-based composer classification. arXiv preprint arXiv:2010.14805 (2020)
17. Kostka, S.: Materials and Techniques of Twentieth-Century Music, 3rd ed. Pearson Prentice Hall (2006)
18. Micchi, G.: A neural network for composer classification. In: International Society for Music Information Retrieval Conference (ISMIR) (2018)
19. Miller, H.M.: History of Music. Barnes & Noble Books (1973)
20. Molnar, C.: Interpretable machine learning: a Guide for Making Black Box Models Explainable. Lulu. com (2019)
21. Murdoch, W.J., Singh, C., Kumbier, K., Abbasi-Asl, R., Yu, B.: Definitions, methods, and applications in interpretable machine learning. Proc. Natl. Acad. Sci. **116**(44), 22071–22080 (2019)
22. Proença, H.M., Leeuwen, M.: Interpretable multiclass classification by MDL-based rule lists. Inf. Sci. **512**, 1372–1393 (2020)
23. Van Spijker, B.: Classifying classical piano music into time period using machine learning. Master's thesis, University of Twente (2020)
24. Velarde, G., Weyde, T., Chacón, C.C., Meredith, D., Grachten, M.: Composer recognition based on 2d-filtered piano-rolls. In: International Society for Music Information Retrieval Conference (ISMIR), pp. 115–121. International Society for Music Information Retrieval (2016)
25. Weiß, C., Mauch, M., Dixon, S., Müller, M.: Investigating style evolution of Western classical music: a computational approach. Music Sci. **23**(4), 486–507 (2019)
26. Won, M., Chun, S., Serra, X.: Toward interpretable music tagging with self-attention. arXiv preprint arXiv:1906.04972 (2019)
27. Yang, D., Tsai, T.: Composer classification with cross-modal transfer learning and musically-informed augmentation. In: International Society for Music Information Retrieval Conference (ISMIR), pp. 802–809 (2021)
28. Yu, H., Varshney, L.R., Garnett, G.E., Kumar, R.: Learning interpretable musical compositional rules and traces. In: ICML Workshop on Human Interpretability in Machine Learning (WHI) (2016)

Toward Empirical Analysis for Stylistic Expression in Piano Performance

Yu-Fen Huang[1(✉)] and Li Su[2]

[1] Department of Music, National Taiwan University of Arts, Taipei, Taiwan
yfhuang@iis.sinica.edu.tw

[2] Music and Culture Technology Lab (MCTL), Institute of Information Science, Academia Sinica, Taipei, Taiwan
lisu@iis.sinica.edu.tw

Abstract. In the performance of Western art music, musicians apply various strategies to manipulate the sound performed and communicate their musical interpretations through these subtle acoustic variations. It is a common practice for musicians to use typical conventions to express each compositional style (e.g., Baroque, Classical, or Romantic compositions). However, such stylistic expressive conventions have yet to be fully discussed in previous research. In this initial foray, we systematically compare the expressive strategies for different piano compositions. A series of piano performances are recorded in a controlled experimental setting (3 compositions $\times$ 8 pianists $\times$ 3 repeated trials = 72 recordings), and expressive acoustic elements are derived using Music Information Retrieval techniques. In our analysis, we reveal that expressive manners in music performance exhibit stable and systematic features corresponding to each music composition, and those stylistic trends serve as empirical observations for typical performance conventions in different music styles.

Keywords: expressiveness · performance style · piano performance · computational musicology · music information retrieval

1 Introduction

In the past decades, the way how music audiences approach, appreciate, and get to understand music has been evolved with the revolution of digital technologies. From attending physical concerts, purchasing audio/video medium (e.g. CD, DVD), to getting access to large amount of digitized performance recordings via online streaming services, audiences embrace the opportunities to explore the variety of music performance. In the context of Western art music, musicians have the privilege to interpret the written composition and to communicate their understanding of the music piece via intricate variations in their performance (e.g. micro-timing, dynamic, timbral, and articulation arrangement). Audiences also enjoy the process to contemplate and compare diverse artistic variations

S. Ystad et al. (Eds.): CMMR 2023, LNCS 15236, pp. 252–266, 2026.
https://doi.org/10.1007/978-3-032-02042-0_19

in different performance versions, and through which process to discover potential insights for classical repertoire. The artistic, expressive variations in music performances therefore serve as an essential communicative vehicle to deliver musical ideas in the cultured convention.

Recently, systematic studies for large-scale music performance corpus have been advanced with the facilitation of Music Information Retrieval (MIR) techniques. Computational models have been established to map general connections between musical attributes (e.g. note length, note pitch, phrase position) and expressive variations in performance [12,16]. From musicological aspect, scholars focus on specific genres (e.g. Baroque music) and examine how particular aesthetic styles in music are shaped by artistic variations in performance [9]. Musicians also contribute their unique and creative interpretations in the execution process of the performance. [18,34]. The execution of music performance is therefore a complex and interactive process across the aforementioned factors - the composition, stylistic convention, and individual musicians. However, the relationships between these aspects and how they interact together have not yet been fully discussed in previous research, particularly with systematic analysis of individual factors.

In this study, our objective is to provide context-valid observations in terms of the interactions between different factors leading to musical expressiveness. A piano performance corpus is collected under a controlled experimental setting, and Music Information Retrieval (MIR) techniques are applied to retrieve expressive variations in tempo and dynamics. Performance variations are analyzed in conjunction with compositional elements through statistical and time-series methods. We identify important factors to induce unique music expression, and then subsequently investigate how those factors interact in different performing contexts. The contribution of this work is threehold:

- To compile a new piano performance dataset with controlled experimental design for comparison;
- To identify different key factors affecting music expression in individual scenario via statistical analysis;
- To provide empirical observations of how different factors interact together in a time-series process.

In the next section, we will discuss previous studies regarding musical expressiveness. The data collection and data processing procedure of this study will be reported in Sect. 3. In Sect. 4, we will investigate stylistic expressive trends found in individual compositions, and distinctive expressions bound for different compositional elements. In Sect. 5, our analysis results will be discussed in conjunction with findings in previous research, and we therefore suggest that our analysis can be implemented as an empirical approach to describe systematic variations for different expressive styles in music performance.

2 Related Work

The expressiveness in music performance is shaped by complex interactions among diverse factors. In the context of Western art music, composers follow conventional rules to construct the melodic, rhythmic, and harmonic configurations of music (*compositional factor*) [1,24], and each composer's work would exhibit distinctive character according to the composer's preference (*stylistic factor*) [6]. During the performance process, musicians have their unique fashion to communicate personal musical interpretations, and control the variations in performed acoustic sound (e.g., micro-timing, dynamic, and articulation variations) (*musician factor*) [26,27]. GERMS model systematically categorized different origin of musical expressiveness including: generative rules, emotional expression, random variations, motion principles, and stylistic unexpectedness [20]. We will review related works regarding three different origin of musical expressiveness in this section.

2.1 Compositional Factors in Music Performance

In previous studies, rule-based models are established to describe the connection between compositional elements and expressive variations. The KTH model combines generative rules in melodic, harmonic, rhythmic, and phrase aspects to predict the timing, dynamics, and articulation execution in performance [12]. For piano performance, rule-based models and linear Gaussian models can be applied to jointly predict the tempo, dynamic, and articulation variations in performance according to multiple attributes in melodic, rhythmic, and harmonic aspects of performance [11]. Based on large amounts of jazz performance data, inductive logic rules for expressive elements (note onset deviation, dynamic variation, and ornamentation) are found in jazz music [14]. It is also found that tempo and dynamic variations interact together in music performance, and the tempo-loudness trajectory is an effective description to illustrate distinctive features of performance style [4].

Another cluster of studies apply machine learning approach to explore potential relationships between compositional elements and expressive variations. The connection between expressive tempo variations and musical phrase is mapped using Gaussian Mixture Models (GMMs) [25]. Models with transitional hidden state are applied to predict expressive variations according to score-informed attributes. For instance, Hidden Markov Model (HMM) and Hierarchical HMM are used to estimate the expressive variations in piano performance [17]. Conditional random fields (CRFs) are applied to predict expressive elements based on melodic and harmonic components [21]. Feed Forward Neural Networks (FFNNs) are used to predict the dynamic variations based on local-level score-informed attributes including the pitch, duration, and the note's relative interval with neighboring notes [3]. Linear and non-linear models for musical expression are systematically evaluated in [2], and it is concluded that compared to linear models, non-linear models have better performance to estimate the tempo and dynamic changes in music performance.

2.2 Stylistic Factors in Music Performance

Computational models are also built to explore specific performance styles. Restricted Boltzmann Machines (RBMs) are capable of predicting expressive accentuations in piano performance [19]. For solo violin performance, long-term dynamic variations can be successfully modelled using Random Forest, k-nearest neighbors (k-NN), and Support Vector Machine (SVM) [15]. For string quartet, the timing deviation, dynamic level, and the extent of vibrato in performance can be estimated based on melodic (e.g. relative interval) and rhythmic (e.g. metrical hierarchy) descriptors using model trees, k-NN, and SVM [22]. For jazz music, Decision Tree, SVM, and Neural Network (NN) are developed to formulate the stylistic deviations in jazz performance, and the improvised embellishments can be predicted from attributes including the chord type, note duration, and phrase [14].

2.3 Musician Factors in Music Performance

Musicians have their personal expressive manners in music performance. In order to compare different performance versions for the same composition, entropy-based deviation measures are used to describe expressive timing patterns in individual performance versions [26]. Hierarchical clustering is also an useful implement to distinguish different trends of performing styles for orchestral works [27]. For violin performance, individual violinists have their own expressive strategies to convey melodic patterns and phrase structure in the composition [30]. For jazz music, different performance styles by individual musicians can be successfully distinguished based on their intra-note features (e.g. note's attack level, sustain duration, amount of legato, spectral centroid, spectral tilt), inter-note features (e.g. relative pitch and duration to the neighboring notes), and note-to-note transition (pitch contour) [35].

The style of music performance is highly idiosyncratic according to the music genre, the music composition, and the musician. In particular, in Western art music, it is a common practice for pianists to play compositions in Baroque, Classical, and Romantic period following distinctive conventions. Aforementioned studies tends to explore a specific aspect of musical expression (i.e. either compositional, stylistic, or musician factor alone). Yet in music performance, the interactive, dynamical process among different factors work together to shape diverse variations. Based on the foundation of previous research, this work collects a series of piano performance data, and systematically analyze how individual factors interplay together to shape the overall musical expressiveness.

3 Method

In order to systematically examine how different factors affect the expressive variations in piano performance, a series of piano performance data are collected in this study. In this section, we report the procedure for data collection, and the data processing methods to extract expressive variations from recorded performance audio.

3.1 Data Collection

Eight pianists are recruited to participate the recording sessions. The recruited participants are graduate/undergraduate students majoring in piano in music department at university (male = 4, female = 4). We reached out the participant pool via personal contact of music department staff. Participants are all right-handed, with the average age of 21.63 (SD = 0.70). They have learnt piano for 14.88 years in average (SD = 2.42), and practice for 3.75 h in average per day at the time of data collection (SD = 1.84).

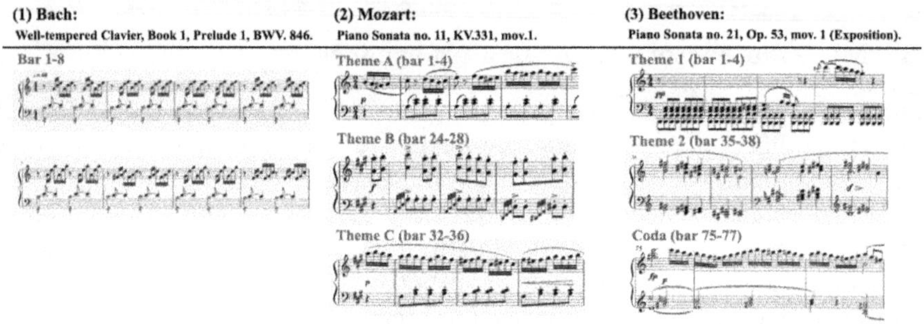

Fig. 1. The repertoire for data collection: three piano solo works by Bach, Mozart and Beethoven.

In order to compare different performance styles, piano solo works written by different composers are selected as materials (Fig. 1). Repeated measures design is used to observe if pianists show stable features when performing the same piece of music multiple times. The three music pieces selected for data collection are Bach Well-tempered Clavier, Book 1, Prelude 1, BWV.846; Mozart Piano Sonata no. 11, KV. 331, mov.1, and Beethoven Piano Sonata no. 21, Op. 53, mov.1 (bar 1–86, Exposition). In our experiment, each pianist played each music piece for 3 times in a random order, which resulted in 72 performance recordings (3 music pieces × 3 performances × 8 pianists). The recording sessions took place at the Motion Analysis Lab (National Yang Ming Chiao Tung University, Taiwan), where the performances were recorded on Yamaha digital piano P-115. In order to accurately align each notes in the performance with the music scores in the subsequent stage of data analysis, the performance is recorded as both midi and audio formats. During recording sessions, participants' body were also attached to optical markers to record 3-d motion capture data for their performance body movement, which will be further analyzed elsewhere.

3.2 Data Processing

The dynamic and tempo variations in piano performance are the two expressive features to be analyzed in our subsequent investigation. In order to derive our target features, the first step is to perform audio-to-score alignment and to obtain the time stamp for each note in the performance. The audio-to-score alignment for polyphonic music, particularly with casual playing errors and asynchrony between two hands in piano performance, has been considered as a challenging task in Music Information Retrieval [5,13,31]. We applied an automatic alignment method to align recorded midi files and music scores files, in which Viterbi algorithms are used to exclude playing error regions and alignment errors in a pre-alignment process, and then hidden Markov models are applied to divide notes playing by two hands and accurately re-align each note based on the merged information [32] (see Fig. 2).

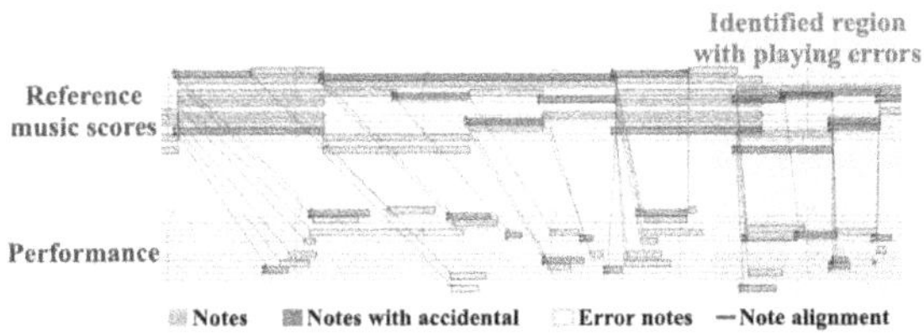

Fig. 2. The automatic audio-to-score alignment process to extract note timing from performance.

In order to associate expressive variations with the overall compositional structures, we analyze the dynamic and tempo variations at bar-level instead of instant dynamics and tempo. For tempo variations, the timing for each beat is extracted from the audio-to-score alignment data. The note information (e.g. the note pitch, duration, bar and beat position) is extracted from xml files using Python library Music21 [7], and such information from music scores serves as the reference to locate corresponding onset timing for each beat in the performance. In case of absent note on downbeat, linear interpolation is performed based on the timing of neighboring beats; in case of the asynchrony between two hands, the note with the lowest register is taken as the reference. The ***tempo*** per bar is then defined as the average bpm (beat per minute) per bar. For dynamic data, the decibel is computed from the input audio (sampling rate = 22050 Hz) using Python library Librosa [29]. In order to eliminate the disturbance of local noise, moving average (window size = 220 samples, roughly 0.01 s) is used to smooth the original data. Since each note has a natural ADSR (attack-decay-sustain-release) curve, and the maximum volume on the attack is the main feature concerned, the ***dynamic*** level per bar is defined as the maximum decibel within a bar duration. Conventional music analysis is performed on the music scores, and structural features of music works including the harmonic progression, phrase and sectional boundaries are analyzed to be compared with features extracted from performance audio.

4 Analysis Results

Through the data collection and processing procedure, a series of piano performance data are collected, and expressive tempo and dynamic variations are extracted. In this section, we report our analyses and observations for stylistic expression in three aspects: 1) the general expressive manners, 2) the interaction between different compositional elements and expressive features, and 3) the time-series expressive trends found in individual compositions, which can be regarded as individual stylistic expressive strategies attached to the composition.

4.1 General Expressive Manners

In our analysis, it appears that pianists use different strategies to express each composition. In Fig. 3, different tendencies of pianists' expressive manners can be observed in the distributions and statistics of tempo (the upper panel) and dynamics (the lower panel). In order to distinguish the influence from compositions versus from pianists, We perform statistical tests on two factors (composition and performer). Since the distributions of both tempo and dynamic data violate the assumption of homogeneity in Levene's test, non-parametric tests (Kruskal-Wallis tests) are performed instead of regular ANOVA, and Bonferroni correction is applied to post hoc analysis [10]. Regarding the tempo data, the statistical analyses yield significant differences between all three compositions, while the performances for Mozart's and Beethoven's pieces have more similar average tempo (126.77 and 136.30 bpm) compared to Bach's piece (69.70 bpm). Comparing the performances for Mozart's and Beethoven's compositions, Beethoven's composition possesses higher variations (SD = 14.58, range = 124.67) than Mozart's work (SD = 10.85, range = 96.27). It is worth noted that according to the statistic analyses on the pianist factor, some pianists have distinctive expressive strategies, which can be distinguished from other pianists' expressive trend.

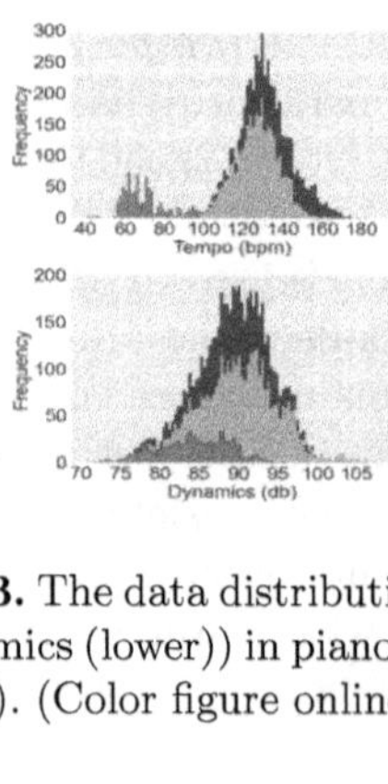

Tempo statistics				K-W test	
Composition	Mean	SD	Range	Composition factor	Pianist factor
Bach	69.70	10.93	57.22	p< .001 All pairs are significant	p<.001 Not significant pairs: P1-P2, P1-P8, P3-P5, P3-P7, P5-P7
Mozart	126.77	10.85	96.27		
Beethoven	136.30	14.58	124.67		

Dynamics statistics				K-W test	
Composition	Mean	SD	Range	Composition factor	Pianist factor
Bach	84.23	4.54	24.87	p< .001 All pairs are significant	p<.001 Not significant pairs: P1-P3, P2-P3, P2-P8, P4-P7, P5-P8
Mozart	90.97	4.77	31.82		
Beethoven	89.26	4.34	24.47		

Fig. 3. The data distribution and statistics for two expressive elements (tempo (upper), dynamics (lower)) in piano works written by Bach (red), Mozart (green), and Beethoven (blue). (Color figure online)

4.2 Interactions Between Compositional and Expressive Elements

Pianists perform individual compositions with diverse expressive manners, and they may use different expressive strategies to communicate each compositional element. In this section, we further analyze the interaction between different compositional elements and expressive features. We focus on the phrase, section, and harmony aspects of composition, and manually-annotate five different features for each musical bar in each composition: 1) section boundary (on section boundary/ non-boundary), 2) phrase boundary (on phrase boundary/ non-boundary), 3) section position (in the first /middle/ last one third of a section), 4) phrase position (in the first/ middle/ last one third of a phrase), 5) harmony (I/ V/ other types of chord). We contemplate both the boundary and relative position for section/phrase, since in our preliminary observation, we found that musicians tend to show different manners at section/phrase boundaries, and their expressive tendencies also vary when they initiate a new section/phrase versus when they are approaching the end of section/phrase. For the harmonic aspect, we only compare three types of chord to simplify the analysis process, since it is not straight forward to observe the overall general tendency in the comparisons of many groups (e.g. comparing all 7°C of chord lead to $C_2^7 = 21$ combinations). In many chord types, we choose tonic and dominant chords to analyze, considering that those two chords take essential position in Western tonal music and are often used to signify structural location in music (authentic or half cadence).

For statistic analyses, we take the expressive measurements (tempo/ dynamics) in each bar, and then split the data into groups according to their compositional elements. Figure 4 (A0 and B0) shows all the 26 comparison groups for statistic analysis. We first perform normality tests for all groups, and subsequently carry out homogeneity tests for three-group comparisons (section position, phrase position, and harmony type). For groups violating the normality or homogeneity assumptions, the non-parametric counterpart is performed instead of parametric test (i.e. t-test or Mann-Whitney U test for two-group comparisons; one-way ANOVA or Kruskal-Wallis test for three-group comparisons). For three-group comparisons, we further carry out post hoc tests to compare different combinations. Aforementioned procedure is performed three times for the three compositions individually.

In Fig. 4, the general expressive tendencies (column 0) and differences between compositions (column 1 - 3) can be observed. For tempo variations (Fig. 4, A0), musicians generally incline to slow down at section and phrase boundaries, as well as at the bars with tonic and dominate chords, since those chords may coincide with cadence. But different expressions emerge when comparing three compositions. For the section position, in Bach's and Mozart's music piece (Fig. 4, A1 and A2), musicians' tempo variation exhibits a U-shape curve, in which they tend to perform with faster tempi at the beginning and end of section, and slightly slow down in the middle of section, whereas in Beethoven's music piece (Fig. 4, A3), musicians' tempo curve tilts toward the end of section, in which they apply a ritardando to highlight the end of section. For dynamic variations (Fig. 4, B0), it is shown that pianists tend to perform with softer

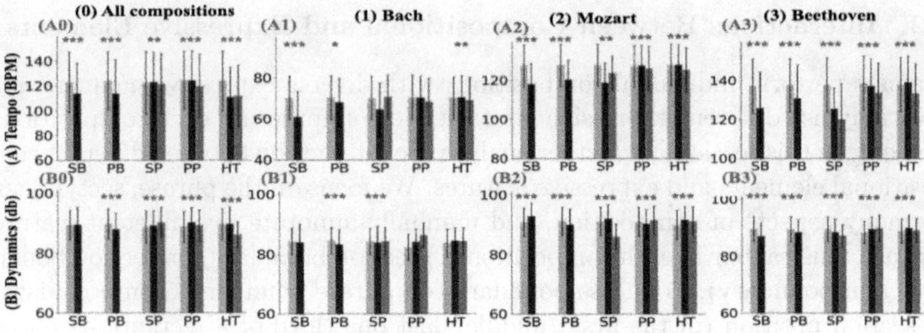

Fig. 4. The statistic analyses for 2 expressive elements (tempo (row A), dynamics (row B)), with 5 compositional elements in 3 music pieces (Bach (column 1), Mozart (column 2), Beethoven (column 3)), including the means (bars), standard deviations (error bars), and significance level (stars). Comparison groups are: section boundary (SB), phrase boundary (PB) (non-boundary (pink), boundary (blue)), section position (SP), phrase position (PP) (the first 1/3 (pink), the middle 1/3 (blue), the last 1/3 (green)), harmony types (HT) (others (pink), I (blue), V (green)). (Color figure online)

dynamic levels when they are approaching the end of section or phrase. The softer dynamic level sometimes incorporate with ritardando to be used as the expressive strategy to shape 'the sense of direction toward the end of phrase/ section' in performance. We can observe that most of comparisons yield significant difference between groups, which indicates that musicians generally jointly use the combination of different expressive variations (tempo and dynamics) to deliver compositional traits in music, whereas in Bach's music piece, the section, phrase, and harmonic structures sometimes are not manifest in expressive variations.

4.3 Stylistic Time-Series Expressions in Compositions

In addition to the comparison between different compositional elements, in music performance, both expressive variations and compositional elements are revealed during the course of time. We therefore take a step further in this section to discuss the time-series connection between expressive and compositional elements. In Fig. 5, the time-series curve of average tempo (Row A) and dynamics (Row B) per bar (for all trials performed by all pianists) are aligned with musical elements in compositions including phrases (Row C), sectional boundaries (Row D), and harmonic progression (Row E). In our analysis, the expression curves show that pianists tend to adopt different patterns of variation in their performance to convey distinctive traits in each composition.

In Bach's work, pianists perform with a steady tempo, except an obvious ritardandos indicating the cadence at the end of the piece (Fig. 5, 1A). The dynamic variation in Bach shows distinct features corresponding to the phrase structure and the harmonic progression (Fig. 5, 1B). For the phrase structure, the dynamic curve exhibits an inverted U-shape matching with phrase boundaries

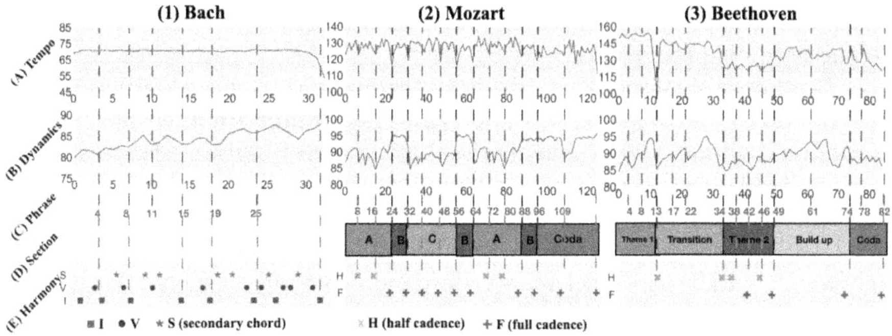

Fig. 5. Time-series trends of tempo and dynamic variations in piano performance. The expressive curves of mean tempo (bpm) (Row A) and the mean dynamics (db) (Row B), aligned with compositional elements including phrases (Row C), sectional boundaries (Row D), and harmonic progression (Row E) in Bach's (Column 1), Mozart's (Column 2), and Beethoven's (Column 3) compositions.

per 4 to 6 bars, which shows that pianists tend to perform a crescendo for the first half of the phrase, and then perform a decrescendo for the second half of the phrase. For the harmonic progression, louder performance dynamics are applied to emphasize harmony with higher tension such as secondary chords (red markers), whereas softer dynamics associate with tonic chord (blue markers), which often coincides with the boundary of phrase and represents the release of harmony tension.

In Mozart's composition, the tempo and dynamic curves in pianists' performances exhibit different traits compared to Bach's work. In contrast with the smooth tempo curve in Bach's work, pianists apply tempo variations to express the phrase structure when performing Mozart's work, in which their tempi tend to slow down at phrase boundaries (Fig. 5, 2A). For dynamic variations, in Bach's work, pianists use dynamic variations (crescendo-decrescendo patterns) to express phrase structure, whereas dynamic variations in Mozart's work serve as the means to convey higher-level music structure (Fig. 5, 2B). In Mozart's work, the regions with relatively louder dynamic levels often coincide with the appearance of theme B. In Mozart's this composition, theme A and theme C possess contrasting characters compared to theme B. Theme A and theme C mostly consist of rapid sixteenth notes, whereas the main components of theme B are unison chords played by both hands simultaneously. It would be a natural practice for pianists to perform theme B with a louder dynamic level in this case. An interesting observation is that given the contrasting dynamic levels between different themes (theme A, C versus theme B), the dynamic variations in Mozart's work still reflect the harmonic progression at the local-level. As shown in (Fig. 5, 2B), within individual themes, the valleys of dynamic curve at local regions often coincide with the release of harmonic tension, such as half cadences (pink markers) or full cadences (purple markers). Those observations indicate that the dynamic curve in Mozart's work is formed by complex interactions between diverse musical components, including the theme arrangement and the harmonic progression.

In Beethoven's composition, pianists accentuate the musical structure using different strategies compared to the previous two compositions. It appears that pianists tend to focus on the higher-level structure of music rather than local-level details in this composition, and employ combinative strategies to emphasize their interpretation of the overall musical structure. For the tempo variation, Bach's work has a smooth tempo curve, and in Mozart's work, pianists apply tempo variations (accelerando-ritardando pattern) to express local phrase boundaries. On the other hand, in Beethoven's composition, obvious valleys in tempo curve tend to coincide with the end of structural sections rather than local phrase boundaries (Fig. 5, 3A), which indicates that pianists employ a noticeable ritardando to signify the end of the section. The dynamic variations in Beethoven's work exhibit multi-layered musical features in the composition (Fig. 5, 3B). The global trend in dynamic variation shows inverted U-shapes corresponding to the high-level section structure of different themes, which suggests that pianists' performances exhibit the crescendo-decrescendo global pattern for each structural section. In addition, the dynamic curve within local regions still reflects detailed local-level features in the composition, in such a way that occasional fluctuations with limited range match with phrase boundaries, and the curve valleys are usually consistent with the locations with lower harmonic tension (half or full cadences).

To summarize general time-series trends observed in the tempo and dynamic variations, pianists employ diverse strategies to communicate the harmonic, phrase, and sectional structure in the three music compositions. Pianists generally utilize dynamic variations (crescendo-decrescendo pattern) to convey the phrase and harmonic structure in Bach's work. In contrast, in Mozart's work, dynamic variations are the means to communicate higher-level sectional structure rather than local phrase boundaries, and the phrase structure is more manifest in the tempo variation curve (ritardando at phrase end). In Beethoven's composition, tempo and dynamic variations exhibit complex influences from diverse musical features. The sectional structure is evident in both tempo (ritardando at section end) and dynamic variations (crescendo-decrescendo pattern), and the dynamic fluctuations are affected by global features in sectional structure, as well as by local features in phrase and harmony.

5 Discussion

In the previous section, we reported our findings regarding tempo and dynamic variations in performances of three piano pieces, and how pianists apply different expressive variations to communicate distinctive musical structures in the composition. We will further incorporate our findings with previous research in this section.

According to our analysis, musical phrase appears to be one of the main components for musicians to express in their performance. Previous research reported that the arching pattern in tempo curve [9,36] and dynamic variations [15] are attached to phrase formation. In our analysis, we further found that pianists apply diverse strategies to express phrase structure when they are performing different compositions. For instance, the dynamic variations indicate the phrase structure in Bach's composition (crescendo-decrescendo pattern per phrase), whereas tempo variations are mostly used to express phrase in Mozart's composition (slow down at phrase end). Different expressive strategies also reflects diverse compositional characters in these two music pieces. Bach's composition holds an invariant rhythmic pattern, which is expressed by a stable tempo in pianists' performances. In contrast, pianists are more likely to emphasize the dynamic change in order to highlight the tension-release process for the harmonic progression in Bach's composition, and such harmonic progression usually conforms with phrase structure (e.g. cadence at the end of phrase). The compositional structure in Baroque period mostly focuses on the development of short motives, whereas compositions in Classical period emphasize clear formation of phrase. In Mozart's composition, pianists therefore apply the accelerando-ritardando pattern in the tempo curve to shape the direction of the phrase.

Regarding the combination of local music elements and the global structure of music, previous studies suggest that the expressive manner in music performance is affected by both local elements (e.g. melodic peak, rhythmic grouping) [23, 33] and global structure (e.g. sectional arrangement) [9]. In our analysis, we found that pianists apply different strategies to stress local and global elements. For instance, Beethoven's composition exhibits an interesting combination of local and global factors, in which the general curve in both tempo and dynamic variations remain mostly consistent with global sectional arrangement, while the variations still show small-range fluctuations corresponding to local phrase boundaries. Compared to Bach's and Mozart's works, Beethoven's composition has sophisticated theme transformation accompanied by frequent modulation, and the manifest harmonic tension build-up process is one of the key features in Beethoven's compositions. Pianists may therefore manipulate both tempo and dynamic variations in their performance to communicate this important structural character.

It emerges from our analysis that in piano performance, expressive variations in tempo and dynamics exhibit systematic variations consistent with musical structures. Such systematic variations can be regarded as typical components to shape distinctive performance style, in which we generally expect that pianists should apply different expressive conventions when they are performing different styles of music in Western art music (e.g. Baroque, Classical, Romantic compositions). Our analysis method and results can serve as empirical means and provide observations for diverse performance styles in Western art music. Our current analysis is limited to piano performances for several selected compositions, and this analysis procedure can be further applied to the investigation for wider range of repertoire and for different instrument's performances.

6 Conclusion

In this paper, we show that pianists' performances exhibit systematic expressive variations corresponding to diverse compositional styles in Western art music. We collected 72 piano performance recordings for three compositions, and derived expressive variations in tempo and dynamics using automatic audio-to-score alignment and MIR techniques. Statistical and time-series analyses are performed to clarify the relationship between different compositional and expressive element, as well as their time-series connections during the course of performance. It is found that pianists apply stylistic expressive variations to communicate musical components at both global (e.g. sectional arrangement, harmonic progression) and local (e.g. phrase boundaries) levels, and they choose different expressive strategies according to distinctive traits of each composition. We suggest that those systematic variations in expressive elements constitute the core of distinctive performance style, and the complex interaction among diverse expressive elements (e.g. tempo and dynamic variations) at multi-layered musical structures (local and global levels) can compose an empirical approach to describe and compare idiosyncratic music performance styles.

References

1. Aldwell, E., Schachter, C., Cadwallader, A.: Harmony and Voice Leading. Cengage Learning (2018)
2. Cancino-Chacón, C.E., Gadermaier, T., Widmer, G., Grachten, M.: An evaluation of linear and non-linear models of expressive dynamics in classical piano and symphonic music. Mach. Learn. **106**(6), 887–909 (2017). https://doi.org/10.1007/s10994-017-5631-y
3. Cancino-Chacón, C.E., Grachten, M.: An evaluation of score descriptors combined with non-linear models of expressive dynamics in music. In: Proceedings of International Conference on Discovery Science (2015)
4. Cancino-Chacón, C.E., Grachten, M., Goebl, W., Widmer, G.: Computational models of expressive music performance: a comprehensive and critical review. Front. Digit. Hum. **5**, 25 (2018)
5. Chen, C.T., Jang, J.S.R., Liou, W.: Improved score-performance alignment algorithms on polyphonic music. In: Proceedings of IEEE International Conference on Acoustics, Speech and Signal Processing (2014)
6. Cook, N.: A Guide to Musical Analysis. Oxford University Press, USA (1994)
7. Cuthbert, M.S., Ariza, C.: Music21: a toolkit for computer-aided musicology and symbolic music data. In: Proceedings of International Society for Music Information Retrieval Conference (2010)
8. Dodson, A.: Expressive asynchrony in a recording of Chopin's Prelude No. 6 in B Minor by Vladimir de Pachmann. Music Theory Spectrum **33**(1), 59–64 (2011)
9. Fabian, D.: A Musicology of Performance: Theory and Method Based on Bach's Solos for Violin. Open Book Publishers (2015)
10. Field, A.: Discovering Statistics Using IBM SPSS Statistics, 4th edn. Sage (2013)
11. Flossmann, S., Grachten, M., Widmer, G.: Expressive performance rendering with probabilistic models. In: Kirke, A., Miranda, E.R. (eds.), Guide to Computing for Expressive Music Performance, pp. 75–98. Springer, London (2013). https://doi.org/10.1007/978-1-4471-4123-5_3

12. Friberg, A., Bresin, R., Sundberg, J.: Overview of the KTH rule system for musical performance. Adv. Cogn. Psychol. **2**(2–3), 145–161 (2006)
13. Gingras, B., McAdams, S.: Improved score-performance matching using both structural and temporal information from MIDI recordings. J. New Music Res. **40**(1), 43–57 (2011)
14. Giraldo, S., Ramirez, R.: A machine learning approach to ornamentation modelling and synthesis in jazz guitar. J. Math. Music **10**(2), 107–126 (2016)
15. Giraldo, S., et al.: Automatic assessment of tone quality in violin music performance. Front. Psychol. **10**, 334 (2019)
16. Grachten, M., Widmer, G.: Linear basis models for prediction and analysis of musical expression. J. New Music Res. **41**(4), 311–322 (2012)
17. Grindlay, G., Helmbold, D.: Modeling, analyzing, and synthesizing expressive piano performance with graphical models. Mach. Learn. **65**(2), 361–387 (2006)
18. Héroux, I.: Creative processes in the shaping of a musical interpretation: a study of nine professional musicians. Front. Psychol. **9**, 665 (2018)
19. Van Herwaarden, S., Grachten, M., De Haas, W.B.: Predicting expressive dynamics in piano performances using neural networks. In: Proceedings of The Conference of International Society for Music Information Retrieval (2014)
20. Juslin, P.N.: Five facets of musical expression: a psychologist's perspective on music performance. Psychol. Music **31**(3), 273–302 (2003)
21. Kim, T. H., Fukayama, S., Nishimoto, T., Sagayama, S.: Statistical approach to automatic expressive rendition of polyphonic piano music. In: Kirke, A., Miranda, E.R. (eds.) Guide to Computing for Expressive Music Performance, pp. 145–179. Springer, London (2013). https://doi.org/10.1007/978-1-4471-4123-5_6
22. Kosta, K., Ramírez, R., Bandtlow, O.F., Chew, E.: Mapping between dynamic markings and performed loudness: a machine learning approach. J. Math. Music **10**(2), 149–172 (2016)
23. Leech-Wilkinson, D.: Cortot's Berceuse. Music. Anal. **34**(3), 335–363 (2015)
24. Lerdahl, F., Jackendoff, R.: A Generative Theory of Tonal Music. MIT Press (1983)
25. Li, S., Dixon, S., Plumbley, M.D.: Clustering expressive timing with regressed polynomial coefficients demonstrated by a model selection test. In: Proceedings of International Society for Music Information Retrieval Conference (2017)
26. Liem, C. C., Hanjalic, A.: Expressive timing from cross-performance and audio-based alignment patterns: an extended case study. In: Proceedings of International Society for Music Information Retrieval Conference (2011)
27. Liem, C.C., Hanjalic, A.: Comparative analysis of orchestral performance recordings: an image-based approach. In: Proceedings of International Society for Music Information Retrieval Conference (2015)
28. Llorens, A.: Brahmsian articulation: ambiguous and unfixed structures in op. 38. Music Theory Online **27**(4) (2021)
29. McFee, B., et al.: Librosa: audio and music signal analysis in python. In: Proceedings of the 14th Python in Science Conference (2015)
30. Molina-Solana, M., Lluis-Arcos, J., Gomez, E.: Identifying violin performers by their expressive trends. Intell. Data Anal. **14**(5), 555–571 (2010)
31. Nakamura, E., Ono, N., Saito, Y., Sagayama, S.: Merged-output hidden Markov model for score following of MIDI performance with ornaments, desynchronized voices, repeats and skips. In: Proceedings of International Computer Music Conference (2014)
32. Nakamura, E., Yoshii, K., Katayose, H.: Performance error detection and post-processing for fast and accurate symbolic music alignment. In: Proceedings of International Society for Music Information Retrieval Conference (2017)

33. Ornoy, E., Cohen, S.: Analysis of contemporary violin recordings of 19th century repertoire: identifying trends and impacts. Front. Psychol. **9**, 22–33 (2018)
34. Payne, E.: Creativity beyond innovation: musical performance and craft. Music Sci. **20**(3), 325–344 (2016)
35. Ramirez, R., Maestre, E., Serra, X.: Automatic performer identification in commercial monophonic jazz performances. Pattern Recogn. Lett. **31**(12), 1514–1523 (2010)
36. Spiro, N., Gold, N., Rink, J.: Musical motives in performance: a study of absolute timing patterns. In: Chew, E., Assayag, G., Smith, J.B. (eds.) Mathemusical Conversations: Mathematics and Computation in Music Performance and Composition, pp. 109–128. World Scientific (2016)
37. Windsor, W.L., Desain, P., Penel, A., Borkent, M.: A structurally guided method for the decomposition of expression in music performance. J. Acoust. Soc. Am. **119**(2), 1182–1193 (2006)

deepGTTM-IV: Deep Learning Based Time-Span Tree Analyzer of "A Generative Theory of Tonal Music"

Masatoshi Hamanaka[1(✉)], Keiji Hirata[2], and Satoshi Tojo[3]

[1] RIKEN, Tokyo, Japan
masatoshi.hamanaka@riken.jp
[2] MIRAI SHARE, Yokohama, Japan
[3] Asia University, Tokyo, Japan

Abstract. This paper describes our development of a deep learning based time-span tree analyzer of the Generative Theory of Tonal Music (GTTM). Construction of a time-span tree analyzer has been attempted several times, but most previous analyzers performed very poorly, while those that performed relatively well required parameters to be manually adjusted. We previously proposed stepwise reduction for a time-span tree, which reduces the branches of the tree one by one, and confirmed that it can be learned by using the Transformer model. However, stepwise reduction could not obtain a time-span tree because it does not know to which notes the reduced notes were absorbed. Therefore, we improved the encoding for learning stepwise reduction and specified which notes are absorbed by which notes. We also propose a time-span tree acquisition algorithm that iterates stepwise reduction by representing the time-span tree as a matrix. As a result of experiments with 30 pieces, correct time-span trees were obtained for 29 pieces.

Keywords: generative theory of tonal music (GTTM) · time-span tree · melody reduction · transformer model

1 Introduction

We have developed a time-span tree analyzer that is based on the Generative Theory of Tonal Music (GTTM) by using deep learning called deepGTTM-IV. The GTTM was proposed by Leardahl and Jackendoff in 1983, and the time-span tree is a binary tree with each branch connected to each note [12].

Many time-span tree analyzers have been proposed, but most have many analytical errors [3–6,14]. The time-span tree analyzer that had the highest analytical performance required parameters to be manually adjusted [8].

The reason previous time-span tree analyzers performed insufficiently is that they analyzed in a bottom-up manner using only local information. [3–6,8,14]. Therefore, we considered learning the raw data of the entire piece by deep learning. Our deepGTTM-IV has four features.

S. Ystad et al. (Eds.): CMMR 2023, LNCS 15236, pp. 267–275, 2026.
https://doi.org/10.1007/978-3-032-02042-0_20

Stepwise reduction: The Ground Truth data of a time-span tree is insufficient to directly learn the relationship between a piece and its time-span tree. To enable learning, we set the learning target as the process of reducing one note.

Branch priority: To make possible the stepwise reduction, the priority order of branches needs to be defined. The maximum time span is used as the branch priority.

Encoding: By encoding the score into text, stepwise reduction can be learned in the framework of automatic translation. This makes it possible to reduce notes at designated positions in a piece as if words are omitted in a sentence.

Time-span-tree matrix: The time-span tree has been handled in XML and Json formats, making coding difficult [7]. We made coding easier by expressing the information necessary for reduction (i.e., pitch, duration, time-span-tree shape, and branch priority) in a matrix.

We performed an experiment in which 270 items from a GTTM analysis corpus consisting of 300 pieces and their time-span trees were used to learn the Transformer model with the remaining 30 used for evaluation and found that our analyzer was able to obtain correct time-span trees for 29 out of 30 pieces. The remainder of the paper is as follows. Section 2 presents problems of time-span tree analysis based on deep learning, Sect. 3 describes the data for learning and evaluation, and Sect. 4 describes the implementation of the analyzer. Section 5 describes the experimental results, and Sect. 6 gives a summary and mentions future plans.

2 Problems of Time-Span Tree Analysis Based on Deep Learning

In GTTM analysis, the relationship between structurally important notes and other notes in a score is expressed by a binary tree called a time-span tree. The time-span tree in Fig. 1 is the result of analyzing Melody A on the basis of GTTM. Reduced melodies can be extracted by cutting this time-span tree with a horizontal line and omitting the notes connected below the line. In melody reduction with GTTM, decorative notes are absorbed by structurally important notes.

There are the following three problems in the deep learning of time-span tree analysis.

2.1 Low Number of Ground Truth Data

As ground truth data of the time-span tree, 300 classical melodies and their time-span trees are published in the GTTM database [7,10]. However, the number of datasets (300) is extremely small for learning deep neural networks (DNNs) [1]. In the case of a small number of pieces of learning data, over-fitting is inevitable, and an appropriate value cannot be output when unknown data is input.

In the time-span analysis by musicologists, the entire time-span tree cannot be acquired at once but is gradually analyzed from the bottom up. Therefore,

Fig. 1. Time-span tree

the minimum process of analysis is set as one dataset, and then the number of datasets is increased. For example, if the DNN directly learns the relationship between a four-note melody and its time-span tree, the number of datasets is only one. On the other hand, if we consider the process of reducing one note to one dataset, the number of datasets will be three, as shown in Fig. 2(a).

The trained DNN estimates the melody consisting of $n - 1$ notes that is reduced to one note when a melody consisting of n notes is input. A time-span tree for a melody consisting of four notes can be constructed by estimating four to three notes, three to two notes, and two notes to one note, and combining the results (Fig. 2(b)).

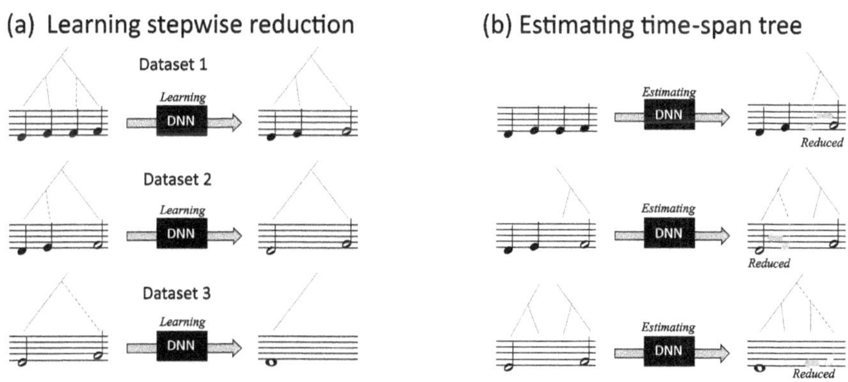

Fig. 2. Stepwise reduction

2.2 Ambiguity of Reduction Process

Time-span reduction removes decorative notes by pruning from the leaves at the tip of the tree, leaving only structurally important notes in the melody. To implement the stepwise reduction, the priority of branches must be obtained in a total order.

However, when it comes to GTTM itself, there are only a few examples of reduction using the time-span tree, and there is no detailed explanation on the reduction procedure [12]. For example, in Fig. 1, we can see two levels of reduction results, but it is not clear how many levels are actually necessary.

Marsden *et al.*. [13] suggested a way to determine the salience of two note events (a and b), neither of which are descendants of the other. They proposed defining the salience of an event as the duration of the maximum of the time spans of the two children at the branching point when the event is generated, or where it is reduced.

In contrast, in this study, the DNN needs to learn the relationship before and after the reduction than it is to reduce the order of the notes to close to that of human cognition. We use a time-span tree leveled by the duration of the time span for a simple reduction order that it is easy for the DNN to learn [9].

2.3 Long Note Sequence

The previous time-span tree analyzers performed poorly because they analyzed in a bottom-up manner using only local information [3,5,8,14]. In contrast, we propose using the entire note sequence before and after stepwise reduction for learning the DNN.

When a recurrent neural network (RNN) [16] or long short-term memory (LSTM) [11] is used as the DNN, the DNN can learn using note sequence, but when a long note sequence is input, the DNN forgets the beginning of it, and then the DNN cannot make use of the whole information of the note sequence.

The Transformer model [17] can learn and predict using the information of the entire note sequence. Moreover, the Transformer model has an additional layer of position information independently and uses the absolute position.

3 Data for deepGTTM-IV

This section describes the data for training the Transformer model. The Transformer model, which is an automatic translation tool, uses text for both input and output. Also, the Transformer model can learn the task of adding two values [2]. The duration of a note after reduction is the sum of the durations of the two notes before reduction, and we thought that this task could also be done with Transformer.

3.1 Learning and Evaluation Data

The preparation of the dataset for stepwise reduction is as follows. First, the priority of each branch of the time-span tree is evaluated on the basis of the duration of the maximum time span [9]. We refer to the longest temporal interval when a given pitch event becomes most salient as the maximum time span for the event. Next, stepwise reduction is applied to the least important note. A learning dataset of stepwise reduction is then created using the data before stepwise reduction as input data and the data after reduction as output data.

3.2 Encoding

Learning data are created from MusicXML and time-spanXML in the GTTM database. Since all melodies in the GTTM database are monophonic, the reduction method is limited to monophony. The notes in the melodies are made into a one-character string with the pitch and duration concatenated. The pitch is represented as 12 types without distinguishing between different octaves. By multiplying by 4, the duration of most notes becomes an integer, but since there are melodies containing only a few triplets, quintuplets, sextuplets, and septuplets, the duration is rounded up to an integer. The placeholders "l" or "r" are inserted at positions where notes disappeared due to the reduction. The "l" (left) is inserted when the reduction is absorbed into the left note, and "r" (right) is inserted when it is absorbed into the right note. In our previous work, we were unable to reconstruct the time-span tree because we did not distinguish between "l" and "r" [9]. Figure 3 is an example of learning data.

Before reduction. → After reduction.

c14 c16 d30 **c14 c12** c16 d20 c16 . → c14 c16 d30 **c26 l** c16 d20 c16.
c14 c16 d30 c26 **c16 d20** c16 . → c14 c16 d30 c26 **r d36** c16.
c14 c16 d30 **c26 d36** c16 . → c14 c16 d30 **r d62** c16.
c14 c16 d30 d62 c16 . → **c30 l** d30 R2 d62 c16.
c30 d30 d62 c16 . → **c60 l** d62 c16.
c60 **d62 c16.** → c62 **r c78.**
c60 c78. → r c138.

Fig. 3. Learning data for melody reduction

As a result of preparing the datasets, 7362 stepwise reduction training datasets are generated from 270 music pieces from the GTTM database consisting of 300 pieces and 849 stepwise reduction evaluation datasets are generated from the remaining 30 pieces for evaluation.

3.3 Data Augmentation

The 7362 training datasets are not enough to train the Transformer model, so we carry out data augmentation. Each note is shifted 11 times by a semitone and the amount of training data is augmented by 12 times. The durations of notes are 2–16 times and rounded up to the nearest integer, then the amount of data is augmented by 16 times. Finally, we prepare 1,432,704 ($= 7362 \times 12 \times 16$) learning datasets.

4 Implementation of deepGTTM-IV

A time-span tree is obtained by iterating stepwise reduction. We expressed time-span trees in XML or Json, but they were difficult to handle with programs because of their deep hierarchical tree structure. Representing a time-span tree as a matrix makes melody reduction easier to implement in a program.

4.1 Matrix Representation of Time-Span Tree

In Fig. 4(a), the first row of the matrix is the encoded pitch and duration and the second row is the connected parent branch number. The root branch has no parent branch to which to connect, so the parent branch number is set to 0. Both the 2nd and 4th branches are connected to the 1st branch, but the branches of the time-span tree do not cross [12], indicating that the 4th is connected to the 1st at a position closer to the root. Notes that are missing due to reduction have blank pitches and durations on the matrix.

The 3rd row of the matrix is the branch priority. Since the branch priority is obtained from the time-span tree and the note duration, it is redundant information, but it is differentiated in this paper for clearer explanation.

4.2 Generation of Stepwise Reduction Data

Stepwise reduction data is generated by performing stepwise reduction in the order from the lowest priority branch. Applying a step-wise reduction to Fig. 4(a) reduces the notes in the 3rd branch, which has the lowest priority, to the 4th branch. The input of the Transformer model is "d8 e8 e8 f8." The output is "d8 e8 r f16." because the third note is absorbed on the right side. Next, when stepwise reduction is applied to Fig. 4(b), the note on 2nd branch with the second lowest priority is reduced to the note on 1st branch, and the input and output of the Transformer model are "d8 e8 f16 ->d16 l f16.". Stepwise reduction data is created by repeating stepwise reduction until there is only one note left.

4.3 DeepGTTM-IV: Reduction System

Figure 5 shows an overview of the reduction system. First, the input melody is converted into Matrix Representation of the time-span tree. In the initial state, no branches are connected, so the matrix has all 0 in the second row (Fig. 5(a)). Then the note sequence in the first row is sent to the Transformer model (Fig. 5(b)). The output of the Transformer model is reflected in the matrix in which the 3rd note is absorbed in the 4th note (Fig. 5(c)). Then (a) to (c) are

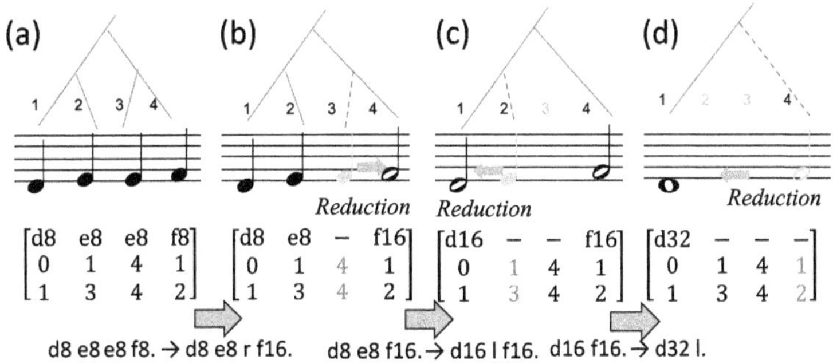

Fig. 4. Generation of stepwise reduction data

iterated until there are no notes for reduction (Fig. 5(d)). Finally, a time-span tree is output (Fig. 5(e)).

The Transformer model may produce unexpected outputs from untrained inputs. In such a case, it may be difficult to proceed with the reduction process and our method multiplies the initial duration of one note by a randomly chosen value between 2 and 16 and restarts the reduction process.

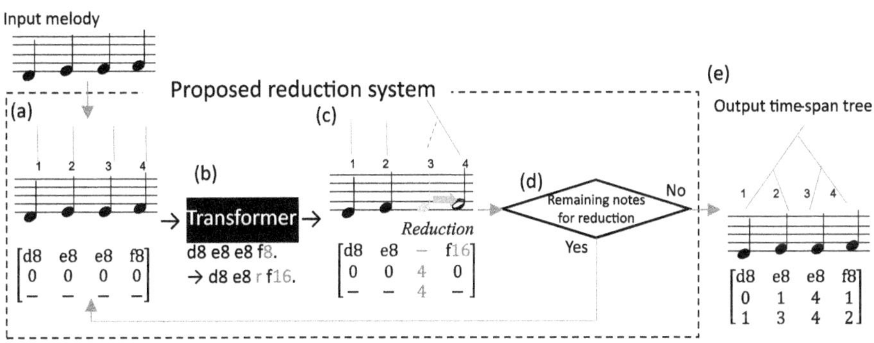

Fig. 5. Overview of reduction system

5 Experimental Results

We trained the Transformer model using 1,432,704 ($= 7362 \times 12 \times 16$) learning datasets created by data augmentation of 7362 stepwise reductions made from 270 pieces out of 300 pieces in the GTTM database. Accuracy was 0.99 when evaluated with 849 Stepwise reductions made from the remaining 30 pieces. Learning was carried out using Nvidia Quadro RTX5000 for laptops [15], and the learning time was seven hours.

We tried to acquire time-span trees for the remaining 30 pieces with deepGTTM-IV using the trained Transformer model, and we were able to acquire time-span trees for 29 pieces. The one remaining piece contained quintuplets and the output of the Transformer model was unexpected, so the notes could not be reduced.

6 Conclusion

Previous time-span analyzers could hardly obtain time-span trees without analysis errors, but we dramatically improved the analysis performance by learning step-wise reduction with the Transformer model. At the time of encoding the training data, by specifying which note to be reduced to the left or right will be absorbed, decoding becomes possible and a time-span tree can be obtained. As a result of experiments with 30 pieces, all time-span trees were obtained except one piece that contained quintuplets. We plan to conduct evaluation experiments with more pieces. In the case of quintuplets, septuplets, and higher multituplets, there is little data in the GTTM database and it is difficult to learn by the Transformer model, so we plan to increase the data of multituplets by data augmentation to improve performance.

Acknowledgements. This work was supported by JSPS KAKENHI Grant numbers 24H00748 and 21H03572.

References

1. Amari, S.I., Ozeki, T., Karakida, R., Yoshida, Y., Okada, M.: Dynamics of learning in MLP: natural gradient and singularity revisited. Neural Comput. **30**(1), 1–33 (2018). https://doi.org/10.1162/neco_a_01029
2. Brown, T.B., et al.: Language models are few-shot learners. In: Proceedings of the 34th International Conference on Neural Information Processing Systems. NIPS '20, Red Hook, NY, USA. Curran Associates Inc. (2020)
3. Groves, R.: Automatic melodic reduction using a supervised probabilistic context-free grammar. In: Proceedings of the 17th International Society for Music Information Retrieval Conference (ISMIR2016), pp. 775–781 (2016). https://archives.ismir.net/ismir2016/paper/000274.pdf
4. Hamanaka, M., Hirata, K., Tojo, S.: ATTA: automatic time-span tree analyzer based on extended GTTM. In: Proceedings of the 6th International Conference on Music Information Retrieval Conference (ISMIR2025), pp. 358–365 (2005). https://ismir2005.ismir.net/proceedings/1015.pdf
5. Hamanaka, M., Hirata, K., Tojo, S.: Implementing "a generative theory of tonal music. J. New Music Res. **35**(4), 249–277 (2006). https://doi.org/10.1080/09298210701563238
6. Hamanaka, M., Hirata, K., Tojo, S.: FATTA: full automatic time-span tree analyzer. In: Proceedings of the 2007 International Computer Music Conference (ICMC2007), vol. 1, pp. 153–156 (2007). https://api.semanticscholar.org/CorpusID:17056478

7. Hamanaka, M., Hirata, K., Tojo, S.: Musical structural analysis database based on GTTM. In: Proceedings of the 15th International Society for Music Information Retrieval Conference (ISMIR2014), pp. 325–330 (2014). https://gttm.jp/hamanaka/wp-content/uploads/2015/12/ISMIR2014-hamanaka.pdf
8. Hamanaka, M., Hirata, K., Tojo, S.: σGTTM III: learning-based time-span tree generator based on PCFG. In: Kronland-Martinet, R., Aramaki, M., Ystad, S. (eds.) CMMR 2015. LNCS, vol. 9617, pp. 387–404. Springer, Cham (2016). https://doi.org/10.1007/978-3-319-46282-0_25
9. Hamanaka, M., Hirata, K., Tojo, S.: Time-span tree leveled by duration of time-span. In: Music in the AI Era: Proceedings of The 15th International Symposium on Computer Music Multidisciplinary Research (CMMR 2023), Revised Selected Papers, pp. 47–58. Springer (2023). https://doi.org/10.1007/978-3-031-35382-6_5
10. Hamanaka, M., Isono, Y., Hirata, K., Tojo, S.: Web-based time-span tree editor and analysis database. In: Proceedings of the 17th Sound and Music Computing Conference (SMC2020), pp. 338–343 (2020)
11. Hochreiter, S., Schmidhuber, J.: Long short-term memory. Neural Comput. **9**(8), 1735–1780 (1997). https://doi.org/10.1162/neco.1997.9.8.1735
12. Lerdahl, F., Jackendoff, R.: A Generative Theory of Tonal Music. The MIT Press, Cambridge (1983)
13. Marsden, A., Tojo, S., Hirata, K.: No longer 'somewhat arbitrary': calculating salience in GTTM-style reduction. In: Proceedings of the 5th International Conference on Digital Libraries for Musicology. DLfM '18, New York, NY, USA, pp. 26–33. Association for Computing Machinery (2018). https://doi.org/10.1145/3273024.3273037,
14. Nakamura, E., Hamanaka, M., Hirata, K., Yoshii, K.: Tree-structured probabilistic model of monophonic written music based on the generative theory of tonal music. In: 2016 IEEE International Conference on Acoustics, Speech and Signal Processing (ICASSP), pp. 276–280. IEEE Press (2016). https://doi.org/10.1109/ICASSP.2016.7471680
15. Nvidia: NVIDIA RTX in Professional Laptops — nvidia.com (2024). https://www.nvidia.com/en-us/design-visualization/rtx-professional-laptops. Accessed 13 Feb 2025
16. Pineda, F.J.: Generalization of back-propagation to recurrent neural networks. Phys. Rev. Lett. **59**, 2229–2232 (1987). https://doi.org/10.1103/PhysRevLett.59.2229
17. Vaswani, A., et al.: Attention is all you need. In: Proceedings of the 31st International Conference on Neural Information Processing Systems. NIPS'17, pp. 6000–6010, Red Hook, NY, USA. Curran Associates Inc. (2017)

SANGEET: An XML Based Open Dataset for Research in Hindustani Sangeet

Chandan Misra(✉) and Swarup Chattopadhyay

School of Computer Science and Engineering, XIM University, Bhubaneswar, India
{chandan,swarupc}@xim.edu.in

Abstract. It is very important to access a rich music dataset that is useful in a wide variety of applications. Currently, available datasets are mostly focused on storing vocal or instrumental recording data and ignoring the requirement of its visual representation and retrieval. This paper attempts to build an XML-based public dataset, called SANGEET, that stores comprehensive information of *Hindustani Sangeet* (North Indian Classical Music) compositions written by famous musicologist *Pt. Vishnu Narayan Bhatkhande*. SANGEET preserves all the required information of any given composition including metadata, structural, notational, rhythmic, and melodic information in a standardized way for easy and efficient storage and extraction of musical information. The dataset is intended to provide the ground truth information for music information research tasks, thereby supporting several data-driven analysis from a machine learning perspective. We present the usefulness of the dataset by demonstrating its application on music information retrieval using XQuery, visualization through *Omenad* rendering system. Finally, we propose approaches to transform the dataset for performing statistical and machine learning tasks for a better understanding of *Hindustani Sangeet*. The dataset can be found at https://github.com/cmisra/Sangeet.

Keywords: Hindustani Sangeet · north Indian classical music · XML · music dataset · classification · XQuery · music rendition

1 Introduction

Having access to free, well-maintained databases of music is a crucial resource for researchers. In the case of Indian Classical Music, this is also true since it has been shown to be important for high-quality research in music information retrieval (MIR) [8, 11, 15, 21] and musicological analysis using machine learning [18, 22, 23], deep learning [12, 16, 19, 20], etc. Several high-quality datasets, [1, 2] for example, for research in MIR and computational musicology can be found in the published literature.

Although audio recording-based music corpora are essential in certain types of music applications, studies of existing literature reveal a dearth of substantial research related to the varied domains of *Sound and Music Computing* (SMC), especially in the design and development of interfaces for expressing Indic Music on an electronic medium. One of the domains that interest us is the creation of an Indian music environment through the transcription and rendering of an Indic music piece using Indic

S. Ystad et al. (Eds.): CMMR 2023, LNCS 15236, pp. 276–283, 2026.
https://doi.org/10.1007/978-3-032-02042-0_21

notation systems and Indic language script. The ability to compose music electronically entirely in an Indian music environment necessitates the emergence of research in different domains in SMC. This requires a musicological analysis of the grammar and structure of the music sheets presently in use and the consequent development of musical fonts and rendering engines ([5] for staff notation for example). Needless to say, such endeavors would motivate the research community to create models for Indic music notation systems and their language bases [14] and provide ample opportunities to work in building interfaces for music expressions on an electronic medium.

The mere enabling of music practitioners in composing music electronically is insufficient unless we have tools to exchange such musical information seamlessly across applications. Consequently, this establishes the need for the development of a common music exchange format to communicate music independent of any genre, notation system, language script, and music sheet structure [13]. XML-based formats for exchanging musical information have existed for quite some time [7, 10, 13] and are being adopted by extremely robust and popular notation software like *Finale* [3], *Sibelius* [6], *MuseScore* etc. Additionally, the ability to store musical information in XML solves the problem of archiving our historic musical art form as an electronic database.

One of the most authentic sources of Hindustani Sangeet is the compositions published in the book *Hindusthani Sangeet Paddhati-Kramik Pustak Malika* which comprises of approximately 1900 compositions belonging to North Indian Classical Music penned by *Pt. Vishnu Narayan Bhatkhande* (1860 - 1936). In order to reach a greater number of music students and scholars, the first volume of *Kramik Pustak Malika* has been translated to *Hindi* language in 1953 by prominent music scholar *Dr. Laxminarayan Garg*. This paper introduces SANGEET, arguably the first XML-based music corpora that try to capture comprehensive musical information contained in these rich music sources to apply in various music applications like music transcription, visualization, MIR, computational musicology, etc. We begin the preparation of the dataset with the second volume of *Kramik Pustal Malika* book series and our objective is to store compositions of different genres in a carefully crafted XML database to preserve comprehensive musical information in a single format. This will provide the users to obtain a standard framework for efficient and easy access to the dataset that can be easily transformed to apply to various applications. We refer to three music applications related to visualization, MIR, and machine learning in support of the coverage, quality, and accessibility of SANGEET.

2 The Organization and Access of SANGEET

Pt. Vishnu Narayan Bhatkhande is the pioneer for providing a comprehensive theoretical foundation of Hindustani Sangeet in a published form in his six-volume book series titled *Hindustani Sangeet Paddhati, Kramik Pustak Malika* written in *Marathi* language in 1920. His book contains a comprehensive description of music symbols for realizing musical components including notes (Svar), time signatures (Lay), beats (Taal), ornaments (Alankar) etc. The dataset created in the current work has been taken from the Hindi translation of the second volume of the series. The second volume of the book series contains a total of 319 compositions belonging to 10 different raags. The present work takes these written compositions as a source of musical information to create the database for Hindustani Sangeet to be used in various applications.

We have taken 116 compositions of the three highest frequent raags i.e. raag *Bhairav* (42), *Todi* (39), and *Poorvi* (35) respectively, from the entire collection of 319 compositions for performing our experimental analysis. Eventually, the entire collection of compositions from all six volumes will be preserved in the dataset for applications related to music information retrieval, music-sheet visualization, etc.

The dataset consists of a number of XML documents that is equal to the number of compositions in the dataset i.e. each XML document represents a single composition of the dataset. The XML documents are equipped with meaningful tags to store all the necessary musical information for the compositions. The format of the XML files is validated against a schema definition document so that the format of the dataset or compositions are preserved. The schema definition document is an XML Schema Definition (XSD) file against which each XML document is checked and validated for legal elements and attributes. The XSD consists of four parts namely *info*, *taal*, *raag*, and *sheet* responsible for storing metadata, rhythmic, melodic, structural, and notational information in the XML files.

The metadata linked to the musical composition is represented by the *info* portion. It contains information on the catalog, the genre, and the notational system as shown in Listing 1.1 describing the first composition of the second volume of the book.

```
<INFO>
  <TITLE>Composition 1 Volume 2 Kramik Pustak Malika</TITLE>
  <AUTHOR>Pt. Vishnu Narayan Bhatkhande</AUTHOR>
  <NOTATION_SYSTEM>Bhatkhande</NOTATION_SYSTEM>
  <DATE_TIME>1923</DATE_TIME>
  <GENRE>Hindusthani Sangeet</GENRE>
  <ADDITIONAL>
    <ENTRY>http://ndl.iitkgp.ac.in/document/
    R2pPWGRxdkRWWnlvOVdPYzdzaWpTV0pYYTFITOVnNTB6V1dnR1dJVW1kUT0</ENTRY>
  </ADDITIONAL>
</INFO>
```

Listing 1.1. Info Part of XML file depicting metadata

The rhythmic foundation of Indian music is provided by *taal*. Indic music has nearly hundreds of Taals, each with its own specific composition that includes the name, *Bibhaga* or measure, *Maatra* or the number of beats, *Avartana* or the number of cycles per line, etc. Additionally, Taal has two designated beat indices, known as *Taali* and *Khali*, to signify stressed or unstressed strokes in addition to a specific beat pattern to uniquely identify a Taal. These patterns, which are required to portray the Taal graphically or as a music sheet accompanied by an Indian percussionist, have been illustrated as a series of numbers (seen in Listing 1.2). Additionally, the regular expression specifies the expression for a beat pattern, making it easier to query the Taal's structure.

```
<TAAL>
  <TAAL_NAME>Tritaal</TAAL_NAME>
  <BIBHAGA>4</BIBHAGA>
  <MAATRA>16</MAATRA>
  <AVARTANA>1</AVARTANA>
  <BEAT_PATTERN>4-4-4-4</BEAT_PATTERN>
  <ALTERNATE_BEAT_PATTERN>NA</ALTERNATE_BEAT_PATTERN>
```

```
    <TAALI_COUNT>3</TAALI_COUNT>
    <KHALI_COUNT>1</KHALI_COUNT>
    <TAALI_INDEX>1-5-13</TAALI_INDEX>
    <KHALI_INDEX>9</KHALI_INDEX>
</TAAL>
```

Listing 1.2. Taal Part of XML file depicting Taal and its sub-components

Raag provides the melodic framework to Hindustani Sangeet and each raag can be identified by characteristics like *Arohana* and *Avarohana*, which are ascending or descending movements made up of a series of notes, *Vadi* and *Samvadi*, which are consonant and dissonant notes, and classification forms like *Pakad* and *Jaati*. These characteristics are note sequences and have been encoded using *Ome Swarlipi* [4], the same rendition we use for storing notes in our dataset.

```
<RAAG>
    <RAAG_NAME>Yaman</RAAG_NAME>
    <THAAT>Kalyan</THAAT>
    <AROHANA>n-r-g-M-d-n-su</AROHANA>
    <AVAROHANA>su-n-d-p-M-g-r-s</AVAROHANA>
    <VADI>g</VADI>
    <SAMVADI>n</SAMVADI>
    <JAATI>Sampoorna</JAATI>
    <PAKAD>nlrgr-s-pMg-su</PAKAD>
</RAAG>
```

Listing 1.3. Raag Part of XML file depicting Raag and its sub-components

Sheet, which is based on the 2D matrix model *Swaralipi* [14], specifies the layout of the music sheet and the placement of the notation symbols. As a result, it replicates the entirety of the contents as a rectangular row-column arrangement. Even though we haven't yet transcribed the beat markings and lyrics, the model has the provision to include them in the future. The format cleverly transforms row and column models into helpful tags that make it easier to develop various applications, such as real-time note playback, producing music sheets, and retrieving score data.

For example, part of the first line of the original composition (shown in Fig. 1a) has been converted into the sheet part (shown in Fig. 1b and 1c).

3 Applications of the Dataset

Visualization of Music-Sheets: One of the primary applications of any music dataset is to visualize it or render it using a notation system in which it is preserved. We have encountered several difficulties in visualizing the composition in the Bhatkhande notation system since there is no standard font system for rendering Bhatkhande music symbols in any language script. The closest rendition we have found is the *Ome Swarlipi* [4] system which is a compact version of the Bhatkhande notation system and easy to use. In order to visualize in HTML format, the system provides the necessary styling information to render it in *Devanagari* script. Therefore the pre-processing step for this application is a converter that takes an XML file as a standalone composition and transforms it into equivalent HTML with the *Ome Swarlipi* rendition of the score. The source code of the converter has been given in the online repository link and the corresponding rendition is shown in Fig. 2.

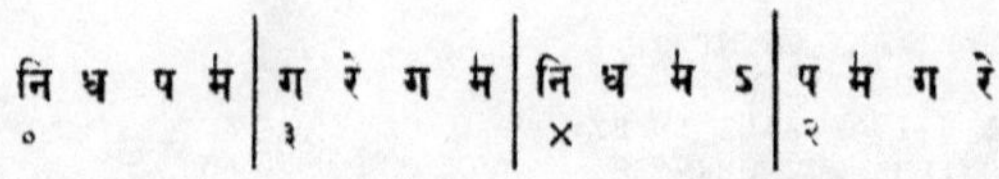

(a)

```
<SHEET>
  <TOTAL_LINE></TOTAL_LINE>
  <LINES>
    <LINE INDEX="1">
      <ROW INDEX="1">
        <COL INDEX="1">
          <NOTE_COUNT>1</NOTE_COUNT>
          <CONTENT>n</CONTENT>
        </COL>
        <COL INDEX="2">
          <NOTE_COUNT>1</NOTE_COUNT>
          <CONTENT>d</CONTENT>
        </COL>
        <COL INDEX="3">
          <NOTE_COUNT>1</NOTE_COUNT>
          <CONTENT>p</CONTENT>
        </COL>
        <COL INDEX="4">
          <NOTE_COUNT>1</NOTE_COUNT>
          <CONTENT>M</CONTENT>
        </COL>
      </ROW>
      ......
```

(b)

```
<LINE INDEX="2">
      <ROW INDEX="1">
        <COL INDEX="1">
          <NOTE_COUNT>1</NOTE_COUNT>
          <CONTENT>g</CONTENT>
        </COL>
        <COL INDEX="2">
          <NOTE_COUNT>1</NOTE_COUNT>
          <CONTENT>M</CONTENT>
        </COL>
        <COL INDEX="3">
          <NOTE_COUNT>1</NOTE_COUNT>
          <CONTENT>p</CONTENT>
        </COL>
        <COL INDEX="4">
          <NOTE_COUNT>1</NOTE_COUNT>
          <CONTENT>M</CONTENT>
        </COL>
      </ROW>
    </LINE>
  </LINES>
</SHEET>
```

(c)

Fig. 1. Sheet part of the XML file (b) and (c) depicting part of the original music sheet (a).

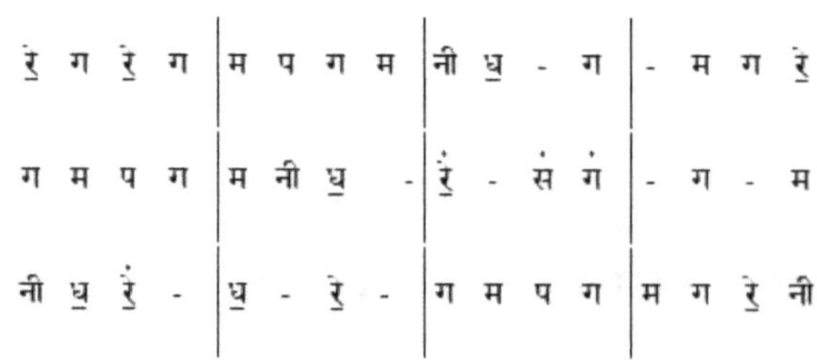

Fig. 2. Music-sheet web visualization using Ome Swarlipi.

Query and Retrieval of Musical Information: This is the application where we can appreciate the power of XML as a means to build the music dataset. XML has brought with it a number of tools and technologies to efficiently process the information contained inside it. For the present application, we have used two tools, namely *XPath* and *XQuery*. XPath, the XML Path Language, uses path expressions to parse through the elements and attributes of an XML document and select node elements to extract the contents inside it. This language is also used in another query language XQuery to query an XML database and retrieve required information from it much like the SQL that does the same on a relational database.

```
(: List of compositions having Meend :)
for $songs in collection ("
    Bhatkhande-Database")//swarlipi
let $title := $songs/INFO/TITLE/text()
let $contents := $songs/SHEET/LINES/
    LINE/ROW/COL/CONTENT/text()
let $notes := (for $song in $songs
return $song/SHEET/LINES/LINE/ROW/COL/
    CONTENT/text())
return if (contains(string-join($notes
    , ""),"g")) then
$title
```

(a)

```
(: List of compositions having a
    particular Arohana subsequence :)
for $songs in collection ("
    Bhatkhande-Database")//swarlipi
let $title := $songs/INFO/TITLE/text()
let $aroha := $songs/RAAG/AROHANA/text()
return if (contains($aroha, "s-R-g"))
    then
$title
```

(b)

```
(: Note frequency distribution of each composition :)
for $song in collection("Bhatkhande-Database")//swarlipi
let $raag := $song/RAAG/RAAG_NAME/text()
let $contents := $song/SHEET/LINES/LINE/ROW/COL/CONTENT/text()
let $joined_str := string-join(data($contents), ',')
let $joined_str := replace($joined_str, "<sup>|</sup>|@|u|1|\)|\(|-|,|\s+", "")
let $notes := (115,82,114,71,103,109,77,112,68,100,78,110)
let $code_points := string-to-codepoints($joined_str)
let $result := (for $i in $notes
    return count(index-of($code_points, $i))  )
let $result := normalize-space(string-join($result, ","))
return $result
```

(c)

Fig. 3. XQuery to retrieve the (a) list of compositions having Meend, (b) List of compositions having a particular *Arohana* subsequence and (c) Note frequency distribution of each composition.

The *preprocessing* stage for this application is to create an XML database created from the XML documents. We have used *BaseX* database engine to create the database from our dataset and XQuery to efficiently and easily perform complex queries and retrieve information from it and therefore, can be extremely useful for data-intensive complex web applications. This also provides a single-point query and retrieval system, as opposed to the current search and retrieval platforms [9,17] used for querying and browsing musical data. Figure 3 provides a few interesting and complex queries that satisfy the fine-grained information needs of the user. For example query 3c can be used to generate dataset for raag classification as described in the following section.

Table 1. Performance measure of Logistic Regression, K-Nearest Neighbors with varying values of k, and Decision Tree. The dataset is divided into 70:30 as training and test set to calculate the accuracy score of different classification models.

Accuracy Score of Classification Models				
Logistic Regression	K-Nearest-Neighbors (KNN)			Decision Tree
	$k = 3$	$k = 5$	$k = 7$	
0.9143	0.9714	0.9428	0.9428	0.9714

Raag Prediction Through Machine Learning: This application refers to the musicological analysis of various musical components present in Hindustani Sangeet. It covers statistical and structural analysis, data mining, and inference using machine learning and deep learning techniques. As an example of the application, we apply machine learning techniques on the dataset for the task of raag prediction. The *preprocessing* step for raag prediction is to convert the XML dataset into a tabular data-frame containing a number of features and a target variable. For raag prediction, we take features as the frequencies of individual notes and the corresponding raag as a target variable for any composition. Instead of taking the note-frequency distribution of 36 notes for a composition spanning across three octaves, we merge the notes to obtain the frequency distribution of 12 notes. Since, the positions of the notes of the *Arohana* and *Avarohana* of any particular composition in different octaves do not affect the raag of the composition, we map corresponding notes of three octaves and make a sum of frequencies of corresponding notes to obtain 12 note-frequency distribution (can be obtained from 3c given in GitHub). Table 1 shows the measure of performance of different machine learning techniques for raag prediction for our dataset. We have transformed our dataset into a three-class classification problem by taking the three most frequent raags i.e. *Bhairav*, *Todi*, and *Poorvi*, and applied the different classification models to generate the accuracy scores. Since each classifier examined shows high accuracy score the dataset can be considered as a robust dataset for raag classification. Table 1 shows that KNN with $k = 3$ and decision tree classifier gives better accuracy scores than the logistic regression model.

4 Conclusions and Future Works

This paper presents SANGEET, a Hindustani Sangeet dataset based on XML to provide easy and efficient access to a music corpora to perform various applications including music visualization, MIR, and Raag prediction using machine learning techniques. Backed by a robust music-sheet framework and a structured XSD, SANGEET provides a comprehensive repository for rich musical information to be shared seamlessly across applications. We have shown that SANGEET is quite efficient for accessing and transforming musical data into a format suitable for various musical applications. Our future objective is to extend SANGEET with the compositions of Bhatkhande's other five volumes of *Kramik Pustak Malika* and update the structure of the XML dataset with taal markings and lyric information. This will provide better music-sheet rendition and richer queries to fulfill the user's information needs.

Acknowledgments.. We would like to thank the undergraduate students of School of Computer Science & Engineering for helping create the dataset.

References

1. Annotated compmusic datasets. https://compmusic.upf.edu/datasets. Accessed 6 May 2022
2. Dunya. https://dunya.compmusic.upf.edu/. Accessed 6 May 2022

3. Finale—music notation software that lets you create your way. https://www.finalemusic.com/. Accessed 6 May 2022
4. Fonts for writing Indian music - Omenad fonts. https://omenad.github.io/fonts/. Accessed 6 May 2022
5. Lilypond... music notation for everyone. http://lilypond.org/. Accessed 23 Feb 2022
6. Music notation software - sibelius - avid. https://www.avid.com/sibelius. Accessed 6 May 2022
7. Baggi, D., Haus, G.: IEEE 1599: music encoding and interaction. Computer **42**(3), 84–87 (2009)
8. Chithra, S., Sinith, M., Gayathri, A.: Music information retrieval for polyphonic signals using hidden markov model. Procedia Comput. Sci. **46**, 381–387 (2015)
9. Ghosh, S., Dasgupta, A., Mukhopadhyay, D., Datta, D.: Tagoreweb: the complete works of Rabindranath Tagore (2020). http://tagoreweb.in/. Accessed 6 May 2022
10. Good, M., et al.: Musicxml: an internet-friendly format for sheet music. In: XML Conference and Expo, pp. 3–4. Citeseer (2001)
11. Kirthika, P., Chattamvelli, R.: A review of raga based music classification and music information retrieval (MIR). In: 2012 IEEE International Conference on Engineering Education: Innovative Practices and Future Trends (AICERA), pp. 1–5. IEEE (2012)
12. Madhusudhan, S.T., Chowdhary, G.: Deepsrgm-sequence classification and ranking in Indian classical music with deep learning. In: Proceedings of the 20th International Society for Music Information Retrieval Conference, pp. 533–540 (2019)
13. Misra, C.: Sangeetxml: an xml format for score retrieval for Indic music. In: ACM Multimedia Asia, pp. 1–5 (2021)
14. Misra, C., Chakraborty, T., Basu, A., Bhattacharya, B.: Swaralipi: a framework for transcribing and rendering Indic music sheet (2016)
15. Murthy, Y.S., Koolagudi, S.G.: Content-based music information retrieval (CB-MIR) and its applications toward the music industry: a review. ACM Comput. Surv. (CSUR) **51**(3), 1–46 (2018)
16. Nag, S., Basu, M., Sanyal, S., Banerjee, A., Ghosh, D.: On the application of deep learning and multifractal techniques to classify emotions and instruments using Indian classical music. Phys. A **597**, 127261 (2022)
17. Society for Natural Language Technology Research, G.O.W.B.: Rabindra-Rachanabali (1905). https://rabindra-rachanabali.nltr.org. Accessed 6 May 2022
18. Patel, E., Chauhan, S.: Raag detection in music using supervised machine learning approach. Int. J. Adv. Technol. Eng. Explor. **4**(29), 58 (2017)
19. Pendyala, V.S., Yadav, N., Kulkarni, C., Vadlamudi, L.: Towards building a deep learning based automated Indian classical music tutor for the masses. Syst. Soft Comput. **4**, 200042 (2022)
20. Sharma, A.K., et al.: Classification of Indian classical music with time-series matching deep learning approach. IEEE Access **9**, 102041–102052 (2021)
21. Sridhar, R., Geetha, T.: Raga identification of Carnatic music for music information retrieval. Int. J. Recent Trends Eng. **1**(1), 571 (2009)
22. Sridharan, A., Moh, M., Moh, T.S.: Similarity estimation for classical Indian music. In: 2018 17th IEEE International Conference on Machine Learning and Applications (ICMLA), pp. 814–819. IEEE (2018)
23. Ujlambkar, A.M., Attar, V.Z.: Mood classification of Indian popular music. In: Proceedings of the CUBE International Information Technology Conference, pp. 278–283 (2012)

Music Analysis Through Mathematical Logic

Matteo Bizzarri(✉)

Scuola Normale Superiore, Pisa, Italy
matteo.bizzarri@sns.it
https://matteo.bizzarri.net

Abstract. Music and mathematics have a long-standing relationship, but what about music and logic? Only recently have some authors started to explore the relationship between logic and music analysis, thanks to developments in both fields. The aim of this paper is to analyze this relationship, by developing a system capable of analyzing chord sequences using a logical presentation as well as create new harmonic structures. The logical presentation draws heavily from proof theory and its dual, i.e. tableuax. Also if music is not a proof, its adaptability makes it effective for this purpose. The attempt here proposed will try to apply proof theory to a brief, but important part of music: chord sequence analysis.

Keywords: music analysis · logic · proof theory · chords analysis

1 Introduction

Logic is primarily used in mathematics to formalize human reasoning, and the study of the relationship between mathematics and music has a long-standing tradition. This work aims to explore the connection between logic and music, which has not been studied extensively. Specifically, the idea arose from my personal interest in proof theory and its ability to simplify complex sentences into simpler propositions. The objective of this paper is to make a preliminary attempt in this direction, by exploring the possibility of applying proof theory techniques to chord analysis[1].

The method presented in this paper it is inspired by Neo-Riemannian and Tonfeld theories, which are systematic approaches to the musical structures' analysis, albeit not in a formal logical sense. The main goal of this paper is to introduce a rule-based logic method for chord analysis, which shares some similarities with structural proof theory (e.g., Troelstra's Basic Proof Theory [12]) in its logical foundations.

Something similar to this method has been presented in various articles, such as Rohrmeier: extended harmony [10], Granroth-Wilding, Mark and Steedman, Mark: Statistical Parsing for Harmonic Analysis of Jazz Chord Sequences [6] and

[1] Similar attempts were done in [1–4].

S. Ystad et al. (Eds.): CMMR 2023, LNCS 15236, pp. 284–296, 2026.
https://doi.org/10.1007/978-3-032-02042-0_22

Satoshi: modal logic music [11], but this contribution takes a different approach. Instead of decomposing a chord progression through grammar syntax, it presents a set of rules that can reduce the total number of chords, making the analysis simpler.

The method is as follows:

- we begin with a given chord progression;
- we apply rules that can *reduct* a certain set of chords into a smaller one;
- repeat the process until no further reductions are possible.

The corresponding method in proof theory is the decomposition of a proposition into a set of simpler ones to understand easier if the proposition is a tautology or not. But in the case of music analysis the final set of chords, that can't be simplified, will be called the *core set* and it will be associated with a particular type of chord set according to Tonfeld theory. The rules, once explained, can be analyzed both bottom-up and top-down, revealing the application of each rule at each level of the decomposition. The invertibility of each rule can also be used to compose new chord progressions, providing a mechanical method for choosing between different chords.

The paper is organized as follows: in the second section, we provide a description of Tonfeld and the Circle of Fifths; in the third section, we present our motivations for choosing structural proof theory and a very brief presentation of it is given; in the fourth section, we present the method for analysis in detail; in the fifth section, we outline the inverse process of composition using the rule-based method. Throughout the paper, we provide examples to help illustrate the motivations and the methods being discussed.

2 Tonfeld and Circle of Fifths

The Tonfeld theory [8] provides a visual depiction of the relationships between chords in tonal harmony using an infinite plane graph where each node represents a unique pitch class. Notes are understood as points in the graph, and chords are depicted by their relationships. The theory identifies three fundamental types of relationships: octatonic, hexatonic, and stacks of fifths, which are cyclic and sufficient to describe all other cyclic groups (Fig. 1).

Instead of explicitly defining the octatonic and hexatonic sets for each note (see for example [9]), it is possible to specify only three octatonic and four hexatonic sets, because the others are permutations of these, thanks to the limited transposition modes ([7]). This allows for a more efficient and compact representation of the harmonic relations within the Tonfeld theory:

$$Oct_0 = \{C, D\ , E\ , E\ , G\ , G\ , A, B\ \} \tag{1}$$

$$Oct_1 = \{D\ , D, E\ , F, G, A\ , B\ , C\ \} \tag{2}$$

$$Oct_2 = \{C, D, E\ , F, G\ , A\ , A\ , B\} \tag{3}$$

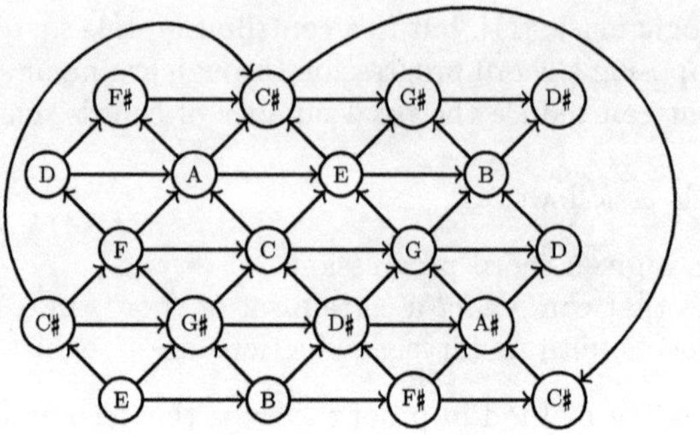

Fig. 1. A part of the Tonfeld. The lines outside the figure outline the relation between the same chords throughout the plane.

$$Hex_0 = \{C, E\ , E, G, A\ , B\} \tag{4}$$

$$Hex_1 = \{C\ , E, F, G\ , A, C\} \tag{5}$$

$$Hex_2 = \{D, F, F\ , A, B\ , C\ \} \tag{6}$$

$$Hex_3 = \{E\ , F\ , G, B\ , B\ , D\} \tag{7}$$

The stack of fifths is not a mode of limited transposition, so it is necessary to enumerate them for each note and for each expansion. This means that all possible stacks of fifths need to be explicitly listed, unlike the octatonic and hexatonic sets which can be represented with a little number of sets due to the limited transposition modes.

$$Fif_{C,1} = \{C, G\} \tag{8}$$

$$Fif_{C,2} = \{C, G, D\} \tag{9}$$

$$\vdots$$

This enumeration of every component, as is well-known, can be easily deduced thanks to the circle of fifths. Furthermore, this system simplifies the work with the proof-theoretic platform that will be presented later.

3 Why Structural Proof Theory?

Proof theory is a branch of mathematical logic that studies the nature of mathematical proofs and their properties. The central questions in proof theory concern the nature of proof, the relationship between syntax and semantics, and the role of proofs in the development of mathematics. It is a fundamental component of mathematical logic, and has important applications in computer science, philosophy, and other fields. Proof theory aims to understand the nature of formal systems and develop techniques for analyzing and manipulating them; there are several approaches to proof theory, but the one we want to emphasize here is *structural proof theory.*

The origins of structural proof theory [12] can be traced back to the early 1930s when Gerhard Gentzen (1909–1945) introduced the concept in his doctoral thesis titled "Untersuchungen über das logische Schließen" [5]. in 1933. In this thesis, Gentzen presented two primary systems of logical rules: natural deduction and sequent calculus. The former system aimed to closely align with the way theorems are typically proven in practice, while the latter system provided the framework through which Gentzen arrived at his main finding, often referred to as Gentzen's "Hauptsatz". This theorem states that any proof in classical logic can be transformed into a specific "cut-free" form, which means that the proof can be obtained without detours. Additionally, the cut-free proof has the subformula property, which states that all the premises used in the proof are contained in the conclusions. From this, general conclusions about proofs can be drawn, such as the consistency of the system of rules. The method has the following structure: the top formulas, also called *leaves*, represent the *starting point* of the proof ($q \vdash q$ and $p \vdash p$), while on the bottom we find the proven formula (i.e., $\vdash (p \wedge q) \rightarrow (q \wedge p)$).

$$\dfrac{\dfrac{\dfrac{\dfrac{q \vdash q \qquad p \vdash p}{q, p \vdash q \wedge p}\,(\wedge_{R,I})}{p, q \vdash q \wedge p}\,(ex.)}{p \wedge q \vdash q \wedge p}\,(\wedge_{L,I})}{\vdash (p \wedge q) \rightarrow (q \wedge p)}\,(\rightarrow_{R,I})$$

In this context, R and L denote the side of the rule to be applied; I represents the *introduction* of a rule; *ex.* represents the exchange rule, which enables swapping of the terms in the proof. The symbol $\wedge$ represents conjunction, which can be interpreted in English as *and*, and $\rightarrow$ represents implication, interpreted as *if... then...*

We believe that this system's clarity and duality make it an effective way to represent not only propositions but also chords. In proof theory, it is possible to use not only trees like the one presented earlier but also trees constructed *from the bottom* known as *tableaux.* These trees are constructed from the proposition to be proved, as shown below:

$$\vdash (p \wedge q) \rightarrow (q \wedge p)$$

$$|$$

$$p \wedge q \vdash q \wedge p$$

$$|$$

$$p, q \vdash q \wedge p$$

$$/ \quad \backslash$$

$$p, q \vdash q \qquad p, q \vdash p$$

The dual approach of the system, allowing for progression from the axioms or the propositions, will be useful in presenting the two-fold perspective we aim to convey in this article: analyzing chords from one direction and creating new harmonic structures from the other.

4 Rule Based Presentation

In proof theory, specifically in the style developed by Gentzen [12], a set of rules is used to introduce and eliminate certain logical connectives $(\wedge, \vee, \rightarrow, \neg)$ in order to determine whether the topmost nodes of a proof correspond to axioms, i.e., whether $p \vdash p$ (*p proves p*). The purpose of this section is to provide a more systematic account of the application of certain harmonic rules, using the rules of harmony, the Tonfeld theory, and a proof-theoretic framework.

While music is not a proof, a set of fundamental rules can still be outlined and adapted by adding or removing rules. This article focuses on jazz tonal harmony and presents a construction using a limited set of rules, but it can be hopefully expanded. Our attempt is to find a way to combine the generative theory of tonal music (GTTM) [10] with the ability of proof theory to explicitly indicate when and where a certain rule must or can be applied. This aims to provide a more systematic and logical approach to understanding and analyzing harmony in tonal music. It must be stressed that this attempt will not adhere to all of the structural rules typically found in proof theory. In fact, the only structural rule that we will use is the Contraction Rule, which will play a crucial role.

$$\frac{\vdash p, p}{\vdash p} \; (Contraction)$$

but there is no place for weakening, because we don't want that new chords can appear spontaneously:

$$\frac{\vdash p}{\vdash p, q} \; (Weakening)$$

and exchange, because we don't want that chords change position:

$$\frac{\vdash p, q}{\vdash q, p} \; (Exchange)$$

4.1 The First Rules

In a Gentzen's style presentation a rule has the following form:

$$\frac{\vdash p \qquad \vdash q}{\vdash p \wedge q}\,(\wedge_I)$$

where the letter *I*, indicates the *introduction* rule. The reason for erasing a chord in the presented version of the rule is to identify the essential components of the harmonic sequence during harmonic analysis. Therefore, the objective is to isolate the *core* set of harmonies. In fact here the presentation is as follows:

Authentic Cadence:

$$\frac{\text{V7} \qquad \text{I}\textsc{ma}^7}{\text{I}\textsc{ma}^7}\,(Fif_{I,1})$$

This kind of cadence can be expanded with the stack of fifths:

$$\frac{\text{IIm7} \qquad \text{V7} \qquad \text{I}\textsc{ma}^7}{\text{I}\textsc{ma}^7}\,(Fif_{I,2})$$

$$\frac{\text{VIm7} \qquad \text{IIm7} \qquad \text{V7} \qquad \text{I}\textsc{ma}^7}{\text{I}\textsc{ma}^7}\,(Fif_{I,3})$$

$$\vdots$$

Another rule is the *Plagal Cadence*, which is extensively used in ancient as well as modern pop music. *Plagal Cadence* is a type of cadence that goes from the fourth scale degree to the first one. It can be schematized in three main ways, to also explicitly show the movement from the fourth minor scale degree to the first one. It can be interpreted as a particular case of the circle of fifths: from the last instances to the first one.

Plagal cadence :

$$\frac{\text{IV}\textsc{ma}^7 \qquad \text{I}\textsc{ma}^7}{\text{I}\textsc{ma}^7}\,\text{P.C.} \quad \frac{\text{IVm7} \qquad \text{I}\textsc{ma}^7}{\text{I}\textsc{ma}^7}\,\text{P.C.} \quad \frac{\text{IV}\textsc{ma}^7 \qquad \text{IVm7} \qquad \text{I}\textsc{ma}^7}{\text{I}\textsc{ma}^7}\,\text{P.C.}$$

To explicitly explain the other types of cadences, like the *Deceptive Cadence*, it must be noted that the tonic and the submediant have a lot of notes in common, which allows for their mutual substitution. For example, an authentic cadence can be transformed into a deceptive one by substituting the tonic with the submediant. Something similar occurs between the tonic and the mediant.

Inversions:

$$\frac{\text{VI}}{\text{I}}\,(i.) \qquad \frac{\text{III}}{\text{I}}\,(i.) \qquad \frac{\text{I}}{\text{III}}\,(i.) \qquad \frac{\text{I}}{\text{IV}}\,(i.)$$

In jazz and classical music, another rule is deduced: the tritone substitution. This rule allows for the substitution of a dominant chord with its relative tritone. This is particularly useful in the context of jazz improvisation and the creation of complex harmonic progressions in classical music. The tritone substitution adds more dissonance to the progression, and is one of the most important feature of jazz harmony. It can be used to create tension and dissonance and it is an essential tool to understand the harmonic language of jazz.

$$\frac{\text{V}}{\text{I}}\,(tr)$$

From the Authentic Cadence and its inversions, it is possible to also obtain the Deceptive Cadence and the Authentic Cadence with the subdominant scale degree instead of the supertonic:

- Deceptive Cadence: V-VI;
- Authentic Cadence with subdominant: IV-I;

These variations help to create a more rich and complex harmonic language and can be used to create a different emotional or stylistic effect in the music.

$$\frac{\text{V7} \qquad \dfrac{\text{VIm7}}{\text{I}\textsc{ma}^7}\,(i)}{\text{I}\textsc{ma}^7}\,(Fif_{I,2})$$

$$\frac{\dfrac{(\text{IV}\textsc{ma}^7)}{\text{IIm7}}\,(i.) \qquad \text{V7} \qquad \text{I}\textsc{ma}^7}{\text{I}\textsc{ma}^7}\,(Fif_{I,2})$$

4.2 Examples

Example 1. The following example is taken from "But not for me" by George Gershwin. The structure is divided into sections, because the tree was too long.

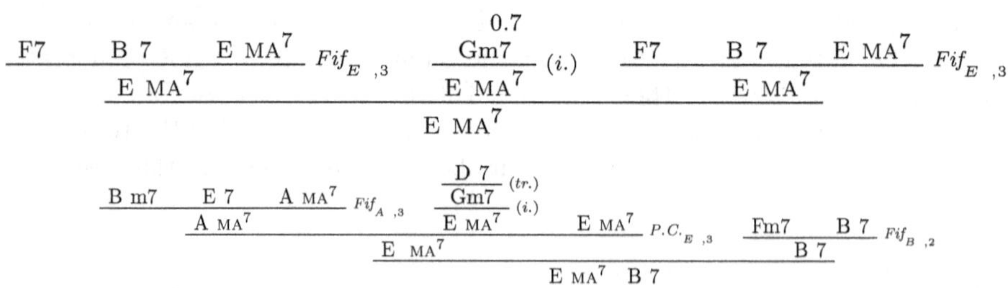

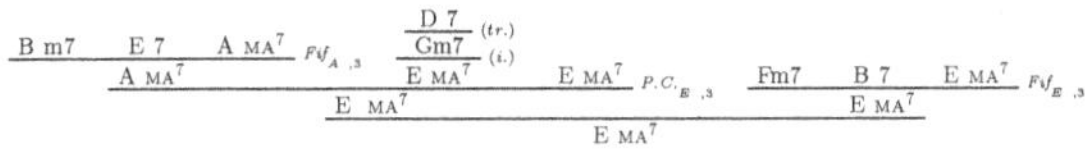

As we can see the main chord is E MA^7, that is always the main chord.

5 Composition of New Musical Structures Through a Rule Based Presentation

This method uses invertible rules to create novel harmonic tonal structures. The process is straightforward and involves selecting a fundamental node, determining the desired length of the structure, and applying the rules to expand the system until the required number of chords is reached. By using this systematic and logical approach based on the invertibility of the rules, it's possible to compose original harmonies.

5.1 Tableux

The inversion of the rules made in Sect. 4.1 can be inverted thanks to the dual of proof theory: tableux.

Generation of the Authentic Cadence:

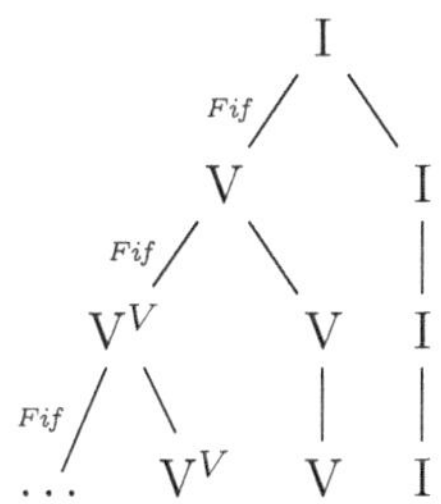

Generation of the Plagal Cadence:

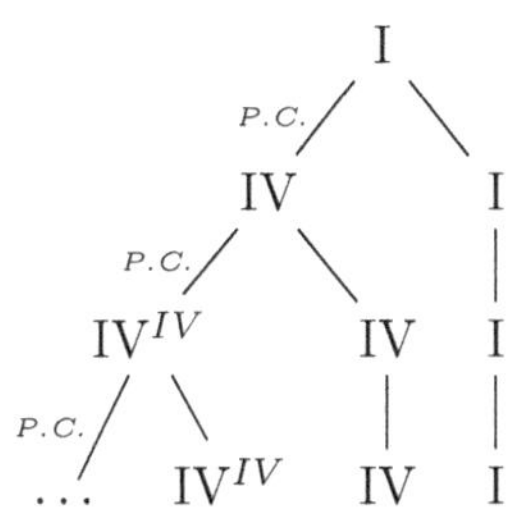

The inversions:

I
i. |
VI

III
i. |
I

I
i. |
III

VI
i. |
I

Triton substitution:

V
tr. |
I

Example 2. Firstly, we'll form a basic arrangement of three notes taken from the initial Octatonic set. Then, we'll establish a preferred duration for the arrangement, say 8 measures. We'll utilize various techniques, such as stack of fifths, plagal cadence, and tritone substitution, to extend the pattern following certain guidelines until we attain the desired number of chords. Consequently, we'll obtain 11 distinctive chords, resulting in an 8-measure arrangement with increased intricacy and musical appeal.

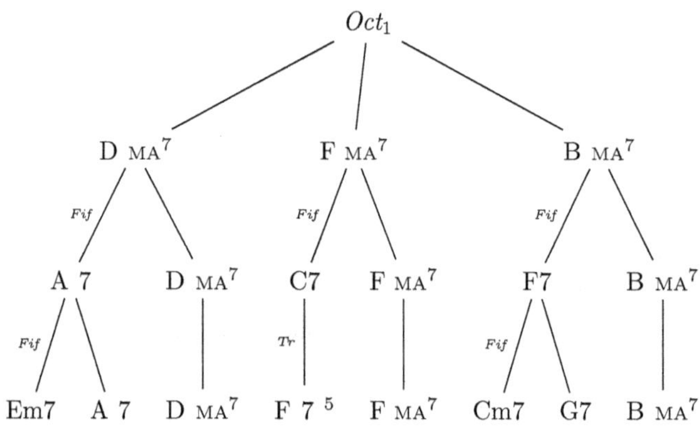

This way of composition can be automatized to create new and different harmonic structures, always remaining into a tonal configuration, but what if we want to create a non-tonal structure?

5.2 New Rules

One of the interesting thing about our system is that it is possible to add new rules giving flexibility to the system. Music and harmony, in fact, can change between ages and the rule-based system can be expanded with new rules if they are considered useful for a certain kind of analysis or a certain kind of composition. Suppose that the analyzed piece is taken from the baroque period and so it is important to explicit the *picardy third.* Then it is easy to add a rule that could be something like:

$$\frac{\text{Im} \qquad \text{V} \qquad \text{I}}{\text{Im} \qquad \text{I}}\ P.T.$$

This could seem redundant in respect of the rule of the stack of fifths, but the attempt here is to create something general that could be useful also in specific cases. In the baroque chorals, for example, understand when there is an authentic minor cadence or a picardy third could be useful, because a picardy third indicates the end of a phrase or of the piece.

Fig. 2. J.S. Bach's Jesu, meine Freude; mm. 11-13

Example 3. Let's consider, for example, J.S. Bach's Jesu, meine Freude (Fig. 2), this is an example of picardy third.

To analyze these bars it is possible to use the new rule:

$$\dfrac{\dfrac{\text{Em} \qquad \text{Am} \qquad \text{Em}}{\text{Em}}\ P.C. \qquad \dfrac{\text{F 7} \qquad \text{B7} \qquad \text{E}}{\text{E}}\ P.T.}{\text{Em} \qquad \text{E}}$$

New Rules in Composition In addition to their traditional use in tonality, add rules can also be employed in composition to generate unconventional results. For instance, a new rule could be introduced to mandate the inclusion of the third degree of a chord in any dominant chord that appears. This rule might read as follows: "Whenever a dominant chord is encountered, it must contain also the third degree" and let's call that *Th.*.

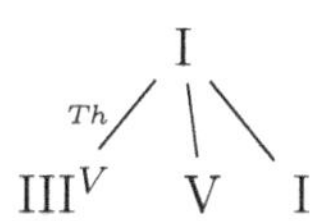

Incorporating this additional layer would introduce an added level of intricacy and diversity to the harmonic arrangements produced by the system, leading to a greater potential for novel and unforeseen outcomes. It is crucial to acknowledge that the regulations you integrate will shape the final composition to align with your specific requirements.

Example 4. For example try to write a new harmonic form using this rule with also some other rule:

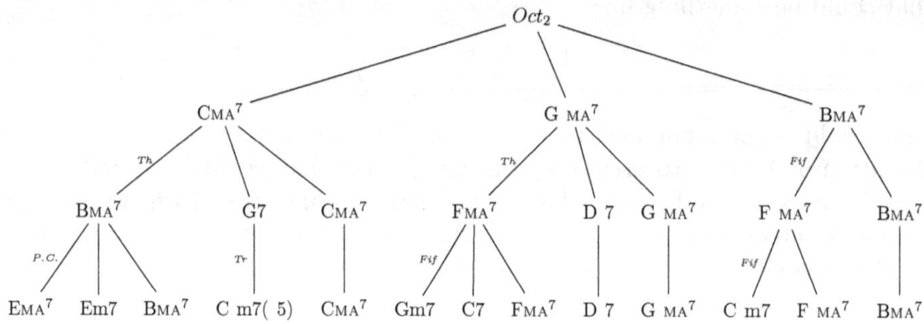

5.3 Proof Theory Method and CCG

The presented method shares similarities with the one presented in [6] that uses Combinatorial Category Grammar (CCG), but there are some notable differences. On one hand, the reduction method we propose is more flexible than the one presented in [6]. On the other hand, our method is not currently linked to machine learning or automatic analysis, which are areas that we plan to explore in the future. It's worth noting that the two methods are not in conflict and can ideally be combined in the future.

The contraction method we propose is particularly useful because it's malleable: we can add new rules to analyze and stress different musical aspects, and we can even invert the method to create new harmonic structures. In contrast, the method presented in [6] relies on a statistical machine learning technique that may not be as straightforward to implement using our proof theoretic presentation. Moreover, our proof theoretic presentation can be inverted to create new harmonic structures, which CCG can only achieve by working on the rules. However, this inversion process is not as straightforward as it is with our method. A common point between CCG and our method is the philosophical and musicological idea that chord progressions are driven by the listener's *expectations* of progression, based on the same harmonic Riemannian concept. However, our method can be expanded due to its ability to incorporate new rules.

6 Conclusions

The presented method is a different approach to understanding chord progressions, drawing inspiration from proof theory. While music cannot be proven, this rule-based method simplifies and clearly demonstrates the invertibility of the rules between analysis and composition. The approach's advantage is that new rules can be added to the system to emphasize specific structures or introduce new ones.

This approach to harmonic analysis offers several advantages for students and professionals alike. Firstly, its visual representation can aid in better understanding the underlying principles of harmony. By breaking down complex harmonic structures into their component parts and representing them as a tree-like structure, students can more easily grasp the relationships between chords and the rules that govern them. Secondly, this approach can be helpful in promoting creativity when composing new harmonic structures by providing the opportunity to choose new rules and leading to unexpected solutions and unique harmonic progressions. Lastly, this method can help shed light on a particular harmonic structure that may otherwise go unnoticed. By approaching a harmonic structure several times, each time with a different lens, an analyst can highlight a particular composer's choice over another, revealing the nuances and subtleties of their harmonic language. Overall, this approach to harmonic analysis offers a powerful tool for understanding and creating harmonic structures, and its potential applications are wide-ranging, from the classroom to the automatic composition.

Future researches should explore practical applications, incorporating additional examples and use cases. A deeper understanding of cut admissibility within this method is imperative. Moreover, the method presented holds potential for automated harmonic generation, which could be harnessed for an automatic theorem prover centered on harmonic structures. In summary, this method transforms chord comprehension through proof theory insights. While music eludes formal proof, this approach helps in understanding of rule dynamics in analysis and composition. Its adaptability and visual lucidity aid learners and creators alike, finding relevance from education to composition.

Acknowledgments. I would like to express my sincere gratitude to Professors Satoshi Tojo, Mario Piazza, and Fabio De Sanctis De Benedictis for their invaluable assistance in writing and developing this essay. Additionally, I extend my appreciation to the two reviewers for their insightful suggestions, which greatly contributed to the enhancement of both the method and the overall paper. Their recommendations on potential research directions have also been immensely valuable.

References

1. Bizzarri, M.: Music and Logic: a connection between two worlds. In: Proceedings of The 16th International Symposium on Computer Music Multidisciplinary Research (CMMR) (2023)
2. Bizzarri, M., Tojo, S.: A Formal Proof-Theoretic Approach to Music Analysis using Labelled Lambek Calculus, SIGMUS (2024)
3. Bizzarri, M., Tojo, S. : Chord Progression Analysis by Labelled Lambek Calculus (2024)

4. Bizzarri, M., Tojo, S.: Foundations of LLCM: Labelled Lambek Calculus for Music Analysis. In: Proceedings of 14th International Conference on Artificial Intelligence in Music, Sound, Art and Design (EvoMUSART) (2025)
5. Gentzen, G.: Untersuchungen über das logische Schließen. I. Math Z **39**, 176–210 (1935)
6. Granroth-Wilding, M., Steedman, M.: Statistical parsing for harmonic analysis of Jazz chord sequences. ICMC 2012: Non-Cochlear Sound - Proceedings of the International Computer Music Conference 2012, pp. 478-485 (2012,1)
7. Messiaen, O.: Technique de mon langage musical. Alphonse Leduc (1944)
8. Polth, M.: The Individual Tone and Musical Context in Albert Simon's Tonfeldtheorie. Music Theory Online. **24** (2018)
9. Rohrmeier, M.: Towards a generative syntax of tonal harmony. J. Math Music **5**, 35–53 (2011)
10. Rohrmeier, M., Moss, F.: A formal model of extended tonal harmony. In: Proceedings of the 22nd International Society for Music Information Retrieval Conference, pp. 569–578 (2021)
11. Tojo, S.: Modal logic for tonal music. In: Perception, Representations, Image, Sound, Music: 14th International Symposium, CMMR 2019, Marseille, France, October 14–18, 2019, Revised Selected Papers, pp. 113–128 (2019)
12. Troelstra, A., Schwichtenberg, H.: Basic Proof Theory. Cambridge University Press (2000)

Global Prediction of Time-Span Tree by Cloze Task

Riku Takahashi(✉), Risa Izu, Yoshinari Takegawa, and Keiji Hirata

Future University Hakodate, Hakodate, Japan
g3124004@fun.ac.jp

Abstract. Time-span trees in A Generative Theory of Tonal Music (GTTM) have global and local relationships. However, no analysis based on global relationships has been done, and higher-order mechanisms have not been clarified. Therefore, in this research, we will clarify this mechanism by masking the time-span tree as it is and using it as a cloze task. To experiment with the cloze task, we vectorized and embedded the tree structure. We also extended the data by changing the pitch and masking. As a result of experiments, it is possible to predict higher layers when masking a small maximum time-span.

Keywords: generative theory of tonal music (GTTM), time-span tree, LSTM, Seq2Seq, blockview, skip-thought

1 Introduction

In cognitive science, how humans listen to music is an important factor. When listening to music, people do actively listen while predicting the next melody, harmony, and rhythm. Emotional arousal during listening to music is said to be related to betrayal of the listener's conscious and unconscious predictions [9]. It has been reported that when an unpredictable change in pitch occurs while listening to a melody, people react psychologically and physiologically [2]. It has also been found that the memorability of a melody is related to the predictability [1]. For these reasons, we find that human perception of music is simultaneously analyzing and predicting. Therefore, music analyzers are required to be able to perform multiple analysis and prediction.

In addition, music theory shows that there are not only local relations but also global relations. A Generative Theory of Tonal Music (GTTM) [7], which is a cognitive music theory, describes local and global relationships, and is implemented on computers. In particular, GTTM's time-span tree implementation has been attempted [4,5]. So far, however, there has been little research about how to implement higher-order mechanisms. Specifically, the current algorithm inputs scores in specific batches and analyzes the time-span tree based on local relationships. However, when humans listen to music, they analyze and make predictions at some point. We never listen to the whole music and analyze it in

S. Ystad et al. (Eds.): CMMR 2023, LNCS 15236, pp. 297–309, 2026.
https://doi.org/10.1007/978-3-032-02042-0_23

batches. In fact, referring to Fig. 1, the subtree of C C and the subtree of G G are composed one subtree, so they have a local relationship. Similarly, there is a global relationship between C C and A A. On the other hand, the subtree of G G and the subtree of A A have not local relationship and global relationships. However, the subtree of C C, G G, and A A can be seen as three consecutive syllables of the same two sounds. Therefore, there is also a relationship between G G and A A as syllables. However, due to the reduced subtrees of the GTTM rules, it is difficult to find hidden global relations for subtrees of such syllables and phrases.

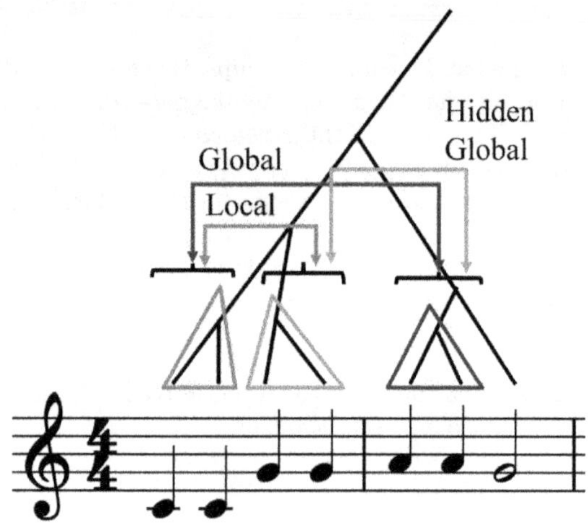

Fig. 1. Local and global relations in time-span tree

In this paper, we consider local and global analyzes of time-span trees. In detail, this paper reproduces the analysis and prediction of human music listening by taking missing time-span trees as inputs and complemented time-span trees as outputs. It enables local and global analysis and prediction using Sequence to Sequence (Seq2Seq) models and cloze tasks. The Seq2Seq model uses LSTM, and the recursive processing of LSTM enables analysis and prediction at the same time. Also, the input must be a tree structure. However, although previous research has discussed the analysis of tree structures [8,10], using the tree structure itself as data has not been previously considered. In this research, based on the representation proposed in ON-LSTM, a tree structure input is realized by factoring in the hierarchical direction and horizontal directions. It predicts complemented time-span trees from missing time-span trees. In conclusion, this paper proposes local and global time-span tree filling tasks for analyzing time-span trees based on human music perception.

This paper is divided into five sections as follows. First, the definition of the time-span tree used is explained. Section 2 reviews previous studies using time-span tree and deep learning models for tree-structured data. Section 3 details the dataset and data augmentation and embedding used in this paper. Section 4 introduces the Seq2Seq model used for the cloze task in this paper. Section 5 presents results from experiments to predict subtrees from subtrees. Section 6 presents a discussion of the results. Section 7 describes conclusions and future prospects.

2 Prerequisites and Related Work

Hamanaka et al. [4] analyzed time-span tree obtained by GTTM using deep learning. At low-level boundaries, the accuracy is 0.03 points higher than the conventional method, and the metrical structure has almost the same performance as the conventional method. However, this method is analyzed based on the theory of GTTM, and it shows that it cannot be analyzed without analyzer of GTTM. Hamanaka et al. [5] realized time-span analysis and melody morphing using deep learning. The research makes it possible to analyze time-span trees by learning the order of melody reduction. However, it does not take a tree structure as input, and also requires a melody input.

Ordered Neurons LSTM (ON-LSTM) [10] showed a function called Cumax. This function allows deep learning to learn the composition of the hierarchical structure. Then, the paper demonstrated that the function is effective in unsupervised learning. It shows that it is similar to analyzing a tree structure by a person who does not know the rules. However, it is not extended from tree structure to learning tree structure. Pyraformer [8] investigated whether hierarchical attention mechanisms are effective for long-term dependencies on time-series data. In addition, Pyraformer reduced the amount of calculation compared to the conventional method. However, it requires a large amount of data, well exceeding the number of pieces of music that a human being can listen to in a lifetime.

In conclusion, there is no model that predicts a tree structure from another tree structure, and either rules are used, or a large amount of data is required to acquire the hierarchical structure. Therefore, it is necessary to research a model that predicts and analyzes tree structure with a small amount of data without knowing the theory, similar to people listening to music.

3 Create the Experimental Dataset

The size of the tree structure varies greatly both vertically and horizontally. This tendency is particularly strong in the case of binary trees. There are two cases of extreme tree structures. One is when every possible reduction always occurs at each layer. In this case, since there are many tones, the sequence length is long, but the number of layers is relatively small. On the other hand, there are cases where the reduction is done only once at each Layer. In this case, even if the number of tones is small and the sequence length is short, the number of layers increases in proportion to the number of tones. As a result, when a tree structure is used as input, the size of the data differs greatly. Therefore, by using different learning methods for the vertical and horizontal directions, the effects of each are reduced and, with the implementation of deep learning, learns rules related to time-span trees. In the following, four procedures for solving the subtree filling problem of a time-span tree with Seq2Seq.

3.1 Data Collection

A dataset analyzing time-span trees of 300 songs has been published [3]. The time-span tree of the dataset is 8 bars long. Time-span trees are excluded that are ambiguous and subject to multiple analyzes due to preference rules. Furthermore, excluding the time-span tree whose sequence is long and sparse, the number of songs analyzed in this research is 279. The number of minimum layers is 5 and the maximum is 10. Also, the number of minimum notes is 10 and the maximum is 80.

3.2 Splitting the Dataset and Data Augmentation with Transposition

279 songs are divided into 8 to 2, and divided into 223 songs as learning data and 56 songs as test data. After that, the learning data is split 8 to 2 into training data and validation data, resulting in 178 songs in training data and 45 songs in validation data. Additionally, as a data augmentation, the training and validation data pitches are changed +2, +4, +5, +7, +9, +11. This multiplies the original data by 7.

3.3 Vectorization of Time-Span Tree

The tree structure is constructed so that it is easy for humans to understand. However, it is a format that is difficult to handle for Artificial Intelligence such as deep learning. Therefore, blockview was proposed by ON-LSTM [10] as a vector representation of the tree structure. This research extended blokview, which normally analyzes in parse trees, to time-span trees. This research extends time-span trees to blockview. Also, smaller parts are zero-padded. In detail, vectorization is performed so that the maximum lengths in the vertical and horizontal directions can be obtained.

In the original time-span tree, the duration becomes the total value as it is simplified. But in this research, it is not the total value in order to avoid the prediction becoming deterministic due to the duration. In addition, when using the total value, it is possible that the accuracy of the prediction will be greatly affected. The reason is that all durations that appear must be labeled, and with the current number of data, the data will be sparse. For these two reason, duration is not a total value in this research.

Figure 2 shows the original time-span tree and the time-span tree vectorized by the blockview. Note id 1 wins the most, so only notes with note id are vectorized in fourth layer. Originally, the simplification of note id 4 and 5 is ambiguous whether it is the second layer or the first layer. But for the sake of simplification, it is the first layer that can be considered. For note id 1, the duration is 0.75, 1.5, 3, but as We said earlier, we can't consider all combinations of numbers, so we consider it only as 0.75.

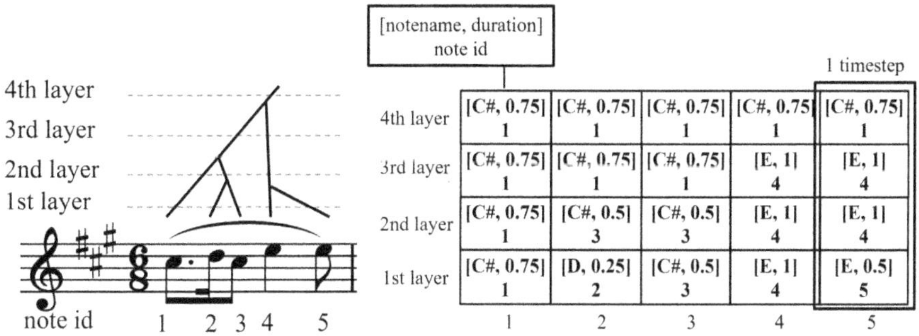

Fig. 2. The original time-span tree and corresponding blockview

3.4 Vertical Embedding

To predict the tree structure, the tree structure needs to be embedded into the latent space. Time-span trees vectorized by blockview are split vertically. This split vector is called a timestep. Timesteps have more similarity in elements as they go up in the layer. To take advantage of this feature, we use skip-thought [6]. Skip-thought captures a latent space from some sentence that predicts the sentences before and after it. Figure 3 shows the skip-thought architecture for embedding timestep vectors. In addition, it is a Seq2Seq model that outputs a timestep vector with the latent space by skip-thought as input. Therefore, information above the maximum time-span must also be masked for a complete gap-filling task.

3.5 Data Augmentation and Create Cloze Tasks by Masking Blockview

By creating the experimental dataset, the training data is 1246 songs and the training data is 315 songs. Also, the test data is 56 songs. However, if one mask is applied to one song, the data is insufficient for deep learning.Therefore, we create all possible masked time-span trees. For example, if a time-span tree has n notes, n-1 time-span trees are obtained as masked time-span trees by subtracting the head of the time-span tree. Using Fig. 2 as an example, mask all but the maximum time-span with note id=1. Two examples are shown below.

If the note id is 2 in Fig. 4, the maximum time-span is only the first layer, so only the time step with note id 2 is masked. On the other hand, if the note id

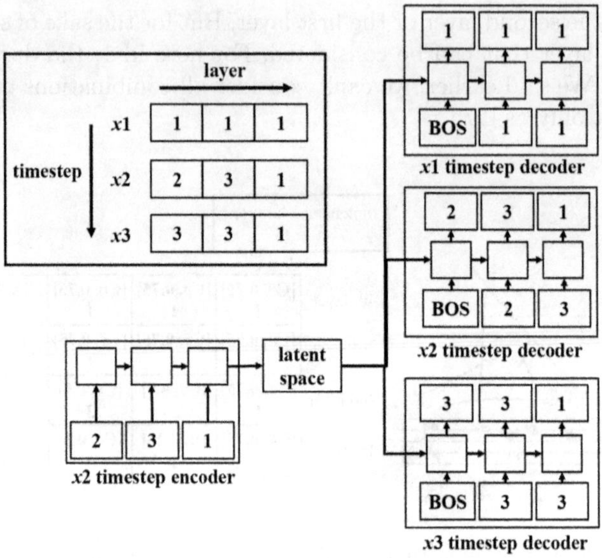

Fig. 3. Embedding x2 timestep by skip-thought

is 4 in Fig. 4, the maximum time-span is the second layer, so the timestep with note id 4 and the timestep with note id 5 that is reduced to 4 will be masked. In addition, in this research, since the latent space by skip-thought is input and the time step vector is output, it is necessary to mask the information above the maximum time-span tree in order to complete the blank filling task.

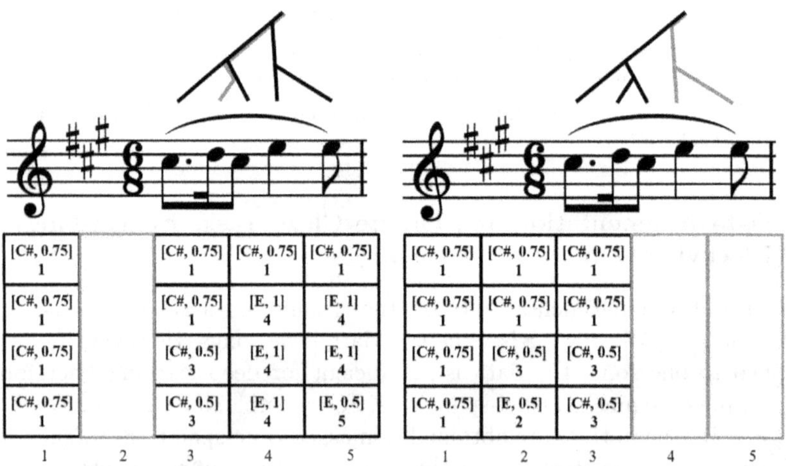

Fig. 4. (*left*) Masking the maximum time-span with note id 2, (*right*) Masking the maximum time-span with note id 4.

By masking, we obtained 43253 training data, 10780 validation data, and 1833 test data. For training and validation data, we obtained 34 times as many as original ones, and for test data, 32 times as many as original one.

4 Overview of the Seq2Seq Model

The purpose of this paper is to clarify the local and global relationships of time-span trees as a high-level analysis. To realize the implementation of this relationship, it is necessary to do analysis and prediction at the same time. To analyze and predict at the same time, we propose a Seq2Seq model with LSTM. The Seq2Seq model realizes analysis and prediction at the same time by recursive processing of LSTM. In addition, it learns local and global relationships through a time-span tree fill-in task. Also, by using single-head attention, learn the relationship between local and global. Specifically, the decoder in the Seq2Seq model adds attention and computes the relationship between the masked time-span tree and the hole-filled time-span tree.

The Seq2Seq model used in this experiment takes skip-thought embedding as input and outputs a timestep vector as output. At this research, by solving the cloze task, it learns the global tree structure relationships. The LSTM used for the Seq2Seq model is bidirectional in the encoder and unidirectional in the decoder. Also, decoder use attention to help them learn global relationships. Figure 5 shows the outline of the Seq2Seq model when attention is used.

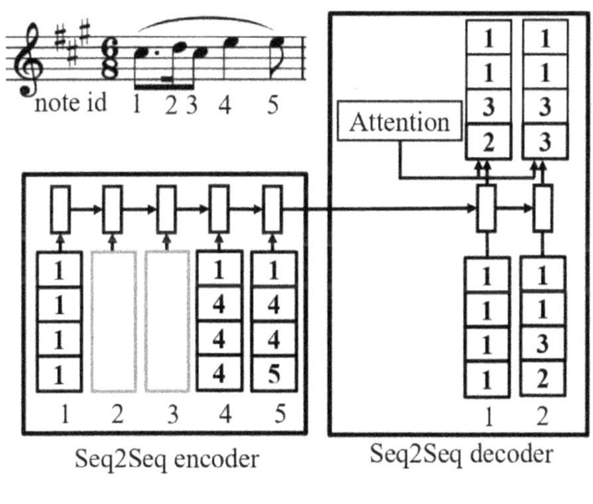

Fig. 5. Outline of Seq2Seq model using attention

Conventionally, attention takes all correspondences, but since cloze task, it does not calculate the masked timesteps. Figure 6 shows the attention calculation in this research. This avoids the state where the correct answer data paired with the masked timesteps are visible due to attention. Self-correspondence is not used because the same problem can occur and affect the prediction of other masked time-span trees.

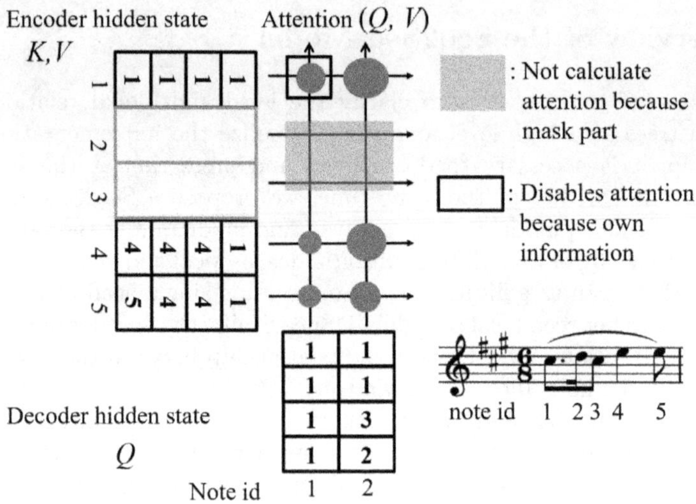

Fig. 6. Calculating the attention of the timestep vector in Fig. 5

Also, this research, each note is a multi-hot vector by combining a one-hot vector for note name, a one-hot vector for octave, a one-hot vector for duration, a label indicating padding, and a label indicating mask. In addition, when outputting, padding labels are combined with note name, octave, and duration,

Table 1. multi-hot vector ravel

category	contents of label	number
mask	mask or not	1
padding	BOS, EOS, padding for sequences, padding for layers	4
note name	C, C♯, D, E♭, E, F, F♯, G, G♯, A,B♭, B	12
octave	4, 5, 6, 7, 8	5
duration	0.125, 0.1667, 0.25, 0.3333, 0.375, 0.5, 0.625, 0.6667, 0.75, 0.875, 1.0, 1.167, 1.25, 1.333, 1.5, 1.625, 1.75, 2.0, 2.25, 2.5, 2.75, 3.0, 3.5, 3.75, 4.0, 4.5, 5.0, 6.0	28

and softmax is calculated as a one-hot vector. After that, the loss is calculated using the categorical cross-entropy as the loss function. Details of each category are shown in Table 1. The masked parts are note id 2 and 3 in Fig. 5, backpropagation is performed to reduce the loss of note id 2 and 3.

5 Experiment Results

Using the data set prepared in Sect. 3, we show the results of training with the model in Sect. 4. To see if attention is valid for local and global information, we compare it with a normal Seq2Seq model without attention.

5.1 Parameter Tuning of Seq2Seq Model

Deep learning requires learning with optimal parameters, but learning with all data requires a huge amount of computation for skip-thought and learning with Seq2Seq models. Therefore, we decided to find the optimal parameters for 178 training data and 45 validation data before data augmentation, and use those parameters when learning with all data.

To determine the parameters of the Seq2Seq model, the parameters were tested four dimensions: 200, 300, 400, 500, in the latent space of skip-thought and the hidden layer of the Seq2Seq model. Also, the seq2seq parameter tried three learning rates: 0.001, 0.0001, 0.00001. We trained Seq2Seq over 50 epochs and compared the loss function with the validation data. As a result, the loss value was lowest at 2.697 with a skip-thought dimension of 300, a hidden layer dimension of 200, a learning rate of 0.0001, and a batch size of 64. The top 10 losses are shown in Table 2. 6 of the top 10 losses no longer had a loss update within 10 epochs. Also, the loss was not updated when the learning rate was high, and the loss value was large when the learning rate was low.

Table 2. Validation loss value

thought dim	hidden layer	learning rate	batch size	epoch	validation loss
300	200	0.001	32	5	2.730
		0.0001	32	39	2.732
			64	29	2.697
400	400	0.0001	32	17	2.748
	500	0.001	32	3	2.765
500	200	0.0001	32	43	2.759
	300	0.0001	64	8	2.742
	500	0.001	32	2	2.760
			64	2	2.7576
		0.0001	64	7	2.761

As a result, for the cloze task, the best parameter skip-thought dimension was 300, the hidden layer was 200, and the learning rate was 0.0001. The batch size was 256, that it will be multiplied by 7.

5.2 Cloze Task Results

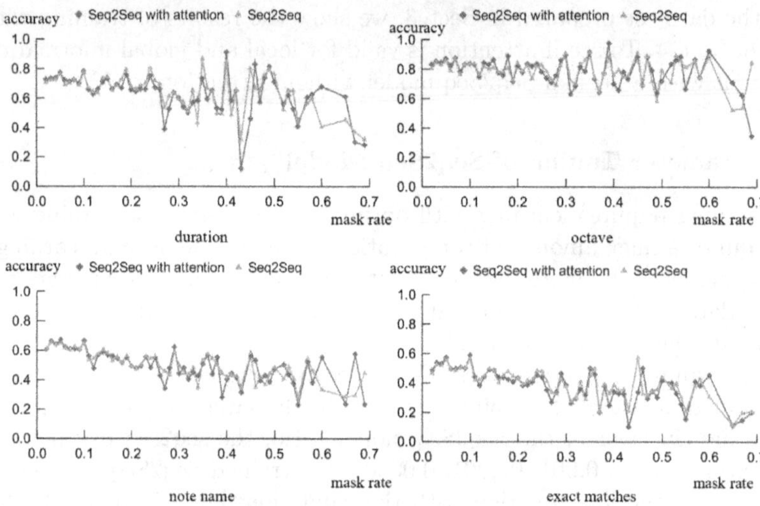

Fig. 7. Accuracy of mask rate in four conditions

First, since the timestep was masked as a cloze task, we calculated the accuracy rate for the test data for each masking rate of the timestep including padding. In other words, in a time-span tree with a maximum layer of 5, the remaining 5 layers are padding. The mask rate is calculated by dividing the masked timestep by the total timestep. Figure 7 four accuracy for each mask rate. As a result, the prediction for the pitch name had the lowest accuracy without exact matchs. The duration was the worst when the mask rate was 0.43, the accuracy was 0.1208 with attention, and the accuracy was 0.3208 with the normal model.

Next, we show the result of whether the prediction was correct as a layer. Figure 8 shows the four accuracy for each n th layer. In the graph, padding has been removed to show how well the predicted timesteps restore the original time-span tree. Therefore, the total number of predictions made decreases with each layer. As a result, we were able to confirm the pure accuracy for each layer. In all four results from first to fifth layer, Seq2Seq with attention is equal to or better than normal Seq2Seq. For sixth layer, Seq2Seq with attention gave better results for note names and octaves. However, normal Seq2Seq performed better in all results from seventh to tenth layer. For ninth layer, the duration was 0.4036 for Seq2Seq with attention and 0.6539 for normal Seq2Seq. The result

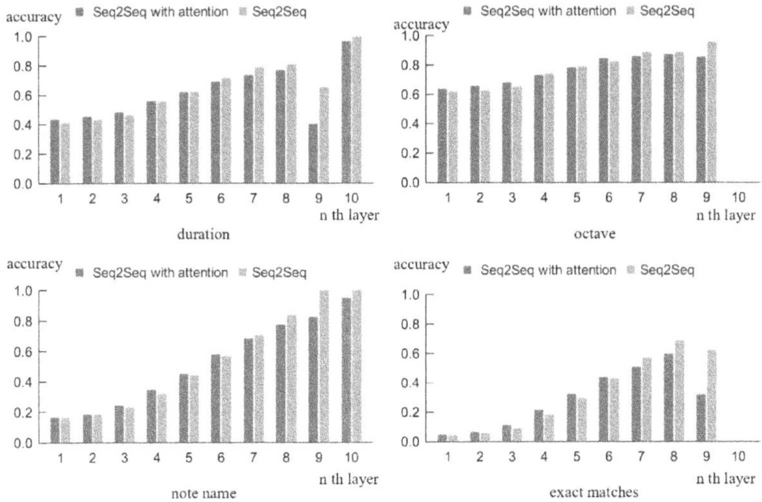

Fig. 8. Accuracy for each n th layer in four conditions

was 0.3677 lower with attention and 0.1515 lower with normal, than eighth layer. In particular, Seq2Seq with attention, the accuracy was the lowest for all layers. Octaves were not predictable at all for tenth layer. Along with that, the exact matches was also completely unpredictable in the case of tenth layer.

6 Discussion

Let us discuss the following four issues.

- The parameter tuning of the Seq2Seq model : The top 10 losses were presented, and 6 of them completed training within 10 epochs. The learning has not converged from the general case of deep learning. It is necessary to devise more evaluation functions.
- The treatment of duration : In GTTM rules, simplification is performed using the total value of duration. Due to the number of labels, this study did not use total values. However, this method is not to learn the higher the hierarchy. To discuss this issue, we implement a loss function that recursively predicts the duration and compares the lengths.
- The data size is small : In fact, the most predicted factor was octave, and the next was duration. This is thought to be due to data augmentation for the pitch during learning. It is necessary to increase the total number of time-span trees and learn the data with a suitable distribution. In addition to the number of data, it is also necessary to discuss for labeling. This time, the note names are simply labels, but we should also consider the difference in how many notes are separated from each other.

– Using attention : The reason why there was no difference between Seq2Seq with attention and normal Seq2Seq is that attention was single-headed. Single-headed attention takes only one relationship. On the other hand, multi-head attention takes multiple relationships. Therefore, multi-head attention may improve subtree-to-subtree prediction.

7 Conclusion

We proposed learning a global tree structure by a cloze task of a time-span tree. As a result, Small subtrees within a time-span tree can now be predicted based on local and global relationships. However, the larger the subtree, the lower the accuracy. In addition, it is now possible to make predictions about the upper layers. However, the lower the layer, the more difficult the prediction, and the first layer could hardly be restored. Also, using attention did not show any significant improvement in accuracy.

The points to be improved in the future are as follows. Since the blockview is divided vertically as a timestep and the skip-thought is used as an embedded expression, it is possible that the constraints before and after are not completely predicted. This could be improved by changing the Seq2Seq decoder activation function to Cumax, which is used in ON-LSTM. Also, by taking the relationship between attentions like pyraformer, it may be possible to take the relationship in units of subtrees.

Acknowledgements. This work was supported by JSPS KAKENHI Grant number 21H03572.

References

1. Agres, K., Abdallah, S., Pearce, M.: Information-theoretic properties of auditory sequences dynamically influence expectation and memory. Cogn. Sci. **42**, 43–76 (2018)
2. Egermann, H., Pearce, M. T., Wiggins, G. A., McAdams, S.: Probabilistic models of expectation violation predict psychophysiological emotional responses to live concert music. Cogn., Affect. Behav. Neurosci. **13**(3), pp.533—553 (2013)
3. GTTM Database. https://gttm.jp/gttm/ja/database/
4. Hamanaka, M., Hirata, K., Tojo, S.: deepGTTM III: multi task learning with grouping and metrical structures. In: The 13th International Symposium on Computer Music Multidisciplinary Research, pp. 161–172 (2018)
5. Hamanaka, M., Hirata, K., Tojo, S.: Time-span tree leveled by duration of time-span. In: The 15th International Symposium on Computer Music Multidisciplinary Research, pp. 155–164 (2021)
6. Kiros, R., et al.: Skip-thought vectors. In: Advances in Neural Information Processing Systems, vol. 28, Montreal (2015)
7. Lerdahl, F., Jackendoff, R.: A Generative Theory of Tonal Music. The MIT Press, Cambridge (1983)

8. Liu, S., et al.: Pyraformer: low-complexity pyramidal attention for long-range time series modeling and forecasting. In: International Conference on Learning Representations, Online, (2022)
9. Meyer, L.B.: Meaning in music and information theory. J. Aesthet. Art Critic. **15**(4), 412–424 (1957)
10. Shen, Y., Tan, S., Sordoni, A., Courville, A.: Ordered neurons: integrating tree structures into recurrent neural network. In: Proceedings of International Conference on Learning Representations, New Orleans (2019)

Music Recognition and Creation Tools

Design of a Music Recognition, Encoding, and Transcription Online Tool

David Rizo[1,2](✉), Jorge Calvo-Zaragoza[1], Juan C. Martínez-Sevilla[1], Adrián Roselló[1], and Eliseo Fuentes-Martínez[1]

[1] Universidad de Alicante, San Vicente del Raspeig, Spain
[2] Instituto Superior de Enseñanzas Artísticas de la Comunidad Valenciana (ISEA.CV), Valencia, Spain
drizo@dlsi.ua.es

Abstract. In recent years, Optical Music Recognition (OMR) technologies have experienced a notable boost thanks mainly to the use of new pipelines based on machine learning, especially on deep neural networks. These methods are usually studied just from the point of view of the accuracy of the output of the networks. However, from a practical perspective in a real-world context, this is not enough. In this paper, we present a design of a tool devised for allowing the scientific study of the complete OMR workflow in different scenarios and notations, including both the possibility of analyzing the real impact of improvements in automatic recognition models and how they are integrated for practical purposes in the work of the transcriber.

Keywords: optical music recognition · encoding · transcription · user experience

1 Introduction

Digitizing sheet music and other music-related documents can provide several benefits, including easier access for researchers, music practitioners, musicologists, and the general public, as well as preservation of musical heritage. Digitized sheet music can be searched, played, analyzed, and annotated using specialized software tools, allowing for new discoveries and insights into musical history and culture.

One notable example of an effort to digitize music collections into digital images is the International Music Score Library Project[1] (IMSLP), which aims to create a virtual library of public domain sheet music. The IMSLP has digitized thousands of scores from various composers and genres, making them freely available for download and use. Other organizations and institutions, such as libraries, museums, and universities, are also scanning their music collections into image files to increase access and preserve musical heritage.

[1] https://www.imslp.org (accessed April 13th, 2024).

S. Ystad et al. (Eds.): CMMR 2023, LNCS 15236, pp. 313–328, 2026.
https://doi.org/10.1007/978-3-032-02042-0_24

As a matter of fact, having the musical content information, i.e., the audio and the scans, not digitally encoded ends up being a waste of resources given that current music information retrieval pipelines require it. By this means, we cannot consider a score digitization process as finished until the digital score version encoding is produced.

Alfaro-Contreras et al. [2] showed that the most efficient way to obtain these digital scores is to resort to an automated reading of documents by using the so-called Optical Music Recognition (OMR) [4]. This technology has achieved different levels of recognition accuracy depending on the type of documents, the quality of the medium, and the type and complexity of the notation. But still, in most cases, the OMR does not yield perfect results. The need for post-editing depends on the tasks to be performed on the recognized content. Some projects such as F-Tempo[2] directly use—possibly with errors—OMR output to approximate performing searches. When requiring a curated transcription, a manual correction process has to be done. For instance, this pipeline was used to encode a large number of files of the KernScores repository.[3]

The low accuracy of OMR is not the only obstacle in real use-cases. There is no OMR system yet able to process the whole set of symbols found in early notations. The processing of orchestral scores of varying layout, the presence of *ossias*, or dealing with works where the different parts are written in separate sheets, makes it even more challenging. This is why, in many real projects, the encoding process is eventually performed by transcribers using computerized notation tools such as Finale[4], Dorico[5], MuseScore[6], or Sibelius[7]. In projects such as Didone [28], around 4 000 Eighteenth-Century Italian Opera arias are being manually copied in Finale to be later stored into MusicXML files [12]. The same approach was used to obtain the encodings of the modern version of the renaissance works from the "Josquin Research Project" (JRP).[8]

In this scenario, the main advances in OMR are achieved by modern artificial intelligence techniques based on machine learning, namely deep learning [4]. Improvements are attained through the correct selection of neural network architectures and the availability of training data in sufficient quantity and quality for those architectures. The research-oriented OMR tool "Music Recognition, Encoding, and Transcription" (MuRET) [19] was introduced to push the development of both OMR techniques and the creation and curation of datasets. This tool was developed with JavaFX[9] as a desktop application. It included our first OMR models [7], which allowed for the curation of a number of training sets and the development of new OMR approaches [8,26].

---

[2] https://f-tempo.org (accessed April 13th, 2024).

[3] http://kern.ccarh.org/ (accessed April 13th, 2024).

[4] https://www.finalemusic.com (accessed April 13th, 2024).

[5] https://www.steinberg.net/dorico (accessed April 13th, 2024).

[6] https://musescore.org (accessed April 13th, 2024).

[7] https://www.avid.com/sibelius (accessed April 13th, 2024).

[8] https://josquin.stanford.edu (accessed April 13th, 2024).

[9] https://www.oracle.com/es/java/technologies/javase/javafx-overview.html (accessed April 13th, 2024).

Once the usefulness of MuRET became clear, we decided to port it to a web application for two main reasons. The first is that the technology is continuously evolving, which made it difficult to deploy the application on a daily basis. The second, and more important, is to naturally maintain a growing repository of both ongoing transcription documents and trained OMR models shared among all users. Having evaluated this research-oriented OMR online tool in real scenarios, in this paper the main decisions to build it are described with which we expect to contribute to the improvement of ongoing and future OMR investigations.

The paper is organized as follows. Section 2 details other alternatives to MuRET that, due to the fact that this tool is eminently research-oriented, may be most suitable to be used in transcription projects. Next, the requirements taken into account in Sect. 3 and decisions made during the development of the current online version are discussed in Sect. 4 that may be useful for other similar projects. Finally, conclusions will be drawn and future works outlined in Sect. 6.

2 State of the Art

There are several Optical Music Recognition (OMR) tools available to transcribe Common Western Modern Notation (CWMN). Only one open-source tool, Audiveris[10] is available, and a number of commercial packages such as SmartScore[11], PhotoScore[12], or PlayScore 2[13]. The effectiveness of each tool can vary depending on the complexity and quality of the sheet music being analyzed. A brief analysis of them for recognizing music theory books can be found in [13], that shows how far they are from retrieving successful results in complex scenarios.

The transcription of notations other than CWMN is very restricted to very few applications. In the context of the SIMSSA project [10], two applications in the past years have been used to automatically extract musical information from images, although they are no longer maintained: Gamut and Aruspix [16]. In addition, within this project, an OMR meta-workflow called Rodan was built in which users can create their own systems using predefined image processing and machine learning blocks [11]. Although not designed for any specific notation, most of the existing blocks are intended for neume recognition. More recently, another approach based on convolutional neural networks was developed specifically for mensural notation, which reported high accuracies [27].

Given this context, to the best of our knowledge, no tool ready to deal both with handwritten and printed sources of several kinds of notation is available other than our proposal MuRET.

[10] https://github.com/Audiveris/audiveris (accessed April 13th, 2024).
[11] https://www.musitek.com (accessed April 13th, 2024).
[12] https://www.neuratron.com/photoscore.htm (accessed April 13th, 2024).
[13] https://www.playscore.co (accessed April 13th, 2024).

3 Requirements

The ultimate goal of MuRET is to facilitate OMR research from a holistic perspective. This means that the tool must support the research of all individual steps of the workflow to obtain a final digital score from the different images, considering both the automatic processes and user manual interactions. Being this a research tool, it must be prepared to be scaled to any possible scenario in terms of notation type, parts arrangement, document layout, calligraphies and fonts, and transcription purposes.

From an end-user point of view, the user should be first allowed to manage collections of works made of digital images of any format and resolution. For transcribing a new work, the constituent elements in each image such as pages, staves, and lyrics must be identified. Then, in the case of being a polyphonic work, they must be assigned to the different instruments, voices, or parts. The contents in staves and text regions must be recognized using a variety of approaches that, after being combined, will make up a final digital score that will be exported to standard encoding formats. All possible aids that the machine can compute, such as displaying early notations in modern forms, or hints in the final scoring-up, should be provided. Additionally, the tool must incorporate process-oriented functionalities, as an aid to account for the current status of work on several simultaneous works, or the inclusion of comments both for the whole work or elements inside it.

Ultimately, the system must be able to perform all processes in an assisted manner, so that the output of the various automatic classifiers is corrected when necessary by the user as quickly as possible.

From the OMR process research perspective, the tool must be ready to accommodate different approaches to convert a set of input images into a digital score. For each of those approaches, in the case of being based on machine learning, the extraction of new training sets from the already processed works and the posterior training, upload, and use of new models, must be supported. For analyzing the actual behavior of any paradigm and model besides the usual model performance metrics, all actions of the user must be recorded and categorized for being later analyzed.

Several non-functional requirements arise that can influence the design of the tool. It must allow the simultaneous transcription of the same work by different, possibly remote, users. To allow the accommodation of new repertories with a minimum amount of effort, and to make the user unconcerned about formats and resolutions, the use of IIIF framework[14] for exchanging the processed works to other external tools is recommended. Finally, the system must be usable with a standard computer setup.

[14] https://iiif.io (accessed April 13th, 2024).

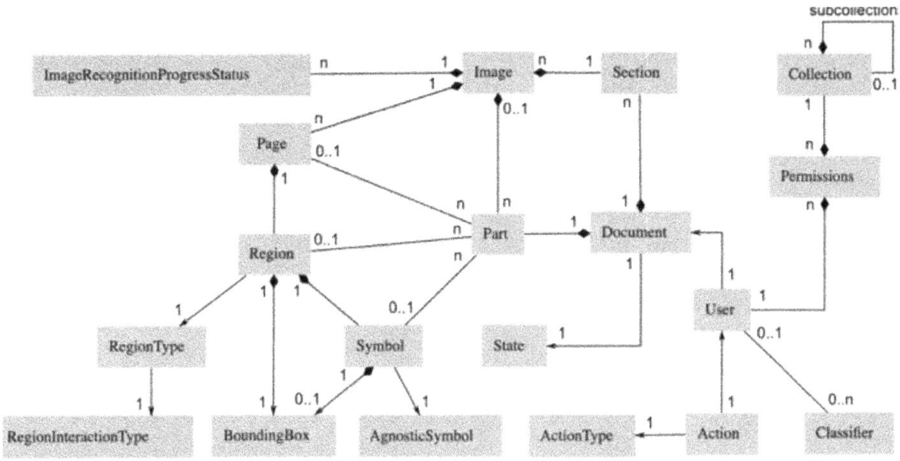

Fig. 1. Domain model. Some classes and relations, and all attributes have been omitted for easier reading.

4 Solution Design

The current online version of MuRET[15] presents a possible approach to solve all the requirements detailed above. In order to implement it, several decisions have been made that will be described in this section.

The system has been structured using a three-tier web architecture style. The *presentation layer* has been solved using Angular with the Redux pattern[16], the *application layer* has been implemented using Spring Boot[17], and the *data layer* served by a MariaDB[18] relational database.

All the system data is eventually stored in records of the database that is converted to the object-oriented hierarchy shown in Fig. 1 through the Hibernate Object-Relation Mapping (ORM)[19]. The names of the classes can be easily understood from the explanation in the following lines.

4.1 User Collections and Images

Users must be registered by a system administrator to work on the tool. No self-registering process is offered. All works are organized into collections and sub-collections, whose access is granted by the administrator.

A document is the core entity of a transcription project. After being uploaded as individual image files or inside a PDF document, the images of a document to

[15] https://muret.dlsi.ua.es/muret.
[16] https://angular.io and https://redux.js.org (accessed April 13th, 2024).
[17] https://spring.io/projects/spring-boot (accessed April 13th, 2024).
[18] https://mariadb.org (accessed April 13th, 2024).
[19] https://hibernate.org/orm/ (accessed April 13th, 2024).

be transcribed are grouped, at least, into one default section. This is useful for dealing with compound works such as masses and operas. Images and sections can be deleted, edited, and reordered. Images that contain cover sheets, or non-musical content, can be hidden for subsequent automatic recognition processes. Users are allowed to assign to each work metadata such as the notation type, manuscript type (printed or handwritten), composer and printer.

For the purpose of helping the user in daily work tasks, the work in progress and image recognition annotations stages can be marked up to the final transcription (see buttons to mark this progress below in the bottom-right of Fig. 5c).

4.2 Document Analysis

After organizing the images, the first step to transcribe a work, known as *document analysis*, is to segment each image into separate components, a series of regions of different types such as staves and lyrics are identified (Fig. 2). Usually, each image contains just one page, but it is also usual to receive scans of books where images contain several pages, as in the case of the image in that figure. This process can be performed either manually by drawing bounding boxes on top of the image and assigning a region type to each drawn box, or by using an automatic classifier that identifies the different segments in the image. Across MuRET, when an operation can be performed automatically, the user can select and apply a classifier (see the two available models of the drop-down control at the top-right of the Fig. 2), and correct the output if necessary. Classifiers are run currently in the user browser using TensorFlow.js.[20] This decision has the advantage that it allows avoiding collapsing the server machine when several users are using MuRET at the same time running different models that have to be loaded in memory. The main drawback is that the used models have had to be tuned to keep their size at the minimum for being used in standard computers.

4.3 Part Management

Most of the sources to be processed are polyphonic, consisting of several voices, instruments, or parts. There is a variety of arrangements, such as works made of parts distributed across pages (the image in Fig. 2 corresponds just to a part), choir-books where the same page contains two voices (Fig. 3b), ensembles or orchestral scores (Fig. 3a). The kind of book to transcribe could be of a totally different nature. For instance, it can be a compilation of songs not related to any instrument, such as a jazz *Real Book*, or be a catalog containing lists of incipits. In some cases, the volume to be transcribed describes music theory as it is the case of music treatises [13], where most of the content is textual with some illustrative music examples. The process of dealing with parts is performed currently manually. In all cases, the internal implementation of all those situations is reduced to the case where the whole image or page is linked to a part, or when each region must be assigned to a part. The system is also prepared

[20] https://www.tensorflow.org/js (accessed April 13th, 2024).

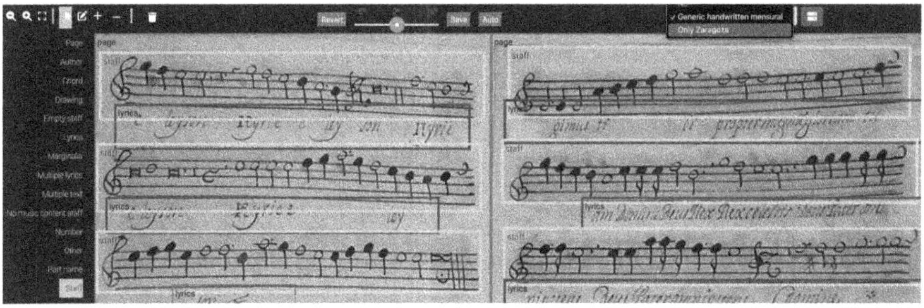

Fig. 2. Document analysis screenshot. In this example, only the staves and lyrics regions are segmented. The snapshot shows two possible classifiers to perform a document analysis (top-right), and controls to rotate, manually or automatically, the image (top-center). The current catalog of region types shown at the left of the image can be easily modified.

to deal with chorale layouts with two staves for four voices. In that case, each individual symbol inside the region must be linked to each part. For reducing user effort, the system offers aids to manage the set of instruments and to reuse the different layouts between pages.

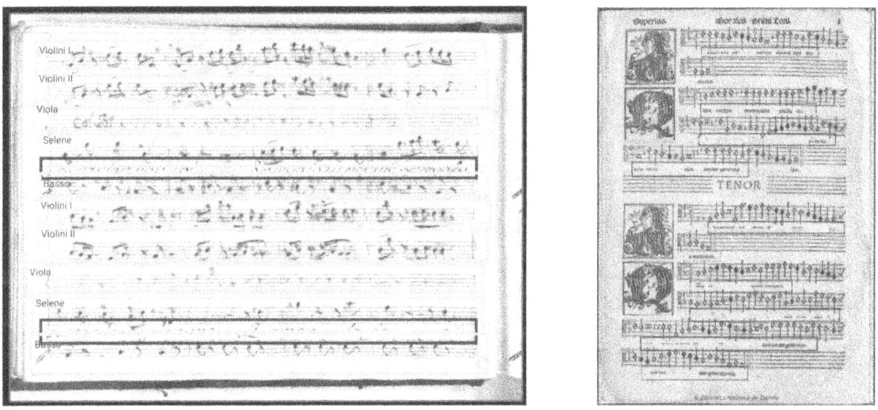

(a) Parts in orchestral score (b) Parts in choir book

Fig. 3. Different parts and arrangements. All regions must be attributed to a part.

4.4 Region Contents Recognition

Once the different staves are identified and assigned to the part they belong to, the musical contents inside the image crop that corresponds to each region must be recognized and encoded. Currently, lyrics can be encoded as text but they are just stored in the database without any further treatment (Fig. 4a). New region types can be easily incorporated in the future. There are several approaches that can be followed to obtain an encoding from the image, either manually or by applying an automatic classifier. The first consists of manually tracing the graphic symbols so a classifier [7], by using both the stroke (Fig. 4b) and the image obtained from the bounding box that encloses the stroke, identifies each symbol among a set of possible *agnostic symbols* [6] (i.e. graphical symbols without an attributed musical meaning yet), and the vertical position in the staff as an absolute value regardless the clef. Although we use this *symbol-agnostic* concept where we identify complete glyphs, we could easily adapt it to recognize primitives (note head, stem, etc.) as proposed in [15].

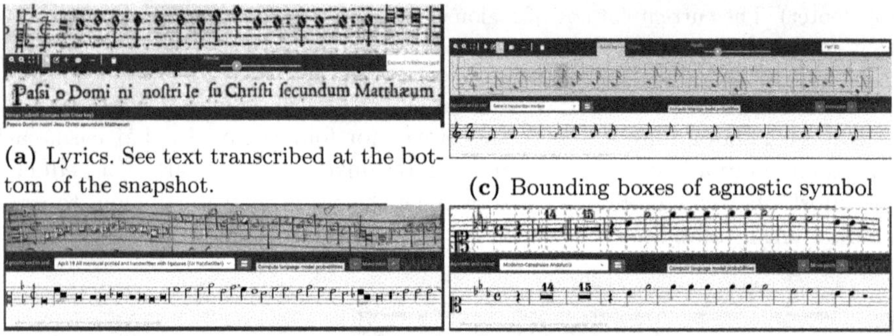

(a) Lyrics. See text transcribed at the bottom of the snapshot.

(c) Bounding boxes of agnostic symbol

(b) Strokes

(d) Staff-level end-to-end

Fig. 4. Transcription of regions.

An alternative is just to draw the bounding box surrounding each symbol to use just the image clipping as input information for the classifier [14] to identify the agnostic symbol type (Fig. 4c). In either of the two options, an agnostic symbol sequence is obtained, i.e., a sequence of symbols ordered from left to right, top to bottom. For instance, the beginning of the agnostic sequence in Fig. 4c is: `clef.G2:L2 digit.2:L4 digit.4:L2 note.8th:L1 note.8th:S1 verticalLine:L1`. The rendering of the bottom staff is performed by using fonts that have a glyph for each agnostic symbol that are just placed in the position of the symbol in the image. For white mensural notation, the Capitan [20] font is used that was developed on-purpose, and for modern notation, Petaluma font[21] has been utilized.

The next possibility is to use a staff-level end-to-end classifier that identifies the agnostic symbols in the image in such a way that the sequence order is respected but the bounding boxes of each symbol are not detected but their approximate horizontal position [6] (dashed lines in Fig. 4d show those approximate positions). The user can move and correct any of the symbols. In that

[21] https://www.smufl.org/fonts/ (accessed April 13th, 2024).

case, to take advantage of the interaction for obtaining a new training sample, the bounding box is drawn (see the second flat in the key signature in Fig. 4d).

4.5 Music Encoding of Individual Staves

The agnostic sequence must be converted to a meaningful music encoding denoted as *semantic encoding* [6]. For example, the sequence of three flats at the beginning of the agnostic sequence in Fig. 4d must be converted to a E major (or its relative minor) key. When encoding the pitch of the notes, this key signature must be taken into account for correctly assigning if necessary the right accidental. This translation from *agnostic* to *semantic* (Fig 5a) can be performed either using a rules-based automaton transducer [20], or translation technologies based on machine learning approaches [24][22]. For early notations, a valid conversion into modern notation is performed with any consideration of transposition or metric change (Fig. 5c). The rendering of the bottom staff is delegated to Verovio [17], through a previous conversion of our internal format introduced below into MEI (Fig. 5b). If the staff to convert is not the top staff, the contextual information from previous staves, such as the previous time signature, is propagated. The conversion to Plaine and Easie Code [3] for cataloging in RISM[23] is performed by that library as well.

It is important to note that MEI or Verovio do not always support all required features. For instance, bar-lines crossing a note in late mensural notations or the rendering of *signum congruentiae*. In those cases, our principle has been to internally store a specific tag for each unsupported feature and print text marks to visualize them.

A key decision taken to design MuRET was the method to store those semantic sequences. We have not chosen any standard format as the internal encoding, but an ad-hoc representation extended from the Humdrum [25] formats **kern and **mens [21] in what we name **skm. Later, when exporting the final encoding, standard formats are used. This has allowed us to adapt the format to encode specific situations that were not possible with standard **kern/**mens when we required it (e.g. *custos* symbol, the position of rests, canceling accidentals in mensural notation, or dots after a barline). This encoding contains also information about the agnostic symbol each semantic element is related to, which allows for later exporting this kind of graphical information to formats such as the *facsimile* element in MEI. The choice of extending Humdrum formats and not other more comprehensive ones such as SCORE [25], MusicXML [12] or MEI [23], is the ease with which users can fully manually encode or correct the output of the classifiers. In any case, the translation process generates a sequence of objects of a musical object-oriented hierarchy that are just converted into **skm in order to serialize them allowing its presentation in the interface and storage.

[22] Note that there is an agnostic representation for dealing with more complex situations such as the presence of chords [1]. In any case, the workflow is the same regardless of the agnostic encoding.

[23] https://rism.info/ (accessed April 13th, 2024).

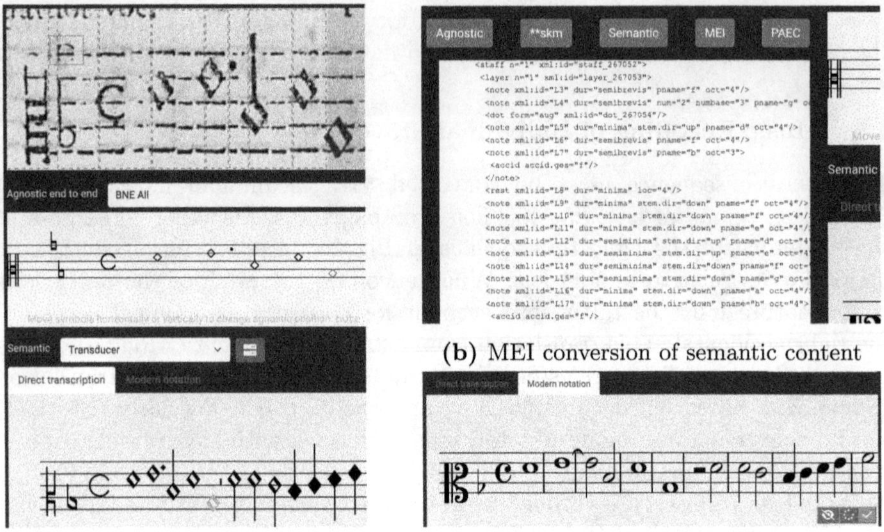

(a) Agnostic to semantic

(b) MEI conversion of semantic content

(c) Modern transcription

Fig. 5. Semantic contents recognized from the image.

MuRET does not include yet the direct recognition from the image to the **skm encoding because we have experimented to be faster and more accurate to use this intermediate representation as shown in [5]. If a classifier was proven to yield better results, both the transcription and correction processes, it could be easily introduced into the application.

4.6 Scoring Up and Exporting

Finally, when all previous steps have been finished, the user can select the images (Fig. 6a) that they they want to be used to generate a final score (Fig. 6b). This operation is accomplished by concatenating all the staves in the selected images grouped by the parts they belong to, exporting them from our internal format to MEI, and letting Verovio engrave the score. In order to share the transcription with external services, the previous MEI can be exported as it is rendered by Verovio. MuRET also is able to convert to a parts-based MEI format including graphical information in the facsimile element (Fig. 6c). This functionality was included for exchanging information with specialized tools such as MP-Editor to perform scoring-up processing in mensural notation [9].

4.7 Model Training

As mentioned above, the classifiers that support the automatic processes use machine learning models that need training data for being built. The system allows downloading different training sets from selected collections and works.

(a) Image selection

(b) Score preview

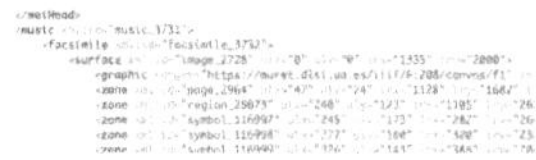

(c) Parts based MEI including facsimile (see more details in [9]).

Fig. 6. Previsualizing and exporting

This training data is just a set of JSON files containing an export of the objects in our internal data model (Fig. 1). After being trained offline, these models can be uploaded again to the system. This incremental workflow, i.e., fixing the output of the different classifiers, downloading datasets with corrected data, building new models, and uploading them to improve the performance of the system, is being shown in our transcription projects to be a proper way to proceed. Using this approach for transcribing a work by Jacob van Eyck, printed by Paulus Matthijsz in 1649, the recognition and post-editing effort were reduced by a factor of 10, allowing the end user to obtain a complete and correct encoding of a standard book page in under one minute per page.

4.8 User Action Logging and User Experience

Some models perform better than others in a theoretical way, but the corrections required to fix their outputs lead to a higher effort by the user. This can be measured by analyzing the actions each individual user performs on the tool that is logged and conveniently categorized into meaningful operations, such as the editing of regions, symbols, semantic content, part management or classifier use (see Fig. 7). The timestamps of all operations are also registered, as well as the document, region or symbol involved in each operation. Currently, we have stored more than 300 000 actions from different users.

These action logs have helped us to improve the user experience of the system by evincing many operations that are frequent and repetitive, decreasing the final throughput. These issues, such as those related to the feedback of the system in error messages, long actions, or the graphical design of interaction controls, have been gradually corrected or taken into account to include new capabilities to the system.

5 Qualitative and Quantitative Evaluation

MuRET was recently used to transcribe a large corpus of white mensural music preserved at the National Library of Spain. This effort spanned 63 volumes and approximately 12,000 images, requiring around 18 person-months to complete. While the primary objective was to produce high-quality digital encodings in

ActionID	User	Phase	Action type	Duration in seconds	DocumentID	SectionID	ImageID	PageID	RegionID	SymbolID	ClassifierID
240971	davidrizo	d	Open document		323						
240972	admin	d	Upload file	2074	323						
240973	davidrizo	d	Open document		323						
240974	davidrizo	d	Open image	8	323		11934				
240975	davidrizo	da	Automatic document analysis	10	323		11934				
240976	davidrizo	da	Clear document analysis	11	323		11934				
240980	davidrizo	d	Open document		323						
240981	admin	d	Upload file	43	323						
240982	davidrizo	d	Open document		323						
240983	davidrizo	d	Open image	2	323		11935				
240984	davidrizo	da	Automatic document analysis	7	323		11935				
240985	davidrizo	d	Open image	6	323		11935				
240986	davidrizo	a	Agnostic end-to-end	4	323		11935	9614	88708		
240987	davidrizo	a	Region symbols clear	8	323		11935	9614	88708		

Fig. 7. User action logs

MEI from historical sources, the project also served as a comprehensive evaluation of MuRET's performance from both quantitative and qualitative perspectives [18].

5.1 Quantitative Results

As introduced in Sect. 4.8, all user actions were systematically recorded, enabling a precise measurement of the time required for each stage of the workflow. Comparisons with purely manual encoding workflows demonstrated that MuRET significantly reduced transcription time.

In a case study focusing on a 126-page volume of *Magnificat* by Cristóbal Morales, a purely manual method required approximately 49 min per page to achieve an agnostic (symbol-only) representation. In contrast, using MuRET for the same step reduced the average processing time to about 15 min per page.

One of the most challenging examples is "Psaumes de David" (see Fig. 8), which stands out due to its unique page layout consisting of two columns—the only instance of this format found in the collection. In addition to its elongated shape, which differs from the standard vertical or landscape layouts of other books, it contains an exceptionally dense amount of musical information, with approximately 40 staves per page, tightly packed characters, and minimal spacing between them. Combined with the low quality of the provided images, these factors significantly increased the manual effort required, making some actions that were automatic in other works up to five times more labor-intensive in this case. This example serves as a paradigm of the effectiveness of an incremental OMR training approach. Given how distinct this collection was from the others, meaningful agnostic sequences could only be obtained by training a dedicated model specifically for this manuscript. Initially, tagging the first pages to adapt the models to this source took up to 50 min per page. However, after sufficient training on the corpus, the transcription effort decreased to approximately 4–5 min per page.

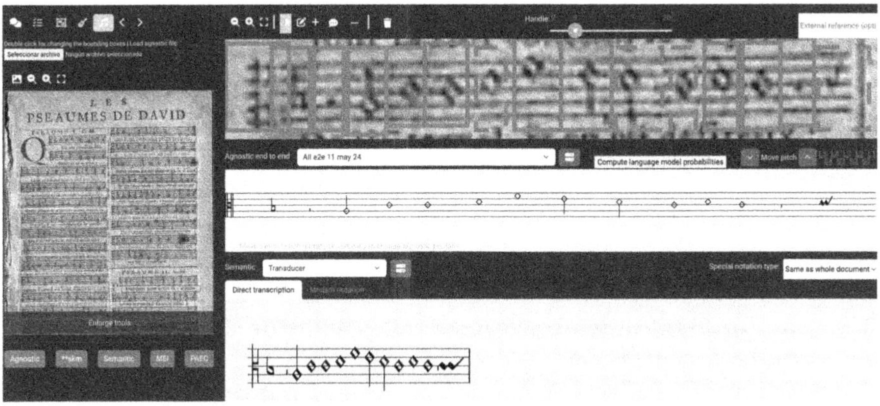

Fig. 8. Processing of "Les Pseaumes de David", printed by Weduwe van Jan Jacobsz Schipper in 1683.

The results presented in [18] highlight that the time required for OMR-based recognition of musical symbols was not the only significant factor. Additional processes, such as setting up metadata, filtering out non-musical pages, assigning parts, and reviewing alignment in multi-voice works, also contributed to the overall effort. However, these steps still proved considerably faster than fully manual transcription. Furthermore, the iterative retraining of MuRET's models led to continuous improvements in recognition accuracy for new pages. As the annotated dataset expanded, the average number of user edits per page decreased, and the system's symbol-level predictions for mensural ligatures, accidentals, and note shapes became increasingly reliable.

5.2 Qualitative Insights

From a user-experience perspective, MuRET's interface and workflow design are just as crucial to productivity as the core recognition algorithms. The separation of the process into agnostic transcription followed by semantic encoding proved particularly effective for early notation sources. This approach allowed non-specialist transcribers to quickly check and correct basic graphical issues, while more advanced musicologists focused on the complex rules of mensural notation.

Despite these efficiencies, the study identified areas for further refinement. For example, automatically detecting non-musical pages (e.g., textual indices or blank pages) could save significant time, as could more advanced part-assignment tools for choirbooks. Additionally, while MuRET's interface allows for symbol-by-symbol correction, users emphasized the need for batch operations to reuse region or staff annotations across similar pages.

Another recurring challenge was the handling of special symbols, such as ligatures or plicas in older notations. Enhancements in the model's ability to process ligatures—by reducing the generation of unnecessary sub-symbols [22]—significantly decreased correction time.

Finally, qualitative feedback emphasized the importance of MuRET's real-time highlighting of corresponding elements in the manuscript image and the final encoded score, which greatly facilitated the detection and correction of errors.

6 Conclusions and Future Work

This paper has outlined the key components required to develop an OMR system that is both scalable and adaptable to different notations and transcription scenarios. Beyond its practical applications for real transcription projects, such a system also contributes to advancing OMR research.

In a large-scale project, MuRET has demonstrated its ability to significantly accelerate the transcription of complex historical sources while reducing user effort. However, expert oversight remains necessary for ambiguous or highly degraded regions. By combining incremental model training with a user-centric interface, the tool effectively balances automation with manual control, providing a scalable solution for digitizing extensive music collections.

MuRET is continuously evolving as new project requirements emerge. Current development efforts focus primarily on enhancing OMR models by leveraging the growing corpus of transcribed works and modern advances in deep learning. Future improvements will address several key areas: integrating new front-end frameworks and formats such as ONNX[24], enabling direct use of IIIF manifests from servers without requiring image uploads, implementing automatic classification of entire works for later correction to complement the current fully interactive workflow, facilitating direct online model training, and continuously refining the tool's user experience.

Acknowledgments. This research was supported by the Spanish Ministry of Science and Innovation through the LEMUR research project (PID2023-148259NB-I00).

References

1. Alfaro-Contreras, M., Calvo-Zaragoza, J., Iñesta, J.M.: Approaching end-to-end optical music recognition for homophonic scores. In: Morales, A., Fierrez, J., Sánchez, J.S., Ribeiro, B. (eds.) IbPRIA 2019. LNCS, vol. 11868, pp. 147–158. Springer, Cham (2019). https://doi.org/10.1007/978-3-030-31321-0_13
2. Alfaro-Contreras, M., Rizo, D., Iñesta, J., Calvo-Zaragoza, J.: OMR-assisted transcription: a case study with early prints. In: Proceedings of the 22nd International Society for Music Information Retrieval Conference, pp. 35–41. ISMIR, Online (Nov 2021)

[24] https://onnx.ai/ (accessed April 13th, 2024).

3. Brook, B.: The simplified plaine and easie code system for notating music: a proposal for international adoption. Fontes Artis Musicae **12**(2-3), 156–160 (jan 1965)
4. Calvo-Zaragoza, J., Hajič, J., Pacha, A.: Understanding optical music recognition. ACM Comput. Surv. (CSUR) **53**(4), 1–35 (2020)
5. Calvo-Zaragoza, J., Rizo, D.: Camera-PrIMuS: neural end-to-end optical music recognition on realistic monophonic scores. In: Proceedings of the 19th International Society for Music Information Retrieval Conference, ISMIR 2018, Paris, 2018, pp. 248–255 (2018)
6. Calvo-Zaragoza, J., Rizo, D.: End-to-end neural optical music recognition of monophonic scores. Appl. Sci. **8**(4) (2018)
7. Calvo-Zaragoza, J., Rizo, D., Iñesta, J.: Two (note) heads are better than one: pen-based multimodal interaction with music scores. In: International Society for Music Information Retrieval Conference (2016)
8. Calvo-Zaragoza, J., Toselli, A., Vidal, E.: Hybrid hidden Markov models and artificial neural networks for handwritten music recognition in mensural notation. Pattern Anal. Appl. **22**(4), 1573–1584 (2019)
9. Desmond, K., Pugin, L., Regimbal, J., Rizo, D., Sapp, C., Thomae, M.E.: Encoding polyphony from medieval manuscripts notated in mensural notation. In: Music Encoding Conference Proceedings 2021, pp. 197–219. Humanities Commons (May 2022)
10. Fujinaga, I., Hankinson, A., Cumming, J.: Introduction to SIMSSA (single interface for music score searching and analysis). In: Proceedings of the 1st International Workshop on Digital Libraries for Musicology, pp. 1–3. DLfM '14, Association for Computing Machinery, New York, NY, USA (2014)
11. Fujinaga, I., Vigliensoni, G.: The art of teaching computers: the SIMSSA optical music recognition workflow system. In: 27th European Signal Processing Conference, EUSIPCO 2019, A Coruña, Spain, September 2-6, 2019, pp. 1–5. IEEE (2019)
12. Good, M., Actor, G.: Using MusicXML for File Interchange. Web Delivering of Music, International Conference on **0**, 153 (2003)
13. Moss, F., Nápoles-López, N., Köster, M., Rizo, D.: Challenging sources: a new dataset for OMR of diverse 19th-century music theory examples. In: Proceedings of the 4th International Workshop on Reading Music Systems (WoRMS 2022) (November 2022)
14. Nuñez-Alcover, A., Ponce de León, P., Calvo-Zaragoza, J.: Glyph and position classification of music symbols in early music manuscripts. In: Proceedings of the 9th Iberian Conference on Pattern Recognition and Image Analysis, LNCS vol. 11867, pp. 159–168. AERFAI, APRP, Springer, Madrid, Spain (July 2019)
15. Pacha, A., Choi, K., Coüasnon, B., Ricquebourg, Y., Zanibbi, R., Eidenberger, H.: Handwritten music object detection: open issues and baseline results. In: 2018 13th IAPR International Workshop on Document Analysis Systems (DAS), pp. 163–168. IEEE (2018)
16. Pugin, L., Hockman, J., Burgoyne, J., Fujinaga, I.: Gamera versus aruspix: two optical music recognition approaches. In: 9th International Conference on Music Information Retrieval, Drexel University, Philadelphia, USA, September, 2008, pp. 419–424 (2008)
17. Pugin, L., Zitellini, R., Roland, P.: Verovio - A library for engraving MEI music notation into SVG. In: International Society for Music Information Retrieval (Jan 2014)
18. Rizo, D., Calvo-Zaragoza, J.: Lessons learned from a project to encode Mensural music on a large scale with optical music recognition. In: Proceedings of the

25th International Society for Music Information Retrieval Conference. ISMIR (nov 2024)
19. Rizo, D., Calvo-Zaragoza, J., Iñesta, J.: MuRET: A music recognition, encoding, and transcription tool. In: Proceedings of the 5th International Conference on Digital Libraries for Musicology, pp. 52–56. DLfM '18, Association for Computing Machinery, New York, NY, USA (2018)
20. Rizo, D., Pascual, B., Iñesta, J., Ezquerro, A., González, L.: Towards the digital encoding of Hispanic white mensural notation. Anu. Music. **72**, 293–304 (2017)
21. Rizo, D., Pascual-León, N., Sapp, C.S.: White mensural manual encoding: from humdrum to mei. Cuadernos de Investigación Musical **6**, 373–393 (2018)
22. Rizo, D., Calvo-Zaragoza, J., Martínez-Sevilla, J.C., Madueño, A., García-Iasci, P., Delgado-Sánchez, T.: Encoding in human centered machine learning workflows: case study on mensural ligature recognition. In: Joint MEC and TEI Conference: Encoding Cultures Conference. Paderborn (2023)
23. Roland, P.: The music encoding initiative (MEI). In: Proceedings of the First International Conference on Musical Applications Using XML. pp. 55–59 (Jan 2002)
24. Ríos-Vila, A., Esplá-Gomis, M., Rizo, D., Ponce de León, P., Iñesta, J.: Applying automatic translation for optical music recognition's encoding step. Appl. Sci. **11**(9) (April 2021)
25. Selfridge-Field, E. (ed.): Beyond MIDI: The Handbook of Musical Codes. MIT Press, Cambridge, MA, USA (1997)
26. Sober-Mira, J., Calvo-Zaragoza, J., Rizo, D., Iñesta, J.: Pen-based music document transcription with convolutional neural networks. In: Graphics Recognition, Current Trends and Evolutions - 12th IAPR International Workshop, GREC 2017, Kyoto, Japan, November 9-10, 2017, Revised Selected Papers. Lecture Notes in Computer Science, vol. 11009, pp. 71–80. Springer (2017)
27. Stoessel, J., Collins, D., Bolland, S.: Using optical music recognition to encode 17th-century music prints: The canonic works of paolo agostini (c.1583–1629) as a test case. In: 7th International Conference on Digital Libraries for Musicology, pp. 1–9. DLfM 2020, Association for Computing Machinery, New York, NY, USA (2020)
28. Torrente, A., Llorens, A.: The musicology lab: teamwork and the musicological toolbox. In: Music Encoding Conference Proceedings 2021, pp. 9–20. Humanities Commons (2022)

Automated Arrangements of Multi-part Music for Sets of Monophonic Instruments

Matthew McCloskey[1], Gabrielle Curcio[1], Amulya Badineni[1], Kevin McGrath[1], Georgios Papamichail[2], and Dimitris Papamichail[1](✉)

[1] The College of New Jersey, Ewing, NJ 08618, USA
papamicd@tcnj.edu
[2] New York College, Athens, Greece

Abstract. Arranging music for a different set of instruments that it was originally written for is traditionally a tedious and time-consuming process, performed by experts with intricate knowledge of the specific instruments and involving significant experimentation. In this paper we study the problem of automating music arrangements for music pieces written for monophonic instruments or voices. We designed and implemented an algorithm that can always produce a music arrangement when feasible by potentially transposing the music piece to a different scale, permuting the assigned parts to instruments/voices, and transposing individual parts by one or more octaves. We also published open source software written in Python that processes MusicXML files and allows musicians to experiment with music arrangements. Our software can serve as a platform for future extensions that will include music reductions and inclusion of polyphonic instruments.

Keywords: music arrangement · music algorithms

1 Introduction

Music arrangements involve the adaptation of a piece of music for different instruments or ensembles. This allows the music to be performed in a variety of settings, enhances the repertory of musicians, and can also help to bring new life to a piece that may have been composed for a specific instrument or ensemble [16]. Additionally, arrangements can help to showcase the unique strengths of different instruments or even create entirely new interpretations of a piece. The process of arranging a piece of music can be a creative endeavor in itself, giving the arranger the opportunity to put their own spin on a familiar work, greatly enhancing the listening experience for audiences [1,5,12].

The computational complexity of arranging music written for a set of instruments toward a target single instrument, often employing reasonable reductive constraints, has been examined in the work of Moses and Demaine [4]. Complexities of dealing with polyphonic instruments, such as piano and guitar, include the need of considering possible fingerings as well as reductions, the elimination of certain notes for playability of even feasibility. Most research in automating music arrangements has concentrated on the piano, primarily concerning orchestral pieces [2,8,10,11,13,14]. Much of that work involves reductions to enable feasibility. Other work in the field has examined arrangements for the guitar [6,7,15], wind ensembles [9], and other orchestral instruments [3].

S. Ystad et al. (Eds.): CMMR 2023, LNCS 15236, pp. 329–336, 2026.
https://doi.org/10.1007/978-3-032-02042-0_25

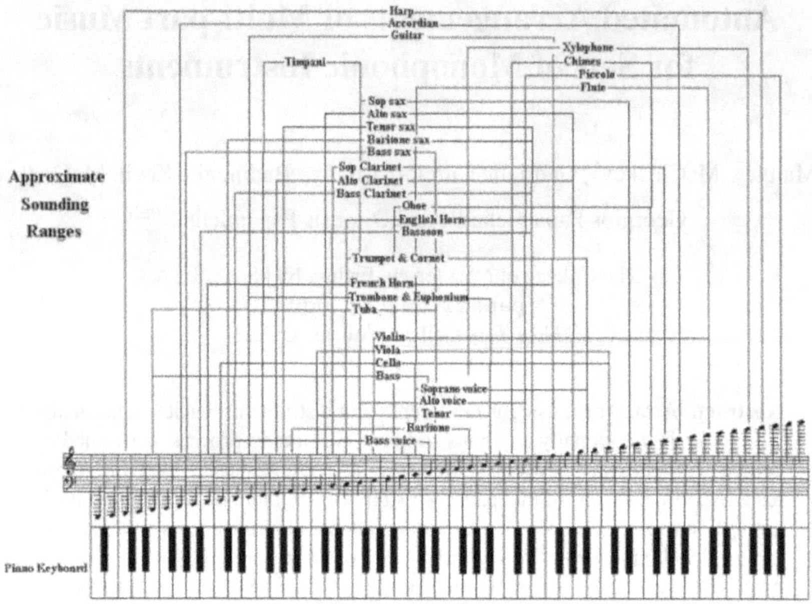

Fig. 1. Approximate sounding ranges of instruments and voices. Figure reproduced with permission from Dr. Brian Blood (dolmetch.com)

Despite its obvious benefits, we are not aware of any published algorithm or widely available software that allows for the automated arrangement of a given music piece to a different set of instruments that it was originally written for in the general case. Working toward filling that need, we designed and implemented an algorithm that arranges music written for monophonic instruments and guarantees a successful outcome when an arrangement is possible without score reduction. Our recursive backtracking algorithm exhaustively examines all feasible assignments of parts to available instruments and all possible transpositions of the piece, including independent octave transpositions of individual parts, to determine a successful arrangement that minimally affects the musicality of the piece. The use of memoization, storing partial results for reuse, further enhances the time efficiency of our software and allows processing of most music pieces in a matter of seconds.

2 Methods

2.1 Definitions

For the purposes of our research, a music piece is written in a chromatic scale and notes are separated by the interval of a semitone. We will assume that all notes fall within a total range of 88 semitones, the notes of a traditional piano, from A0 to C8. We will assign an integer to each note in the range, such that all notes can be represented by an integer from 1 to 88. For our discussion, a monophonic instrument is one that can only play one pitch at a time, such as the flute, the oboe, or a voice. Polyphonic instruments can play multiple notes simultaneously, such as the piano, guitar, or harp. A polyphonic instrument can always play a monophonic part within its range.

For our study an input music piece will consist of n parts, each being assigned to a single monophonic instrument or voice. Such parts are presented in the sheet music representation of the piece in an equal number of staves each. Our algorithm preserves the rhythm, rhythmic values of notes and rests, as well as bar lines of the music piece. Clefs, key signatures and accidentals are adjusted based on the scale of the transposed music and the instruments/voices that parts are assigned to. Our algorithm does not control for instrument timbre that may be expected in any part of the music; similarly, the thickness of the piece is not being necessarily maintained.

We will assume that an input music piece is originally written for n instruments $I_1, I_2, \cdots, I_n$, each assigned to play a part P_i of the piece, with $1 \leq i \leq n$. We seek to arrange the music for n output instruments $O_1, O_2, \cdots, O_n$. The range of each part i is an integer interval $R_i = [\![a_i, b_i]\!]$, where a_i is the integer value corresponding to the lowest frequency note and b_i to the highest frequency note played by instrument I_i in part P_i, $1 \leq i \leq n$. Likewise, the playing range of each output instrument O_i will be denoted by OR_i, $1 \leq i \leq n$, indicating the integer interval of values corresponding to the notes the instrument is able to play. Approximate ranges for a set of instruments and voices can be seen in Fig. 1.

2.2 Monophonic Instrument Set Arrangement Algorithm

Our Monophonic Music Arrangement (MMS) algorithm performs a nearly comprehensive search of possible permutations of parts. The music is transposed to all twelve keys, and the algorithm runs on each key, unless a solution has been found so far that results in fewer sharps/flats over all keys for each part. This is designed to prevent the "ideal" transposition from having a complex key signature if not necessary. Other than that, the search is fully comprehensive. For each part, the algorithm finds all possible transpositions of each part in the source piece that can be played by at least one available instrument. All permutations of these possible transpositions are then examined. If all parts can be played by at least one instrument, the algorithm then checks if there exists a set of part assignments that is valid. This is performed by a recursive function that is memoized to improve performance. If a transposed key yields valid permutations, the transposition with the least total deviation from the original composition is selected. Once all twelve keys have been checked, all permutations are tried using the selected transposition, unless there is no selected transposition, in which case the algorithm fails. All permutations are checked, and for those that are valid in the given transposition, the best arrangement is selected based on how closely the average pitch of each part matches the median pitch of the instrument's range.

The MMA algorithm implementation consists of four main function described in pseudocode below.

Algorithm 1. Find Transposed Options

```
procedure FINDTRANSPOSEDOPTIONS(originalStream, arrangementParts, semitones)
    stream ← originalStream transposed by given semitones
    parts ← new list
    for part in stream do
        choices ← new list
        for each transposition do
            set ← the subset of arrangementParts that can play at this transposition
            add (semitones + transposition, set) to choices
        end for
        if choices is empty then
            return null
        end if
        add choices to parts
    end for
    return parts
end procedure
```

Algorithm 2. Run Transposed

```
procedure RUNTRANSPOSED(stream, parts, semitones)
    selections ← new list
    for option in all possible transpositions from FINDTRANSPOSEDOPTIONS(stream, parts, semitones) do
        partsCovered ← new list
        selection ← new list
        for transposition in option do
            add set of parts covered to partsCovered
            add deviation of transposition to selection
        end for
        allPartsCovered ← the union of all sets in partsCovered
        if allPartsCovered contains all parts and ValidateArrangement(parts, partsCovered, allPartsCovered) then
            add selection to selections
        end if
    end for
    return selections
end procedure
```

2.3 Implementation

The MMA algorithm was implemented in Python utilizing the Music21 library and the MuseScore software. Our program requires two input files and produces a single output file with the music arrangement. The required input files consist of the original piece of music in MusicXML format and a TOML file listing the instrument set to arrange for, where an assigned value of k to an instrument indicates k parts should be arranged for that instrument. An example of a TOML file with an input instrument set consisting of one clarinet, two tenor saxophones, and two alto saxophones is shown in Fig. 2a.

Algorithm 3. Find Best Choice

```
procedure FindBestChoice(stream, parts)
    bestChoice ← null
    bestSharps ← ∞
    for semitones from −6 through 5 do
        sharps ← the total number of sharps/flats that would appear in the key signature for each part
        if sharps ≤ bestSharps then
            thisBestChoice ← element from RunTransposed(stream, parts, semitones) with the least deviation
            if thisBestChoice ≠ null and either sharps < bestSharps or deviation of thisBestChoice < deviation of bestChoice then
                bestChoice ← thisBestChoice
                bestSharps ← thisBestSharps
            end if
        end if
    end for
    return bestChoice
end procedure
```

Algorithm 4. MMA Algorithm

```
procedure MMA(stream, parts)
    bestChoice ← FindBestChoice(stream, parts)
    if bestChoice = null then
        return null
    end if
    transpose each part by the resulting transposition
    bestFit ← ∞
    for each permutation of newParts do
        if all parts are valid in the given permutation then
            fit ← the total absolute difference between the average pitches and the median pitch of each part
            if fit < bestFit then
                bestFit ← fit
                bestPermutation ← this permutation
            end if
        end if
    end for
    return bestPermutation
end procedure
```

Metadata about each instrument, consisting of its key in notation and a reasonable note range, is defined in a separate TOML file which is loaded separately by the program and is populated with common music instruments. An example of an entry for the alto saxophone in the instrument metadata file is shown in Fig. 2b.

```
clarinet = 1
tenor-sax = 2
alto-sax = 2
```

(a) An example arrangement file

```
[alto-sax]
name = "AltoSaxophone"
minimum = "Db3"
maximum = "Bb5"
key = "Eb"
```

(b) An entry in the instrument metadata file

Fig. 2. Examples of input instrument set and instrument information files

During execution our program checks whether the number of input instruments matches the number of parts in the piece, and then attempts to arrange for the given instruments as previously described. If arrangements are found, the best arrangement based on the criteria described in Sect. 2.2 is output as a MusicXML file. If no feasible arrangement is found, or if the number of instruments does not match, then an error message is displayed and no output file is produced.

3 Results

(a) Original Score **(b)** Arranged score

Fig. 3. Three measures from an arrangement of 'Puttin' on the Ritz' from piano to saxophone quartet

We tested our software on a variety of music pieces written for monophonic instruments. In Fig. 3 we show three measures, starting at measure 16, of the *Puttin' on the Ritz* song by Irving Berlin. Part (a) shows the input score composed of four monophonic parts. Part (b) displays the arranged piece for saxophone quartet, consisting of a soprano, alto, tenor, and baritone saxophones. Similarly, in Fig. 4 we display three measures of *Carol of the Bells*, as arranged and performed by the Pentatonix voice group, starting at measure 18 of the piece.

Complete input/output files for three test cases of our software, including the *Puttin' on the Ritz* and *Carol of the Bells* above, can be examined at: https://owd.tcnj.edu/~papamicd/music/mma/examples/

The software repository for this project can be found at: https://github.com/spazzylemons/music-arrangement/

(a) Original Score **(b)** Arranged score

Fig. 4. Three measures from an arrangement of 'Carol of the Bells' from voices to saxophone quartet

4 Conclusions and Future Work

Our monophonic music arrangement algorithm and its software implementation create a platform for automating music arrangements with minimal user input. Although currently basic in its functionality, it is now being extended in a number of different directions. For accommodating arrangements for a smaller sets of instruments than the number of parts in the music, we are examining score reduction techniques to eliminate certain parts or at least reduce the number of simultaneous notes that are played throughout the piece, while maintaining faithfulness to the original. To allow for the inclusion of polyphonic instruments in the arrangements, we are looking into analyzing and decomposing polyphonic parts into monophonic ones and inversely, while adhering to constraints related to fingerings and other instrument and player restrictions.

Acknowledgments. The authors acknowledge use of the ELSA high performance computing cluster at The College of New Jersey for conducting the research reported in this paper. This cluster is funded in part by the National Science Foundation under grant numbers OAC-1826915 and OAC-1828163.

References

1. Baker, D.: David Baker's Arranging and Composing: For the Small Ensemble, Jazz, R & B, Jazz-rock. Alfred Publishing Company (1988). https://books.google.com/books?id=Le0EnwEACAAJ
2. Chiu, S.C., Shan, M.K., Huang, J.L.: Automatic system for the arrangement of piano reductions. In: ISM 2009 - 11th IEEE International Symposium on Multimedia (2009). https://doi.org/10.1109/ISM.2009.105
3. Crestel, L., Esling, P.: Live orchestral piano, a system for real-time orchestral music generation. In: Proceedings of the 14th Sound and Music Computing Conference 2017, SMC 2017 (2019)
4. Demaine, E.D., Moses, W.S.: 364computational complexity of arranging music. In: The Mathematics of Various Entertaining Subjects: Research in Games, Graphs, Counting, and Complexity, Volume 2. Princeton University Press (09 2017). https://doi.org/10.23943/princeton/9780691171920.003.0019
5. Elder, J.: The Art of Arranging and Orchestration. Independently Published (2018). https://books.google.com/books?id=mOQKugEACAAJ
6. Hori, G., Kameoka, H., Sagayama, S.: Input-output HMM applied to automatic arrangement for guitars. J. Inform. Process. (2013). https://doi.org/10.2197/ipsjjip.21.264
7. Hori, G., Yoshinaga, Y., Fukayama, S., Kameoka, H., Sagayama, S.: Automatic arrangement for guitars using hidden Markov model. In: Proceedings of 9th Sound and Music Computing Conference (SMC2012), pp. 450–455 (7 2012)
8. Huang, J.L., Chiu, S.C., Shan, M.K.: Towards an automatic music arrangement framework using score reduction. ACM Trans. Multimedia Comput. Commun. Appl. **8**(1) (Feb 2012). https://doi.org/10.1145/2071396.2071404
9. Maekawa, H., Emura, N., Miura, M., Yanagida, M.: On machine arrangement for smaller wind-orchestras based on scores for standard wind-orchestras. In: International Conference on Music Perception and Cognition, ICMPC 2006, pp. 268–273 (2006)
10. Nakamura, E., Yoshii, K.: Statistical piano reduction controlling performance difficulty. APSIPA Trans. Signal Inform. Process. (2018). https://doi.org/10.1017/ATSIP.2018.18
11. Onuma, S., Hamanaka, M.: Piano arrangement system based on composers' arrangement processes. In: International Computer Music Conference, ICMC 2010 (2010)
12. Stefan Kostka, T., Dorothy Payne, T., Almén, B.: Tonal Harmony. McGraw-Hill Education (2017). https://books.google.com/books?id=Cs2UAQAACAAJ
13. Takamori, H., Sato, H., Nakatsuka, T., Morishima, S.: Automatic arranging musical score for piano using important musical elements. In: Proceedings of the 14th Sound and Music Computing Conference 2017, SMC 2017 (2019)
14. Terao, M., Hiramatsu, Y., Ishizuka, R., Wu, Y., Yoshii, K.: Difficulty-aware neural band-to-piano score arrangement based on note- and statistic-level criteria. In: ICASSP 2022 - 2022 IEEE International Conference on Acoustics, Speech and Signal Processing (ICASSP), pp. 196–200 (2022). https://doi.org/10.1109/ICASSP43922.2022.9747615
15. Tuohy, D., Potter, W.: Ga-based music arranging for guitar. In: 2006 IEEE International Conference on Evolutionary Computation, pp. 1065–1070 (2006). https://doi.org/10.1109/CEC.2006.1688427
16. White, G.: Instrumental Arranging. McGraw-Hill (1992). https://books.google.com/books?id=4c2KMwEACAAJ

8 + 8 = 4: Formalizing Time Units to Handle Symbolic Music Durations

Emmanouil Karystinaios[1(✉)], Francesco Foscarin[1], Florent Jacquemard[2], Masahiko Sakai[3], Satoshi Tojo[4], and Gerhard Widmer[1,5]

[1] Institute of Computational Perception, Johannes Kepler University Linz, Linz, Austria
{emmanouil.karystinaios,francesco.foscarin}@jku.at
[2] CNAM Paris, Paris, France
[3] Nagoya University, Nagoya, Japan
[4] Asia University, Taichung City, Japan
[5] LIT AI Lab, Linz Institute of Technology, Linz, Austria

Abstract. This paper focuses on the nominal durations of musical events (notes and rests) in a symbolic musical score, and on how to conveniently handle these in computer applications. We propose the usage of a temporal unit that is directly related to the graphical symbols in musical scores, and pair this with a set of operations that cover typical computations in music applications. We formalise this time unit and the more commonly used approach in a single mathematical framework, as semirings, algebraic structures that enable an abstract description of algorithms / processing pipelines. We then discuss some practical use cases and highlight when our system can improve such pipelines by making them more efficient in terms of data type used and the number of computations.

Keywords: symbolic music · musical score · duration encoding

1 Introduction

In a musical score, the duration of musical events (i.e., notes and rests) is defined by a finite set of symbols, and their temporal position by summing the duration of the previous musical events. Computer applications that deal with musical scores typically work with *Relative Symbolic Duration* (RSD) units, i.e., they choose a reference note duration and model all temporal information as ratios of that reference. For example, for the first four notes of the upper voice in Fig. 1, one can choose a quarter note as a reference and represent the durations in the first two beats as the sequence $[0.5, 0.25, 0.25, 1]$. This kind of encoding shows its limits for certain durations, typically those produced by irregular groupings (also called tuplets). The 5th note in the top voice in the figure would have a duration of $2/3$, which is a periodic number not representable as a floating point value in computer applications, thus requiring a truncation. This introduces an

S. Ystad et al. (Eds.): CMMR 2023, LNCS 15236, pp. 337–348, 2026.
https://doi.org/10.1007/978-3-032-02042-0_26

error that propagates to all subsequent musical events and creates a number of problems for applications that require exact matching of temporal positions.

Two main approaches have been proposed to solve this problem. The first is the *fraction approach*, implemented, for example, by the Python library Music21 [3]. It involves the representation of durations with specific Python objects made to mimic a fraction. This eliminates the rounding problems, but the fraction object is inefficient to handle with respect to native Python types and is not supported by libraries for heavy computations such as Numba, Pytorch, or TensorFlow. The second method, the *common divisor* approach, consists of setting the aforementioned reference duration to a value that is a common divisor of all durations appearing in a given piece or set of pieces. All temporal information can then be expressed with natural numbers, enabling very efficient computations. This solution is adopted by the Python library Partitura [2], in some musical score storage formats such as MIDI, MEI, MusicXML, and in other computer music frameworks (e.g., [6]). However, this solution is still problematic for real-time scenarios when we do not know all duration in advance or when the piece can be modified. When a new duration is added that is not a multiple of the reference, the reference must be recomputed and all values updated.

Fig. 1. A musical score example with two problematic configurations: a tuplet and an incomplete bottom voice.

Example 1. Let us consider a toy application on the score of Fig. 1. We are interested in importing it from an MEI file, splitting the third note (the C) in the top voice into two, and producing a pianoroll representation. The notes in the top voice have durations, in RSD units (with a quarter note as reference), of $[\frac{1}{2}, \frac{1}{4}, \frac{1}{4}, 1, \frac{2}{3}, \frac{2}{3}, \frac{2}{3}]$. In the common division approach, we first need to compute as reference value δ a common divisor of all absolute note durations, the largest (i.e., the greatest common divisor GCD) if we want to optimize memory usage. In this case, this is $\frac{1}{12}$ of a quarter note. We then express each duration as a multiple of the reference, i.e., $[6, 3, 3, 12, 8, 8, 8]$. If we want to split the third note, we need to recalculate the value of δ as $1/24$, update the durations to $[12, 6, 6, 24, 16, 16, 16]$, and finally split the third note in two notes with duration 3. We can produce the pianorolls of the two voices independently and then perform an element-wise sum to obtain the score pianoroll. However, the second voice is logically incomplete in the score, missing an explicit half-note rest.[1] Thus, we first need to compute the maximum between the total duration of the two voices and insert the missing rests in the second voice. We compute the onset of each note by summing the durations of all previous notes in the same voice. ◊

[1] Ideally, both voices will have the same duration, but in real scores, this is often not the case; see [7,8] for a discussion about score quality.

This paper discusses an alternative approach to handling durations: the use of *Absolute Symbolic Duration* (ASD) units. The core idea is to consider the integers implied by the names of the graphical symbols. For example, a quarter note as 4, an eight note as 8, a 16th note as 16, and so on. Durations produced from irregular groupings are also expressed as integers (see Table 1). ASD units are already used by the Humdrum **kern file format, and (in a mixed representation with the divs approach) by MEI and MusicXML. However, they are only used to encode single note/rest durations. The typical pipeline procedure is to translate this duration format into relative symbolic durations, as a preprocessing step before any other operation.

Table 1. Examples of music symbols and corresponding durations in RSD and ASD units. Notes with "3" on top are notes that are part of a triplet.

Music Symbol				3		3	
Relative Symbolic Duration (1 =)	4	2	1	$0.\bar{6}$	0.5	$0.\bar{3}$	0.25
Absolute Symbolic Duration	1	2	4	6	8	12	16

On the contrary, we explore the usage of ASD, as "standalone" units to manipulate musical score durations. To make this practicable, we define two operations that cover typical use cases and we prove that, like RSD, ASD units form a *semiring*, an algebraic structure that enables a more abstract general description of processing pipelines. The actual computations can later be performed in ASD or RSD (or a mixture of the two), depending on the situation. This is enabled by an isomorphism that we provide to translate between the two units. Finally, we discuss some practical cases where one unit is to be preferred over the other to make the pipeline more efficient in terms of the number of operations and data types that are considered. We implement some algorithms that use ASD units in the Python library Partitura [2].

2 Definitions

In this section, we first introduce the semiring; then we formally define *ASD* and *RSD* units and a morphism between them. Our goal with the introduction of this formalism is to give a general, abstract way of describing algorithms on music durations which is valid for both ASD and RSD units. Such algorithms can practically be performed in one unit or the other (or a mix of the two) depending on the specific application (see Sect. 3).

2.1 Semiring

Formally, a *semiring* $\mathcal{S} = \langle \mathbb{S}, \oplus, \otimes \rangle$ is an algebraic structure that consists of a domain $\mathbb{S} = dom(\mathcal{S})$, and two associative binary operators $\oplus$ and $\otimes$. Some properties must be verified: $\oplus$ is commutative, and $\otimes$ distributes over $\oplus$, i.e., $\forall x, y, z \in \mathbb{S}$, $x \otimes (y \oplus z) = (x \otimes y) \oplus (x \otimes z)$.

Note that there is no complete agreement in the literature over the exact definition of a semiring. Other research (e.g., [15]) defines the two operations of a semiring with a neutral element ($\mathbb{0}$ and $\mathbb{1}$ respectively), such that $\mathbb{0}$ is absorbing for $\otimes$: $\forall x \in \mathbb{S}$, $\mathbb{0} \otimes x = x \otimes \mathbb{0} = \mathbb{0}$. Then the semiring without neutral elements is called *hemiring*. However, similarly to [5,17], we just use the term semiring, without including neutral elements (and in particular the absorbing propriety of $\mathbb{0}$). The motivation is that verifying the absorbing propriety requires changes that would take our framework further away from its use for practically useful operations on music duration (more on this in Sect. 2.3). Components of any semiring $\mathcal{S}$ may be superscripted by $\mathcal{S}$ when needed. By abuse of notation, we write $x \in \mathcal{S}$ to denote $x \in \mathbb{S}$.

A semiring $\mathcal{S}$ is *commutative* if $\otimes$ is commutative. It is *idempotent* if for all $x \in \mathcal{S}$, $x \oplus x = x$. It is *monotonic* w.r.t. a partial ordering $\leq$ iff for all x, y, z, $x \leq y$ implies $x \oplus z \leq y \oplus z$, $x \otimes z \leq y \otimes z$ and $z \otimes x \leq z \otimes y$. Every idempotent semiring $\mathcal{S}$ induces a partial ordering $\leq_{\mathcal{S}}$ called the *natural ordering* of $\mathcal{S}$ and defined by: for all x and y, $x \leq_{\mathcal{S}} y$ iff $x \oplus y = x$. It holds then that $\mathcal{S}$ is monotonic w.r.t. $\leq_{\mathcal{S}}$. $\mathcal{S}$ is called *total* if it is idempotent and $\leq_{\mathcal{S}}$ is total, i.e., when for all x and y, either $x \oplus y = x$ or $x \oplus y = y$.

Given the particular algebraic properties above, semirings can be used as a weight domain for optimization problems such as the search for shortest paths in weighted graphs or hypergraphs [12,14]. Indeed, the theory of semirings and in particular the min-plus and max-plus Tropical Algebras [10] is commonly applied in decision theory and operational research, performance evaluation and control of dynamic systems, and also formal language theory, for quantitative extensions of formal computation models [4] (weighted automata and grammars). They have also been recently used for the formalization of musical elements, e.g., harmonic/melodic intervals by Albini [1], and to describe algorithms for musical tasks, e.g., music transcription by n-best parsing [6], and melodic distance computation [11].

This work focuses on formalisations of musical duration that form idempotent and commutative semirings. Intuitively, in the applications presented in this paper, $\oplus$ selects the longest duration and $\otimes$ aggregates two durations in a single one.

2.2 Absolute Symbolic Durations

Let us define the semiring of Absolute Music Duration units $\mathcal{A} = \langle \mathbb{Q}^+ \cup \{\infty\}, \oplus, \otimes \rangle$ by detailing its domain and the two operations.

The Domain. The domain $dom(\mathcal{A}) = \mathbb{Q}^+ \cup \{\infty\}$ of $\mathcal{A}$ contains (but is not limited to) non-null integers implied by the graphical symbol of notes and rests, e.g., quarter notes, eight notes, 16th notes, 32th notes, etc. Intuitively, larger values correspond to shorter notes. The limiting case is the null musical duration (used, for example, for grace notes), which is denoted by ∞. $dom(\mathcal{A})$ also includes other values that can result from the use of *duration modifiers* in the musical score, such as dots and tuplets, and will be described later in this section. We define $\prec^{\mathcal{A}}$ to be the strict order of absolute musical durations on the domain of $\mathcal{A}$. Elements of $\mathcal{A}$ are defined such that $\forall a, b \in dom(\mathcal{A}), a \prec^{\mathcal{A}} b \iff a > b$.

Operations. We are interested in two operations: a *selection* operation to find the longest duration, and a *concatenation* to combine two or more musical durations. We define $\oplus^{\mathcal{A}}$ such that $a \oplus^{\mathcal{A}} b = \min(a, b)$, as the selection operation. Practically, this operation can be used to select the longest voice within a measure, when their durations do not correspond, like in Example 1.

The concatenation operation $\otimes^{\mathcal{A}}$ is defined as $a \otimes^{\mathcal{A}} b = \frac{ab}{a+b}$. This operation expresses mathematically the well-known musical rules about aggregating durations. For example, the concatenation of two eighth notes yields a quarter note, which in our framework can be written as $8 \otimes^{\mathcal{A}} 8 = 4$. A more advanced usage for ties and dots is also exemplified in Sect. 2.4. Readers who are not familiar with the semiring formalisms may find confusing that this concatenation operation, which looks very much like a sum, is denoted with the symbol $\otimes$, but this is what is commonly used and we keep it for consistency.

To prove that $\mathcal{A}$ is a semiring we need to prove that we have closure for both operations and that the multiplication distributes over additions. We go slightly further than proving closure and prove that both operations are commutative monoids (i.e. that they are commutative, associative, and there is an identity element) since this could be useful for further extension of our framework. Remember that for simplicity we write $x \in \mathcal{A}$ to denote $x \in dom(\mathcal{A})$.

Lemma 1. *$\langle dom(\mathcal{A}), \oplus^{\mathcal{A}} \rangle$ is a commutative monoid.*

Proof. Let $a, b, c \in \mathcal{A}$. By definition $a \oplus^{\mathcal{A}} b = \min(a, b)$.

Then from the commutativity and associativity properties of the min operation, $\oplus$ is also commutative and associative. The closure is trivial for min. The identity element is ∞, i.e., $\forall a \in \mathcal{A}, a \oplus \infty = a$.

Lemma 2. *$\langle dom(\mathcal{A}), \otimes^{\mathcal{A}} \rangle$ is a commutative monoid.*

Proof. Let $a, b, c \in \mathcal{A}$. By definition $a \otimes^{\mathcal{A}} b = \frac{ab}{a+b}$. By the commutativity of addition and multiplication, it follows that $\otimes^{\mathcal{A}}$ is also commutative and associative. Closure is also verified for the same reason. Let us investigate if the relationship also holds for the case of the null durations, i.e. ∞. We define $a \otimes^{\mathcal{A}} \infty$ as the limit $\lim_{b\to\infty} \left(a \otimes^{\mathcal{A}} b\right)$.

$$a \otimes^{\mathcal{A}} \infty = \lim_{b\to\infty} \left(a \otimes^{\mathcal{A}} b\right) = \lim_{b\to\infty} \left(\frac{ab}{a+b}\right) = a \lim_{b\to\infty} \left(\frac{b}{a+b}\right) = a \lim_{b\to\infty} \left(\frac{1}{\frac{a}{b}+1}\right) =$$

$$= a \left(\frac{\lim_{b\to\infty} 1}{\lim_{b\to\infty} \frac{a}{b}+1}\right) = a \left(\frac{1}{\lim_{b\to\infty} \frac{a}{b}+1}\right) = a \left(\frac{1}{0+1}\right) = a$$

Since $\otimes^{\mathcal{A}}$ is commutative, this also holds for the case $\infty \otimes^{\mathcal{A}} a$. We also proved that ∞ is the neutral element of $\otimes^{\mathcal{A}}$. $\Diamond$

We will now prove some Lemmas that will be useful for the proof of Theorem 1.

Lemma 3. *Let $a, b, c \in \mathcal{A}$, then $b < c \iff a \otimes^{\mathcal{A}} b < a \otimes^{\mathcal{A}} c$.*

Proof.

$$b < c \overset{a>0}{\iff} ab < ac \overset{bc>0}{\iff} ab + bc < ac + bc \iff b(a+c) < c(a+b) \overset{a>0}{\iff}$$
$$ab(a+c) < ac(a+b) \overset{a+c>0,\, a+b>0}{\iff} \frac{ab}{a+b} < \frac{ac}{a+c} \equiv a \otimes^{\mathcal{A}} b < a \otimes^{\mathcal{A}} c$$

◊

Lemma 4. *$\otimes^{\mathcal{A}}$ is left and right distributive over $\oplus^{\mathcal{A}}$.*

Proof. Let $a, b, c \in \mathcal{A}$: By induction on the order relation between b, c:

- $b = c$:
  Trivial.
- $b < c$:

$$a \otimes (b \oplus c) = \frac{a \min(b,c)}{a + \min(b,c)} \overset{\text{by IH}}{=} \frac{ab}{a+b} = a \otimes b \tag{1}$$

$$(a \otimes b) \oplus (a \otimes c) = \min((a \otimes b),\ (a \otimes c)) \overset{\text{by Lemma 3 and IH}}{=\!=} a \otimes b \tag{2}$$

  Then our proof is completed by using reflexivity on 1 and 2.

- $b > c$:
  Similar to $b < c$.

The right side distributivity follows by the commutativity properties of the operations. ◊

Theorem 1. *$(dom(\mathcal{A}), \oplus^{\mathcal{A}}, \otimes^{\mathcal{A}})$ is a semiring.*

Proof. We have all the elements to conclude the proof:

- $(dom(\mathcal{A}), \oplus^{\mathcal{A}})$ is associative and satisfies the closure property (by Lemma 1);
- $(dom(\mathcal{A}), \otimes^{\mathcal{A}})$ is associative and satisfies the closure property (by Lemma 2);
- Multiplication distributes over addition (by Lemma 4)

◊

When dealing with multiple equal durations in music, it is practical to extend the $\oplus$ operation to define a scalar multiplication. For a duration $a \in \mathcal{A}$ and a scalar $n \in \mathbb{Q}$, it is denoted by the function $\text{repeat}^{\mathcal{A}}(a, n) = a/n$.

2.3 Relative Symbolic Durations

We define the semiring of Relative Symbolic Duration units $\mathcal{R}^{\delta} = (\mathbb{Q}^{+} \cup \{0\}, \oplus, \otimes)$ relative to the reference duration δ.

The Domain. The domain $dom(\mathcal{R}^\delta) = \mathbb{Q}^+ \cup \{0\}$ of $\mathcal{R}$ contains durations measured relative to a reference duration value. Intuitively, smaller values correspond to shorter notes. The limiting case is the duration 0, which can be used, for example, for grace notes. We define $\prec^\mathcal{R}$ to be the strict order of absolute musical durations on the domain of $\mathcal{A}$. Elements of $\mathcal{R}$ are defined such that $\forall a, b \in dom(\mathcal{R}), a \prec^\mathcal{R} b \iff a < b$.

Operations. Similarly to $\mathcal{A}$, $\oplus^\mathcal{R} \equiv \max$ is used to select the larger duration and $\otimes^\mathcal{R} \equiv +$ is used to add two durations together. The repeat operation can be defined as $\text{repeat}^\mathcal{R}(a, n) = a * n$.

We skip the proof of $\mathcal{R}$ being a semiring for brevity. It can also be noted that the operations and domain we defined are equivalent to those of a tropical semiring [15], so the proof for tropical semirings is also valid for our case. Differently from a tropical semiring, however, we don't have the absorption property of the $\otimes$ neutral elements $\mathbb{0}$, i.e., $\forall x \in \mathcal{R}$, $\mathbb{0} \otimes x = x \otimes \mathbb{0} = \mathbb{0}$. In order to verify this, we would need to swap the min with the max (and vice-versa) for the $\otimes$ in our two semirings, but this would make for a non-musically useful operation, violating the ultimate objective of this research.

2.4 A General Duration Framework

Table 2 summarises our formalization of ASD and RSD units. In the following, we introduce a morphing function to convert between these two units. Finally, we include in our framework the duration modifiers that are used in musical scores, i.e., ties, dots, and tuplets.

Morphing Between Time Units. Given a reference duration value δ, we define the reciprocal function $f(x) = \delta/x$ that maps every element $x \in dom(\mathcal{A})$ to its correspondent in $\mathcal{R}^\delta$, and vice-versa. It is trivial to see that this function is isomorphic and order-preserving (it preserves the ordering in the respective source/target domains, even though the order in $\mathcal{A}$ is reversed with respect to $\mathcal{R}$); it follows that f is a *Homomorphism*, i.e. $\forall a, b \in dom(\mathcal{R})$, $f(a \otimes^\mathcal{R} b) = f(a) \otimes^\mathcal{A} f(b)$. The choice of δ has interesting practical implications. For example, by setting it to a beat duration (which depends on the time signature), we obtain units typically used in music research to reduce the dependency on the time signature. By setting it to a quarter note duration we obtain the so-called *quarter length* durations, commonly used for general applications since they do not depend on other score parameters.

Duration Modifiers. In a musical score, there are some graphical symbols, i.e., ties, dots, and tuplet groupings, that modify the duration of the notes/rests they are assigned to. In this section, we will define ties, dots, and tuplets as functions applied to elements of either $\mathcal{A}$ or $\mathcal{R}$. We use the symbol $\mathcal{X}$ to refer to either of the structures $\mathcal{A}$ or $\mathcal{R}$.

Table 2. Table comparing the semirings of Absolute and Relative Symbolic Durations.

	$\mathbb{S}$	$\oplus$	$\otimes$
ASD $\mathcal{A}$	$\mathbb{Q}^+ \cup \{\infty\}$	$\min(a, b)$	$\frac{ab}{a+b}$
RSD $\mathcal{R}$	$\mathbb{Q}^+ \cup \{0\}$	$\max(a, b)$	$a + b$

First, let us consider the ties between notes. The total duration of two tied notes $a, b \in \mathcal{X}$ can be easily captured by the $\otimes$ operation.

Definition 1. *The total duration of two tied notes $a, b \in \mathcal{X}$ is given by function tie* : $\mathcal{X} \times \mathcal{X} \to \mathcal{X}$

$$\text{tie}(a, b) = a \otimes^{\mathcal{X}} b \tag{3}$$

Another musical concept that can prolong the duration of a musical note is the dot. A dotted note a can be seen as a function dot applied to the note a. This can be generalized for an arbitrary number of dots:

Definition 2. *The function dot* : $\mathcal{X} \times \mathbb{N} \to \mathcal{X}$ *applied to a note $a \in \mathcal{X}$ is inductively defined as follows:*

$$\text{dot}(a, 0) = a \tag{4}$$

$$\text{dot}(a, n+1) = \text{repeat}(a, \frac{1}{2^{n+1}}) \otimes^{\mathcal{X}} \text{dot}(a, n) \tag{5}$$

Another function that can be used to construct musical duration is the tuplet function. The duration of a note in a tuplet of total duration $a \in \mathcal{X}$ can be seen as a function with two parameters, the base note duration a and the type of tuple γ (in this case 3 for triplet).

Definition 3. *Let $a \in \mathcal{X}$, $\gamma \in \mathbb{N}_{>2}$. The tuplet function,t* : $\mathcal{X} \times \mathbb{N}^* \to \mathcal{X}$, *is defined as:*

$$t(a, \gamma) = \text{repeat}(a, \frac{2}{\gamma}) \tag{6}$$

Example 2. We use the formalisms introduced in this section on the problem of Example 1, where the goal was to import the score from an MEI file, split the third note (the C) in the top voice into two, and produce a pianoroll representation. This process can abstractly be described solved as: (1) read all durations $[d_1, d_2, \ldots, d_n]$ from the input MEI file; (2) compute the values of the notes under the triplet with Definition 3; (3) split the third note into two notes with duration $d_{\text{new}} = \text{repeat}(d_3, 1/2)$; (4) find each note onset and offset position by $[d_1 \otimes d_2 \otimes \cdots \otimes d_n]$; (5) for the last note offset of each voice, compute the maximum with the $\oplus$ operator; (6) output the pianoroll representations for the two voices, using the start times and durations thus calculated.

3 From Abstract Description to Algorithm Implementation

In the previous section, we introduced an abstract formalism to describe algorithms on music sequences. We now discuss cases where it is more efficient to perform such algorithms in ASD units or in RSD units.

3.1 Advantages and Disadvantages

The use of ASD units can bring advantages in terms of data types because it can give a prevalence of integers over floating point (and periodic) values. For this to be the case, we need to deal with durations that span a maximum of a whole note. In a 4/4 piece, this will correspond to durations of one measure. This does not mean that algorithms implemented in ASD units cannot handle multiple measures, but rather that they should follow a "divide et impera" principle where every measure is handled independently. This is already quite common in file-parsing systems since scores are encoded measure by measure in file formats such as MusicXML and MEI.

In terms of the number of computations, ASD units are ideal for applications that concern the graphical symbols used in the score, for example, changing the pitch of a note, changing a duration, or segmenting a musical score. Such applications can skip the costly computation of common divisor, and conversion to RSD units altogether. Instead, when the measure is not specified (which could be the case, for example, in handling a MIDI file), or when we want to do operations that don't follow the measure segmentation (e.g., segmenting a score between measures), the usage of RSD units is preferred.

Example 3. Let us consider the problem of Example 1. By considering ASD units, we can parse the input score file simply by copying the values for the note graphical durations. The splitting of the third note of duration 16 in two parts yields two notes of duration $16 * 2 = 32$.

A big limit in the efficiency of ASD units is posed by time signatures where the beat is a dotted note, for example, 6/8. A dotted note will make the duration assume noninteger, or even periodic, values. A possible solution to this problem is given in the next section.

3.2 The Lazy Evaluation Case

It is common for systems that deal with musical scores to have a generic import function, where the score file is converted to some internal representation. If in In this step, the user did not yet specify the set of operations they intend to perform, the choice of whether to use ASD or RSD cannot be performed made. In order to let the system choose between ASD and RSD to exploit the advantages described in the previous section, we suggest using a *lazy evaluation* parsing strategy. First, we propose to reduce the domain by considering only the *ASD* values $\{2^n \mid \forall n \in [0..7]\}$ (i.e. only single graphical note/rest symbols). Duration modifiers such as dots or tuplets are imported as functions dot or tuple without being computed. Only when the user specifies a task, will these functions be resolved to actual values, and the task is performed either in ASD or RSD units, depending on what would allow for the most efficient computation. From a functional programming perspective, this can be viewed as a Monad transformation [18] of the parsed elements.

3.3 Implementation

We provide a proof of concept of the practical utility of the methods introduced in this paper, by implementing some functions in the Python library Partitura [2]. The core of this library, i.e., the *Timeline* object, uses RSD units, in particular on the common divisor technique described in the introduction. However, some functions in the file parsing module are modular enough to make it possible to run them in ADS without the need of making major changes to the rest of the library. These are: (1) the functions to compute the common divisor for integer encoding of RSD durations, (2) the function to find the longest voice in a measure, and (3) the computation of the actual duration for a note inside a tuplet. We also implement an alternative (still partial) parser of **Kern files that leverages a lazy evaluation approach.

4 Conclusions and Discussion

In this paper, we proposed an alternative approach to handling the symbolic music durations from musical scores, that is based on absolute symbolic duration (ASD) units. We formalized ASD, and the (typically used) relative symbolic duration (RSD) units, in a single mathematical framework, and paired them with two operations. The result is two semirings: algebraic structures that enable an abstract description of algorithms on symbolic durations. We then moved to a more practical discussion and described some use cases where one unit is more efficient than the other, in terms of data types (integers vs floating point) and number of calculations. Finally, we advocated a functional parsing of symbolic music formats that can select the most efficient way of performing the various operations in an algorithm and enable considerable speed-up for common use cases.

It is clear that the proposals in this paper are mostly of theoretical interest, and belong to the research branch that formalizes musical elements with mathematical structures [1,13,16]. However, our interest in this topic started from our practical experience with parsing and processing musical score files to use their information as input for music information retrieval (MIR) systems. While the improvement in efficiency that our methods may enable is negligible for a single score, large deep-learning models have to load thousands of scores, thus making each small optimization much more useful. For example, we will probably soon see some general tokenization techniques for musical scores (similar to the multiple ones that have been proposed for MIDI files [9]); in this context, a tokenization that focuses on the graphical symbols using only ASD, could enable major speedups in computing time.

Acknowledgments. This work was supported by the European Research Council (ERC) under the EU's Horizon 2020 research and innovation programme, grant agreement No. 101019375 (*Whither Music?*), the Federal State of Upper Austria (LIT AI Lab), and JSPS Kaken 20H04302, 21H03572.

References

1. Albini, G., Bernardi, M.P.: Tropical generalized interval systems. In: Montiel, M., Gomez-Martin, F., Agustin-Aquino, O.A. (eds.) Mathematics and Computation in Music, pp. 73–83. Springer International Publishing (2019)
2. Cancino-Chacón, C.E., Peter, S.D., Karystinaios, E., Foscarin, F., Grachten, M., Widmer, G.: Partitura: A Python package for symbolic music processing. In: Proceedings of the Music Encoding Conference (MEC2022). Halifax, Canada (2022)
3. Cuthbert, M.S., Ariza, C.: Music21: a toolkit for computer-aided musicology and symbolic music data. In: Proceedings of the International Society for Music Information Retrieval Conference (ISMIR), pp. 637–642 (2010)
4. Droste, M., Kuich, W.: Semirings and formal power series. In: Handbook of Weighted Automata, pp. 3–28. Springer (2009)
5. Dudek, W.A., Shabir, M., Anjum, R.: Characterizations of hemirings by their h-ideals. Comput. Math. Appl. **59**(9), 3167–3179 (2010)
6. Foscarin, F., Jacquemard, F., Rigaux, P., Sakai, M.: A parse-based framework for coupled rhythm quantization and score structuring. In: Proceedings of the International Conference on Mathematics and Computation in Music (MCM), pp. 248–260. Springer (2019)
7. Foscarin, F., McLeod, A., Rigaux, P., Jacquemard, F., Sakai, M.: ASAP: a dataset of aligned scores and performances for piano transcription. In: Proceedings of the International Society for Music Information Retrieval Conference (ISMIR), pp. 534–541 (2020)
8. Foscarin, F., Rigaux, P., Thion, V.: Data quality assessment in digital score libraries: the gioqoso project. Int. J. Digit. Libr. **22**, 159–173 (2021)
9. Fradet, N., Briot, J.P., Chhel, F., El Fallah Seghrouchni, A., Gutowski, N.: MidiTok: A python package for MIDI file tokenization. In: Late-Breaking Demo Session of the International Society for Music Information Retrieval Conference (2021)
10. Gaubert, S., Plus, M.: Methods and applications of (max,+) linear algebra. In: Reischuk, R., Morvan, M. (eds.) STACS 1997. LNCS, vol. 1200, pp. 261–282. Springer, Heidelberg (1997). https://doi.org/10.1007/BFb0023465
11. Giraud, M., Jacquemard, F.: Weighted automata computation of edit distances with consolidations and fragmentations. Inform. Comput. **282** (2022)
12. Huang, L.: Advanced dynamic programming in semiring and hypergraph frameworks. In: International Committee on Computational Linguistics Conference (COLING) (2008)
13. Mazzola, G.: The topos of music: geometric logic of concepts, theory, and performance. Birkhäuser (2012)

14. Mohri, M.: Semiring frameworks and algorithms for shortest-distance problems. J. Autom. Lang. Comb. **7**(3), 321–350 (2002)
15. Pin, J.E.: Tropical Semirings. Cambridge Univ. Press, Cambridge (1998)
16. Popoff, A., Agon, C., Andreatta, M., Ehresmann, A.: From k-nets to PK-nets: a categorical approach. Perspect. New Music **54**(2), 5–63 (2016)
17. Sen, M., Maity, S., Shum, K.: Some aspects of semirings. Southeast Asian Bull. Math. **45**(6) (2021)
18. Wadler, P.: The essence of functional programming. In: Proceedings of the ACM SIGPLAN-SIGACT Symposium on Principles of Programming Languages, pp. 1–14 (1992)

DiffVel: Note-Level MIDI Velocity Estimation for Piano Performance by a Double Conditioned Diffusion Model

Hyon Kim(✉) and Xavier Serra

Music Technology Group, Universitat Pompeu Fabra, Barcelona, Spain
{hyon.kim,xavier.serra}@upf.edu

Abstract. In any piano performance, expressiveness is paramount for effectively conveying the intent of the performer, and one of the most significant aspects of expressiveness is the loudness at the individual key or note level. However, accurately detecting note-level loudness poses a considerable technical challenge due to the polyphonic nature of piano performances, wherein multiple notes are played simultaneously, as well as the similarity of harmonic elements.

MIDI velocity is crucial for indicating loudness in piano notes. This study conducted experiments for estimating a note-level MIDI velocity expanding the DiffRoll model: the Diffusion Model for piano performance transcription. By adopting double conditioning–audio and score information–and implementing noise removal as a post-processing, our findings highlight the model's potential in estimating note level MIDI velocity.

Keywords: MIDI velocity estimation · diffusion model · conditioned deep neural network · FiLM conditioning

1 Introduction

The assessment of piano performance can be attributed to three key factors, namely loudness, rhythm, and accurate key strokes [15]. Owing to the polyphonic nature of piano performances, multiple auditory streams coexist, such as melody line and accompaniment. This intricate aspect allows for enhanced distinguishability in the interpretations of expert pianists [28]. The expressiveness of a musical piece is significantly influenced by the series of loudness values associated with each note in the score, which contribute to the dynamic alterations throughout the composition [8].

Within the realm of music education, research has demonstrated the effectiveness of utilizing visual feedback in enhancing students' abilities [9,10]. In this regard, the comprehension and management of loudness become especially significant [15] when it is visualised. The employment of techniques for estimating and visualizing loudness fulfills the crucial system requirement, enabling the provision of valuable feedback to learners.

[19–21] researched mapping from perceptual loudness value in dB scale to dynamic symbols for piano performance such as *forte*, *mezzoforte*, *piano*,

S. Ystad et al. (Eds.): CMMR 2023, LNCS 15236, pp. 349–361, 2026.
https://doi.org/10.1007/978-3-032-02042-0_27

pianissimo, *crescendo*, etc. Note that using MIDI velocity, we predict loudness at a lower granularity, i.e. finer scale than the dynamic markings which are explicitly written in most of music scores and indicate how loud the piece should be played. Furthermore, each note in a piano performance may have a different loudness depending on the texture of the music [7,17]. Therefore, the note-level loudness itself has special meaning in piano performance, considering its polyphonic characteristics.

To prevent ambiguity, we use the term "loudness" to denote the combined MIDI velocities within a specific time frame as measured by an electronic piano device. On the other hand, "intensity" refers to the maximum value of the frequency sum for a note frame, as defined in [12]. It is essential to recognize that MIDI velocity does not have a direct correlation with loudness as experienced by the human auditory system. Studies have been conducted to explore the relationship between MIDI velocity and loudness measured in decibels (dB) [4]. While the research demonstrates a consistent increase in perceived loudness (in dB) with increasing MIDI velocity, it also reveals that this relationship is non-linear [27].

Since this research aims to detect MIDI velocity on each note performed, automatic piano performance transcription is a closely related area for this purpose. Piano performance transcription is also an actively researched topic [2,16]. However, these studies primarily focus on detecting individual notes, rather than note loudness or dynamic symbols in a score. Additionally, the transcription process is not yet fully accurate and reproducible of performance.

Several studies have explored the note-level loudness estimation task [5,6,12–14]. These researchers employed NMF and DNN methods to isolate piano performance audio into 88 distinct keys and estimated MIDI velocity or intensity for each note. We consider this area of research as an application of Automatic Music Transcription (AMT) and to be applied to expressiveness performance modeling. The piano note-level MIDI velocity estimation task involves solving a two-fold problem. One aspect is a regression problem, requiring the estimation of numbers within the 0–127 range for MIDI velocity. The other issue is audio classification, which involves sorting audio into each piano key, typically consisting of 88 keys. To address these challenges, we propose the DiffVel as an expansion of DiffRoll [3], a diffusion model for AMT, and Feature-wise Linear Modulation (FiLM) conditioning layers [26] to incorporate score information into the DNN. We conducted experiments to estimate the MIDI velocity using this approach.

2 Related Work

2.1 Automatic Music Transcription

The piano performance transcription is one of the closest problems for classification from audio input. [18] proposed a CNN-GRU combined acoustic model which branches into four outputs: velocity regression, onset, offset, and note frame estimation. The note frame estimation is the final goal of this model and the other three estimations are gathered as input to another acoustic model to estimate the notes at the frame level. Therefore, the estimated MIDI velocity regression is not evaluated in the paper since it is out of the scope.

Recently, diffusion models have been explored as an alternative approach. DiffWave, a state-of-the-art generative model for audio synthesis, leverages the diffusion probabilistic framework and exhibits remarkable capabilities in generating high-quality audio samples from various sources. The core idea behind DiffWave involves employing a series of de-noising score matching steps, iteratively refining the generated audio samples to achieve accurate and precise output. Building upon DiffWave, DiffRoll has been researched [3]. DiffRoll expands DiffWave into a two-dimensional representation of sound and output, taking Mel Spectrogram as a condition and forming the two-dimensional Gaussian noise input into MIDI roll. The generative model's characteristics offer considerable potential to simultaneously address classification and regression problems by tuning conditions. Exploring conditions with not only one but also multiple conditions would contribute to estimating MIDI velocity more accurately. However, the model disregards velocity estimation in the model evaluation.

For conditioning, existing research utilizes score information to inform musical instrument separation in polyphonic music [22,23,29]. These works employ score or video information to enhance source separation results by creating an additional neural network to extract features from the supplementary data, which are then fed into the original DNN.

2.2 Feature-wise Linear Modulation (FiLM)

In this paper, we utilized the FiLM conditioning [26] to insert score information in order to estimate note-level MIDI velocity for piano performance. FiLM conditioning is used in the image processing area and has gained improved results on object detection [26]. In previous research, natural language is used as an external condition to indicate the existence of target objects to be detected. This idea has been applied to audio source separation tasks by conditioning audio with video and score information [29].

The FiLM comprises a set of neural network layers that generate an affine transformation for a given input layer in a neural network. It consists of a base DNN which is trained in a supervised fashion and a condition generator which takes conditions such as score as input and generates β and γ to make an element-wise affine transformation in the latent space of the base DNN. In the math formula, it is described as follows;

$$FiLM(\boldsymbol{x}) = \gamma(\boldsymbol{z}) \cdot \boldsymbol{x} + \beta(\boldsymbol{z}) \tag{1}$$

where vector $\boldsymbol{z}$ is a conditional vector.

The Fig. 1 shows the architecture of FiLM conditioning. This condition embedding model generates parameters, β and γ, to make an affine transformation on the latent vector $\boldsymbol{x}$ from the base DNN.

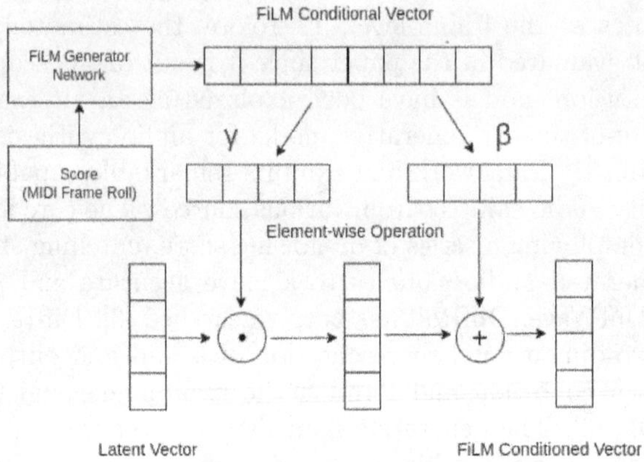

Fig. 1. The diagram illustrates the operation flow for inserting a FiLM condition into a latent vector

2.3 Note Level MIDI Velocity Estimation with Score Information

Only three papers have considered note-level MIDI velocity in music performance, employing NMF [12,13] and DNN methods [14]. NMF methods have been used for source separation problems and effectively applied to music source separation as well [12,24] examined an NMF method with score information to estimate note-level intensity before creating a linear regression model to obtain note-level MIDI velocity estimation. This research provided a detailed analysis of NMF method errors and their causes. The DNN method attempted to address the estimation problem by applying the AMT method and score conditioning. The DNN architecture involves stacking convolution blocks and GRU block and inserting a FiLM conditioning generated by a fully connected linear layer. Although it did not surpass the results of the NMF method, it was the first attempt to estimate MIDI velocity using a DNN method and to generalize the model for unseen classical music inputs, as opposed to the NMF method which optimizes parameters for each test data. [6] aimed to estimate the note level intensity, rather than MIDI velocity, from the spectrogram by filtering it according to the frequency of each note.

In our study, we compare our results with the NMF method proposed in [12] and the DNN method [14] as our benchmark.

3 Method

There are two models experimented in this study: the diffusion models with and without score information by FiLM conditioning. The entire architecture is based on the DiffRoll model and the conditions, Mel Spectrogram and score, are inserted as an expansion. We used the MIDI velocity data on note frame level as supervised data for training for both models. Score information is represented in a note frame roll in the MIDI roll.

For the training data, we used the Maestro dataset [11]. The data segmentation is 20 s, and the number of data frames is 31 in one second. Therefore, each output from the models is a (620, 88) matrix containing onset, offset, and velocity information.

3.1 Model Architecture

The simplified overall model architecture is illustrated in Fig. 2. In the diffusion model, each residual layer takes the conditions. The Mel Spectrogram transformed from input audio is added as another condition to each residual layer before the FiLM conditional vector insertion.

For the purpose of inserting the score information, we also added a FiLM conditioning layer as it is introduced in Sect. 2. We have tested the element-wise operations for multiplication and addition. However, the scalar multiplication and addition gave us better results. The FiLM generator is designed as a fully connected layer to generate conditioning parameters, and it is inserted after Mel Spectrum conditioning in each residual layer, i.e. the generated conditional vectors are sliced for each residual layer for the affine transformation.

For the parameter setup for DiffVel, the original setup is employed from DiffRoll: 15 residual layers, sampling rate 16000 Hz, the hop size 512, the drop rate 0 to be fully supervised learning fashion, and the convolutional kernel size 9 for the residual layers. The loss function is L2 (mean square error) loss for the entire data segment, not note-level MIDI velocity error. We have tried Binary Cross Entropy (BCE) for better classification and L1 loss for MIDI velocity estimation. However, they did not work well in this diffusion model setup. Due to the limitation of computational resources, the epoch is stopped at 2000 for each training.

In the task of MIDI velocity estimation, which aims to get a number as value from the output, dealing with the input Gaussian noise is crucial. When the Gaussian noise is generated, it has a mean value of 0 and variance of 1. The diffusion step to denoise the Gaussian noise is set to 200 steps. However this noise is not perfectly removed after the diffusion steps and we need to perform denoising to each output by the post-processing.

During the post-processing, Gaussian noise removal is performed, which remained after the diffusion steps. This remainder causes a problem that it is considered as velocity during the evaluation process and causes 100% of the recall score and its note level estimation error is calculated high since the error is calculated where the note is not actually detected by the model. In this research, velocity estimation evaluation is made only on correctly detected notes. This evaluation constraint is applied to the other two models to be compared, the DNN [14] and NMF [12] models.

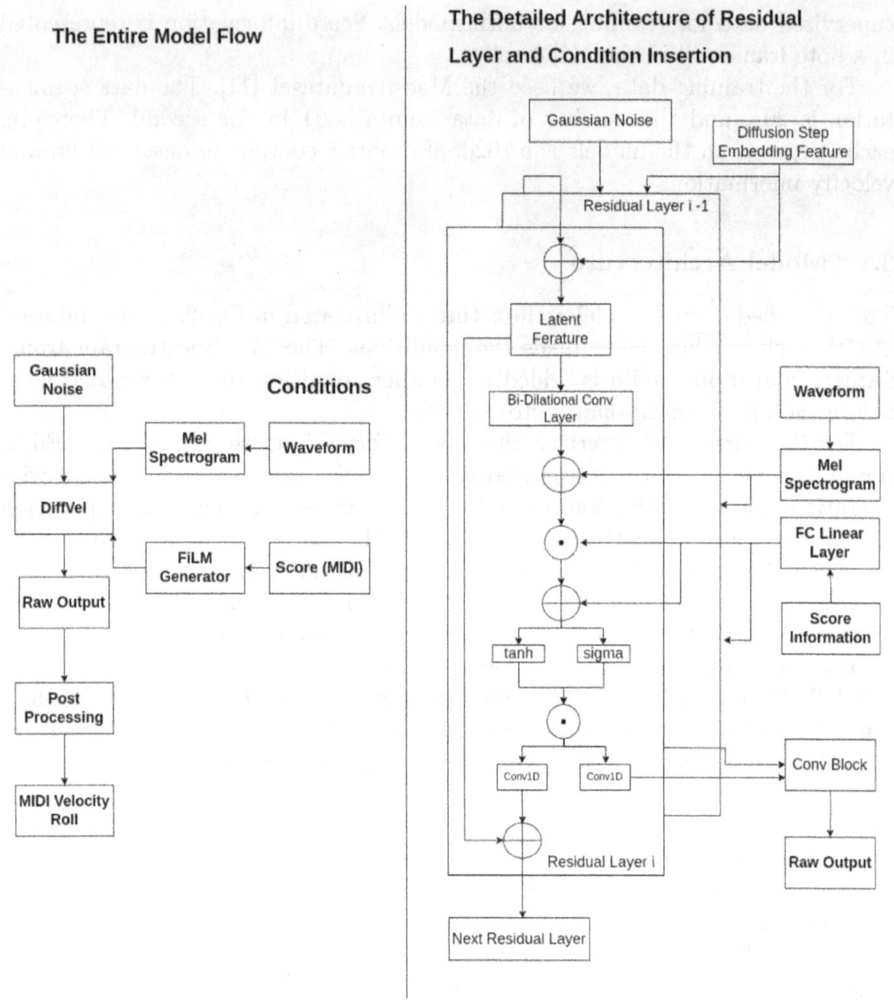

Fig. 2. The simplified overall process (left) and the detailed condition insertion into each residual layer (right)

In order to remove the remaining noise, three methods are considered; one is to increase the diffusion steps since each step of diffusion step reduces the Gaussian noise. The second way is using a post-processing method employed by SegDiff, which averages the output from multiple inferences [1], at the expense of computational resources. However, these methods were not chosen due to the limitation of computational resources. In the process of removing the remaining Gaussian noise in the output, we calculated the distribution where the note does not exist in the ground truth score and defined a threshold to set output value 0. More precisely, a right Z-score is set based on the distribution in order to find a threshold to set the output value to 0. Z-score is a number derived by following equation;

$$Z = \frac{x - \mu}{\sigma} \tag{2}$$

where x is observed value, μ and σ are mean and standard deviation of all output values for each score.

The reason why the right Z-scores is chosen, rather than taking the highest value in the area where the note does not exist in the ground truth, is that there are wrongly detected extra notes which have proper values to represent a MIDI velocity. These values are considered above the Z-score in the distribution of the remaining noise and do not affect the correctly detected values during the post-processing by not setting them to 0.

After removing the remaining Gaussian noise, we normalized the output to be in the range $[0, 1]$ looking at entire output value of each excerpt, not just for each output, and then scaled back to $[0, 127]$.

3.2 Evaluation

For testing purposes, we used the Saarland Music Data (SMD) dataset [25], which is also used for testing in previous researches [12,14]. The dataset consists of students' piano performances, both audio data and MIDI data, which are perfectly aligned. The amount of data includes 50 classical piano excerpts, performed on Yamaha Disklavier. The original sampling frequency is 44.1kHz and down-sampled to 16kHz. We chose 49 excerpts from this dataset which are used in the score-informed NMF method by [12].

The model evaluation is made by taking an $L1$ distance of MIDI velocities for each note between ground truth and inference by the models, similarly to the previous research [12].

$$Error = \frac{\sum_i |V(i)_{\text{ground truth}} - V(i)_{\text{inference}}|}{N} \tag{3}$$

where i is each note and N is the number of correctly detected notes in the score.

The inferred MIDI velocity is the maximum value within the interval of each detected and classified velocity frame against the ground truth velocity frame for each note. This is because the detected velocity tends to fade after having the maximum value in the estimated MIDI velocity in a note frame as if depicting attack and fades of loudness of each note.

To evaluate the classification accuracy, recall score is chosen as the evaluation metric. This is because the estimation is masked by the given score, and recall is considered as the most appropriate evaluation metric for this classification problem when score is informed, as it takes into account both true positive and false negative. It measures the proportion of the total actual positive cases that are correctly identified by the classifier.

In this study, only correctly detected notes are evaluated, since we separate the MIDI velocity estimation accuracy and note detection accuracy as different research problem statements; the AMT and the MIDI velocity estimation as mentioned in the Sect. 2.

4 Results and Analysis

As we can see from the Table 1, FiLM conditioning to incorporate score information helped the estimation accuracy among the two models we have tested. The results show that FiLM conditioning improved MIDI velocity estimation but did not help with note detection for any setup. The result represents all note-wise errors inferred on the SMD dataset.

In terms of Gaussian noise removal, the right Z-score $= 3$ improved the overall accuracy significantly by sorting output values to correctly detected notes and the remaining noise after the diffusion steps. When post-processing is not performed and the noise remains, the evaluation method considers MIDI velocity detected and recall score is always 100%.

Table 1. The mean and standard deviation (SD) of the MIDI velocity estimation error for the models are based on Z-score for noise removal

	Single Conditioning			Double Conditioning with Score		
Z-score	Mean	SD	Recall	Mean	SD	Recall
Raw Output	32.8	20.5	100%	28.6	19.2	100%
1	24.7	16.7	60%	21.0	14.5	56%
2	24.0	16.1	58%	20.2	13.6	54%
3	23.7	15.8	56%	**19.7**	**13.1**	53%

The Fig. 4 shows an example of the remaining Gaussian noise removal. The pale red color shown in the raw output is the remaining Gaussian noise from the input to the model, and setting Z-score determines the threshold to set the value to zero, attempting not to touch the detected notes. It can be intuitively seen that the remaining noise is removed without changing the value of the detected note velocities based on Z-score values.

We also compared the results to the previous models that have the same setup: a score-informed MIDI velocity estimation task. The Table 2 displays the mean and standard deviation (SD) values for proposed and previously researched models. The proposed model exhibited a mean value of 19.7 and an SD of 13.1, indicating the poorest performance among the three methods. In contrast, the Conv-FiLM DNN with Score approach achieved a mean of 15.1 and an SD of

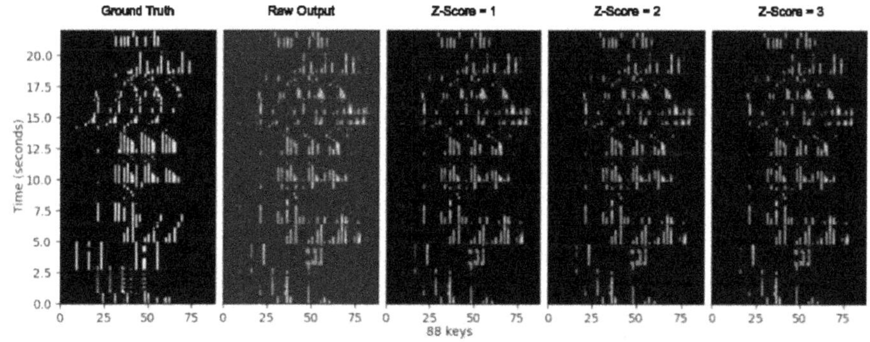

Fig. 3. The visualization and comparison of Gaussian noise removal for raw output and after removal are based on Z-score = 1, 2 and 3.

Table 2. The comparison of results for the proposed model and previous research

Proposed Model		Conv-FiLM with Score [14]		NMF with Score [12]	
Mean	SD	Mean	SD	Mean	SD
19.7	13.1	15.1	12.3	4.1	5

12.3, while the NMF with score method demonstrated the best performance with the lowest mean and SD values, at 4.1 and 5, respectively. Although the proposed model currently underperforms compared to the other models, it is important to note that the difference between their mean values is not substantial and we do not know significance in the sense of perceptual loudness yet.

Figure 4 displays the deviation of the error in each range of MIDI velocity, pitch, and sustain pedal activation respectively for both models. The box-charts for pitch and sustain pedal are similar figure for both models. These charts demonstrate that the more training data notes you have, the more accurate your MIDI velocity estimation will be, looking at the note ratio in the training dataset. This implies that data augmentation, such as pitch shifting, is necessary for low and high pitch notes in the training data. When looking at the error based on the MIDI velocity group, it is interesting to observe that FiLM conditioning improved the model's estimation for lower velocity notes, but resulted in worse estimation for higher velocity notes compared to the model without score information. It was also observed that both models tend to estimate MIDI velocity lower than the ground truth. Further analysis is required to interpret this phenomenon.

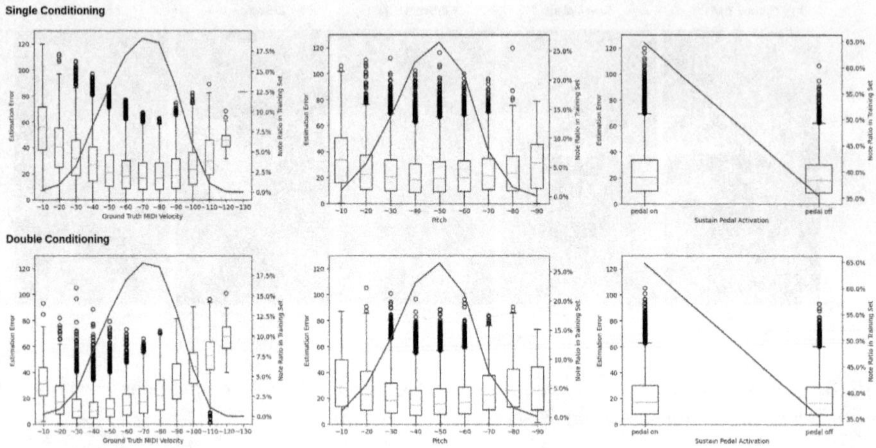

Fig. 4. The error analysis is based on ground truth MIDI velocity, pitch and sustain pedal activation. The box charts in the upper row display results for the single-conditioned model. Similarly, the box charts in the lower row show the results of the model with score information.

5 Discussion and Future Work

In this study, experiments on a diffusion model with double conditions for note level MIDI velocity estimation for piano performance have been conducted. We discovered that FiLM conditioning for score information insertion improved the estimation error and standard deviation on the overall test data.

We need to investigate the how the MIDI velocity error gives us the human perceptual sense to give the true evaluation of the model. As is mentioned in the introduction, there is still no research has been conducted for creating mapping from MIDI velocity to perceptual loudness. This will be one of our future works to keep this research move forward.

One of the downside of the models is they take significant amount of time and computational cost for an inference and model convergence in training phase. In this study, for example, it took about 2.5 min for 20 s of MIDI velocity roll output. This problem would be a blocker for a use case which requires real time processing.

The model achieved a similar result to the DNN used in a previous study [14], which indicates that the direction of this research is promising, and further exploration is warranted. Due to computational limitations, the training was stopped at 2000 epochs. However, the losses on validation set are still showing the trend of decrease on each model. This indicates that further training could improve accuracy within a short period of time with high confidence. Moreover, the recent rapid development and evolution on generative models including the diffusion model will improve its transcription accuracy, and at the same time, it would lead more attention to the FiLM conditioning to realize multi-modality for certain use-case scenarios such as education purposes which needs score and audio information.

Since it has been observed that FiLM conditioning improves the estimation results, further investigation into the condition generator is necessary for better estimation and note detection, rather than a simple fully connected linear layer. Moreover, the proposed diffusion model is adaptable to multiple conditioning techniques, making feature engineering a particularly suitable strategy for optimization within the DiffVel setup. By refining the features used in the model, it may be possible to extract more meaningful patterns and relationships from the data, ultimately leading to improved results. Additionally, incorporating more data and extending the training process could potentially enhance the proposed model's performance. Therefore, future research can focus on these aspects to optimize the proposed model and potentially achieve better performance than the existing approaches.

In real-world use cases, such as music education, score alignment must be taken into account for conditioning. A Dynamic Time Warping will be used to address this issue in a future work.

The code and the dataset used for this research would be provided upon request.

Acknowledgments. This research was carried out under the project Musical AI - PID2019- 111403GB-I00/AEI/10.13039/501100011033, funded by the Spanish Ministerio de Ciencia e Innovación and the Agencia Estatal de Investigación.

References

1. Amit, S., Nachmani, E., Wolf, L.: Segdiff: image segmentation with diffusion probabilistic models. arXiv preprint arXiv:2112.00390 (2022)
2. Benetos, E., Dixon, S., Giannoulis, D., Kirchhoff, H., Klapuri, A.: Automatic music transcription: challenges and future directions. J. Intell. Inform. Syst. **41**(3), 407–434 (2013). https://doi.org/10.1007/s10844-013-0258-3
3. Cheuk, K.W., Sawata, R., Uesaka, T., Murata, N., Takahashi, N., Takahashi, S., Herremans, D., Mitsufuji, Y.: Diffroll: Diffusion-based generative music transcription with unsupervised pretraining capability. In: ICASSP 2023 - IEEE International Conference on Acoustics, Speech and Signal Processing. pp. 1–5 (2022)
4. Dannenberg, R.B.: The interpretation of midi velocity. In: International Conference on Mathematics and Computing (2006)
5. Devaney, J., Mandel, M.: An evaluation of score-informed methods for estimating fundamental frequency and power from polyphonic audio. In: IEEE International Conference on Acoustics, Speech and Signal Processing (ICASSP), pp. 181–185 (2017)
6. Ewert, S., Müller, M.: Estimating note intensities in music recordings. In: IEEE International Conference on Acoustics, Speech and Signal Processing (ICASSP), pp. 385–388. IEEE (2011)
7. Goebl, W.: Melody lead in piano performance: expressive device or artifact? J. Acoust. Society America **110**(1), 563–572 (2001)

8. Grachten, M., Widmer, G.: Linear basis models for prediction and analysis of musical expression. J. New Music Res. **41**(4), 311–322 (2012)
9. Hamond, L.: The pedagogical use of technology-mediated feedback in a higher education piano studio: an exploratory action case study. Ph.D. thesis, UCL (University College London) (2017)
10. Hamond, L., Welch, G.F., Himonides, E.: The pedagogical use of visual feedback for enhancing dynamics in higher education piano learning and performance. Opus **25**(3), 581–601 (2019)
11. Hawthorne, C., et al.: Enabling factorized piano music modeling and generation with the maestro dataset. In: International Conference on Learning Representations (2018)
12. Jeong, D., Kwon, T., Nam, J.: Note-intensity estimation of piano recordings using coarsely aligned midi score. J. Audio Eng. Society **68**(1), 34–47 (2019)
13. Jeong, D., Nam, J.: Note intensity estimation of piano recordings by score-informed NMF. In: 2017 AES International Conference on Semantic Audio. Audio Engineering Society (2017)
14. Kim, H., Miron, M., Serra, X.: Score-informed midi velocity estimation for piano performance by film conditioning. In: Proceedings of the International Conference on Sound and Music Computing (2023)
15. Kim, H., Ramoneda, P., Miron, M., Serra, X.: An overview of automatic piano performance assessment within the music education context. In: Proceedings of the 14th International Conference on Computer Supported Education (CSEDU). vol. 1, pp. 465–474 (2022). https://doi.org/10.5220/0011137600003182
16. Kim, J.W., Bello, J.P.: Adversarial learning for improved onsets and frames music transcription. arXiv preprint arXiv:1906.08512 (2019)
17. Kim, S., Park, J.M., Rhyu, S., Nam, J., Lee, K.: Quantitative analysis of piano performance proficiency focusing on difference between hands. PLoS ONE **16** (2021)
18. Kong, Q., Li, B., Song, X., Wan, Y., Wang, Y.: High-resolution piano transcription with pedals by regressing onset and offset times. IEEE/ACM Trans. Audio, Speech, Lang. Process. **29**, 3707–3717 (2021)
19. Kosta, K., Bandtlow, O.F., Chew, E.: Outliers in performed loudness transitions: An analysis of chopin mazurka recordings. In: International Conference for Music Perception and Cognition (ICMPC), pp. 601–604. California, USA (2016)
20. Kosta, K., Bandtlow, O.F., Chew, E.: Dynamics and relativity: practical implications of dynamic markings in the score. J. New Music Res. **47**(5), 438–461 (2018). https://doi.org/10.1080/09298215.2018.1486430
21. Kosta, K., Ramírez, R., Bandtlow, O.F., Chew, E.: Mapping between dynamic markings and performed loudness: a machine learning approach. J. Math. Music **10**(2), 149–172 (2016)
22. Manilow, E., Pardo, B.: Bespoke neural networks for score-informed source separation. arXiv preprint arXiv:2009.13729 (2020)
23. Meseguer-Brocal, G., Peeters, G.: Conditioned-u-net: introducing a control mechanism in the u-net for multiple source separations. arXiv preprint arXiv:1907.01277 (2019)
24. Miron, M., Carabias, J.J., Janer, J.: Improving score-informed source separation for classical music through note refinement. In: Proceedings of the 16th International Society for Music Information Retrieval (ISMIR) Conference. Málaga, Spain (2015)
25. Müller, M., Konz, V., Bogler, W., Arifi-M., V.: Saarland music data (smd) (2011)
26. Perez, E., Strub, F., de Vries, H., Dumoulin, V., Courville, A.: Film: Visual reasoning with a general conditioning layer. arXiv preprint arXiv:1709.07871 (2018). http://arxiv.org/abs/1709.07871

27. Qu, Y., Qin, Y., Chao, L., Qian, H., Wang, Z., Xia, G.: Modeling perceptual loudness of piano tone: Theory and applications. arXiv preprint arXiv:2209.10674 (2022)
28. Simonetta, F., Avanzini, F., Ntalampiras, S.: A perceptual measure for evaluating the resynthesis of automatic music transcriptions. Multimed. Tools Appl. **3**, 1–21 (2022). https://doi.org/10.1007/s11042-022-12476-0
29. Slizovskaia, O., Haro, G., Gómez, E.: Conditioned source separation for musical instrument performances. IEEE/ACM Trans. Audio, Speech, Lang. Process. **29**, 2083–2095 (2021)

Music Information Retrieval

From Sunrise to Sunset: Investigating Diurnal Rhythmic Patterns in Music Listening Habits in India

Geetika Arora, Keyur Choudhari, Ponnurangam Kumaraguru, and Vinoo Alluri(✉)

International Institute of Information Technology Hyderabad, Hyderabad, India
keyur.choudhari@students.iiit.ac.in, {pk.guru,vinoo.alluri}@iiit.ac.in

Abstract. Circadian rhythm is a 24-hour cycle of human physiology that governs various aspects of human behavior and cognition, including attention, mood, and performance. This suggests that daily physiological rhythms may influence an individual's musical preferences and listening habits. The objective of this study is to investigate how musical preferences vary throughout the day and across seasons among the Indian population. To this end, we examined music consumption of the participants in terms of audio features by analyzing their one-year Spotify listening history to identify distinct diurnal patterns in music choices. Unsupervised clustering of musical features suggests that preference can be divided into four distinct time blocks: morning, afternoon, evening, and night. Besides, we extended the analysis by incorporating demographic information of the individuals under study. We also conducted a seasonal analysis to investigate potential differences in music consumption patterns between winter and summer months. It was found that individuals prefer music with positive valence, low arousal, and high danceability post-midnight. Additionally, loudness was recorded as the highest (maximum value) around 12 noon. Gender-based differences were also observed, with females perceiving music as slightly less energetic and less positive in terms of emotional valence compared to males, but showing a preference for higher acousticness. Age-based differences revealed that older individuals prefer music that is less energetic, less danceable, less loud, and more acoustic. These findings suggest that music preferences and perceptions vary based on gender and age, and that diurnal patterns play a role in shaping musical choices and listening habits. The findings can have significant implications for the music industry, particularly in creating tailored playlists and curating music to suit different times of the day. Furthermore, the analyses provide a framework for understanding the role of music in other cultures as well, allowing for cross-cultural comparisons, thereby showing how diurnal patterns and other physiological factors may influence culture-specific musical traditions.

Keywords: diurnal variation · musical preferences · online streaming platforms · cultural factors · acoustic features

S. Ystad et al. (Eds.): CMMR 2023, LNCS 15236, pp. 365–377, 2026.
https://doi.org/10.1007/978-3-032-02042-0_28

1 Introduction

Chronobiologists have discovered that humans tend to perform activities according to the time of day, modulated by circadian rhythms. These rhythms are endogenously generated and persist without external cues such as light or temperature change. On the other hand, a diurnal pattern could be either a natural or man-made cyclic pattern of behavior, activity, or other phenomena occurring within a 24-hour period [19]. During the past few decades, it has also been demonstrated that cognitive and emotional states display regular diurnal rhythms [3]. For example, production of cortisol [10], also known as the stress hormone, also follows a diurnal pattern, with its level increasing to 50–60% after waking up and declining slowly for the rest of the day [11]. Cortisol levels tend to increase during a stressor; hence, it's often linked with higher negative affect characterized by feelings of psychological distress, such as nervousness and irritability. Consequently, it can be considered an indicator of psychological and physiological states.

Nowadays, there is a growing reliance on digital technologies for regulating moods, and music has emerged as the most common choice for many [16]. With the shift of music listening to the digital and online sphere, as evidenced by the 59.4 million users of paid music streaming in India in 2021 [18], music has taken on an increasingly prominent role in people's everyday lives. For instance, it is often used as background music while working or during physical activity. Interestingly, the emotional impact of music may also vary depending on the time of day, as seen in the strong association between time and each raga in Hindustani (Indian) music [2]. It has been observed that people may be more or less receptive to a particular raga during different parts of the day, indicating that the time of day could influence the emotional response to music. However, it remains to be determined whether this phenomenon also applies to popular music beyond Indian classical music. This trend presents an exciting opportunity to identify diurnal patterns in music usage and explore their potential association with psychological well-being. Previous research by Heggli et al. [6] quantified distinct diurnal patterns of musical preferences using the music streaming sessions dataset (MSSD), which contains over 2 billion music streaming events. As per their observation, the morning features higher loudness, valence, and energy, but lower tempo. Afternoon time saw a significant increase in tempo with beat strength and danceability reaching average values. Highest tempo along with peaks in beat strength and danceability were recorded in the evening, indicating tracks associated with dancing and partying. The limitation of the study is that the dataset was randomly sampled over an eight-week period for the analysis, and it does not include demographic or individual-level data.

In this study, we aim to analyze diurnal patterns of musical preferences in the Indian population. India is known for its incredibly diverse and rich culture, one of the oldest and most unique in the world due to its unparalleled diversity and richness, stemming from its ancient civilization and history that spans thousands of years. Additionally, India's diverse geography and climatic conditions give rise to multiple seasons, such as Spring, Autumn, Summer, Winter, and

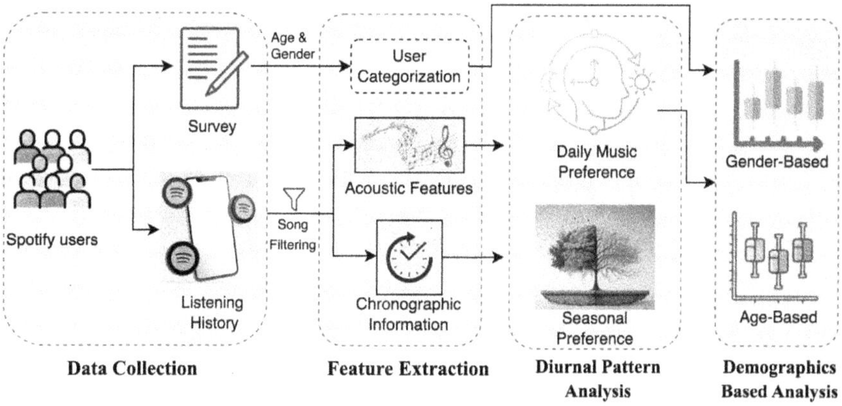

Fig. 1. The research methodology consists of four modules: Data Collection, Feature Extraction, Diurnal Pattern Analysis, and Demographics-Based Analysis. The process starts by collecting Spotify listening history from active users. The collected data is preprocessed by keeping only the songs that have been listened to for more than 45 s and extracting their audio features. Chronographic data such as date, time of the day, day of the week, and month are also extracted for each song. These features are utilized to examine diurnal and seasonal trends in the musical preferences of the Indian population. Diurnal patterns are also analyzed for different gender and age groups to find if they are a factor of influence in musical preferences on daily basis.

Monsoon [7]. Therefore, observing how musical preferences vary in a day in such a diverse culture and according to the different seasons would be worthwhile. To this end, we analyzed one year of Spotify listening history of Indian participants. We additionally examined differences in diurnal patterns in music consumption specific to age and gender. We added unique dimension to our study by examining the effect of seasons on diurnal pattern in music listening to understand the interplay between seasonality and music preferences in Indian specific context. This analysis could offer unique insights into population-level musical preferences throughout the day. Inferences from the study have the potential to make a significant impact in the field of Music Information Retrieval (MIR), specifically in the areas of developing customized playlists and curating music to align with a culture at different times of the day. Moreover, understanding how these factors contribute to diurnal patterns in music can provide insights into the relationship between culture, geography, and musical preferences, with potential implications for the music industry.

2 Methodology

The methodology encompasses four modules: data collection, feature extraction, diurnal pattern analysis for the entire year and across seasons, and demographic-based analysis of daily diurnal patterns. A block diagram illustrating the proposed methodology is shown in Fig. 1. Each of these modules is elaborated upon in the subsequent subsections.

2.1 Data Collection

Hundred and one Indian citizens (mean age = 21 years, std = 2.44; 88 males) volunteered to participate in exchange for monetary compensation. For the study, a 'call for participation' was disseminated through various social media platforms, including Instagram, LinkedIn, and Twitter, as well as email. Ethical approval was taken for the study from the Institute Review Board (IRB) of the affiliated institute before publishing the same. Eligible participants were required to be Indian citizens and residents, as well as active users of the music streaming service Spotify, for at least one year at the time of the call. Participants were requested to obtain and upload their listening history data from their Spotify accounts, which typically takes 3–5 d to be delivered by Spotify via email in the form of a JSON file. Participants were also asked to complete supplementary questionnaires, including the Kessler's psychological distress scale, Healthy Unhealthy Music Scale (HUMS), Highly Sensitive Person Scale (HSPS), and Inter-Personal Reactivity Index (IRI). However, these questionnaires are not utilized in the current analysis and can be used in the future for analyzing diurnal patterns in various categories of people.

2.2 Feature Extraction

Data Filtering and Pre-processing. Data preprocessing step provided valuable temporal information that was used for further analysis and interpretation of the music listening patterns in our study. The JSON file obtained from Spotify contained track-level information, including attributes such as track name, artist name, endTime, and msPlayed, representing the song name, artist of the song, the chronological information, and the number of milliseconds for which the track was played, respectively. To facilitate further analysis, we converted this JSON file to a CSV format. We extracted the chronological components such as, date, hour, day of the week, and month, from the endTime information, which was in the format "yyyy-mm-dd hh:mm". The milliseconds information was utilized to filter out songs that were played for less than 45 s, indicating that they were skipped. The milliseconds information was utilized to filter out songs that were played for less than 45 s, as they were considered skipped tracks. On average, each participant listened to 510 songs in one year, with each one being listened to for more than 45 s.

Audio Features. To gather audio features of the songs, we utilized the Spotify Web API [17], which allows users to retrieve multiple audio features based on track names. These features include Valence, Energy, Acousticness, Danceability, Loudness, Tempo, and Instrumentalness, and are derived from advanced calculations using algorithms proposed by Echo Nest.[1] These audio features provide

[1] https://blog.echonest.com/.

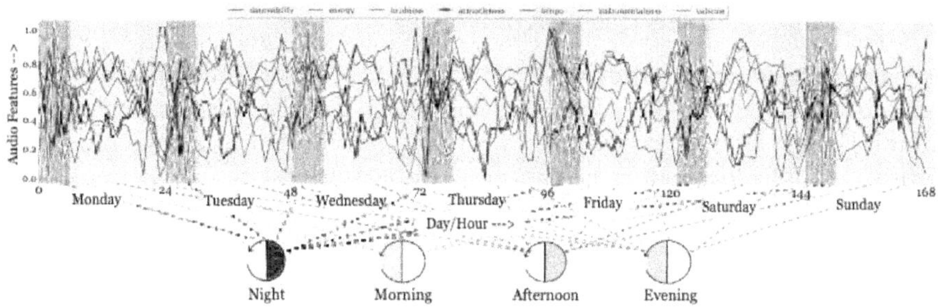

Fig. 2. Diurnal patterns in audio features mapped to four subdivisions of the day using k-means clustering. Normalized audio features are plotted across the entire week with optimal division into distinct clusters represented by colored overlays. Clusters label is based on descriptive terms for time of day.

a comprehensive and multi-dimensional understanding of music content, capturing both basic and more nuanced aspects of the music. For each participant in our study, we computed an average of the considered audio features on an hourly basis. This resulted in an seven-dimensional feature vector representing the average audio feature values for each hour of the day for each participant. The obtained 24×8 feature vectors for each participant were then clustered to find optimal sub-divisions in the day, as explained in the next section.

2.3 Chronological Sub-divisions

K-means clustering [8] was utilized to identify recurring patterns in the data and to partition the data into k clusters with minimized within-cluster variance. Clustering was performed on normalized audio features data for a range of k values from 2 to 24 using the KMeans function from the sklearn library, with a maximum of 300 iterations per k. Varying the value of k in the k-means clustering algorithm and observing the resulting clusters, helps in identifying which value of k yields meaningful and interpretable clusters that align with diurnal patterns in music preferences. The "elbow knee method" is a common approach to determine the optimal value of k, where the inertia (i.e., within-cluster sum-of-squares) is plotted against various values of k and the point where the decrease in inertia flattens out, resembling an elbow or knee shape, is visually identified. This point indicates the optimal partitioning of the dataset into clusters and for our dataset, we could identify four clusters. Data normalization was performed using the MinMaxScaler [15] function from scikit-learn [13]. The MinMaxScaler function individually scales each feature to a given minimum and maximum value, with a default range of 0 and 1. Following selection of $k = 4$, we used an inverse transformation on the normalized cluster centroids to get the mean and standard deviation of audio features in each cluster.

2.4 Age and Gender-Based Analysis

We further delved deeper to identify if there are potential differences in diurnal music listening patterns based on gender and age. Initially, we assess whether the variables under investigation follow a normal distribution using the ShapiroWilk test [14]. This evaluation helps us determine whether to employ parametric or non-parametric statistical tests in our subsequent analyses. For the variables which do not exhibit a normal distribution, we apply the Box-Cox transformation technique [1], which aims to convert non-normal variables into normal ones. We then perform the ShapiroWilk test again to verify if the transformation has achieved normality, as it is not always guaranteed. The variables under consideration were following a normal distribution and thus, for each chronological subdivision obtained through k-means clustering, we conducted a two-way repeated measures analysis of variance (RM-ANOVA) for the considered features to assess if there were significant differences because of the sources of variation, including gender, time of the day, and the interaction between gender and time of the day. Additionally, we employed a similar approach to examine differences based on three age groups (i.e., 18–20, 21–25, and > 25 years) with 55, 39, and 7 participants, respectively.

2.5 Seasonal Patterns

Inspired by previous research by Part et al. [12], we conducted a seasonal analysis to investigate potential differences in music consumption patterns between winter and summer months. We selected two months from each season, specifically December and January for winter and April and May for summer, which represent the respective seasons in the Indian region. Using a similar approach as our diurnal analysis, we analyzed the variations in music listening patterns by conducting an in-depth analysis of the acoustic features for each sub-division during different times of the day in both winter and summer months.

3 Results

3.1 Diurnal Patterns: Chronological Sub-divisions

The k-means clustering algorithm identified four sub-divisions in a day. The cluster labels of the audio features for each hour of the week exhibited a sequence over 168 h, in which a recurring cycle was found to occur on a 24-hour day. The first sub-division 'Night' covers the duration from midnight (denoted by 00 h) to 6 a.m., followed by 'Morning' (6 a.m. to 12 noon), 'Afternoon' (12 noon to 6 p.m.), and 'Evening' (6 p.m. to 12 midnight). This differed from what was obtained in the previous study on the MSSD dataset [6], which reported five sub-divisions in the day- morning (6 a.m.–noon), afternoon (noon - 8 p.m.), evening (8 p.m.–1 p.m.), night (11 p.m.–4 a.m.), and early morning (4 a.m.–6 a.m.). Figure 2 illustrates the diurnal pattern exhibited by normalized audio features across these four sub-divisions of the day and across the days of the week.

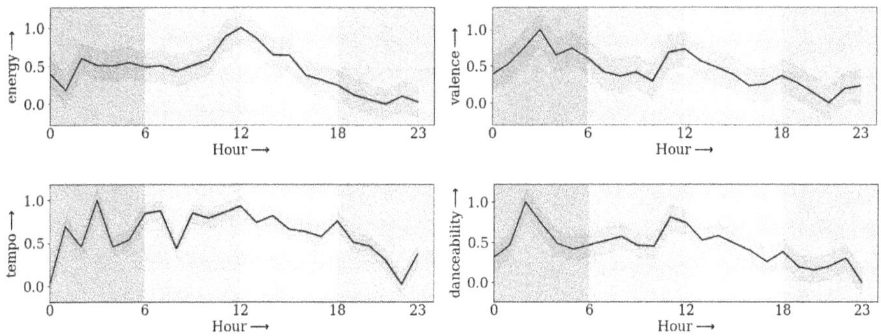

Fig. 3. Plots demonstrating diurnal patterns exhibited by the selected four audio features across a day, from 12 midnight to 2359 h. The shaded area indicates the standard deviation of the considered acoustic feature.

The diurnal pattern of music listening behavior, as revealed through song-level analysis, showed a peak in the number of songs being listened to during the afternoon (33.48%), followed by the morning (30.98%) and evening (20.03%) periods with slightly lower percentages, and the lowest percentage during the night (15.51%). This pattern may be influenced by various factors such as daily routines, activities, and energy levels. For instance, during the afternoon and morning, people may be engaged in work, study, or other activities that are conducive to listening to music using streaming platforms. Specifically, since our sample was predominantly university students, listening to music at these hours is indeed predictable. Interestingly, the diurnal pattern in music listening behavior was found to be consistent when analyzing streams for weekdays and weekends separately, suggesting that it is a stable feature of music preferences among the Indian population and not influenced by external factors such as work schedules or other obligations.

3.2 Hourly Diurnal Patterns: Granular Analysis of Audio Features

The analysis of audio features revealed distinct diurnal patterns, showcasing how various musical elements change over the course of the day with a high level of granularity. Figure 3 provides a detailed representation of how the emotional content of music may vary throughout different times of the day, ranging from morning to evening, and how people's listening preferences may reflect these changes. Among the seven features analyzed, four of them, that is, energy, valence, tempo and danceability can be seen in the figure. The remaining features were found to be highly correlated with these four. Specifically, we observed a strong positive correlation of loudness with energy and danceability, while instrumentalness and acousticness were highly but negatively correlated with the energy of the song.

Peak energy levels were observed during late morning to early afternoon, which could be due to people seeking an energy boost during those times to stay alert and focused, or to match their activities. On the other hand, the gradual

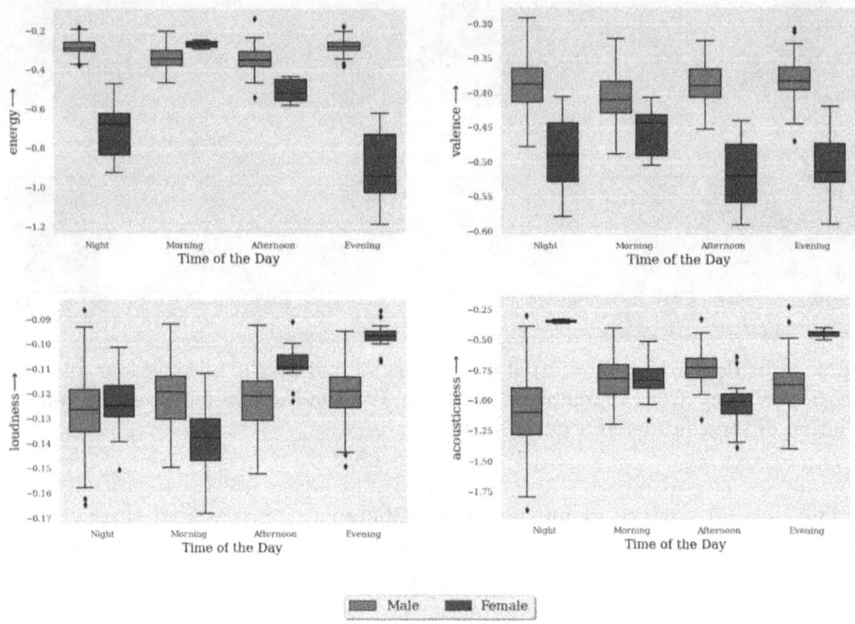

Fig. 4. Box plots showing the distribution of energy, valence, loudness, and acousticness for male and female participants across the four proposed sub-divisions of the day.

dip in energy levels for the reminder of the day could be deemed indicative of their need to counteract the evening fatigue or stress. Peak valence was observed during late night/early hours followed by a gradual decrease. Variations in danceability values have been observed throughout the day which could be reflective of people's activities and preferences, with increased danceability during late-night hours possibly indicating preferences for more upbeat and danceable music during parties or social events, and a shift towards more relaxed music during the late-night and daytime hours as people wind down or engage in different activities. Loudness shows an overall upward trend during the night. This could be attributed to preferences for stimulating or energetic music during the night for studying. Potential spikes are reported during daytime hours which possibly reflects a desire for stimulating music during daytime hours. However, after 12 noon, loudness values start to decrease rapidly until midnight, which could indicate a shift towards more mellow or relaxing genres as the day progresses. Tempo remains almost constant throughout most of the day, with a peak at 3 a.m. and a dip at 4 a.m., which could be reflective of people's preferences for more upbeat music before shifting to more relaxed music to wind down.

In line with the previous study done on MSSD dataset [6], the peaks in energy, loudness, danceability, and tempo were observed around the same time of the day (i.e., 12 noon, 2 a.m. and 3 a.m. respectively). However, they observed that the peak in valence starts around noon and remains fairly constant throughout the day while we observe the peak around 3 a.m.

To summarise, the acoustic features exhibit distinct patterns of fluctuation over the course of a day. Valence and energy tend to be higher at night and lower during the day, with energy slightly increasing in the morning. Loudness increases until noon and then decreases rapidly until midnight. Danceability shows a peak in the night and then decreases until early morning, after which it decreases till midnight. Tempo shows a generally consistent trend throughout the day, with some fluctuations, but it tends to decrease in the evening before increasing again after 11 p.m.

3.3 Gender Based Analysis

RM-Anova revealed significant main effects of gender and time of the day and demonstrated significant interactions (all $p < .001$) on the audio features. The F-statics and partial eta squared values for the variables are reported in Table 1. This suggests that the effect of the time of day on the kind of music consumed, represented here by audio features depend demonstrates gender-specific patterns. Highest effect was observed for energy, danceability, and valence as demonstrated by the partial eta square (ηp^2).

Figure 4 shows box plots to depict differences in the four audio features for male and female participants at different times of the day. As can be seen, on average, females prefer music that is less energetic and negatively valenced when compared to males. On the contrary, the preference for higher acousticness was observed in females in the Indian population. The findings of this study are in line with Greenberg's research on the relationship between music preferences and the Empathizing-Systemizing (ES) theory [5]. According to the ES theory, females tend to be empathizers and thus have a preference for music that is mellow and has a negative valence. In contrast, males tend to be systemizers and prefer music that is more upbeat and positive in valence. These gender-based differences in music preferences observed in our study support the ES theory.

3.4 Age Based Analysis

The RM-Anova analysis showed that there were statistically significant differences in all the audio features among different age groups for four specific time periods of the day. The F-statics and partial eta squared values for the variables are reported in Table 1. This suggests that the effect of the time of day on the kind of music consumed, represented here by audio features, depend demonstrates age-specific patterns. Highest effect was observed for valence, loudness, and tempo as demonstrated by the partial eta square (ηp^2).

As shown in Fig. 5), individuals in Group 3, who were over 25 years of age, tend to prefer music with lower valence, energy, danceability, loudness, and acousticness. There could be several reasons for the observed preferences. One possible explanation is that music is becoming more danceable and louder [4],

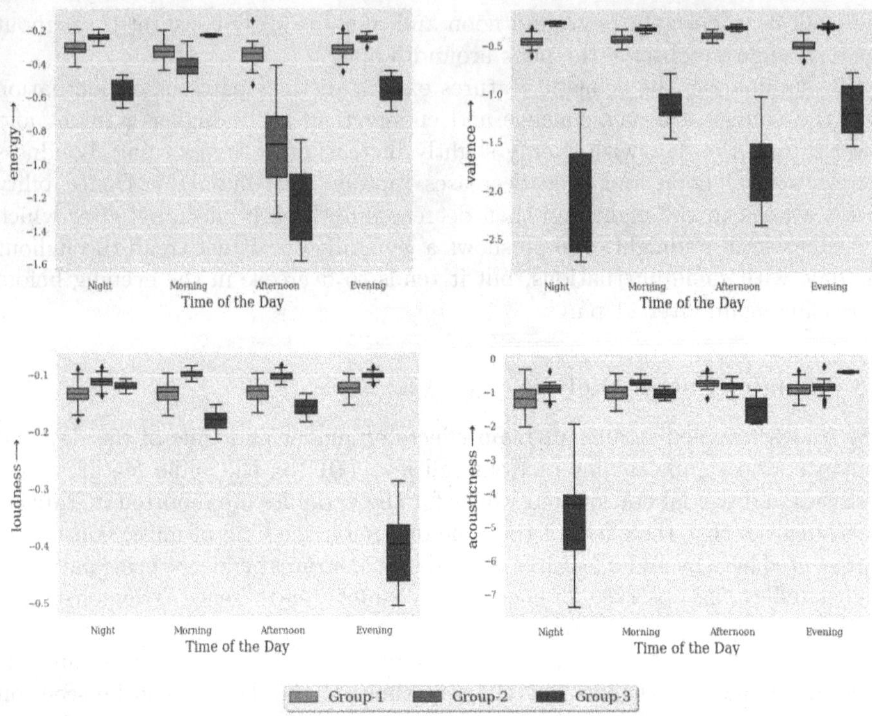

Fig. 5. Box plots showing the distribution of energy, valence, loudness, and acousticness for three age group participants (below 20 years, 21–25 years and more than 25 years) across the four proposed sub-divisions of the day.

which implies that the older group would indeed gravitate towards music that aligns with their past musical experiences. While previous studies have demonstrated that sentiments in lyrics of English songs are decreasing in valence over time [9], this does not seem to hold in the Indian context where people engage in music in various Indian languages too.

3.5 Seasonal Analysis

Analysis of audio features in relation to winter and summer months, as well as different times of day, revealed potential differences in musical preferences. During winter nights, mornings, and afternoons, lower valence values but higher energy values were observed, suggesting a preference for more energetic and stimulating music with potentially introspective or reflective moods. In contrast, during winter evenings, lower energy and valence values were observed, indicating a preference for more calming and relaxing music to wind down after a day of activities.

Furthermore, higher loudness values were observed during winter months, except for evenings, indicating a preference for potentially energizing and stim-

Table 1. RM-ANOVA results (F-statics and partial eta-squared (ηp^2) for energy, valence, loudness, tempo, danceability, and acousticness by gender, time of day (g_tod) and their interaction (gender*g_tod) and age, time of day (a_tod) and their interaction (age*a_tod).

Variable→	gender	g_tod	gender*g_tod	age	a_tod	age*a_tod
			Energy			
F-statistics	1005.200	8.090	286.540	204.200	280.010	157.140
ηp^2	0.720	0.060	0.690	0.510	0.680	0.710
			Valence			
F-statistics	367.250	5.280	13.400	1358.310	3.230	58.170
ηp^2	0.480	0.040	0.090	0.880	0.020	0.470
			Loudness			
F-statistics	8.340	9.420	19.960	526.430	14.730	197.790
ηp^2	0.020	0.070	0.130	0.730	0.100	0.750
			Tempo			
F-statistics	84.030	58.720	14.590	265.380	32.850	217.260
ηp^2	0.180	0.310	0.100	0.580	0.200	0.770
			Danceability			
F-statistics	856.970	65.220	536.690	254.690	35.860	235.730
ηp^2	0.690	0.330	0.800	0.570	0.220	0.780
			Acousticness			
F-statistics	48.320	22.770	52.070	138.790	57.100	110.670
ηp^2	0.110	0.150	0.280	0.420	0.310	0.630

ulating music. Danceability values were generally lower during winter months, suggesting a preference for less physically active music. Higher tempo values during winter months indicated a potential preference for faster-paced and more lively music, while lower acousticness values in nights, mornings, and afternoons could indicate a preference for more electronic or synthesized sounds. In contrast, higher acousticness values in evenings could suggest a preference for more natural or organic music.

Overall, these findings suggest that during winter months, people may prefer music that is more energetic and potentially introspective or reflective in the night, morning, and afternoon, while seeking more calming and relaxing music in the evenings to wind down after a day of activities. Further research is needed to better understand the underlying factors driving these seasonal differences in musical preferences.

4 Conclusion

This study on circadian rhythms and music preferences among the Indian population sheds light on how daily physiological rhythms may influence listening habits. The analysis of audio features revealed distinct diurnal patterns in music choices, with variations in audio features depending on the time of day. The k-means clustering algorithm identified four sub-divisions in a day, in contrast to the previous study [6] that reported five sub-divisions. While similarities were observed in the arousal dimension represented by energy in addition to loudness and tempo, valence on the other hand, demonstrated distinct peak at a different time of the day. Furthermore, we identified significant gender-based and age-related differences in music preferences, with females perceiving music as slightly less energetic and less positive in valence compared to males, and older individuals showing preferences for music with lower valence, energy, danceability, loudness, and acousticness. Our findings also highlight potential seasonal differences in music choices, with preferences for different types of music during winter and summer months. These demographic differences emphasize the need to consider psychological, social, and cultural factors in understanding music preferences. Our findings not only have practical implications for the music industry in terms of tailoring music recommendations to a specific time of day and season but also contribute to our understanding of the role of music in different cultures. Further research in this area could deepen the understanding of the complex relationship between music, physiology, culture, and human behavior.

References

1. Box, G.E., Cox, D.R.: An analysis of transformations. J. Roy. Stat. Soc.: Ser. B (Methodol.) **26**(2), 211–243 (1964)
2. Brabant, O., Toiviainen, P.: Diurnal changes in the perception of emotions in music: does the time of day matter? Music Sci. **18**(3), 256–274 (2014)
3. Forsling, M.L.: Diurnal rhythms in neurohypophysial function. Exp. Physiol. **85**(s1), 179s–186s (2000)
4. Georgieva, E., Kaneshiro, B.: Using Spotify audio features to study the evolution of pop music
5. Greenberg, D.M., Baron-Cohen, S., Stillwell, D.J., Kosinski, M., Rentfrow, P.J.: Musical preferences are linked to cognitive styles. PLoS ONE **10**(7), e0131151 (2015)
6. Heggli, O.A., Stupacher, J., Vuust, P.: Diurnal fluctuations in musical preference. Royal Soc. Open Sci. **8**(11), 210885 (2021)
7. Kuriqi, A., et al.: Seasonality shift and streamflow flow variability trends in central India. Acta Geophysica **68**, 1461–1475 (2020)
8. Likas, A., Vlassis, N., Verbeek, J.J.: The global k-means clustering algorithm. Pattern Recogn. **36**(2), 451–461 (2003)
9. Napier, K., Shamir, L.: Quantitative sentiment analysis of lyrics in popular music. J. Pop. Music. Stud. **30**(4), 161–176 (2018)

10. Ockenfels, M.C., Porter, L., Smyth, J., Kirschbaum, C., Hellhammer, D.H., Stone, A.A.: Effect of chronic stress associated with unemployment on salivary cortisol: overall cortisol levels, diurnal rhythm, and acute stress reactivity. Psychosom. Med. **57**(5), 460–467 (1995)
11. Otto, L.R., Sin, N.L., Almeida, D.M., Sloan, R.P.: Trait emotion regulation strategies and diurnal cortisol profiles in healthy adults. Health Psychol. **37**(3), 301 (2018)
12. Park, M., Thom, J., Mennicken, S., Cramer, H., Macy, M.: Global music streaming data reveal diurnal and seasonal patterns of affective preference. Nat. Hum. Behav. **3**(3), 230–236 (2019)
13. Pedregosa, F., et al.: Scikit-learn: machine learning in Python. J. Mach. Learn. Res. **12**, 2825–2830 (2011)
14. Royston, P.: Approximating the shapiro-wilk w-test for non-normality. Stat. Comput. **2**, 117–119 (1992)
15. Saranya, C., Manikandan, G.: A study on normalization techniques for privacy preserving data mining. Int. J. Eng. Technol. (IJET) **5**(3), 2701–2704 (2013)
16. Smith, W., et al.: Digital emotion regulation in everyday life. In: Proceedings of the 2022 CHI Conference on Human Factors in Computing Systems, pp. 1–15 (2022)
17. Spotify: Spotify for developers. https://developer.spotify.com/. Accessed 2022
18. Statista: Statista- music users statistics in India (2023). https://www.statista.com/outlook/dmo/digital-media/digital-music/music-streaming/india. Accessed 24 Mar 2023
19. Wirz-Justice, A.: Diurnal variation of depressive symptoms. Dialogues in clinical neuroscience (2022)

A Novel Local Alignment-Based Approach to Motif Extraction in Polyphonic Music

Tiange Zhu[1(✉)], Danny Diamond[2], James McDermott[2], Raphaël Fournier-S'niehotta[1], Mathieu d'Aquin[3], and Philippe Rigaux[1]

[1] CNAM Paris, Paris, France
tiange.zhu@lecnam.net
[2] University of Galway, Galway, France
d.diamond1@universityofgalway.ie
[3] Université de Lorraine, Nancy, France

Abstract. Repetition is ubiquitous in music across cultures and time periods, and the study of repeated music patterns offers insight into composition, structure, and evolution of musical works. In this paper, we propose a novel motif detection approach for polyphonic music. A local alignment-based segmentation method is designed to investigate the interrelationship between voices within a composition. For motif selection, we offer a musicologically-informed model that compares repeated patterns and evaluates their significance in the opus. Our method has been evaluated with the JKUPDD dataset, a Western classical music dataset with expert motif annotations. The evaluation results demonstrate strong performance, comparable to other state-of-the-art methods in music pattern discovery.

Keywords: music information retrieval · pattern discovery · computational musicology

1 Introduction

Repetition is a fundamental aspect of music, present across a great variety of time periods and cultures. Repeated patterns have been extensively studied, as they provide valuable insights into composition, structure, and the evolution of musical works. In Western classical music theory, patterns often refer to motives and themes, where a motif is "*the smallest structural unit possessing thematic identity*" within a piece of music [35]. Depending on music genre or tradition, music patterns may be referred to by varying names and definitions [20]. Previously, Music Information Retrieval researchers have studied automatic detection of music patterns in various traditions [8, 10, 11, 15, 19, 25–27, 32]. Some of these works attempt to facilitate automatic analysis of certain genres from musicological perspectives, while others consider patterns as compressed music representations that help retrieval or generation systems.

In this paper, we propose a motif extraction method for classical polyphonic music, and consider motives as short melodic patterns recurring within a piece of music which contain significant or characteristic thematic materials. Some works [25, 32] adopt a two-step framework for pattern (e.g., motif, theme or section) detection: they first

S. Ystad et al. (Eds.): CMMR 2023, LNCS 15236, pp. 378–389, 2026.
https://doi.org/10.1007/978-3-032-02042-0_29

extract melodic features, segment a musical piece into fragments based on these features, then select a set of patterns by identifying the most frequent or salient fragments. Our method follows the same framework, while introducing a novel investigation into the interrelationship between voices for segmentation. In polyphonic music, the interplay between different voices is crucial to its structure; however, to the best of our knowledge, we are the first to explore this aspect for intra-opus motif discovery.

We adopt pairwise local alignment between melodically similar voice pairs within a single piece for segmentation. Local alignment techniques, originally employed for comparative analysis of nucleic acid and protein sequences in computational biology [31], have been successfully applied to assess melodic similarities between musical compositions as shown in [3,14,17,30,34]. Particularly, we are inspired by the discovery of Bountouridis et al. [3] that local alignment is effective in preserving motif alignments between related monophonic music pairs.

For post-segmentation motif selection, we propose a graph-based model for similarity scoring to measure the overall significance of obtained music fragments. These fragments are ranked, and further filtered according to musicological analysis from rhythmic perspectives, to produce a focused set of motives as the final output.

This work provides novel perspectives in motif extraction from polyphonic music, and is of importance in use cases which range from thematic analysis of the piece of music, or musicological study of the body of work of a composer [13], to characterization of a musical tradition, genre or period. Apart from being applied to polyphonic melodies as in this paper, our method can also be applied to detect motives between multiple related monophonic scores, which is potentially of use in the study of tune families or regional styles within folk traditions [33]. For evaluation, we test our method for motif extraction from classical music pieces in the JKUPDD dataset [6], comparing the identified motives with expert annotations. The results validate our work, demonstrating a high degree of accuracy, comparable to the state-of-the-art.

2 State of the Art

Music pattern detection tasks can be either "*intra-opus*" (within a single piece of music) and/or "*inter-opus*" (across multiple pieces of music). Computational methods for intra-opus pattern detection generally fall into three broad categories of 1) string or sequence-based, 2) geometric-based, and 3) data-driven (e.g., machine learning, deep learning).

String-based methods are the most common, which treat music as a string of symbols, often applied to melodic pattern detection in monophonic music. Among the earliest, Conklin et al. [10] introduced viewpoints as functions that extract features (e.g., pitch, duration, interval between notes) from symbolic music, which transform musical events into sequences. Their method builds a suffix tree for viewpoints, and uses a set of rules to select patterns from the suffix tree.

Best-in-class geometric models include the family of "point-set" geometric compression algorithms set out in [21–24], which converts a piece of music into a set of points, presenting note events as points in a multi-dimensional space. Meredith et al. [24] proposed the SIA algorithm to compute vectors that map points onto other points in the dataset, and select the maximally repeated patterns. A series of methods have evolved from this work using point-set representation, namely the COSIATEC and SIATECCompress proposed in [22], which compress a music piece into a union of translational equivalence classes of maximal translatable patterns. Both COSIATEC and SIATECCompress use this approach but differ in selection criteria. Collins et al. [8] sought to improve the SIA algorithm by eliminating the false positives and facilitating inexact pattern matching through allowance for rhythmic variations, and ranking the discovered patterns in order of importance. This family of algorithms have performed well on tasks ranging from intra-opus pattern detection in classical music [22], to Dutch folk song classification [23].

Despite the lack of sizable pattern annotation data being a significant obstacle for applying and evaluating data-driven methods for pattern detection, possibilities have been explored in some previous work [26,27]. Nuttall et al. [26] proposed a Natural Language Processing-inspired method for Arab-Andalusian music by extracting pitch sequences, converting them into a set of n-grams, and detecting the most salient melodic patterns combining TF-IDF and the SIA algorithm. Pesek et al. [27] developed a compositional hierarchical model that learns statistics of pattern occurrences to provide a hierarchical representation for pattern detection. Velarde et al. [32] explored wavelet transform-based method for melodic pattern recognition. They extracted melodies as sequences of pitch signals filtered with the continuous wavelet transform using the Haar wavelet, then segmented the sequences and compared them based on similarity. After clustering the fragments, they ranked the clusters by occurrences to produce a selection of themes and section. Nieto et al. [25] adopted Gestalt-principles-based rules to extract potential patterns, and applied clustering and filtering to locate motives and themes. Ren et al. [28] leveraged two data fusion methods, namely a pattern polling algorithm (PPA) and Time Indexed Novelty algorithm (TINA), to analyze dissimilarities between the output by a selection of state-of-the-art algorithms. This work points out noticeable inconsistency and distinctiveness in the patterns found by these algorithms, highlighting opportunities for advancement and refinement in automatic music pattern recognition.

3 Methodology

3.1 Pre-processing

A polyphonic music score is processed as follows. From each voice, we first extract a melodic pitch sequence represented as MIDI note numbers, and estimate its key using the Krumhansl-Schmuckler algorithm [18] provided in music21 [12]. To compute diatonic intervals, MIDI numbers are resolved to note names using pitch spelling with the algorithm incorporated in music21. Each note is then mapped to its scale degree within the extracted key (e.g., in C major, C = 1, D = 2, ..., B = 7). Diatonic intervals are calculated as the difference between consecutive scale degrees, normalized to a single octave, reflecting their position within the diatonic scale.

Definition 1 (Melody). *Let the kth voice in a score be v_k, and the estimated key of v_k be key_k. Let $M(v_k) = [m_1, ...m_n]$ be the melody of v_k, where m_i denotes the MIDI pitch of the ith note.*

Definition 2 (Diatonic Intervals). *Let* $dia(v_k) = [d_1, ...d_{n-1}]$ *be a sequence of key-invariant diatonic intervals for* v_k*, where* d_i *is the interval between consecutive notes* m_i *and* m_{i+1}*. Resolve* m_i *and* $m_i + 1$ *to note names within the context of* key_k *using pitch spelling, and map* m_i *and* m_{i+1} *to its scale degrees* s_i *and* s_{i+1} *in the diatonic scale. To compute* d_i*:*

$$d_i = (s_{i+1} - s_i)\%7 \tag{1}$$

For example, from the incipit of the first voice of the Bach fugue BWV889 in Fig. 1, the key-invariant diatonic interval sequence $dia(v_1)$ can be extracted as $[-2, +3, -6, +4, -2, +3, -2, -2, -2, +5, -2, -2, -2, +5]$. The diatonic intervals are then encoded into alphabetic sequences for music segmentation, following the encoding rules:

Definition 3 (Encoding). *A function Dict(x) presents rules for encoding, which maps an integer in [-6, 6] to a distinctive character. To specify in detail,* $Dict(-6) = A$, $Dict(-5) = B$, $Dict(-4) = C$, $Dict(-3) = D$, $Dict(-2) = E$, $Dict(-1) = F$, $Dict(0) = M$, $Dict(1) = G$, $Dict(2) = H$, $Dict(3) = I$, $Dict(4) = J$, $Dict(5) = K$, $Dict(6) = L$.

Let an encoded sequence of $dia(v_k)$ *be* $enc(dia(v_k))$*,*

$$enc(dia(v_k)) = [Dict(d) : d \in dia(v_k)] \tag{2}$$

For instance, a diatonic interval sequence $[-1, +2, +1, -4, +2]$ can be encoded as $FHGCH$.

Fig. 1. Incipit of the first voice of Bach fugue BWV889 with annotation given by our encoding.

3.2 Music Segmentation

For each pair of voices v_x, v_y, a Smith-Waterman local alignment [31] between $enc(dia(v_x))$ and $enc(dia(v_y))$ is generated. This step detects locally-aligned fragments between $enc(dia(v_x))$ and $enc(dia(v_y))$, and outputs an alignment of the two sequences. We calculate the similarity score between v_x, v_y, and only consider pairs with a similarity score greater than 0.2 for further segmentation, as we are unlikely to detect meaningful melodic patterns from alignments between pairs that lack correlation in melody.

Figure 2 presents the alignment between the openings of voices 1 and 2 of the Bach BWV889 fugue, with locally-aligned fragments identified by the Smith-Waterman algorithm boxed in red. In this representation, characters represent encoded diatonic interval sequences, where "-" represents a gap due to a mismatch between the sequence pair, and

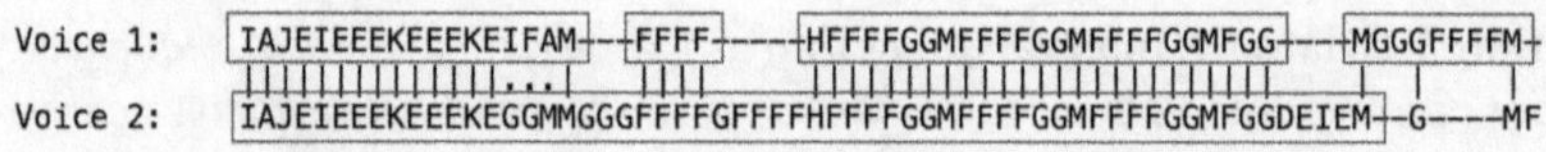

Fig. 2. Alignment between the openings of voice 1 and 2 of Bach BWV889 fugue

"." represents a permitted mismatch. From the alignment of each pair of voices v_x, v_y, we extract all contiguous fragments (i.e. break the sequences on each "-" character) to obtain a set of fragments. Furthermore, a filter is implemented to remove all fragments of less than 3 elements in length, according to the common belief that a motif should contain at least 4 notes.

Definition 4 (Pattern). *Let a set of fragments obtained from local alignment between* v_x, v_x *be* $A(enc(v_x), enc(v_y))$. *An element in* $A(enc(v_x), enc(v_y))$ *is defined as a pattern* p.

Definition 5 (Pattern set). *Let a score of* m *voices be* $S = [v_1, ..., v_m]$. *From the alignment between voice pairs in* S, *we obtain a set of patterns:*

$$P(S) = \bigcup_{(v_x, v_y) \in S \times S} A(enc(v_x), enc(v_y)) \tag{3}$$

In the course of the segmentation process, we count the occurrences of every pattern p in P, and define the sum of p's occurrences as $occ(p)$.

3.3 Intra-pattern Discovery of Motives

Fig. 3. Intra-pattern discovery example (from Bach BWV889 fugue)

We adopt a string-based approach to uncover additional motives which are not well-captured in the segmentation process, including those which occur exclusively in one voice. From patterns of greater than 11 intervals in length in P, we extract the longest frequent substring which occurs more than once. The choice of the length threshold has been suggested by a previous use case in [36]. As the aim of this paper is to discover short motives, we favor relatively short patterns over longer patterns, which potentially correspond more to musical sections or themes than motives. The lengths of such musical structural units are not defined in absolute terms, so the threshold we adopt is proposed as a working heuristic, rather than a formal definition of maximum motif length. Figure 3 illustrates a case where a pattern repeatedly appears in a sequence of intervals.

The longest frequent substring extracted from a long pattern becomes its substitution for motif selection, according to the following rules:

Definition 6 (Pattern substitution). *Let* p *be a pattern of length* $|p|$, *and let* $sub(p)$ *of length* $|sub(p)|$ *be the longest substring that repeated at least two times in* p. *Let* $r_{sub(p),p}$ *be the number of times* $sub(p)$ *appears in* p *without overlapping.* $sub(p)$ *takes the place of* p *in* P *if certain conditions are met, specifically:*

$$p \rightarrow \begin{cases} sub(p), & \text{if } |sub(p)| > 3 \text{ and } |sub(p)| * r_{sub(p),p} >= 0.6|p| \\ p, & \text{otherwise} \end{cases} \tag{4}$$

In Definition 6, $|sub(p)| > 3$ ensures that $sub(p)$ is a non-trivial substring, with the aim of removing frequent-but-insignificant short patterns. $|sub(p)| * r_{sub(p),p} >= 0.6|p|$ ensures that $sub(p)$ meets the required threshold to substitute for p. Considering that $sub(p)$ could substitute for more than one pattern in P, let p_i be one of the patterns in P that is substituted by $sub(p)$, then

$$occ(sub(p)) = \sum_{p_i \in \mathcal{P}} occ(p_i) \times r_{sub(p),pi} \tag{5}$$

3.4 Inter-pattern Discovery of Motives

Definition 7 (All possible pairs of long patterns). *Let* (p_i, p_j) *be a distinctive pair of patterns in* P, *and the set of all possible pairs of patterns in* P *that are longer than 11 elements be* $longpairs(P)$, *then*

$$longpairs(P) = \{(p_i, p_j) | p_i, p_j \in P \text{ and } |p_i| > 11, |p_j| > 11\} \tag{6}$$

We take the longest common substrings (LCSS) of each pattern pair in $longpairs(P)$. Unique substrings discovered in this step are added as patterns for further selection.

3.5 Selection of Patterns

Pattern Importance Measure. The overall importance of a pattern is measured based on its occurrence frequency and influence through the relationship with other detected patterns. In order to measure the latter, we construct a weighted graph to capture the relationship between patterns. From a set of patterns P, we construct a graph where each pattern p in P is a node, and a directed edge indicates the existence of substring relationship between two patterns. The weight of the edge reflects the strength of the relationship, given by the occurrences of a pattern in its related pattern.

Let $G = (P, E, w)$ be a graph, P be a set of nodes, E be a set of directed edges, and w be the weight function. For each pair of patterns p_i and p_j, if p_i is a substring of p_j, both a directed edge e_{ij} from p_i to p_j and a directed edge e_{ji} from p_j to p_i are added to G, as the relationship is mutual. However, the edges e_{ij} and e_{ji} are weighted differently, according to the function w defined as follows:

The weight of the edge e_{ji} from p_j to p_i is defined as the frequency of non-overlapping occurrences of p_j in p_i. When p_j is a substring of p_i, the weight of the

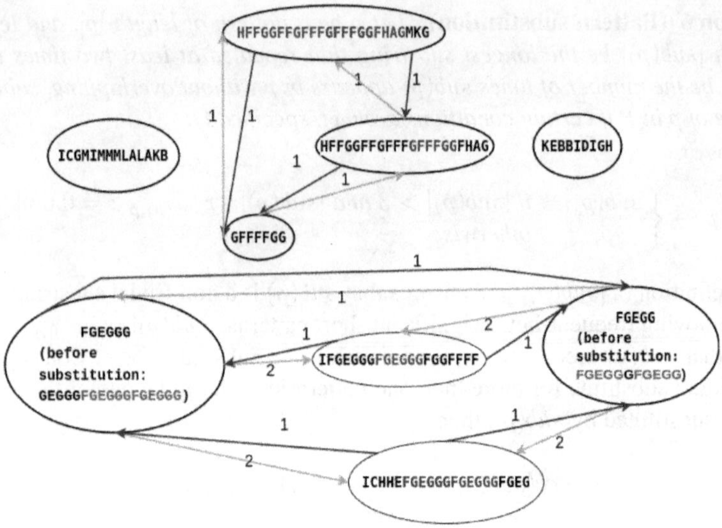

Fig. 4. A weighted graph constructed from 9 example patterns from Bach's BWV889 fugue. Each node is a pattern represented as an encoded sequence (characters correspond to diatonic intervals), and an edge between two nodes represents a present substring relationship. The green edges are edges from patterns to their superstrings, and the purple edges are edges from superstring patterns to their substrings. The weight of an edge indicates the strength of the relationship.

edge e_{ij} from p_i to p_j is defined as 1. Let $I(p_i)$ be the custom importance measure of a pattern p_i, and $[e_{i1}, ..., e_{in}]$ be the set of directed edges from p_i, where:

$$I(p_i) = occ(p_i) + \sum_{k=0}^{n} \pi(e_{in}) \tag{7}$$

Figure 4 shows an example of a graph constructed from a set of 9 different patterns. Edges are added when two patterns have a substring relationship. The green edges are edges from substrings to their superstrings, with a number representing their weight, while the purple edges are from superstrings to their substring. Pattern "FGEGGG" is a substring of "IFGEGGGFGEGGGFGGFFFF" which appeared 2 times, thus the edge from the former to the latter is weighted as 2. Both "FGEGGG" and "FGEGG" have the highest out-degree of 4, suggesting their significance among the set of patterns that constructed the graph in Fig. 4.

Rhythmic Perspectives. In addition to fundamental music attributes like pitch duration, we analyze the rhythmic feature of patterns by measuring their onset metrical strength (i.e., metrical strength of the beginning note) for pattern filtering. Metrical strength refers to the perceived intensity or the degree of rhythmic emphasis, and strong beats are emphasized beats that provide stability and hierarchy within a rhythmic structure, typically guiding the listener's perception of time. For example, the first note of every bar is heavily rhythmically accented, and is assigned the highest value by default.

Patterns beginning on strong beats align with the metric structure of the piece of music, as well as the natural cognitive tendency to group and organize musical information around strong pulses, thus making patterns easier for listeners to process and remember. For motif selection, we only obtain the patterns that start at strong beats. Furthermore, as it is often the case that motives occur at or near the beginning of a score, we only keep patterns which occur in the opening 8 bars of a score regardless of their onset metrical strength. The threshold of 8 bars is chosen as this is the most common length for the opening period (the opening two phrases) in common Western musical practice.

In short, we measure the significance of patterns (according to the rules presented in Sect. 3.5), obtain the top 20 ranked patterns, and filter out the less rhythmically-emphasized ones based on onset metrical strength (except the ones appear at the beginning of a piece), to obtain the final selected set of motives.

4 Experiments

We apply our method to extract motives from the JKUPDD dataset [6], which has been previously used for evaluation of other pattern detection work, notably as input data for the Music Information Retrieval Evaluation eXchange (MIREX) Discovery of Repeated Themes & Sections challenge [9]. The dataset includes 5 polyphonic classical music scores with ground-truth annotation of repeating patterns drawn from academic sources [1,4,29]. The pattern annotation in the dataset covers a wide variety of pattern types, including motives, themes, phrases, and sections. They range in length from three elements to more than 150 elements. As our method specializes towards detection of short motif patterns, we elect to omit long annotated periods and sections.

5 Evaluation

5.1 Results

The results are presented in Table 1, and our methodology is proven to be effective in motif extraction from the JKUPDD dataset. For evaluation, diatonic interval sequences are extracted from the labeled ground truth patterns, and compared with the output of our algorithm. The scores are manually checked to identify and annotate the exact diatonic interval occurrences of the ground truth patterns. According to documentation of the JKUPDD dataset, patterns are labeled with alphabetic identifiers: "A", "B" and so on for each score, named in order of their importance. We will make reference to this hierarchical ordering in the discussion (see Sect. 5.2 below).

Table 2 compares our work with other studies tested on the JKUPDD dataset. The precision and recall reported in [5,27,32] are establishment precision and recall, which allows for the validity of a partial match (see definition in MIREX task guidelines [7]), aligned with our definition (positive scoring of partial matches). It is important to note that the results in Table 2 only allow an informal comparison, due to our use of diatonic interval sequences rather than MIDI pitch sequences, our omission of sections from the ground truth given research focus in motif extraction, and our use of standard precision/recall all differ from the approach set out in the MIREX task documentation.

Table 1. Evaluation results of our method for motif extraction from scores in the JKUPDD dataset.

Work	Precision (%)	Recall (%)
Bach: BWV889 fugue	66.7	61.5
Beethoven: Op. 2, No. 1, Mvt. 3	100.0	45.0
Chopin: Op. 24, No. 4	50.0	50.0
Gibbons: The Silver Swan	87.5	84.6
Mozart: K282, Mvt. 2	60.0	100.0
Average	**72.8**	**68.2**

Table 2. Comparison between our results with the average establishment precision and recall for previous work evaluated on the JKUPDD dataset.

Study	Precision (%)	Recall (%)
VM1 [32]	84.0	89.0
VM2 [32]	76.0	80.0
SymCHM [27]	67.9	45.4
SymCHMMerge [27]	68.0	51.0
Chen & Su [5]	50.0	69.6
Zhu & Diamond	**72.8**	**68.2**

5.2 Discussion

Fig. 5. Exact match of ground truth pattern "A", occurrence 4, in Bach BWV889 fugue

Bach: BWV889 Fugue. Patterns A and B are the most frequent and most significant patterns in this score. The algorithm returned A exactly. It is the opening musical motif of the entire piece and the key musical idea behind the composition. The result is illustrated in Fig. 5, and detailed in the following sections. Although B matched only partially, the matching subsequence repeats twice within B. This may suggest we are capturing a core or fundamental motif within pattern B, per Fig. 6.

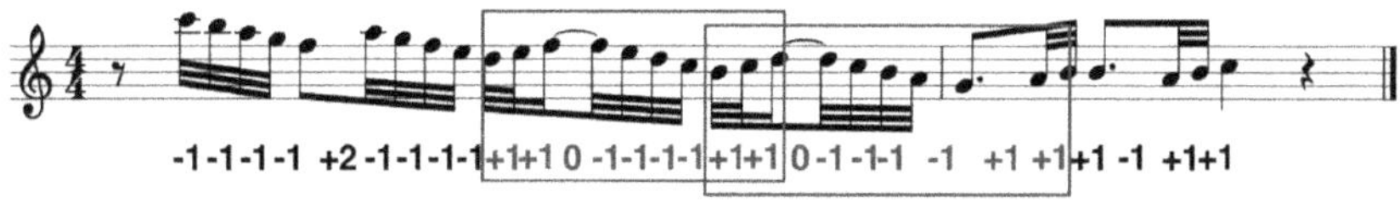

Fig. 6. Pattern "B" from Bach BWV889 fugue with two overlapping partial matches highlighted and boxed in red. (Color figure online)

Beethoven: Op. 2, No. 1, Mvt. 3. We fail to identify pattern A, but match the opening 11-element subsequence of pattern B, which is the second most important music pattern in the piece according to the annotation.

Chopin: Op. 24, No. 4. We found a robust partial match to ground truth pattern A. The found motif occurs at the start of pattern A and repeats twice within it, in a similar manner to 6 above. Thus, the motif may be core content within pattern A, which is the most musically important/distinctive in the piece.

Gibbons: The Silver Swan. Pattern A, which occurs early and repetitiously in 4 of the 5 voices, has been detected in full. Overall, our precision and recall scores are very high for this composition.

Mozart: K282, Mvt. 2. The sole ground truth pattern detected is a significant subsequence of pattern A. This is an incomplete but positive result, capturing the last 6 notes of this 10-note pattern. The detected pattern does not appear in the "definitive" opening occurrence of pattern A, but occurs in 10 of the 11 other noted variant occurrences of pattern A in the course of the score.

6 Contribution and Future Work

This paper presents a method for automatic motif extraction from polyphonic classical music. We introduce a novel use of local alignment for segmentation, inspired by the observed correlating relationship between voices in polyphonic music. We further develop a graph-based model for pattern similarity scoring, combined with music analysis in rhythmic perspective to help measure music pattern significance. Our method proves useful by yielding promising results in the evaluation of motif detection in the JKUPDD dataset, broadly comparable to other state-of-the-art algorithms. The proposed method supports related musicological tasks, such as analysis of characteristic motives in composition styles, or classification of music corpora, and is potentially of use for other MIR applications like guiding automatic music generation.

In the future, we plan to improve the algorithm via encoding more musicological knowledge. We also intend to apply the algorithm to inter-opus pattern detection in a corpus of monophonic Irish traditional folk tunes on *The Session* [16], which may help gain insight into the role of motives in defining *tune families* [2] within the corpus.

Acknowledgments. This work is part of a project that has received funding from the European Union's Horizon 2020 research and innovation programme under grant agreement No 101004746 (Polifonia: a digital harmoniser for musical heritage knowledge, H2020-SC6-TRANSFORMATIONS).

References

1. Barlow, H., Morgenstern, S.: A Dictionary of Musical Themes. Crown Publishers (1948)
2. Bayard, S.P.: Prolegomena to a study of the principal melodic families of British-American folk song. J. Am. Folklore **63**(247) (1950). https://doi.org/10.2307/537347, publisher: University of Illinois Press
3. Bountouridis, D., Brown, D.G., Wiering, F., Veltkamp, R.C.: Melodic similarity and applications using biologically-inspired techniques. Appl. Sci. **7**(12) (2017). https://doi.org/10.3390/app7121242, https://www.mdpi.com/2076-3417/7/12/1242
4. Bruhn, S.: J.S. Bach's Well-Tempered Clavier: in-depth analysis and interpretation. Mainer International (1993)
5. Chen, T.P., Su, L.: Discovery of repeated themes and sections with pattern clustering. https://www.music-ir.org/mirex/abstracts/2017/CS3.pdf
6. Collins, T.: The Johannes Kepler university patterns development database. https://www.music-ir.org/mirex/wiki/2017:Discovery_of_Repeated_Themes_%26_Sections
7. Collins, T.: Mirex 2017: Discovery of repeated themes & sections results. https://www.music-ir.org/mirex/wiki/2017:Discovery_of_Repeated_Themes_%26_Sections
8. Collins, T., Arzt, A., Flossmann, S., Widmer, G.: SIARCT-CFP: improving precision and the discovery of inexact musical patterns in point-set representations. In: International Society for Music Information Retrieval Conference (2013)
9. Collins, T., Janssen, B., Hao, Y.: Mirex 2017: discovery of repeated themes & sections results. https://www.music-ir.org/mirex/wiki/2017:MIREX2017_Results
10. Conklin, D., Anagnostopoulou, C.: Representation and discovery of multiple viewpoint patterns. In: Proceedings of the International Computer Music Conference (2003)
11. Conklin, D., Bergeron, M.: Feature set patterns in music. Comput. Music. J. **32**(1), 60–70 (2008)
12. Cuthbert, M.S., Ariza, C.: music21: a toolkit for computer-aided musicology and symbolic music data. In: Proceedings of the 11th International Society for Music Information Retrieval Conference (ISMIR 2010), pp. 637–642 (2010)
13. Giraud, M., Groult, R., Levé, F.: Subject and counter-subject detection for analysis of the well-tempered clavier fugues. In: Aramaki, M., Barthet, M., Kronland-Martinet, R., Ystad, S. (eds.) From Sounds to Music and Emotions. Springer, Berlin Heidelberg (2013). https://doi.org/10.1007/978-3-642-41248-6_24
14. Hillewaere, R., Manderick, B., Conklin, D.: Alignment methods for folk tune classification. In: Spiliopoulou, M., Schmidt-Thieme, L., Janning, R. (eds.) Data Analysis, Machine Learning and Knowledge Discovery. SCDAKO, pp. 369–377. Springer, Cham (2014). https://doi.org/10.1007/978-3-319-01595-8_40
15. Janssen, B., Haas, W.B., Volk, A., Kranenburg, P.: Finding repeated patterns in music: state of knowledge, challenges, perspectives. In: Aramaki, M., Derrien, O., Kronland-Martinet, R., Ystad, S. (eds.) CMMR 2013. LNCS, vol. 8905, pp. 277–297. Springer, Cham (2014). https://doi.org/10.1007/978-3-319-12976-1_18
16. Keith, J.: The session. https://thesession.org
17. van Kranenberg, P.: A computational approach to content-based retrieval of folk song melodies. PHD thesis, Utrecht University (2010)

18. Krumhansl, C.L.: Cognitive foundations of musical pitch. Music Percept. Interdiscip. J. **9**, 476–492 (1992). https://doi.org/10.2307/40285567
19. Lartillot, O.: Multidimensional motivic pattern extraction founded on adaptive redundancy filtering. J. New Music Res. **34**, 375–393 (2005). https://doi.org/10.1080/09298210600578246
20. Melkonian, O., Red, I.Y., Swierstra, W., Volk, A.: What constitutes a musical pattern? In: Proceedings of the 7th ACM SIGPLAN International Workshop on Functional Art, Music, Modeling, and Design, pp. 95–105. FARM 2019 (2019)
21. Meredith, D.: Point-set algorithms for pattern discovery and pattern matching in music. In: Content-Based Retrieval. Dagstuhl Seminar Proceedings (DagSemProc), vol. 6171, pp. 1–23. Schloss Dagstuhl – Leibniz-Zentrum für Informatik (2006)
22. Meredith, D.: COSIATEC and SIATECCompress: pattern discovery by geometric compression. In: Music Information Retrieval Evaluation eXchange (MIREX 2013). International Society for Music Information Retrieval (2013)
23. Meredith, D.: Compression-based geometric pattern discovery in music. In: 2014 4th International Workshop on Cognitive Information Processing (CIP), pp. 1–6 (2014)
24. Meredith, D., Lemström, K., Wiggins, G.A.: Algorithms for discovering repeated patterns in multidimensional representations of polyphonic music. J. New Music Res. **31**(4), 321–345 (2002)
25. Nieto, O., Farbood, M.M.: Perceptual evaluation of automatically extracted musical motives. In: Proceedings of the 12th International Conference on Music Perception and Cognition, ICMPC, pp. 723–727 (2012)
26. Nuttall, T., Casado, M.G., Ferraro, A., Conklin, D., Repetto, R.C.: A computational exploration of melodic patterns in Arab-Andalusian music. J. Math. Music **15**(2) (2021)
27. Pesek, M., Leonardis, A., Marolt, M.: SymCHM–an unsupervised approach for pattern discovery in symbolic music with a compositional hierarchical model. Appl. Sci. **7**, 1135 (2017)
28. Ren, I.Y., Koops, H.V., Volk, A., Swierstra, W.: In search of the consensus among musical pattern discovery algorithms. In: International Society for Music Information Retrieval Conference (2017)
29. Schoenberg, A.: Fundamentals of musical composition. Faber and Faber (1967)
30. Serra, J., Gomez, E., Herrera, P., Serra, X.: Chroma binary similarity and local alignment applied to cover song identification. IEEE Trans. Audio Speech Lang. Process. **16**(6), 1138–1151 (2008). https://doi.org/10.1109/TASL.2008.924595
31. Smith, T.F., Waterman, M.S.: Identification of common molecular subsequences. J. Mol. Biol. **147**, 1 (1981)
32. Velarde, G., Meredith, D.: A wavelet-based approach to the discovery of themes and sections in monophonic melodies
33. Volk, A., Van Kranenburg, P.: Melodic similarity among folk songs: an annotation study on similarity-based categorization in music. Musicae Scientiae **16**, 317–339 (2012)
34. Walshaw, C.: Tune classification using multilevel recursive local alignment algorithms. In: The 7th International Workshop on Folk Music Analysis (2017)
35. White, J.D.: The Analysis of Music. Prentice-Hall (1976)
36. Zhu, T., Fournier-S'niehotta, R., Rigaux, P., Travers, N.: A framework for content-based search in large music collections. Big Data Cognit. Comput. **6**(1), 23 (2022)

Predicting Audio Features of Background Music From Game Scenes

Ryusei Hayashi(✉) and Tetsuro Kitahara(✉)

Nihon University, Tokyo 156–8550, Japan
ryusei@kthrlab.jp, kitahara.tetsuro@nihon-u.ac.jp

Abstract. We propose a system to retrieve background music (BGM) for game scenes. BGM plays an important role in creating a particular atmosphere in game scenes, so studies have investigated the relationship between game scenes and BGM. However, none of the existing studies attempted to predict the audio features of BGM directly from a sequence of images expressing game scenes. In our system, the user inputs a sequence of images of a game scene, then our machine learning model, trained with gameplay videos, predicts the audio features from the input. Finally, the system retrieves the closest musical piece to the predicted audio features. Experimental results show both positive and negative tendencies: the predicted audio features for fight scenes are closer to the features of actually used BGM in fight scenes than those in other scenes (positive); the same musical piece was retrieved for different scenes (negative).

Keywords: CNN-LSTM · video game music (VGM) · role-playing game (RPG) · speedrun video · copyright-free music

1 Introduction

Background music (BGM) plays a role in creating the atmosphere of a video game. In particular, musical pieces used in different scenes (e.g., talk, fight) would be carefully composed to make different atmospheres that different scenes have. Therefore, we suppose a strong relationship exists between the atmosphere of a scene, and the feature of the BGM used there. For example, the BGM in a fight scene of a role-playing game (RPG) may tend to create a tense atmosphere with strong beats, while the BGM used in a talk scene may tend to create a calm atmosphere with soft timbres and rhythm.

The final goal of our study is to establish a technology that makes it possible to recommend the BGM that fits each of the various scenes in a game. This technology is intended to be used by indie game creators. After they create various scenes of their own game, they will give each scene (a sequence of screen images) to our system. Then, the system recommends the musical piece that fits each scene as BGM based on a machine learning model.

Some researchers have investigated the relationship between game scenes and BGM. Yamauchi et al. developed a system that retrieves music from game

S. Ystad et al. (Eds.): CMMR 2023, LNCS 15236, pp. 390–401, 2026.
https://doi.org/10.1007/978-3-032-02042-0_30

scenarios [17]. Nemoto et al. investigated the relationship between the emotional state of a character and BGM [12]. Choi et al. created a game music database with emotion labels and a model to generate a baseline [2]. Kim et al. developed a game that records BGM's and the player's moods simultaneously and analyzed their relationship [6]. Ishikawa et al. developed a system that retrieves BGM from visual scenes through impression words [5]. Zeng et al. developed a system that retrieves movies from music [18]. "AmBeat" is an application that adds generated music to a video when the video is input [1]. "Deep12" searches for similar music when music is input [3]. They did not deal with directly predicting musical features of BGM for games from those games' visual scenes.

In this paper, we develop a method for predicting audio features of BGM that fits given game scenes from a sequence of screen images. Because there are many gameplay videos on Web-based video hosting services, we can quickly obtain large-scale data consisting of pairs of a sequence of screen images of a game and audio signals of its BGM. By learning those data, we will achieve the prediction of the audio features of BGM from screen images.

2 Proposed Method

We propose a system that outputs the audio features of BGM suitable for the input game scene. The system is intended to be used when the user creates his/her own game and finds musical pieces for adding to the game as BGM. First, the user inputs a sequence of images of a scene (e.g., Fight, Talk) included in the created game. Then, the system predicts a sequence of the audio features that are considered to fit the given scene. Finally, the system outputs the musical piece with the closest audio features to the predicted ones from the music collection prepared in advance.

It is generally challenging to find a universal relationship between scenes and BGM. We assume that the user creates a game referring to an existing game (called a *referred game* here), and they are similar to each other. Therefore, we let the user specify the referred game and learn the relationship between scenes and BGM.

2.1 Input and Output Data

The input and output data were taken from speedrun videos posted on YouTube. First, we saved videos in MP4 format. Next, we classify the video frame by frame using k-means [10]. Finally, we extracted one hundred 12-second segments from the video to avoid including multiple classes.

Then, we applied the following pre-processing. We divide the input and output data obtained by these processes in half and use them as training and test data.

Input Data. We loaded a 12-second video using the OpenCV library and converted the color space of images from BGR to HSV. The image size was also changed to 80×80. We accordingly obtained tensor data of dimensions $80 \times 80 \times 3$.

Output Data. We extracted the audio tracks from the videos mentioned above and saved them in WAV format. The audio features described in Table 1 were extracted using the LiBROSA library. Some of these audio features can be selected and used.

Table 1. Audio features to be extracted

	Feature	Outline
01	cqt	Semitone power spectrogram using constant-Q transform
02	iirt	Semitone power spectrogram using a multirate filter bank consisting of IIR filters
03	chroma_stft	12-dimensional features representing the power of each pitch class, calculated from the STFT-based power spectrogram
04	chroma_cqt	12-dimensional features representing the power of each pitch class, calculated from the CQT-based power spectrogram
05	chroma_cens	12-dimensional features with smoothed temporal variations in chroma_cqt
06	melspectrogram	Mel-scaled spectrogram
07	mfcc	Mel-frequency cepstral coefficients
08	mfcc_delta2	Temporal second-order differentials of MFCCs
09	nmf	Activations obtained by non-negative matrix factorization from the spectrogram

2.2 Model Architecture

Our model is based on CNN-LSTM [14,15], in which the CNN [8] part reduces the image data of the given game scene video while the LSTM [4] part models the temporal features contained in the scene video and BGM. The overview of this model is shown in Fig. 1. The CNN part consists of multiple convolution layers and max pooling layers. The LSTM part consists of two LSTM layers to make it possible to consider long temporal dependencies.

As mentioned above, we assume that the user has a *referred game*, an existing game that he/she referred to when creating a game. Therefore, our model is trained individually on each training game, and the model trained on the referred game is intended to be selected by the user.

This model has been implemented with the Keras library of Tensorflow. We use ADAM [7,13] as an optimizer and the mean squared error as the loss function. The batch size is 16. The number of epochs is 500 for chromagrams and 100 for other audio features. They were experimentally determined to make the loss function less than 0.01.

2.3 Retrieval of Musical Pieces From Predicted Audio Features

After the audio features for BGM are predicted, the system retrieves the musical piece with the closest audio features to the predicted ones from a pre-made music collection. This process includes the following two phases.

Extraction of 12-Second Representative Segment. First, the system extracts a 12-second representative segment from each piece included in the collection. This is because a sequence of audio features extracted from each piece in the collection should have the same duration as the predicted audio features.

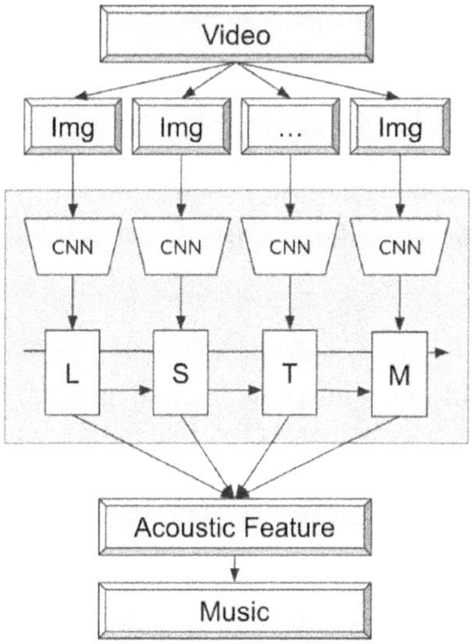

	Layer type	Details	Activation
01	Convolution	Filters: 16, Size: 3 × 3	ReLU
02	Max pooling	Size: 2 × 2	—
03	Convolution	Filters: 32, Size: 3 × 3	ReLU
04	Max pooling	Size: 2 × 2	—
05	Convolution	Filters: 64, Size: 3 × 3	ReLU
06	Max pooling	Size: 2 × 2	—
07	Flatten	—	—
08	Full connect	Nodes: 128	ReLU
09	Full connect	Nodes: 128	—

Fig. 1. Architecture of our model. The right-hand table shows the details of the CNN layers

Although extracting the first 12-second segment may be the simplest way, it may not capture the characteristics of the entire music. Therefore, we extract the segment that captures the characteristics of the music as follows:

1. A sequence of MFCCs is extracted from the target audio signal. Let $\mathbf{x} = [x_1, x_2, \cdots, x_N]$ be the sequence of the MFCCs.
2. All MFCC vectors $x_1, x_2, \cdots, x_N$ are clustered with the k-means algorithm [11]. The number of clusters is set to 4. Let c_i be the cluster ID of x_i. Then, the most frequent cluster ID, c_{mode}, is obtained.
3. Let $\mathbf{x}_i = [x_i, x_{i+1}, \cdots, x_{i+n}]$ be a 12-second segment beginning at x_i, where n is the number of elements for a 12-second segment. Then we compute $\hat{i}$ that satisfies the following equation:

$$\hat{i} = \operatorname*{argmax}_{i \in [0, N-n]} \mathrm{count}(c_{\mathrm{mode}}, [c_i, c_{i+1}, \cdots, c_{i+n}]),$$

   where $\mathrm{count}(a, A)$ counts how many elements in a sequence A equals a.
4. $\mathbf{x}_{\hat{i}}$ is regarded as the 12-second representative segment.

Search of Musical Piece. Next, we extract audio features from the extracted 12-second representative segment for every piece in the collection. The audio features to be extracted, listed in Table 1, are the same as those used in the prediction with the CNN-LSTM model. Then, the Earth Mover's Distance [9,16] of the extracted audio features from the predicted ones is extracted for every piece in the collection. Finally, the piece that has the minimal distance is searched.

3 Experiments

We conducted the following experiments.

1. Determination of referred and test games
2. Prediction of audio features
3. Retrieval of musical pieces from the predicted audio features

3.1 Dataset

We made a dataset from speedrun videos of the games in Table 2 posted on YouTube. We divided them into 12-second scenes and extracted two fight scenes, two walk scenes, and two talk scenes. We created a music collection for BGM from the copyright-free music sites in Table 3. We downloaded 99 WAV files from free music sites.

Table 2. Games used in the experiment as referred and test games

	Game	Usage	Outline
01	Ghost of Tsushima	Test game	A samurai joins a battle on a quest to protect Tsushima Island during the first Mongol invasion of Japan
02	OFF	Test game	An enigmatic humanoid entity called *Batter* travels the world on a *sacred mission* to *purify* the world
03	OMORI	Test game	The player explores both the real world with Sunny and the dream world with his alter-ego "OMORI" in the dream, overcoming his secrets
04	Undertale	Referred game	The player controls a child who has fallen underground and adventures back to the surface while meeting various monsters
05	Chrono Trigger	Referred game	The player controls a group of adventurers on a journey through time to prevent a global catastrophe
06	It's a Wonderful World	Test game	Players are deprived of what is most precious to them and forced to participate in the Reaper's Game for the survival of Shibuya
07	NieR: Automata	Test game	Players take on the role of human-made androids in a proxy war against an invading army of Machines from another world
08	PERSONA5	Test game	The player and his friends awaken their persona abilities and become the Phantom Thieves of Hearts to steal malevolent intent from the hearts of adults
09	MONSTER HUNTER STORIES	Test game	Players explore the world after the village where they live with the monsters they were born into is hit by a disaster
10	Romancing Saga 3	Test game	Rise of Morastrum occurs again, and the player ends up involved in the hunt for the Child of Destiny as eight main characters
11	WILD ARMS	Test game	Players control a boy who wields ARMS to prevent an otherworldly threat from reviving their lost leader and destroying the world
12	Okami	Test game	The player becomes Amaterasu and embarks on a journey to fulfill people's wishes to defeat Yamata no Orochi and restore the world

Table 3. Copyright-free music websites used to create a music collection

	Site	URL
01	bensound	https://www.bensound.com/
02	DOVA-SYNDROME	https://dova-s.jp/
03	MusMus	https://musmus.main.jp/
04	PeriTune	https://peritune.com/
05	Solitary Sound	https://az-ho.org/
06	Devil Soul	https://maou.audio/

3.2 Determination of Referred and Test Games

As mentioned above, we assume that the user selects a referred game and uses the model trained with that game. To simulate this situation, we adopt the following three-step approach. To reduce the computation time for learning models, we first choose a referred game and then decide the test game which is closest to the referred game.

1. Choose a referred game.
2. Find the game with the most similar visual scenes to the chosen one. This game is regarded as a test game.
3. The model trained with the referred game's data is used for predicting audio features.

Step 2 is calculated based on the average of the image hash value differences. The average hash value difference is calculated in the following steps.

2–1 Load the videos of the two games as images.
2–2 Compute hash values of all images.
2–3 Compute the difference between the hash values of the two games for all combinations.
2–4 Compute the average of hash value differences.

The results of the calculated dissimilarities are shown in Fig. 2. For "Undertale" (referred game), "OMORI" (test game) was selected. For "Chrono Trigger" (referred game), "Romancing Saga 3" (test game) was selected. Figure 3 shows some excerpts of the visual scenes of those games.

3.3 Evaluation on Prediction of Audio Features

We experimented with evaluating audio feature prediction through our CNN-LSTM model. This evaluation compares the dissimilarity between the predicted audio features and those of actually used BGM. Because the effectiveness of the prediction would be different among audio feature categories, the effects of each feature category are evaluated individually, as well as their combinations.

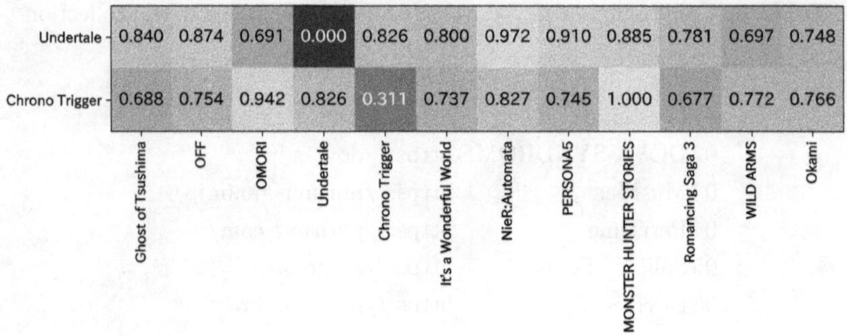

Fig. 2. Dismilarity of visual scenes between games to determine test games

(a) Toby Fox: "Undertale", 2015

(b) OMOCAT: "OMORI", 2020

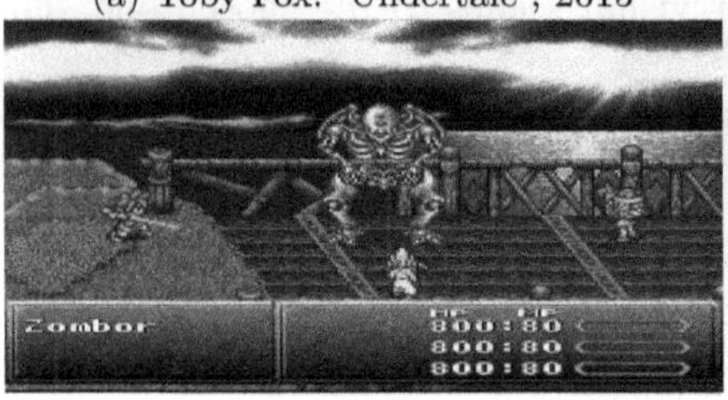

(c) SQUARE: "Chrono Trigger", 1995

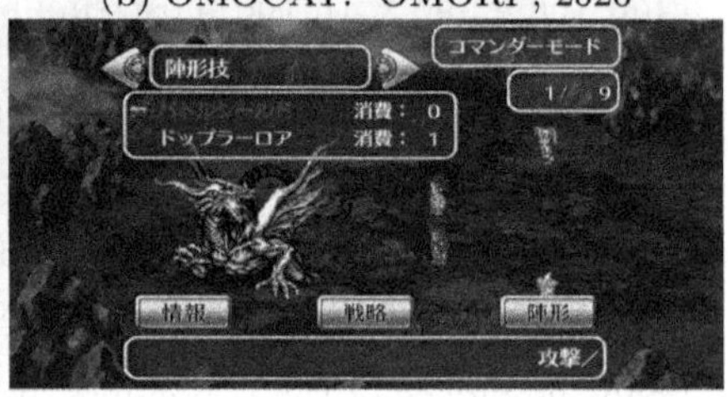

(d) SQUARE: "Romancing Saga 3", 1995

Fig. 3. Excerpts of visual scenes in the used games

Method. We trained models with each feature category to evaluate the effects of each audio feature category individually. Because we have nine feature categories (Table 1) and two games ("Undertale" and "Chrono Trigger") as referred games, we trained 18 models. Then, we gave the models six scenes S (two fight, two walk, and two talk scenes) from each of the two games ("OMORI" and "Romancing Saga 3") as test games. Hence, we obtained the predicted audio features $y_i^{\text{pred}}(s)$ and compared them with the audio features $y_i^{\text{true}}(s)$ of actually used BGM (i: audio feature type, $s (\in S)$: scene).

Because BGM for different scenes should have different audio features, we identified that the audio features have inter-scene variations. Specifically, we calculate i that maximizes the following equation:

$$\sum_{s \in S} \sum_{s' \in S \setminus \{s\}} \{\mathrm{dist}(y_i^{\mathrm{true}}(s'), y_i^{\mathrm{pred}}(s)) - \mathrm{dist}(y_i^{\mathrm{true}}(s), y_i^{\mathrm{pred}}(s)\}$$

where $\mathrm{dist}(y_i^{\mathrm{true}}(s), y_i^{\mathrm{pred}} s)$ represents the distance between the predicted and actual audio features of the same scene.

Results. For "OMORI" (referred game: "Undertale"), the use of only chroma_cqt maximized the inter-scene variations of the audio features. For "Chrono Trigger' (referred game: "Romancing Saga 3"), the combination of chroma_stft, chroma_cqt, chroma_cens, and mfcc_delta2 maximized the inter-scene variations.

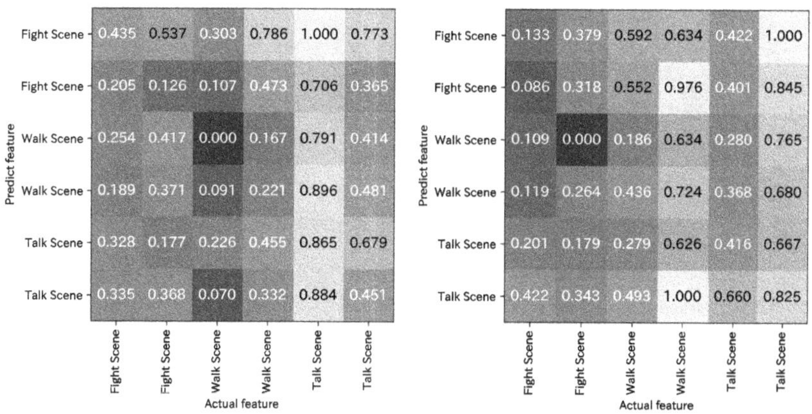

Fig. 4. Distance matrix of predicted vs. actual audio features (Left: "Undertale", Right: "Chrono Trigger")

Discussion. Figure 4 (Left) shows the distance between the predicted features and actual features of each scene for "OMORI" (referred game: "Undertale"). Observations from this figure can be summarized as follows:

- When we focus on Fight Scene 1's predicted features, the distance from the actual features of the same scene should have been the smallest, but the distance from Walk Scene 1's actual features was the smallest. Also, for Fight Scene 2, the distance of its predicted features from Walk Scene 1's actual features was the smallest. These results imply that "Undertale" fight scenes and "OMORI" walk scenes may have similar features in BGM.
- When we focus on the two walk scenes, both Walk Scene 1's and Walk Scene 2's predicted features had the smallest distance from Walk Scene 1's actual features. It means that our models well predicted the walk scenes' audio features.

- For the two talk scenes, the distances between their predicted and actual features were the largest. In general, talk scenes' actual features tended to have large distances from all scenes' predicted features. This could be why "Undertale" tended to have few talk scenes.

Figure 4 (Right) shows the distance between the predicted features and actual features of each scene for "Chrono Trigger" (referred game: "Romancing Saga 3"). Observations from this figure are summarized as follows:

- When we focus on the two fight scenes, the scenes with the actual features with the minimal distance from the fight scenes' predicted features were fight scenes. These results imply that "Chrono Trigger"'s fight scenes may have similar features BGM to each other.
- The walk scenes' predicted features were closer to the fight scenes' actual features than the walk scenes' ones. Similarly, the talk scenes' predicted features were also closer to the fight scenes' actual features than the talk scenes' actual features. As well as "OMORI", the distance from the talk scenes' actual features tended to be large in general. This could be why "Chrono Trigger" tended to have many fight scenes.

3.4 Evaluation on Retrieval of Musical Pieces From the Predicted Audio Features

We experiment with music output. If the same music is output, even if different scenes are input, it goes against the purpose of the research. Therefore, we verify which audio features are suitable for outputting different music.

Method. We prepared six scenes from each of the 12 games listed in Table 2 (72 scenes in total). Let $S = \{s_1, s_2, \cdots, s_J\}$ be a set of the prepared scenes. For BGM retrieval, we used the music collection described in Sect. 3.1, which consists of 99 musical pieces taken from copyright-free music collection websites. Here, $M = \{m_1, m_2, \cdots, m_K\}$ be the music collection. For each scene s_i in S, we retrieved the musical piece that best fits the given scene. Here, the retrieved musical piece for scene s_i is represented by $\mathrm{output}(s_j)$.

The important point is that retrieved musical pieces should differ for different scenes. In other words, for s_i and s_j $(i \neq j)$, it should be $\mathrm{output}(s_i) \neq \mathrm{output}(s_j)$. Therefore, for each musical piece m_k, we calculated the number of scenes $s_j (1 \leq j \leq J)$ satisfying $m_k = \mathrm{output}(s_j)$. This number is denoted by $X_i(m_k)$ (i: the audio feature category). When the condition mentioned above is satisfied, $X_i(m_k)$ should equal 0 or 1 (as long as M has a sufficiently large number of pieces compared to the number of scenes), and its expected value is J/K. Therefore, we evaluated the appropriateness of the BGM retrieval by calculating the mean squared error between $X_i(m_k)$ and J/K. That is, we identified the most effective audio feature category $\hat{\imath}$ that minimizes the following equation:

$$\hat{\imath} = \operatorname*{argmin}_{i \in I} \sum_{k=1}^{K} \left(X_i(m_k) - \frac{J}{K} \right)^2$$

Results. Experimental results show that chroma_cqt is the most effective audio feature category for learning "Undertale". Table 4 lists the retrieval results obtained by inputting the scenes of "OMORI" into the model trained by "Undertale" with chroma_cqt. This shows that the same musical piece was output for different scenes (the two walk scenes and one talk scene).

For "Chrono Trigger", chorma_stft is the most effective audio feature category. Table 5 lists the retrieval results obtained by inputting the scenes of "Romancing Saga 3" into the model trained by "Chrono Trigger" with chroma_stft. It shows that the same musical piece was output for Walk Scene 1 and Talk Scene 2. Otherwise, different musical pieces were output for different scenes.

Table 4. Musical pieces retrieved for scenes from "OMORI" (features: chroma_cqt, referred game: "Undertale")

	Scene	EMD	Music title	Artist	URL
01	Fight Scene 1	0.132	Catch!!	watson	https://musmus.main.jp/music_game.html
02	Fight Scene 2	0.075	And then we ran	watson	https://musmus.main.jp/music_game.html
03	Walk Scene 1	0.044	Pursuer	watson	https://musmus.main.jp/music_game.html
04	Walk Scene 2	0.024	Pursuer	watson	https://musmus.main.jp/music_game.html
05	Talk Scene 1	0.125	And then we ran	watson	https://musmus.main.jp/music_game.html
06	Talk Scene 2	0.051	Pursuer	watson	https://musmus.main.jp/music_game.html

Table 5. Musical pieces retrieved for scenes from "Chrono Trigger" (features: chroma_stft, referred game: "Romancing Saga 3")

	Scene	EMD	Music title	Artist	URL
01	Fight Scene 1	0.078	And then we ran	watson	https://musmus.main.jp/music_game.html
02	Fight Scene 2	0.067	Pursuer	watson	https://musmus.main.jp/music_game.html
03	Walk Scene 1	0.033	Sonorously Box	watson	https://musmus.main.jp/music_game.html
04	Walk Scene 2	0.036	The Chuckling Witch	Hibiki Abe	https://az-ho.org/a-smiling-witch
05	Talk Scene 1	0.088	Mid-range Strength	watson	https://musmus.main.jp/music_game.html
06	Talk Scene 2	0.086	Sonorously Box	watson	https://musmus.main.jp/music_game.html

4 Conclusion

In this paper, we proposed a system that retrieves BGM that fits game scenes given as a sequence of screen images. Using gameplay videos taken from YouTube, we learned a CNN-LSTM-based transformation model from a sequence of screen images to audio features of BGM. Next, the system uses this model to predict the audio features that match the given game scene as BGM. Finally, the system retrieves the musical piece with the closest audio features to the predicted ones.

To confirm the effectiveness of this system, we conducted some experiments. In particular, the comparisons of the predicted audio features and those used in actual BGM show that the predicted features for fight scenes are close to those of the actual BGM. In contrast, the predicted features of walk scenes and talk scenes are not close to those of the same scenes' actual BGM. Also, we discussed retrieved musical pieces for each scene. Retrieved musical pieces should be different for different scenes. It was partly achieved, even though the same musical piece was output for some scenes.

This research is based on a strong assumption that screen images and BGM in games have explicit dependencies on each other. We believe this assumption is partly true but has not yet been fully confirmed. In the future, we will verify the appropriateness of our ideas with larger-scale data as well as the system's usability tests.

References

1. AmBeat. https://tollite.yamaha.com/Ambeat/
2. Choi, E., Chung, Y., Lee, S., Jeon, J., Kwon, T., Nam, J.: YM2413-MDB: a multi-instrumental FM video game music dataset with emotion annotations. In: Proceedings of the 23rd ISMIR Conference, pp. 100–108. ISMIR, India (2022)
3. Deep12. https://www.sonycsl.co.jp/tokyo/14621/
4. Hochreiter, S., Schmidhuber, J.: Short-term memory. Neural Comput. **9**(8), 1735–1780 (1997)
5. Ishikawa, T.: Background music search system to an input video using factor analysis for impression words. Inst. Image Electron. Eng. Jpn. **9**(2), 69–77 (2023)
6. Kim, Y., Schmidt, E., Emelle, L.: Moodswings: A collaborative game for music mood label collection. In: 9th International Conference on Music Information Retrieval, pp. 231–236. ISMIR, Philadelphia (2008)
7. Kingma, D., Ba, J.: Adam: a method for stochastic optimization. In: International Conference on Learning Representations (2015)
8. Lecun, Y., Bottou, L., Bengio, Y., Haffner, P.: Gradient-based learning applied to document recognition. Proc. IEEE **86**(11), 2278–2324 (1998)
9. Logan, B., Salomon, A.: A music similarity function based on signal analysis. In: International Conference on Multimedia and Expo, pp. 745–748. IEEE, Japan (2001)
10. MacQueen, J.: Some methods for classification and analysis of multivariate observations. In: Proceedings of the Fifth Berkeley Symposium on Mathematical Statistics and Probability, vol. 1, pp. 281–297 (1967)
11. McFee, B., Ellis, D.: Analyzing song structure with spectral clustering. In: Proceedings of the 15th Conference of the International Society for Music Information Retrieval, pp. 405–410. ISMIR, Taiwan (2014)
12. Nemoto, S., et al.: Extraction of relationship between character's emotional state and bgm in story scene. J. Jpn. Soc. Inf. Knowl. **30**(2), 63–269 (2020)
13. Reddi, S., Kale, S., Kumar, S.: On the convergence of Adam and beyond. In: International Conference on Learning Representations (2018)

14. Rial, R., Ramadhan, R., Hyun-Jin, L.: A review on deep learning models for forecasting time series data of solar irradiance and photovoltaic power. Energies **13**(24), 6623 (2020)
15. Somu, N., Gauthama, R., Krithivasan, R.: A deep learning framework for building energy consumption forecast. Renew. Sustain. Energy Rev. **137**, 110591 (2021)
16. Xiao, Q., Tsuge, S., Kita, K.: Music retrieval method based on filter-bank feature and earth mover's distance. In: Seventh International Conference on Natural Computation, pp. 1845–1849. IEEE, China (2021)
17. Yamauchi, T., et al.: Game BGM selection based on scenario and emotional state. In: 34th Annual Conference of the Japanese Society for Artificial Intelligence, pp. 4C2GS1304–4C2GS1304. Japan (2020)
18. Zeng, D., Yu, Y., Oyama, K.: Audio-visual embedding for cross-modal music video retrieval through supervised deep CCA. In: International Symposium on Multimedia, pp. 143–150. IEEE, Taiwan (2018)

A Music Exploration Interface Based on Vocal Timbre and Pitch in Popular Music

Tomoyasu Nakano[1(✉)], Momoka Sasaki[2], Mayuko Kishi[2], Masahiro Hamasaki[1], Masataka Goto[1], and Yoshinori Hijikata[2,3]

[1] National Institute of Advanced Industrial Science and Technology (AIST), Tsukuba, Japan
{t.nakano,masahiro.hamasaki,m.goto}@aist.go.jp
[2] School of Business Administration, Kwansei Gakuin University, Nishinomiya, Japan
[3] Graduate School of Information Science, University of Hyogo, Kobe, Japan
contact@soc-research.org

Abstract. This paper proposes an interface that enables users to conduct music explorations focusing on two aspects of singing voices, vocal timbre and pitch, that are useful in finding singing voices that match users' preferences. The interface includes a two-dimensional map to visualize the songs being explored. The map plots songs according to timbre or pitch similarities of their singing voices. Since similar songs are located nearby each other on the map, users can visually find singing voices similar to their favorite singing voices. In addition to locating songs on the map, the interface colors each song in order to visualize additional aspects related to characteristics of singing voices, such as acoustic features or words describing singing voices (*e.g.*, "Clear"). Prior to developing the interface, we conducted a questionnaire survey with twenty participants and confirmed that both vocal timbre and pitch are important when listening to music. We then implemented an interface with 102 songs and conducted a user study with 60 participants.

Keywords: music information retrieval · vocal timbre · pitch histogram · singing descriptors · music exploration interface

1 Introduction

Vocals are a major aspect of many kinds of music [1], and music information retrieval (MIR) technologies focusing on singing voices are beneficial to a wide range of users [5]. In fact, MIR methods and interfaces that focus on various aspects of singing voices—such as vocal timbre [3,15–17], vocal range profile (*i.e.*, pitch and intensity) [11,24], lyrics [14,17,20,25,28], singing style [18,30,31], and gender [4]—have been proposed for the purpose of listening to songs or finding songs to sing. As a new direction for such academic studies, this paper proposes a novel interface that enables exploratory music retrieval focusing on multiple aspects of singer voices.

S. Ystad et al. (Eds.): CMMR 2023, LNCS 15236, pp. 402–418, 2026.
https://doi.org/10.1007/978-3-032-02042-0_31

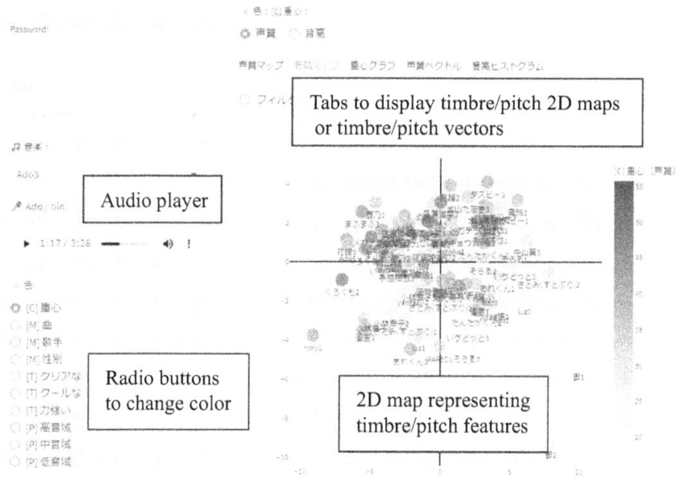

Fig. 1. Screenshot of the proposed interface.

Singing voices have various aspects, so a music exploration interface that allows switching between visualizations of them would be convenient for a variety of purposes. For instance, users who are interested in finding singers having similar vocal timbres may find visualizing the vocal timbre useful, whereas users who are interested in finding songs having similar vocal pitch (technically, pitch distribution) may find visualizing the vocal pitch useful. The aspects to be focused on thus depend on the purpose of the exploration.

We targeted the aspects of vocal timbre and pitch for our interface. We consider these two aspects to be effective for music exploration for two reasons. First, as a result of our survey (explained later) in which participants were asked to describe their favorite singing voices, many responses included descriptions of vocal timbre and pitch. Second, it is helpful for users who want to find songs with their favorite singing voices to use or combine vocal timbre and pitch. These days, a lot of people enjoy singing existing songs as cover versions and sharing their cover songs online. Users who enjoy listening to such songs would be able to find songs with their favorite singing voices even if they do not know those songs or singers.

Here, we developed a music exploration interface that visualizes vocal timbre and pitch and enables users to switch between the visualized factors to find songs having their favorite singing voices. A screenshot of our interface is shown in Fig. 1. On the right side, each song is depicted as a circular dot on a two-dimensional map representing the similarities of vocal timbre or vocal pitch, and the user can switch between vocal timbre and vocal pitch maps. Since similar songs are located nearby each other on the map, users can easily find songs having vocal timbres that are similar, *e.g.*, to those of their favorite singers on the map focusing on the vocal timbre similarity. The user can see the song title and singer name by mousing over a song. Each song has an identifier (ID) based on the singer name (e.g., *Ado3* means the third song of singer *Ado* in our dataset used for the interface), and the user can play back a song by specifying its ID from a pull-down menu on the left sidebar of the screen. The interface uses color to indicate one of the following: singer name, song title, singer gender, center of gravity of the average mel spectrum, center of gravity of the pitch histogram, and singing descriptors (*e.g.*, "High-Range" and "Clear"). This color helps users understand the characteristics of the singing voices in finding their favorite songs, and the combination of the map location and color enables multiple aspects (factors) of singing voices to be visualized. To the best of our knowledge, such a flexible music exploration interface that leverages both vocal timbre and pitch factors has not been proposed.

2 Related Work

Related to this research are studies on music visualization interfaces for finding one's favorite singers or lyrics. Fujihara *et al.* [3] proposed VocalFinder, an interface that retrieves songs having similar singing voices by modeling vocal timbre and singing style with a Gaussian mixture model. Hamasaki *et al.* [4] proposed Songrium, a music browsing assistance interface that has a function to analyze and visualize singing voices. It uses a circle to visualize a song, and the color and size of the circle indicate the singer's gender and number of play counts, respectively. Sasaki *et al.* [20] proposed LyricsRadar, an interface that estimates topic distributions from lyrics text by using latent Dirichlet allocation and locates lyrics on a two-dimensional map by using t-SNE [10]. Tsukuda *et al.* [25] proposed Lyric Jumper, an interface that visualizes lyric topic distributions for each singer as a donut chart to let users find singers with similar topics. Watanabe *et al.* [28] proposed Query-by-Blending, an interface that enables users to find songs by a query combining lyrics, song acoustic signals, and artists.

Map-based music browsing interfaces that locate songs on a two- or three-dimensional map have also been proposed [9]. Shen *et al.* [23] not only used such a map-based interface for the latent representation of audio spectrograms, but also visualized the latent vectors by using a heatmap and parallel coordinates plot. In addition, as MIR methods targeting pitch, Tzanetakis *et al.* [27] used a pitch histogram to automatically classify music genres. Moreover, to recommend songs appropriate for the user's singing ability, a feature called vocal range profile (VRP) has been studied (*e.g.*, [11]). The VRP indicates the range of intensity for each pitch that a singer can sing.

Words that describe singing voices can help to determine vocal characteristics that people are likely to pay attention to when listening to songs. There have been studies on emotional expressions of singing voices [21,22]. Scherer *et al.* [22] studied the correlation of acoustic features to "anger", "fear", "tenderness", "joy", "sadness", and "pride" when eight professional opera singers sang musical scales. There have also been studies that determined a set of words that express impressions of singing and used them to annotate songs [6,8] for their automatic estimation methods. Kanato *et al.* [6] defined a set of 47 words conveying impressions of singing voices. A factor analysis revealed three factors, "power," "politeness," and "brightness," as well as 12 words (*e.g.*, "clear" and "cute") that comprise the singing impression scale. Kim *et al.* [8] defined a vocabulary of 70 words to describe solo singers. They had five musically sophisticated listeners use that 70-word vocabulary to annotate actual songs, and from those annotations, they selected 42 and classified them into five categories: pitch (range), timbre, gender, genre, and technique.

The key contribution of this paper is to develop a music exploration interface that uses a combination of vocal timbre and pitch. Another contribution is the analysis of the results of a questionnaire survey showing the appropriateness of using vocal timbre and pitch for music exploration.

3 Survey of Preference for Singing Voices When Listening to Music

Prior to developing the interface, we conducted a questionnaire survey with 20 participants, males and females in their twenties, who had sufficient conversational ability in Japanese. The purpose of the survey was to investigate users' impressions of vocals and their preferences when listening to music. Note that, although there have been previous studies [6,8] that defined impression words describing the characteristics of vocals in popular music, they did not focus on preference for singing voices when listening to music.

The questionnaire consisted of three sections:

S1: a section to measure the participants' musical ability based on the Goldsmiths Musical Sophistication Index (Gold-MSI) [13],
S2: a section in which participants were asked to write freely about their favorite singing voices, favorite artists/songs, and the reasons for their favorites, and
S3: a section in which participants were asked to rate fourteen aspects on a 7-point scale, including three related to vocal pitch and timbre (pitch height, pitch range, and timbre), which they are aware of when listening to music in their daily life.

3.1 S1: Musical Sophistication of Participants

In the Gold-MSI, participants answer questions such as "I am able to hit the right notes when I sing along with a recording." on a 7-point scale from 1 (Completely Disagree) to 7 (Completely Agree). In this paper, we asked participants to answer questions on "Active Engagement" and "General Sophistication" because we thought they are relevant to music appreciation in general. Moreover, since the survey focused on singing, we also asked participants to answer questions on their "Singing Abilities."

The scores for "Active Engagement," "General Sophistication," and "Singing Abilities" are shown in Fig. 2. Each score was obtained by averaging the raw score values for the relevant questions for comparisons independent of the number of questions. In the scatter plot, differences in Singing Abilities score are represented by different colors. The results show that all median values of the

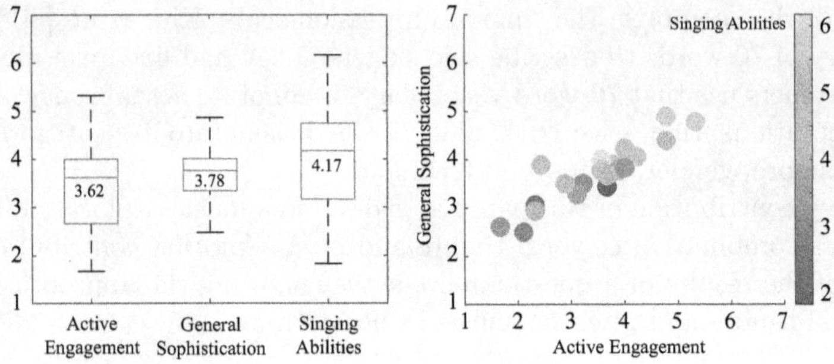

Fig. 2. Distribution of scores for Active Engagement, General Sophistication, and Singing Abilities in Gold-MSI. Differences in Singing Abilities score are indicated by the color in the scatter plot. Higher scores indicate more sophistication in the measured aspect.

scores were around 4. The correlation between Active Engagement and General Sophistication was high, at 0.90, and their medians were slightly below 4, indicating a distribution towards slightly lower scores. On the other hand, the median for Singing Abilities was slightly above 4, with a balanced distribution of high and low scores. The correlation between Singing Abilities and Active Engagement was 0.59, and that between Singing Abilities and General Sophistication was 0.74. These results indicate that the participants had an average interest and ability in music, and the high correlation between Active Engagement and General Sophistication indicated a certain degree of reliability in their answers.

3.2 S2: Preference for Singing Voices When Listening to Music

The analysis focused on two open-ended questions.

Q1 "Please describe as many characteristics as possible of your favorite singing voice when you listen to music."
Q2 "Please describe the artist whose voice you like to listen to. Please also describe what you like about that artist's voice."

The words and phrases used by the participants to describe singing voices in their answers to Q1 and Q2 are shown below. These words are hereafter referred to as "singing descriptors." The number of participants who used each is shown in parentheses. Each singing descriptor was classified according to Kim *et al.* [8]'s classification: pitch, timbre (voice quality, singing style, emotion), gender, and singing ability (singing technique).

- **Pitch**: High-pitched (10), Low-pitched (6), Not too high (1), Mid-low range (1), Not too low (1), Very low (1), Wide range (1)

- **Timbre (voice quality, singing style, emotion)**[1]: Clear/Transparent (14), Beautiful (6), Unique (6), Tender (4), Powerful (4), Calm (4), Fluffy/Airy/Floating (3), Cute (3), Comfortable (3), Cool (2), Sexy (2), Sweet (2), Cheerful/Energizing (2), Likable (2), Rough (2), Soft (2), Deep (2), Delicate (2), Distinctive (2), Healing (2)
- **Gender**: Female (3), Male (2), Neutral (1)
- **Singing ability (singing technique)**: Expressive (3), Falsetto (2), Large inflection (2), Vibrato (2), Strong (2), Accurate pitch control (2), Long tones without hoarseness (1), Comfortable high tone (1), Breathy (1), Head voice (1), Sound on inhalation (1), Precise control (1), Unstrained (1), Emotional variation (1), Steady (1), Kobushi[2] (1), Growl (1), Sing out from the diaphragm (Sing with abdominal support) (1)

The above results show that singing descriptors related to pitch and timbre were frequently mentioned. Pitch-related descriptors "High-pitched" and "Low-pitched" were included in 10 and 6 answers, respectively. Timbre-related descriptors "Clear/Transparent" and "Beautiful" were included in 14 and 6 answers, respectively. On the other hand, singing descriptors related to gender and singing ability (singing technique) were not frequently mentioned. These results suggest that pitch and timbre are important for preferred characteristics of singing voices.

3.3 S3: Aspects of Singing to Be Aware of When Listening to Music

Using a 7-point Likert scale, we asked participants to rate fourteen aspects of music—vocal pitch height, vocal pitch range, lyrics, harmony, vocal gender, vocal timbre, singing style, singing ability, visual appearance of the artist, rhythm/beat/tempo, type of instruments used, instruments' timbre, mood/atmosphere, and emotion of vocal/lyrics—as music elements they are aware of when listening to music, without limiting themselves to specific songs. Fig. 3 shows the number of participants and their scores for each question related to vocals. The average scores for vocal pitch height and vocal pitch range were 4.15 and 4.35, respectively, indicating that the degree of awareness was greater than 4. The average score for vocal timbre was high, at 6.1. In addition, singing style and emotion, which are related to timbre, had high average scores, at 5.7 and 5.85, respectively.

The average scores for lyrics and singing ability exceeded 5. This aspects could also be valuable for music exploration although we did not target them in the interface development. Also, four aspects other than vocal—harmony, rhythm/beat/tempo, instruments' timbre, and mood/atmosphere—had average scores of 4 or more, suggesting that they too would be useful for future developments.

---

[1] Since there were too many singing descriptors answered for the timbre category, only singing descriptors answered by two or more participants are shown.

[2] A singing technique that uses two or more notes in a single syllable.

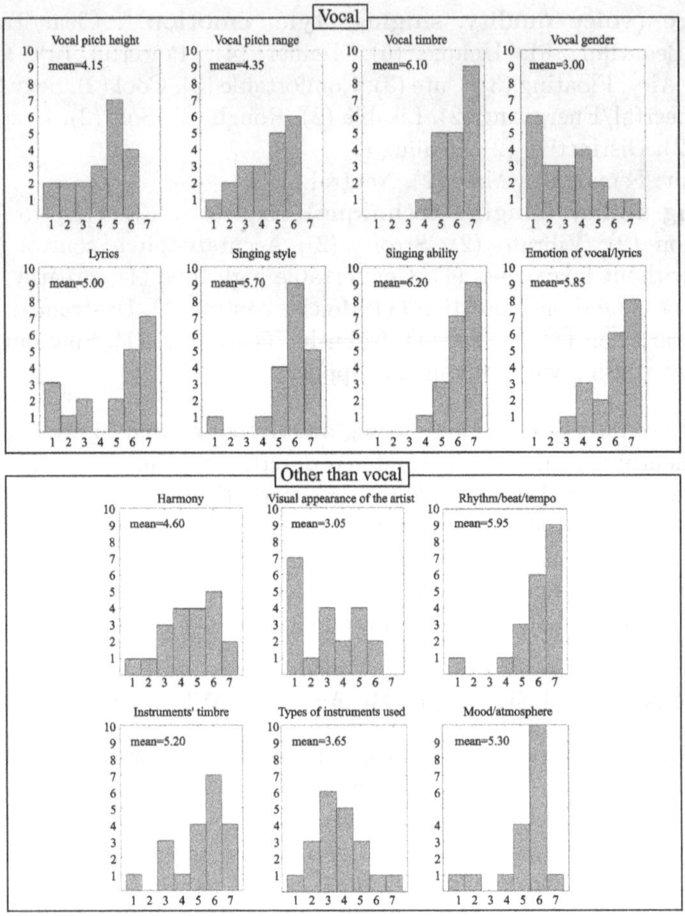

Fig. 3. S3: Answers to questions related to eight aspects of vocal and six aspects for other than vocal on a 7-point Likert scale. The higher the score, the more aware the participant is of the factor when listening to music.

3.4 Discussion

The results of this survey suggest that vocal pitch and timbre played important roles when participants with average musical sophistication determined their favorite singing voices. This conclusion is supported by previous studies in which pitch and timbre categories were used as vocal tags defined by Kim *et al.* [8] and music tags defined by Turnbull *et al.* [26]. We therefore believe that developing a music exploration interface focusing on vocal pitch and timbre is worthwhile and effective.

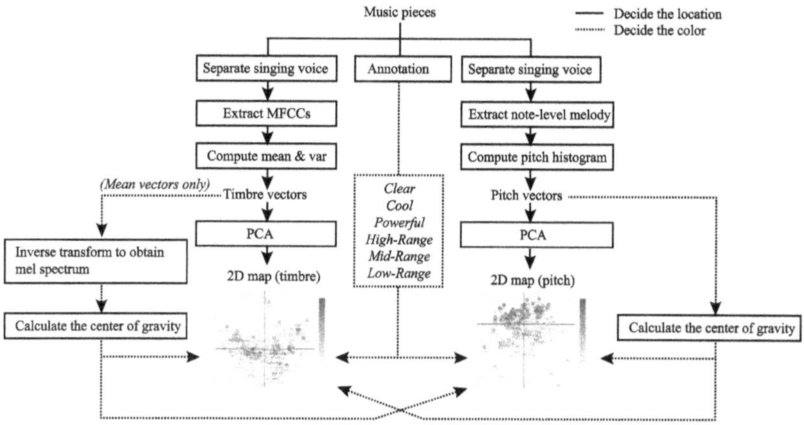

Fig. 4. Overview of the back-end processing of the proposed interface.

4 Interface

In order to visualize the similarities in vocal timbre and pitch and to enable exploratory searches, we implemented a map-based interface (Fig. 1), which has often been proposed in the past [9]. The interface estimates the timbre and pitch feature vectors of vocals from audio signals of each song and uses them to locate each song as a single circular point on a two-dimensional map.

4.1 Data and Back-End Processing

The songs used for the interface development consisted of 51 songs with 17 female singers (3 songs for each singer), and 51 songs with 17 male singers (3 songs for each singer), for a total of 102 songs. All the songs had at least 10,000 views on YouTube as of December 2022 even though they are cover versions of 36 original pieces of Japanese popular music (2 or 3 covers per song).

An overview of the back-end processing is shown in Fig. 4. First, the singing voices were separated from all 102 songs by using Hybrid Demucs [2], which was ranked 1st in the Music Demixing (MDX) Challenge 2021 [12]. Next, pitch and timbre features were extracted and used for mapping and coloring. To estimate the pitch histograms, a note-level pitch sequence in the separated singing voice was estimated by using Omnizart [29]. The pitch histograms were standardized by song to eliminate the effect of song length and then standardized by dimension and referred to as pitch vectors.

Timbre features were obtained by calculating the mean and variance of each dimension of the MFCCs from the separated singing voice by using librosa[3] To calculate the MFCCs, the STFT was calculated for a music signal with a sampling frequency of 22,050 Hz, with a window length of 2048 and a shift width

[3] https://librosa.org/.

of 512. The number of mel frequency bins was 128 and the MFCC dimension was 12, excluding DC components. Here, the vocal activity segments were determined by utilizing the note-level pitch information from Omnizart, and only the MFCCs for those vocal segments were used to calculate the mean and variance. Finally, the mean and variance of the MFCCs for all 102 songs were standardized by dimension and referred to as timbre vectors.

As a last step, we performed principal component analysis on these timbre and pitch vectors, and located them to a two-dimensional timbre map and a two-dimensional pitch map. The performance of Hybrid Demucs was high enough, but even if there were errors, they were unlikely to affect the histograms and mean vectors.

4.2 Annotate Singing Descriptors

For the purpose of improving the user's understanding of the map, manually annotated singing descriptors were also used for coloring. To determine appropriate singing descriptors for each song, the 102 songs were tagged by six annotators, three male and three female. Three annotators per song were assigned to tag the singing voice, and at least one of the three was of a gender different from that of the singer of the song.

The singing descriptors used in this paper were determined on the basis of previous studies [6–8] in which inter-annotator agreement, intelligibility, or synonymity were taken into account. First, 33 descriptors were selected from the tags used in the KVT dataset [8], three descriptors—High-Range, Mid-Range, and Low-Range—related to pitch range and 30 descriptors—Breathy, Bright, Clear, Dark, Energetic, Husky/Throaty, Mild/Soft, Relaxed, Rich, Rounded, Sharp, Stable, Thick, Thin, Warm, Charismatic, Compressed, Cute, Delicate, Dynamic, Embellishing, Emotional, Lonely, Pretty, Passion, Pure, Robotic/Artificial, Sad, Sweet, and Young—related to timbre. Nine other descriptors were added, including seven descriptors—Powerful, Nasal, Calm, Weak, Sexy, Resonant, and Dosu (Threatening/Frightening)—that were selected from previous studies on singing impression [6] and speech timbre [7], and two descriptors—Beautiful and Cool—that were from previous studies of singing impression [6]. As a result, a total of 42 different descriptors were selected.

The number of annotations for the pitch descriptors and the number of annotations for the timbre descriptors are shown in Table 1 and Table 2, respectively. Since using all 42 descriptors would give too much information, we used only the top-three timbre descriptors—"Clear," "Cool," and "Powerful"—on the basis of how often they were annotated. These descriptors were used 176, 119, and 102, respectively (three annotators tagged 102 songs, so the maximum number of descriptors was 306). As for the pitch descriptors, we used all three descriptors for pitch ranges: "High-Range," "Mid-Range," and "Low-Range."

Table 1. Pitch descriptor counts for female and male vocals. If three annotators assigned a descriptor to a song, it was counted as 3.

Descriptor	Female	Male	Both
High-Range	78	65	143
Mid-Range	60	62	122
Low-Range	14	24	38

Table 2. Timbre descriptor counts for female and male vocals.

Descriptor	Female	Male	Both
Clear	107	69	176
Cool	49	70	119
Powerful	41	61	102
Emotional	49	50	99
Calm	48	44	92
Relaxed	51	33	84
Breathy	56	25	81
Energetic	24	54	78
Dynamic	24	48	72
Passion	18	53	71
Resonate/Resonant	43	27	70
Delicate	50	16	66
Beautiful	53	8	61
Robotic/Artificial	26	32	58
Husky/Throaty	23	33	56
Sweet	25	31	56
Sexy	30	24	54
Young	28	26	54
Bright	27	26	53
Stable	23	28	51

Descriptor	Female	Male	Both
Nasal	12	36	48
Mild/Soft	25	21	46
Sharp	19	27	46
Cute	32	10	42
Pure	26	15	41
Embellishing	15	24	39
Rich	24	14	38
Weak	28	10	38
Warm	19	15	34
Charismatic	21	13	34
Compressed	14	18	32
Lonely	23	9	32
Rounded	21	10	31
Dark	18	11	29
Thin	20	7	27
Pretty	24	3	27
Sad	17	8	25
Thick	8	13	21
Dosu	7	13	20

4.3 Interaction

The user can select either the timbre map or the pitch map, and can change the color of the songs by assigning the color to one of the following: singer name, song title, singer gender, center of gravity of timbre vector, center of gravity of pitch vector, and singing descriptor (the number of annotators who assigned it). Discrete coloring is applied to the singer name, song title, and vocal gender, and continuous coloring (*i.e.*, gradation) is applied to the rest. The singer name, song title, and vocal gender are taken from metadata of the songs.

Figure 5 shows the timbre and pitch maps, each of which is colored using either the center of gravity of the timbre vector or that of the pitch vector. Figures 6 and 7 also show the timbre and pitch maps, respectively, colored using vocal gender and the corresponding singing descriptors. In addition, the correlation coefficients between the principal components, gender (0 or 1), the center

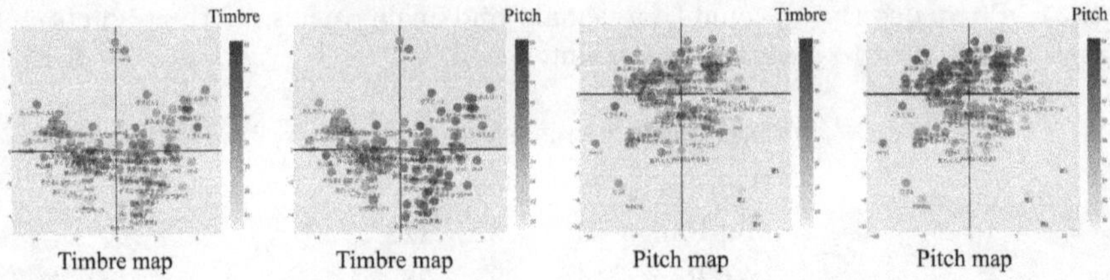

Fig. 5. Timbre maps and pitch maps colored using either the center of gravity of the timbre vector or that of the pitch vector.

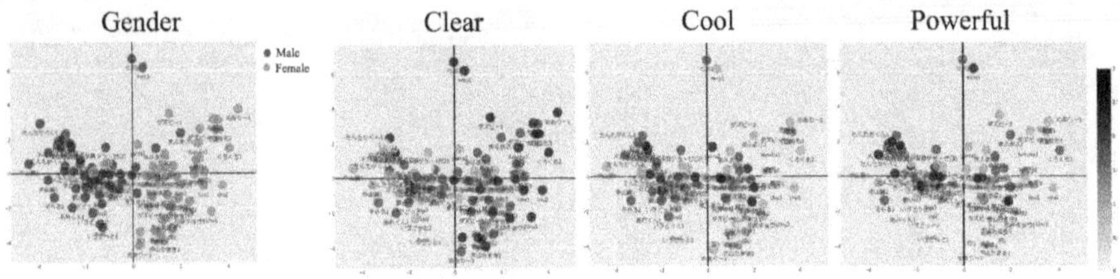

Fig. 6. Timbre maps colored based on gender and three singing descriptors, "Clear," "Cool," and "Powerful." Continuous coloring for each of the three descriptors depends on the number of annotators who labeled it.

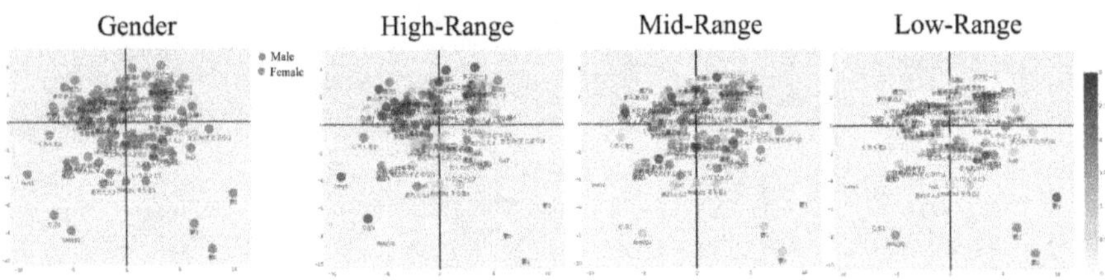

Fig. 7. Pitch maps colored based on gender or three singing descriptors, "High-Range," "Mid-Range," and "Low-Range." Continuous coloring for each of the three descriptors depends on the number of annotators who labeled it.

of gravity, and the count of descriptors (*i.e.*, number of annotators) for singing descriptors related to pitch and timbre are shown in Table 3.

We can see that the horizontal axis of the timbre map is correlated with gender (the correlation coefficient was 0.80) in the first map of Fig. 6, placing female songs on the right and male songs on the left, as well as the center of gravity of the pitch vector (0.62) in the second map of Fig. 5. It is also correlated with the number of annotators of "Clear" (0.57) in the second map of Fig. 6, though the vertical axis of the timbre map is weakly correlated with the number of annotators of "Powerful" (0.34) in the fourth map of that figure.

Table 3. Correlation coefficients between the principal components, gender (0 or 1), the center of gravity, and the number of annotators for singing descriptors related to timbre and pitch. The horizontal axis represents the 1st principal component, and the vertical axis represents the 2nd principal component.

	Timbre map		Pitch map	
	Horizontal axis	Vertical axis	Horizontal axis	Vertical axis
(1) Gender	0.80	−0.17	−0.18	0.51
(2) The center of gravity (Timbre)	0.18	0.39	−0.37	0.32
(3) The center of gravity (Pitch)	0.62	0.03	−0.47	0.84
(4) Clear (Timbre)	0.57	0.03	−0.18	0.32
(5) Cool (Timbre)	−0.26	0.08	0.08	−0.26
(6) Powerful (Timbre)	−0.22	0.34	−0.35	−0.11
(7) High-Range (Pitch)	0.38	0.32	−0.41	0.38
(8) Mid-Range (Pitch)	−0.23	−0.40	0.18	−0.09
(9) Low-Range (Pitch)	−0.30	−0.02	0.44	−0.48

	(1)	(2)	(3)	(4)	(5)	(6)	(7)	(8)	(9)
(1)	1.00								
(2)	−0.04	1.00							
(3)	0.55	0.46	1.00						
(4)	0.40	0.20	0.43	1.00					
(5)	−0.20	−0.07	−0.29	−0.18	1.00				
(6)	−0.18	0.34	0.06	−0.20	0.40	1.00			
(7)	0.11	0.49	0.59	0.38	−0.14	0.17	1.00		
(8)	−0.02	−0.29	−0.22	−0.13	−0.04	−0.26	−0.76	1.00	
(9)	−0.13	−0.40	−0.64	−0.40	0.28	0.09	−0.59	−0.05	1.00

The vertical axis of the pitch map is also correlated with gender (0.51) in the first map of Fig. 7 as well as the center of gravity of the pitch vector (0.84) in the fourth map of Fig. 5. It is also weakly correlated with the number of annotators of "High-Range" (0.38) and "Low-Range" (−0.48) in the second and fourth maps of Fig. 7, though the horizontal axis of the pitch map is weakly correlated with the center of gravity of the timbre vector (−0.37) in the third map of Fig. 5.

As shown in these examples, the proposed interface enables flexible changes in location and coloring with respect to timbre and pitch as well as related singing descriptors. In addition to the two-dimensional map, the user can also visualize the sorting results based on the center of gravity and compare the timbre vector and pitch vector across multiple songs.

5 Evaluation

Since the proposed interface has functions for people who like music, we evaluated its effectiveness in terms of entertainment and knowledge discovery rather than efficiency and accuracy. Sixty participants, males and females in their teens or twenties, were assigned to the following groups, G1 through G3, each with 20 participants.

- **G1 (proposed)**: Used the music exploration interface based on vocal timbre and pitch
- **G2**: Used the music exploration interface based on pitch only
- **G3**: Used the music exploration interface based on timbre only

G2 and G3 are comparison groups to evaluate the effectiveness of the proposed interface. Participants assigned to G2 could not use the timbre map, the center of gravity of the timbre vector, or the singing descriptors for timbre. Participants assigned to G3 could not use the pitch map, the center of gravity of the pitch vector, or the singing descriptors for pitch. The experiment was conducted in the form of a laboratory experiment. Prior to the start of the experiment, the experimenter verbally explained the procedure to the participants in Japanese and also verbally confirmed that each of the participants consented to participate in the experiment. This interaction confirmed that each participant had sufficient hearing ability and conversational ability in Japanese to participate in the experiment. The experiment was conducted on a laptop computer, and the participants listened to the music through canal-type wired earphones. Participants were paid 1,800 JPY and each spent approximately 1 h and 45 min in the experiment.

Participants first completed a questionnaire that measured their level of interest in music and then they watched a video explaining the interface. The explanation was made as easy to understand as possible for participants who are not familiar with music technologies, using as little technical terminology as possible. Next, while recording the screen operation, participants were asked to explore their favorite music until they got bored within the duration of the experiment. After the experiment, each participant answered a questionnaire and was interviewed. In the post-experimental questionnaire, we assessed focused attention (FA), perceived usefulness (PU), aesthetic appeal (AE), and reward factor (RW) using questions from the User Engagement Scale (UES-LF) [19] on a 7-point scale. Participants also answered open-ended questions about the pros and cons of the interface. In addition, participants in G1 answered whether they felt that vocal timbre or pitch was more suitable for them when exploring the music.

5.1 Results

First, the data of three participants (two in G2 and one in G3) were filtered out because the data were inappropriate (*e.g.*, the map was not used). Using the data from G1 to G3 after filtering, each score in the UES-LF was calculated.

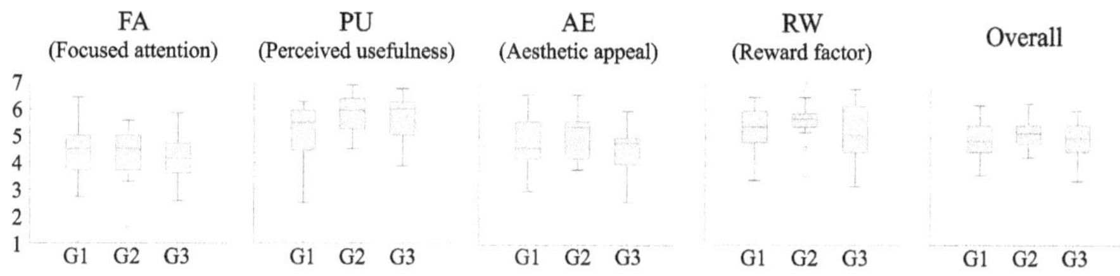

Fig. 8. Box plots of the scores in UES-LF.

The average screen recording time for the remaining 57 participants was 28.8 min (ranged from 11.8 to 53.1 min).

Their distribution is shown in Fig. 8, where "Overall" is the overall engagement score, obtained by averaging the other four scores. A one-way ANOVA confirmed a significant difference only in PU at the 5% level ($p = 0.037$). The results of Bonferroni's multiple comparison test based on Wilcoxon's rank-sum test showed no significant differences in all combinations. This suggested that the type of interface did not affect user engagement.

Regarding the answers to the experimental questionnaire, 13 of the 20 participants in G1 answered that the vocal timbre feature was more suitable when searching for music, while seven answered that the pitch feature was more suitable. This confirmed the need for our interface that allows searching from multiple factors since the vocal timbre feature worked best for some users and the pitch feature worked best for others. Moreover, in the interview, seven participants in G1 commented that the combination of vocal timbre and pitch facilitated their exploration. Some participants in G1 to G3 understood their own preferences for vocal timbre and pitch, while others found that they unexpectedly liked timbres and pitches that they had thought they did not like.

The top three functions mentioned as pros by all 57 of the participants were the timbre and pitch maps by 29 participants and the timbre and pitch vectors by 16 participants. 11 participants mentioned the design and usability of the interface, and 11 participants mentioned the identification or change of their preferences. Moreover, 20 participants expressed that they found the interface enjoyable, fun, and interesting. On the other hand, since the design and usability were also mentioned as cons by 50 participants, we conclude that it is necessary to improve the usability of the implementation in the future. Eight participants also commented that they did not understand the meaning of the axes of the two-dimensional map and that the differences in color according to acoustic features and singing descriptors did not match their own perception. Therefore, there is a possibility of developing a better interface to help users grasp the meaning of acoustic features and singing descriptors.

5.2 Discussion

The following can be considered as reasons for the small differences in UES-LF between G1 and G2 and between G1 and G3.

- Exploring music from the visualization of pitch and timbre was a novel experience for the participants. Even for G2 and G3, the participants may have felt that it was enough for them to find preferred songs from a new point of view. In fact, some understood their own preferences for pitch and timbre and discovered new or unexpected preferences during the use of the interface.
- This may be due to the doubling of the amount of information and manipulation. The interface has become more complex, which probably increased the time and effort required for participants to become familiar with the interface operation.

Three participants in G2 commented that while they felt the pitch information was effective, they also wanted information on vocal timbre. Therefore, some users are expected to be more satisfied with our interface that allows for both pitch and timbre.

6 Conclusion

We proposed a music exploration interface that flexibly visualizes vocal timbre and pitch as well as singing descriptors. The questionnaire survey results indicated that vocal timbre and pitch can be utilized to explore music. In the present analysis based on the UES-LF, no significant differences were identified between the proposed interface and the comparison interfaces. However, the results of the questionnaire and interviews indicated that music exploration based on vocal timbre and pitch not only provides enjoyment and fun but also leads to the discovery of preferences regarding timbre and pitch. Future work will include building an interface that improves usability and taking into account the singer's singing style.

Acknowledgments. This work was supported in part by JST CREST Grant Number JPMJCR20D4 and JSPS KAKENHI Grant Number JP21H04917, Japan.

Disclosure of Interests. The authors have no competing interests to declare that are relevant to the content of this article.

References

1. Demetriou, A., Jansson, A., Kumar, A., Bittner, R.: Vocals in music matter: the relevance of vocals in the minds of listeners. In: Proceedings of the 19th International Society for Music Information Retrieval Conference (ISMIR 2018), pp. 514–520 (2018)
2. Défossez, A.: Hybrid spectrogram and waveform source separation. In: Proceedings of Music Demixing Workshop (MDX 2021), pp. 1–11 (2021)
3. Fujihara, H., Goto, M., Kitahara, T., Okuno, H.: A modeling of singing voice robust to accompaniment sounds and its application to singer identification and vocal-timbre-similarity-based music information retrieval. IEEE Trans. Audio, Speech Lang. Process. **18**(3), 638–648 (2010)

4. Hamasaki, M., Goto, M., Nakano, T.: Songrium: a music browsing assistance service with interactive visualization and exploration of a web of music. In: Proceedings of the 23rd International World Wide Web Conference (WWW 2014) (2014)
5. Humphrey, E., et al.: An introduction to signal processing for singing-voice analysis: high notes in the effort to automate the understanding of vocals in music. IEEE Signal Process. Mag. **36**, 82–94 (2019)
6. Kanato, A., Nakano, T., Goto, M., Kikuchi, H.: An automatic singing impression estimation method using factor analysis and multiple regression. In: Proceedings of the 40th International Computer Music Conference and 11th Sound and Music Computing Conference (Joint ICMC SMC 2014 Conference), pp. 1244–1251 (2014)
7. Kido, H., Kasuya, H.: Representation of voice quality features associated with talker individuality. In: Proceedings of the 5th International Conference on Spoken Language Processing (ICSLP 1998), pp. 1–4 (1998)
8. Kim, K., Lee, J., Kum, S., Park, C., Nam, J.: Semantic tagging of singing voices in popular music recordings. IEEE/ACM Trans. Audio Speech Lang. Process. **28**, 1656–1668 (2020)
9. Knees, P., Schedl, M., Goto, M.: Intelligent user interfaces for music discovery. Trans. Inter. Soc. Music Inform. Retrieval **3**(1), 165–179 (2020)
10. Van der Maaten, L., Hinton, G.: Visualizing data using t-SNE. J. Mach. Learn. Res. **9**(11) (2008)
11. Mao, K., Fan, J., Shou, L., Chen, G., Kankanhalli, M.S.: Competence-based song recommendation: matching songs to one's singing skill. IEEE Trans. Multimedia **17**(3), 396–408 (2015)
12. Mitsufuji, Y., et al.: Music demixing challenge. In: Proceedings of Music Demixing Workshop (MDX 2021), pp. 1–8 (2021)
13. Müllensiefen, D., Gingras, B., Musil, J., Stewart, L.: The musicality of non-musicians: an index for assessing musical sophistication in the general population. PLOS One **9**(2) (2014)
14. Nakano, T., Goto, M.: LyricListPlayer: a consecutive-query-by-playback interface for retrieving similar word sequences from different song lyrics. In: Proceedings of the 13th Sound and Music Computing Conference (SMC 2016), pp. 344–349 (2016)
15. Nakano, T., Mochihashi, D., Yoshii, K., Goto, M.: Musical typicality: how many similar songs exist? In: Proceedings of the 17th International Society for Music Information Retrieval Conference (ISMIR 2016), pp. 695–701 (2016)
16. Nakano, T., Yoshii, K., Goto, M.: Vocal timbre analysis using latent dirichlet allocation and cross-gender vocal timbre similarity. In: Proc. the 39th IEEE International Conference on Acoustics, Speech and Signal Processing (ICASSP 2014), pp. 5239–5343 (2014)
17. Nakano, T., Yoshii, K., Goto, M.: Musical similarity and commonness estimation based on probabilistic generative models of musical elements. Inter. J. Semantic Comput. (IJSC) **10**(1), 27–52 (2016)
18. Ohishi, Y., Goto, M., Ito, K., Takeda, K.: A stochastic representation of the dynamics of sung melody. In: Proceedings of the 8th International Conference on Music Information Retrieval (ISMIR 2007), pp. 371–372 (2007)
19. O'Brien, H., Cairns, P., Hall, M.: A practical approach to measuring user engagement with the refined user engagement scale (UES) and new UES short form. Intl. J. of Hum.-Comput. Stud. **112**, 28–39 (2018)
20. Sasaki, S., Yoshii, K., Nakano, T., Goto, M., Morishima, S.: LyricsRadar: a lyrics retrieval system based on latent topics of lyrics. In: Proceedings of the 15th International Society for Music Information Retrieval Conference (ISMIR 2014), pp. 585–590 (2014)

21. Scherer, K.: Vocal communication of emotion: a review of research paradigms. Speech Commun. **40**, 227–256 (2003)
22. Scherer, K., Sundberg, J., Fantini, B., Trznadel, S., Eyben, F.: The expression of emotion in the singing voice: acoustic patterns in vocal performance. J. Acoust. Soc. Am. **142**(4), 1805–1815 (2017)
23. Shen, J., Wang, R., Shen, H.: Visual exploration of latent space for traditional Chinese music. Vis. Inform. **4**, 99–108 (2020)
24. Shou, L., Mao, K., Luo, X., Chen, K., Chen, G., Hu, T.: Competence-based song recommendation. In: Proceedings of the 36th International ACM SIGIR conference (SIGIR 2013), pp. 423–432 (2013)
25. Tsukuda, K., Ishida, K., Goto, M.: Lyric Jumper: a lyrics-based music exploratory web service by modeling lyrics generative process. In: Proceedings of the 18th International Society for Music Information Retrieval Conference (ISMIR 2017), pp. 544–551 (2017)
26. Turnbull, D., Barrington, L., Torres, D., Lanckriet, G.: Semantic annotation and retrieval of music and sound effects. IEEE/ACM Trans. Audio Speech Lang. Process. **16**(2), 467–476 (2008)
27. Tzanetakis, G., Ermolinskyi, A., Cook, P.: Pitch histograms in audio and symbolic music information retrieval. J. New Music Res. **14**(2), 143–152 (2003)
28. Watanabe, K., Goto, M.: Query-by-Blending: a music exploration system blending latent vector representations of lyric word, song audio, and artist. In: Proceedings of the 20th International Society for Music Information Retrieval Conference (ISMIR 2019), pp. 144–151 (2019)
29. Wu, Y., et al.: Omnizart: a general toolbox for automatic music transcription. J. Open Source Softw. **6**(68), 3391 (2021)
30. Yakura, H., Watanabe, K., Goto, M.: Self-supervised contrastive learning for singing voices. IEEE/ACM Trans. Audio Speech Lang. Process. **30**, 1614–1623 (2022)
31. Yamamoto, Y., Nam, J., Terasawa, H.: Analysis and detection of singing techniques in repertoires of J-POP solo singers. In: Proceedings of the 23rd International Society for Music Information Retrieval Conference (ISMIR 2022), pp. 384–391 (2022)

Exploring Diverse Sounds: Identifying Outliers in a Music Corpus

Le Cai[1(✉)], Sam Ferguson[1], Gengfa Fang[2], and Hani Alshamrani[1]

[1] Creativity and Cognition Studios, Faculty of Engineering and IT, University of Technology Sydney, 15 Broadway, Ultimo, NSW 2007, Australia
{le.cai-1,hani.alshamrani}@student.uts.edu.au, samuel.ferguson@uts.edu.au

[2] The Hong Kong University of Science and Technology (Guangzhou), No. 1 Du Xue Road, Guangzhou, Nansha District, China
gengfafang@hkust-gz.edu.cn

Abstract. Existing research on music recommendation systems primarily focuses on recommending similar music, thereby often neglecting diverse and distinctive musical recordings. Musical outliers can provide valuable insights due to the inherent diversity of music itself. In this paper, we explore music outliers, investigating their potential usefulness for music discovery and recommendation systems. We argue that not all outliers should be treated as irrelevant data, as they can offer unique perspectives to contribute to a richer musical understanding. We attempt to identify 'Genuine' music outliers, which may reveal unique aspects of an artist's repertoire and serve to enhance music exploration and discovery.

Keywords: Music Outlier · Music Outlier Detection · Audio characteristics · Music discovery

1 Introduction

In the field of music information retrieval, a primary focus is often on finding similarities among digital musical recordings, to enable recommendation systems and facilitate music discovery [5,10,14,23]. Given this context, analysis of outliers has attracted less research attention [18], as they are often considered irrelevant data and removed during preprocessing, or are naturally scored lower by most similarity-focused algorithms [7]. However, outliers in the context of music can provide interesting insights and reveal unique patterns, as music inherently exhibits great diversity [13,20].

In this paper, we explore the identification and categorization of music outliers, with an aim to ultimately enhance music discovery and recommendation systems. We propose a method to describe and discover genuine musical outliers based on audio characteristics, such as tempo and loudness. By doing so, we aim to identify outliers that can provide valuable information for music discovery

S. Ystad et al. (Eds.): CMMR 2023, LNCS 15236, pp. 419–432, 2026.
https://doi.org/10.1007/978-3-032-02042-0_32

while not being non-musical. We present a definition of what constitutes a 'Genuine' music outlier and investigate its characteristics. Genuine outliers exhibit unique characteristics that set them apart from an artist's main style, providing insightful information for music discovery.

This paper is structured as follows: The introduction presents the motivation of our study, followed by a comprehensive literature review, which discusses the relevant background and prior research. Next, the aims and objectives are followed by the methodology section which outlines our proposed definition of Genuine music outliers and the subsequent dataset and algorithm developed for the detection. The results and discussion section evaluates the effectiveness of our algorithm based on the dataset and provides insights into its performance. Finally, the conclusion summarizes our findings and highlights the implications of our work, while also suggesting potential avenues for future research in the realm of music outlier detection and analysis.

2 Related Work

2.1 What Makes a Song Different from Audio?

Understanding outliers in the context of music recommendation systems necessitates a thorough examination of their diverse nature and the ability to differentiate actual music from other forms of audio. Mller [17] provides a comprehensive overview of music structure analysis, focusing on techniques for segmenting and organizing music into meaningful sections, laying the foundation for understanding the key aspects of music structure and demonstrating how various representations and algorithms can be used to analyze and compare music pieces. A system for finding structural descriptions of musical pieces defines the structure of a piece as segments with specific time ranges and labels, with segments sharing the same label considered occurrences of a particular structural part [21]. In another study, a multi-task deep learning framework is introduced for directly modeling structural semantic labels in music, such as "verses" and "choruses", from audio signals. This approach proposes a 7-class taxonomy that includes intro, verse, chorus, bridge, outro, instrumental, and silence, and consolidates annotations from four different datasets [27]. A large-scale analysis of songs in 315 different societies has found that songs share universal features like tonality, rhythm, and repetitive structures [16]. A study conducted by Shuqi et al. [8]. analyzes the significance of repetition and structure in music, specifically in popular music, and demonstrated that deep learning models often struggle to identify these essential elements, which are crucial for generating coherent and appealing musical pieces. Subsequently, Sargent et al. [22]. introduced a fourth principle: regularity. This principle posits that musical segments possess a certain degree of regularity, which can be leveraged to better understand and analyze the structure of the music.

2.2 Outlier Detection Approaches

The purpose of outlier detection algorithms is to identify patterns and samples that deviate significantly from the normal characteristics of a group of data [12]. The reason to detect outliers is it can providing interesting insights contribute to a richer understanding of an artist's work. General outlier detection methods can be categorized into 4 categories based on an overview conducted by [26]:

Clustering-based methods: use a clustering algorithm to classify the majority of the elements of the set, while also clearly defining the outlying elements of the set.

Density-based methods: identifying outliers as points in low-density regions within a data set.

Distance-based methods: determining the distance between points, and considering outliers to be points with a large distance from their nearest neighbors.

Statistical methods: using measures such as mean, median and standard deviation to identify data points that fall outside of a defined range.

Clustering-based methods, exemplified by [2], utilize subspace cluster analysis to construct classification trees while addressing dataset scarcity. A deep learning model using a Clustering Augmented Learning Method (CALM) classifier improves genre classification by extracting deep time series features [11]. In contrast, density-based methods like DBSCAN [9] and OPTICS [1] identify outliers in low-density regions within a dataset, as demonstrated by the OPTICS algorithm applied to traditional Chinese folk music [28]. In the exploration of automatic outlier detection methods on music genre datasets, Lu et al. [15] characterized outliers using their musical attributes, demonstrating the potential of these techniques to unveil unique insights into music structure and diversity within genre classification. Distance-based methods, including K-means [4] and CLARANS [19], examine the distance between data points and their nearest neighbors, considering outliers as points with large distances from the nearest neighbors. This approach has been successfully applied to traditional Irish music in [24]. Meanwhile, statistical-based methods employ measures such as mean, median, and standard deviation to identify data points outside a defined range to reveal patterns in cluster structure dynamics in popular music data [25]. However, while these studies focus on detecting outliers based on their statistical properties, the potential of the outliers themselves for music discovery has not been as extensively investigated.

3 Aims and Objectives

In this paper, our aims center around exploring the potential of music outliers for music discovery. To achieve this, we propose the following objectives:

Propose an approach to describe musical outliers: by examining various attributes that distinguish them from an artist's typical style, facilitating their identification and analysis. This implies establishing a clear definition to describe 'Genuine' music outliers as a distinct category of outliers that exhibit meaningful deviations from a set of existing digital musical recordings.

Categorise music outliers: into meaningful categories based on their distinguishing characteristics to create a meaningful interpretation, that also can help find the outliers that are helpful to understanding and discovering interesting music while excluding outliers that hold little data.

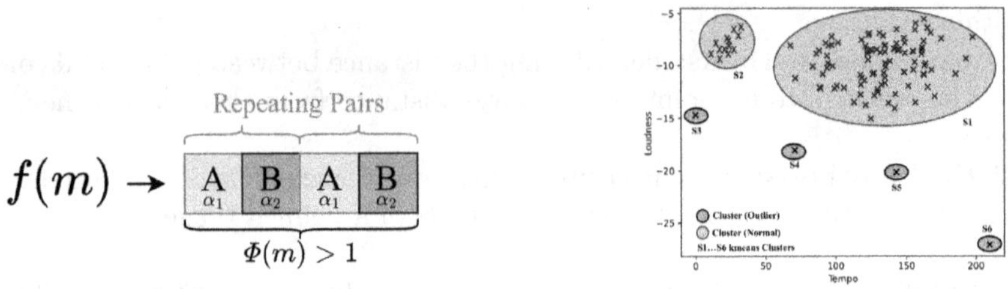

(a) Example of a subsequence of audio forms a complete song

(b) Example of a k-means cluster with identified outlier

Fig. 1. The Definition of Genuine Music Outliers

4 Method

We introduce the concept of genuine outliers within the context of music data and explore their potential value in recommendation systems. To accomplish this, we first propose a definition for genuine outliers, then create a labelled dataset for evaluation, and finally, apply an outlier detection algorithm to validate our definition.

4.1 Definition of Genuine Music Outliers

A "Genuine" music outlier is a complete song that maintains an artist's typical musical structure while distinctly diverging in sound and style from their predominant body of work, due to the complex nature of music, in our scenario, we consider pop music only.

To achieve this, a genuine outlier must satisfy the following constraints: 1): Forms a complete song, this distinguishes the identified outlier must be a song, not something else, e.g. speech, or sound effect, shown in fig.1a. To ensure this, audio must satisfy these conditions: a): The length of music structure ϕ must be greater than one in a subsequence, this means the input recordings must at least have one or more music structures otherwise it is not music. b): The identified music structure must at least has one unique pair. e.g. a music structure in $(A{-}B)$ is a song that can identify at least one unique pair, not $(A{-}A)$ or $(B{-}B)$. c): The identified music structure must contain repeated parts, as repetition is a crucial element in music. A piece of audio that forms music should exhibit repeating sections, such as $(A - B - A - B)$ patterns. The formal definition of a Genuine outlier is as follows:

Let M represents the set of all recordings produced by a specific artist. For a finite set S_M, suppose function $\Phi : M \to \mathbb{N}^+$ that maps a recording to a finite integer and a function $f_\Phi : M \to S_M^{\Phi(M)}$ that maps a recording $m \in M$ to a finite length sequence. A recording $m \in M$ is defined as a "Genuine" music outlier if the following conditions is satisfied:

1. Forms A Complete Song: For any recording $m \in M$, the sequence $f_\Phi(m)$ and number $\Phi(m)$ should satisfy the following:

1. $\Phi(m) > 1$,
2. There exist a subsequence $a_{k_1}...a_{k_p}(k_1 < ... < k_p, p > 1)$ from $f_\Phi(m)$ that, at least one repeated subsequence from $f(m)$ can be found, i.e., there exist $a_{k_1'}...a_{k_p'}(k_1' < ... < k_p', p > 1)$ that $k_1 \neq k_1'$ and $k_p \neq k_p'$.

For any given recording $m \in M$, if the previous condition satisfied, for given constant $C_G \in (0, 1]$, κ and a positive integer N_d, either of the following conditions must be satisfied,

2. Distinctiveness: Define $F : M \to \mathbb{R}^n$ be a function that maps each recording to an n-dimensional feature space, where n is a positive integer representing the number of musical features being considered. Define $\mathrm{Card}(\cdot)$ as the Cardinality of a set, $\|\cdot\|$ as the 2-norm and κ-means cluster sets $\boldsymbol{\Omega} = \{\Omega_1, ..., \Omega_\kappa\}(1 \le \kappa \le \mathrm{Card}(M))$ that

$$\begin{aligned} \boldsymbol{\Omega} &\in \arg\min_{\bar{\boldsymbol{\Omega}}} \sum_{i=1}^{\kappa} \sum_{\mathbf{x}\in\bar{\Omega}_i\subset M} \|F(\mathbf{x}) - \boldsymbol{\mu}_i\|^2 \\ \text{s.t.} \quad \boldsymbol{\mu}_i &= \frac{1}{\mathrm{Card}(\bar{\Omega}_i)} \sum_{\mathbf{y}\in\bar{\Omega}_i\subset M} F(\mathbf{y}), \text{for } 1 \le i \le \kappa. \end{aligned} \tag{1}$$

For any given integer $N_d > 0$, for any $m \in M$, if $m \in \Omega_i$ and $\mathrm{Card}(\Omega_i) < N_d$, we say that recording m is distinct with respect to M.

3. Non-adherence: For a given positive number $C_G \in (0, 1]$. We define

$$R_M(m) := \frac{\mathrm{Card}(\{m' | f_\Phi(m') = f_\Phi(m) \text{ for all } m' \in M\})}{\mathrm{Card}(M)}. \tag{2}$$

If $R_M(m) < C_G$, we say m is not adhere to set M.

In conclusion, if recording m does form a complete song, either the song m is distinct with respect to M or m is not adhere to set M, with given C_G, κ, and N_d, then we say song m is an outlier (Fig. 2).

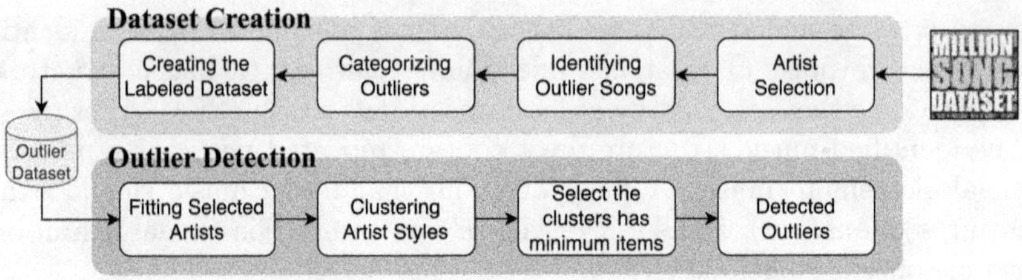

Fig. 2. Dataset Creation Process

4.2 Dataset Creation and Outlier Selection Algorithm

In order to evaluate our above-proposed definition for Genuine music outliers, we created a dataset specifically designed to examine our hypothesis, To achieve this goal, the following steps were carried out:

Artist Selection: From the Million Song Dataset[1], a smaller sample consisting of 10,000 songs extracted from the MSD, we randomly chose 20 artists using a random number generator to pick artist IDs. For each of the selected artists, we identified a list of all the songs contained in the dataset with the particular artist id.

Identifying Outlier Songs: To identify and categorize outliers within the selected artists' music, we conducted a manual listening and labeling process for these songs by ear. First, we acquainted the artist's typical styles. To achieve that, we listened to about 20%-30% songs in this artist's main cluster. After establishing the primary styles, we listened to these songs once with selected artists again, focusing on identifying tracks that significantly deviated from the typical style. Attention was paid to musical elements, such as tempo, melody, harmony, instrumentation, and song structure.

Categorizing Outliers: We then listened to the characteristics of the identified outliers, focusing on specific attributes such as tempo, melody, harmony, instrumentation, and song structure that differentiate them from the artist's dominant style. By examining these properties, we classified outliers into five categories: Error, Speech, Intro, Sound Effect, and Genuine. Each identified outlier was assigned to one of the categories based on a two-step process. First, we selected songs with a Euclidean distance greater than 3 times the z-score threshold from the main cluster. Second, we manually reviewed these outliers, focusing on listening to their distinctive features such as tempo, loudness, melody, and the composition of instruments.

Creating the Labeled Dataset: Finally, After identifying and categorizing outliers, we compiled a list of all songs from the selected artists, along with their corresponding outlier categories. This list included each song's title, artist, genre, and other metadata. Utilizing the pre-extracted audio features from the MSD

[1] Million Song Dataset [6] is available at: http://millionsongdataset.com.

Subset, such as tempo, loudness, key, and mode, we created a dataset compiled with data including outlier categories and the MSD pre-extracted features.

We consider this to be a classification problem where each artist typically consists of 1 main distinct style. Note we only considered the case for 1. Distinctiveness and 2. Non-adherences for the current approach, the case of forms a complete song is discarded due to the complexity of the anlysis of music structures.

Let M be a set of recordings under an artist. Let $x_i \in \mathbb{R}^d$ to denote a d-dimensional feature vector for the i-th song from $M(1 \leq i \leq \text{Card}(M))$. Suppose K is an integer that $1 \leq K \leq \text{Card}(M)$. For $1 \leq k, k^{'} \leq K$, define C_k as a subset of M, such that $C_k \cap C_{k'} = \emptyset$ for $k \neq k^{'}$, and $\cup_{1 \leq i \leq K} C_i = M$. In our case, $d = 2$. We adopt k-means algorithm [3] to partition set M that satisfies such conditions. In the next section, we first delineate the outlier categorization, followed by the presentation of outlier detection results.

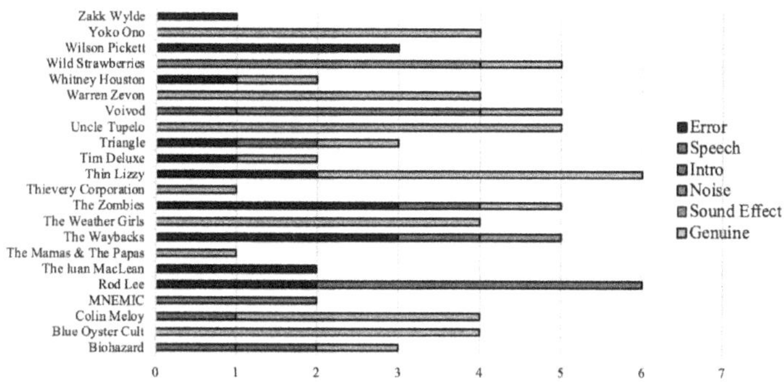

Fig. 3. Outlier Dataset: Categorisation of Outliers by Artists

5 Results

5.1 Outlier Categorisations

We found 34 genuine outliers from 29 artists in 320 songs as well as 17 errors, 5 speeches, 1 intro, 5 noise, and 3 sound effects from 29 artists shown in Fig. 3, they can categorize into 5 types: *a)* **Error:** such as erroneous data value, e.g. doubling tempo due to feature extractor failure, incorrect data type, such as text entered as a numeric type. *b)* **Noise:** unintentional sounds such as non-musical noise, jitter, or glitches in a recording, often due to recording issues or equipment quality. e.g. a live performance recording with excessive audience noise. *c)* **Speech:** such as some spoken words, or a short story integrated into the music to enhance the atmosphere of the listening experience. these types of practices commonly occur in certain music genres, such as hip and electronic music. *d)* **Sound Effect:** This type of recording is used to create a certain mood, it can build tension and add extra impact to certain sections of the song. Particularly, sound effect is used in certain genres of music such as electronic & rock music to add extra depth and interest to music. *e)* **Intro:** A very short track is often less than 30 s in length and serves as an introduction or a brief to establish the identity of the album. *f)* **Genuine:** a musical piece that deviates significantly from an artist's typical style or the norm within a genre, exhibiting unique characteristics. These outliers are not classified as errors, noise, or other non-musical categories.

Table 1. The Result of Automatic Outlier Detection

Artist Name	TPR	FPR	TNR	FNR
Zakk Wylde	0	0.455	0.545	1
Blue Oyster Cult	1	0	1	0
Biohazard	0.5	0.381	0.619	0.5
Yoko Ono	0.25	0.049	0.951	0.75
Wilson Pickett	1	0.316	0.684	0
Wild Strawberries	1	0.087	0.913	0
Whitney Houston	0.5	0	1	0.5
Warren Zevon	1	0.356	0.644	0
Voivod	0.833	0	1	0.167
Uncle Tupelo	0.4	0.217	0.783	0.6
Triangle	0.75	0	1	0.25
Tim Deluxe	1	1	0	0
Thin Lizzy	0.429	0.37	0.63	0.571
Thievery Corporation	0.667	0.299	0.701	0.333
The Zombies	1	0.378	0.622	0
The Weather Girls	1	0.344	0.656	0
The Waybacks	0.5	0.214	0.786	0.5
The Trammps	N/A	0.136	0.864	N/A
The Subhumans	N/A	0.133	0.867	N/A
The Skatalites	N/A	0.317	0.683	N/A
THERION	0	0.275	0.725	1
The Mutton Birds	N/A	0.269	0.731	N/A
The Mission	N/A	0.324	0.676	N/A
The Mamas & The Papas	1	0.206	0.794	0
The Juan MacLean	N/A	0.324	0.676	N/A
Zee Avi	N/A	0.231	0.769	N/A
MNEMIC	1	0.043	0.957	0
Rod Lee	1	0.167	0.833	0
Colin Meloy	0.333	0.062	0.938	0.667

5.2 Automation Outlier Detection Result

The outlier detection algorithm was applied to the dataset, and the results obtained were analyzed to assess the performance of the method. The Table 1 summarizes the performance of the outlier detection for various artists in the dataset. **True Positive Rate (TPR)** and **False Positive Rate (FPR)** represent the proportion of outliers that were correctly and incorrectly identified as outliers, respectively. **True Negative Rate (TNR)** and **False Negative Rate (FNR)** represent the proportion of non-outliers that were correctly and incorrectly identified as non-outliers, respectively. **Not Applicable (N/A):** indicates no outliers being identified for a particular artist.

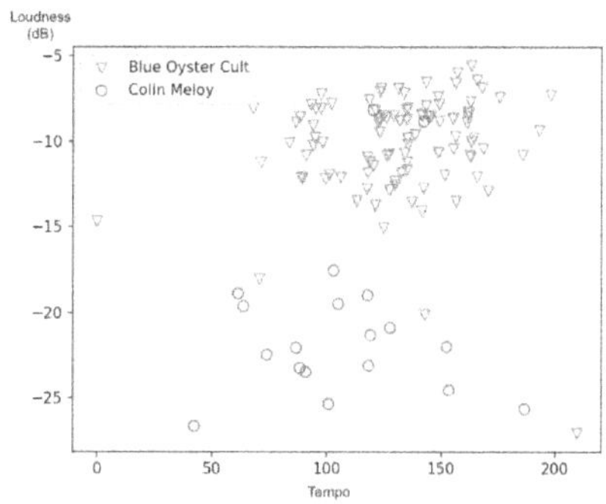

Fig. 4. Outlier Overlap: Shared characteristics between two artists' outliers.

6 Discussion

6.1 Outlier Categorisation

Genuine outliers are complete songs that adhere to an artist's typical musical structure but differ in sound and style. Often custom-made for specific events, they incorporate unique elements like distinct percussion. For instance, Colin Meloy's "Lazy Little Ada" is situated at the center of Blue Oyster Cult's cluster (Fig. 4), deviating from Meloy's usual style yet resembling Blue Oyster Cult's. In comparison, Meloy's cluster exhibits lower loudness, potentially due to less percussion. When percussion is added to Meloy's outliers, they show similarities to Blue Oyster Cult's cluster. Conversely, most of Blue Oyster Cult's songs form a well-defined cluster, but 4 outliers incorporate synthesizers and lack percussion, producing similarity to Meloy's cluster.

In contrast, non-genuine outliers can be categorized into four types: Error, Speech, Sound Effect, and Intro. 1) Error tracks result from feature extractor misinterpretations or exceptions, such as doubling tempo or missing audio features. 2) Speech is often used in albums for storytelling, setting narrative themes, or as interludes to create a narrative flow between musical pieces, e.g., Kendrick Lamar's "To Pimp a Butterfly." 3) Sound effects enhance the musical narrative, especially in concept albums like Pink Floyd's "The Trial." 4) Intros are short tracks that set the tone, introduce themes, or provide transitions between songs. However, these tracks do not follow typical musical structures (e.g., ABAB, ABAC), so we consider them non-genuine outliers.

6.2 Outlier Detection Result

The overall results of the outlier detection algorithm show that it is capable of identifying outliers in an artist's body of work. The algorithm performs exceptionally well on some artists by correctly classifying all outliers and non-outliers. However, varying performance among artists suggests the need for refining the algorithm with additional constraints. In summary, we can obtain these insights from the following results:

The consideration of distinctiveness in the algorithm has worked well on artists that primarily have one style, for example, Blue Oyster Cult, The Mamas & The Papas, and Wild Strawberries had a perfect TPR and TNR, indicating that the definition works well for this artist even without considering the constraints of whether it forms a complete song. Furthermore, we find the distinctiveness constraint effective in identifying genuine music outliers in some artists. For example, the algorithm isolated outliers in artists such as Blue Oyster Cult (TPR: 1.0, FPR: 0, TNR: 1, FNR: 0) and Warren Zevon (TPR: 1.0, FPR: 0.356, TNR: 0.644, FNR: 0).

However, the varied performances across different artists suggest that discarding the consideration of constraints 1. Forms A Complete Song and 2. Non-adherence may lead to the algorithm's inability to accurately determine whether an outlier is genuine, as it lacks the capacity to assess the music structure of input recordings. The reasons causing these varying performances can be summarized as follows:

Mixed Content: Recordings may contain various non-musical elements, including intros with predominantly speech content (e.g., "Rod Intro" by Rod Lee), live recordings featuring audience applause or speech interactions with the audience (e.g., "Dracula's Daughter" by Colin Meloy), or studio chats consisting solely of speech (e.g., "The Way I Feel Inside/Studio Chat" by The Zombies). These non-musical segments may introduce noise and impact the algorithm's performance.

Noise and Artifacts: The presence of noise, artifacts, or other non-musical elements within a recording might lead to it being classified as an outlier, even if it does not constitute a genuine outlier in terms of musical content. Such factors can interfere with the algorithm's capability to accurately assess a song's structure.

Transitional Pieces: Some artists release tracks with transition pieces containing sound effects or ambient sounds, which can be difficult for the algorithm to categorize as genuine outliers. Notable examples include "Catalepsy I" by Voivod and "The Audio Injection" by MNEMIC.

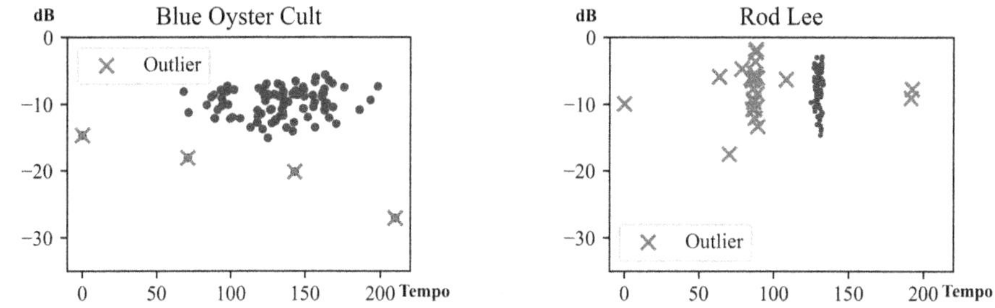

(a) Artist (Blue Oyster Cult)

(b) Artist (Rod Lee)

Fig. 5. Automatic Outlier Detection Using k-means: Demonstrating the algorithm works well on single-style artists (a) but fails for multi-style artists (b). (Color figure online)

6.3 Limitations and Future Work

Overall, the findings of this study highlight the importance of considering outliers and their potential impact on the audio characteristics of different genres and artists in music production. It suggests several avenues for future research, including:

Integration of more Music Features: Expanding the range of music features integrated into the algorithm can potentially improve its performance in detecting genuine outliers. The current features, such as loudness and tempo, may not fully capture the characteristics and the style of music. Therefore, incorporating additional features like timbre, harmony, and chroma could enhance the algorithm's effectiveness in distinguishing genuine outliers from the rest of an artist's work.

Consideration of "Forms a Complete Song" and "Non-adherence" constraints: Incorporating the "Forms A Complete Song" constraint ensures that the detected outliers are actual pieces of music. This guarantees that the outliers are indeed genuine musical outliers and not artifacts or other irrelevant audio content. The 'Non-Adherence' constraint ensures detected outliers distinctly deviate from an artist's typical musical structure. This helps to identify unique songs that stand out from an artist's typical style. Furthermore, music segmentation techniques can be considered to extract musical parts from audio pieces that may contain both speech and music. This will aid in ensuring the detected item actually is music.

Handling Artists with more than One Style: The current outlier detection approach may struggle with artists exhibiting multiple styles, such as Rod Lee (shown in fig.5). Addressing this limitation would result in a more representative understanding of an artist's work and improve the accuracy of outlier detection. One possible solution is to consider an artist's stylistic diversity when detecting outliers, thereby accounting for the various styles present within their body of work.

Exploration of Other Clustering Models: In this study, only the k-means clustering algorithm was considered for the clustering model. However, k-means is based on circular data, which can lead to suboptimal results. Exploring other clustering models that may better handle the complexities of music data could further enhance the performance of the outlier detection algorithm and yield more accurate results.

7 Conclusion

In conclusion, this study has proposed a definition for genuine music outliers and explored the application of an outlier detection algorithm in music genre datasets. The results have demonstrated that the consideration of distinctiveness is a reasonable starting point for detecting music outliers. However, the current approach lacks the ability to detect the music structure and struggles when handling artists with more than one style. To overcome these limitations, future work should focus on integrating more music features, such as timbre, harmony, and chroma, and considering the constraints of "Forms A Complete Song" and "Non-Adherence." Furthermore, music segmentation techniques should be explored to extract musical parts from audio pieces containing both speech and music. Handling artists with multiple styles and exploring alternative clustering models, such as those that can better accommodate non-circular data, are other avenues for improvement. By addressing these limitations and incorporating these suggestions, the proposed outlier detection approach can be further refined and made more robust for detecting genuine music outliers in diverse music genre datasets.

Acknowledgements. We would like to acknowledge the support received from Assoc. Prof. Sam Ferguson, In Addition, Le Cai wants to thank his partner Hanyu Meng for her unwavering patience and constant presence in his life.

References

1. Ankerst, M., Breunig, M.M., Kriegel, H.P., Sander, J.: Optics. ACM SIGMOD Rec. **28**(2), 49–60 (1999). https://doi.org/10.1145/304181.304187
2. Ariyaratne, H.B., Zhang, D.: A novel automatic hierachical approach to music genre classification. In: 2012 IEEE International Conference on Multimedia and Expo Workshops. IEEE (2012). https://doi.org/10.1109/icmew.2012.104
3. Arthur, D., Vassilvitskii, S.: How slow is the k-means method? In: Proceedings of the Twenty-Second Annual Symposium on Computational Geometry, SCG 2006, pp. 144–153. Association for Computing Machinery, New York (2006). https://doi.org/10.1145/1137856.1137880
4. Azcarraga, A., Flores, F.K.: A study on self-organizing maps and k-means clustering on a music genre dataset. In: Theory and Practice of Computation. World Scientific (2017). https://doi.org/10.1142/9789813234079_0017

5. Bello, J.P.: Measuring structural similarity in music. IEEE Trans. Audio Speech Lang. Process. **19**(7), 2013–2025 (2011). https://doi.org/10.1109/TASL.2011.2108287
6. Bertin-Mahieux, T., Ellis, D.P.W., Whitman, B., Lamere, P.: The million song dataset. In: International Society for Music Information Retrieval Conference (2011)
7. Bountouridis, D., Koops, H.V., Wiering, F., Veltkamp, R.C.: Music outlier detection using multiple sequence alignment and independent ensembles. In: Amsaleg, L., Houle, M.E., Schubert, E. (eds.) Similarity Search and Applications, pp. 286–300. Springer International Publishing, Cham (2016). https://doi.org/10.1007/978-3-319-46759-7_22
8. Dai, S., Yu, H., Dannenberg, R.B.: What is missing in deep music generation? a study of repetition and structure in popular music. In: What is missing in deep music generation? A study of repetition and structure in popular music. arXiv (2022). https://doi.org/10.48550/ARXIV.2209.00182
9. Deng, D.: Dbscan clustering algorithm based on density. In: 2020 7th International Forum on Electrical Engineering and Automation (IFEEA), pp. 949–953 (2020). https://doi.org/10.1109/IFEEA51475.2020.00199
10. Fathollahi, M.S., Razzazi, F.: Music similarity measurement and recommendation system using convolutional neural networks. Inter. J. Multimedia Inform. Retrieval **10**(1), 43–53 (2021). https://doi.org/10.1007/s13735-021-00206-5
11. Ghosal, S.S., Sarkar, I.: Novel approach to music genre classification using clustering augmented learning method (calm). In: AAAI Spring Symposium Combining Machine Learning with Knowledge Engineering (2020)
12. Hawkins, D.M.: Identification of Outliers. Springer Netherlands (1980). https://doi.org/10.1007/978-94-015-3994-4
13. Herskind Sejr, J., Christiansen, T., Dvinge, N., Hougesen, D., Schneider-Kamp, P., Zimek, A.: Outlier detection with explanations on music streaming data: a case study with danmark music group ltd. Appli. Sci. **11**(5) (2021). https://doi.org/10.3390/app11052270
14. Knees, P., Schedl, M.: A survey of music similarity and recommendation from music context data. ACM Trans. Multimed. Comput. Commun. Appl. **10**(1), 1–21 (2013). https://doi.org/10.1145/2542205.2542206
15. Lu, Y.C., Wu, C.W., Lerch, A., Lu, C.T.: Automatic outlier detection in music genre datasets. In: International Society for Music Information Retrieval Conference (2016)
16. Mehr, S.A., et al.: Universality and diversity in human song. Science **366**(6468) (2019). https://doi.org/10.1126/science.aax0868
17. Müller, M.: Fundamentals of music processing: audio, analysis, algorithms, applications. Springer International Publishing (2015). https://doi.org/10.1007/978-3-319-21945-5
18. Neubarth, K., Conklin, D.: Identification and description of outliers in the densmore collection of native american music. Appli. Sci. **9**(3) (2019). https://doi.org/10.3390/app9030552
19. Ng, R., Han, J.: Clarans: a method for clustering objects for spatial data mining. IEEE Trans. Knowl. Data Eng. **14**(5), 1003–1016 (2002). https://doi.org/10.1109/TKDE.2002.1033770
20. Panteli, M., Benetos, E., Dixon, S.: A computational study on outliers in world music. PLoS ONE **12**(12), e0189399 (2017). https://doi.org/10.1371/journal.pone.0189399

21. Paulus, J., Klapuri, A.: Music structure analysis by finding repeated parts. In: Proceedings of the 1st ACM Workshop on Audio and Music Computing Multimedia. ACM (Oct 2006). https://doi.org/10.1145/1178723.1178733
22. Sargent, G., Bimbot, F., Vincent, E.: A regularity-constrained Viterbi algorithm and its application to the structural segmentation of songs. In: International Society for Music Information Retrieval Conference (ISMIR), Miami, United States (Oct 2011)
23. Schedl, M., Gómez, E., Urbano, J.: Music information retrieval: recent developments and applications. Foundations Trends® Inform. Retrieval **8**(2-3), 127–261 (2014). https://doi.org/10.1561/1500000042
24. Shingte, G., d'Aquin, M.: Unsupervised learning approach for identifying subgenres in music scores. In: Irish Conference on Artificial Intelligence and Cognitive Science (2019)
25. Singh, R., Nakamura, E.: Dynamic cluster structure and predictive modelling of music creation style distributions. Royal Soc. Open Sci. **9**(11) (2022). https://doi.org/10.1098/rsos.220516
26. Smiti, A.: A critical overview of outlier detection methods. Comput. Sci. Rev. **38**, 100306 (Nov 2020). https://doi.org/10.1016/j.cosrev.2020.100306
27. Wang, J.C., Hung, Y.N., Smith, J.B.L.: To catch a chorus, verse, intro, or anything else: Analyzing a song with structural functions. In: ICASSP 2022 - 2022 IEEE International Conference on Acoustics, Speech and Signal Processing (ICASSP). IEEE (May 2022). https://doi.org/10.1109/icassp43922.2022.9747252
28. Zhang, L., Jiang, F.: Visualizing symbolic music via textualization: an empirical study on chinese traditional folk music. In: Mobile Multimedia Communications, pp. 647–662. Springer International Publishing (2021). https://doi.org/10.1007/978-3-030-89814-4_47

Audio Signal Processing and HCI in Music

Co-creation and Deep Listening Between Humans and Machines in a Telematic Workshop Environment

Rory Hoy(✉) and Doug Van Nort

DisPerSion Lab, York University, Toronto, Canada
{hoy,vannort}@yorku.ca
https://dispersionlab.org/

Abstract. This paper presents *dispersion.eLabOrate(D)*, a networked performance system which augments and supports Deep Listening workshop experiences through an environment that integrates human and machine collaboration. The sonic materials used for the machine voices are provided by the vocal activity of human participants, which are continually added to an audio corpus of past content for resynthesis. Each participant experiences their own spatial sonic reality within a shared virtual audio space, as relative placement to other collaborative sources provide a unique vantage point via an accompanying virtual acoustics system. Responses from public play sessions are analyzed using a grounded theory approach to report on salient qualitative data resulting from performances with the system.

Keywords: Telematic Performance · Networked Audio · Interactive Agents · Deep Listening

1 Introduction

Network-based communal activity and connection in the area of telematic music grew dramatically throughout the global COVID-19 pandemic [13], as musicians turned to software solutions in order to continue their regular performance sessions at a distance. During this period the DisPerSion Lab produced over 40 telematic performance events, involving more than 40 performers from around the world. Research and development in our current "post-pandemic" context continues to foster distributed musical practice and telepresence, for ourselves and many others, through various systems capable of low latency and high quality audio. One distinct performative practice that was impeded by the lack of in person events, both in our own local lab context and more broadly, was Deep Listening – described as "a practice that is intended to heighten and expand consciousness of sound in as many dimensions of awareness and attentional dynamics as humanly possible" [18], by its creator Pauline Oliveros. Public engagement with the typically in-person and group-based Deep Listening workshop events were therefore put on hold until restrictions had lightened.

S. Ystad et al. (Eds.): CMMR 2023, LNCS 15236, pp. 435–447, 2026.
https://doi.org/10.1007/978-3-032-02042-0_33

Continuing this trajectory of research-creation work conducted on telematic performance, Deep Listening practice and human/machine co-creation, the system outlined in this paper was developed to explore the results of augmenting a well-known Sonic Meditation-style [20] text piece by Oliveros from the Deep Listening literature called The Tuning Meditation. In particular, this augmentation introduces non-human agents directly performing alongside human participants. Entitled *dispersion.eLabOrate(D)*, this project is a conceptual reconstruction and extension of a previous system by the authors, entitled *dispersion.eLabOrate* [10] - with the updated name reflecting that the system, and the practice that it fosters, is now *(D)istributed.* Vocalizations made by human performers during this piece are captured in an audio corpus which is then used both as raw material for the synthesis of new tones by the machine agents, as well as functioning as their running memory of past sonic events. The population of agents is variable and each acts autonomously according to the score for The Tuning Meditation (which will be outlined in Sect. 2). While physically dispersed, players and machine agents are placed within a singular virtual acoustics space to be heard within the same environmental conditions.

One challenge for this project, something faced by most telematic-based performances, is the collapse of spatial qualities to a (typically) stereo mix of all performers. This flattens any variance in positioning of local sound sources one would find within an in-person event, which can provide contextual information or sonic material to react to. Systems that can support spatial representations of source placement typically orient sound to a particular "sweet-spot" in the centre of the virtual space, which all sources are placed relative to. For *dispersion.eLabOrate(D)*, we develop and present a spatial audio setup which allows for unique sonic perspectives tied to relative placement within the virtual acoustics environment.

Following the completion of the system, Deep Listening workshop sessions were held to gather qualitative feedback on various elements of the experience. These responses are presented and analyzed with a grounded theory approach in Sect. 5. Key categories of responses are discussed, which were found to focus on immersion and communal space, diversity of machine voices, and strategies for human/machine collaboration.

2 Related Work

Our previous work on augmenting Deep Listening practices emerged over the course of a 12-week DisPerSion Lab seminar that posed the question: "Can we imagine ways that interactive systems might synergize, entangle with, and augment - but not distract from - Deep Listening practice?" This resulted in our performance system *Dispersion.eLabOrate*, created for collective listening and sounding in a shared physical space. This system can detect and react to player vocalizations as well as ambient sound within an environment. Like this newer project, *eLabOrate* was designed to engage and augment group performances of The Tuning Meditation (TM), placing the output of the system as a machine agent which engages with the vocal and collaborative dynamics of the human participants. The TM asks participants to focus on their breath – inhale deeply, exhaling on a tone of their choice for one full breath. On the following exhalation, match a tone currently being sung by another player. Then on the next vocalization, sing a new tone that hasn't been sung yet. This cycle continues until a natural end point is reached where each player has stopped, and is depicted in (Fig. 1).

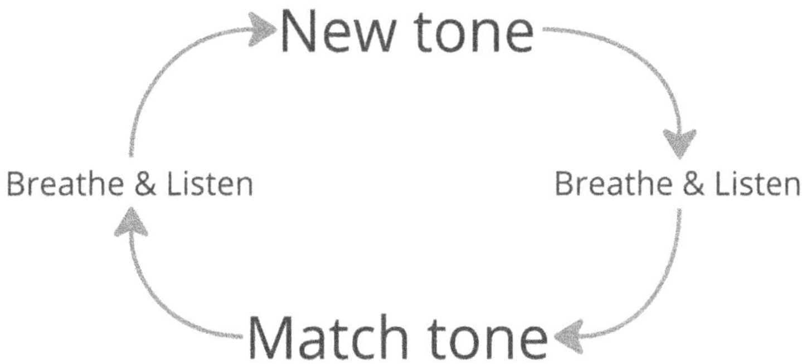

Fig. 1. Breathing and sounding cycle of participants for the Tuning Meditation from the practice of Deep Listening. Particpants alternate new and matching tones on each exhalation.

Building upon this past work, we once again begin from the position that the machine voice/participation is not an element which should conceptually or perceptually dominate the piece, but rather should work in tandem alongside human performers to facilitate broadened sonic potentials. We investigated the past system through the lens of "Sonic Ecosystems", foregrounding resonance, feedback, and autonomous behaviour inside/outside the direct influence of human action. Building upon related works in the field, Sonic Ecosystems are framed here as performative contexts – ones which establish environments that in turn adapt to agents, which define their own self-regulating populations and their own ambience. This ambience may be naturally-occurring within the acoustic space facilitating the system, or could be generated as a result of the sonic ecosystem's behaviour. These systems rely on self-monitoring techniques both virtually and physically, often including microphones or other sensing devices within the space in order to enact and react to these recurrent activity loops [6]. Musick (2016) [16] provides a thorough look at the theory and practice of the field within their Sonic Space Project, and includes assessment strategies of sonic ecosystems within their 2014 paper [15].

In addition to *eLabOrate*, another recent DisPerSion Lab project by Maraj and Van Nort [14] also focused on developing an agent-based system for interactive performance, building upon rules found in a Sonic Meditation-style piece. In this case the text piece "Interdependence" was used as a starting principle for structuring agent interaction, and the focus was on gestural performance with an interactive system rather than collective vocalization in a workshop setting. Both projects emerge from and sit at the intersection of two larger DisPerSion Lab projects that engage this broader area, entitled Deeply Listening Machines and Deep Listening Entanglements [7], both of which build upon past work on intersecting machine improvisation and Deep Listening principles [24].

3 System

eLabOrate(D) allows for more complex, refined, and flexible agent behaviour to that of its predecessor *eLabOrate*. Where *eLabOrate* created a pervasive and mirroring-like behaviour for all vocalizations and ambient sound, *eLabOrate(D)* more closely follows the cyclical behaviours of new tones, matching, and most importantly active listening as is requested within the context of The Tuning Meditation. A key concept discussed within the Deep Listening community of practice is the distinction between directed and focused active listening, as opposed to the passive physiological process of hearing [19]. The behaviour for each machine agent in the system enacts this active listening as opposed to the more passive and reflexive hearing and sounding which occurred in our past work. Situating this performance system as a telematic piece, we also investigate the viability of a remote virtual shared space as a facilitator for the characteristics and behaviour of sonic ecosystems.

In practice, the *eLabOrate(D)* system is comprised of modules to capture human signals and generate machine voices created in Max/MSP, which are detailed in the following subsections. These are instantiated at the beginning of a session, with an individual module for each human/machine participant being scripted once the total number of participants is selected. These modules allow captured and generated sound to be sent to an accompanying patch to be spatialized appropriately for each human participant. All participants (both human and machine) are placed in a circle within this virtual acoustics space, which is relevant for machine voice behaviour and will be outlined in Subsect. 3.2.

3.1 Audio Corpus - Sonic Memory

The audio corpus is implemented through the Mubu package [21] in Max, and is used within the system as a running memory of all vocalized tones. Input signals from human players are segmented into audio buffers based on detected onsets, with recording taking place until the signal falls below an established threshold. The system is limited to the last n (default 50) segmented tones in order to avoid memory & processing issues, but could be extended depending on the hardware capabilities of the host computer. This places the corpus as a short term memory of sonic events, as the oldest events are erased when a new buffer is saved to the corpus beyond the limit. Buffer input is held for a short time after vocalization ends, to allow machine voices the opportunity to match without the target voice being explicitly active. This behaviour is similar to human participants matching another tone briefly after a given vocalization has stopped, which happens often in practice. The buffer content is analyzed and segmented through Mubu and is made accessible within the corpus as separated grains.

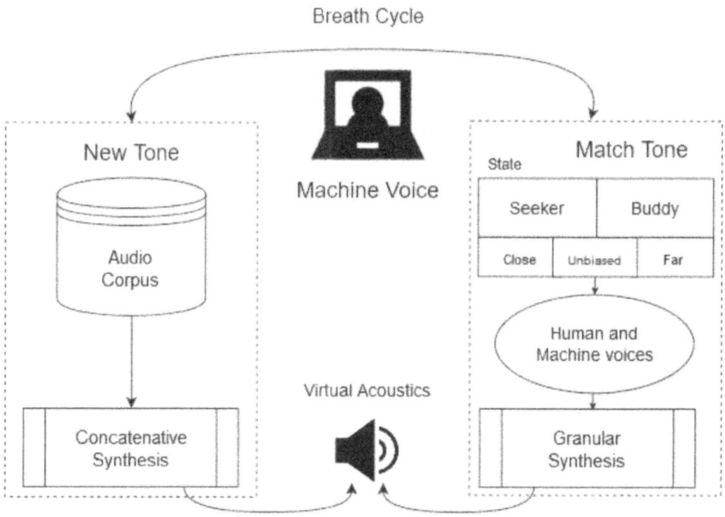

Fig. 2. Machine voice module depicting breath cycle alternating between both vocalization states and synthesis engines

3.2 Machine Module

Each machine module consists of separate logic sub-modules inside. Controlling the movement between matching and new tone behaviours is the breath control module, which mimics a range of human time scale breath cycles (Fig. 2). This approximation of human breath allows the machine agents a voicing and breathing alternation, so as to both avoid continuous output and to better align with the time scales present within a typical performance of the Tuning Meditation.

New tones are made up of grains from the collective audio corpus populated by human participant voices, scrubbed through and resynthesized using a concatenative synthesis [22] method within Mubu. A target frequency area is scrubbed to playback these grains as a continuous voice, with the resulting tone constituting a new voice comprised of grains from various participant sounds.

Machine voices are assigned one of 6 possible states upon instantiation, which define either their matching (Seeker or Buddy) or their spatial biasing (Close, Far, Unbiased) behaviours. Matched tones result from copying a desired target's current voice buffer content into the acting machine voice's buffer. This buffer is then played back with a granular synthesis method to mimic the held tone by another player (both human and machine). The *Seeker* state implements a spatial encoding neural net using ml.spatial [5] to keep track of recently-matched participants. A recent match of a participant would mean that on the next match behaviour, they become the least likely to be chosen. The *Buddy* state chooses a small subset of the total population to use as potential matching targets. A spatial bias of near/far/unbiased for both *Seeker* and *Buddy* skews the likelihood to match a specific subgroup based on angular proximity within the established virtual circle. Participants within a ± 90° degree arc from a given voice or less are deemed "close", while beyond this places a voice as "far". Through these added logic modules, the system possesses possible "listening behaviours" that are above and beyond the basic instructions of the TM piece, thereby providing differing kinds of performative identities for each machine voice.

3.3 Human Module

Human participants are connected to the system and to one another by utilizing JackTrip [1], a software tool for low latency and high quality audio. Depending on the microphone setup of each participant, acoustic characteristics of each player's environment may be sent along with their vocal input allowing for a perceived commingling of ambient sounds within the virtual acoustics space. These various local sonic realities are relayed along with one's intended vocal utterance of a new tone or matched tone, and may therefore become sonic material that a machine voice may pull from to generate its own new tone. In this way, the expanded sense of shared acoustic environments remains present as a point of focus during these sessions - in the spirit of Deep Listening practice that emphases attention to one's sonic environment. These vocalizations can be conceived of as "the performer-instrument articulation", theorized by Waters as

> "[...]result[ing] not only from the physiology of the player, but also from the complex feedback into that player's body of vibrating materials, air, room, and the physiological adaptations and adjustments in that body and its 'software' which themselves feed back into the vibrating complex of instrument and room." [25]

This feedback is additionally facilitated by the networked nature of the system, and in the individual behaviours of each machine voices. Resynthesis of vocal material of participants continually shapes the timbral range of the machine voice, and in turn has influence over the potential tones a human participant may match through the score. This also comes about through the matching behaviour of the machine voices, as they are able to copy another vocalizing machine.

3.4 Multi-spat Virtual - Acoustics

All output is processed and positioned spatially within an accompanying multi-listener spatialization patch developed for this system. Audio from each human

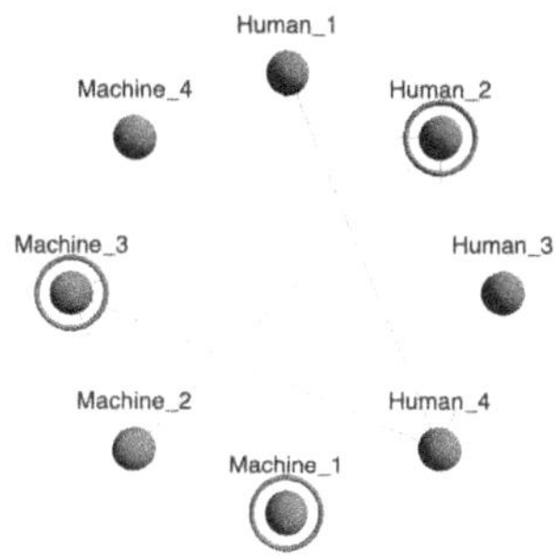

Fig. 3. Layout of human and machine voices (top-down) within the accompanying virtual acoustics space. Lines denote matching behaviour and rings denote new tones being vocalized.

and machine participant is placed at a corresponding source location distributed evenly in a circular pattern around the virtual space. Relative spatial listening mixes are achieved through separate instances of IRCAM's Spat 5 [2], with one virtual space model per human player. In practice, this allows a hypothetical listener 2 to be placed to the left of listener 1, and be heard from that direction by listener 1. The same is true for listener 2; their relative position to 1 would perceptually place listener 1 to their right. Each instance of Spat is run using a binaural panning mode for a stereo output, as headphone based monitoring is encouraged for the performance. Two virtual audio drivers [9,12] are employed to allow for routing to and from JackTrip for each participant and allows a separate and accurate binaural mix to be passed individually back to players in relation to their virtual orientation. An accompanying visual layout of the spatial positions and behaviour of each participant can be displayed to depict current activity of sources (Fig. 3). New tones are depicted as rings around a given source, and matching behaviours point to the target source a voice is matching.

4 Study/Play Sessions

Telematic Deep Listening workshop sessions were held with various sized groups of players in order to explore multiple factors of engaging with machine agents in this setting. The sessions were facilitated by the second author, a certified Deep Listening instructor, and placed focus on performance of the Tuning Meditation in the context of also drawing attention to the shared sonic environment, one's local environment, one's body and to inner listening - all common elements of a Deep Listening workshop session.

Participants were invited through calls sent out to online email lists and social media groups focused on computer music, Deep Listening, sound art/studies and listening more broadly. Based on scheduling alignments, we arrived at 8 total participants who connected from disparate locations in North America and Europe. Multiple sessions were held, which included an equal number of human and machine players at a given time (e.g. 4 human players, 4 machine players in one session). Sessions were an hour in length and included two different performances of the TM, each with a different active state for the machine voices. States were decided randomly (without duplicates) in order to have at least one response to each of the varied matching behaviours across all of the sessions. To recap, these states include:

- Far Seeker, Close Seeker, Non-biased Seeker
- Far Buddy, Close Buddy, Non-biased Buddy

These states introduce a bias towards spatial positioning of participants (far, close, unbiased), and a matching behaviour (Seeker or Buddy) which alters how the machine voices attempt to match another vocalizing participant.

Participants were not primed on several factors of the experience, as we were interested in gathering undirected qualitative data for analysis using a grounded theory approach. Grounded theory is a qualitative methodology aimed at uncovering key information from responses and allowing for central themes to emerge via multiple stages of coding - extracting relevant data and ultimately "Crystallizing the significance of the points" [3]. Our grounded theory-based approach for this study consisted of separate open coding steps each done individually by both authors. After this initial coding pass, cross-checking of codes occurred followed by focused coding - creating larger categories of responses that were synthesized from the resulting codes and will be presented in the following section.

After engaging in two runs of the meditation, players were invited to complete an online form in the (approximately) fifteen minutes remaining within their given session. The questions were designed to allow for open reporting on the experience with the goal of allowing key areas of personal interest and thought processes to come to the forefront. That said, once the session was completed it was clear to participants that there were both human and machine voices present, and so we explicitly asked about the experience relative to these distinct entities. The questions provided were as follows:

1. What are your general thoughts about the session?
2. How would you characterize the various voices (both human and machine)?
3. Could you compare and contrast your experience of the two (human/machine)?
4. What was your strategy for following the TM piece?
5. Could you characterize your relationship to space and describe if (and how) it might have influenced your experience?

To clarify demographic and background information, we also asked participants if they had any previous experience with Deep Listening as a practice, and if they had ever performed The Tuning Meditation.

5 Analysis

Three key categories of focus emerged through our process of coding participant responses and subsequent analysis, which we will discuss in the following subsections.

5.1 Experience of Immersion in a Shared Communal Space

A recurring theme that was prevalent throughout participant responses was a sense of immersion, with this being tied to a characterization of the session as a shared communal space. "I lost all sense of my local space. With eyes closed I was entirely in a shared space with everyone. I forgot we were not physically together", noted one participant with an extensive background in Deep Listening practices. As one might expect, specific mention of the term "sonic ecosystems" was not present in responses, however those characteristics we previously identified as belonging to sonic ecosystems were indeed reported, with one player explicitly noting "I noticed a bit of a back and forth between being influenced by the machines and the other humans in the session". In response to a subsequent question, they evoked metaphors of physical ecosystems:

> "I was visualizing the sound itself a lot more. I felt like I was contributing to a moving stream. I didn't know how loud I was, and so it felt like I was occasionally throwing a bucket of dyed water into the stream as the water flowed by, changing it in ways I wasn't aware of."

This ambiguity of outcome also gestures to the lack of direct control over the system. While each performer is an active participant in seeding the amalgamated voices generated by the audio corpus, there is a blurring of causal human action to machine reaction. This is congruent with the concept of a "floating phenomena/floating piece of art" from Weibel & Dinkla, described by Dixon as "[...] no longer the expression of a single individual. Neither is it the expression of a collective, but it is the state of a 'connective' - a web of influences that are continually reorganized by all participants." [8] This is further emphasized by another participant, in commenting on the influence that the space had on their interaction with others:

> "The relationship with space was expansive, I was travelling across the space to meet the tones. It highly influenced my experience particularly in the second tuning. I was able to go with more ease and pleasure, as the space expanded for me, on the possible tones and voices to tune in."

These performer statements, representative of the broader viewpoints expressed, depict experience within the session as taking part within a shared space which affected their perception of the inter-relational action present within the Tuning Meditation.

5.2 Diversity of Machine Voices Expanding Timbral Content of Meditation

The sense of a diversity of voices from machine agents was reported, and this was characterized as allowing for extended timbral content beyond the human. One participant stated: "[...] it was a great experience to listen to both human and machine voices and respond to them in real time, reflecting my own impression on them. Analyzing various notes of multiple voices was not an easy task but I enjoyed finding atonal harmony in inharmonious sounds." Similarly, conception of collective space was also addressed via perception of the machine voice character, as one participant articulated: "The expansion of tones was really helping me to expand my sense of space and time, and my connection with others, and with my body tuning in." This reinforces sentiment from the previous subsection (5.1) while here being expressed in relation to the "expansion of tones" offered by the machine voices.

One participant characterized the voices taking part within the piece as "diverse, some calmer than others. Most of them steady, but some evolving and agile", which highlights the varied approaches that both human and machine voices took in either matching or new tone vocalizations. Another participant expressed that the character of the machine voices was "[...] radical, refined, with a different atmosphere, pleasant too in a different way." These statements cause us to question if this evolutionary/radical character was a product of the cyclical matching behaviours that are capable within the system, depending on the nature of the machine voices' behavioural states. As one voice matches another, a chain-like effect can occur between both human and machine players that either match that same voice, or a voice that is already matching another (visible in Fig. 3). Once established, this type of chain may build upon and subtly (or not so subtlety) alter the timbres at play and seed new material into the audio corpus which defines the machine voices. If and when this is established, such diversity and "refined" nature of the machine voices may also be a direct result of the concatenative synthesis technique used to derive the new machine tones via the "raw material" of the captured player's voices.

In this complex human/machine network we can only speculate on the specific causalities - though we do note the above as affordances of the *eLabOrate(D)* system that we know to be at play in establishing a sense of evolution and refinement over time. What we can say with more certainty however, is that the machine voices were characterized as diverse, refined and evolving, both in terms of their timbral character and in their behaviours of interaction. This was articulated as a central influence in moving the dynamics of human attention forward in time.

5.3 Reflexive Engagement with Machine Voices and Influence Upon Performance Strategies

An openness towards the involvement of the machine agents was clear in the previously-mentioned responses. For some participants, the overall experience was that all audio was collapsed into a cohesive sounding body: "At a few points, I couldn't tell which were human and which were not."

When they are clearly recognized, the incorporation of accompanying machine agents introduces such Deep Listening sessions to sonic material and gestures which would not occur within a human-only performance. It was reported by some participants that this coaxed out playful transgressions upon the score itself, with one player noting: "I tried to make sound[s] that were machine-like myself. I tried to 'chop' my voice, by tapping my cheek or throat, as I was influenced by the other sounds that were made." Such transgressions certainly can (and do) come about in general during pieces such as the TM by participants who would like to push the limits of what constitutes a held tone, a pitched sound, etc. – and this is an important aspect of the social dynamics of this and similar pieces. Through the interjected behaviours of the machine voices, new timbral and rhythmic components are often introduced into the palette of materials which participants are engaging with. This added dimension of uncertainty and dynamism from this hybrid context is captured by Waters, who states "One of the benefits of hybrid (physical/virtual) systems is their very impurity: their propensity to suggest or afford rich unforeseen behaviours which engage the player (and the listener) at a variety of levels: sonic, tactile, and dynamic." [25].

For some respondents, the incorporation of machine voices changed the conception of their own voice in relation to others. One participant stated, "The machine tones bring a strength from me, fearless voicing. The human voices invite me to listen more, and to engage with care for them, trying to explore the soft voices I haven't listen[ed] to yet." In contrasting human and machine contributions (Q3), another respondent expressed, "The human is easier to follow accurately, the machine leaves more room for interpretation of the note and timbre (which I enjoyed!)", further relating these characteristics to one's own strategy for realization of the score's instructions.

6 Conclusion and Future Work

We have presented our system *dispersion.eLabOrate(D)*, a set of telematic autonomous participants who engage the Tuning Meditation in the context of a Deep Listening workshop setting. An overview of our previous research and a system overview were presented, providing context and structure for relating the design of the system to a set of broader reflections, which were informed by a set of qualitative data that emerged from a series of workshop sessions with the system. Through these sessions, we investigated the potentials for augmenting group Deep Listening practices in a telematic setting via machine participation, and presented an accompanying virtual acoustics system allowing for unique sonic vantage points into the collective virtual performance space.

Responses to play sessions were approached and processed through a grounded theory methodology to parse out key "codes" and broader themes, resulting in the three salient response categories outlined in Sect. 5. These revealed a sense of immersion that was tied to "space", understood as dual conception that was both social and sonic, a sense of evolving diversity that was carried forward by awareness of machine actors, and a set of strategies that articulated human responses towards positioning themselves within this sonic-communal engagement.

In future work, we will look to further explore and assess these perceived dimensions in this Deep Listening performative context, iterating our design (both computational and workshop structure) in light of what we've learned this far. This includes an examination of the concepts of immersion intensity [4] & presence [23]). From a design perspective, future considerations include new and varied implementations of virtual acoustic parameters, and expanding timbral possibilities concerning voices of the machine agents. Both realistic representations of in-person performance spaces and extended potentials for virtual space (physically impossible listening orientations, source positions, room qualities, etc.) offer new potentials for facilitating Deep Listening practices. This virtualized potential for Deep Listening practice is a key component of the *eLab-Orate(D)* project in particular.

More broadly, this work contributes to the larger Deeply Listening Machines and Deep Listening Entanglements lab projects. These sister projects seek to transform and augment the kinds of listening and sounding practices found within the Deep Listening literature, such as that expressed by the Tuning Meditation (or Interdependence, in the case of Intergestura). These existing text scores act as starting points - seed ideas - for an evolving set of structured approaches to collective listening and sounding, both in public workshop and improvised performance settings. Each system such as *eLabOrate(D)* is part of this ecosystem of human/machine engagement in a Deep Listening context. Thus future work for this system is focused on diversity of approaches, such as exploring different methods for machine voice synthesis based on sound analysis and machine learning from human vocal inputs, and on modularity such that these particular machine voices might evolve new listening/sounding rules, and interact with other agents that emerge from the larger project.

References

1. Cáceres, J., Chafe, C.: JackTrip: under the hood of an engine for network audio. J. New Music Res. **39**(3), 183–187 (2010). https://doi.org/10.1080/09298215.2010.481361
2. Carpentier, T.: A new implementation of spat in max. In: 15th Sound and Music Computing Conference (SMC2018), pp. 184–191 (2018). https://hal.science/hal-02094499
3. Charmaz, K.: Constructing Grounded Theory. Sage Publications, Thousand Oaks, Calif (2006)
4. Colsman, A., Aspã., L.: Development of a questionnaire to investigate immersion of virtual acoustic environments. In: DAGA, Aachen, Germany (2016)
5. Day Smith, B.: Ml.* - Machine Learning Toolkit in Max (2017). https://www.benjamindaysmith.com/ml-machine-learning-toolkit-in-max
6. Scipio, A.: Sound is the interface: from interactive to ecosystemic signal processing. Organised Sound **8**, 269–277 (2003). https://doi.org/10.1017/S1355771803000244
7. DisPerSion Lab.: DisPerSion Lab Research Areas (2023). https://dispersionlab.org/research/
8. Dixon, S.: Digital Performance : A History of New Media in Theater, Dance, Performance Art, and Installation. The MIT Press, Cambridge (2007). http://archive.org/details/digitalperforman0000dixo.561

9. ExistentialAudio: BlackHole. C (2019). https://github.com/ExistentialAudio/BlackHole
10. Hoy, R., Nort, D.: Augmentation of sonic meditation practices: resonance, feedback and interaction through an ecosystemic approach. In: Kronland-Martinet, R., Ystad, S., Aramaki, M. (eds.) CMMR 2019. LNCS, vol. 12631, pp. 591–599. Springer, Cham (2021). https://doi.org/10.1007/978-3-030-70210-6_38
11. Hoy, R., Van Nort, D.: A technological and methodological ecosystem for dynamic virtual acoustics in telematic performance contexts. In: Audio Mostly 2021, virtual/Trento Italy, pp. 169—74 (2021). https://doi.org/10.1145/3478384.3478425
12. Ingalls, M.: SoundFlower. Objective-C (2014). https://github.com/mattingalls/Soundflower
13. Keller, D., Costalonga, L., Messina, M.: Editorial: ubiquitous music making in COVID-19 times. In: Proceedings of the 10th Workshop on Ubiquitous Music (UbiMus 2020) (2020). https://halshs.archives-ouvertes.fr/halshs-03035034
14. Maraj, K., Van Nort, D.: Intergestura: a gestural agent based on sonic meditation practices. In: 13th International Conference on Computational Creativity, Bozen-Bolzano, Italy (2022)
15. Musick, M.: Examining the analysis of dynamical sonic ecosystems: in light of a criterion for evaluating theories. In: ICMC 2014, Athens, Greece, pp. 154–161 (2014)
16. Musick, M.: Practice-Led Research / Research-Led Practice Identifying the Theory and Technique of Sonic Space Ecosystems. Ph.D., New York University (2016). https://www.proquest.com/docview/1871306234/abstract/9000417E723B4A90PQ/1
17. Neidhardt, A., Schneiderwind, C., and Klein, F.: Perceptual matching of room acoustics for auditory augmented reality in small rooms - literature review and theoretical framework. Trends in Hearing **26**, 233121652210929 (2022). https://doi.org/10.1177/23312165221092919
18. Oliveros, P.: Deep Listening: A Composer's Sound Practice. iUniverse, Lincoln (2005)
19. Oliveros, P.: Quantum listening: From Practice to Theory (to practice practice). Culture and Humanity in the New Millennium: The Future of Human Values, pp. 27–41 (2002)
20. Oliveros, P.: Sonic Meditations. Smith Publications, Baltimore, MD (1974)
21. Schnell, N., Röbel, A., Schwarz, D., Peeters, G., Borghesi, R.: MuBu & friends - assembling tools for content based real-time interactive audio processing in Max/MSP. In: ICMC 2009, Montreal, Canada, pp. 423–426 (2009)
22. Schwarz, D.: Corpus-based concatenative synthesis. IEEE Signal Process. Mag. **24**(2), 92–104 (2007)
23. Støckert, R., Bergsland, A., Xambó, A.: The notion of presence in a telematic cross-disciplinary program for music, communication and technology. In Music Technology in Education, pp. 77—101. Cappelen Damm Akademisk/NOASP (2020). https://doi.org/10.23865/noasp.108.ch3
24. Nort, D., Pauline, O., Braasch, J.: Electro/acoustic improvisation and deeply listening machines. J. New Music Res. **42**(4), 303–324 (2013). https://doi.org/10.1080/09298215.2013.860465
25. Waters, S.: Touching at a distance: resistance, tactility, proxemics and the development of a hybrid virtual/physical performance system. Contemporary Music Rev. **32**(2–03), 119–134 (2013)

Estimating Interaction Time in Music Notation Editors

Matthias Nowakowski[1(✉)] and Aristotelis Hadjakos[2]

[1] KreativInstitutOWL (KIO), University Paderborn, Paderborn, Germany
matthias.nowakowski@uni-paderborn.de

[2] Center for Music and Film Informatics (CeMFI), University of Music Detmold, Detmold, Germany

Abstract. Modern music notation software is extensive and so can be a comparative analysis. Since they employ a lot of different interactions to write scores, due to the mass of different symbols and their combinations, we developed a method to estimate the time spent by the user in interacting with the software interface in order to perform fundamental operations. For this we applied and extended the Keystroke-Level Model by analyzing interaction percentages in MusicXML files. Our findings contribute to modeling interaction and usability/ user experience research about interaction in music notation editors. These findings can be then transferred to analyze other editors and we expect to use the method in formative analyses to reduce user studies and thus development time in the long run.

Keywords: Human Computer Interaction · Music Notation Editor · Keystroke Level Model

1 Introduction

Score editors allow users to create, edit and play musical scores. They are widely used by composers, musicians, teachers and students for various purposes, such as composing music, arranging songs, transcribing audio, or learning music theory. However, developing score editor interfaces with good usability and user experience is hard. User interface design is a complex task in general, as evidenced by the documents of the extensive ISO standard 9421 [3], which provides various guidelines for interface design. In the context of score editors, it is necessary to identify the needs and context of use for the score editors, to specify the design criteria as well as functional and non-functional requirements, to produce design solutions, create prototypes and test them with users or experts. Implement the design solutions and evaluate the use of the score editors in real or simulated situations.

Another important challenge is media specificity by which we mean the purpose for which a software is created and by which means the (editable) medium can be accessed. For example, a word processor is created for the purpose of writing and editing text documents. In the case of text editing, consensual interactions and modalities with mouse and keyboard were established which are based on the metaphor of the type

S. Ystad et al. (Eds.): CMMR 2023, LNCS 15236, pp. 448–460, 2026.
https://doi.org/10.1007/978-3-032-02042-0_34

writer. These interactions are familiar and so feel intuitive to most users. Transferring the input modality to another medium—namely sheet music, music creation and music editing in general—may cause conceptual dissonance simply because of mismatch of input and output symbols and gestures. This means that users may find more difficult to match interactions that rely on a text-based keyboard to interact with musical symbols. In lack of consensual metaphors, it is symptomatic that widely used notation editors such as Sibelius, MuseScore, Dorico and Finale often employ vastly different interaction paradigms combining mouse and keyboard interaction in idiosyncratic ways. We could already show that standard questionnaires yield mostly low ratings for usability and user experience [16]. Moreover, we found in that study that most users used the score editors mainly for practical purposes and tend not to require features that are specifically supporting the creative process.

By visualizing a distribution profile of task-specific interaction times, we can gain insight into how long different tasks take and which ones are particularly time-consuming. With this approach we analyze six widely used score editors as well of our web-based score editor for Learning Management Systems, which uses the Verovio[1] engraving packet to render musical scores.

2 Related Work

To our knowledge there is no systematic and comparative work which deals with usability and user experience of notation editors. Nevertheless, Human Computer Interaction (HCI) is a prevalent topic in music research especially in the context of New Instruments for Musical Expression (NIME) [7] and Education [19]. Dealing with music production specifically Nash et al. [13–15] were interested in the creative involvement of the user with trackers and sequencers based on the concepts of Cognitive Dimensions [8] and Flow [6]. Although score editors are not explicitly analyzed they employ the same feedback loops as trackers, albeit by using different symbols. Based on this we also applied these metrics to analyze characteristics of usage of different score editors and isolate significant items by which they can be best described and most efficiently assessed [16]. Peterson et al. [17] approached the quality of creative outcome in digital media and on paper respectively by measuring interaction times.

A good starting point to research interaction times in general is to refer to the earliest of HCI research relating to text editors which can be adjusted and applied to music notation editors which we could view as text editors with special requirements. First wave HCI methodology in the 1980s was concentrated on operations which could be modeled as simple reactions in order to operate a system, ignoring such factors as emotions or the personality of the user. Card et al. [4] introduced the Keystroke-Level model which was intended to model expert user interactions with text editing software on a low level, consisting of operations such as "Keystroke", "Button Press" and "Pointing". However, mental operations were also introduced and with higher complexity of software core tasks had to be defined [20] to focus on the most relevant interactions, i.e. tasks which every software with the same purpose should have it implemented. We will discuss how we defined these operators and core tasks for our research in Sect. 3.

[1] https://www.verovio.org/index.xhtml.

In contrast to this, the GOMS (Goals, Operators, Methods, Selection rules) Model tries to explain a users behavior from a top-down perspective. It takes the actual goal of the action into account and fragments it into the actions that have to be taken to accomplish it [5]. This is useful in analyzing the procedural knowledge users and why they might use a certain interaction path. It is also useful to model new tasks around the given goals, since it is not based on an existing system [11].

Today the Keystroke-Level model remains a viable tool for fundamental research with new input modalities and situations, e.g. with touch screens [1, 10], in virtual reality [9], device interaction while driving [18] or exploring interactions with non-western writing systems [12]. Of course, the list of operators was adapted, where necessary to accommodate for new input devices and gestures [2].

3 Method

3.1 Program Selection

To decide for which music notation editors to compare we referenced to a previously conducted study in which we analyzed the most used ones [16]. From the 29 mentioned programs six were viable for statistical analysis, being Capella, MuseScore, Dorico, Finale, Sibelius and Lilypond. For the paper at hand we were not able to make a KLM analysis for Lilypond, since it is entirely text based and cannot be adequately compared to graphical user interfaces (GUI) we implicitly had in mind for the study. Since MuseScore had a major update during the preparation of the data, we also decided to integrate the KLM of MuseScore Versions 3 and 4, giving us the opportunity to discuss recent changes in their interaction design.

3.2 Data Collection and Evaluation

First we agreed on a set of unit tasks, meaning any atomic tasks that can be accomplished with a music notation editor. Encoding these tasks then was then performed by three people according to Card et al. [4]. We did not expect the encoders to know every program, but they must have worked with music score editors in the past. We are aware that each encoder might have more experience with a certain program and to ensure an average view on the multiple interaction paths we have taken the following measures:

- Multiple people explored each software for the same unit task. This accounts for different ways to solve a task in the case the software has different paths.
- Encodings were taken for different modalities, i.e. major keyboard and major mouse use respectively. This represents people with different ways of working. Although many people might prefer a mix of both, we have a potential range and a basis to interpolate between those values.
- The resulting times of all encoders were averaged for each software and modality.

The KLM provides encodings and already fixed times for series of actions (operators) as "methods" that are necessary to perform a certain task. The operators can be mental preparation (M), keystroke (K), button click (B), homing (H), pointing (P) and selecting from a pull down menu (pd) in different combinations which are empirically determined and applied in our study. The encoders worked on their own computers. We regard the variability of screen sizes as negligible, since the KLM already provides times which are insensitive to this factor.

We also aim to incorporate actions involving multiple inputs that lead to valid changes in the score, such as composing compound elements like tempi or chords. To achieve this, in the following section we calculated average sequence lengths, which we utilized as factors for encoding interaction methods.

As we cannot anticipate every potential context in which a task might arise, the encoding process may result in tasks being coded with slightly slower execution times than they would exhibit in actual scenarios. For instance, consider the scenario where a specific palette must be accessed before adding an articulation, and typically, the palette remains open when multiple articulations are added in sequence. However, in our encoding approach, the act of opening the palette is always included. Consequently, it's important to acknowledge a margin of error, which could extend up to 20% according to previous research [4].

3.3 Task Selection

KLM describes existing systems on a single level by taking inventory of interaction durations and so making tasks comparable between systems. Since not all tasks are used with equal frequency, we decided to perform four steps that helped us to access interaction times for relevant tasks:

1. Define all unit tasks that are found in at least one music notation editor.
2. Analyze MusicXML data to find frequencies of all elements that result from interactions.
3. Apply the frequencies from step 2 as weights to compute distributions for all unit tasks.
4. Filter unit tasks with the help of step 2 that account for 95% of interactions. Include interactions that are necessary to write a valid music score to get a more manageable number of tasks to discuss. All these tasks we will be denoted as "core tasks".

In total we defined 234 unit tasks first. These are actions that lead to a visual and/or sound change in the GUI (including score and menus). This effectively filters out all subordinate system interactions which only indirectly contribute in visual outcome. Unit tasks do not have to be solely tasks that change sound events such as notes, chords or articulations. This can be annotations of every kind, as well as lyrics, but also the act of selecting elements, since they add highlighting to the score, and playing the music which adds automatic highlighting to the currently sounding events.

According to Roberts et al. [20] core tasks consist of a cross product of the following operations and objects as seen in Table 1. We had to do some accommodations for musical syntax, since some operations like "transpose" have different meanings in music. We also omitted "swapping", "splitting" and "merging" for which we found no scenarios in the described GUIs. Also the number of objects is much larger than in linguistic text, so that we had to group symbols in a similar hierarchical manner (Table 2).

Table 1. Operations and objects according to [20].

Operations	*Objects*
insert delete replace move copy transpose (≈ swap) split merge	character word line sentence paragraph section

Table 2. Adjusted operations and objects for music notation editors.

Operations	*Objects*
add delete replace move/displace rebind copy paste	primitives (notes, rests, lines, clefs, marks, etc.) diacritic signs (beams, articulations, ornaments, etc.) compounds (chord, measures, key signatures, tempo, etc.) semantic structures (parts, voices, lyrics, annotations, etc.)

Some operations are only applicable to some objects such as transposing can only be applied to chords and notes while rebinding (bind an anchor to a new event and so making also a change in the synthesized sound) is mostly associated with elements which modify the sound on larger time scales such as crescendo/ decrescendo, tempi, slurs, dynamics, etc.

To get a more concise view of the frequencies of occurrence of all elements we analyzed freely available MusicXML files by simply counting the elements and mapping them to their corresponding tasks. We also counted sequences of inputs to account for unit tasks that require multiple consecutive inputs, like writing a sequence of notes with the same duration, writing a chord, writing chord symbols or textual tempo instructions. For durations this value lies at 1.4, word length is 5.7 on average. The mean of all found sequences in the analyzed pieces is 3.6 which we will use as a multiplier to compute individual task related times.

As a base for our model we took four pieces from different time periods, with different instrumentation to cover a wide range of quantities of used symbols:

- Johann Sebastian Bach: Orchestral Suite in D Major (BWV 1068)
  20897 elements

- Wolfgang Amadeus Mozart: Clarinet Concerto in A Major (KV 622)
  81844 elements
- Frédéric Chopin: Three Waltzes (Op. 64)
  13209 elements
- Frederik Pfohl: Symphonic Phantasy for great Orchestra *The Sea*, Movement 5 *Frisian Rhapsody* (PWV 24)
  92519 elements
- Gabriel Fauré: Piano Quintet No. 2 (Op. 115)
  75591 elements

Table 3 shows the most used elements in the MusicXML that account for ≈ 95% of interaction according to the weighted means. These percentages are representing the weights which we will apply to the tasks resulting in the distribution in Fig. 1.

In the table "type" is referring to the symbolic duration (quarter, 16th, etc.), which by itself accounts for 35.72% of interactions in a notation program, followed by pitch with 29.25%. Slurs and articulations are child elements of "notations" element and can include further symbols that modify the note such as ornaments, arepeggios etc. "Dot" represents the prolongation of a note.

We decided to base our evaluation on the weighted mean, since we have wide differences in element numbers per piece. By this we assume that the selected pieces are somewhat representative for scores produced for music of this period.

The ranks of the elements for each piece follow the ranks of th arithmetic and the weighted mean in general. The arthmetic mean has some shifted numbers, only the ranks for "slur" and "accidentals" are swapped. Higher shares of accidentals are found for Chopin, Fauré and Pfohl, whose pieces may include extended harmonic development which can likely occur in 19th century pieces. Rests have higher percentages in the large orchestra pieces (Mozart and Pfohl), where entire instruments could stop playing for long times which results in a relatively high standard deviation of 4.8%.

However, these elements do not encompass the entirety of essential functionalities found in music notation editors. The editor must include specific features for initializing and managing information necessary for reading and playing from a score, as these aspects are imperative for its validity. We have meticulously selected these features and refer to them as "essential tasks". Table 4 summarizes the number of relevant tasks over

Table 3. Percentages of MusicXML elements that are found in all of the analyzed pieces and account for ≈ 95 % of the interaction with the score. sd = standard deviation, mad = mean absolute deviation, wt ... = weighted ...

element name	BWV 1068	Chopin Op.64	Fauré Op.115	PWV 24 (Mvt 5)	KV 622	mean	sd	mad	wt mean	wt sd	wt mad
type (= symbolic duration)	38.98	41.24	34.01	34.54	36.92	37.14	3.03	3.52	35.72	1.96	1.77
pitch	33.88	39.44	29.76	27.49	27.94	31.70	5.01	3.37	29.25	2.83	1.20
rest	5.10	2.03	5.68	13.20	11.98	7.60	4.78	5.42	9.73	3.75	3.74
beam	14.16	2.99	7.06	1.63	7.32	6.63	4.89	6.03	5.70	3.50	3.41
slur	0.58	2.94	5.16	4.72	5.48	3.78	2.04	1.12	4.67	1.27	0.51
accidental	1.38	5.65	7.93	2.82	2.39	4.04	2.69	2.13	4.08	2.44	0.83
articulations	0.22	0.11	0.99	8.06	3.73	2.62	3.37	1.30	3.98	3.09	4.15
dot (= prolongation)	2.94	0.91	3.22	2.86	1.92	2.37	0.95	0.52	2.60	0.63	0.44

the 12 most central unit task areas according to the combination scheme of operations and objects mentioned in Table 2 and Table 3.

Table 4. Number of core tasks accounting for most relevant interactions in music notation editors.

unit task area	correspondences in XML elements	number of core tasks
duration	type, dot, rest, chord	16
pitch	pitch	6
accidental	accidental	5
beam	beam	3
notations	slur	5
	articulations	6
initial score configuration	essential tasks comprising various compounds of XML elements	2
time signatures		5
key signatures		6
tempo		7
clefs		6
playback		1
staff/ measure		11
	tasks total	101

4 Results

4.1 General

In Fig. 1 we show all accumulated KLM values that we encoded for all accessible functionalities, separated by using (if possible) only keyboard or only mouse. It is not surprising that mouse interaction is much slower than pure keyboard interaction in general. The distributions are already weighted according to Table 4. Mouse modality has less outliers in general which points to more equally distributed data. The violin plots now mostly remind hi-hats, meaning that interaction times of core tasks cluster around different regions with few tasks in between. Despite some variations between the graphs one can clearly identify peaks in the lower portions which mostly represent core tasks. Tasks that could be subsumed under "notations" as well as pitch and duration related tasks have usually similar speeds within the software and modality and so forming distinguishable peaks.

The descriptive statistics in Table 5 show that most of the tasks are performed in very similar speeds. Overall Sibelius is slowest for mouse interaction with 6.89 s. MuseScore4 is the fastest in key interaction with 3.22 s. Dorico, Finale and MuseScore 3 are significantly faster in mouse interaction than the rest. In general most tasks are performed in between 3 to 9 s.

Table 5. Descriptive statistics for Fig. 1. q1 = first quartile, q3 = third quartile, iqr = interquartile range, mad = median absolute deviation, sd = standard deviation, se = standard error, ci = 95% confidence interval.

software	modality	min	max	median	q1	q3	iqr	mad	mean	sd	se	ci
Capella	key	2.08	13.58	3.56	2.96	4.46	1.51	1.3	4.14	1.66	0.01	0.01
	mouse	2.55	14.89	6.86	5.34	8.1	2.75	1.84	6.6	2.17	0.01	0.02
Dorico	key	1.95	15.17	3.58	2.95	4.01	1.06	0.74	3.81	1.33	0	0.01
	mouse	1.95	15.17	4.46	3.75	8.01	4.26	1.48	5.88	2.56	0.01	0.02
Finale	key	1.75	16.26	3.91	3.7	4.66	0.96	0.78	4.24	1.08	0	0.01
	mouse	2.52	19.18	4.94	3.76	8.32	4.56	1.76	5.96	2.85	0.01	0.02
MuseScore 3	key	1.68	15.62	3.47	2.86	4.04	1.19	0.85	3.64	1.15	0	0.01
	mouse	2.42	16.36	4.93	3.75	7.86	4.11	2.79	5.96	2.66	0.01	0.02
MuseScore 4	key	1.75	15.15	3.22	2.72	4.15	1.43	0.94	3.54	1.33	0	0.01
	mouse	2.15	14.25	6.58	3.75	7.79	4.04	3.8	5.99	2.51	0.01	0.02
Sibelius	key	1.68	13.67	3.7	3.2	4.2	1	0.75	4.05	1.42	0	0.01
	mouse	2.35	15.92	6.89	4.56	8.67	4.12	3.46	7.17	3.07	0.01	0.02

Comparing MuseScore 3 and 4 we can see, that the later Version tends to make some interactions slower especially with mouse interaction. Pitch and duration related tasks are clearly visible in the peaks. For mouse interaction the times in both editors are similar, but MuseScore4 having a higher median despite having a similar interquarile range. This indicates that non-essential tasks have become faster, which are not heavily weighted. Comparing the peaks around 7 s with Sibelius we can find mostly tasks for "notations" like in MuseScore 3 and 4 but Sibelius also includes many tasks about various changes about staves and element displacement which is usually faster in other editors. Many similar peaks over a wide range resulting in a mostly symmetric shape can be an indicator that some core tasks may be inconsistently modeled, also more coherent plots over a wide range can show special treatment of some methods that are less consistent with similar tasks and should be examined in more detail.

4.2 Outliers

As a rule it is not problematic having many outliers in the set of interactions. Since most of the editors have low third quartile boundaries in the key modality, interactions with lengths of 5 to 7 s can already count as outliers in these cases.

From the perspective of the software designer this might point to concentration on faster speeds in interaction design and addressing specific problems that have to be solved in order to appeal to a certain user group. Also, this does not mean, that one program is more preferable over the other due to interaction speed differences. As mentioned our previous study [16] Capella has the best usability and user experience ratings in our experiments, while from a KLM perspective there are more peaks in higher regions in both modalities. With this method it is more important to analyze

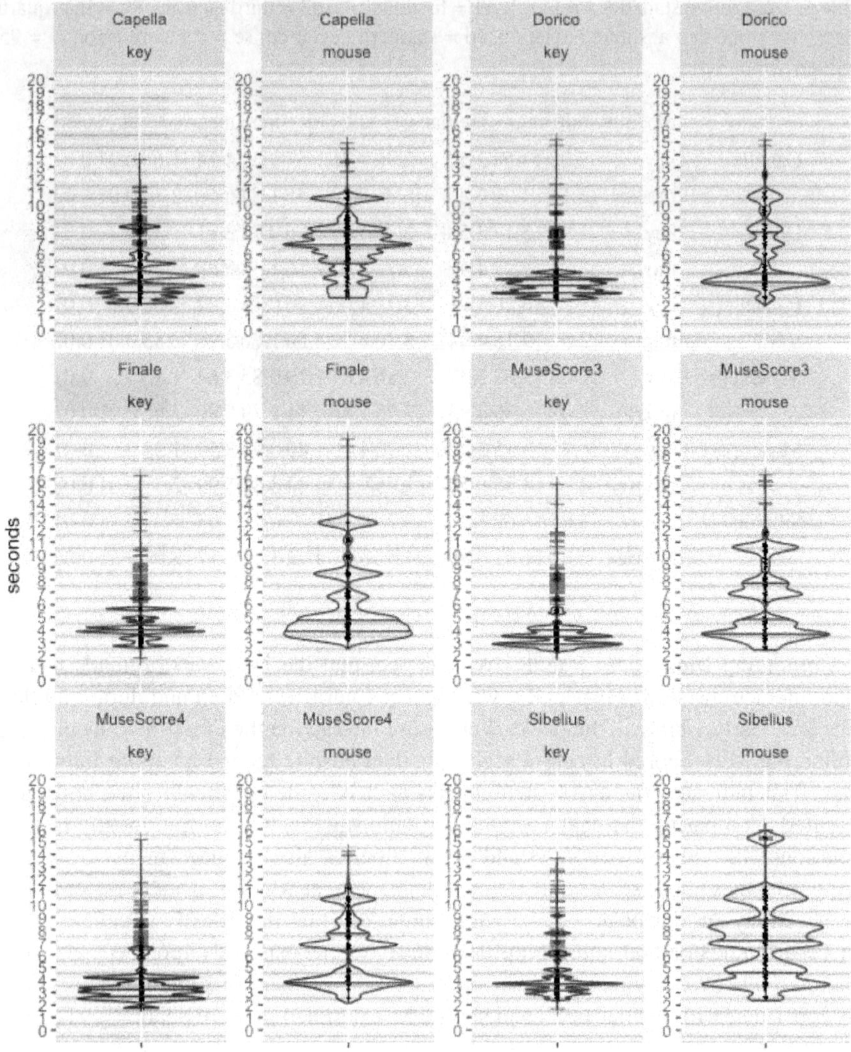

Fig. 1. Violin plots with quartiles of the weighted Keystroke-Level Model of the six music notation score editors. The red '+'-Symbols mark outliers. The width on the x-axis is not

different peculiarities, like for example having mostly core tasks hidden behind slow or dissimilar interactions.

In Dorico we can see, that the data is much wider distributed using a mouse than using solely keys. Only changing the instrument for a specific staff, transfer notes between voices and creating multiple bars at the end were considered to be very slow. In contrast we have 38 outliers for key interaction, most of them including tasks that immediately result in a different layout, especially adding and deleting measures. But we can also find frequently used objects as described in Table 3, like beams and staves, while 101 Tasks can be completed between 3 to 4 s.

Finale has a very characteristic peak at 12.5 s for the mouse modality, which consist of some layout and MIDI operations. Also there seems to be no simple way to paste notes, chords or rests—objects which are highly weighted—by mouse which in turn is better handled by keyboard interaction.

In general keyboard interactions across all editors are especially slow making major changes to the layouts or creating scores. Most outliers consist of these since there are seldom adequate methods so that here are no options despite using the mouse. These are actions that one might access rarely are not among outliers in any mouse interaction. This also applies for more fine grained interactions considering changes around staffs and notes, like beams, meter changes or barline related tasks like creating repetitions. It is debatable, if fast keyboard access is necessary if such actions account for less than 2% of the total. Outliers in mouse interactions are mostly idiosyncratic and revolve around elements outside the staff like tempi and charts. Here especially Sibelius, MuseScore3 and Finale seem to have deficits.

4.3 Application

The results shown above provide guidelines for monitoring the ongoing development of our music notation interface called **VIBE** (Verovio Interface for Browser-based Editing)[2], as well as for assessing its performance in comparison to other solutions. While the method presented above entails a summative analysis, we are confident that it can also be adapted to formative scenarios. These scenarios can then be employed at different stages throughout the development process.

VIBE currently implements 41 of the 101 listed core tasks (see Table 4), most of them use mouse interactions which are better explorable visually when using the program for the first time. Mostly "notations" and "dynamics's' have to be implemented yet, as well as several actions of copying, pasting and rebinding. Main development dealt with actions around adjusting durations, interacting with the identity of a note directly and creating a valid score. Additionally we were also interested in handling annotations and chord symbols since these are important features for analyzing a score and make information accessible for other persons in a teaching environment, as required by the underlying project for which it is developed. This added possible 14 unit tasks of which 10 are implemented, combining to 51 implemented unit tasks in total.

In Fig. 2 we can see, that most of the interactions are around 3.75 s (with the median at this point and a very narrow third quartile) which belong to the relevant core tasks handling durations and pitch. Although we concentrated on mouse interaction first, the results can keep up with other editors sometimes even with fast keyboard inputs. In our case especially creating time signatures is slow, since it is currently required to choose always from two drop down menus to create a combination of count and unit which then has to be dragged to the intended position. Generally actions that include dragging and dropping items (clef, key, time) are found among the outliers, as well as actions which

[2] Source Code: https://github.com/mnowakow/VerovioScoreEditor.
Demo: https://mnowakow.github.io/.

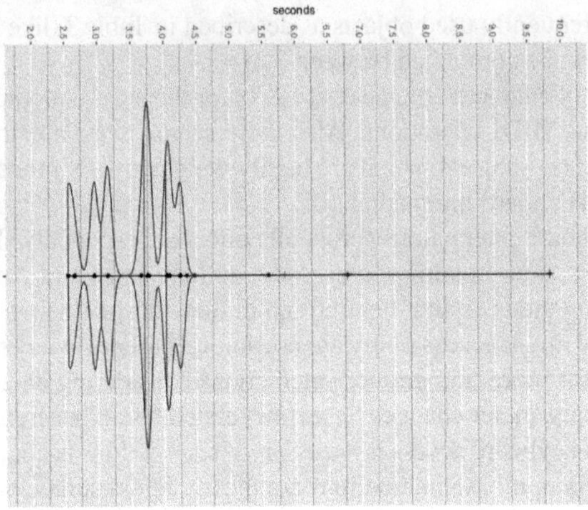

Fig. 2. Violin plot of VIBE. The red '+'-Symbols mark outliers.

have to be performed multiple times to accomplish the intended result, like deleting or adding multiple measures at the end of the score.

5 Discussion

In this paper we presented an approach to evaluate music notation editors objectively by simulating and comparing their interaction times. We oriented our research on the original publications about the KLM and applied them to editors by several annotators. By defining unit tasks and model their weights after element occurrence in MusicXML we can find slow and fast interactions and especially locate relevant ones in the resulting distributions. Same speeds usually point to similar sequences of operators. Horizontally symmetric plots over a wide range might point to inconsistencies in the interaction modeling. This helps us to evaluate different music notation editors and model interactions in new interfaces according to access times. These times do not represent rigid metrics but a way do identify potential shortcomings fast.

By listing and ranking core tasks, this paper also contributes to monitor the process of development and functional completeness of notation editors as shown in Sect. 4.3. New editors will at least have to implement the core tasks presented here, but might have different requirements for working more creatively or making elaborate editions. In these cases the list of unit tasks can be extended as presented in Sect. 3.3. KLM is flawed when it comes to evaluating user responses. In our case we approached the topic by modeling methods which are not informed by the user manual, but by exploration and restriction to input modalities which might represent a user with average skills. We did not expect a perfect and efficient user, but did assume a perfectly set score. So still questions remain about the system and user behavior in case of errors: How fast can users correct their errors? What methods does the system provide to make corrections? That is why most research using KLM is concerned with user tests to verify interaction times with new interaction modalities such as touch, pen or VR. In our case, we adopted an established model, as we focused on mouse and keyboard interactions. We then extended its application to a domain within HCI that has received limited scientific attention until now. However, since we base our method on informed assumptions, we still would like to verify these results with actual user tests. This will also help us to bring the results from this paper closer to the field of user experience. When conducting user tests it will be also fruitful to combine it with discussions and questionnaires to evaluate specific usability issues, which could not be represented by the KLM directly.

Acknowledgements. We would like to thank Claudia Cecchinato, Árpad Kovács and Juan Sebastian Mora Lopez for creating the KLM encodings and giving valuable input for task description and selection.

This research was supported by the Ministry of Culture and Science of the State of North Rhine-Westphalia, Germany.

Disclosure of Interests. The authors have no competing interests to declare that are relevant to the content of this article.

References

1. Abdulin, E.: Using the keystroke-level model for designing user interface on middle-sized touch screens. In: CHI 2011 Extended Abstracts on Human Factors in Computing Systems, pp. 673–686 (2011)
2. Al-Megren, S., Khabti, J., Al-Khalifa, H.S.: A systematic review of modifications and validation methods for the extension of the keystroke-level model. Adv. Human-Comput. Interact., 1–26 (2018)
3. Bevana, N., Kirakowski, J., Maissela, J.: What is usability? In: Proceedings of the 4th International Conference on HCI, pp. 1–6 (1991)
4. Card, S.K., Moran, T.P., Newell, A.: The keystroke-level model for user performance time with interactive systems. Commun. ACM **23**(7), 396–410 (1980)
5. Card, S., Moran, T., Newell, A.: Computer text-editing: an information-processing analysis of a routine cognitive skill. Cogn. Psychol. **12**(1), 32–74 (1980)
6. Csikszentmihalyi, M.: Flow and the Psychology of Discovery and Invention. Harper Perennial, vol. 39 (1997)
7. Fasciani, S., Goode, J.: 20 NIMEs: twenty years of new interfaces for musical expression. In: Proceedings of the International Conference on New Interfaces for Musical Expression (2021). https://doi.org/10.21428/92fbeb44.b368bcd5
8. Green, T., Petre, M.: Usability analysis of visual programming environments: a 'cognitive dimensions' framework. J. Visual Lang. Comput. **7**(2), 131–174 (1996)
9. Guerra, E., Kurz, B., Bräucker, J.: An Extension to the Keystroke-Level Model for Extended Reality Interactions. Mensch und Computer (2022)
10. Holleis, P., Otto, F., Hussmann, H., Schmidt, A.: Keystroke-level model for advanced mobile phone interaction. In: Proceedings of the SIGCHI Conference on Human Factors in Computing Systems (CHI 2007), pp. 1505–1514 (2007). https://doi.org/10.1145/1240624.1240851
11. Kieras, D., Butler, K.: Task analysis and the design of functionality. Comput. Sci. Eng. Handbook **23**, 1401–1423 (2014)
12. Myung, R.: Keystroke-level analysis of korean text entry methods on mobile phones. Int. J. Hum Comput Stud. **60**(5–6), 545–563 (2004)

13. Nash, C., Blackwell, A.: Tracking virtuosity and flow in computer music. In: Proceedings of the International Computer Music Conference (ICMC) (2011)
14. Nash, C., Blackwell, A.: Liveness and flow in notation use. In: Proceedings of the International Conference on New Interfaces for Musical Expression (NIME) (2021). http://www.nime.org/proceedings/2012/nime2012217.pdf
15. Nash, C., Blackwell, A.: Flow of Creative Interaction with Digital Music Notations. Oxford University Press (2014). https://doi.org/10.1093/oxfordhb/9780199797226.013.023
16. Nowakowski, M., Hadjakos, A.: Online survey on usability and user experience of music notation editors. In: Proceedings of the First International Conference on Technologies for Music Notation and Representation (TENOR 2023) (2023), in press
17. Peterson, J., Schubert, E.: Music notation software: some observations on its effects on composer creativity. In: Proceedings of International Conference on Music Communication Science (ICoMCS), vol. 127-130 (2007)
18. Pettitt, M., Burnett G., Karbassioun D.: Applying the keystroke level model in a driving context. In: Contemporary Ergonomics 2006. Taylor & Francis (2006)
19. Repenning, A., Basawapatna, A.R., Escherle, N.A.: Principles of computational thinking tools. In: Rich, P.J., Hodges, C.B. (eds.) Emerging Research, Practice, and Policy on Computational Thinking. ECTII, pp. 291–305. Springer, Cham (2017). https://doi.org/10.1007/978-3-319-52691-1_18
20. Roberts, T.L., Moran, T.: P: the evaluation of text editors: methodology and empirical results. Commun. ACM **26**(4), 265–283 (1983)

Challenging Beat Tracking: Tackling Polyrhythm, Polymetre, and Polytempo with Human-in-the-Loop Adaptation

António Sá Pinto[1,2(✉)], Gilberto Bernardes[1,2], and Matthew E. P. Davies[1,2]

[1] Faculdade de Engenharia da Universidade do Porto, Porto, Portugal
asapinto@fe.up.pt

[2] INESC TEC, Porto, Portugal

Abstract. Deep-learning beat-tracking algorithms have achieved remarkable accuracy in recent years. However, despite these advancements, challenges persist with musical examples featuring complex rhythmic structures, especially given their under-representation in training corpora. Expanding on our prior work, this paper demonstrates how our user-centred beat-tracking methodology effectively handles increasingly demanding musical scenarios. We evaluate its adaptability and robustness through musical pieces that exhibit rhythmic dissonance, while maintaining ease of integration with leading methods through minimal user annotations. The selected musical works—Uruguayan *Candombe*, Colombian *Bambuco*, and Steve Reich's *Piano Phase*—present escalating levels of rhythmic complexity through their respective *polyrhythm*, *polymetre*, and *polytempo* characteristics. These examples not only validate our method's effectiveness but also demonstrate its capability across increasingly challenging scenarios, culminating in the novel application of beat tracking to polytempo contexts. The results show notable improvements in terms of the F-measure, ranging from 2 to 5 times the state-of-the-art performance. The beat annotations used in fine-tuning reduce the correction edit operations from 1.4 to 2.8 times, while reducing the global annotation effort to between 16% and 37% of the baseline approach. Our experiments demonstrate the broad applicability of our human-in-the-loop strategy in the domain of Computational Ethnomusicology, confronting the prevalent Music Information Retrieval (MIR) constraints found in non-Western musical scenarios. Beyond beat tracking and computational rhythm analysis, this user-driven adaptation framework suggests wider implications for various MIR technologies, particularly in scenarios where musical signal ambiguity and human subjectivity challenge conventional algorithms.

Keywords: User-Centred · Transfer Learning · Beat Tracking · Computational Ethnomusicology

S. Ystad et al. (Eds.): CMMR 2023, LNCS 15236, pp. 461–479, 2026.
https://doi.org/10.1007/978-3-032-02042-0_35

1 Introduction

As a fundamental aspect of music, rhythm has emerged as a critical focus of computational analysis within Music Information Retrieval (MIR). This area involves numerous tasks, such as tempo extraction, rhythmic pattern recognition, and metre determination [12]. Algorithmic beat tracking, the automatic detection of a musical signal's pulse, plays an essential role in various MIR applications that require the parsing of musical *time*, i.e., the beat. In the past decade, beat tracking has seen significant progress, with state-of-the-art methods achieving accuracy levels over 90% on benchmark datasets [2,6,9,15]. However, even these advanced methods can face challenges with complex rhythms, especially if they differ from the features of their training data. These challenges are amplified in specialized areas like Computational Ethnomusicology (CE) [33]. In this domain, the availability of annotated datasets is limited, and the need for specialized cultural knowledge to annotate unique rhythmic examples is crucial. Due to these limitations, many musical traditions remain under-represented in MIR research. This gap highlights a known issue in MIR systems: a primary focus on Western (or *Eurogenetic*) music at the expense of diverse global genres and expressions [5,13].

To overcome these obstacles, various methods have been proposed to improve rhythmic analysis tasks. Informed methods have been developed for tasks such as beat tracking [10] and metre determination [31]. These approaches leverage a priori knowledge about rhythmic content, which, while effective in specific genres, lack generalizability. Transfer learning methods have also been explored, such as adapting beat tracking knowledge from mainstream Western to Greek music [8]; however, this approach, besides being computationally intensive, performed worse than training from scratch and yielded unsatisfactory results on challenging examples. Human-in-the-Loop strategies have emerged as an alternative, with reported applications ranging from iterative frameworks for sound event labelling [18] to interactive beat-tracking systems that adapt to individual users and specific musical content [34].

Following a human-centred direction, we leverage minimal user annotations to refine an existing state-of-the-art beat tracker, enabling adaptation to diverse musical contexts. This methodology provides a general and streamlined solution that aligns with interactive principles while incorporating elements of transfer learning. Our initial research explored system customization through high-level parameters [26,27], while subsequent work developed model fine-tuning based on minimal annotated examples [23]. Results have demonstrated superior performance compared to established techniques across multiple datasets, proving particularly effective for complex cases as found in the *SMC* dataset [14].

In this study, we further challenge our system by expanding its scope beyond Western music. We evaluate its performance using demanding datasets such as the Uruguayan *Candombe* and the Colombian *Bambuco*, both distinguished by their respective polyrhythm and polymetre features. These musical traditions serve as a rigorous test bed to assess the system's adaptability and robustness. Additionally, we extend our analysis to Steve Reich's *Piano Phase*, a composition renowned for its innovative use of concurrent *tempi*. Analysing this piece presents a formidable test: to our knowledge, it is the first reported attempt at beat tracking a polytempo composition. Our findings indicate that our system effectively manages diverse rhythmic dissonances[1] across a spectrum of styles and genres.

2 Rhythmic Dissonance Challenges

Rhythm serves as a foundational scaffold for many musical traditions. Particularly, within African heritage cultures, there is a notable use of complex rhythmic techniques such as polyrhythms, polymetres, and to a lesser extent, polytempi [1]. While these rhythmic intricacies contribute to the distinctiveness of these traditions, they introduce unique challenges in Music Information Retrieval (MIR). In this section, we explore the rhythmic dissonances found in *Candombe*, *Bambuco*, and Steve Reich's *Piano Phase*.

Fig. 1. Interaction of the main *Candombe* patterns and the resulting metric structure levels (adapted from [22]).

2.1 Polyrhythm in Uruguayan *Candombe*

Candombe is an African-origin rhythm prominent in Uruguay and, to a lesser extent, in other South American countries [30]. Musically, as illustrated in Fig. 1, it is characterised by the interplay of three percussion instruments: the *chico*, the *repique*, and the *piano*, with an additional time-line pattern called *clave*, shared

[1] Rhythmic dissonance is used here as a general term referring to the specific manifestations of polyrhythm in *Candombe*, polymetre in *Bambuco*, and polytempo in Steve Reich's *Piano Phase*. In musicological literature, *metrical dissonance* [19] encompasses polyrhythm and polymetre.

by the three drums [17]. Such combination produces a typical rhythmic structure consisting of a four-beat measure evenly divided into 16 tatums, typically played at a tempo of about 110–150 bpm. *Candombe* distinguishes itself from other rhythms through two features that connect it to Afro-Atlantic music traditions: a) the pulse pattern emphasizes the second tatum rather than the one on the beat, and b) the clave divides the 16-tatum cycle irregularly (3+3+4+2+4), with only two of its five strokes synchronized with the beat. This interplay creates an overall polyrhythmic texture. Moreover, in actual performances, the primary pattern of *repique* leans towards a triplet feeling, and although the *chico* drum establishes the metrical foundation, its pattern exhibits a contraction of inter-onset intervals (IOIs) [22]. These unique characteristics of *Candombe* present challenges for both untrained listeners and standard beat-tracking algorithms, making it a compelling test case for evaluating our user-driven approach.

2.2 Polymetre in Colombian *Bambuco*

Bambuco is a Colombian traditional music genre known for its rhythmic complexity, characterised by heavy syncopation, odd accents, and a certain degree of rhythmic freedom, including tempo variations and micro-timing [3]. Its most distinctive aspect is the polymetric nature, resulting from the superposition or alternation of musical elements in two metres: a simple metre (3/4) and a compound one (6/8), as illustrated by Fig. 2. Such phenomenon, commonly known as "hemiola" or the equivalent Latin term "sesquialtera", appears in various South American musical genres [30] and presents significant challenges for *Bambuco*'s metre and beat-tracking analysis. As illustrated by the guitar voice, depending on the simple or compound metre interpretation, the beats' locations do not align, except for the downbeat, highlighting a close relationship between the tasks of metre analysis and beat tracking. Essentially, it implies that we can deduce the metric interpretation from the placement of the beats. These properties make *Bambuco* an ideal test case for our approach. More specifically, while

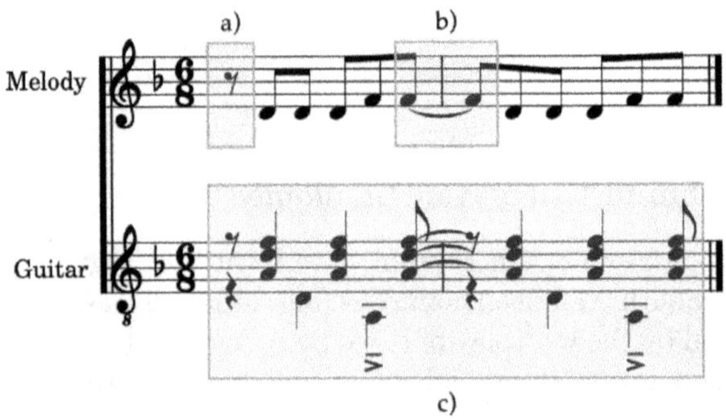

Fig. 2. Colombian *Bambuco* pattern showing a) downbeat in a rest; b) caudal syncopation; and c) guitar pattern suggesting 6/8 at the top voice and 3/4 at the bass voice (adapted from [3]).

primarily targeting beat tracking, our method also informs metre analysis due to the interconnected nature of these rhythmical facets.

2.3 Polytempo in Steve Reich *Piano Phase*

Steve Reich's *Piano Phase* represents a notable case of polytempo, a phenomenon mostly absent from mainstream music genres and entirely missing from datasets used to train deep-learning beat-tracking models. The effect presents a significant challenge for general-purpose beat trackers, as it involves concurrent and isochronous pulses within the same music piece. This compositional technique is primarily found in avant-garde Western music, with Charles Ives's *Symphony no. 4* being considered the earliest formalized work featuring polytempo [32]. Later, composers such as Conlon Nancarrow or György Ligeti expanded upon this rhythmic framework [11]. Steve Reich's *phasing* is a unique manifestation of polytempo, where identical phrases are played simultaneously at slightly different tempi, creating a gradual phase shift. *Piano Phase* brings Reich's technique to live performance (a rendition of the original score is shown in Fig. 3), complete with a detailed set of instructions for performance, which we briefly summarise:

1. *One performer starts, the other fades in unison (bars* 1–2*), and both continue playing the pattern over and over again*;
2. *The first performer keeps a constant tempo. The other performer gradually increases his tempo, until he is one note ahead of the first performer (bar* 3*)*;
3. *After playing in synchronisation for a while, the second performer begins increasing his tempo, and the phase shifting process starts again (bars* 3-4*)*;
4. *In the first part of the piece, this procedure is repeated twelve times.*

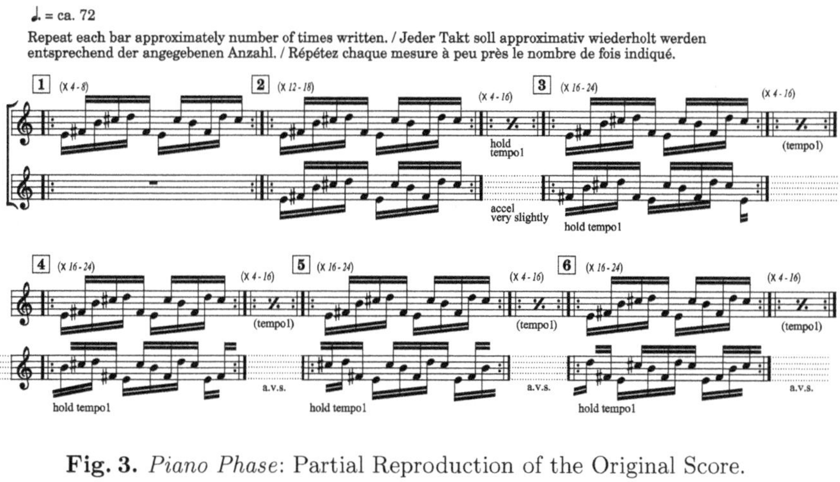

Fig. 3. *Piano Phase*: Partial Reproduction of the Original Score.

3 Methodology

Building on our earlier contributions [23,27], our approach integrates user knowledge with an established beat tracker [2], enabling direct, content-specific adaptation. Through minimal manual annotation, we tailor this system to the unique characteristics of a musical piece and the user's own subjective musical judgement. Our strategy addresses a fundamental challenge: adapting systems when state-of-the-art techniques prove insufficient. To overcome this limitation, user knowledge provides the key to rapid adaptation of leading MIR methods, enhancing their performance on challenging musical examples.

The selected baseline for adaptation is the temporal convolutional network (TCN) model proposed by Böck and Davies [2], a system pre-trained for beat, downbeat, and tempo tracking which held state-of-the-art status when this research began [25]. While more advanced algorithms have since emerged (e.g.,[4,9,15,35]), for challenging music signals, performance improvements have been modest, as exemplified by the *SMC* dataset [14], where the F-measure has progressed from 0.552 to 0.627 in what is currently the most advanced method [9]. Moreover, this model's compact architecture makes it optimal for in-situ adaptation. This aligns with our preference for general methods over specialized approaches, despite the latter's potential advantages in specific scenarios—for instance, the work by Maia et al. [20] achieved remarkable results in the *Candombe* dataset.

Given these considerations, our choice of baseline remains methodologically sound, offering both experimental consistency and a streamlined framework, while maintaining competitive performance in challenging scenarios.

3.1 Retraining and Inference

To ensure this paper stands as a self-contained resource, we provide a concise overview of our user-centred approach to model fine-tuning and parameter customization. For an in-depth understanding, readers are directed to consult [23].

Fine-tuning is allowed for all layers of the baseline network. Given the present task is beat-tracking, the losses for tempo and downbeat tasks on the underlying multitask network [2] are masked. Common practice in transfer learning is followed, thus reducing the learning rate to one fifth of the rate used in the base training [2]. To control network adaptation, we divide the fine-tuning segment into two adjacent, disjoint regions for (re)training and validation, setting a maximum of 50 epochs, and employing learning rate reduction and early stopping strategies. To account for the limited data in the fine-tuning region, target widening and data augmentation are employed. The user-annotated region also serves to parameterise the post-processing Dynamic Bayesian Network (DBN), which extracts beat positions from the Temporal Convolutional Network's likelihood output. For DBN parameterisation, we employ two strategies: 1) adjusting the transition-λ parameter for the adaptive processor type (`pt`), and 2) setting a tempo tolerance window using user annotations as the tempo guide (`tg`). While fine-tuning (`ft`) and data augmentation (`da`) are general user-driven techniques, strategies like the adaptive processor type and tempo guide are specific to networks employing DBN.

A key experimental consideration is that in real-world applications, the length and characteristics of the annotated region would be determined by end-users, significantly impacting the final performance. For experimental consistency, we simulated this user-driven process by defining a standardized protocol: using a quarter of each file's length as the fine-tuning region.

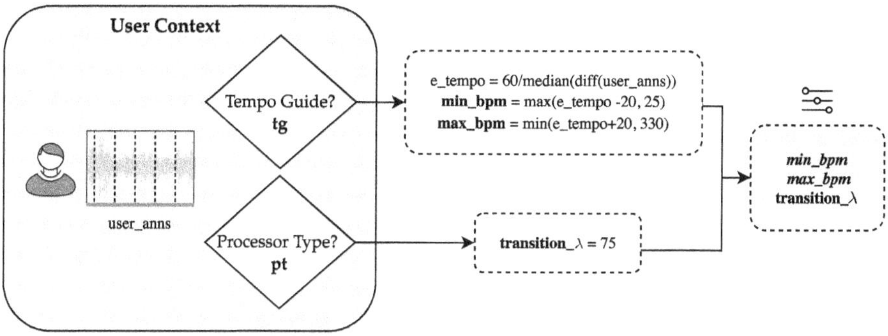

Fig. 4. DBN parameterisation (default values of `min_bpm`:50, `max_bpm`:215, `transition_`λ:100).

3.2 Scope of Evaluation

The evaluation considers two complementary scenarios: a controlled evaluation that excludes the user-annotated segment (`testRes`) and a comprehensive assessment of the entire signal (`fullRes`). We examine key combinations of user-driven techniques: fine-tuning (`ft`), data augmentation (`da`), and DBN customisations (`tg` and `pt`).

To minimise variability, we adapt the data augmentation procedure from [23] to a deterministic sampling approach based on a uniform distribution with a $\pm 30\%$ deviation from the local tempo, calculated using the median inter-beat interval across the annotated region. Addressing the stochastic effects from applying dropout on the TCN, results are averaged over three iterations, except for the *Piano Phase* analysis, which consists of a single run.

While there are 11 combinations of user-driven beat-tracking configurations, our evaluation focuses on the primary configurations: `ft+da`, `ft+da+pt`, `ft+da+tg`, and `ft+da+tg+pt`. These are compared with the underlying beat tracker, denoted as baseline (`bsl`). Occasionally, we reference results from configurations that highlight the standalone application of specific techniques, namely `ft`, `pt`, and `tg`.

In all figures, configurations follow a consistent colour scheme: baseline in blue, primary configurations in orange, and standalone configurations in white.

For tabulated results, best-performing values are emphasized using bold font for metrics where higher values are preferable (e.g., F-measure) and italics for metrics where lower values are optimal (e.g., correction operations #ops).

3.3 Evaluation Metrics

We employ both the standard F-measure and the E-measure [24,28] for beat-tracking evaluation. This latter metric, which we introduced to address practical annotation considerations, conceptualises the evaluation process from a user workflow perspective, framing it in terms of the effort necessary to modify a series of detected beats to align with the ground-truth annotations. This approach aims to provide a more intuitive understanding and better alignment with real-world annotation practices. The metric is quantified by counting the number of edit operations, specifically insertions and deletions, but also–contrarily to the F-measure–, including the *shifting* of poorly localized individual beats, a very common operation in annotation workflows.

$$E_m = \frac{t^+}{t^+ + shf + f^+ + f^-} = \frac{det}{det + shf + del + ins} \tag{1}$$

Additionally, we utilize the *Annotation Efficiency* (*Ae*) metric [24] to evaluate the efficiency of our approach with respect to the user annotation effort, applicable only to results that include the annotated part of the input signal (`fullRes`). The *Ae* quantifies the reduction in correction operations achieved through fine-tuning relative to the number of user annotations required:

$$Ae = \frac{ops_{bsl} - ops_{ft}}{ft_{anns}} \tag{2}$$

where ops_{bsl} represents the number of correction operations needed for the baseline output, ops_{ft} the corrections needed for the fine-tuned output, and ft_{anns} the number of user annotations provided for fine-tuning. The total correction operations are computed as $ops = shf + del + ins$.

This dual evaluation framework provides complementary perspectives on beat tracking performance. While the F-measure offers a traditional accuracy assessment, the workflow-oriented metrics address distinct aspects of user interaction: the E-measure captures the practical demands of annotation correction, while the *Ae* specifically quantifies the return on investment of user annotations during fine-tuning. Together, these metrics enable a more nuanced assessment of beat tracking systems, particularly in adaptive user-centred settings.

3.4 Datasets

This study employs three datasets: two existing collections (*Candombe* and *Bambuco*) and a custom-developed dataset for Steve Reich's *Piano Phase*.

The first consists of 35 full-length recordings, accumulating nearly 2.5 hours of audio [17]. The second, from the "Rhythm Set" of the ACMUS-MIR (V1.1) [21], contains more than 70 short musical excerpts, each approximately 30 s in duration. It includes two separate sets of ground-truth beat annotations, corresponding to the two predominant meters in this genre: 3/4 and 6/8, referred to as *Bambuco (simple)* and *Bambuco (compound)*, respectively.

Fig. 5. Musical score of the simplified version of *Piano Phase.*

The analysis of Steve Reich's *Piano Phase* required developing our own dataset. The piece features two identical melodic lines played at unequal tempi, gradually shifting out of alignment. Automatic transcription of real performances proved infeasible for such polytempo material. Likewise, traditional MIDI-related software lacked the capability to generate a faithful rendition of this composition, due to limited support of concurrent tempi in both MIDI sequencing and notation tools [16]. Leveraging the procedural nature of Reich's composition, we generated a simplified version of *Piano Phase*(as depicted in Fig. 5) using *PureData*(*Pd*)[29].

Our *Pd* patch (see Fig. 6) generates two independent streams of 12 MIDI notes, corresponding to the main motif of *Piano Phase.* Each stream follows a slightly different tempo: =72 bpm for stream A and =73 bpm for stream B[2]. The resulting two-minute-long audio was created via a MIDI-driven piano synthesizer, and solo renditions of streams A and B were also produced to complement evaluation. To establish ground-truth beat annotations, we assumed a 6/8 time signature, defining the dotted quarter note ( ) as the beat—an inference based on the score[3]. This dataset serves as an experimental benchmark to assess whether our beat tracker can synchronize with the independent tempi present in the music. The main files in this dataset are `pianophaseM_A` and `pianophaseM_B`, which contain the mixed audio of both streams with ground-truth annotations for streams A and B, respectively, each with a duration of 2 min. Additionally, `pianophaseA_A` and `pianophaseB_B` provide solo renditions of streams A and B, with corresponding annotations, and are included for testing purposes.

All audio files, annotations, and the *PureData* patch used for dataset generation are freely available in our GitHub repository[4].

[2] Following the original score's instructions, we computed the inter-onset intervals as 138.8 ms (A) and 136.9 ms (B), rounding them to the nearest integer.

[3] Reich's *Clapping Music* performance notes suggest avoiding explicit time signatures to prevent metrical accents.

[4] https://github.com/asapsmc/PolyrhythmicChallenges.

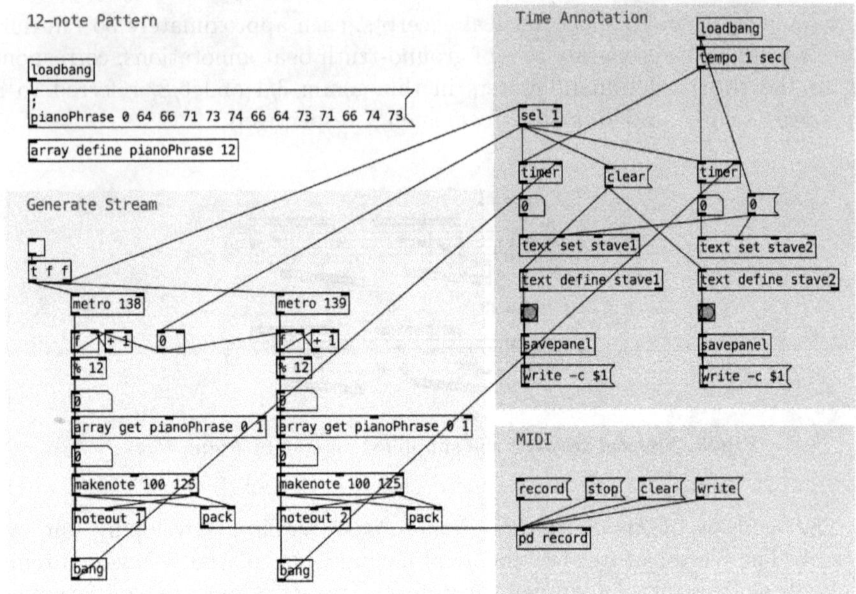

Fig. 6. *Pd* patch - generation of a simplified version of Steve Reich *Piano Phase*.

4 Results

4.1 Beat Tracking in Uruguayan *Candombe*

Fig. 7 provides a summary of the overall results. A clear improvement in accuracy scores is observed across all fine-tuning configurations when compared to the baseline (`bsl`). Exceptions arise with configurations exclusively utilising DBN-parameterisation techniques (`pt` and `tg`), which yield scores similar to the baseline. This is expected for the adaptive processor type (`pt`) given the mostly stable tempo within each recording, while constraining the DBN's tempo range (`tg`)–beneficial only when erroneous beat estimates fall outside this range–shows marginally better performance than both baseline and the former. Quantitatively, the best-performing configuration (`ft`) raises the mean F-measure score from 0.280 to 0.952 when excluding the fine-tuned region (`testRes`), and from 0.334 to 0.956 when considering the entire file extent (`fullRes`). We observe that combining fine-tuning with data augmentation (`ft+da`) performs worse than fine-tuning alone. We hypothesize this may be due to two factors: first, *Candombe*'s characteristic steady tempo range (110–150 bpm) potentially limiting the utility of tempo variations; second, the dataset's substantial duration (averaging 4 min per recording, with fine-tuning regions exceeding 1 min) possibly providing sufficient beat information for model adaptation without augmentation. However, additional experiments would be needed to conclusively establish these relationships.

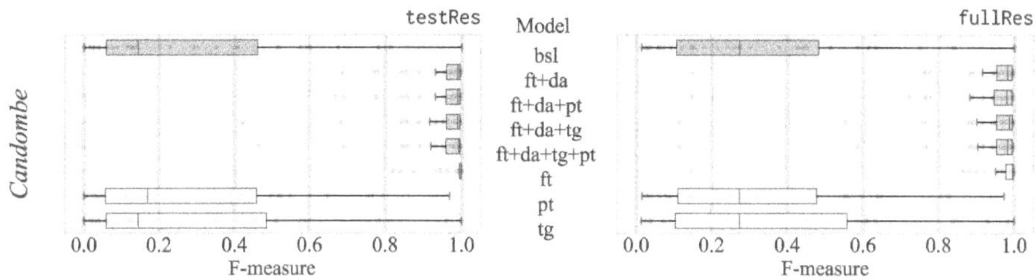

Fig. 7. Distribution of F-measure scores by configuration for the *Candombe* dataset.

When examining the annotation-correction workflow detailed in Table 1, it is observed that the E-measure improvements are marginally less than those of the F-measure, an inherent consequence of the E-measure's single weighting of true positives (i.e., detections) compared to the F-measure's double weighting. Most importantly, the results demonstrate that our method significantly enhances efficiency. The number of operations (#ops) required to correct beat detections drops from 12,912 in the baseline to just 1,904 with the `ft` configuration. Given that there are 19,136 total beat annotations in the *Candombe* dataset, this means that the `ft` configuration requires only about 10% of the total beats to be corrected, achieving a reduction of approximately 85% from the baseline. Even accounting for the required user annotations for fine-tuning (which amount to 4,757 in the current experimental scenario), the results demonstrate a compelling decrease in manual annotation effort, reaching an annotation efficiency (Ae) of 2.557, indicating that each beat annotation provided for fine-tuning saves more than two and a half correction operations in the subsequent analysis.

Table 1. Mean E-measure and Ae scores, and sum of edit operation counts for the *Candombe* dataset. Best values per metric highlighted: bold (maximization), italics (minimization). (`fullRes`)

Dataset	Model	E-measure	#det	#ins	#del	#shf	#ops	Ae
Candombe	bsl	0.319	6,316	2,901	92	9,919	12,912	–
	ft+da	0.919	16,688	1,885	181	561	2,632	2.439
	ft+da+pt	0.915	16,575	1,997	178	563	2,739	2.420
	ft+da+tg	0.922	16,892	*1,504*	190	739	2,437	2.444
	ft+da+tg+pt	0.923	16,903	*1,504*	188	726	2,421	2.449
	ft	**0.949**	**17,330**	1,565	98	*242*	*1,904*	**2.557**
	pt	0.319	6,319	2,821	100	9,996	12,917	–
	tg	0.369	7,498	1,567	*90*	10,071	11,728	–

4.2 Beat Tracking in Colombian *Bambuco*

As summarised in Fig. 8, all primary configurations outperform the baseline (`bsl`). Results are consistent across both settings (`testRes` and `fullRes`), revealing notable F-measure improvements: around 25% points (p.p.) for the simple metre and close to 30 p.p. for the compound metre datasets. The `ft+da+tg` configuration emerges as the standout performer in both scenarios. Although each of the techniques (`ft`, `pt`, and `tg`) yields different contributions individually, their combined implementation is what truly augments performance. The effectiveness of combined techniques aligns with the characteristics of the dataset, which exhibits wider tempo variations and expressive timing. While fine-tuning provides a base accuracy improvement, data augmentation and DBN parameterisation strategies further enhance performance. Given the heterogeneity of the musical signals, a more detailed analysis would require examining performance variations at the individual file level.

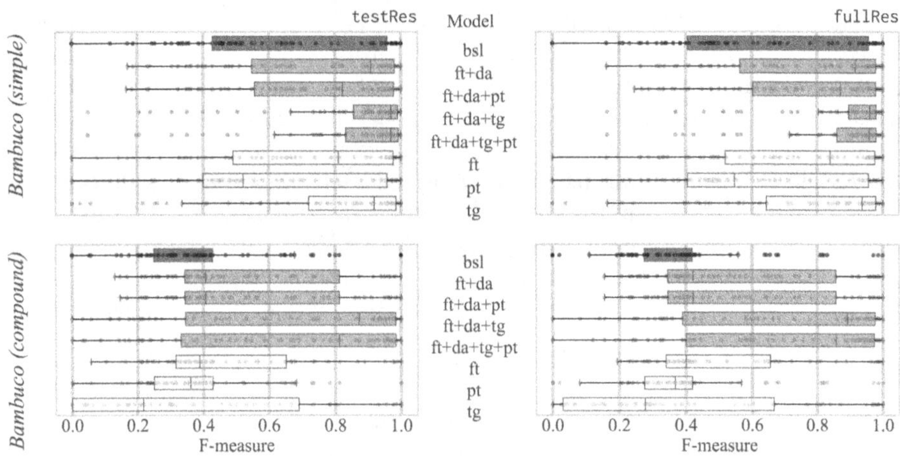

Fig. 8. Distribution of F-measure scores by model for the *Bambuco* datasets.

Results in Table 2 show the `ft+da+tg` setup in simple metre achieves a two-thirds reduction in beat estimate correction operations (#ops) compared to baseline (455 *vs* 1,610). For the compound subset, correct detections (#det) almost double in the optimal setting (from 899 to 1,665). The annotation efficiency (Ae) differs between metrical types, reaching 1.139 for simple and 1.814 for compound patterns, reflecting the method's increased effectiveness in handling more complex metrical structures.

4.3 Beat Tracking in Steve Reich *Piano Phase*

The primary experimental objective is to evaluate the capability of our beat-tracking method in synchronising with distinct tempi present in this musical

Table 2. Mean E-measure and Ae scores, and sum of edit operation counts for the *Bambuco* datasets. Best values per metric highlighted: bold (maximization), italics (minimization). (fullRes)

Dataset	Model	E-measure	#det	#ins	#del	#shf	#ops	Ae
Bambuco (simple)	bsl	0.556	1,756	1,110	*60*	440	1,610	–
	ft+da	0.726	2,439	602	91	*265*	957	0.631
	ft+da+pt	0.718	2,428	588	94	291	972	0.599
	ft+da+tg	**0.869**	**2,990**	*12*	138	306	*455*	**1.139**
	ft+da+tg+pt	0.866	2,978	*12*	137	316	465	1.130
	ft	0.683	2,306	703	88	297	1,088	0.473
	pt	0.544	1,726	1,102	*60*	478	1,640	–
	tg	0.768	2,582	24	139	700	863	–
Bambuco (comp.)	bsl	0.338	899	424	410	947	1,781	–
	ft+da	0.509	1,319	285	340	665	1,292	0.743
	ft+da+pt	0.513	1,322	285	332	663	1,282	0.785
	ft+da+tg	**0.685**	**1,665**	*63*	62	*541*	*667*	**1.814**
	ft+da+tg+pt	0.671	1,640	73	61	557	691	1.757
	ft	0.441	1,188	322	416	759	1,499	0.383
	pt	0.335	895	422	416	953	1,791	–
	tg	0.364	898	107	*59*	1,265	1,431	–

piece. When referencing stream A or stream B, we are essentially assessing the beat tracker's ability to tune into each stream's tempo. This task, which is already immensely challenging for most humans, i.e., allowing themselves to align with one tempo while ignoring conflicting ones, presents an even more formidable test for an automatic beat tracker. Given this complexity, any advancement in performance, even if slight, warrants interest. With this perspective, we now delve into the results obtained from our experiments.

Results shown in Fig. 9 demonstrate improvements across all fine-tuning configurations when compared to the baseline for both streams (A and B). The F-measure score rises from approximately 0.2 to 0.7 across the main configurations. The role of fine-tuning (ft) is prominent, emerging as a key factor in performance enhancement. However, a more constrained adaptation to stream B is also apparent, an aspect we currently lack comprehensive data to fully elucidate. Another aspect worth further investigation is the observed efficiency of the adaptive processor type (pt) over the tempo guide (tg). This observation is somewhat counterintuitive, given that the primary goal of this beat tracking method aims to synchronize with conflicting, yet stable, tempi.

Examining specific musical segments of stream A in Fig. 10 allows comparison between the baseline approach and our best-performing configuration (ft+da).

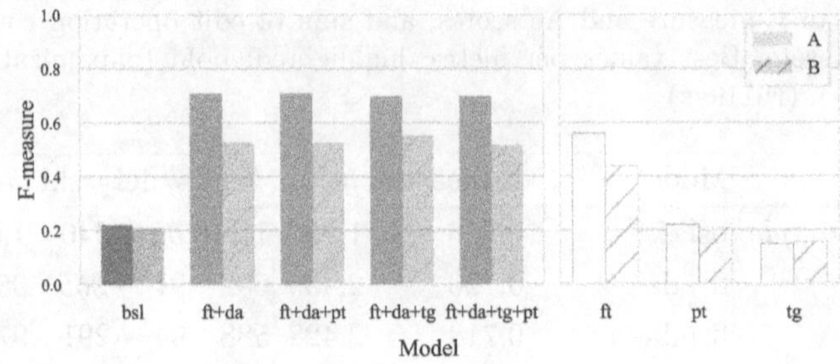

Fig. 9. F-measure *vs* model for *Piano Phase.* Each model is evaluated with ground-truth from stream A (pianophaseM_A: unhatched, left) and stream B (pianophaseM_B: hatched, right).

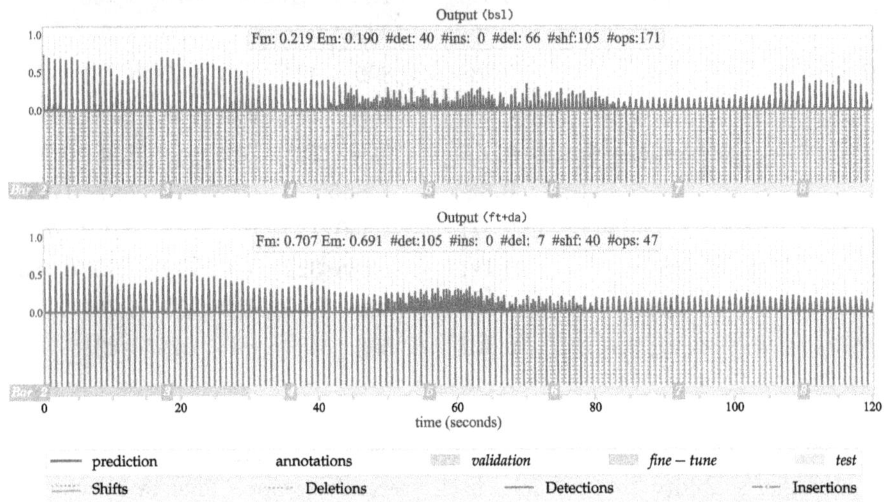

Fig. 10. Detailed analysis for *pianophaseM_ A* (Mixed audio and beat annotations for stream A).

The fine-tuned configuration shows improved accuracy across most parts of the musical segment. Notably, the beat estimates are accurate up to 68 s (near bar *6*). However, around this location, signs of desynchronisation emerge, with the imprecise predictions persisting until bar *8*. In this specific range, the baseline method manages to hold a slight edge over our approach by correctly identifying certain beats. In terms of the annotation-correction workflow, the base model correctly estimates 40 beats, while our fine-tuned configuration achieves 105 correct estimates. Considering that this improvement requires only 19 user annotations for the fine-tuning segment, the results are particularly noteworthy given the material's complexity.

A crucial factor to consider when evaluating beat tracking in *Piano Phase* is the choice of tolerance window size for the F-measure. While all previous results were based on the standard 70 ms for beat tracking [7], this setting becomes problematic in polytempo music. In Reich's *phasing* technique, where two near-identical tempi drift in and out of phase, the temporal offset between streams oscillates between unison and the inter-beat interval. Critically, the coarseness of the tolerance window conflates beats from the two streams when their temporal offset falls within its range, rendering the metric unable to discriminate between them. This issue is inherent to the compositional technique: as the phase relationship evolves, beats from both streams repeatedly enter and exit the tolerance window, making definitive discrimination impossible. To disentangle this effect, we supplement our analysis with an F-measure sensitivity study across tolerance windows ranging from 5 ms (included for completeness, since the TCN network's resolution is 10 ms) to 70 ms, in 5 ms increments. As shown in Fig. 11, our method's improvement over the baseline remains consistent across all window sizes. At stricter thresholds, such as 20 ms, the fine-tuned configuration (`ft+da`) achieves an F-measure of 0.539 for stream A, compared to the baseline's 0.135. These results confirm that performance gains reflect improved accuracy rather than evaluation artifacts, even in scenarios where the tolerance window overlaps both streams.

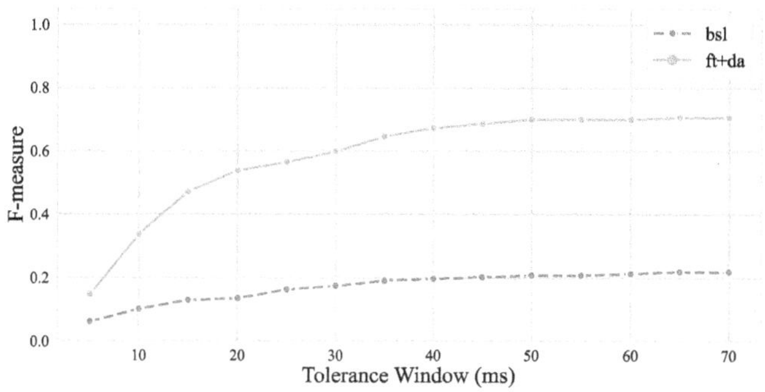

Fig. 11. F-measure *vs* tolerance window for *Piano Phase* (`pianophaseM_A`).

Beyond the methodological considerations of evaluation metrics, it is important to recognize that comparing our method with non-adaptive beat trackers, including the state of the art, is not an even comparison. Traditional beat trackers are designed for music adhering to a single tempo, and this type of rhythmic dissonance, as exemplified by Reich's *Piano Phase*, is naturally absent from standard training datasets. Conversely, while we could have optimized for polytempi scenarios, for example by customizing the DBN to synchronize with each stream's tempo, we deliberately avoided such task-specific modifications in favour of generality, achieving improvements without compromising broader applicability. Still, we present this comparison to demonstrate the versatility of our approach in face of an extremely challenging case, one that defies the conventional definition of beat tracking. By leveraging minimal user input, our method adapts the model's general knowledge to synchronize with each conflicting tempo, showcasing its capability in diverse and structurally complex musical scenarios. This highlights the potential of adaptive systems to address niche yet significant challenges that lie beyond the scope of traditional tools.

5 Conclusions

In this study, we presented a user-centric approach to beat tracking designed specifically for challenging music signals. By leveraging concise user-annotated regions, our method significantly enhanced the performance of leading beat tracking methods, especially in environments dominated by complex rhythms. We examined three representative cases of such complexity: Colombian *Bambuco*, Uruguayan *Candombe*, and Steve Reich's *Piano Phase*, each exemplifying distinct rhythmic phenomena: polyrhythm, polymetre, and polytempo, respectively.

Our experimental protocol focused on dataset-averaged results using predefined fine-tuning regions and systematic evaluation of different analysis techniques combinations. However, in practical applications, users would select both the annotated regions and the appropriate configuration, informed by the specific characteristics of each musical signal. For instance, while the steady tempo and extended fine-tuning regions of *Candombe* showed no benefit from data augmentation or DBN parameterisation, the more heterogeneous *Bambuco* demonstrated varying benefits from different configurations across its diverse signals. This underscores the importance of user-driven adaptation of our methodology to signal-specific characteristics in real-world scenarios.

Among the notable results, for *Candombe*, our approach achieved an excess of 3-fold improvement over existing techniques. In *Bambuco*, performance improved by approximately 25 p.p. for simple metre and neared 30 p.p. for compound metre dataset. With Reich's *Piano Phase*, even though the F-measure score escalated 50 p.p., our primary objective was to demonstrate our method's capability in handling the extreme polytempo challenges, breaking new ground in computational analysis of such compositional techniques.

While these results are promising, it is essential to interpret accuracy variations carefully and circumscribe them to the scope of our investigation. Looking forward to future research directions, the exploration of extended musical segments, enriched with a diverse set of fine-tuning parameters, could provide more profound insights into adaptability to complex rhythmic structures. Despite its defined scope, this investigation establishes methodological foundations for scenarios where traditional techniques prove insufficient.

In summary, our research demonstrated the potential of transfer learning and user-driven adaptation for beat tracking in rhythmically complex musical contexts. Using minimal user feedback, we enhanced a state-of-the-art model, enabling its adaptability to challenging musical scenarios and underscoring its utility for specific applications, notably musicological analysis. Our research reach extends past beat tracking, touching upon rhythm-focused tasks such as metre determination and downbeat tracking. Yet, our user-centred approach suggests even wider application across various MIR tasks, beyond computational rhythm analysis. Given the inherent ambiguity in music signals, incorporating the user perspective is crucial for attaining accuracy while respecting human subjectivity.

While our findings represent an encouraging step forward, much remains to explore. We hope this study serves as a starting point for future endeavours in refining adaptive strategies and the human-in-the-loop paradigm. Ultimately, our goal is to promote open, user-friendly MIR tools capable of handling diverse musical traditions, fostering inclusivity and a deeper appreciation of global musical heritage.

Disclosure of Interests. The authors have no competing interests to declare that are relevant to the content of this article.

References

1. Agawu, K., Agawu, V.K.: African Rhythm: A Northern Ewe Perspective. Cambridge University Press (1995)
2. Böck, S., Davies, M.E.P.: Deconstruct, analyse, reconstruct: how to improve tempo, beat, and downbeat estimation. In: Proceedings of the 21st International Society for Music Information Retrieval Conference (ISMIR), pp. 574–582 (2020)
3. Cano, E., et al.: Sesquialtera in the Colombian Bambuco: perception and estimation of beat and meter - extended version. Trans. Int. Society Music Inform. Retrieval **4**(1), 248–262 (2021)
4. Cheng, T., Goto, M.: Transformer-based beat tracking with low-resolution encoder and high-resolution decoder. In: Proceedings of the 24th International Society for Music Information Retrieval Conference (ISMIR), pp. 466–473 (2023)
5. Cornelis, O., Lesaffre, M., Moelants, D., Leman, M.: Access to ethnic music: advances and perspectives in content-based music information retrieval. Signal Process. **90**(4), 1008–1031 (2010)
6. Davies, M.E.P., Böck, S.: Temporal convolutional networks for musical audio beat tracking. In: Proceedings of the 27th European Signal Processing Conference (EUSIPCO) (2019)
7. Dixon, S.: Automatic extraction of tempo and beat from expressive performances. J. New Music Res. **30**(1), 39–58 (2001)
8. Fiocchi, D., Buccoli, M., Zanoni, M., Antonacci, F., Sarti, A.: Beat tracking using recurrent neural network: a transfer learning approach. In: 26th European Signal Processing Conference (EUSIPCO), pp. 1915–1919. IEEE (2018)
9. Foscarin, F., Schlüter, J., Widmer, G.: Beat this! accurate beat tracking without DBN postprocessing. In: Proceedings of the 25th International Conference on Music Information Retrieval (ISMIR) (2024)
10. Fuentes, M., et al.: Tracking beats and microtiming in Afro-latin American music using conditional random fields and deep learning. In: Proceedings of the 20th International Society for Music Information Retrieval Conference (ISMIR), pp. 251–258 (2019)
11. Gann, K.: The Music of Conlon Nancarrow, Music in the 20th Century, vol. 7. Cambridge University Press (2008)
12. Gouyon, F., Dixon, S.: A review of automatic rhythm description systems. Comput. Music. J. **29**(1), 34–54 (2005)

13. Gómez, E., Herrera, P., Gómez-Martin, F.: Computational ethnomusicology: perspectives and challenges. J. New Music Res. **42**(2), 111–112 (2013)
14. Holzapfel, A., Davies, M.E.P., Zapata, J.R., Oliveira, J.L., Gouyon, F.: Selective sampling for beat tracking evaluation. IEEE Trans. Audio Speech Lang. Process. **20**(9), 2539–2548 (2012)
15. Hung, Y.N., Wang, J.C., Song, X., Lu, W.T., Won, M.: Modeling beats and downbeats with a time-frequency transformer. In: ICASSP 2022 - 2022 IEEE International Conference on Acoustics, Speech and Signal Processing (ICASSP), vol. 2022-May, pp. 401–405. IEEE (2022)
16. Hunt, S.J.: Exploring polyrhythms, polymeters, and polytempi with the universal grid sequencer framework. In: Proceedings of the 15th International Audio Mostly Conference, pp. 101–106. ACM (2020)
17. Jure, L., Rocamora, M.: Microtiming in the rhythmic structure of Candombe drumming patterns. In: Fourth International Conference on Analytical Approaches to World Music (AAWM 2016), pp. 1–5 (2016)
18. Kim, B., Pardo, B.: A human-in-the-loop system for sound event detection and annotation. ACM Trans. Interact. Intell. Syst. **8**(2), 1–23 (2018)
19. Krebs, H.: Some extensions of the concepts of metrical consonance and dissonance. J. Music Theory **31**(1), 99–99 (1987)
20. Maia, L.S., Rocamora, M., Fuentes, M.: Adapting meter tracking models to Latin american music. In: Proceedings of the 23th International Society for Music Information Retrieval Conference (ISMIR) (2022)
21. Mora-Ángel, F., Gil, G.L., Cano, E., Grollmisch, S.: ACMUS-MIR: A new annotated data set of Andean Colombian music. In: 7th International Conference on Digital Libraries for Musicology (DLfM) (2019)
22. Nunes, L., Rocamora, M., Jure, L., Biscainho, L.W.: Beat and downbeat tracking based on rhythmic patterns applied to the Uruguayan candombe drumming. In: Proceedings of the 16th International Society for Music Information Retrieval Conference (ISMIR), pp. 264–270 (2015)
23. Pinto, A., Böck, S., Cardoso, J., Davies, M.: User-driven fine-tuning for beat tracking. Electronics **10**(13), 1518–1518 (2021)
24. Pinto, A.S.: Towards Human-in-the-Loop Computational Rhythm Analysis in Challenging Musical Conditions. Ph.D. thesis, Universidade do Porto (2023)
25. Pinto, A.S., Bernardes, G.: Bridging the rhythmic gap : a user-centric approach to beat tracking in challenging music signals. In: 16th International Symposium on Computer Music Multidisciplinary Research (CMMR), pp. 1–12 (2023)
26. Pinto, A.S., Davies, M.E.P.: Towards user-informed beat tracking of musical audio. In: 14th International Symposium on Computer Music Multidisciplinary Research (CMMR), pp. 577–588 (2019)
27. Pinto, A.S., Davies, M.E.: Tapping along to the difficult ones: leveraging user-input for beat tracking in highly expressive musical content. In: Kronland-Martinet, R., Ystad, S., Aramaki, M. (eds.) Perception, Representations, Image, Sound, Music - 14th International Symposium, CMMR 2019, Marseille, France, October 14–18, 2019, Revised Selected Papers, Lecture Notes in Computer Science, vol. 12631, pp. 75–90. Springer (2021)
28. Pinto, A.S., Domingues, I., Davies, M.E.P.: Shift if you can: counting and visualising correction operations for beat tracking evaluation. In: Extended Abstracts for the Late-Breaking Demo Session of the International Society for Music Information Retrieval Conference (ISMIR) (2020)

29. Puckette, M.S.: Pure Data. In: Proceedings of the International Computer Music Conference (ICMC), pp. 224–227. International Computer Music Association (1997)
30. Schechter, J.M., Sheehy, D.E., Smith, R.R.: Latin America. Ethnomusicology **29**(2), 317–317 (1985)
31. Srinivasamurthy, A., Holzapfel, A., Serra, X.: Informed automatic meter analysis of music recordings. In: Proceedings of the 18th International Society for Music Information Retrieval Conference (ISMIR), pp. 679–685 (2017)
32. Thoegersen, P.A.: Polytempic Polymicrotonal Music: A Road Less Traveled. Ph.D. thesis, University of Illinois at Urbana-Champaign (2012)
33. Tzanetakis, G., Kapur, A., Schloss, W., Wright, M.: Computational ethnomusicology. J. Interdiscip. Music Stud. **1**(2), 1–24 (2007)
34. Yamamoto, K.: Human-in-the-loop adaptation for interactive musical beat tracking. In: Proceedings of the 22nd International Society for Music Information Retrieval Conference (ISMIR) (2021)
35. Zhao, J., Xia, G., Wang, Y.: Beat transformer: demixed beat and downbeat tracking with dilated self-attention. In: Proceedings of the 23rd International Society for Music Information Retrieval Conference (ISMIR) (2022)

Algorithms for Roughness Control Using Frequency Shifting and Attenuation of Partials in Audio

Jeremy Hyrkas(✉)

University of California San Diego, San Diego, USA
jhyrkas@ucsd.edu

Abstract. Though synthesis algorithms frequently use parameters to change the produced sound, it is not always the case that these parameters have a direct (or intuitive) correlation to the change made to the perceptual attributes—the more meaningful sound descriptors for the listener and/or musician. In this work we explore two strategies by which a perceptual descriptor, roughness, can be parameterized directly on a scale, much like how interactive sound allows for control of pitch and/or loudness. Here, roughness (often tied to dissonance) is controlled by changing either the frequency or amplitude of partials that lie within a critical band. Audio examples are provided to demonstrate use in audio mixing, sound (re)synthesis and audio effects, with two implementations made available: one for offline use and another for real-time interactive synthesis using Max/MSP.

Keywords: auditory roughness · additive synthesis · assistive audio production

1 Introduction

This work presents two algorithms for controlling the roughness of sound by adjusting the frequency or amplitude of individual partials or harmonics of the sound. Auditory roughness is a perceptual feature of sound that is often linked with an experience of dissonance, making it a particularly salient sonic parameter that a composer may want to manipulate. Roughness has historically been studied in relation to musical consonance with regards to interval choice and tuning. Consequently, previous approaches that manipulate the roughness of sound often utilize pitch shifting. The approaches described here avoid pitch shifting, favoring subtle changes to the spectrum to control roughness while maintaining as much of the original signals as possible. A brief history of roughness and musical applications is presented in Sect. 2. Algorithms for roughness control are described generally in Sect. 3. Finally, implementations for audio files and additive synthesis are presented in Sect. 4. Implementations of the algorithms and audio examples are available online.

S. Ystad et al. (Eds.): CMMR 2023, LNCS 15236, pp. 480–493, 2026.
https://doi.org/10.1007/978-3-032-02042-0_36

2 Auditory Roughness, Musical Consonance and Tuning

Auditory roughness is a psychoacoustic and physical phenomena that occurs when sinusoidal components of sound fall within the same critical band of the ear. Sinusoidal components that are very close in frequency (separated by less 10 Hz) are heard as a single partial with slow beating, a special case of amplitude modulation where the modulating sinusoid (acting as the amplitude envelope) is sufficiently low in frequency that the sound is brought in and out of prominence on a perceptible time scale. While such sounds are generally considered to be *consonant*, increasing the modulation frequency or, equivalently, the difference in frequency between the two components, increases the rate of beating, eventually prohibiting the listener's ability to track the beats. The tone then takes on a more steady amplitude but with a distinct quality known as *roughness*, an attribute often associated with *dissonance*. Increasing the modulation frequency still, so that the frequency separation approaches the critical bandwidth, the listener begins to recognize the sound as separate tones, at which point discomfort decreases and eventually disappears.

2.1 Psychoacoustic Models of Roughness

Auditory roughness relates the experience of dissonance to the presence of sound partials that fall within a critical band of the human ear. Theories relating musical consonance and the proximity in frequency of sound partials date at least as far back as Helmholtz, who credited consonance to the lack of beating partials when harmonic instruments play intervals related by integer ratios [4].

Plomp and Levelt tested the perception of dissonance and proposed a general model of dissonance of sinusoidal tones based on critical bandwidth [12]. The resulting data informed a model by Sethares [15] who calculates the dissonance between partials with frequencies f_1 and f_2 having amplitudes a_1 and a_2 as

$$r(f_1, a_1, f_2, a_2) = a_1 a_2 \cdot \left[e^{-b_1 sx} - e^{-b_2 sx}\right], \tag{1}$$

where $b_1 = 3.5$ and $b_2 = 5.75$ are chosen by fitting the exponent sx to Plomp and Levelt's standard dissonance curve.

In (1), $x = f_2 - f_1$ (where $f_1 < f_2$) is the frequency difference between the two partials and s scales the frequency difference to fit Plomp and Levelt's standard curve, which was originally plotted with respect to critical bandwidth. The frequency difference is scaled by

$$s = \frac{d^*}{s_1 f_1 + s_2}, \tag{2}$$

where $d^* = 0.24$ is the position of maximum dissonance and $s_1 = 0.021$ and $s_2 = 19$ are obtained using a least-squares fit. Equation 1 accounts for partials having different amplitudes, so softer components contribute less to dissonance. Figure 1 demonstrates how (1) varies across the frequency domain. We will later

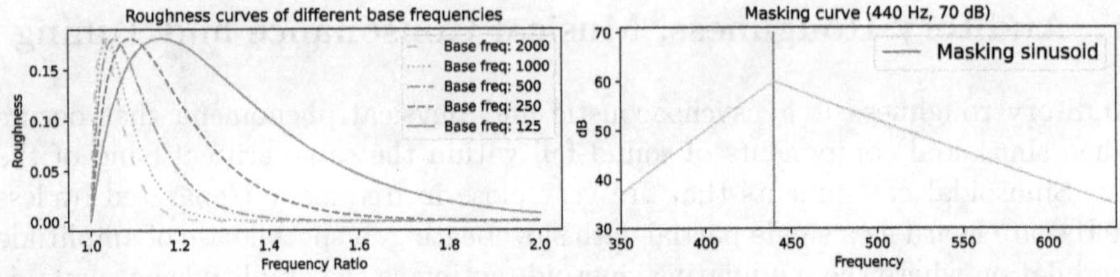

Fig. 1. Left: the roughness of partials with equal amplitude plotted against their frequency ratio at different regions of the frequency domain (1). **Right**: a plot of (3), a simple model for estimating the masking curve of a tone given its frequency and sound pressure level in dB. A second tone on or below the sloped lines will be masked.

use (1) to calculate the roughness of sound partials and choose new frequencies to reduce roughness.

Kameoka and Kuriyagawa extended Plomp and Levelt's experiments and investigated the role of masking [5]. The perception of dissonance when two partials have different amplitudes was found to differ from the pattern found in masking curves. While a louder sinusoid will more easily mask a quieter sinusoid of higher frequency, pairs of sinusoids were found to be more dissonant when the tone with lower frequency was louder than the tone of higher frequency. Nevertheless, perceived dissonance dropped when one was completely masked by the other, suggesting that masking plays a role in perceived dissonance. A simple model for estimating the masking curve of a partial based on difference in Barks [7] can be computed as

$$mask(x|f, dB) = \left\{ \begin{array}{l} dB - 10 - 27\left[B_{Hz}(f) - B_{Hz}(x)\right], \text{if } x < f \\ dB - 10 - 15\left[B_{Hz}(x) - B_{Hz}(f)\right], \text{if } x \geq f \end{array} \right\}, \quad (3)$$

which we will later use to computationally control roughness by amplitude changes informed by masking. B_{Hz} converts from Hz to Bark using Traunmüller's model [18]. A plot of this masking curve is shown on the right side of Fig. 1.

Concepts of consonance and dissonance have many definitions in the context of music. The sensation caused by beating partials in a critical band, which can also be described as the presence of amplitude modulation within a critical band, is now referred to as *roughness* in psychoacoustics to disambiguate it from compositional definitions. Based on the work of Plomp and Levelt, more sophisticated models of roughness have been developed. Sethares's model of Plomp and Levelt accounts for the amplitude of partials (see Eq. 1). Vassilakis [19] additionally accounts for the role of amplitude modulation in an extension to (1)[1]. The roughness of a signal is usually defined as the sum of roughness between all pairs of partials.

[1] Vassilakis's model more thoroughly accounts for the role of loudness and amplitude modulation to roughness. However, this equation is more complex and was not found to improve synthesis in this study, so the simpler model from Sethares is used.

2.2 Applications to Tuning, Mixing and Synthesis

While roughness can be measured outside the context of musical applications, it has been supposed to be related to musical consonance [4] and has been used as a metric in tuning, mixing and composition. Sethares developed the Adaptive Tuning algorithm, which adjusts the fundamental frequencies of notes based on their spectra to minimize the expected roughness of the sound. Sethares's algorithm can be approximated in real-time on spectra that are known ahead of time [16] or computed exactly on mixtures of spectra in the full implementation [17]. Adaptive Tuning is based on minimizing (1) with respect to fundamental frequency (as opposed to individual partial frequency) and has been used in other musical contexts (for example, to control the pitch of a Therein implementation in real-time using Pure Data [13]).

The roughness of an audio mix can be a useful metric to measure and control for in sound engineering. Vassilakis used an extension of (1) to analyze and annotate the roughness of sound files [19]. Real-time roughness estimators have been implemented in Pure Data [8,20], each of which use sinusoidal modeling to estimate partials of an incoming mix to determine the roughness. These real-time algorithms have difficulty detecting sinusoidal peaks that are nearby (e.g., less 20 Hz difference) due to their reliance on FFT-based peak-picking. Vassilakis's software, on the other hand, can use a larger FFT analysis window and smaller hop size, in addition to frequency reassignment methods, to obtain finer resolution of nearby partials at the expense of operating offline.

The roughness of a sound can be used as a parameter to be increased or reduced in some synthesis or resynthesis methods. Molina et al. modeled audio signals of chords using sinusoid-plus-residual analysis and reduced beating partials in resynthesis by forcing partial frequencies be an integer multiple of one of the fundamental frequencies of the chord [9]. Roughness was found to be the most impactful feature when pitch shifting one track to be consonant with another in the context of DJing [2,3]. When synthesizing impact sounds using additive synthesis, roughness has been used as a parameter to create convincing sound examples [1]. Finally, Park et al. created software to manipulate psychoacoustic features such as spectral slope or inharmonicity when composing using sound material [11]; auditory roughness control was not implemented in the software but may be another candidate for compositional control.

3 Roughness Control by Individual Partial Adjustment

Previous approaches to roughness control have focused on changing fundamental frequencies (and therefore all partials) of notes [16], pitch shifting audio tracks [3], or quantizing partial frequencies to strict integer harmonics [9]. An unexplored approach is the selective adjustment of partials independent of tuning to control roughness while leaving the majority of the signal intact. Such an approach gives the composer options for reducing or increasing roughness in subtle ways that preserve the essence of the original material as much as possible. The methods developed here explore this approach in both a real-time and offline process. Real-time methods change either the frequency or amplitude of additive synthesis parameters in the Max/MSP computer music environment, while offline approaches selectively filter and resynthesize certain partials in audio files while preserving the remaining portions of audio, which may produce higher fidelity output than methods that use sinusoidal resynthesis [9]. Section 3.1 presents an algorithm for frequency adjustment and Sect. 3.2 presents an algorithm for amplitude adjustment. Offline and online implementations are described in Sect. 4.

3.1 Changing Roughness by Partial Tuning

Here we define *frequency bashing*, a greedy algorithm for reducing or increasing roughness by changing the frequency of partials that lie within a critical band. Pairs of partials that overlap in time and cause roughness are selected and iteratively changed to adjust roughness. A partial may contribute to roughness in more than one pair of nearby partials, so as the algorithm iterates, partials that have already been adjusted are skipped.

In the algorithm, partials pairs are analyzed for their contribution to the overall roughness of the sound using (1), with the most rough partial pairs processed first. The quieter partial has its frequency changed to be the frequency that either minimizes or maximizes roughness with respect to the louder partial within a predefined distance. We restrict movement to a specified range in Barks due to the shape of (1), which would otherwise set partials to have the same frequency when bashing for minimized roughness; we also aim to keep partials within their original critical band to avoid drastically altering the nature of the original sound. Based on the maximum dissonance of (1), distance in Barks is typically set to between 0.05 and 0.4 in our experiments, but the distance is exposed as a user parameter.

Frequency bashing for consonance is computed mathematically as

$$f_2^* = \underset{f_{\min} \leq f^* \leq f_{\max}}{\arg\min} \quad r(f_1, a_1, f^*, a_2) \tag{4}$$

with constraints defined as

$$f_{\min}, f_{\max} = Hz_B(B_{Hz}(f_1) + B_L), Hz_B(B_{Hz}(f_1) + B_H)\,. \tag{5}$$

Hz_B and B_{Hz} convert from Bark to Hz and vice versa [18], and B_L and B_H define the allowable distance in Barks. In (4) and (5), f_1 is the louder partial whose frequency remains constant, while frequency f_2 is the quieter partial whose frequency will be bashed to a new value. When increasing roughness instead of decreasing, the argmin operation in (4) is replaced by argmax. (5) assumes $f_1 < f_2$; when $f_1 > f_2$ the Bark range is defined below f_1 instead of above.

Figure 2 shows potential adjustments for sinusoid pairs. Note that for partials with identical differences in frequency, their position along the roughness curve and solutions for maximum consonance and dissonance will change depending on their location in the frequency domain. The partial pairs depicted (440 Hz

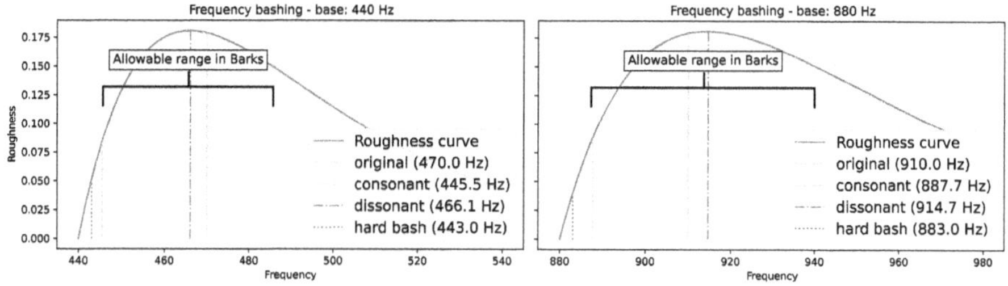

Fig. 2. Frequency bashing two pairs of partials with frequencies (440 Hz, 470 Hz) on the left and (880 Hz, 910 Hz) on the right. The partials with higher frequencies are adjusted. The original frequency of the higher partial is depicted in the long-dashed red line, the most consonant in the specified allowable range of movement in Barks is shown in the short-dashed yellow line and the most dissonant in the dash-dotted green line. Hard-bashing the partial to a difference 3 Hz is shown in the dotted purple line. Hard-bashing ignores the roughness curve and allowable range. (Color figure online)

470 Hz 880 Hz 910 Hz) have unequal differences in their maximally consonant and dissonant solutions, even though they begin with the same difference 30 Hz per pair.

Another option is *hard-bashing*, where the quieter partial is adjusted to be a specified difference in Hz from the unchanged partial. An advantage of hard-bashing is that when multiple partials are adjusted within a sound, they will have identical frequency difference from their neighboring partial, creating a slow-beating (tremolo) effect but only in certain frequency ranges of the signal. However, consonance and dissonance as defined by roughness models are disregarded. In Fig. 2, hard-bashing partials to have a difference 3 Hz maintains the equal difference between partial pairs after bashing and both new frequencies result in lower roughness. However, they now fall on different positions along the roughness curve due to their different critical bandwidths.

Frequency bashing is implemented as described for offline processing of audio files, with further modifications described in Sect. 4.1. Simplifications made to this algorithm for real-time implementation are described in Sect. 4.2.

3.2 Changing Roughness by Amplitude Adjustment

Another approach to roughness control is changing the amplitude of partials, as the absolute and relative loudness of partials contributes to roughness. A simple technique would be to lower the amplitude of the quieter partial in a pair that contributes roughness to the sound. However, lowering the amplitude of a partial will reduce the power of the signal. Instead, the quieter partial must have its amplitude decreased while the louder partial's amplitude is increased to maintain the original signal power. This seesaw effect of amplitude adjustments may remind the reader of the children's arcade game "whack-a-mole," and is therefore named *amplitude whacking.*

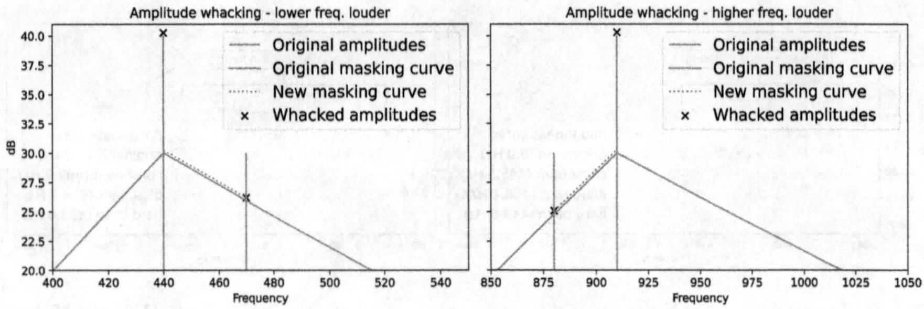

Fig. 3. Amplitude whacking pairs of partials with frequencies (440 Hz, 470 Hz) on the left and (880 Hz, 910 Hz) on the right. Original amplitudes are shown as red solid lines, with whacked amplitudes depicted as black X's. Despite each pair being equidistant in Hz, the example on the right requires more attenuation of the quieter partial due to the asymmetry of the masking curve.

Whacking can be performed using a user parameter w_p between 0.0 (no change) and 1.0 (maximum amplitude change). At $w_p = 1$, the algorithm adjusts amplitudes so that the quieter partial is fully masked by the louder partial. When adjusting the amplitudes of a pair of partials to reduce roughness, the resulting difference in dB (Δ_{dB}) should be the masking threshold specified by (3) multiplied by w_p. The original power of the signal should also be retained. If a_1 is the amplitude of the louder partial and a_2 the amplitude of the quieter partial, these constraints are specified as

$$20\log_{10}(a_1^*) - 20\log_{10}(a_2^*) = \Delta_{dB}\ , (a_1)^2 + (a_2)^2 = (a_1^*)^2 + (a_2^*)^2 \tag{6}$$

respectively, where a_1^* and a_2^* are the new amplitudes of the partials. Solving the system of equations algebraically leads to the solutions:

$$a_2^* = \sqrt{\frac{(a_1)^2 + (a_2)^2}{1 + 10^{\frac{\Delta_{dB}}{10}}}},\ a_1^* = \sqrt{(a_1)^2 + (a_2)^2 - (a_2^*)^2}\ . \tag{7}$$

Amplitude whacking proceeds identically to frequency bashing, with pairs of partials that contribute the most roughness processed first and partials that have already been adjusted skipped in later iterations. Figure 3 shows potential adjustments for amplitudes of partial pairs to reduce the roughness of a sound. Offline and real-time implementations of the algorithm are further described in Sects. 4.1 and 4.2, respectively.

4 Algorithm Implementations

The algorithms for frequency bashing and amplitude whacking can be performed offline on mixes of audio files or in real-time in additive synthesis. Each approach requires certain tweaks and optimizations. The implementations are described below, followed by a discussion of potential applications with accompanying examples available online.

4.1 Offline Implementations on Audio Files

Auditory roughness occurs maximally when partials fall very close to each other (e.g., on the order of 20–40 Hz difference). Finding individual partials with such resolution in one signal is difficult using only FFT-based methods [19], and isolating one partial from another with a similar frequency using digital filters also presents challenges. Taking these limitations into account, and following previous application of roughness control on combinations of sounds [2, 9, 16], we use the algorithms defined in Sect. 3 to control the roughness of audio files that are intended to be combined in a mix.

Given a collection of audio files, each file is analyzed using sinusoidal modeling [14] to find the top N partials of each frame of audio. N can be a small number (on the order of 10) because the sinusoidal tracks will not be used for resynthesis and are instead used to identify the most prominent partials at a given time. When a partial from signal x_i and a partial from signal x_j overlap in time and cause roughness as calculated using (1), the partials are collected as candidates for frequency bashing or amplitude whacking with new frequencies or amplitudes determined using (4) and (7).

To adjust partials of a signal x, the offending partials are removed from x and in parallel isolated, altered, and added back in. The mean frequency and frequency range of a partial are used to set the center frequency f_c and quality factor Q of an amplitude-complimentary pair of H_N, a notch filter, and H_P, a peaking bandpass filter, such that

$$H_N(f_c, Q) \cdot X + H_P(f_c, Q) \cdot X = X \ . \tag{8}$$

If a signal has k partials to be adjusted, the output signal x' is computed as

$$X' = X \cdot \prod_{i=1}^{k} H_{N_i}(f_{c_i}, Q_i) + \sum_{i=1}^{k} \Delta_i(H_{P_i}(f_{c_i}, Q_i) \cdot X) \ , \tag{9}$$

where Δ_i changes either the amplitude or frequency of the partial isolated in the peaking filter. H_N and H_P are biquad filters with coefficients derived in [10] and implemented as the *iirnotch* and *iirpeak* functions in MATLAB and scipy.

Figure 4 depicts the audio processing of partials. Forward and backward filtering is used for zero-phase filtering. When frequency bashing, the output of a peaking filter is frequency shifted using single sideband modulation; when amplitude whacking, gain is applied so that the mean amplitude of the bandpassed signal matches the value derived using (7). The processed signals are then added to the output of the series of notch filters. Cross-fades are applied so that processed signals with adjusted partials are only heard during the lifetime of the partial. When partials that cause roughness are not present, the original signals are used unaltered.

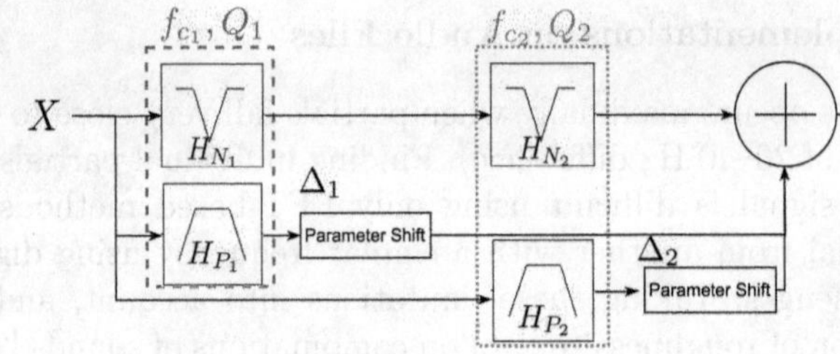

Fig. 4. Partials of a signal x are adjusted by removing them using notch filters, and in parallel, isolating them from x using amplitude-complimentary peaking bandpass filters. Complimentary filters share the same center frequency f_{c_k} and quality factor Q_k. The output of the peaking filters are processed to adjust either the frequency or the amplitude by some amount Δ_k.

4.2 Real-Time Implementations for Additive Synthesis Parameters

Frequency bashing and amplitude whacking can be performed more straightforwardly on additive synthesis parameters, as no audio analysis is inherently required. In additive synthesis, frequency and amplitude pairs are used to control an oscillator bank, with each oscillator receiving one frequency and amplitude per synthesis step. Roughness control on additive synthesis parameters can be more easily performed in real-time due to the lack an audio analysis step, although some simplifications to the algorithms are required to reduce computational load.

Two externals for the Max/MSP computer music environment were created to control roughness of additive synthesis parameters. The externals are control rate objects that take as input a list of frequency/amplitude pairs and output one list of frequencies and one list of amplitudes. In the *basher* object, frequencies are adjusted using (4) while amplitudes are passed through unchanged, while amplitudes are adjusted by the *whacker* object using (7) with the frequencies unchanged. The outputs can be connected to multichannel Max objects for additive synthesis (see the associated code for examples). The input list of sinusoidal parameters can come from an analysis-resynthesis system for sinusoidal modeling [6,14], but composers are free to use any method for generating sinusoidal parameters. Other algorithmic parameters include the Bark range of search and adjustment (see Eq. 5), a toggle to change from decreasing roughness to increasing roughness, and the percent of movement from the original sinusoidal parameters to the adjusted parameters. These parameters can be fixed or adjusted by the user algorithmically or manually on-the-fly as a musical effect.

Equation 1 is expensive to compute in real-time for every potential pairwise combination for every frame. When searching for potential candidates for parameter adjustment in the Max objects, partial pairs are sorted by frequency instead of by overall roughness to reduce computational load. Pairs are processed in ascending order of frequency, short-cutting whenever pairs start to fall outside of the defined Bark range. In many cases there will not be many partials lying within a fraction of a critical band of each other, but in general results may differ from the offline implementation.

When changing amplitudes in Max, the user parameter for whacking amount maximally transfers all power from the quietest partial to the loudest partial to avoid computing (3) at every frame. As a result, the audible effect of the parameter will stop before reaching the maximum value once quieter partials are fully masked. This issue could be avoided by precomputing and quantizing masking curves. Finally, while offline methods change the parameters of partials across time, sinusoidal parameters here are adjusted at every frame in a memoryless fashion. This change reduces computation and computer memory necessary to track previous changes, but makes the objects more susceptible to rapid fluctuation in the case where two nearby partials are nearly the same amplitude and fluctuate between which one is louder.

4.3 Audio Examples and Observations

Audio examples of frequency bashing and amplitude whacking on audio files and additive synthesis parameters are available on the supplemental website[2]. The algorithms are demonstrated on the sinusoidal examples in Figs. 2 and 3 where the effect of each algorithm and parameter choice is most obvious. More complex examples showcase various use cases of the algorithms in more realistic musical contexts.

The effects of frequency bashing and amplitude whacking on synthesized notes is shown in Fig. 5. Each algorithm is applied to an equal tempered major triad of sawtooth waves with 10 partials. The original spectrum is shown on the left side of the figure, alongside the adjusted partials in each algorithm in a zoomed region of the spectrum. Three pairs of partials are found to be nearby in a critical band and contribute to roughness. Although the algorithms only adjust a handful of partials, there is a noticeable difference in beating between the original and processed examples while the characteristic of the sound is largely intact. In contrast, an accompanying audio example demonstrates the chord in just intonation, which an algorithm such as Adaptive Tuning [16] may offer as a solution. The retuned example also contains less roughness than the original but sounds fundamentally different. This example demonstrates the difference in philosophy between our methods for roughness control versus tuning-based approaches, as the goal of our algorithms is to only change the perceived auditory roughness while maintaining as much of the original signal as possible.

More examples of roughness reduction include frequency bashing a slightly detuned major chord and amplitude whacking a horn line. The horn line is depicted in Fig. 6, with a spectrogram of the original on the left and a spectrogram of the difference signal after amplitude whacking on the right. This example again demonstrates the very subtle changes made to the signal, as well as the preservation of the original signal during periods of time where no roughness is present. Another example demonstrates the effect of simply filtering partials that contribute to roughness without reintroducing them to the mix with a different frequency or amplitude, which can be effective in mixes where very few

[2] https://jeremyhyrkas.com/cmmr2023.

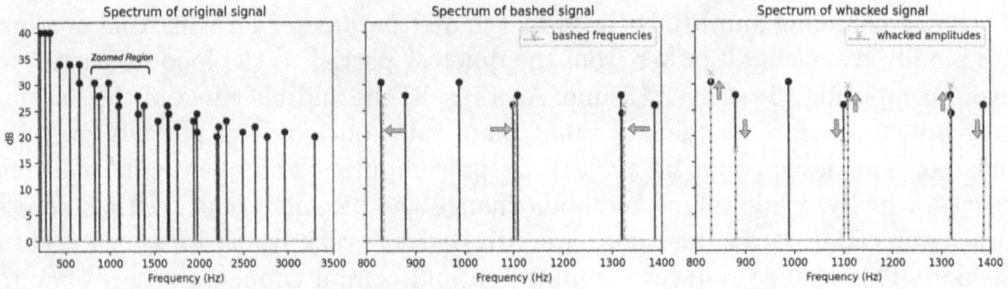

Fig. 5. **Left**: the spectrum of a major triad of sawtooth waveforms in equal temperament tuning. **Center**: zoomed region of the spectrum after frequency bashing. Three partials have been moved. **Right**: the same zoomed region of the spectrum after amplitude whacking. Three pairs of nearby partials (six partials total) have had their amplitudes adjusted.

partials contribute to roughness. These examples demonstrate a potential use case of reducing roughness when mixing a track without the use of retuning or manually intensive EQing. Finally, a creative example demonstrates roughness control on trumpets playing a chord with dissonant intervals (root, minor second and minor third). The processed output contains far less roughness than the original mix but is still musically dissonant. This example demonstrates the potential for separating musical consonance from auditory roughness as musical parameters in a composition.

Two examples are presented where frequency bashing is used to introduce more roughness into a sound mix than was originally present. A sawtooth major seventh chord is used, as is a recording of a choir singing a chorale. This use case shows frequency bashing as an audio effect that may be useful for a composer who wishes to introduce dissonance without detuning or modulating the entire signal. Finally, an example is presented using hard-bashing where pairs that contribute roughness are moved to be 3 Hz apart from one another. The effect is similar to a tremolo audio effect, but the modulation is only heard when roughness is present and only in some parts of the frequency domain. All examples described can be found on the accompanying website.

The Max externals described in Sect. 4.2 are demonstrated in videos using harmonic and inharmonic drones, as well as a dynamic sinusoidal reconstruction of the horn line described previously. The reconstruction requires playback of an offline analysis using the SPEAR modeling software [6]. Preliminary versions of these Max externals that control the amplitude, frequency and spatial panning of additive synthesis parameters were used to create the composition "The Hearing Test," which musically investigates the perception of roughness, tuning and the experience of participating in a listening test[3].

[3] This piece piece was presented at ICMC 2024. A binaural version is available online.

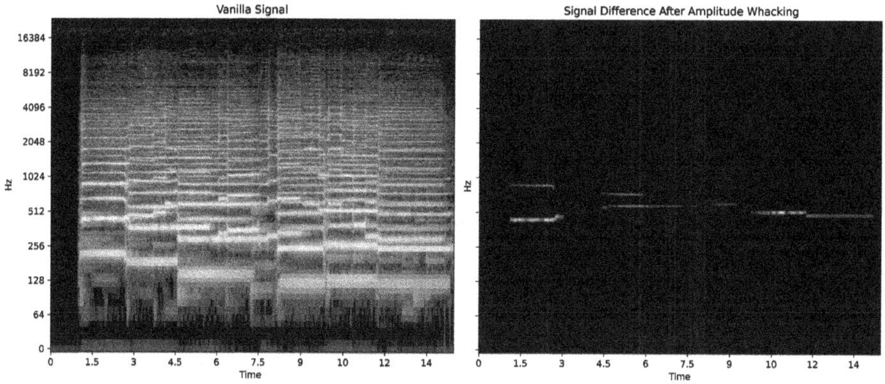

Fig. 6. **Left**: a spectrogram of a dynamic horn line featuring audio of three players performing. **Right**: the spectral difference of an amplitude whacked version of the horn line and the original. Amplitudes of partials are only adjusted in areas of roughness, after which point the original signals are faded back in. This example is time-varying and demonstrates subtle changes that achieve a reduction in roughness without retuning any notes.

5 Conclusion and Future Work

We present two algorithms for controlling auditory roughness by targeted sound partial adjustment. Frequency bashing modifies the frequencies of neighboring partials, while amplitude whacking modifies their amplitude. Considerations are made based on previous work modeling listener perception of roughness, auditory masking, and previous approaches to roughness reduction. Offline implementations of both algorithms are provided for audio files intended to be mixed in time[4], and control-rate objects for additive synthesis are provided for the Max/MSP environment[5]. The accompanying audio examples demonstrate potential use cases in mixing and composition.

The algorithms reduce roughness as calculated by the roughness models by their definition, but listening tests would be beneficial to confirm the intended effect on listeners, as the perception of consonance and dissonance is affected by context in ways not accounted for in these models. Additionally, a VST implementation of the audio processing algorithms would assist sound engineers in incorporating them into their workflow. While these algorithms do not currently work on incoming audio streams, a plug-in implementation may be beneficial for use on processed tracks before final mixing and mastering. Finally, simplifying certain portions of the audio implementations may make them viable for use in real-time applications.

[4] https://github.com/jhyrkas/audio-bashing.

[5] https://github.com/jhyrkas/basher_max.

Acknowledgments. Special thanks to Miller Puckette and Tamara Smyth for advising portions of this project.

References

1. Aramaki, M., Gondre, C., Kronland-Martinet, R., Voinier, T., Ystad, S.: Thinking the sounds: an intuitive control of an impact sound synthesizer. In: Proceedings of the 15th International Conference on Auditory Display (ICAD) (2009)
2. Gebhardt, R., Davies, M., Seeber, B.: Harmonic mixing based on roughness and pitch commonality. In: Proceedings of the of the International Conference on Digital Audio Effects (DAFx) (2015)
3. Gebhardt, R., Davies, M., Seeber, B.: Psychoacoustic approaches for harmonic music mixing. J. Appl. Sci. **6**(5), 123–143 (2016)
4. Helmholtz, H.: On the Sensations of Tone as a Physiological Basis for the Theory of Music. Longmans, Green and Co. (1877)
5. Kameoka, A., Kuriyagawa, M.: Consonance theory Part I: consonance of dyads. J. Acoust. Soc. Am. **45**(6), 1451–1459 (1969)
6. Klingbeil, M.: Software for spectral analysis, editing, and synthesis. In: Proceedings of the International Computer Music Conference (ICMC) (2005)
7. Lagrange, M., Marchand, S.: Real-time additive synthesis of sound by taking advantage of psychoacoustics. In: Proceedings of the International Conference on Digital Audio Effects (DAFx) (2001)
8. MacCallum, J. and Einbond, A.: Real-time analysis of sensory dissonance. In: Computer Music Modeling and Retrieval. Sense of Sounds. 4th International Symposium, CMMR 2007, Copenhagen, Denmark, August 2007, Revised Papers (2007)
9. Molina, E., Barbancho, A., Tardón, L., Barbancho, I.: Dissonance reduction in polyphonic audio using harmonic reorganization. IEEE/ACM Trans. Audio Speech Lang. Process. **22**(2), 325–334 (2013)
10. Orfanidis, S.J.: Introduction to Signal Processing. Prentice Hall, Upper Saddle River (1996)
11. Park, T.H., Biguenet, J., Li, Z., Richardson, C., Scharr, T.: Feature modulation synthesis (FMS). In: Proceedings of the International Computer Music Conference (ICMC) (2007)
12. Plomp, R., Levelt, W.: Tonal consonance and critical bandwidth. J. Acoust. Soc. Am. **38**(4), 548–560 (1965)
13. Porres, A., Manzolli, J.: A roughness model in PD for an adaptive tuning patch controlled by antennas. In: Proceedings of the Pure Data Convention (2007)
14. Serra, X.: A system for sound analysis/transformation/synthesis based on a deterministic plus stochastic decomposition. Dissertation, Stanford University (1990)
15. Sethares, W.: Local consonance and the relationship between timbre and scale. J. Acoust. Soc. Am. **94**(3), 1218–1228 (1993)
16. Sethares, W.: Real-time adaptive tunings using max. J. New Music Res. **31**(4), 347–355 (2002)
17. Sethares, W.: Tuning, Timbre, Spectrum, Scale. Springer, London (2005). https://doi.org/10.1007/b138848
18. Traunmüller, H.: Analytical expressions for the tonotopic sensory scale. J. Acoust. Soc. Am. **88**(1), 97–100 (1990)

19. Vassilakis, P., Fitz, K.: SRA: a web-based research tool for spectral and roughness analysis of sound signals. In: Proceedings of the Sound and Music Computing Conference (SMC) (2007)
20. Villegas, J., Cohen, M.: "Roughometer": realtime roughness calculation and profiling. In: Proceedings of the Audio Engineering Society Convention 125 (AES) (2008)

NUFluteDB: Flute Sound Dataset with Appropriate and Inappropriate Blowing Styles

Sai Oshita(✉) and Tetsuro Kitahara

Graduate School of Integrated Basic Sciences, Nihon University Setagaya-ku, Tokyo, Japan
{ohshita,kitahara}@kthrlab.jp

Abstract. This paper describes a dataset of flute sounds with appropriate and inappropriate blowing styles. The flute is known as a difficult instrument to learn. We, therefore, have been developing a support system that automatically identifies the appropriateness of blowing in flute performances. To develop such a system, we need a dataset that consists of various sounds with various blowing styles, including both appropriate and inappropriate ways, but there are no such datasets. In this paper, we present the dataset that we have been developing. This dataset consists of sounds played by various players with various blowing styles, and also it has annotations of each sound's subjective evaluation.

Keywords: Flute · Dataset · Subjective evaluation

1 Introduction

The flute is an instrument whose sound changes greatly when the breath's direction and the mouth's size are changed. Therefore, it is necessary to carefully control the size of the mouth and the direction and strength of the breath to play the flute with appropriate tone quality. However, although many books on the market instruct how to play the flute, only a few clearly describe these points. Therefore, even if one reads a detailed book, it is not easy for a beginner to listen to their sound and judge how to improve it by themselves.

To facilitate beginners' practice of the flute, we have been developing a system that analyzes users' flute sounds and feeds back on how inappropriate their sounds are and/or why they are inappropriate. To achieve such technologies, we need a lot of flute sounds played by various players with different skill levels.

Several studies have been conducted on flute performance support systems. Yoonchang [11] created a system to judge whether the player was playing appropriate sounds by evaluating the head-tube relationship, air pressure, and fingering from the sounds. Kuroda et al. [5] created a dataset that includes sounds played by a robot and human players to control the blow's strength and direction strictly. After creating their dataset called *Good Sounds*, Romani et al. [9] created a system to analyze the acoustic characteristics of flute sounds.

S. Ystad et al. (Eds.): CMMR 2023, LNCS 15236, pp. 494–503, 2026.
https://doi.org/10.1007/978-3-032-02042-0_37

Datasets of flute sounds have also been developed recently. Brum [1] created a dataset commprising performances of four pieces with different directions. Cantos [2] created a dataset of flute sounds to research automatic music transcription; it contains monophonic and polyphonic flute sounds, their MIDI transcriptions, and objective evaluations of the transcription accuracy. Goto et al. [3] created a dataset of sounds of various instrument by different performers with different intensities. In addition, multiple datasets of sounds other than flute performances have been developed [4,6,8,10]. However, a dataset has not been developed that includes various sounds played with both appropriate and inappropriate blowing styles with annotations of their subjective evaluation.

In this paper, we describe a dataset we have created for a flute performance support system. This dataset is a combination of flute-playing sounds and their ratings.

2 Dataset

Because this dataset aims to develop a support system of flute practice, the dataset has to include various sounds ranging from novice-level to advanced ones. In addition, each sound should have an annotation representing how it sounds well. Therefore, we can summarize the issues in designing the dataset as follows:

- **The skill level of players**
  Various players ranging from novices to experts should participate in our recording. In particular, asking novice players to participate is essential because such players may hesitate to record their flute sounds, even though it is crucial to analyze sounds played by such players.
- **Playing styles**
  The dataset should include sounds played in inappropriate styles, such as too large mouth, too small mouth, too upward breath, and too downward breath. In particular, it would be adequate to ask skillful players to play in such styles intentionally.
- **The number of sounds to be collected**
  The dataset should include as many sounds as possible. It is helpful to collect sounds on the Web because participants record their sounds without restrictions on the place and time. It was also significant because our lifestyle was strongly influenced by COVID-19 when we made the dataset.
- **Annotations of subjective evaluation**
  To evaluate the appropriateness of flute sounds played by various players on a computer, we need an annotation of the subjective evaluation of each sound. We have to ask sufficiently advanced players to do subjective evaluations to keep the evaluations reliable.

This strategy has some limitations. One is a lack of uniformity in the recording quality. Because participants record their sounds and send them to us via the Web, they are assumed to be recorded via their own devices (such as smartphones). Also, the recording environment (e.g., the distance between the

Fig. 1. Note performed by participants

microphone to the flute) cannot be unified. The lack of uniformity may have negative influences on sound analysis.

Another is that we cannot check if participants follow our instructions. Even if they are asked to play in the "too large mouth" style, no one can check if they are genuinely opening their large mouth.

Even though it has such limitations, we made a dataset based on this strategy. Below, we mention the details of the dataset. The dataset is available at the following URL:

https://github.com/5418010saiohshita/dataset

2.1 Audio Recordings

We collected flute sounds played in various blowing styles, including both appropriate and inappropriate ones. As inappropriate ways, we focused on mouth size and breath direction. Due to COVID-19, we asked performers to record their performances themselves and collected them on a crowdsourcing site. The performers were asked to play the score shown in Fig. 1 without vibrato. To reduce the burden on individual performers, we asked either of the following two patterns:

1 [Normal] [Large mouth] [Small mouth] [Breath upward]
2 [Normal] [Breath downward]

The details of the performers and the number of collected sounds are listed in Tables 1 and 2, respectively. To compensate for the fact that the sound volume varies depending on the recording conditions, we corrected the amplitudes so that the temporal mean values of the amplitudes are equal.

Figure 3 shows acoustic features of the collected flute sounds: the averages of temporal variations in amplitude and fundamental frequency (F0). Regarding both the amplitude and F0, sounds played in non-normal blowing styles tend to have more considerrable temporal variations.

2.2 Subjective Evaluation

To each sound collected above, we annotated its blowing appropriateness. To obtain such annotations, we conducted subjective evaluations of the collected sounds using a web-based crowdsourcing service. Participants were limited to current or former students of flute majors in music colleges or high school music departments and those who have played the flute for at least 12 months. As a result, six participants listed in Table 3 participated. The number of participations is different among the participants because we allowed them to participate several times as they would like.

Table 1. Details of musical experience etc. of performers

Per-formers	Age	Exp.* [yrs.]	Gap in exp. [yrs.]	Non-flute experience	Max non-flute exp. [yrs.]	Self-determined flute level
P01	46	2	5	Trumpet	9	Beginner
P02	34	10	3	piano, Guitar	5	Intermediate near beginner
P03	55	2	0	Piano	7	Beginner
P04	29	3	0	Piano	5	Intermediate near beginner
P05	33	2	1	Tenor sax, soprano sax, alto sax	12	Beginner
P06	51	0.8	2	Piano, alto sax, clarinet, bass clarinet	11	Almost no experience
P07	21	3	10			Intermediate near beginner
P08	21	0.1				Intermediate near beginner
P09	46	5	10	Piano	12	Beginner
P10	16	8				Intermediate near advanced
P11	24	10	2			Intermediate near beginner
P12	30	10	5	Piano	16	Intermediate near advanced
P13						
P14						

Exp.: experience
Empty cells mean unanswered.
*Some performers may have answered years of experience excluding the gap.

When each participant opened the designated web page, 20 randomly selected sounds were displayed. They listened to them individually and entered their answers to the questions in Table 4. The choices for choice-type questions are listed in Tables 5 and 6.

Figure 3 shows the distribution of subjective evaluation 1 (overall quality) for the collected sounds. In general, sounds played in the normal-blowing style were given higher ratings than those in the non-normal-blowing style.

3 Examples of the Use of This Dataset

In this section, we present examples using the dataset we created[1].

3.1 Predicting Subjective Evaluation from Acoustic Features

We conducted the prediction of subjective evaluation from acoustic features. This would help develop support system for flute practice. Here, we used linear regression. From each audio signal included in the dataset, 10 acoustic features listed in Table 7 are extracted. Then, these features are applied to linear regression. In linear regression, the objective variable is subjective evaluation 1 (overall quality), while the explanatory variables are those features. Half data were assigned to the training data and the rest to the test data.

Figure 4 compares the subjective evaluation's predicted and actual values. The figure shows that even though the actual value of the highest subjective

[1] These have been presented in our previous paper [7].

Table 2. Number of Experiments for flute sound collection

Performers	Blowing styles					Total
	Normal	Larger	Smaller	Upward	Downward	
P01	1	1	1	1	0	4
P02	2	1	1	1	1	6
P03	10	5	5	5	5	30
P04	1	0	0	0	1	2
P05	1	1	1	1	0	4
P06	10	5	5	5	5	30
P07	2	1	1	1	1	6
P08	7	4	4	4	4	23
P09	7	7	7	7	6	34
P10	3	3	3	3	3	15
P11	2	1	1	1	1	6
P12	1	1	1	1	0	4
P13	1	0	0	0	1	2
P14	1	0	0	0	1	2
Total	49	30	30	30	29	168

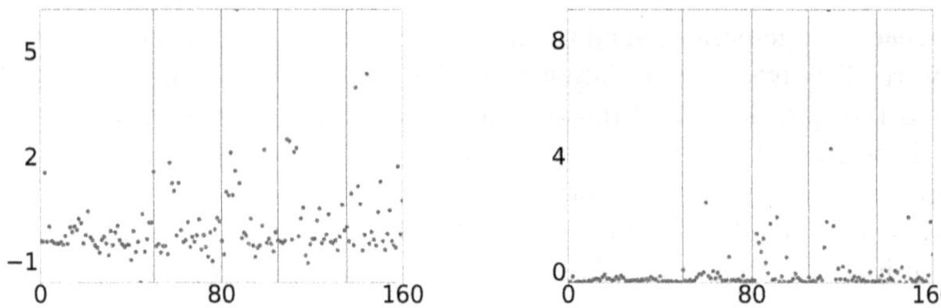

(a) Average of temporal variation in amplitude (d_v)

(b) Average of temporal variation in F0 (d_f)

Fig. 2. Acoustic features of the collected flute sounds. Horizontal: sound ID (from left to right: [Normal], [Large mouth], [Small mouth], [Breath upward], [Breath downward]), Vertical: standardized feature values

Table 3. Participants (evaluators) for subjective sound evaluation

Participant	# of participation	Flute experience [yrs.]	Non-flute experience
S01	1	3	Sax, piano
S02	10	5	Piano, harp
S03	1	6	Electric organ, percussion, etc.
S04	1	22	Piano, percussion, piccolo, etc.
S05	1	28	Piano
S06	1	28	Piano

Table 4. Questions used in the subjective evaluation

1	Overall quality	Response type 1
2	Clearness of the tone	Response type 1
3	Stability of the intensity	Response type 1
4	Stability of the pitch	Response type 1
5	Smallness of the breathy noise	Response type 1
6	Which in the blowing problems apply? (one or more)	Response type 2
7	Write anything else you noticed	Description

Table 5. Response type 1 for subjective evaluation

1	Below beginner level. Seen as just starting level.
2	Beginner level. There are some areas that need improvement.
3	Intermediate level. Some improvement is needed. In general, the student's performance is satisfactory.
4	Intermediate to advanced level. There are some points to be improved, but the performance is acceptable for an amateur concert.
5	Advanced level. There is nothing to be improved at all.

Table 6. Response type 2 for subjective evaluation

1	Breathing too strong
2	Breathing too weak
3	Mouth size too large
4	Mouth too small
5	Breath too upward
6	Breath too downward
7	No problem
8	I don't know

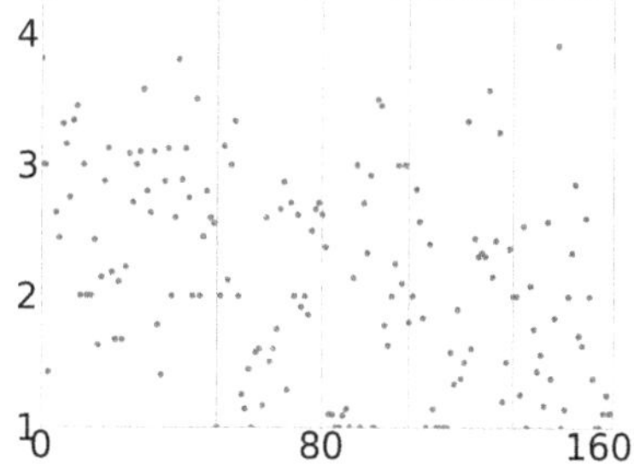

Fig. 3. Distribution of subjective evaluation 1 (overall quality) of collected sound. Horizontal: sound ID (from left to right: [Normal], [Large mouth], [Small mouth], [Breath upward], [Breath downward]), Vertical: ratings

Table 7. Acoustic features extracted from flute sounds

Feature	Feature description
d_v	Average of time variation of amplitude
d_f	Average of time variation of fundamental frequency
r_v	Amplitude range
r_f	Fundamental frequency range
o_s	Number of harmonic components (including fundamental frequency components) at the beginning of blowing
f_s	Percentage of overtones (non-fundamental components) in all harmonics at the beginning of blowing
n_s	Percentage of overtones in the entire spectrum at the beginning of blowing
o_c	Number of overtones (calculated from the middle interval)
f_c	Percentage of non-fundamental frequency components in all overtones (calculated from the middle interval)
n_c	Percentage of overtone components in the whole spectrum (calculated from the middle interval)

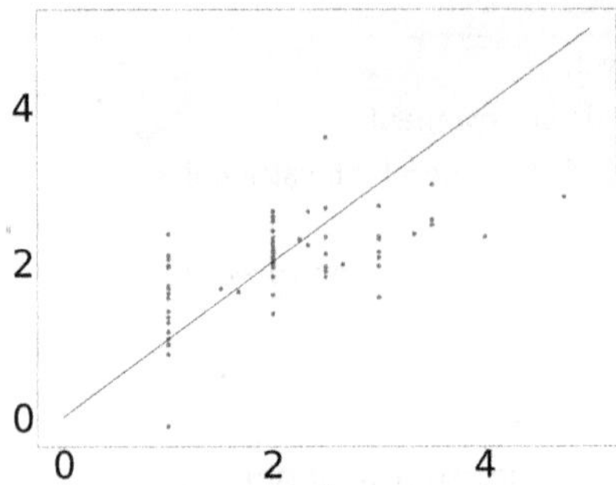

(a) (a) Outliers included

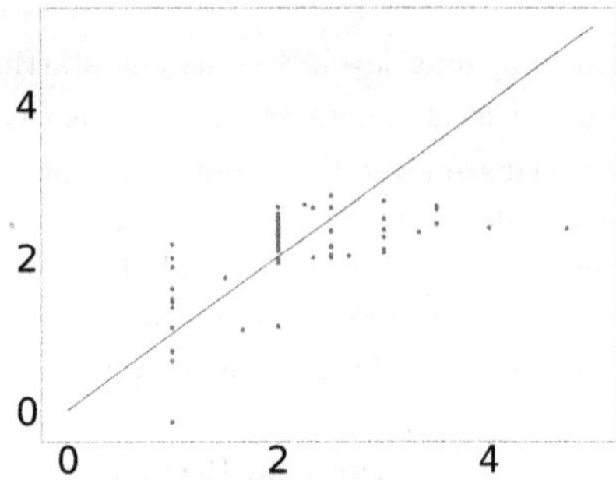

(b) (b) Outliers removed

Fig. 4. Actual subjective evaluation (horizontal) and its prediction (vertical) with linear regression

evaluation is 4.75, and its predicted value is 2.38. When the outliers are removed, the sounds where the actual subjective evaluation is greater than 3 have lower predicted values than the actual evaluation. The root mean square error (RMSE) of the prediction is 0.670. When the outliers are removed, the RMSE is 0.642.

We also attempted the same prediction with decision trees (DTs) after the subjective evaluation was discretized into two or three classes (that is, we conducted it as two-class or three-class classification). The objective feature and explanatory features are the same as above. Table 8 lists the classification accuracy and the depth of the trees acquired. An example of the trees is shown in Fig. 5.

Table 8. Accuracy of predicting subjective evaluation with DT (in parentheses: outliers removed)

Classification	Maximum(Depth 2)	Maximum
Two-class (Lower than 2 / 2 or higher)	0.93 (0.94)	0.93 (0.94)
Three-class (Lower than 2 / 2 to 3 / 3 or higher)	0.83 (0.84)	0.86 (0.84)

Table 9. Accuracy of predicting blowing styles with DT (in parentheses: outlier removal)

Classification	Maximum (Depth 2)	Maximum
Two-class (Normal, Others)	0.70 (0.41)	0.71 (0.75)
Three-class (Normal, Oral, Breath)	0.39 (0.31)	0.49 (0.44)
Five-class (Each blowing style)	0.36 (0.19)	0.36 (0.19)

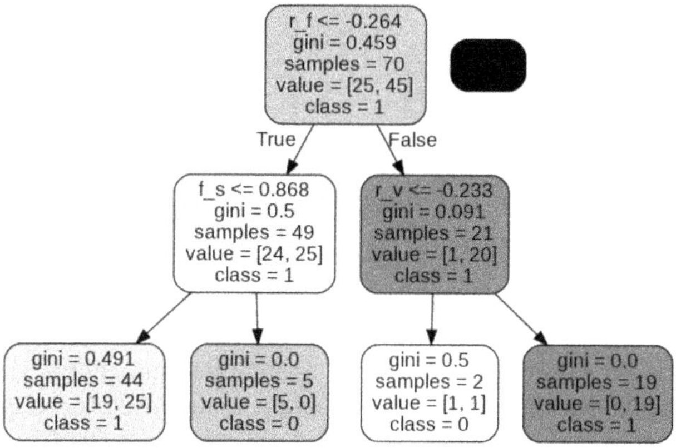

Fig. 5. DT for predicting subjective evaluation

3.2 Predicting Blowing Styles from Acoustic Features

When the performers recorded a sound, they were asked the blowing style from [Normal], [Large mouth], [Small mouth], [Breath upward], and [Breath downward]. We attempted the prediction of this blowing style from the acoustic features. We conducted different classification tasks with DTs: two-class [Normal / Other], three-class [Normal / Mouth-size-related / Breath-direction-related], and five-class: each style. Table 9 lists the classification accuracy. An example of the acquired trees is shown in Fig. 6.

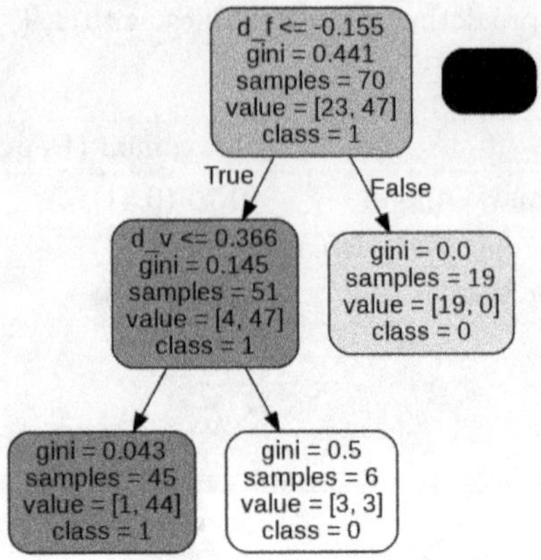

Fig. 6. DT for predicting blowing styles

4 Conclusion

We presented a flute sound database consisting of sounds played in appropriate and inappropriate blowing styles. This dataset is intended to be used for developing a support system of flute practice by analyzing how inappropriate the user's sounds are and why. To help such analysis, we annotated the subjective evaluation to each sound.

In addition, we presented examples of flute sound analysis using our dataset. Even though the prediction of subjective evaluation using linear regression and DTs showed promising results to some extent, the accuracy for predicting blowing styles was low. One possible reason could be that the performer could not strictly control the mouth size and breath direction.

In the future, we would like to improve how to collect sounds. For example, we will ask advanced players to control their mouth size and breath direction strictly and will check them via video recordings. Through this, we would like to develop technologies that help novice flute players improve their skills.

Acknowledgments. This work was supported by JSPS Kakenhi Nos. JP22H03711 and JP21H03572.

References

1. Brum, J. P. B.: Traditional Flute Dataset for Score Alignment (2018). https://www.kaggle.com/jbraga/traditional-flute-dataset
2. Elena A. C.: Flute Audio Labelled Database for Automatic Music Transcription (2018). https://doi.org/10.5281/zenodo.1408985
3. Goto, M., Hashiguchi, H., Nishimura, T. and Oka, R. : RWC Music Database: Music Genre Database and Musical Instrument Sound Database, ISMIR (2003)

4. Ito, K., Johnson, L.: The LJ Speech Dataset (2017). https://keithito.com/LJ-Speech-Dataset/
5. Jin, K., Gou, K.: Sensing control parameters of flute from microphone sound based on machine learning from robotic performer, Sensors **22** (2022)
6. John, K., Alan, W. B.: CMU ARCTIC Databases for Speech Synthesis, CMU-LTI-03-177 (2003)
7. Oshita, S., Kitahara, T.: Automatic Classification of Blowing Properness in Flute Sounds, ICA, ABS-0467 (2022)
8. Paul, B.: Automatic Prosodic Analysis for Computer Aided Pronunciation Teaching, PhD thesis, University of Edinburgh, UK (1994)
9. Romani, O., et al.: A real-time system for measuring sound goodness in instrumental sounds. In: 138th Audio Engineering Society Convention (2015)
10. Vassil, P., Guoguo, C., Daniel, P., and Sanjeev, K.: LibriSpeech: an ASR Corpus Based on Public Domain Audio Books, ICASSP (2015)
11. Yoonchang, H., Kyogu, L.: Hierarchical Approach to Detect Common Mistakes of Beginner Flute Players, ISMIR (2014)

Author Index

S. Ystad et al. (Eds.): CMMR 2023, LNCS 15236, pp. 505–506, 2026.
https://doi.org/10.1007/978-3-032-02042-0

GPSR Compliance
The European Union's (EU) General Product Safety Regulation (GPSR) is a set of rules that requires consumer products to be safe and our obligations to ensure this.

If you have any concerns about our products, you can contact us on

ProductSafety@springernature.com

In case Publisher is established outside the EU, the EU authorized representative is:

Springer Nature Customer Service Center GmbH
Europaplatz 3
69115 Heidelberg, Germany

www.ingramcontent.com/pod-product-compliance
Lightning Source LLC
Chambersburg PA
CBHW071409211025
34252CB00026B/451
* 9 7 8 3 0 3 2 0 2 0 4 1 3 *